CHARITY LAW IN NORTHERN IRELAND

AUSTRALIA

LBC Information Services
Sydney

CANADA AND the USA

Carswell

NEW ZEALAND

Brooker's
Wellington

SINGAPORE AND MALAYSIA

Thomson Information (S.E. Asia)
Singapore

Charity Law in Northern Ireland

KERRY O'HALLORAN

B.A., LL.B., MSc., LL.M.,
BL (King's Inns),
Ph.D. (Trinity College Dublin).

and

RONAN CORMACAIN

LL.B., LL.M. (Queen's University Belfast),
of the Inn of Court of Northern Ireland, Barrister at Law.

DUBLIN
ROUND HALL SWEET & MAXWELL
2001

Published in 2001 by
Round Hall Ltd
43 Fitzwilliam Place
Dublin 2

Typeset by
Gough Typesetting Services
Dublin

Printed by
MPG Books, Cornwall

ISBN 1-85800-212-5

A catalogue record for this book
is available from the British Library.

The Authors

Kerry O'Halloran is an academic lawyer who has had several law books published. He is currently employed as Assistant Director (Research) in the Centre for Voluntary Action Studies at the University of Ulster on the Coleraine campus. He is a member of the Irish Association of Law Teachers, secretary of the Association of Voluntary Action Research in Ireland and a member of the editorial board of the International Journal for Non-Profit Law (Washington, U.S.A.).

Ronan Cormacain is a practising barrister at the Bar of Northern Ireland. He has recently completed a review of charity law in Northern Ireland as part of a research project being conducted by the Centre for Voluntary Action Studies. He is the author of two publications on Housing Law in Northern Ireland. He is also currently a part-time tutor at Queen's University Belfast in Company Law, Contract Law and Property Law. His main interests are in Charity Law and Human Rights Law.

To Mary Campbell

Table of Contents

Part 1: The Law and Practice

The Principles, the Law and the Courts

Administration

Charitable Purposes

Charities

Part 2: The Procedures

Inland Revenue Procedures

Charities Branch Procedures

Appendices

Foreword

In recent years there has been a welcome increase in the number of new text books relating to law and practice in Northern Ireland. Up until now there has been little published material on charity law in this jurisdiction. This new book more than adequately fills that lacuna.

Charity law has developed in a piecemeal and at times illogical and incoherent way over the centuries, many of the governing principles finding their origins in bygone times with very different values and norms. As Lord Simons pointed out in *Gilmour v Coats*:[1]

> "It is a trite saying that the law is life, not logic. But it is, I think, conspicuously true of the law of charity that it has been built up not logically but empirically."

This book will greatly assist those involved in the interpretation, application and administration of charity law to see that law in its historical context, understand the modern law and pick their way through the rather difficult and at times treacherous terrain which charity law represents. The text sets out in as structured and coherent a way as is possible with the subject the guiding legal principles and helpfully brings the reader up-to-date with recent developments in case law and statute law.

As the text makes clear charity law in this jurisdiction differs in some respects from the law applied in other jurisdictions in these islands particularly in its administration. These differences are highlighted and discussed in the text and there is thought provoking discussion of shortcomings in the law in practice as it currently stands. Those whose task it is to keep the adequacy of the modern law under review will find much food for thought in the pages of this book.

Mr Justice Girvan
Royal Courts of Justice

November 2000

---

[1] [1949] A.C. 426 at 448–449.

Acknowledgments

Many people in many agencies, charitable and otherwise, have made this book possible. Constraints of space make it unrealistic to render a full account of the debt owed to them. However, it would be very wrong not to attempt a brief if wholly inadequate mention of those whose contributions have been particularly helpful. Their contributions, of course, are without any liability on their part. We must take full responsibility for all mistakes, omissions and opinions expressed.

This book owes a great deal to the example set by those who in the past have written on charity law in Northern Ireland. In particular, the many published works of J.C. Brady[1] together with that of Keeton and Sheridan[2] have been instructive. In other jurisdictions, the contemporary work of J. Warburton assisted by D. Morris,[3] together with L.A. Sheridan,[4] H. Picarda[5] and C. Barker[6] *et al*, have all been of great assistance. From further afield, the publications of L. Irish and K. Simon[7] have also been influential. A number of busy practitioners gave generously of their time either to discuss charity law issues or to read and offer comments on draft chapters. We are particularly indebted to the Honourable Mr Justice Girvan[8] for his most kind Foreword and for undertaking the considerable task of reading through the entire text. We are indebted also to Denis Cathcart[9] who provided much information, a willing ear to hear our queries and offered comments upon the text as it emerged chapter by chapter. The assistance provided by Roger Yates[10] was helpful as

---

[1] See, for example, Brady, J C., *Charitable Purposes and Ratings Exemption in Ireland* (1968) 3 Ir. Jur. (N.S.) 114; *House of Lords, Charities and Rating Relief in Northern Ireland* (1973) 24 N.I.L.Q. 106; *Religion and the Law of Charities in Ireland* (W & S Magowan, Belfast, 1975).

[2] Keeton, G.W., and Sheridan, L A., *The Modern Law of Charities,* (2nd ed., N.I.L.Q., Belfast, 1971).

[3] See Warburton J., *Tudor on Charities,* (8th ed., 1995) Sweet & Maxwell, London.

[4] See Sheridan, L A., *The Modern Law of Charities* (1992) Barry Rose, Chichester.

[5] See Picarda, H, *The Law and Practice Relating to Charities,* (2nd ed., 1995) Butterworths, London.

[6] See Barker, CR., Ford, P.J., Moody, S.R. and Elliot, RC., *Charity Law in Scotland* (1996) W Green/Sweet & Maxwell, Edinburgh.

[7] See the International Centre for Not-for-Profit Law, and the *International Journal of Not-for-Profit Law* both of Washington, D.C., USA.

[8] The High Court, Royal Courts of Justice, Belfast.

[9] Director, Charities branch, Dept for Social Development, Belfast.

[10] Technical Adviser (Charity), Inland Revenue.

were the comments offered by Michael Curry[11] and Alan Beaney[12] on the draft chapter "Rates Exemption" and those made by Janet Stevenson[13] and Peter Loughlin[14] on the "Fundraising" chapter.

The Centre for Voluntary Action Studies at the University of Ulster provided the stimulus and support necessary for this project.[15] The support of Arthur Williamson[16] is warmly acknowledged as is the encouragement provided by Jimmy Kearney,[17] Nick Acheson[18] and Derek Bacon.[19]

The support and efficiency of the publishers, particularly the trust and patience shown by Thérèse Carrick,[20] are gratefully acknowledged.

---

[11] The Lands Tribunal, Belfast.

[12] The Valuation and Lands Agency, Belfast

[13] Secretary, The Institute of Charity Fundraising Managers.

[14] Inspector, Staff Officer to the Assistant Chief of Police, Castlereagh RUC Station.

[15] As it did for its sister publication; see, O'Halloran, K., *Charity Law* (Round Hall Sweet & Maxwell, Dublin, 2000).

[16] Director, Centre for Voluntary Action Studies, Faculty of Social and Health Sciences and Education, University of Ulster, Cromore Rd., Coleraine, Northern Ireland.

[17] Visiting Professor, Centre for Voluntary Action Studies

[18] Research Officer, Centre for Voluntary Action Studies.

[19] Research Officer, Centre for Voluntary Action Studies.

[20] Commissioning editor, Round Hall Sweet & Maxwell, Dublin.

Table of Cases

Table of Statutes

Charities Act (N.I.) 1964—*contd.*

Statutory Rules and Orders (Northern Ireland) (1921 to date)

Introduction

The quattro-centennial anniversary of the foundation stone of our charity law, the Statute of Charitable Uses 1601,[1] is an appropriate time to reflect on how well that law has served the needs of our society and to review its relevance for the future. Other jurisdictions equally indebted to the 1601 Act, mainly those left with the colonial legacy of the common law, have been similarly engaged in a review process.[2] But, it has been in these islands, from which the common law was initially exported, that the progenitor of modern charity law has been facing most scrutiny. It would be fitting if the work currently being done independently in each of the jurisdictions of these islands could be co-ordinated and the results used to inform and re-vitalise practice in the wider common law world.

In England and Wales, the work commenced by the Deakin Commission[3] is being continued by the National Council for Voluntary Organisations[4] and by the Charity Commission.[5] In Scotland the report of the Charity Law Research Unit at Dundee University[6] has prepared the ground for further legislative reform. In Ireland the Department of Justice, Equality and Law Reform has been conducting a review of charity law and is about to introduce new legislation. In Northern Ireland, the Charities Branch carried out its own review[7] but, when faced with opposition from the voluntary sector, it dropped its modest proposals for reform. The case for resuming and completing that unfinished business is now pressing.

Charities form part of the voluntary sector (or third sector, or not-for-profit

---

[1] 43 Eliz. 1, Cap. 4. In Ireland, the equivalent legislation was the Statute of Pious Uses 1634 (10 Car. 1, Sess. 3, Cap. 1).

[2] See, for example, the Ontario Law Reform Commission, *Report on the Law of Charities*, 1997.

[3] See the Deakin Commission, *Meeting the Challenge of Change, Voluntary Action into the 21st Century*, NCVO, 1996; see also, the Goodman Committee, *Charity Law and Voluntary Organisations* (1976) Bedford Square Press.

[4] See Report of the Charity Law Reform Advisory Group (draft), London, 2000.

[5] See the on-going review of the register of charities (E&W).

[6] See the Charity Law Research Unit at the University of Dundee: *Scottish Charity Legislation: an Evaluation*, Scottish Executive Central Research Unit (Legal Studies Research Findings No. 26), 2000 and the work of the Scottish Charity Law Review Commission, established in March 2000.

[7] See DHSS, *Consultation Document on Charity Law in Northern Ireland*, Charities Branch, Belfast, 1995.

sector). This sector makes an important contribution to the socio-economic fabric of our society. In Northern Ireland, it has been estimated that there are approximately 5,000 voluntary and community organisations providing employment to some 33,500 people. Collectively there are more people engaged in this sector than are employed in manufacturing. The gross annual income for the sector is estimated to be around £500 million.[8] It is difficult to estimate the part played by charities but, given that there are at least 3,000 charities in Northern Ireland and that many of the larger voluntary organisations are charities, it may not be overstating their significance to suggest that they constitute the cutting edge of the voluntary sector.

The legal context within which charities operate is also that which prevails generally in the voluntary sector. Much of the law governing the sector applies equally to all voluntary and community organisations whether or not they are charities. In recent years the pressures of the market place have been such as to force a creeping conformity upon all third sector organisations. In practice, many of the traditional distinctions between friendly societies, mutual benefit societies, co-operatives, charities and others have become fudged; the authenticity, autonomy and appropriateness of these legal forms in relation to the current activities of their respective organisations can no longer be assumed. For charities in particular this has been a period of uncertainty and change. For charity law in Northern Ireland it has been a period of protracted inertia.

Law must relate to its contemporary social context. Although for some centuries charity law remained, to a remarkable degree, able to retain its integrity as a discrete coherent sphere of jurisprudence it nevertheless always demonstrated a capacity to adjust to accommodate relevant social developments. This was due to judicial rather than legislative initiative.

In Northern Ireland, for the past few decades, neither legislative initiative nor judicial intervention have been brought to bear on the law governing charities. It may now be difficult for legislators to reach, isolate and amend aspects of charity law without at the same time having to deal with the implications arising more generally for the voluntary sector and for ancillary legislation such as company law, tax law, rates etc. The blurring of the distinction between state and charity in the delivery of social care services has, for example, brought with it enormous complications regarding elasticity of charitable objects, accountability of trustees and has necessarily grafted on to charity law swathes of company and tax law. Again, the widespread incorporation of charitable organisations has made them subject to company law and to the requirements of professional and fiduciary practice in the same way as many other

---

[8] See Department for Social Development, *Consultation Document on Funding for the Voluntary and Community Sector*, the Voluntary Activity Unit, Belfast, April 2000, para 1.

voluntary organisations. Some charities are now very large companies with assets of many millions of pounds and employing hundreds of professional staff. Their management and administration functions are not readily distinguished from those of other companies. They share the same strategic concerns of all companies in terms of "branding" products, mergers and take-overs, competing for market share etc. Fundraising, advocacy, paid volunteers and the demands of the "contract culture" have all stretched the coping capacity of charities and brought their operational activities into closer alignment with those of other voluntary sector organisations. Such developments have also served to reveal the inadequacies of the current legal framework.

Charities share in common a number of distinguishing characteristics allowing them to form a distinctive part of the voluntary sector. A charity must demonstrably benefit the public, maintain independent governance, be properly constituted, non-profit distributing and not engage in political activity. Of these, the single most important and overriding feature which sets charities apart from the myriad of voluntary organisations constituting the voluntary sector is the requirement that they benefit the public. In this jurisdiction it would be difficult to overestimate the importance of the very considerable and sustained contribution to the common good made by many thousands of charities over hundreds of years.

The law has typically recognised this contribution by adopting a facilitative rather than an interventionist approach to the work of charities. The absence of a comprehensive safety net of care services prompted the State to leave the development of many hospital, residential and community based care facilities to charities and to place as few legal obstructions in their way as possible. More recently, the development of a mixed economy of service provision has become evident whereby State initiated partnerships are formed with leading charities to deliver care, education and other services. Arguably, this has resulted in a vibrant voluntary sector with charities able to negotiate from a position of strength and independence with government bodies on the development and implementation of social inclusion strategies to address the needs of the disadvantaged. Unarguably it has also resulted in this jurisdiction having the most dated, least relevant and non-interventionist legislation relating to charities within the United Kingdom.

In Northern Ireland, the need to reform the law relating to charities is now becoming urgent. Any such reform should begin with a recognition that our knowledge of the organisations engaged in charitable activity is poor. It should be informed by research which establishes the dimensions, characteristics, dynamics and problems of those organisations constituting the charitable part of the voluntary sector. While there are some studies on charitable giving and volunteering activity, a fuller profile is required – including data on the legal form, size, duration, governance and management, inputs and outputs – of charities in Northern Ireland. Information is needed on trends that have emerged in recent years: the distribution of charitable giving under each of the four

Pemsel heads;[9] legal forms adopted; funding sources; fundraising and involvement of professional fundraisers; cross-jurisdiction activity; impact of the "contract culture"; the nature and extent of trading activities etc. The details illustrating the need for reform will become apparent later in the book. At this stage it is sufficient just to note the main reasons why charity law in Northern Ireland is now unsatisfactory and the type of problems urgently requiring legislative attention.

The evolution of charity law has never quite overcome the constraints imposed by initial legislation. The Preamble to the Statute of Charitable Uses 1601, the legislative progenitor of charity law in all common law nations, consisted largely of a list of activities which were then considered charitable. This common law approach of listing subjects for legal redress, permitting subsequent empirical extension by analogy, has itself proved problematic as it has prevented the emergence of unifying principles which could have brought more coherence to charity law. Some listed items, such as the repair of highways and bridges, would now be clearly recognised as responsibilities attributable to public service agencies. Other items on the list included a reference to dowries for poor maids carrying the implication that a gift, not to alleviate poverty but to subsidise adherence to prevailing social norms, is thereby worthy of charitable status. This has a modern resonance, for example, in the acceptance that such status is appropriate for socially elite institutions as private schools and theatres.

Charity law has failed to keep abreast of social change. Charitable status, itself a misleading term in this jurisdiction, is determined by charitable purpose which is only ascertainable by reference to the prevailing social context. Some of the social pressures conditioning charity legislation in the years following the Reformation were fundamentally different from those now requiring a legislative response. It is not just that today's social problems are no longer appropriately addressed by the charitable purposes listed in the Preamble; the problems, and the answers provided by the State, are now sometimes construed entirely differently from the way they appeared in the early seventeenth century. Charities, for example, are no longer necessarily distinct from the State and are recognisable by the fact that they fill gaps in State service provision; not inclusive of self-help organisations; and charity workers may now be salaried professionals, indistinguishable from their counterparts in government agencies, rather than dedicated unpaid volunteers.

There is a need to reconsider certain elements of charity law. The distinction between charitable purposes and public service needs to be examined; the convergence between some large public service bodies and some traditional charities can be seen in their funding arrangements, activities, use of salaried professional staff etc. It is not always clear where public service ends and charitable activity begins. Focussing on a charity's objects or intentions, to

---

[9] *Commissioners for Special Purposes of Income Tax v. Pemsel* (1891) A.C. 531.

determine whether or not these conform to one of the charitable purposes within the *Pemsel* umbrella, is arguably less instructive than examining the charity's activities and outputs. Poverty, a relative term in any western society, may need to be re-interpreted to facilitate charitable activity directed at reducing unemployment, bolstering community development and forging alliances with public and private bodies within a social partnership framework. The variation in the burden of proof across the four *Pemsel* heads is questionable; consideration could be given to making the test more rigorous and then applying it uniformly to all organisations seeking to acquire or retain charitable status. The restrictions on trading may place charities at a disadvantage in today's commercial environment. The advantages in permitting charities, particularly those dedicated to serving the interests of socially excluded groups, to campaign, lobby or otherwise engage in political activities on their behalf may outweigh the disadvantages. The presumption that gifts to advance religion are charitable is open to question in an increasingly secular society and may serve to harden underlying divisions in a society struggling to cope with a legacy of religious turmoil. Many of these matters spring from a fundamental and increasingly pressing difficulty facing many areas of law – how to discriminate between public and private interests?

Currently, at least three agencies mediate on different aspects of this distinction. The Charities Branch provides the guidance necessary to become properly constituted as a charity, the Inland Revenue affords the recognition required for tax exemption and the Valuation and Lands Agency considers eligibility for rates exemption. Other agencies, such as the Companies Registry Office, the Friendly Societies Registry Office and the Royal Ulster Constabulary may also have a part to play in the common task of considering whether an organisation is sufficiently addressing the public interests rather than private or mutual benefit interests. Their respective terms of reference, however, do not promote a seamless and co-ordinated continuity among the formal processes for screening charities and charitable activities. Moreover, they are all responsive rather than regulatory in their mode of intervention. There is now a pressing need for a single body to be statutorily charged with the duty to determine whether or not an organisation is a charity, and if it is, to then require compliance with fixed standards of fiscal probity, transparency and public accountability. This body should bear responsibility for adding and removing charities from a central register and for maintaining a supervisory brief in respect of charitable activities. The absence of a statutory body with over-arching registration and regulatory duties is a particular obstacle to building coherence in charity law and public confidence in charities.

Legislative inertia is a particular feature of modern charity law in Northern Ireland. This single conspicuous fact tends to distract attention from the corollary that the legal system as a whole is relatively inert in its treatment of charities. This may have some advantages in terms of leaving greater room for judicial discretion to interpret charitable purpose in the light of changes in social context. But considerable disadvantages arise from the legal system's lack of response to the contemporary issues affecting charities. The legislation is very dated and tends to be procedural rather than formative in nature. In practice, the law generates little litigation and very few substantive judgments. It is probable that one reason for this is the considerable expense involved in commencing proceedings in the High Court. The ethos associated with charities possibly inhibits litigation. Paradoxically, the usefulness of intermediary fora in filtering out and determining issues which would otherwise feed into the court system, may also be contributing to the general problem that the judiciary rarely have opportunities to deliberate on contemporary charity law dilemmas. The occasional reported cases are mostly concerned with issues relating to rateable valuation; the absence of any consideration of matters of substantive law is noticeable.

These and other characteristic aspects of contemporary charity law in Northern Ireland are given full consideration in the following chapters. This book is in two parts. The first consists of twenty-two chapters of text dealing with the substantive and administrative aspects of charity law. The second is brief and practice oriented. It outlines some of the more common procedures, provides useful addresses and a selected bibliography.

Part One, Section One, "The Principles, the Law and the Courts" consisting of four chapters which introduces the governing principles, the legal framework and processes and the implications arising from Human Rights and other legislation. Section Two, "Administration" in three chapters, deals with the responsibilities of the considerable range of agencies, the distinctiveness of charitable trusts, and the powers and duties of trustees. Section Three, "Charitable Purposes" moves on to consider in eight chapters the subjects traditionally held to constitute the heartland of charity law. Finally, Section Four, "Charities" consisting of seven chapters, examines and explains the matters most likely to attract the attention of those with management responsibility for charities, their formation, activities and cessation. The second Part mainly outlines various procedures and provides specimen forms for making application to certain agencies.

PART ONE

The Law and Practice

The Principles, the Law and the Courts

CHAPTER 1

Charity: Origins and Principles

1.1 INTRODUCTION

According to section 35 of the Charities Act (N.I.) 1964:

> "'Charity' means any institution, corporate or not, which is established for charitable purposes and is subject to the control of the Court in the exercise of the Court's jurisdiction with respect to charities."

The same section provides further, somewhat circular definitions:

> "'Charitable gift' means a gift for charitable purposes;

> 'Charitable purposes' means purposes which are exclusively charitable according to the law of Northern Ireland."

The concept of charity and the related functions of the law have never been wholly satisfactorily defined. This necessarily leads to considerable difficulties for those who set out to explain charity law. It defies logic and requires a systemic approach.

There are inherent problems in any attempt to depict the law governing charities as a discrete and coherent body of jurisprudence. To begin with, the origins of charity law are ancient and rooted in cultures distant in time and place from contemporary life in Northern Ireland.[1] Then there is the problem of boundaries. Charity law shares many of its principles and doctrines with the general law of trusts (see further, Chapters 6 and 7). Increasingly, it is becoming subject to the laws governing revenue, tax and rates (see Chapters 20 and 21), while the range of legal structures available require compliance with company law or perhaps the rules of friendly societies, etc. (see Chapters 16 and 17). Primarily, the uncertainty as to coherence may be attributed to the fact that charity law is largely judge made law. For four centuries, an ever spreading spectrum of activity has been assimilated within the generic term "charitable" as a benign judicial disposition towards philanthropy has filled the space left by a lack of legislative definition. This has proceeded on an *ad hoc* basis as the courts respond to changing social pressures. The results can

---

[1] See, for example, the Preamble to the Statute of Charitable Uses 1601 for illustrations of the type of activity then recognised in England as charitable and subsequently transferred with the armies of that nation to provide the foundations for charity law throughout the common law world.

be seen, for example, in the burgeoning range of activities being accommodated under the fourth *Pemsel* head of charity.

This chapter begins the book by briefly examining the origins of charity
law. It would not be appropriate in a book dealing with the modern law and
practice to attempt more than a brief synopsis noting the main milestones. It
then identifies and considers the core characteristics of charities: charitable
purposes, the public benefit, and exclusivity.

1.2 DEFINITIONS

Flexibility is the hallmark of equity. The permissive and discretionary use of
judicial power has enabled equity to respond to issues unfettered by statutory
constraints and to thereby bridge legislative gaps. This has proved invaluable,
for example, in relation to the wardship of minors. It has also characterised the
application of the law relating to charity.

1.2.1 A charity

1.2.1(i) Legislative definition

As noted above, legislation has done little more than allow judicial discretion
to be the ultimate arbiter of what constitutes a charity. This is a jurisdictional
definition – an entity is a charity if it comes under the charitable jurisdiction of
the court. In this respect, the legislative definition merely reiterates the ancient
jurisdiction of the court over the affairs of charities (see further, Chapter 3).

1.2.1(ii) Judicial definition

The courts have given substance to the terms "charity" and "charitable purposes". They have established the fundamental threefold test for charitable
status: that a body must be established for what are recognised as charitable
purposes, that it must be for the public benefit, and that it must be exclusively
charitable. A good (if not entirely orthodox) definition was given by Fitzgibbon
L.J. a century ago in the leading Irish case of *Re Cranston*[2]:

> "The essential attributes of a legal charity are, in my opinion, that it shall be
> *unselfish* – i.e. for the benefit of other persons than the donor – that it shall be
> *public*, i.e. that those to be benefited shall form a class worthy, in numbers of
> importance, of consideration as a public object of generosity, and that it shall be
> *philanthropic* or *benevolent* – i.e. dictated by a desire to do good."

---

[2] [1898] I.R. 431. Also, see comments of Lord Sterndale M.R. in *Re Tetley* [1923] 1 Ch.
     258 at 266.

1.2.1(iii) Other definitions

For practical purposes a charity may be understood as any organisation, established for and giving effect to charitable purposes, which is recognised by the Inland Revenue as qualifying for charitable exemption from tax liability. Whether constituted as an unincorporated association, a charitable trust or as a charitable company, it may be recognised as a charity by the Inland Revenue. Whether established for centuries or for a few months, operating from a one room office with part-time volunteers or from a multi-storey company building with hundreds of professional staff, servicing need in a local housing estate or across several continents, it may still be a charity.

However, two points need to the made. Firstly, the courts are the ultimate arbiters of charitable status; they can accept or reject a decision of the Inland Revenue as to a body's status. The Inland Revenue only rule that a body is charitable for tax purposes. Secondly, Inland Revenue status is not comprehensive. There are bodies which are charitable but which are not recognised as such by the Inland Revenue. This can be because they either do not produce an income and therefore have no need for contact with the tax authorities, or because they choose on a point of principle not to apply for tax exemption.[3]

In Northern Ireland, there is no official body charged with responsibility for verifying, registering or thereafter inspecting the bona fides of an organisation claiming to be a charity. There is however, a body, the Charities Branch, which is charged with assisting and monitoring charities (see further, Chapter 5).

1.2.2 Difficulties of definition

In the absence of legislative definition and regulation, the judicial treatment of charities has evolved in response to different social pressures. The merits of this approach have been endorsed in *Charities: a Framework for the Future*[4] where the view was expressed that:

> "... the government consider that any attempt to define charity by any of (the suggested means) would be fraught with difficulty and might put at risk the flexibility of the present law which is both its greatest strength and its most valuable feature."[5]

The price of flexibility has been a prevailing uncertainty. On this island, the difficulty in discovering any integrating logic to the law relating to charities

---

[3] For example, some self-help groups disclaim charitable tax status as it detracts from their self-help ethos. Other groups advocating separation of church and state may find it hypocritical to accept tax concessions due to their status.

[4] (1989), Cmnd. 694, paras. 2.07-2.17.

[5] *ibid.,* para. 2.11.

was memorably alluded to by Gavan Duffy J. in *Re Howley's Estate*:[6]

> "'Charity' is in law an artificial conception, which during some 300 years, un-
> der the guidance of pedantic technicians, seems to have strayed rather far from
> the intelligent realm of plain common sense; thus, the textbooks tell us that
> charity in the eyes of the law includes a bequest for a 'Home for Lost Dogs', as
> an institution for domestic animals must benefit the human race which they
> serve. . . . There are decisions extant in the charitable domain which suggest
> that in Ireland ... we must proceed with great circumspection where 'charity' is
> concerned."

Significantly, for the best part of four hundred years, both legislature and judiciary have chosen to ignore opportunities to define the precise legal meaning
of "charity".

1.2.3 Charity recognition and contemporary law

In this jurisdiction, it remains the case that "charitable status", carrying an
inference of *locus standi*, is not an entirely appropriate term to use in reference to charities. Charities do not have legal status as such. Nor is there a
definitive checklist of criteria to determine whether or not an organisation is
eligible for formal recognition as a charity. Official recognition is extended to
charities by the Inland Revenue purely as a technical device to clarify eligibility for charitable tax exemption.

1.3 HISTORICAL BACKGROUND

Any enquiry into the origins of the law relating to charities must be directed
towards the pragmatic decisions made by secular rulers in response to the
uncertain religious climate of early medieval England. Charity law on this
island, a legacy of military conquest by its neighbour, initially wholly reflected
the concerns of English royalty.

1.3.1 The law of mortmain[7]

Feudalism was established in England and extended, imperfectly, to Ireland in
the years following the Norman conquest. It was a centralised system based
on land ownership and became the basis for determining the loyalty, services
and tithes due to rulers. For centuries, land tenure underpinned feudalism and
provided the basis for ordering society.

---

[6] [1940] I.R. 109 at 114. Also, see comments of Lord Sterndale M.R. in *Re Tetley* [1923]
1 Ch. 258 at 266.

[7] See further, Jones, *History of the Law of Charity 1532-1827* (Cambridge University
Press, 1969).

From the perspective of the rulers, a significant threat to the feudal system arose from the growing practice of mortmain. This Norman French term *morte meyn* or "dead hand" referred to the practice whereby a donor would tie-up his lands in perpetuity by gifting them to the Church. This had the effect of robbing the state of many feudal dues and, to some extent, can be compared to the modern use of charities as tax avoidance devices. In both England and Ireland, it was customary for a penitent donor to make a gift to the Church for a pious use coupled with a request that prayers or masses be offered for the salvation of the donor's soul. Such gifts for pious uses were recognised as charitable gifts in the years prior to the Reformation. As Coke has explained:[8]

> "The lands were said to come to dead hands ... for ... by alienation in mortmaine they lost wholly their escheats and in effect their knights services for the defence of the realme; wards, marriages, reliefes and the like; and therefore was called a dead hand, for that a dead hand yeeldeth no service."

Once property passed into the "dead hand of the Church" it remained there as the latter prohibited any alienation of its property. Ultimately, in order to placate government concerns that the church would gradually acquire a large proportion of all land available, parliament introduced the Mortmain Act 1736 to prohibit charitable bequests of land unless by a full and proper conveyance executed 12 months before the death of the donor.

1.3.1(i) Frankalmoigne

Much land came to be owned by the Church on the basis of "tenure by frankalmoigne", the gift of property having been made subject to a condition that it be held for the use of specified persons, usually the donor and/or his family. This has been described as follows:

> "Tenant in frankalmoigne is where an abbot, or prior, or another man of religion or of Holy Church, holdeth of his lord in frankalmoigne that is to say in Latin, *in liberam eleemosinam*, that is, in free almes; and such tenure beganne first in old time."[9]

The statute *Quia Emptores* defined the services owed by a tenant in frankalmoigne to their feudal lord:

> "S. 135(b). And they which hold in frankalmoigne are bound of right before God to make orisons, prayers, masses and other divine services for the soules of their grantor or feofforn and for the soules of their heires which are dead, and for the prosperity and good life and good health of their heires which are alive. And therefore they shall do no fealty to their lord, because that this divine

---

[8]   See Coke, Co.Litt. 2B; quoted by V.T.H. Delany, *The Law Relating to Charities in Ireland* (revised ed., 1962, Dublin), p. 1.

[9]   See Littleton S 133; Co Litt, 93(b).

service is better before God than any doing of fealty; and also because that these words (frankalmoigne) exclude the lord to have any earthly or temporal service, but to have only divine and spiritual service to be done for him."

Feudal rulers, not surprisingly, regarded a grant of land to the Church by a subject as incompatible with the latter's feudal duties and sought to curtail this practice through successive statutes.[10] The systematic avoidance of statutory constraints allowed the Church and particularly the religious orders to acquire power, land and political influence.

1.3.2 The Reformation

The growing breach between Church and State culminated eventually in the action by Henry VIII against the Catholic Church and its powerful land-owning religious orders. In Ireland, although the English sphere of control was restricted to the "Pale", the power of the great monasteries was considerable. The ensuing struggle between monarchy and papacy resulted in Henry VIII taking vigorous action in Ireland to suppress the Church, dissolve the monasteries and confiscate their property. By mid-sixteenth century a large number of Irish abbeys and monasteries had been dissolved and their lands appropriated by the Crown.

Dissolution of the monasteries had several important consequences for charities. Firstly, it had the immediate effect of removing the single most important source of housing, care and education for the poor; the homeless and destitute were left to roam the towns in search of alms and shelter. Secondly, it ended the possibility of making grants of property to the Church in exchange for spiritual benefits. By the end of the seventeenth century much of its power, land and monasteries had been stripped from the Catholic Church. The Elizabethan era began with the attempt to establish a new and comprehensive national Protestant religion regulated by statute. Other religions were not to be tolerated.

This in turn led directly to the two statutes of fundamental importance; in England, the Statute of Charitable Uses (1601), 43 Eliz. 1 Cap 4 (also known as the Statute of Elizabeth) and, in Ireland, the Statute of Pious Uses (1634) 10 Car. 1 Sess. 3 Cap. 1, (also known as the Statute of Charles).

1.3.3 Equity

The jurisdiction of the King as *parens patriae* was exercised by the Court of Chancery in relation to the wardship of minors and lunatics and also in rela-

---

[10] See Statutes of Henry III, 1217, of Marlborough 1267, of Edward I in 1279 and 1285, Richard II in 1391 leading eventually to Poynings Law in 1495.

tion to charitable trusts. This was noted by Macclesfield L.J. in *Eyre v. The Countess of Shaftesbury*[11] when as he then explained:

> "The Court of Chancery, having always exercised jurisdiction in matters of charity, derived from the Crown as *parens patriae*, has proceeded as I have done."

The use of judicial discretion, a hallmark of this jurisdiction, allowed the judiciary to formulate a body of principles to guide the determination of matters affecting trusts and charitable trusts (see also, Chapters 3 and 6). This was quietly developed and consolidated during and following the protracted period of struggle between Church and State. A general power to enforce trusts was recognised and additional common law powers were also used in relation to charities.[12] In *Attorney General v. Tancred*[13] Lord Northington acknowledged that even before the Statute of Charitable Uses 1601 the Court of Chancery would have given aid to a defective conveyance in favour of a charity.

It has to be admitted that prior to 1601 the law relating to charities is extremely obscure. Subsequently, for nearly four centuries, it gradually developed as a discrete body of law loosely attached to the law of trusts. Only in relatively recent decades has the law relating to charity, like its relationship to wardship, been judicially revitalised to become a modern, flexible and sophisticated means for supplementing statutory provision in response to the complex problems typical of contemporary practice. Its capacity to do so owes a good deal to judicial initiative in drawing from case law principles forged in other common law jurisdictions. Just as the principle of the "welfare of the child" in the context of wardship has been judicially tested and applied in common law courts across the world, so too has the principle of "public benefit" in a charity law context. Importing into the jurisprudence of Northern Ireland the results of painstaking judicial deliberations in the courts not only of England and Wales but also of countries such as Canada, New Zealand and Australia has done much to broaden the application of charity law in this jurisdiction.

1.3.4 Statutory foundations for charity law

The foundations of modern charity law were laid by two Elizabethan statutes.

---

[11] 2 P. Wms. 118; quoted with approval by Lord Manners in *Attorney-General v. Flood* Ha. & Jones Ap. 30. But also see, *Attorney-General v. The Skinners' Company* 9 Ross 420, *per* Lord Eldon.
[12] See, for example, *Porter's Case* (1592) 1 Co 22b, *Partridge v. Walker* (1595) 4 Co. 116b and *Martidale v. Martin* (1593) Cro. Eliz. 288. But also see *Eyre v. Shaftesbury* (1722) 2 P. Wms. 119.
[13] (1757) Amb. 351.

1.3.4(i) The Statute of Charitable Uses 1601[14]

This legislation is of fundamental importance to charity law. Entitled "An Act to redress the Mis-employment of Lands, Goods, and Stocks of Money heretofore given to Charitable Uses" its intent was quite explicit. The Preamble sets out the following charitable purposes:

> "The relief of aged, impotent and poor people; the maintenance of sick and maimed soldiers and mariners, schools of learning, free schools and scholars of universities; the repair of bridges, havens, causeways, churches, sea banks and highways; the education and preferment of orphans;the relief, stock or maintenance of houses of correction; marriages of poor maids; supportation, aid and help of young tradèsmen, handicraftsmen and persons decayed; the relief or redemption of prisoners or captives and the aid or ease of any poor inhabitants concerning payments of fifteens, setting out of soldiers, and other taxes."[15]

The charitable trusts enumerated fell into two broad categories: for the poor; and for public works. The fault-line running between the two continues to attract controversy: should charities do the work of the State by providing such public service facilities as bridges, or public toilets, etc.?

From the outset these charitable purposes were treated as being illustrative rather than definitive; though initial judicial uncertainty prevailed as to whether the words in certain parts of the Preamble should be construed disjunctively or conjunctively. The courts would not regard a purpose as charitable unless it could be defined as coming within "the spirit and intendment" of the Preamble. An element of "public benefit" was also crucial. A broad interpretation of the purposes identified in the Preamble continues to provide the basis for modern charity law not only in England but elsewhere in the common law world.

This statute suffered a series of partial repeals until being finally expunged from the statute book by the Charities Act 1960.

1.3.4(ii) The Statute of Pious Uses 1634[16]

This statute, from the reign of Charles 1, entitled "An Act for the Maintenance and Execution of Pious Uses", provided the legislative foundation stone for charity law in Ireland. Although not a carbon copy of the equivalent Eliza-

---

[14] Statute of 43 Eliz. 1 Cap. 4.

[15] As noted in *Tudor, op. cit.* at p. 3, the wording of the preamble closely resembles a passage in *The Vision of Piers Plowman* a fourteenth-century poem. In it, those seeking salvation are enjoined to spend their money charitably, "And therewith repair hospitals / help sick people / mend bad roads / build up bridges that had been broken down / help maidens marry or make them nuns / find food for prisoners and poor people / put scholars to school or to some other craft / help religious orders and / ameliorate rents or taxes".

[16] 10 Car. 1 Sess. 3 Cap. 1.

bethan statute, 43 Eliz. 1 Cap. 4 (the Statute of Charitable Uses 1601), it was judicially held to fulfil exactly the same functions.[17] The Preamble to the 1634 Act sets out the following list of objects:

> "The erection, maintenance, or support of any college, school, lecture in divinity, or in any of the liberal arts and sciences, or for the relief or maintenance of any manner of poor, succourless, distressed, or impotent persons, or for the building, re-edifying or maintaining in repair any church, college, school or hospital, or for the maintenance of any minister and preacher of the Holy Word of God, or for the erection, building, maintenance, or repair of any bridges, causeyes, cashes, paces, and highways within this realm, or for any other lawful and charitable use and uses, warranted by the law of this realm now established and in force. . . ."

Again, the list was never judicially regarded as definitive, a "public benefit" element was vital and a gift could be judged charitable if it fell within the "spirit or intendment" of the statute.[18] As the words "for the relief or maintenance of any manner of poor, succourless, distressed, or impotent persons" were framed disjunctively no judicial controversy ever arose regarding this aspect of their interpretation.

This statute was repealed by the Statute Law Revision Act (Ireland) 1878.

1.3.5 Effect of the statutes

The intention of these statutes, as Lord Morton noted in *Royal College of Surgeons of England v. National Provincial Bank Ltd,*[19] was to reform abuses in the application of property devoted to charitable uses rather than to define the concept of a charity. During the following years the related case law shows

---

[17] But, see *Attorney General v. Corporation of Limerick* (1816) Beat. 563; *Attorney General v. Corp of Dublin* (1827) 1 Bligh. N.S. 312; *Powerscourt v. Powerscourt* (1824) 1 Moll. 616; *Attorney General v. Flood* (1816) H. & J. 21; and *Incorp. Soc. v. Richards* (1841) 1 Dr. and War. 258.

[18] As explained by the Master of the Rolls, Sir William Grant in *Morice v. Bishop of Durham* (1804) 32 E.R. 656, 9 Ves. J. 399:

> Do purposes of liberality and benevolence mean the same as objects of charity? That word in its widest sense denotes all the good affections men ought to bear towards each other; in its most restricted and common sense, relief of the poor. In neither of these senses is it employed in this Court. Here its signification is derived chiefly from the Statute of Elizabeth (Stat. 43, Eliz. c.4). Those purposes are considered charitable, which that Statute enumerates, or which by analogies are deemed within its spirit and intendment; and to some such purpose every bequest to charity generally shall be applied.

> See, also, *Commissioner of Inland Revenue v. Medical Council of New Zealand* [1997] 2 N.Z.L.R. 297, *per* Thomas J. at p. 314 for a modern view of how the 'spirit and intendment' should be applied; viz. with more attention to contemporary circumstances than to case precedents.

[19] [1952] A.C. 631 at 650–651.

the judiciary repeatedly reaffirming that only those charitable purposes corresponding to the statutory definition could be recognised in law. It has remained the case that for a purpose to be recognised as charitable it must broadly come within the scope of the Preamble.

1.3.6 Judicial classification

During the ensuing two centuries neither statute nor judiciary intervened to classify the charitable purposes listed in the Elizabethan statutes. When such classification came it ordered the judicial approach to charities and to charitable activity thereafter.

1.3.6(i) The ruling in Morice v. The Bishop of Durham

A first judicial attempt to classify charitable purposes was undertaken by Sir William Grant M.R. in *Morice v. The Bishop of Durham*[20] when he stated that a fixed principle existed in the law of England that purposes deemed to be charitable are those "which that Statute enumerates" and those "which by analogies are deemed within its spirit and intendment".[21] A taxonomy was formulated by Samuel Romilly (later Sir Samuel Romilly) who served as counsel in that case. He suggested to the Lord Chancellor on appeal that:

> "... there are four objects, within one of which all charity, to be administered in this court, must fall: 1st, the relief of the indigent; in various ways: money: provisions: education: medical assistance; etc: 2nd, the advancement of learning, 3rd the advancement of religion; and 4th, which is the most difficult, the advancement of objects of general public utility".[22]

1.3.6(ii) The ruling in Commissioners for Special Purposes of Income Tax v. Pemsel

Lord Macnaghten accepted Sir Samuel Romilly's classification but added some significant refinements. In *Commissioners for Special Purposes of Income Tax v. Pemsel*[23] he classified all recognised charitable purposes under four heads and added that to be charitable, a gift must also be "beneficial to the community".[24] He ruled as follows:

---

[20] (1804) 9 Ves. 399 before the Master of the Rolls, (1804) 10 Ves. 521 before the Lord Chancellor, Lord Eldon.

[21] See, also, *Kendall v. Grainger* (1842) 5 Beav. 302, *per* Lord Langdale M.R. and *Dolan v. MacDermott* (1868) LR 3 Ch. App. 678.

[22] (1804) 10 Ves. 521 at 532.

[23] [1891] A.C. 531.

[24] See, the caveat entered by Lord Cave in *Attorney General v. National Provincial & Union Bank Ltd.* [1924] A.C. 262.

> "'Charity' in its legal sense comprises four principal divisions: trusts for the relief of poverty; trusts for the advancement of education; trusts for the advancement of religion; and trusts beneficial to the community not falling under any of the preceding heads. The trusts last referred to are not any the less charitable in the eye of the law, because incidentally they benefit the rich as well as the poor, as indeed, every charity that deserves the name must do directly or indirectly."[25]

To be considered charitable in law a trust must fall into one of these four separate but not necessarily mutually exclusive categories. The courts have recognised that these four divisions are not straitjackets by which charitable purposes must be constrained. They are guides, and the profligate nature of philanthropic activity means that one discrete purpose can straddle two or more categories. For example, Lord MacDermott L.C.J. in the Northern Ireland Court of Appeal recognised a particular charitable body as serving "one comprehensive purpose rather than a series of distinct purposes capable of being regarded in isolation".[26]

The Macnaghten ruling has been habitually followed not only in England but also in all common law jurisdictions and still forms the basis of charity law in Ireland. Its limitations were noted by Lord Wilberforce in *Scottish Burial Reform & Cremation Society v. Corp*:[27]

Lord Macnaghten's grouping of the heads of recognised charity in *Pemsel's* case is one that has proved to be of value and there are many problems which it solves. But three things may be said about it, which its author would surely not have denied. Firstly, since it is a classification of convenience, there may well be purposes which do not fit neatly into one or other of the headings; secondly, that the words used must not be given the force of a statute to be construed; and thirdly, that the law of charity is a moving subject which may well have evolved even since 1891.

1.3.6(iii) Other classifications

The *Pemsel* classification is not the only one possible. More recently, Slade J. drew attention to a different category:

> "… a genus or division of charity not mentioned by Lord Macnaghten, of which poverty is merely a species, this genus includes the relief of human suffering and distress in all the various forms enumerated."[28]

---

[25] *op. cit.* at p. 583.
[26] *Trustees of the City of Belfast Young Men's Christian Association v. Commissioner of Valuation* [1969] N.I. 3 at 10.
[27] [1968] A.C. 138.
[28] *McGovern v. Attorney General* [1982] 1 Ch. 321 at 333.

1.3.6(iv) The ruling in Williams' Trustees v. IRC[29]

In this case the House of Lords made a statement regarding the legal limits of charity. It indicated that two propositions must be borne in mind: a trust is not charitable unless it is within the spirit and intendment of the Statute of Elizabeth 1; and the classification of charity in its legal sense into four principal divisions in the *Pemsel* must be read subject to the qualification that every object of public general utility is not necessarily charitable:

> "If the purposes are not charitable *per se*, the localisation of them will not make them charitable."

This case reiterated the principle that demonstrating public benefit remained a vital component of the test for charitable status.

1.3.7 Judicial classification in Ireland and Northern Ireland

The *Pemsel* and *Bishop of Durham* cases were English and were not necessarily binding on the courts in pre-partition Ireland or in Northern Ireland. However, the courts in Northern Ireland adopted the fourfold *Pemsel* taxonomy and consequently the law in this jurisdiction now corresponds closely to that prevailing in the rest of the United Kingdom. There is, however, a hint of regional difference which suggests that the definition of charity may be slightly broader here than in the rest of the U.K.

1.3.7(i) Common sense argument

Different words are used to define charity in the 1601 and the 1634 statutes. Sometimes the same words are used, but they are used in a different context or a different order. How can it be said that charity means the same in both jurisdictions? Many cases in other fields of law have been determined by very minor differences in the wording of statutes. It is illogical to argue that two very different statutes could both produce exactly the same result.

   To counter this argument it could be said that the judges in their definitions of charity do not rely upon the precise wording of these statutes. The important factor is the legislative spirit and intendment. Minor semantic differences do not affect the essence of these two statutes, and their essence is a common definition of charity. Indeed the statutes have long been repealed and are no longer law. They survive not as a narrow, technically constrained aid to construction, but as a broad conceptual framework upon which can be hung diverse charitable activities. This broad framework of both statutes remains uniform both in Northern Ireland and the rest of the United Kingdom.

---

[29] [1947] A.C. 447.
[30] *Incorporated Society in Dublin for Promoting English Protestant Schools in Ireland v. Richards* (1841) 1 Dr. & War. 258.

This argument can itself be countered. The courts have at times relied upon the precise wording of the statutes. For example, witness the debate over whether "aged, impotent and poor" should be construed conjunctively or disjunctively. Those cases relied upon a tight construction of the actual words used in the statute. It is not logical to talk about broad common frameworks when the facts of cases have relied upon narrow, specific definitions.

1.3.7(ii) Weight of authority argument

The weight of authority is that an English charity is exactly the same as a Northern Ireland charity. In Ireland, Sugden L.C. ruled that, for all intents and purposes, the statutes of 1601 and 1634 were to be regarded as identical:

> "The Statute of Charles seems ... an almost exact pattern of the Statute of Elizabeth and I have little doubt but that its framers had the latter Act before them at the time they were preparing it."[30]

In *Attorney General v. Delaney*[31] it was held:

> "... for the purposes of the present case we may deem a charitable purpose in Ireland to be identical with that which ... would be a charitable purpose in England under the Act 43 Eliz. Cap.4."

In *Pemsel* itself, it was stated that the meaning of charity was the same in both jurisdictions. No judge has ever explicitly stated that there is a jurisdictional difference in the meaning given to charity.

However, there is evidence of some judicial reluctance to accept a common definition. William Moore K.C. argued in *Shillington v. Portadown Urban District Council* that "the statute of 10 Car. I Sess. 3 c. 1 is wider in its terms than the corresponding statute of Elizabeth".[32] The court did not rule out this argument. Delany[33] argues that *Attorney General v. Delaney* stated that the law in Ireland and England was analogous as regards mechanisms for preventing fraud, but not as regards the definition of charity. A closer reading of the judgment in *Delaney* reveals an inclusive approach; Irish charities included everything that English charities included, but they may also contain further and wider charitable objects. The court held that:

> "... the analogy of the statute of 43 Eliz. c.4 has been so applied as to include everything comprised within the larger words of the statute of Charles I".[34]

In Northern Ireland, the *Baptist Union* case[35] approved the above statement in

---

[31] (1875) I.R. 10 C.L. 104.

[32] *Shillington* at p. 253.

[33] *Delaney, op. cit.*

[34] *Delaney* at p. 125.

[35] See, *Baptist Union of Ireland (Northern) Corp. Ltd. v. Commissioners of Inland Revenue* [1945] N.I. 99.

Delaney. The court went on to find that "the English statute is to be regarded as *in pari materia*"[36] to the Irish statute. *Baptist Union* was decided by helpful reference to the Irish statute, *i.e.* "would come within that part of the Statute of Charles which speaks of the maintenance of any minister"[37] and "come well within the intendment of the statutes".[38] The Statute of Charles is not regarded as an irrelevancy, but as providing a vibrant and defining component of charity law in this jurisdiction.

There are other examples of judges looking to both the 1601 and the 1634 statutes. The implicit assumption in both *Attorney-General for Northern Ireland v. Forde*[39] and *Trustees of the Londonderry Presbyterian Church House v. IRC*[40] was that an object would be charitable if it came within the spirit of the Irish act if not within the English one. In *Belfast Y.M.C.A. v. Commissioner of Valuation (Northern Ireland)*[41] the court also looked "to the spirit and intendment of the statutes".[42] Section 6 of the Charitable Bequests and Donations Act (Ireland) 1871 speaks of "charitable or pious" purposes, a clear reference to the titles of both the 1601 and 1634 statutes.

Further authority for a separate definition can be found from the judgements in the *Campbell College* case.[43] The Court of Appeal stated that "the statutes of Elizabeth and Charles are co-terminous".[44] However, the House of Lords noted that the Irish statute:

> "... had provided an almost exact parallel to the Statute of Elizabeth except possibly that it was even more explicit in treating education, religion and the relief of poverty as independent objects."[45]

It was also noted that the statutes "corresponded" but that the Irish statute "is in clearer terms".[46] Furthermore, Viscount Radcliffe observed that "the purpose of science, literature and the fine arts ... may well be coterminous in Ireland with the purposes of charity".[47] Again, in the Lands Tribunal, Harrison stated:

> "... that a trust is not charitable and is not entitled to the privileges which char-

---

[36] *ibid.*, p. 104; meaning "upon an analogous subject".

[37] *ibid.*, p. 105.

[38] *ibid.*, p. 108.

[39] [1932] N.I. 1.

[40] (1945) 27 T.C. 431.

[41] [1969] N.I. 3.

[42] Y.M.C.A. at p. 10.

[43] See *Governors of Campbell College Belfast v. Commissioner of Valuation for Northern Ireland* [1964] 2 All E.R. (H.L.) 705.

[44] *ibid.*, p. 149.

[45] *ibid.*, p. 176.

[46] *ibid.*, p. 188.

[47] *ibid.*, p. 186.

ity confers, unless it is within the spirit and intendment of the preamble to the Statute of Charles I."[48]

Finally, Carswell J. has stated that:

"... for the purposes of this judgment I do not find it necessary to investigate the relationship between that Statute and its Irish analogue of 1634 ... in which the wording of the preamble varies in a number of material respects, not least that concerning poverty.[49]

Carswell J. noted the cases referred to in the first paragraph of this section and, although he did not state the law was different, he left that avenue open to be argued if necessary in any later case.

1.3.7(iii) Conclusion

The statements in *Pemsel et al* that the law is the same in both jurisdictions remain unchallenged. Some Northern Ireland judgments can be construed as allowing a difference in definition. The tenor of all the judgments, however, is that the law is the same in this jurisdiction as in England.

Although there is no separate Northern Ireland charity law, this jurisdiction does have English charity law with a distinct Northern Ireland flavour. The favourable treatment of religious charities, the informal nature of regulation, the miscellaneous statutory and case law differences, all these factors, though not justifying a separate status, do demand recognition of a discernible Northern Ireland current within the broad flow of United Kingdom charity law.

1.4 CHARITY: THE GOVERNING PRINCIPLES

The law relating to charities is not a unified coherent body of jurisprudence. There are few absolute and comprehensive rules to govern and distinguish charities. The concept of a charity has eluded legislative and judicial definition for four centuries. To establish the content and boundaries of contemporary charity law it is still necessary to return to the founding statutes and case law.

There are, however, a few certainties to guide recognition of charities as such in law. Firstly, a charity must have purposes which fit within the spirit and intendment of the founding legislation[50] and under one of the four *Pemsel* heads. Secondly, it must be provided for the benefit of the public. Thirdly, unless exempted by statute, it must be exclusively charitable.

---

[48] *Trustees of the Aquinas Hall v. Commissioner of Valuation* VR/50/1965 at p. 8.
[49] *Re Dunlop* at p. 414.
[50] See, for example, *Re Worth Library* [1994] 1 I.L.R.M. 161, *per* Keane J., p. 191.

1.4.1 Rule against perpetuities

Charitable trusts may be perpetual. Therefore, the rule against inalienability, often used with effect against non-charitable trusts, does not apply. They are, nonetheless, subject to the rule against perpetuities to the extent that the initial vesting must clearly be bound to take place within the relevant perpetuity period; subject to the limited exception that a gift over from one charity to another is not subject to the rule[51] (see further, Chapter 6).

1.4.2 Charitable purposes

These remain as first identified and listed in the two seventeenth century statutes and as classified in *Pemsel*. This listing has always been treated as indicative rather than prescriptive.[52] A charitable purpose has never been strictly defined in law; the courts have tended to interpret this in accordance with contemporary social conditions. As a charitable purpose is defined relative to the prevailing social context, it therefore follows that a trust may lose its charitable status as circumstances change.[53] As explained by Wilberforce L.J. in *Scottish Burial Reform and Cremation Society v. Glasgow Corporation*[54]:

> "The purposes in question to be charitable, must be shown to be for the benefit of the public, or the community, in a sense or manner within the intendment of the Preamble to the statute, 43 Eliz. 1 c.4. The latter requirement does not mean quite what it says; for it is now accepted that what must be regarded is not the wording of the preamble itself, but the effect of decisions given by the courts as to its scope, decisions which have to keep the law as to charities moving according as new ideas arise or old ones become obsolete or satisfied."

Most often, determining the fact and nature of a charitable purpose is accomplished by reference to the objects stated in the relevant governing instrument.

1.4.2(i) Exclusive charitable intent

Where the terms of a gift are expressed unambiguously in favour of a specified charity, then the charitable intent of the donor is clearly stamped on the face of the gift and the court has no difficulty. Initially, the courts looked for such exclusive charitable intent and declined to save gifts as charitable where

---

[51] See, for example, *Christ's Hospital v. Grainger* (1849) 1 Mac. & G. 460; *Re Tyler* [1891] 3 Ch. 252.

[52] See *A.-G. v. Dublin Corp* (1827) 1 Bligh N.S. 312, *per* Lord Redesdale at p. 347 and *Incorporated Society in Dublin for Promoting English Protestant Schools in Ireland v. Richards* (1841) 1 Dr. & War. 258.

[53] See, for example, the anti-vivisection trusts in England and the principles then stated by Lord Simonds; and see further Chapter 11. Also, see, *IRC v. McMullen* [1981] A.C. 115E, *per* Hailsham L.J.

[54] [1968] A.C. 138 at p. 154.

the donor had failed to unequivocally and unambiguously state such intent or had expressed mixed intentions, some charitable and some not. Legislative intervention, in the form of the Charitable Trusts (Validation Act) 1954 and section 24 of the Charities Act (Northern Ireland) 1964, attempted to correct this judicial approach (see further, Chapter 15). However, as Harman J. asserted in *Re Gillingham*,[55] statute law could not authorise a judicial construing of charitable intent regardless of the form of words used by a donor:

> "In my judgment the Act was not intended to produce any such result. It was, as the long title shows, intended to cure dispositions whereby part of the trust fund is devoted to charitable purposes and part to purposes not charitable, or not wholly charitable, so long as the whole of the money could be devoted to charity by excluding words which were too wide or too vague."

In this jurisdiction, the ruling of Lowry J. in *Re McCullough*[56] may be taken as broadly endorsing that approach:

> "The contention that if the words are ambiguous, it would be wrong to give them a more technical and restricted meaning than they demand seems valid. . . ."

Where the objects are not specified, or are inadequately or ambiguously described, then determining charitable purpose rests on ascertaining charitable intention.

1.4.2(ii) Implied charitable intent[57]

There may be cases of a single gift where the court can find in the mind of the testator a general charitable intention. For example, in *Biscoe v. Jackson*[58] the court discovered such a general intention in a bequest to the poor of a parish. Again, in *Duffy v. Doyle*[59] the court concluded that there was no indication that the testator had any intention other than to benefit the recipient.

As an aid to discerning charitable intent the courts have developed a principle of "benignant construction". As stated in Tudor:

> "... the courts seek to save gifts where there is a charitable intention, although there are no clearly defined objects."[60]

For example, in *Re White*[61] a testator left a gift "to the following religious

---

[55] See *Re Gillingham Bus Disaster Fund* [1958] Ch. 300, *per* Harman J., p. 306.

[56] [1966] N.I. 73.

[57] For the constituents of charitable intention see: *Re Lysaght* [1966] Ch. 191 at 201–203; *Re Woodham's* [1981] 1 W.L.R. 493 at 500–502; *Re Stewart's Will Trusts* [1983] N.I. 283 at 297–98.

[58] (1887) 35 Ch. D. 460.

[59] Unreported, McWilliam J., May 9, 1989.

[60] See Tudor, *Charities* (London, Sweet & Maxwell, 1995) at p. 9.

[61] (1893) 2 Ch. 41.

societies *viz.* – to be divided in equal shares among them". No societies were named. The court was able to save the gift by effectuating the donor's charitable intention. It was clear that his intent was charitable, he had merely failed to name the actual objects of charity. In upholding the gift as charitable, Lindley J. explained:

"... a charitable bequest never fails for uncertainty ... the nomination of particular objects is only the mode and not the substance of a gift to charity."[62]

Again, in *Mills v. Farmer*[63] Lord Eldon said:

"... in all cases where the testator has expressed an intention to give to charitable purposes, if that intention is declared absolutely, and nothing is left uncertain but the mode in which it is to be carried into effect, the intention will be carried into execution by this court."

The rule will also be applied if property is left for dispersal among charities selected at the discretion of a specified person.[64]

If the wording of a charitable gift permits a construction which will save it, that construction will be adopted. In *Weir v. Crum-Brown*[65] the difficulty was how to construe a trust for the benefit of aged and indigent bachelors who had "shown practical sympathies either as amateurs or professionals in the pursuits of science in any of its branches". It was argued that such a phrase was so uncertain that the whole gift must be void for uncertainty. The House of Lords adopted the benignant approach and held that the trustees would be able to identify beneficiaries using a common-sense approach. Lord Loreburn L.C. stated that "there is not better rule but that a benignant construction will be placed upon charitable bequests".[66]

This benignant approach was pointedly endorsed by Keane J. in *Re Worth Library*[67] when he referred to what he termed "a principle of general application":

"The court leans in favour of charities and, consequently, will prefer a construction which gives effect to the testator's desire to benefit a stated objective rather than one which leads to a failure of the bequest."[68]

---

[62] (1893) 2 Ch. 41 at 53.

[63] (1815) 1 Mer. 55.

[64] See *Moggridge v. Thackwell* (1802) 7 Ves. 360, *Re Hill* (1909) 53 S.J. 228 and see further Chap. 19 on *cy-près*.

[65] [1908] A.C. 162.

[66] *ibid.*, p. 167, cited with approval in this jurisdiction by Lord Lowry L.C.J. in *Royal British Legion Attendants v. Commissioner of Valuation* [1979] N.I. 138 although Lord Lowry substituted 'beneficent' for 'benignant'.

[67] [1994] 1 I.L.R.M. 161.

[68] *ibid.*, p. 191.

1.4.2(iii) No charitable intent

The principle of "benignant construction" was not always sufficient to save a gift. In a line of cases from *Re Harwood; Coleman v. Innes*[69] to *Re Spence dec'd., Ogden v. Shackleton*[70] the courts in the United Kingdom have held that no charitable intent could be inferred from a testator's will.

1.4.3 Public benefit

The concept of public benefit lies at the heart of charity law. The voluntary redistribution of private wealth for public benefit underpins the history of philanthropy. The moral basis enabling the state to exempt a charitable trust from certain tax and other financial impositions rests on the premise that a donor has chosen not to confer a private benefit upon a personally selected recipient but to instead make an altruistic gift for the public good. Marrying a concept of public benefit broad enough[71] to remain responsive to pressures from an ever-changing social context, with philanthropic intent, and with administrative systems and procedures, to produce an integrated and distinctive body of jurisprudence has always been a central challenge for charity law. This problem was alluded to in *Cross v. The London Anti-vivisection Society*[72]:

> "Charity in law is a highly technical term. The method employed by the Court is to consider the enumeration of charities in the statute, bearing in mind that the enumeration is not exhaustive. Institutions whose objects are analogous to those mentioned in the statute are admitted to be charities; and again, institutions which are analogous to those already admitted by reported decisions are held to be charities. The pursuit of these analogies obviously requires caution and circumspection. After all the best that can be done is to consider each case as it arises, upon its own special circumstances. To be a charity there must be some public purpose – something tending to the benefit of the community."

1.4.3(i) Benefit

There must actually be a "benefit" entailed in the gift i.e. it must have some intrinsic value. The court, for example, in *Re Pinion*,[73] was quite certain that foisting a collection of "worthless junk" on the public would not constitute a benefit. Nor, in the case of *Re Shaw*,[74] did a gift for research into the creation

---

[69] [1936] 1 Ch. 285.

[70] [1979] Ch. 483.

[71] See *Attorney General v. Pearce* (1740) 2 Atk. 87, *per* Lord Hardwicke L.C. who declared that it was extensiveness that constitutes a public charity. See also, *Re McEnery, O'Connell v. Attorney General* [1941] I.R. 323, *per* Gavan Duffy J.

[72] [1985] 2 Ch. 501, *per* Chitty J. at 504.

[73] [1964] 1 All E.R. 890.

[74] [1938] 1 All E.R. 408.

of a new alphabet convince the court that the definition of "benefit" was fully satisfied. Nor would a gift of money to the poor for the purpose of admitting them to dog races be of benefit (*Re Hadji Daeing Tahiro binte Ogening Tedelleh's Estate* (1947) 14 M.L.J. 62 (Singapore CA).

1.4.3(ii) Private and public benefit

The benefit must also be conferred upon a public rather than a private grouping of recipients. Thus, for example, the court has been clear that any benefit entailed in acts of worship conducted by private contemplative religious orders accrues solely to the advantage of those so engaged; it does not benefit the public.[75] The Macnaghten classification, as has been noted, failed to make clear that for a trust to meet the legal requirements of a charity it must first disclose an element of benefit (*e.g.* the relief of poverty) and secondly, demonstrate that this will accrue to an element of the public.[76] The concept of public benefit varies considerably across the four *Pemsel* heads;[77] it is usually presumed for the first three (relief of poverty, advancement of education and advancement of religion) but requires to be proven for the fourth (other charitable purposes).

A great deal of charity law jurisprudence has accumulated around the criteria for differentiating between private and charitable trusts. As stated by Jenkins L.J. in *Re Scarisbrick*[78]:

"It is a general rule that a trust or gift in order to be charitable in the legal sense must be for the benefit of the public or some section of the public. . . ."

This became a statutory rule in England and Wales[79] and in Northern Ireland.[80]

The House of Lords suggested that two conditions should be satisfied before the beneficiaries could be called a "section of the community":

"... [firstly] the possible ... beneficiaries must not be numerically negligible and secondly that the quality which distinguishes them from other members of

---

[75] See *Gilmour v. Coats* [1949] A.C. 426. Note that in Ireland the judiciary have taken quite the opposite view; see, *Re Howley* (1940) I.R. 109. See further, Chap. 10.

[76] See Delany, H., *Equity and the Law of Trusts in Ireland* (Round Hall Sweet and Maxwell, Dublin, 1995), p. 244.

[77] See Lord Simonds in *Gilmour v. Coats* [1949] A.C. 426 at 437; Lord Somervell in *IRC v. Baddeley* [1955] A.C. 572 at 615; and Carswell J. in *Re Dunlop* [1984] N.I. 408 at 425-426.

[78] [1951] Ch. 622, pp. 648-9.

[79] See for example, Recreational Charities Act 1958, s. 1(1): "... the principle that a trust or institution to be charitable must be for the public benefit."

[80] See Recreational Charities Act (Northern Ireland) 1958, s.1(1) which replicates exactly the above provision.

the community so that they form by themselves a section of it, must be a quality which does not depend on their relationship to a particular individual."[81]

1.4.3(iii) Applying the rule

Two requirements are imposed. Firstly, the rule is not that all persons in the relevant class of the public should derive a benefit but only that they should all be eligible to do so. The House of Lords insisted on distinguishing between "a form of relief extended to the whole community yet by its very nature advantageous only to the few" (*e.g.* free surgical supplies would only really be of benefit to doctors) and "a form of relief accorded to a selected few out of a larger number equally willing and able to take advantage of it"[82] (*e.g.*, a bridge which only doctors are allowed to use).

The number constituting a sufficient proportion of "the public" has never been determined. The public benefit test will be met, and the trust in question will have charitable status, when, in the words of Lord Wrenbury in *Verge v. Somerville*,[83] the gift is made:

> "... for the benefit of the community or of an appreciably important class of the community. The inhabitants of a parish or town, or any particular class of such inhabitants may, for instance, be the objects of such a gift, but private individuals, or a fluctuating body of private individuals, cannot."

So, the class of persons who might benefit may be either a section of the public[84] or a class of the community,[85] or a section of the community.[86] The section of the public can be defined by reference to a geographical area which in the past could have been a town or parish (see *Shillington v. Portadown Urban District Council* (1911) 1 I.R. 247) but which today may encompass a housing estate (see, *Northern Ireland Housing Trust v. Commissioner of Valuation* [1970] N.I. 208, *Springhill Housing Action Committee v. Commissioner of Valuation* (1983) 5 N.I.J.B.). Conversely, it will not be met and the trust will not be charitable if those who might benefit are merely "a fluctuating body of private individuals".[87] The basis for this distinction between public and pri-

---

[81] See *Oppenheim v. Tobacco Securities Trust* (1951) A.C. 297 at 306.
[82] See *Inland Revenue Commissioners v. Baddeley* (1955) A.C. 572 at 592.
[83] [1924] A.C. 496 at 499.
[84] See *Re Tree* [1945] 1 Ch. 325 at 327, *per* Evershed J.
[85] See *Verge v. Somerville, op. cit., per* Lord Wrenbury at p. 499 and *IRC v. Baddeley* [1955] A.C. 572, *per* Lord Simmonds L.C. at p. 593.
[86] See, *Trustees of Sir HJ William's Trust v. IRC* (1944) 27 TC 409, *per* Lawrence L.J. at p. 418.
[87] See, *Re Drummond* [1914] 2 Ch. 91, *per* Eve J. at 97; *Verge v. Somerville op. cit., per* Lord Wrenbury at p. 499; *Trustees of Sir HJ William's Trust v. IRC, op. cit., per* Lawrence L.J. at p. 418; *Re Tree, op. cit., per* Evershed J. at p. 327; *IRC v. Baddeley, op. cit. per* Lord Simmonds LC at p. 593; and *Davies v. Perpetual Trustee Co. Ltd.* [1959] A.C. 439, *per* Lord Morton at p. 456.

vate classes is unsatisfactory because in practice fluctuating membership can be a characteristic of both types.

Secondly, the rule does not impose an absolute bar on any private benefit accruing from a charitable gift. It does, however, require that any private benefit conferred must be incidental. Where this is not the case, as in *IRC v. Oldham Training and Enterprise Council*,[88] the court will deny charitable status. In that case the court held that the Council's object of providing support services and advice to new businesses was so wide as to enable it to service the needs of private businesses without necessarily conferring any public benefit on the wider community.

1.4.3(iv) Applying the rule: Private classes

The courts have established that in certain instances a class can be defined as private rather than public, although this approach cannot be applied uniformly across all categories of charitable purpose. As MacDermott L.J. pointed out in *Trustees of the Londonderry Presbyterian Church House v. IRC*[89] there has never been a judicial consensus on what exactly might constitute a "section of the public". His colleague in the same case, Andrews L.C.J., was of the opinion that it was "nothing but a portion or division". It is clear, however, that once a class or section is so closely defined that its membership is fixed then it must be regarded as a private charitable trust.

So, where a class is closed, because it is constituted solely by a number of specified persons, then this is a private trust.[90] Where the class derives from a personal relationship with specified individuals, then this too is private. As explained by Lord Greene in *Re Compton*[91]:

> "A gift under which the beneficiaries are defined by reference to a purely personal relationship to a named *propositus* cannot on principle be a valid charitable gift. And this, I think, must be the case whether the relationship be near or distant, whether it is limited to one generation or is extended to two or three or in perpetuity. The inherent vice of the personal element is present however long the chain and the claimant cannot avoid basing his claim on it."

Again, if a sub-section of the public is so specifically delineated as to form a class within a class, then it must be considered private (see the narrow *Baddeley* rule). Finally, where a section of the public is defined in geographical terms this will be construed as being a public trust, but no other form of limitation is acceptable (see the wider *Baddeley* rule).

---

[88] [1996] S.T.C. 1218.
[89] (1945) 27 T.C. 431 at 439.
[90] See *Re Tree* [1945] 1 Ch. 325 p. 333, *per* Evershed J.
[91] [1945] 1 Ch. 123, [1945] 1 All E.R. 198 (C.A.).

1.4.3(v) Applying the rule: Public classes

The courts have come to recognise that certain restrictively defined classes will nonetheless be sufficiently "public" for the purposes of acquiring charitable status. Where the class is defined by locality, the intended recipients living in the same place, this will be deemed to meet the requirement of being "public".[92] Where the class is defined by its faith then the courts construe this as a non-personal relationship nexus and therefore intrinsically public in nature.[93] A class is often defined by the common relationship of its members as descendants of a named person or as descendants of particular group. The former is open to challenge on the grounds of the personal nexus test.[94] The latter may well satisfy the "public" requirement.[95] If the class is defined by membership of a particular profession then it is likely to be considered too closed.[96] But if members of a profession benefit incidentally, the trust may still be public. In a case concerning the charitable publication of law reports there was still public benefit because:

> "... it is an inevitable and indeed necessary step in the achievement of that benefit that the members of the legal profession are supplied with the tools of their trade."[97]

Common nationality may be sufficient to meet the "public" requirement.[98] Finally, though having been educated at a specified institution has been confirmed by precedent as defining a class as being "public" in nature, it manifestly has a closed membership and as such is open to future judicial or legislative challenge.

1.4.3(vi) The rule in relation to charitable purpose

The courts have inferred with increasing regularity that trusts falling within the first three *Pemsel's* categories will be "assumed to be for the benefit of the community and therefore charitable, unless the contrary is shown".[99] In fact, although this holds good for the first and third categories, trusts for the ad-

---

[92] See *Trustees of the Londonderry Presbyterian Church House v. IRC* [1946] N.I. 178, 183. Also, see the report of the Goodman Committee *Charity Law and Voluntary Organisations*, (1976), para. 40.

[93] See *IRC v. Baddeley, op. cit.* and a class of 'Methodists'.

[94] See *Oppenheim v. Tobacco Securities Trust Co. Ltd.* [1951] A.C. 297 and a maternal relationship.

[95] See *Re Tree, op. cit.* and a group of residents.

[96] See *Trustees of the Londonderry Presbyterian Church House v. IRC* [1946] N.I. 178, 183.

[97] *Incorporated Council of Law Reporting for England and Wales v. Attorney General* (1971) 3 All E.R. 1029 at 1035.

[98] See *Attorney General v. Stewart* (1872) L.R. 14 Eq. 17.

[99] See *National Anti-Vivisection Society v. IRC* [1948] A.C. 31, *per* Lord Simonds at p. 65.

vancement of education have quite often not qualified as charitable trusts because of a failure to satisfy the public benefit requirement. No such presumption applies in respect of gifts within the fourth category which attracts the most stringent application of the public benefit test;[100] in relation to trusts for the promotion of health, however, the test is applied most rigorously.[101] The court will rule that gifts not only to classes of specified individuals but also to those coming within either the "personal nexus" or the "narrow *Baddeley*" rule[102] will fail the public benefit test (see further, Chapter 12).

1.4.3(vii) Relativity of public benefit

Public benefit is a relative concept, ascertainable only in relation to the charitable purpose being served. What might be a section of the public for one purpose may not be for another. Lord Cross gave the following judgement in *Dingle v. Turner*[103]:

> "In truth the question whether or not the potential beneficiaries of a trust can fairly be said to constitute a section of the public is a question of degree and cannot be by itself decisive of the question whether the trust is a charity. Much must depend on the purpose of the trust. It may well be that, on the one hand, a trust to promote some purpose, *prima facie* charitable, will constitute a charity even though the class of potential beneficiaries might fairly be called a private class and that, on the other hand, a trust to promote another purpose, also *prima facie* charitable, will not constitute a charity even though the class of potential beneficiaries might seem to some people fairly to describable as a section of the public."

In particular, the public benefit test is substantially different (and easier) for trusts for the relief of poverty than for other trusts (see further, Chapter 8).

1.4.4 Public benefit and levying charges

Private profit is incompatible with public benefit. The essence of public benefit is that individuals receive benefits due to the bounty of the donor not because of a bargain with him.[104] An organisation which levies a charge for its services will be denied charitable status where the charge is such as to allow for a margin of profit to accrue to individuals in the organisation. However,

---

[100] *ibid.*

[101] See *Trustees of the Londonderry Presbyterian Church House v. IRC* [1946] N.I. 178 at 183.

[102] The effect of the House of Lords ruling in this case was to restrict judicial interpretation of what might constitute a sufficiently "public" section of the community to satisfy the test.

[103] [1972] A.C. 601 at 624.

[104] *Commissioners for Inland Revenue v. Society for the Relief of Widows and Orphans of Medical Men* (1926) 136 L.T. 60 at 65, see further Chap. 8.

there is no prohibition on levying a charge as such;[105] a vast range of charities such as those institutions providing education, entertainment or heath care impose admission fees. Nor is there a prohibition against making a profit provided the surplus proceeds are re-invested to further the charity's purposes. In this jurisdiction, the case of *Valuation Commissioner for Northern Ireland v. Lurgan Borough Council*,[106] which concerned the levying of admission fees to the council's indoor swimming pool, illustrates the effect of this caveat (see further, Chapter 9).

1.4.5 Public benefit: an objective test

The judiciary in this jurisdiction, in common with the rest of the United Kingdom, but unlike Ireland, adopt an objective test in determining whether or not a gift satisfies the public benefit test. The motive of a donor is irrelevant; the courts will focus firmly on deducing the nature of the gift from an objective appraisal of the facts. The relative merits of the objective and subjective approaches were expressly addressed in the anti-vivisection cases. In *Re Fouveaux*[107] Chitty J. had held that the abolition of vivisection was a charitable purpose because the testator's intention was to benefit the community; he ruled that it was not for the court to consider whether the community would in fact benefit. However, the House of Lords in *National Anti-Vivisection Society v. IRC*[108] expressly over-ruled the approach taken by Chitty J. The House declared that it was wrong to treat the intention of the testator as decisive; the public benefit test was to be applied by the court.[109]

The leading Irish case in this context is *Re Cranston, Webb v. Oldfield*[110] where the issue was whether or not a gift to certain vegetarian societies could be construed as charitable. Fitzgibbon L.J. held that if the donor believed it to be so then this view would be endorsed by the court, provided the society's purposes were not immoral or illegal.[111] This view was endorsed by Keane J.

---

[105] See, for example, *Incorporated Council of Law Reporting for England and Wales v. A-G* [1972] Ch. 73 C.A.

[106] [1968] N.I. 104, C.A.

[107] [1895] 2 Ch. 501.

[108] *op. cit.*

[109] But see the finding in *Re Price* (1943) 2 All E.R. 505 which considered a gift to the Anthroposophical Society. Cohen J. may not have found much validity in the views of the Society, but as long as they were not *contra bonos mores*, they would still be charitable. See also the decision in *Thornton v. Howe* (1862) 31 Beav. 14 at 20, "but if the tendency were not immoral, and although this court might consider the opinions sought to be propagated foolish or even devoid of foundation, it would no, on that account declare it void".

[110] [1898] 1 I.R. 431.

[111] See also, *Shillington v. Portadown UDC* [1911] 1 I.R. 247.

in *Re the Worth Library*[112] and illustrates the distinctive subjective approach of the Irish judiciary.

The factors preventing the public benefit test being satisfied, in the context of trusts for the advancement of education, have extended beyond blood ties or a personal nexus to a "nexus of contract". Trusts for the education of persons, or relatives of persons, in common employment have been found not to be charitable in nature.[113] This approach is in line with the recommendations of the Goodman Committee Report on *Charity Law and Voluntary Organisations*[114] (see further, Chapter 9).

1.4.6 Exclusiveness

Case law has long established that for a trust to be charitable its purposes must be confined exclusively to charitable purposes. If a donor's gift included both charitable and non-charitable purposes, and allowed for the possibility of trustees using some or all of the gift for non-charitable purposes, then the courts would refuse to recognise it as charitable.[115] One of the most important of the earlier charity cases was decided on this point. The residue of a will in *Morice v. Bishop of Durham*[116] was left "to such objects of benevolence and liberality as the Bishop of Durham in his own discretion shall most approve". Both Grant M.R. and Eldon L.C. held that "benevolence and liberality" were larger than "charity". Therefore, since the possibility existed of the gift being applied non-charitably, it was not exclusively charitable and therefore not charitable at all.

The exclusivity of charitable purposes continues to be a necessary component of charitable status in the law of England and Wales and in that of Northern Ireland. In the former jurisdiction, according to Tudor:

> "... a trust must not only be declared in favour of objects of a charitable nature, but it must also be expressed that in its application it is confined to such objects."[117]

In the latter, in *Trustees of Cookstown Roman Catholic Church v. Commissioners of Inland Revenue*[118] a trust was created for the purposes of "religious, educational and other parochial requirements" of Roman Catholics in Cookstown. Sheil J. then noted that had the words "and other parochial" been

---

[112] [1994] 1 I.L.R.M. 161.
[113] See *Oppenheim v. Tobacco Securities Trust Co. Ltd.* [1951] A.C. 297; also *George Drexler Ofrex Foundation Trustees v. IRC* [1966] Ch. 673 and *IRC v. Educational Grants Association Ltd.*[1967] Ch. 993.
[114] (1976) paras. 38 and 50(b).
[115] See *Boyle v. Boyle* (1877) I.R. 11 Eq 433.
[116] (1804) 9 Ves. 399, (1804) 10 Ves. 521 on appeal.
[117] Tudor, *Charities, op. cit.* at p. 134.
[118] (1953) 34 T.C. 350.

omitted it would have been possible to construe the uses as charitable. However, since "parochial" purposes could be non-charitable, the entire trust was not a charitable trust. Again, another Northern Ireland case[119] dealt with the "religious, moral, social and recreative life" of Presbyterians in Londonderry. It was held by the Court of Appeal that social and recreative life meant that the purposes were not exclusively charitable, and therefore it was not a charitable trust.

Both Northern Ireland decisions relied on English precedents. In *Dunne v. Byrne*[120] "bishops purposes" were construed as not exclusively charitable. In *Farley v. Westminster Bank*[121] it was held that the words "for parish work" would in their ordinary meaning include objects which were not charitable in the legal sense. The gifts were therefore not charitable. Not until the introduction of the Charitable Trusts (Validation) Act 1954 was this rule relaxed (see also, Chapter 15).

In Ireland the judiciary applied the rule requiring exclusiveness in charitable purposes with some equivocation,[122] particularly where the religious orders or institutions were involved[123] and has since been displaced by legislation. Modern statutory provisions[124] have intervened to relax the exclusivity rule in relation to charitable recognition, particularly under the religion head, although it continues to be fully applied when determining charitable exemption from rates.

This is an area where statute provisions have set charity law in Ireland on a different track from that prevailing in this jurisdiction.

---

[119] See *Trustees of the Londonderry Presbyterian Church House v. Commissioners of Inland Revenue* [1946] N.I. 178.

[120] [1912] A.C. 407.

[121] [1939] A.C. 340.

[122] See for example, *Jackson v. Attorney General* (1917) 1 I.R. 332 and *Moore v. The Pope* (1919) 1 I.R. 316.

[123] See for example: *Phelan v. Slattery* (1887) 19 L.R. Ir. 177; *Bradshaw v. Jackman* (1887) 21 L.R. Ir. 12; *Reichenbach v. Quin* (1888) 21 L.R. Ir. 138; *Armstrong v. Reeves* (1890) 25 L.R. Ir. 325; *Re Gibbons* [1917] 1 I.R. 448; *Re Ryan's Will Trusts* (1926) 60 I.L.T.R. 57; *Re Byrne* [1935] I.R. 782; *Re Keogh's Estate* [1945] I.R. 13.

[124] Charitable Trusts (Validation) Act (N.I.) 1954 and Charities Act (N.I.) 1964, s.24.

CHAPTER 2

The Legislative Framework

2.1 INTRODUCTION

The inherent jurisdiction of the High Court, exercising its traditional protective powers in relation to wards, lunatics and charities, was long considered to offer appropriate and sufficient authority for resolving issues affecting charitable trusts. A paternalistic use of judicial discretion coupled with access to prerogative powers gave this court the flexibility to build a case law structure of principles on the foundations laid by the early seventeenth century statutes. For centuries it seemed that legislation was unnecessary and would be an unjustifiable encroachment upon the protective jurisdiction of the High Court.

When legislative intervention eventually came to Northern Ireland it was only in order to introduce greater clarity to the management and procedures relating to issues affecting charities. That legislation exactly replicated provisions already in place in England and Wales and so brought with it the advantages of a common legislative framework for the two jurisdictions. The subsequent introduction of significant new charity law statutes in England and Wales, and indeed in Scotland, has left Northern Ireland with the most outdated legislative framework for charities in the United Kingdom. This in itself is real cause for concern as is the corollary that the law in Northern Ireland is now left out of alignment with that prevailing in all other U.K. jurisdictions. Northern Ireland has yet to have a formative charity law statute dealing with matters of definition, interpretation and coherence. There is now a pressing need for such legislation. There is also a need to introduce new legal functions to address matters such as registration, regulation and fundraising while also providing for efficient and effective synchronisation of the law governing charities in this and the other jurisdictions of the United Kingdom.

This chapter outlines the historical background of charity legislation. It then sketches the contemporary legislative framework. The current statutory provisions specifically framed to govern charities and related matters are then identified and briefly considered. In particular, attention is drawn to the basis for the continuing fundamental distinction in law between an organisation's eligibility for recognition as a charity and the eligibility of its premises for exemption from rates on charitable grounds. Those provisions which incidentally affect charities are also identified and their significance explained.

This chapter confines itself to identifying the legislative framework and considering the related legislative intent. It leaves to later a more detailed examination of statutory functions. It also alerts the reader to prevailing legal deficiency caused by legislative omission.

2.2 LEGISLATIVE HISTORY

Charity law on the island of Ireland, for most of its history, has been provided within a unified legislative framework. In its initial phase a common baseline was set by the 1601 and 1634 Acts which were judicially construed as legislative equivalents. As explained by Brady[1]:

> "The ... Irish statute of 1634 ... unlike its English counterpart, was primarily concerned with remedying the wholesale misappropriation of funds given for religious uses ... Despite this important difference between the two statutes, the Irish courts subsequently took the view that the Act of Charles was moulded on the 43rd Eliz and Sir Edward Sugden LC held in *Incorporated Society v. Richards* 4 Ir. Eq. Rep. 177 that whatever the latter gave in England was given by the former in this country. Thus the parameters of legal charity in both England and Ireland were drawn by the legislators of 1601."

In the final phase this framework consisted of the Charities Procedure Act 1812 and the Charitable Donations and Bequests (Ireland) Acts 1844, 1867 and 1871. Despite partition into two jurisdictions in 1920, this nineteenth century legislation continued to provide a common governing framework until the 1960s. The legislative history of charity law in this jurisdiction has been thoroughly traced and examined by others.[2] The following account draws from their work to provide a brief synopsis of the main developmental milestones.

2.2.1 The Statutes of Charitable Uses 1601 and 1634

These were reforming statutes imbued with a twofold legislative intent. Firstly, in order to fill the social care gap left by the dissolution of the monasteries and solicit the funds necessary to repair the damage caused by the ravages of war, they sought to channel philanthropic gifts towards identified priorities. Secondly, they aimed to reform the abuse of property donated to charity by listing the type of purposes which would be recognised as charitable. The corollary being a presumption that if a donor's purpose did not approximate to one on the list then it would not be treated in law as charitable.

The judiciary, however, never fully shared the concern of the Crown that

---

[1] See Brady, J.C., 'The Law of Charity and Judicial Responsiveness to Changing Social Need' in *Northern Ireland Legal Quarterly*, Belfast, vol. 27 No. 3 at pp. 200–201.

[2] See in particular: Hamilton, F.A.P., *The Law Relating to Charities*, Dublin, (1881), Brady, J.C., *Religion and the Laws of Charities in Ireland*, N.I.L.Q., Belfast, 1975; Delany, V.T.H., *The Law Relating to Charities in Ireland*, (revised ed.) 1962; and Mr Justice Ronan Keane, *Equity and the Law of Trusts in the Republic of Ireland*, 1988.

statute law should be used restrictively to prevent abuse. Centuries of judicial discretion, in interpreting gifts as coming within the "spirit and intendment" of the statute, served to broaden the range of charitable purposes in an empirical rather than logical fashion; by a process of precedent and analogy the judiciary greatly extended the original list. The Preamble to the 1601 Act, as ordered by the ruling in *Pemsel* and further developed through judicial interpretation, laid a common statutory foundation for charity law in England and in Ireland. For three centuries and more, this foundation facilitated a commonality of judicial approach towards charities on both islands.

2.2.2 Irish Parliament statutes

Before 1800 and the Act of Union, the Irish Parliament had jurisdiction to pass legislation governing the entire island of Ireland. The most important example of this being the Irish Statute of Pious Uses 1634. The Irish Parliament also introduced the Charitable Uses Act (Ireland) 1763 which still provides the necessary authority in certain situations where the governors of charitable institutions resign and are replaced by newly elected governors.[3]

2.2.3 Pre-partition: Westminster statutes

After 1800 until partition, legislation was passed by the British Parliament at Westminster. This took two forms. Firstly, there was legislation which applied to the entire United Kingdom. For example, the Trustee Appointment Act 1850 which provided for the appointment of new trustees of specific types of religious/educational charities.[4] Secondly, there was legislation passed by Westminster specifically for Ireland. For example, the Educational Endowments (Ireland) Act 1885 which set out provisions for regulating and modifying charitable gifts for the purpose of education. A great deal of charity law legislation took the latter form.

2.2.3(i) The Charities Procedure Act 1812

The most usual method of commencing proceedings in respect of a charity was to lodge a petition under the Charities Procedure Act, 1812 ("Sir Samuel Romilly's Act").[5] This statute enabled a petitioner in any case of an actual or alleged breach of a charitable trust to take proceedings for its enforcement. It also allowed petitions to be presented for court assistance in the administration of a charitable trust. The procedure required at least two persons to state such complaint and pray such relief as the nature of the case required. The

---

[3] See s.17, which is the only part of this Act which remains in force today
[4] s. 3 and s. 1.
[5] Statute 52 Geo. 111 Cap. 101. Repealed by the Charities Act (N.I.) 1964.

Lord Chancellor, the Lord Keeper, or the Lords Commissioners for the custody of the Great Seal, could then make such order and award such costs as seemed appropriate.

The application was made by plenary summons, the Attorney-General being joined as a party. The prior consent of the Attorney-General was necessary and could be obtained by sending the summons (with a fee of five guineas) to the office of the solicitor to the Attorney-General, with the certificate of approval to be filed by the Attorney-General. Such consent was not necessary where the application was made by the Commissioners.[6] Two or more persons, with a direct interest in the charity, had to present the summons. The summons was addressed to the High Court and entitled *In the Matter of 52 Geo. III cap. 101 and in the Matter of the X Charity.*

2.2.3(ii) The Charitable Donations and Bequests (Ireland) Acts 1844, 1867, 1871

The Charitable Donations and Bequests (Ireland) Act 1844 was the principal act governing the law relating to charities until 1964. Entitled "An Act for the more effectual application of Charitable Donations and Bequests in Ireland" it was intended to reform abuses in the use of charitable gifts. The legislative intent was to centralise responsibility for responding to charity law issues. Establishing the Commission of Charitable Donations and Bequests (the Commission) proved to be the most important contribution of this legislation. The role and responsibilities of the Commission, as established under the 1844 Act, have continued in Ireland while being transferred to the Charities Branch in Northern Ireland. In neither jurisdiction has their been any fundamental change in the nature and scope of the statutory authority provided. Now as then, throughout the island, that authority is essentially facilitative rather than regulatory in nature. This is apparent from the vesting of powers rather than duties in both Commission and Charities Branch (see, further, Chapter 5).

2.2.3(iii) The Educational Endowments (Ireland) Act 1885

The educational endowments schemes were originally made towards the end of the nineteenth century under the 1885 Act to govern certain educational charities. The subsequent amendment of these schemes has been conducted under the powers provided by the 1885 Act. There are now some 100 such charities which need to be wound up but for which no statutory power is available.

---

[6] Under either ss. 6, 8, 9, or 10 of the 1871 Act. Repealed by the Charities Act (N.I.) 1964.

2.2.4 Post-partition: Westminster and Stormont statutes

After partition in 1920, until the proroguing of the Stormont Assembly in 1972, the two legislatures of Westminster and Stormont contributed to shaping the statutory framework in this jurisdiction. Stormont generated a considerable amount of law affecting charities. Most important was the Charities Act (N.I.) 1964. Other significant legislation included the House to House Charitable Collections Act (N.I.) 1952, the Recreational Charities Act (N.I.) 1958 (which extended slightly the definition of "charitable") and the Charitable Trusts (Validation) Act (N.I.) 1954.[7] Section 1(1) of the latter states the legislative intent as being to save trusts which are only partly charitable.

The provisions of the English Trustee Investments Act 1961 were extended to cover this jurisdiction by the Trustee (Amendment) Act (N.I.) 1962.

Most of these pieces of Stormont legislation virtually replicated corresponding English legislation. For example, the Charities Act (N.I.) 1964 and the Recreational Charities Act (N.I.) 1958 had their counterparts in the English Charities Act 1960 and the Recreational Charities Act 1958. This pattern maintained, to a degree, a level of harmonisation between Northern Ireland and Great Britain in relation to charity law. During this period Westminster also generated legislation which, though affecting the whole of the United Kingdom, proved to have only minimal impact on Northern Ireland charity law.[8]

After Stormont was prorogued in 1972, with all legislative power reverting to Westminster, some legislation was created by Order in Council specifically for Northern Ireland. An example of this was the Charities (N.I.) Order 1987 which made some minor amendments to the Charities Act (N.I.) 1964. This period also witnessed some Westminster generated legislation that applied equally throughout the United Kingdom including Northern Ireland. For example, a small part of the Charities Act 1993 applies in Northern Ireland.[9]

2.3 Contemporary Legislation Governing Charities

The Charities Act (Northern Ireland) 1964 marked a point of departure in this jurisdiction from the common statutory framework shared until then with Ireland. The departure was consolidated by the introduction of the Charities (N.I.) Order 1987. Together they brought sweeping changes and placed charity law in Northern Ireland on a new statutory platform. A raft of previous legislation was repealed. Among the statutes consigned to history were the Charities Pro-

---

[7] Repealed statutes include the Charitable Trustees (Incorporation) Act (N.I.) 1961 whose terms are now subsumed within ss. 10–11 of the Charities Act (N.I.) 1964.

[8] The only real incidents being part of the Finance Act 1960, the Crown Estate Act 1961 and various miscellaneous taxing statutes.

[9] See s. 10 and s. 15(2) by virtue of s. 100 of the Charities Act 1993.

cedure Act 1812, the Charitable Donations and Bequests (Ireland) Acts of 1844, 1867 and 1871, the Working Classes Dwellings Act 1890 and the Charitable Donations and Bequests (Amendment) Act 1955.

2.3.1 The Charities Act (Northern Ireland) 1964

Self-described as:

> "An Act to replace, with new provisions, certain existing enactments relating to charities; to make further provision with respect to gifts to charity and gifts for mixed charitable and non-charitable purposes; and for purposes connected with those matters."

The 1964 Act is in three parts, it largely replicated the provisions of similar legislation enacted in England in 1960 and was based on the recommendations of the Nathan Committee.[10] In recent years the statutory framework thus provided for charities has seemed increasingly inadequate.[11]

2.3.1(i) Part 1: the statutory powers relating to charities

The current role and powers of the Charities Branch, as outlined in Part I of the 1964 Act and amended by the 1987 Order, were then framed in favour of the Ministry of Finance. Subsequently, that statutory authority has been transferred from the Ministry of Finance to the Department of Health and Social Services and most recently to the Department for Social Development, though the powers have remained delegated to and implemented by the Charities Branch. While these powers have been extended they do not differ in any fundamental respect from those conferred on the Commissioners of Charitable Donations and Bequests under the nineteenth century legislation. The current statutory authority of the Charities Branch in Northern Ireland is very similar to that of its counterpart in the adjoining jurisdiction.

The Charities Branch provides its services gratuitously and operates mainly as an advisory body with limited statutory powers to protect and preserve charity funds. Its powers in terms of monitoring and investigation of charities are much more closely circumscribed than those of its English counterpart.

Mostly, Part 1 identifies the circumstances and procedures whereby the Charities Branch should exercise its responsibilities in relation to donors, trus-

---

[10] See *Report of the Committee on the Law and Practice relating to Charitable Trusts*, London, HMSO, 1952, Cmd. 8710 which led to the government White Paper *Government Policy on Charitable Trusts in England and Wales* and then to the introduction of the 1960 Act.

[11] See, for example, the National Council of Social Services, *Charity Law and Voluntary Organisations*, (the 'Goodman Report'), London, Bedford Square Press, 1976 and the Deakin Commission, *Meeting the Challenge of Change, Voluntary Action into the 21st Century*, (the 'Deakin Report'), NCVO, 1996.

tees, the management of charitable gifts and the administration of charities. Particular attention is given to the powers of the Charities Branch where charitable property and *cy-près* schemes are concerned. Coercive involvement in the affairs of a charity is usually made subject to the prior approval of the Attorney-General. In particular, under section 3 of 1964 Act where the Charities Branch has "reasonable grounds to believe that any property belonging to a charity or given for charitable purposes may have been concealed, misapplied or withheld" it may, "with the consent of the Attorney-General", order that related books, records deeds or papers be furnished to it. Under section 2 it falls to the Attorney-General, rather than the Charities Branch, to institute court proceedings in relation to a charity (see further, Chapter 5).

2.3.1(ii) Part II: application of property cy-près, imperfect trusts etc

Under sections 22 to 24 the traditional power to create *cy-près* schemes to save gifts for charitable purposes is extended to include a number of specified circumstances. These powers may be exercised by the court or by the Charities Branch. Other provisions deal with retrieving property the subject of imperfect trusts for charity where practicable. Section 25 deals at some length with common investment funds.

2.3.1(iii) Part III: miscellaneous provisions as to charity trustees

Sections 23 to 29 deal briefly with powers and duties of trustees in certain circumstances, the right to deposit deeds, etc. with the Charities Branch and making certain specific applications to court. In relation to the latter, the capacity of the Charities Branch to make such application without the consent of the Attorney-General, is particularly significant.

2.3.1(iv) Part IV: supplementary

The concluding sections deal largely with matters of interpretation and the consequences of exercising or refusing to exercise the powers provided. Section 30 provides that the Probate Office must annually certify all charitable gifts to the Charities and outlines the procedure to be followed.

2.3.2 The Charities (Northern Ireland) Order 1987

In the words of the accompanying explanatory note:

> "This Order gives the trustees of certain charities additional powers, amends the Charities Act (Northern Ireland) 1964 and makes other changes relating to charities in Northern Ireland."

The note then goes on to explain the powers, amendments and other changes.

Article 3, for example, enables trustees of charities for the relief of poverty to alter the objects of their charity in certain circumstances while Articles 4 and 5 permit trustees of very small charities to transfer property and be exempted from restrictions on capital expenditure, subject to certain conditions. Articles 6, 7 and 8 amend provisions in the 1964 Act, relating to finances, land valuation and annual reports. Article 9 restricts an incorporated charity from altering its instruments and Article 10 provides for an inter-Departmental transfer of certain powers.

These adjustments served primarily to bring the law into closer alignment with that then prevailing in England and Wales.

2.3.3 The Recreational Charities Act (N.I.) 1958

This statute replicates the provisions of its English precursor the Recreational Charities Act 1958. Both were a direct response to the ruling of the House of Lords in *Baddeley* and gave effect to a legislative intent to safeguard the charitable status of recreational facilities such as women's institutes and village halls. There is no equivalent legislation in Ireland (see further, Chapter 14).

2.4 REFORM OF CHARITY LAW IN NORTHERN IRELAND

The legislation governing charities in Northern Ireland is now almost 40 years old and appears quite dated. The scale of change affecting charities throughout the United Kingdom has been such as to require substantive legislative reform in England and Wales and to a lesser extent in Scotland. This process of reform is continuing and further legislation is anticipated. Charities in Northern Ireland have been fully exposed to the same pressures but the law has remained unchanged. It has to be questioned whether a legal framework designed in the 1960s, and found to be deficient elsewhere in the United Kingdom, remains an appropriate and sufficient basis for facilitating and governing charitable activity in Northern Ireland. It is unquestionable that when the current preparations in Scotland and in the Republic of Ireland to introduce new legislation are complete and their charity laws have been modernised, the lax regulatory regime in this jurisdiction will then leave it very vulnerable to abuses prohibited in all other jurisdictions of these islands.

The perceived need to modernise the law of charity[12] has attracted considerable academic and professional attention in recent years. There now exists a

---

[12] See, for example: the report of the Goodman Committee, *Charity Law and Voluntary Organisations* (to the Goodman Report), Bedford Square Press, 1976; the Ontario Law Reform Commission, *Report on the Law of Charities*, Canada, 1995; the report of the Commission on the Future of the Voluntary Sector, *Meeting the Challenge of Change, Voluntary Action into the 21st Century* (or, the Deakin Report), NCVO, London, 1996;

sound body of material to signpost the direction for law reform in Northern Ireland and to provide a more comprehensive source of information than is possible within the confines of this book, for those seeking a detailed examination of the complex issues involved. However, no programme of reform would be adequate if it failed, at the very least, to address matters of registration, regulation, fundraising, trading and public service provision (see also, Chapter 17).

2.4.1 The case for reform: separate charitable status

The issue of what precisely distinguishes charities from other voluntary organisations so as to justify their preferential treatment - in tax and related financial matters, across a range of legislation and within charity law – has attracted attention.[13] It is too complicated a matter for this context, but some aspects may be briefly mentioned. Given that in essence a charity has objects

---

the Charity Law Reform Advisory Group, *Charity Law Reform*, draft report, NCVO, 2000.

[13] See, in particular, the report of the Ontario Law Commission, *ibid.*, Chaps. 6, 7 and 8. The complexity of the issues involved may be judged from the fact that the matter was referred to the Commission in 1989, the resulting report ran to more than 700 pages and was submitted in 1996. The mandate of the Commission, perhaps offering a useful model for charity law review in this jurisdiction, was as follows:

I. To review existing common law and statute enactments governing charities, and, if found necessary, to recommend legislative enactments on any or all issues and all aspects of the law and practice related to charitable organisations operated in Ontario, including:

1. The definition of charity;
2. The method of formation of a charity by incorporation or otherwise, and the jurisdiction to supervise this initial procedure;
3. The control or review of the actions of charities, by whom such reviews should be performed, and through which forum;
4. The rights of charitable organisations to carry on business to earn funds to support their charitable objects;
5. The penalties to be imposed by fine, imprisonment, cancellation of charters or cancellation of the right to operate in Ontario following a failure to comply with legislative enactments;
6. The obligations and responsibilities of officers and directors of charitable organisations and the rights of members;
7. The rights of charitable organisations with respect to the holding, financing, leasing or conveying property, real or personal;
8. Surrender and revival of charitable corporations;
9. The question of disclaimer by charitable organisations;
10. The modification and termination of charitable trusts including corporations, the Variation of Trusts Act, the Accumulations Act, the Perpetuities Act and the Rule in *Saunders v. Vautier*.
11. The application of the doctrine of extra-territoriality;
12. Funding by government grant as compared with contributions or gifts from the public.

which must be fitted under one of the four *Pemsel* heads and also be dedicated to the benefit of the public, is this so different from the work of many state bodies, other voluntary organisations or the Roman Catholic or other Church *per se*? There is also the fact that service provision for the socially disadvantaged increasingly occurs in the context of a "mixed economy of care" where partnerships between charities and other statutory or voluntary bodies necessarily blurs the nature of the charitable contribution. Many charities have spawned trading arms which are in direct competition with private for profit bodies, does this not compromise the integrity of their position? Is there, anyway, a meaningful difference between philanthropy and charity? Should there continue to be a separate status for charities?

Traditionally, the law has rested its case for separate charitable status on a duty owed to the donor to safeguard the integrity of his or her gift and to ensure its use, perpetually, for the purpose intended. This duty was embedded in the law of trusts. Arguably, any attempt to now unravel the complex law of trusts would cause more problems than it would solve. Anyway, each and every charity owes its existence to the gift of a donor and the selflessness of that gesture should continue to attract specific recognition in law. It is one of the distinguishing hallmarks of a democracy that individuals are free to dispose of their property as they choose; when that choice is exercised for the public good it deserves charitable status. The case for separate charitable status continues to rest on the need to encourage and then protect the selfless gifts of donors.

2.4.2 The case for reform: charitable purpose

It is often maintained[14] that charity law is artificially constrained by the straightjacket imposed by the statute of 1601, the *Pemsel* classification and its subsequent common law development by analogous cases. It is argued that the resulting body of law is fatally flawed by the lack of any definition as to what exactly constitutes a "charity", an absence of integrating principles and by the need for a comprehensive code consolidating the distinguishing characteristics and the powers and duties of all charities. How, it is asked, can an Elizabethan statute provide an effective and appropriate basis for governing charities in the twenty first century? The statute's provisions in respect of matters such as dowries for unmarried women and the repair of bridges are simply not relevant to modern social conditions. One response is to point out that four hundred years later charities are flourishing and are undeniably making a significant contribution to improving our society. The law has demonstrated its capacity to evolve in keeping with changing social conditions. But it must be conceded

---

[14] See submissions to the Charity Law Reform Advisory Group established by the NCVO in 1998.

that there are grounds for considering a statutory broadening of matters deemed to constitute charitable purposes.

Again, it is not possible in the context of this book to do justice to the wealth of material available on this debate[15] but some of the more prominent aspects can be briefly mentioned. There is a question as to whether some purposes currently held to be charitable should continue to be so; most usually this discussion focuses on the provision of public utilities, services which benefit the more affluent and on religious purposes. Alternatively, some purposes currently denied such recognition are viewed as meriting charitable status: lobbying for political change, community development, promoting self-help and trading are among those usually cited. In addition, it is argued that subsidiary rules governing matters such as what constitutes "exclusively charitable", "the public" and the application of the "public benefit test" across the four *Pemsel* heads of charity should be statutorily clarified. In keeping with the tenor of the proposals drafted by the NCVO working party[16] the present authors would similarly suggest that a rigorous and uniform application of a statutorily defined 'public benefit test' to all charities would clarify the issue of which can be most appropriately regarded as giving effect to charitable purposes in the context of contemporary social conditions. It should be added, given the fact and nature of social divisions in Northern Ireland, that a strong argument exists for ensuring the application of any such public benefit test is used to promote cross-community initiatives and consolidate the development of civil society.

2.4.3 The case for reform: co-ordination of government agencies

The reform debate most usually focuses on the question of whether a new agency should be introduced with registration and/or regulatory responsibilities (see further, below). However, charities are already required to have dealings with an array of government bodies, each with a different set of administrative rules, which impose time and cost overheads and necessarily detract from charitable activity. Agencies such as the Charities Branch, the Probate Office, the Inland Revenue, the Valuation and Lands Agency, the Customs and Excise and the Registry of Companies are among those with which charities are likely to have on-going negotiations (see further, Chapter 5). At present there is no statutory duty for these agencies to co-ordinate their

---

[15] *ibid.*, also see the Ontario report, *op cit.*, at Chaps. 13 and 14. Note, also, the comment made in this jurisdiction by Keeton, G.W. and Sheridan, L.A. some thirty years ago that:
"... it is desirable, if not essential to preserve a single definition of charity, whether for purposes of validity, rating or taxation; but that does not mean that all charities should necessarily be treated equally for all purposes".
The Modern Law of Charities (2nd ed., Belfast, NILQ, 1971) at p. 51.

[16] *op cit.*

efforts, resulting in charities often having to provide the same information repeatedly to a number of agencies. It should be possible to introduce or streamline inter-agency procedures and thereby avoid duplication of administrative costs being imposed upon charities.

2.4.4 The case for reform: the role of the court

Charity law in Northern Ireland is very obviously administrative law which rarely requires recourse to the courts. The very few reported cases are almost invariably concerned with issues of eligibility for rates exemption. The reasons for this are partly to do with the effectiveness of agencies such as the Charities Branch in filtering out and resolving issues which might otherwise go to court and the prohibitive expense involved for a charity to initiate proceedings in the High Court. As a consequence, the judiciary have been largely excluded from opportunities to shape the evolution of charity law in this jurisdiction. The singular strength of the common law, its capacity to evolve through individual cases to address changing social conditions, is therefore seriously impaired. This, coupled with the absence of any legislative initiative, has resulted in the law remaining particularly inert in Northern Ireland.

If charity law is to retain the value of its case law heritage, escape legislative definition and eventual encoding, then new means must be found for exposing the full range of contemporary practice issues to judicial scrutiny, or perhaps to the type of reported scrutiny undertaken by the Charity Commission in England and Wales (see also, Chapter 3).

2.4.5 The case for reform: registration and regulation

The perceived need for new legislation to modernise charity law in Northern Ireland led to the Charities Branch launching a formal review in 1995. This review, conducted by means of a widely circulated discussion paper,[17] invited comment on the following proposals:

> "A public register of charities, with which all Northern Ireland charities would have to register. Larger charities would have to produce an annual return.
>
> The Department should have power to charge fees for registration.
>
> The Department should have power to exchange information with the RUC, Inland Revenue, and other official bodies.
>
> Charities should be required to produce annual accounts to a specified standard.
>
> Charities should be required to have their annual accounts audited or examined.

---

[17] See Charities Branch, VAU, *Consultation Document on Charity Law in Northern Ireland* (DHSS, Belfast, 1995).

Charities should be required to establish and maintain effective systems of internal controls.

The Department should have power to make regulations specifying the requirements concerning accounts, audits and reports in detail.

Charities should be obliged to furnish copies of their reports and accounts to the public on request.

The Department should have power to require a charity to change its name where it duplicates another charity's or is liable to mislead.

Various persons should be disqualified from acting as charity trustees.

The limits within which small charities can alter their purposes, amalgamate, or expend their capital without undue formality should be relaxed.

In most cases, charities should be allowed to dispose of property without applying to the Department for a power to do so.

The Department should be able to grant a power to dispose of property where one is not strictly required if this is in the charity's interests.

Only one statutory notice should be required in connection with schemes made by the Department, and it may be dispensed with in certain cases.

The Department should have power to transfer untraceable charities' dormant bank accounts to other charities.

The Department should not automatically scrutinise all Wills containing charitable bequests.

The limit of £50,000 on the Department's power to make schemes to change charities' purposes should be removed.

The limit of £2,500 on the Department's power to make schemes to deal with misdescribed charitable bequests should be removed.

Controls should be introduced to prevent professional fundraisers from exploiting charities.

The present systems for licensing street and house-to-house collections should be replaced with a new system covering all public collections.

It should be an offence to fail to carry out a public charitable collection in accordance with the proposed system.

The Department should have power to make regulations prescribing the details of the proposed system.

The RUC should be empowered to identify collectors and seize the proceeds of unauthorised collections, and collecting charities should be required to furnish accounts to the RUC.

The Attorney-General's role should not be altered.

The Department should have the power to vary the limits on Northern Ireland charities' investment powers.

The Department should have the power to wind up charities established under the Educational Endowments (Ireland) Act 1885.

A number of minor technical changes in the charity law are required."

This somewhat conservative list of legal functions identified as requiring up-dating proved to be a step too far for those consulted and, faced with wide-spread resistance, the proposals were dropped (see also, Appendices).

However, the argument for a degree of charity law reform, limited perhaps to the issues of registration and regulation, remains to be addressed. It might be added that although it is customary to link these two functions they could be de-coupled. A system for registration, whether formal or informal, would not necessarily require a system for regulation.

2.4.5(i) Registration

The lifespan of charities varies greatly; some exist for centuries, others for days. In Northern Ireland, many hundreds of new charities appear every year and perhaps as many cease to exist. It would be difficult to design any system which could provide a definitive record of current "live" charities. However, the present situation whereby no responsibility rests upon any government body to maintain a register of such organisations is unhelpful. Aside from those registered as companies or as friendly societies, there is no means of readily identifying charities in Northern Ireland which, after all, are individu-ally eligible for significant tax concessions and cumulatively hold assets and generate income equivalent to the industrial sector. The argument for registra-tion could rest entirely on the point that eligibility for money from the public purse should be accompanied by an obligation to disclose to the public the identity and status of the recipient.

There is also a public confidence argument. The confidence and trust which the general public want to place in charities could only be boosted if a means were available for members of the public to choose, access and challenge charities. They, in turn, have nothing to lose from subscribing to a list of bod-ies engaged in laudable public benefit activity. The issue of whether any such a list should be formal or informal is directly related to the public confidence argument. The list will instil confidence only if it carries the stamp of govern-ment approval; because it has to serve the function of providing a record of "live" and verified charities, it has to be both formal and mandatory. The pub-lic and all relevant agencies will then be able to check the credentials of any organisation engaged, or purporting to be engaged, in charitable activity. Clearly, the degree of public confidence will be proportionate to the standing of the list: the more complete, up-to-date and impartially but thoroughly vet-ted the greater will be the reliance upon it; the fewer categories of "excepted" or "exempt" charities the more public credibility it will attract.

2.4.5(ii) Regulation

In Northern Ireland, many charities are already subject to a regulatory regime. Increasingly, charities are opting for company status and accepting the scrutiny from the Registry that goes with it. However, very many remain unincorporated and even when a charity does become a company it is then scrutinised from the perspective of compliance with company law rather than charity law. Charities, or bodies purporting to be charities, may came to the attention of the RUC, the Inland Revenue, the Valuation and Lands Agency or the Charities Branch for conduct which is particular to the remit of that agency but no one agency holds an inspection brief to detect bad practice in respect of all charities. While all charities are subject to the overview of the Charities Branch, this is essentially a facilitative rather than a regulatory remit; although the agency does have some interventionist powers, they are exercised in a reactive rather than proactive fashion. Currently, there is no regulatory system specifically for charities in Northern Ireland.

Again, the inescapable point is that this jurisdiction is no more immune than any other in the United Kingdom from the type of abuse and irregularity in the affairs of charities that has necessitated the introduction of a regulatory system in those other jurisdictions. Abuses and irregularities have already been detected among some charities in Northern Ireland. It is those remaining undetected and the knowledge that no system exists for their detection which must cause most concern. Arguably, as the existing regulations in England and Wales together with the proposed regulations in Scotland become more effective, so the probability increases of charity abuse being shifted to Northern Ireland. The Charities Branch does much to inform and promote good practice but there is also a clear need for an inspectoral function, perhaps at arm's length remove from the facilitative function, which is focussed squarely on ensuring compliance with the law and with an agreed code of standards.

The practice implications arising from current legislative deficiencies are examined further in the appropriate context (see, for example, Chapters 16, 17 and 18).

2.5 CONTEMPORARY LEGISLATION GOVERNING FUNDRAISING

There is no specific legislative framework designed to govern fundraising for charitable purposes. Such statute law as exists is dated, addresses fundraising for charitable and other purposes and is mostly concerned to outline the authorising procedures rather than to identify and proscribe abuses. The law is to be found in a number of different statutes each dealing with fundraising in a particular setting. So, for example, house to house collections, street collections and small-scale local lotteries continue to be successful methods of fundraising and are the subject of separate statutes. However, such traditional means are now supplemented by more professional and entertaining fundraising techniques with electronic capacity to attract and possibly transfer overseas, within a very short period,.a large volume of funds. Current legislation in Northern Ireland is wholly insufficient and inappropriate to govern modern fundraising for charitable purposes.

2.5.1 The Police, Factories etc (Miscellaneous Provisions) Act 1916

This legislation provides the police with the power to make regulations governing street collections. Under its provisions two sets of regulations governing street collections have been issued and remain in effect; they direct that a street collection can only be carried out after a permit has been obtained from the RUC (see further, Chapter 18).

2.5.2 The House to House Charitable Collections Act (N.I.) 1952

This legislation imposes constraints on fundraising by means of house to house collections whether undertaken for charitable or for non-charitable purposes. This is again largely controlled through the issue of permits for such collections by the RUC (see further, Chapter 18).

2.5.3 The Betting, Gaming, Lotteries and Amusements (N.I.) Order 1985

This statute and its associated subordinate legislation prescribe the circumstances in which gaming and lotteries will be deemed to be lawful for fundraising purposes. The 1985 Order was the subject of a formal Department review in 1997 (see further, Chapter 18).

2.5.4 The Lotteries Regulations (N.I.) 1994

The national lottery was established in the United Kingdom by the National Lottery Act 1993. In keeping with such lotteries in other countries, it offers prizes of much greater value than traditional small-scale local lotteries and does so through draws held at fixed and frequent intervals. It is subject to specific statutory requirements regarding such matters as the proportion of income expended on running costs and the furnishing of accounts. It is not subject to the provisions of the Betting, Gaming, Lotteries and Amusements (N.I.) Order 1985 (see further, Chapter 18).

2.5.5 Professional fundraisers and commercial participants

In England and Wales, specific provisions exist in the Charities Act 1992 to regulate what are termed professional fundraisers and commercial participants.

No legislation exists at all in Northern Ireland to regulate the relationship between charities and fundraisers, or between fundraisers and the public.

2.6 CONTEMPORARY LEGISLATION GOVERNING CHARITABLE EXEMPTION FROM RATES

It is in the legislation governing charitable exemption from rates that the charity law of Ireland and Northern Ireland are most noticeably different. As in both jurisdictions it is this aspect of the law which generates most litigation; the nature of the difference is therefore important.

2.6.1 The Rates (N.I.) Order 1977

The twin problems of 'user' (*i.e.* the nature and degree of the use being made of an hereditament) and "exclusively charitable purposes" (*i.e.* the extent to which the occupying organisation was engaged in charitable purposes) were, for at least a century, the judicial determinants of charitable exemption from rates. In Ireland they continue to be so. In Northern Ireland legislative intervention has removed both problems.

The Rating and Valuation (Amendment) Act (N.I.) 1956 introduced the concept of "apportionment" to rating law in this jurisdiction. This laid to rest the line of case law which held that the entire hereditament in question must be used only for charitable purposes. Subsequently, the Rates (N.I.) Order 1972 granted eligibility for rates exemption for bodies whose main objects, but not necessarily its subsidiary objects, were charitable. This removed the necessity to prove that the occupying organisation was exclusively charitable.

The 1977 Order repealed the Rates (N.I.) Order 1972. It provides a list of exempt hereditaments. It gives 50 per cent exemption for residential use of a hereditament by a member of the charity. It allows for apportionment. It states that any use for profit is non-exempt unless it directly facilitates the charitable ends. It also provides that occupation by a religious office holder in furtherance of his duties is 50 per cent exempt. Finally, it relaxes the test from "exclusively charitable" to "mainly charitable" (see further, Chapter 21).

2.7 CONTEMPORARY LEGISLATION GOVERNING LEGAL STRUCTURES FOR CHARITIES

Charities are subject not only to legislation designed explicitly and solely to govern their activities but may also come within the statutory scope of provisions designed generally for organisations. Most obviously and most frequently the provisions of company law have a bearing on charities.

2.7.1 Legislative framework for commercial activities

Charities have to operate within a commercial environment. For many that has meant launching their organisation from the outset as a company, for others it has meant changing their legal status from unincorporated association or charitable trust to a limited company. Even where they chose not to become incorporated, many charities are still drawn into the commercial world by, for example, employment and trading contracts, by funding arrangements and by internal and external regulatory systems for ensuring probity and accountability. In that context, charities find themselves having to submit to the ever increasing weight of company law which now governs the activities of companies and those organisations with which they are engaged. This is a complex area of law with its own body of professional and academic publications[18] to which reference must be made for more information.

The Companies (N.I.) Order 1986, supplemented by the Companies Orders of 1990, provide the main legislative controls by setting out the relevant constitutional and regulatory requirements of company law. The principal charitable benefits of corporate status are limited liability and perpetual succession. Being subject to the corporate regime also enduces a higher level of professionalism. The drawbacks are usually regarded as lack of privacy and heightened regulation. It may also detract from a charity's philanthropic ethos to adopt a commercial structure. Directors of charitable companies are further subject to the provisions of the Insolvency (N.I.) Order 1989 prohibiting fraudulent and wrongful trading. Corporate law is uniformly applied across the United Kingdom. It is also increasingly subject to the harmonising influence of the European Union.

2.8 THE CRIMINAL LAW STATUTES

The detection and control of activities causing or suspected of causing a criminal offence are governed by general criminal law and enforced by the RUC. There are no statutory provisions directed specifically towards policing offences such as theft, fraud and embezzlement when these occur in a charitable context. Nor are there any specialist police teams with responsibility for charities and their activities. Neither civil nor criminal law provides a totally appropriate framework for regulating charities.

---

[18] See, for example, Inland Revenue, *Trading by Charities; guidelines on the tax treatment of trades carried on by charities*, 1995.

CHAPTER 3

The Courts and the Legal System

3.1 INTRODUCTION

History shows that charity law in these islands has been shaped and adjusted at judicial rather than legislative initiative. For more than three centuries the charity law continuum, with its roots in seventeenth century statutes, escaped any direct legislative attention. Not until the 1960s did Parliament intervene in charitable matters in Ireland and in the United Kingdom and then it was to provide for the better management of charities and their activities rather than make any formative contribution to the development of charity law. Subsequently, Northern Ireland, unlike England and Wales, has continued to rely almost exclusively upon judge made law.

In this jurisdiction, more so than elsewhere in the United Kingdom, the classification of charitable trusts, the formulation of governing principles and the flexible interpretation of the law to meet changing social pressures have been left to judicial discretion. Arguably, this reliance upon judicial common sense rather than legislative prescription has, until relatively recently, proved to be a perfectly adequate means of ensuring that law served the needs of charities.

In Northern Ireland, charity law continues to evade modern legislative constraints. The judiciary, however, now determine only a small proportion of issues. Charity law has become more administrative than judicial in nature (see further, Chapter 5). Nor is the judiciary the sole representative of the legal system to have dealings with charities. The Attorney-General carries a particular brief in relation to charitable trusts. Other elements such as the Probate Office and the Royal Ulster Constabulary also have significant roles.

This chapter examines the different ways in which the courts and the legal system exercise authority in respect of charities and their activities.

3.2 HISTORICAL BACKGROUND[1]

The roots of the current jurisdiction of the courts in relation to charities, their

---

[1] For a history of the legal system in Ireland see, for example: Mr Justice Ronan Keane, "The Historical Background" in *Equity and the Law of Trusts in the Republic of Ireland, op. cit.*; Byrne & McCutcheon, "Development of the Irish Legal System" in *The Irish Legal System*, (3rd ed., 1996), Butterworths, Dublin; Wylie, J.C.W., "Historical Background" in *Irish Land Law* (3rd ed., 1997), Butterworths, Dublin.

property and activities, lie in the ancient *parens patriae* responsibilities of the Crown. The inherent obligation resting on the King to protect the interests of wards and lunatics extended also to charities. The essentially protective nature of this jurisdiction, illustrated most clearly in the exercise of wardship, has consistently characterised the judicial approach throughout many centuries and continues to colour the contemporary relationship between law and charities.

3.2.1 The Court of Chancery

The *parens patriae* responsibilities of the Crown, as exercised by the Lord Chancellor, came to be administered by the Court of Chancery and were used to determine issues relating to trusts, charitable and otherwise, long before Parliament first legislated on such matters. It had also developed the administrative machinery and expertise necessary to resolve, or sometimes supervise, matters relating to financial and property disputes. Chancery exercised an equitable jurisdiction which supplemented the gaps left by a rigid common law system based upon a classification of writs. The approach in Chancery was very different. A petitioner's plea was settled on the basis of principle and good conscience.[2] The following maxims of equity stand as powerful reminders of the principled basis on which Chancery resolved disputes; they continue to inspire lawyers and influence judicial decision-making[3]:

> "Equity follows the law.
>
> Equity will not suffer a wrong to be without a remedy.
>
> Equity acts *in personam*.
>
> He who seeks equity must do equity.
>
> He who comes into equity must come with clean hands.
>
> Delay defeats equity.
>
> Equality is equity.
>
> Equity looks to the intent rather than the form.
>
> Equity looks on that as done which ought to have been done.
>
> Equity imputes an intention to fulfil an obligation.
>
> Where the equities are equal, the first in time prevails.
>
> Where the equities are equal, the law prevails."

---

[2] See, for example, Wylie, J.C.W., *A Casebook on Equity & Trusts in Ireland* (2nd ed., 1998, Dublin, Chap. 1 "Fundamental Principles".

[3] See further, Mr Justice Ronan Keane, "The Maxims of Equity" in *Equity and the Law of Trusts in Ireland, op. cit.* at p. 27.

A defendant could be summoned to appear by the issue of a subpoena. If successful, the plea could be enforced by utilising the prerogative powers, such as the power of injunction or of specific performance, which characterised the traditional authority of the Crown. Chancery, therefore, came to offer an alternative route to justice for petitioners whose cause did not find a remedy in the common law courts. As Mr Justice Ronan Keane has observed,[4] this equitable approach was manifested most clearly in Chancery's treatment of the trust:

> "Where one person – a trustee – held property on behalf of another – a beneficiary – the Chancellor treated the trustee, as did the common law courts, as the legal owner of the property. He did not purport to divest the trustee of that legal ownership and transfer it to the beneficiary. But he did prevent the trustee from acting in breach of the trust he had undertaken. Thus the trustee could be compelled by the intervention of the court in equity to acknowledge that, although the legal ownership was vested in him, he held the property on behalf of the beneficiary."[5]

The application of this equitable approach to charities resulted in the development of the law of charitable trusts (see further, Chapter 6).

Following the statutes of 1601 and 1634, Chancery adopted and applied the Preamble as its guide in determining charity law cases. If a donor's gift or bequest could be defined as coming within the parameters of these seventeenth century statutes, then Chancery would grant it charitable exemption from various rules. For the next two centuries and more the courts of Chancery in both England and Ireland developed a common body of charitable trust jurisprudence.

3.2.2 The common law courts

The common law transferred to Ireland, as it did to other countries, with the armies of the Crown. As it took root it was administered by the courts of King's Bench, Common Pleas and Exchequer.

3.2.2(i) The courts

The court of King's Bench, or Queen's Bench, was closely associated with sovereign authority and became the more important and powerful of the common law courts. It dealt with criminal and civil matters and supervised the lower courts. By the nineteenth century the court of King's Bench comprised the Lord Chief Justice of Ireland and a number of puisne judges.

The court of Common Pleas, as its name suggests, was established to deal

---

[4] *ibid.*
[5] *ibid.*, at p. 4.

with private disputes between 'commoners' rather than criminal matters. By the nineteenth century this court comprised the Lord Chief Justice of Common Pleas and a number of *puisne* judges.

The court of Exchequer was closely associated with the Treasury and largely concerned itself with financial matters, typically with disputes concerning the payment of taxes and other forms of debt owed to the Treasury. By the nineteenth century, this court comprised a Lord Chief Baron and several *puisne* barons.

3.2.2(ii) The common law approach

In common law no writ meant no action. A petitioner could only succeed in lodging a plea in court if he could fit his complaint within the narrowly defined terms of a particular writ; the range of standard form writs available was limited. Once the plea was before the court, the problems facing the petitioner were far from over. As Mr Justice Ronan Keane has noted[6]:

> "The courts in which he sued were so unlike our own that we would have difficulty in recognising them as courts. Not only were the parties unable to give evidence, a feature which persisted in common law courts until well into the nineteenth century: witnesses in the modern sense were unknown in medieval times. The jury, whose verdicts were of paramount importance, arrived at them, not on the basis of evidence as we would understand the word, but from their own knowledge of the parties and the background to the dispute."

On conclusion of the hearing, the range of judicial disposal options was again tightly constrained. Should the plea succeed and the court find in his favour, it quite often lacked the authority necessary to ensure that the plaintiff's rights were enforced.

3.2.3 The Supreme Court of Judicature Act 1873

Legislative intervention eventually ended the continuation of two parallel judicial systems. The 1873 Act unified the court systems of equity and the common law.[7] This statutory fusion of equitable and common law principles included a directive that, in the event of a conflict between them, the principles of equity should prevail. The judicial system for determining issues affecting charities had been set on a new path. The resulting Supreme Court was to consist of a High Court and a Court of Appeal.

The High Court comprised five divisions: Chancery, Queen's Bench, Common Pleas, Exchequer and Probate. The Chancery Division bore responsibility for charities. The body of law and principle accumulated over centuries in

---

[6] *ibid.*, at p. 7.

[7] Extended to Ireland by the Supreme Court of Judicature (Ireland) Act 1877.

the courts of equity continues to guide the determination of issues affecting charitable trusts in Northern Ireland and in other common law jurisdictions.

3.3 THE HIGH COURT

The High Court exercises a broad jurisdiction in respect of charities and ultimate legal accountability for the proper management of a charity's affairs lies to it. In addition to hearing proceedings arising under Charities (N.I.) Order 1987 and the Charities Act (N.I.) 1964, the High Court also exercises the traditional powers available to it under its inherent jurisdiction and it has an appellate jurisdiction. In respect of the latter, the High Court provides final authority for decisions taken within an administrative system consisting of agencies such as the Charities Branch, the Inland Revenue, Her Majesty's Customs and Excise and the Lands Tribunal.

Like the position elsewhere in the United Kingdom, legal business relating to charities is consolidated within the Chancery Division of the High Court and adjudicated accordingly.

3.3.1 Jurisdiction: charitable trusts, etc.

The traditional inherent jurisdiction of the High Court has always been available to allow it to determine issues relating to the validity of dispositions and the administration of trusts for charitable purposes. In the words of Lord Chief Justice MacDermott in *Re Townsend Street Belfast Presbyterian Endowment Trusts*:[8]

> "the jurisdiction of the High Court of Justice in Northern Ireland respecting charitable trusts is an inherent jurisdiction, the salient characteristic of which is that it extends beyond that pertaining to ordinary trusts."[9]

A few years later McVeigh J. made the same point in *McCormick v. Queens University Belfast*[10] when he quoted with approval from *Wallis v. Solicitor General for New Zealand*[11] that:

> "… it has always been recognised as the duty of the law officers of the Crown to intervene for the purpose of protecting charities."[12]

It has at times been argued that the inherent jurisdiction of the High Court is based on trusts and that a trust must be present before the court has power to

---

[8] [1954] N.I. 53.
[9] *ibid.* at p. 57
[10] [1958] N.I. 1.
[11] [1903] A.C. 173.
[12] *Wallis* at p. 181

act. For example, Buckley on behalf of the Attorney-General asserted that "it is the existence of the trust which clothes the court with jurisdiction".[13] However, Vaisey J. in that case ruled that although the court's jurisdiction was mainly based on the existence of a charitable trust, it was not exclusively so based.[14] In the older English case of *Attorney-General v. Skinners Company*[15] the court considered the question of whether this extra jurisdiction was inherent or whether it derived from the Statute of Charitable Uses. It formed the view that the jurisdiction over charities was inherent, and that the said statute was only declaratory of the existing law. The source of this inherent jurisdiction is unclear. It was said in *Moggridge v. Thackwell*[16] that:

> "... where money is given to charity generally and indefinitely, without trustees or objects selected, the King as *parens patriae* is the constitutional trustee."[17]

The Royal prerogative aspect of this inherent jurisdiction is now exercised by the Attorney-General, rather than the monarch, under the Sign Manual procedure (see further, below).[18]

The inherent jurisdiction over charities does not fully extend to foreign charities which carry out some activities in the United Kingdom. In England and Wales, section 33 of the Charities Act 1993 requires that the Charity Commission must authorise the taking of charity proceedings in a court. It did not authorise the taking of proceedings in *Gaudiya Mission v. Brahmachary*[19] by an Indian religious body, recognised as a charity in India but not registered as a charity in the United Kingdom. The Court of Appeal held that foreign charities did not come under the inherent jurisdiction of the High Court, and that consequently, no authority was required from the Charity Commission to allow court proceedings to take place. The reason for debarring foreign charities from the court's inherent jurisdiction is that the court would have no way to control those which were established and governed outside the United Kingdom.[20]

---

[13] *Re Bennett, Sucker v. Attorney General* [1960] Ch. 18 at p. 19.

[14] *ibid.* at p. 26. See also, Picarda (1995) who makes the point that charitable companies are subject to the jurisdiction of the chancery court even though they may not be constituted by trusts.

[15] (1826) 2 Russ. 407.

[16] (1803) 7 Ves. 36.

[17] *Moggridge v. Thackwell* at p. 83

[18] Charities may find strange bedfellows with those who also look to the Crown for special protection:
> ... the King as *parens patriae* took under his special care charitable gifts as he took also infants and lunatics.

See, *National Anti-Vivisection Society v. Inland Revenue Commissioners* (1948) A.C. 32 at p. 63.

[19] [1997] 4 All E.R. 957.

[20] See *Camille and Henry Dreyfus Foundation Inc. v. Inland Revenue Commissioners* (1955) 3 All E.R. 97.

The corresponding section in Northern Ireland is section 29 of the Charities Act (N.I.) 1964 which only requires the consent of the Attorney-General before charity proceedings are instigated. "Charity proceedings" can be broadly defined as proceedings relating to the administration of a charity. For example, in *Mumam v. Nagasena*[21] an internal dispute as to who was the patron and resident monk of a Buddhist charity was deemed to be a charity proceeding. This was so notwithstanding that the action brought was a claim for possession of charity property.

A statutory formulation of this rule was to be found in Romilly's Act 1812.[22] This statute was subtitled "an Act to provide a summary remedy in cases of abuses of trusts created for charitable purposes". It allowed for two or more persons to present a petition to the court on the subject of the abuse of a charitable trust, or seeking directions on the execution of such a trust. It also provided for the court to deal with this petition in a summary way. Romilly's Act was repealed by the Charities Act (N.I.) 1964, but it serves as an illustration of the special jurisdiction of the court in matters affecting charities. In addition, this special jurisdiction is explicitly recognised in the Charities Act (N.I.) 1964. Part of the definition of a charity is that it "is subject to the control of the Court in the exercise of the Court's jurisdiction with respect to charities".[23]

The court in *Re Townsend Street Belfast Presbyterian Endowment Trusts*[24] considered whether or not this inherent charitable jurisdiction could be ousted by statutory provisions, specifically by the Educational Endowments (Ireland) Act 1885. The case concerned privately funded charitable schools established in the nineteenth century. With the advent of state sponsored education, the schools ceased to have any meaningful role. The charity wished to sell the property and apply the funds for different charitable purposes. The difficulty was that the charity was being run under a scheme set up under the auspices of the Educational Endowments (Ireland) Act 1885. Section 18 provided that such a scheme could provide for its alteration by the Commissioners for Charitable Donations and Bequests[25] and such a power was available in respect of the particular scheme in this case. However, the charity applied to the court to allow the scheme to be changed under the Charity Procedure Act 1812 (Romilly's Act). The issue for the court was whether the 1885 Act could oust the court's inherent jurisdiction over charities.

The Court of Appeal did not answer this question conclusively; indeed, it is questionable whether the inherent jurisdiction can be ousted by statute as opposed to its use being restrained by judicial discretion. But, on the particu-

---

[21] (2000) 1 W.L.R. 299; see also *Ex p. Scott* (1998) 1 W.L.R. 226

[22] Also known as the Charities Procedure Act 1812.

[23] s. 35 of the Charities Act (N.I.) Act 1964.

[24] [1954] N.I. 53.

[25] See further Chapter 5 for more information on this body which is now obsolete in Northern Ireland.

lar facts, "no reason has been or can be given why it is necessary to invoke the assistance of the court under Romilly's Act".[26] A power to vary the scheme already existed. This rested with the Ministry of Finance who had inherited the powers of the Commissioners for Charitable Donations and Bequests. Applications to change educational endowments should now be directed to the Charity Branch (current holders of the powers of the Commissioners) rather than the courts.

3.3.2 Jurisdiction: appeals

Appeals from decisions of the Lands Tribunal and from the Inland Revenue will lie to the High Court. Indeed, case law patterns reveal that such appeals constitute a major proportion of the charity related cases heard in that court.

3.3.3 Jurisdiction: framing *cy-près* schemes

Creating a *cy-près* scheme will be necessary in circumstances where a donor has manifested a clear charitable intention and has appointed a trustee, but the charitable purpose of the gift can no longer be given effect. Where a *cy-près* scheme is required in relation to property with a value of £50,000 or more, then the High Court rather than the Charities Branch will have jurisdiction. The statutory authority of the court in relation to the creation of *cy-près* schemes is governed by sections 22 and 23 of the Charities Act 1964. In particular, section 22 permits the property of charitable gifts to be applied *cy-près* in specific circumstances (see further, Chapter 19).

3.3.4 Jurisdiction: the sign manual procedure

The sign manual procedure will be necessary in circumstances where although a donor has manifested a clear charitable intention he or she has not appointed a trustee and the charitable purpose of the gift has been expressed in terms which are too general to allow them to be given effect. Traditionally, the response of the courts was to hold that the gift should devolve to the Crown. This, for example, was the outcome where the donor's gift was simply expressed as being "to charity"[27] or "to the poor".[28]

This point was adjudicated upon relatively recently in *Re Bennett, Sucker v. Attorney General*.[29] In that case a bequest was expressed to be for the Hos-

---

[26] *ibid.* at p. 68.

[27] See *Attorney General v. Syderfen* (1683) 1 Vern. 224; *Attorney General v. Herrick* (1722) Amb. 712; *Legge v. Asgill* (1818) T. & R. 265n; and *Kane v. Cosgrave* (1873) 10 Ir.R.Eq. 211.

[28] See *Ware v. Attorney General* (1843) 3 Ha. 194n.

[29] [1960] Ch. D. 18.

pital for Incurable Women of Brompton Road. No trust was created by the will. No such organisation existed. The court had to decide if jurisdiction lay with the court or with the crown to redistribute the failed gift. Vaisey J. agreed with the Attorney-General's proposition that "the jurisdiction of the court is dependent on the existence of a trust, otherwise the gift is applicable by the Crown under the sign manual".[30] If there was a direct gift to charity with no trust interposed the court did not have jurisdiction.[31]

3.4 THE ATTORNEY-GENERAL

The duties of the Attorney-General include acting as protector of charities and charitable trusts are enforceable by the Attorney-General. In England and Wales, the scope of the Attorney-General's traditional authority in respect of charities has been displaced to some extent by the growth in powers assumed by the Charity Commission.

3.4.1 Jurisdiction

The ancient *parens patriae* jurisdiction of the Crown in relation to charities, and the right to bring proceedings in respect of them, has long been vested in the Attorney-General. It was said in *Ludlow Corpn v. Greenhove*[32] that:

> "... the King is to be considered as the *parens patriae*; that he is the protector of every part of his subjects, and that, therefore, it is the duty of his officer, the Attorney General, to see that justice is done to every part of those subjects."[33]

This official, as guardian of charities, may intervene on evidence of trustee incompetence or malpractice and ensure the court's protection for the interests of the charity.[34] Indeed, a distinguishing characteristic of charitable trusts is that because such a trust is by definition for the public benefit, it thereby acquires an entitlement to protection and enforcement by the Attorney-General. Logical reasons can be given for the Attorney-General's role. All trusts represent a

---

[30] *ibid.* at p. 21.

[31] *Paice v. Archbishop of Canterbury* (1807) 14 Ves. 364 at 372, *Moggridge v. Thackwell* (1802) 7 Ves. 36, *Reeve v. Attorney General* (1829) 3 Hare 191 but see the Irish case of *Re Maguire* L.R. 9 Eq. 632 which held that a direct bequest to a non-existent charity would be applied by the court, not by the crown. Picarda (1995) has stated that the distinction between judicial and royal prerogative over the disposition of charitable gifts has little practical significance today.

[32] (1827) 1 Bli. N.S. 17 at p. 48.

[33] See also *Potts v. Turnley* (1849) 1 Ir. Jur. (o.s.) 57, *Attorney General v. Carlile* (1850) 2 Ir. Jur. (o.s.) 249 and *Re Kelly's Will Trusts* (1862) 7 Ir. Jur. (n.s.) 273.

[34] See, for example, *National Anti-Vivisection Society v. IRC* [1948] A.C. 31 *per* Lord Simonds at p. 62.

division of legal and equitable ownership. With charitable trusts, there are no beneficiaries *per se*, there is only a charitable purpose. Therefore the right to enforce the trust must rest with someone, that someone is the Attorney-General. When so acting, the Attorney-General must be separately advised so as to avoid any possible conflict between the interests of the State and the specific interests of the charity. To ensure such separation, the Attorney-General appoints his own solicitor to advise and act for him on all such matters.

An example of the Attorney-General's role can be seen in *McCormick v. Queens University Belfast*.[35] In that case, the beneficiary of a charitable trust was the university which was happy to consent to a gift being returned to a donor as its purposes could not be fulfilled. However, it had no right to act in this way since the gift was charitable and was "being protected by the Attorney-General who represents the Crown as *parens patriae* to enforce the execution of charitable trusts".[36]

3.4.1(i) Proceedings brought by the Attorney-General

In keeping with the inherent powers of the *parens patriae* jurisdiction, the Attorney-General will initiate proceedings in circumstances where the interests of a particular charity need protection. This may be necessary, for example, where there is evidence that trustees have failed in their duties.[37] It is most likely to be activated where direct intervention is urgently required to prevent or remedy damage to a particular charity. As noted in Tudor[38]:

> "Such proceedings are likely to be brought in the Chancery Division of the High Court and the relief sought may include, *inter alia*, the restitution of charity property, the award of damages and interest for breach of trust, injunctive relief[39] to prevent a breach of trust or its repetition, the appointment or removal of trustees or officers, the appointment of a receiver and manager,[40] the establishment of a scheme or the determination, by means of a declaration or otherwise of questions arising in the administration of the charity or the application of its property."

Whereas in England and Wales an increasing proportion of the above are now likely to be instituted by the Charity Commission, the responsibility to do so in this jurisdiction continues to rest with the Attorney-General.

---

[35] [1958] N.I. 1.

[36] *ibid.* at p. 6.

[37] See *Attorney General v. Brown* (1818) 1 Swan 265, *per* Lord Eldon at p. 291.

[38] See Tudor, *Charities* (8th ed., 1995), Sweet & Maxwell, London at p. 359.

[39] See *Baldry v. Feintuck* [1972] 1 W.L.R. 552.

[40] See *Attorney General v. Schonfeld* [1980] 1 W.L.R. 1182.

3.4.1(ii) Proceedings brought by the Charities Branch and involving the Attorney-General

Where the Charities Branch certifies with particulars, under section 2(1) of the Charities Act 1964, that proceedings should be instigated in relation to any charity then the Attorney-General may, under section 2(2):

> "... if he thinks fit, institute such legal proceedings as he thinks proper."

In any such instance the Attorney-General has a discretion, the inference being that the Attorney-General may reject the Charities Branch request to institute proceedings.

3.4.1(iii) Proceedings brought by others and involving the Attorney-General

The public interest in charities requires notice of proceedings affecting a charity, or charities in general, to be served on the Attorney-General. For example, where a trustee is bringing proceedings affecting a charity, the Attorney-General will normally be cited as a defendant, if not at the outset then he will be later joined as a defendant. In many instances, however, the issues that arise do not become the subject of proceedings and therefore do not require the involvement of the Attorney-General. Even where proceedings are initiated it is not always necessary to join the Attorney-General.[41] The Charities Branch instead of authorising the Attorney-General to commence proceedings may do so itself under section 29(3).

However, the rule is that where proceedings involving a charity are commenced then, if not already a party, the Attorney-General should be joined. As explained in Tudor[42]:

> "By reason of his duty as the Sovereign's representative, protecting all the persons interested in the charity funds,[43] the Attorney General is as a general rule a necessary party to charity proceedings. He represents the beneficial interest;[44] it follows that, in all proceedings in which the beneficial interest has to be before the court, he must be a party.[45] He represents all the objects of the charity, who are thus in effect plaintiffs through him.[46] It was accordingly held that, if all the subscribers to a charitable fund were plaintiffs, the action would still be defective for want of parties, unless the Attorney General was also a party".[47]

---

[41] See *Re Dowling* (1948) 82 ILTR 155.

[42] See Tudor, *Charities* (8th ed., Sweet & Maxwell, London, 1995) at p. 351.

[43] See *Re Sekeford's Charity* (1861) 5 L.T. 488.

[44] See *Wellbeloved v. Jones* (1822) 1 S. & S. 43; and *National Anti-Vivisection Society v. Inland Revenue Commissioners* [1948] A.C. 31.

[45] See *Strickland v. Weldon* (1885) 28 Ch. D. 426.

[46] See *Attorney General v. Brodie* (1846) 6 Moore, P.C.C. 12; *Attorney General v. Bishop of Worcester* (1852) 9 Ha. 361; and *Re King* [1917] 2 Ch. 420.

[47] See *Strickland v. Weldon, op. cit.*

3.4.1(iv) Procedure when involving the Attorney-General

A charitable matter may come before the court on foot of either a plenary or a summary summons, joining the Attorney-General as a party. The Attorney-General should always be brought before the court to protect the interests of the public when any question arises incidental to administration proceedings, such as to the application of a charitable gift, unless the gift be to the trustees of an established charity. In the latter instance his presence might be required where a scheme is to be drawn up on special trusts. This may occur, for example, where the amount which is to form part of the general funds of the charity has not been stipulated.[48] However, the general rule is that the Attorney-General is recognised by the court as plaintiff.

3.5 THE PROBATE OFFICE

The Probate Office is of ancient lineage being a descendant of the common law court of Probate with its jurisdiction in matters relating to wills. Until the Chancery Amendment Act 1858 ("Lord Cairn's Act") and other mid-nineteenth century legislative reforms to the courts of chancery and common law, the granting of probate in respect of wills and letters of administration of the estates of intestates remained the prerogative of the ecclesiastical courts. In 1857 the Prerogative Court was abolished in a programme of reform culminated in England with the Judicature Acts of 1873 and 1875, and in Ireland with the Judicature (Ireland) Act 1877. These statutes abolished the separate courts of equity and common law, establishing in their place a High Court consisting of five divisions (Chancery, Queen's Bench, Common Pleas, Exchequer, and Probate and Matrimonial) of which Probate and Matrimonial was one. Subsequently, this was reduced to four.

3.5.1 Duty to make annual returns to the Board

Under section 30 of the 1964 Act, the Principle Probate Registry of the High Court is required to furnish the Charities Branch annually with:

(1) ... a certified return ... of every charitable gift to be applied or paid in Northern Ireland which is contained in any will entered in that Registry, or of which a copy has been forwarded to him from the district probate registry or from the registrar of the Probate, Divorce and Admiralty Division of the High Court in England, during the year immediately preceding the said 1st July.

(2) The return required under subsection (1) shall specify –
    (a) the name of the testator;

---

[48] See *Wellbeloved v. Jones, op. cit.*

(b) the names of the persons to whom probate of the will or letters of
administration with the will annexed have been granted; and

(c) the date of the will and of the probate or letters of administration.

However, as noted in the Consultation Document, the Charities Branch has
never found this procedure to be a useful way of detecting inappropriate behaviour by executors and has recommended that it be discontinued.

See also section 4 of the 1964 Act and Article 21 of the Wills and Administration Proceedings (N.I.) Order 1994.

3.6 THE ROYAL ULSTER CONSTABULARY

There are no statutory duties placed upon the police specifically in relation to
charities nor are there any organisational arrangements for specific police teams
to be assigned responsibility for offences relating to charities. The duties of
the RUC in respect of charities and charitable activity are of an incidental
nature.

3.6.1 Duties arising under fundraising legislation

The role played by the RUC in regulating fundraising activities is greater in
this jurisdiction than that played by the police in England and Wales. This is
mainly due to the fact that in England and Wales the primary responsibility for
collection rests with the local authorities rather than the police. It is exacer-
bated by the absence in this jurisdiction of any body with powers equivalent to
those of the Charity Commission. In Northern Ireland, an organisation can
apply to the RUC for permission to carry out street collections for "charitable
or other purposes"[49] or house-to-house collections for "any charitable, benevolent or philanthropic purpose".[50] Similarly, under the Betting, Gaming,
Lotteries and Amusements (N.I.) Order 1985, the RUC licence gaming and
lotteries for the purpose of fundraising.

Neither set of legislative provisions is exclusively concerned with charities. Most applicants for fundraising tend to be charitable, but they are not
compelled to be so. In practice, the non-charitable applicants would tend to be
regarded as quasi-charitable by the public. For example, they could be campaigning bodies, or bodies raising funds to help the medical condition of a
particular person (see further, Chapter 18). Licences can be and from time to
time are granted to organisations which are not charities.

---

[49] See s. 5 of the Police, Factories, Etc. (Miscellaneous Provisions) Act 1916.

[50] See s. 8 of the House-to-House Charitable Collections Act (N.I.) 1952.

3.6.2 Duties arising under criminal law

In any case where there is a suspicion that a criminal offence (*e.g.* fraud, theft, obtaining money under false pretences) has been committed by or against a charity or its trustees, or by any body or person falsely claiming to be a charity, this is automatically dealt with by the RUC under the general criminal law. In complex cases, the matter may be referred to the Fraud Squad of the RUC. The powers of the Charities Branch are insufficient to permit the control or supervision of a charity's activities. As explained in the Consultation Document:

> "... most cases where a charity comes under suspicion of malpractice are dealt with by the RUC under the criminal law relating to theft or fraud."[51]

---

[51] See DHSS, *Consultation Document on Charity Law in Northern Ireland*, Charities Branch, Belfast, 1995, at para. 33.

CHAPTER 4

Discrimination and Human Rights

4.1 INTRODUCTION

Human rights concerns are increasingly impacting on all areas of law and charity law is no exception. The Human Rights Act 1998 came into effect in October 2000 and has made human rights a part of the domestic law of the United Kingdom. Legislation outlawing discrimination has also come to the fore in recent years. The Disability Discrimination Act 1995 and the Race Relations (N.I.) Order 1997 have recently added race and disability to the rubric of anti-discrimination legislation in Northern Ireland. They join discrimination on grounds of religious belief, political opinion[1] and gender.[2]

Charities have historically operated on a partisan basis, awarding their benefits on the basis of race, gender or religion. A charity can be viewed as discriminatory when it either explicitly excludes groups of "the public" or when it explicitly favours one such group over all others. In practice it can be difficult to draw the line between discrimination which is prohibited as being in breach of specific rights legislation and discrimination which is permitted because it advances the legitimate interests of a specific group. So far, charities have generally managed to escape the rigours of anti-discrimination by means of specific exemptions from the legislation. It remains to be seen whether the Human Rights Act 1998 will restrict these exemptions.

4.2 DIRECT AND INDIRECT DISCRIMINATION

A distinction can be drawn between direct discrimination and indirect discrimination. The distinction is conceptually clear but cumbersome to state. A standard example is given in the Fair Employment and Treatment (N.I.) Order 1998. A person is guilty of direct discrimination if, on the grounds of religious belief or political opinion he "treats that other less favourably than he treats or would treat other persons".[3] The definition of indirect discrimination is more unwieldy. A person is guilty of indirect discrimination if:

"... he applies to that other a requirement or condition which he applies or

---

[1] Both in the Fair Employment and Treatment (N.I.) Order 1998.
[2] Sex Discrimination (N.I.) Order 1976.
[3] Art. 3(2)(a) Fair Employment and Treatment (N.I.) Order 1998.

would apply equally to persons not of the same religious belief or political opinion as that other but–

(i) which is such that the proportion of persons of the same religious belief or of the same political opinion as that other who can comply with it is considerably smaller than the proportion of persons not of that religious belief, or, as the case requires, not of that political opinion who can comply with it; and

(ii) which he cannot show to be justifiable irrespective of the religious belief or political opinion of the person to whom it is applied; and

(iii) which is to the detriment of that other because he cannot comply with it."[4]

In simple terms, if an employer imposes a condition (*e.g.* working on a Saturday) with which more members of one religion than another can comply (*e.g.* Christians rather than Jews), then, if members of the latter religion suffer a detriment (*i.e.* cannot apply for the job), and there is no justification for that condition, then the employer is guilty of discrimination.

In this chapter, the above definition is given effect in all the anti-discrimination legislation discussed and the distinction between direct and indirect discrimination is similarly adopted. The only exception is the Disability Discrimination Act 1995, which only prohibits direct discrimination.

4.3 RELIGIOUS AND POLITICAL DISCRIMINATION

The Fair Employment and Treatment (N.I.) Order 1998 makes discrimination on the grounds of religious belief or political opinion unlawful. The support of violent methods to attain a political goal is specifically exempted from the definition of political opinion[5].

4.3.1 Types of discrimination deemed unlawful

Discrimination includes both direct and indirect forms.[6] The prohibition on discrimination extends to the fields of employment,[7] further and higher education,[8] the provision of goods, facilities, services and premises[9] and the giving of instructions to barristers.[10]

---

[4] Art. 3(2)(b) Fair Employment and Treatment (N.I.) Order 1998.
[5] Art. 2(4) Fair Employment and Treatment (N.I.) Order 1998.
[6] Art. 3 Fair Employment and Treatment (N.I.) Order 1998.
[7] Part II Fair Employment and Treatment (N.I.) Order 1998.
[8] Art. 27 Fair Employment and Treatment (N.I.) Order 1998.
[9] Arts. 28-31 Fair Employment and Treatment (N.I.) Order 1998.
[10] Art. 32 Fair Employment and Treatment (N.I.) Order 1998.

4.3.2 Exemption for charities

Charities are exempt from parts of this legislation if they can satisfy the requirements of Article 77. There are three requirements:

- The charity is exercising a provision which confers benefits on persons of a particular religious belief/political opinion (disregarding any benefits to persons not of that belief/opinion which are exceptional or relatively insignificant),
- That provision is contained in a statutory provision or other instrument and
- That provision has been enacted or made for purposes which are exclusively charitable.

If charities can gain this exemption, they could, for example, provide educational scholarships for members of only one religion, or provide accommodation on the basis that the occupier attend certain religious services.

It is of course open to charities to voluntarily excise religious discrimination from their constitution. This was done for example in the case of *Incorporated Governors of Riddell Hall*.[11] A *cy-près* scheme was created to delete the requirement "Protestant" from a trust to benefit needy, female, Protestant students at Queens University Belfast. A similar scheme was created to remove a prohibition on Jewish or Roman Catholic students receiving medical scholarships in *Re Lysaght*.[12]

It is important to note that Article 77 does not provide complete exemption for charities from discrimination; it only does so as far as the provision of benefits for beneficiaries of the charity is concerned. Discriminating against employees on the basis of religion, for example, will still be unlawful.

It remains to be seen whether the exemption from the Fair Employment and Treatment (N.I.) Order 1998 will survive the operation of the Human Rights Act 1998.

4.3.2(i) Meaning of "instrument"

The second requirement of the exemption is open to conflicting interpretations which have important repercussions on the scope of the exemption. The crux of the matter is the meaning of the words "statutory provision or other instrument".[13]

The first interpretation is that it refers only to legislative provisions and not private trusts, etc. The strongest argument in support of this is that 'instrument' has been defined by legislation as including "an Order in Council, order or warrant (other than an order made or a warrant issued by a court), scheme,

---

[11] *Incorporated Governors of Riddell Hall*, unreported, Ch. D., February 24, 1972.
[12] *Re Lysaght* [1966] Ch. 191.
[13] Art. 77(2)(a) Fair Employment and Treatment (N.I.) Order 1998.

rule, regulation or bye-law".[14] This indicates that an instrument means a statutory instrument of some description. The second argument in favour of this interpretation is the rule of statutory interpretation known as *ejusdem generis* – where a general word follows a particular one, the general is to be interpreted in the same manner as the particular. Under this argument, the general word "instrument" is preceded by the particular words "statutory provision", therefore, "instrument" should be interpreted as meaning any sort of legislative instrument.

The second interpretation is that "instrument" refers to any formal, written legal document produced either by legislative process or by private individuals, i.e. a will or a trust. There is authority for this interpretation in Halsbury – "usually it applies to a document under which some right or liability, whether legal or equitable, exists".[15] Further authority is available from Stroud's Judicial Dictionary, which offers the interpretation that "an instrument is a writing and generally imports a document of a formal legal kind".[16]

The second argument for this interpretation relies on some other rules of statutory interpretation. The first of these is the intention rule, "our duty in interpreting a statute is to declare and administer the law according to the intention expressed in the statute itself".[17] The intention of the statute is clearly to exempt charities form anti-discrimination legislation. The other rule of statutory interpretation is the mischief rule. This rule requires the courts to look to the situation which the legislation seeks to remedy, "you must look to the mischief which had to be cured as well as to the cure provided".[18] In the context of the Fair Employment and Treatment (N.I.) Order 1998, the mischief is that a wide range of charitable activities could be potentially deemed discriminatory and illegal. Article 77 therefore seeks to ensure that all these laudable public activities remain legal.

It is submitted that the second argument is preferable and that charities with written instruments which provide benefits based on religious belief are not discriminatory under the Order. The final point, however, is that court orders are expressly excluded from the definition of instrument under the Interpretation Act (N.I.) 1954. This could mean that if a court creates a *cy-près* scheme which contains discrimination therein, it will not be exempt by virtue of Article 77 as it is not an instrument.

4.3.2(ii) Timing and retrospective effect

Article 77 does not explicitly state whether it refers to all instruments or only

---

[14] s. 1(f) of the Interpretation Act (N.I.) 1954.
[15] Vol. 12 Halsbury's Laws (4th edition) para. 47.
[16] Stroud's Judicial Dictionary Vol. 3 p. 1315 (3rd ed., 1986), London, Sweet and Maxwell; see also *St. Leonards Trustees v. Charity Commissioners* 10 App. Cas. 304.
[17] *Tasmania v. Commonwealth* [1904] 1 C.L.R. 329.
[18] *Thomson v. Lord Clanmorris* [1900] 1 Ch. 718 at p. 725.

to those made after its coming into operation. Article 77 had a predecessor in section 40 of the Fair Employment (N.I.) Act 1976 so it applies at the very least to instruments created from that date. It is submitted that, in line with the other charitable exemptions from discrimination, as set out below, it applies to all discriminatory provisions whenever the instrument was made. But that it will not render unlawful discriminatory acts carried out before it came into operation.

4.4 RACE DISCRIMINATION

Parliament has enacted legislation outlawing discrimination on the basis of race or racial group in the Race Relations (N.I.) Order 1997. "Racial grounds" means on grounds of "colour, race, nationality or ethnic or national origins".[19] Members of the "travelling community" are specifically mentioned as being a racial group and are defined as:

> "... the community of people commonly so called who are identified (both by themselves and others) as people with a shared history, culture and traditions including, historically a nomadic way of life on the island of Ireland."[20]

It also includes those who have been victimised for initiating or helping a racial discrimination claim.[21] The definition of racial group specifically excludes persons defined by reference to religious belief or political opinion.[22]

4.4.1 Types of discrimination deemed unlawful

Discrimination includes both direct and indirect discrimination.[23] The prohibition on discrimination extends to discrimination by employers,[24] trade unions,[25] vocational training bodies,[26] employment agencies[27] and the police.[28] It also extends to discrimination in the provision of goods, facilities, services and premises[29] and in the instruction of barristers.[30]

It is discriminatory to have a practice which is likely to result in an act of

---

[19] Art. 5(1) Race Relations (N.I.) Order 1997.
[20] Art. 5(2) Race Relations (N.I.) Order 1997.
[21] Art. 4 Race Relations (N.I.) Order 1997.
[22] Art. 5(2)(b) and Art. 5(3) Race Relations (N.I.) Order 1997.
[23] Art. 3 Race Relations (N.I.) Order 1997.
[24] Part II of the Race Relations (N.I.) Order 1997.
[25] Art. 13 Race Relations (N.I.) Order 1997.
[26] Art. 15 Race Relations (N.I.) Order 1997.
[27] Art. 16 Race Relations (N.I.) Order 1997.
[28] Art. 17 Race Relations (N.I.) Order 1997.
[29] Arts. 21-25 Race Relations (N.I.) Order 1997.
[30] Art. 26 Race Relations (N.I.) Order 1997.

discrimination.[31] It is unlawful to instruct any other persons to discriminate,[32] to have discriminatory advertisements,[33] to induce or attempt to induce any person to discriminate[34] or to aid in an act of discrimination.[35]

4.4.2 Exemptions for charities

The exemption is set out in Article 34 of the Order. Charities receive special treatment under the Order depending on the way they discriminate, either on grounds of colour or of race. The exemption requirements are similar to that for the other charitable discrimination exemptions. There are three requirements:

- The charity is exercising a provision which confers benefits on persons of a class defined by reference to colour or racial group.
- That provision is contained in a statutory provision or other instrument; and
- That provision is exclusively charitable according to the law of Northern Ireland.

It is important to note that the exemption for charities is very limited. They are only exempt to the extent that they confer benefits on a person because that person belongs to a racial group as set out below. There is no exemption for practising negative discrimination against certain races, as opposed to positive discrimination in favour of certain races.

As with religious discrimination, charities can voluntarily excise racial discrimination from their constitution. This was done by *cy-près* scheme in *Re Dominion Students' Hall Trust*.[36] In that case a restriction on non-European students using a hostel was removed as it had become contrary to the ethos of the charity.

It remains to be seen if this exemption will be deemed compliant with the prohibition on the grounds of race set out in Article 14 of the European Convention on Human Rights.

4.4.2(i) Discrimination on grounds of colour

If a charitable provision confers benefits on persons defined by reference to their colour, the provision will take effect as if the reference to colour had been removed.[37] The benefit will then be conferred on the grounds of the

---

[31] Art. 28 Race Relations (N.I.) Order 1997.
[32] Art. 30 Race Relations (N.I.) Order 1997.
[33] Art. 29 of the Race Relations (N.I.) Order 1997.
[34] Art. 31 of the Race Relations (N.I.) Order 1997.
[35] Art. 33 of the Race Relations (N.I.) Order 1997.
[36] *Re Dominion Students' Hall Trust* (1947) Ch. 183.
[37] Art. 34(1) of the Race Relations (N.I.) Order 1997.

remaining criteria in the provision[38] or, if no other criteria are present, it will be conferred upon persons generally.[39]

4.4.2(ii) Discrimination on grounds of race

If a charitable provision confers benefits on persons defined otherwise than by reference to their colour (*i.e.* by reference to their race/racial group), it is exempt from the Order.[40] Any act done to give effect to such a provision is also lawful.[41] This type of discriminatory provision is expressed to include a provision which has had the reference to colour in it removed by virtue of the previous section.

4.4.2(iii) Meaning of 'instrument'

The wording of Article 34 is similar to that of Article 77 of the Fair Employment and Treatment (N.I.) Order 1998. The conclusions reached in the above consideration of the former provision apply also to the latter, *viz.* it applies to any formal written legal document, whether or not it is contained in a legislative provision. The comparable English legislation refers to a charitable instrument as meaning "an enactment or other instrument passed or made for charitable purposes".[42] Like its Northern Ireland equivalent, this could be interpreted in one of two ways. However, in discussing the predecessor to that Act,[43] Picarda refers to a "trust instrument"[44] as being an instrument. This lends further authority to the contention that 'instrument' can be either legislative or private.

4.4.2(iv) Timing and retrospective effect

Activities which would have been discriminatory before the coming into operation of the Race Relations (N.I.) Order 1997 are not retrospectively made unlawful. This is explicitly stated in relation to discrimination on the grounds of colour.[45] The full rigour of the Order and the charitable exemptions are applicable after the Order came into force. This is regardless of whether the discriminatory provision was made before or after the coming into effect of the Order.[46]

---

[38] Art. 34(1)(a) of the Race Relations (N.I.) Order 1997.
[39] Art. 34(1)(b) of the of the Race Relations (N.I.) Order 1997.
[40] Art. 34(3)(b) of the Race Relations (N.I.) Order 1997.
[41] Art. 34(3)(b) of the Race Relations (N.I.) Order 1997.
[42] s. 34(4) of the Race Relations Act 1976.
[43] The Race Relations Act 1968.
[44] Picarda (1995) at 754.
[45] Art. 34(2) of the Race Relations (N.I.) Order 1997.
[46] Art. 34(4) of the Race Relations (N.I.) Order 1997.

4.5 SEX DISCRIMINATION

Under the Sex Discrimination (N.I.) Order 1976, discrimination on the grounds of gender is unlawful. This applies to such discrimination against women[47] and against men.[48] It also applies to discrimination against married persons in the field of employment[49] and victimisation of those who have helped or initiated a sex discrimination claim.[50]

4.5.1 Types of discrimination deemed unlawful

Discrimination includes both direct and indirect discrimination.[51] The Sex Discrimination (N.I.) Order 1976 covers discrimination by employers,[52] partnerships,[53] trade unions,[54] vocational training bodies[55] and employment agencies.[56] Special provisions exist for sex discrimination by the police,[57] prison officers,[58] ministers of religion,[59] midwives[60] and mineworkers.[61] Discrimination is also unlawful in the field of education[62] though there are some exemptions for single sex schools.[63] Discrimination on grounds of sex is unlawful in the provision of goods, facilities, services and premises.[64]

4.5.2 Exemptions for charities

The exemption for charities is set out in Article 44 of the Order. As with other discrimination exemptions, there are three requirements:

- The charity is exercising a provision which confers benefits on persons of one sex only (disregarding any benefits to persons of the opposite sex which are exceptional or are relatively insignificant.)

---

[47] Art. 3 of the Sex Discrimination (N.I.) Order 1976.
[48] Art. 4 of the Sex Discrimination (N.I.) Order 1976.
[49] Art. 5 of the Sex Discrimination (N.I.) Order 1976.
[50] Art. 6 of the Sex Discrimination (N.I.) Order 1976.
[51] Art. 3 of the Sex Discrimination (N.I.) Order 1976.
[52] Arts. 8-13 of the Sex Discrimination (N.I.) Order 1976.
[53] Art. 14 of the Sex Discrimination (N.I.) Order 1976.
[54] Art. 15 of the Sex Discrimination (N.I.) Order 1976.
[55] Art. 17 of the Sex Discrimination (N.I.) Order 1976.
[56] Art. 18 of the Sex Discrimination (N.I.) Order 1976.
[57] Art. 19 of the Sex Discrimination (N.I.) Order 1976.
[58] Art. 20 of the Sex Discrimination (N.I.) Order 1976.
[59] Art 21 of the Sex Discrimination (N.I.) Order 1976.
[60] Art. 22 of the Sex Discrimination (N.I.) Order 1976.
[61] Art. 23 of the Sex Discrimination (N.I.) Order 1976.
[62] Arts. 24-29 of the Sex Discrimination (N.I.) Order 1976.
[63] Arts. 27, 28 and see below on the charitable exemption, Art. 78 Sex Discrimination (N.I.) Order 1976.
[64] Arts. 30-36 of the Sex Discrimination (N.I.) Order 1976.

- The provision is contained in a statutory provision or other instrument and
- That provision is for purposes which are exclusively charitable according to the law of Northern Ireland.

The exemption does not apply to all sex discrimination as set out in the Order; it only applies to discrimination on the basis of sex. It does not apply to discrimination on the grounds of marital status. It is therefore arguable that providing benefits for unmarried persons to the exclusion of married persons in the field of employment is now discriminatory. This could conflict with the Statute of Elizabeth with its inclusion in the list of charitable objects of "the marriages of poor maids". Other case law examples are trusts to provide dowries for deserving Jewish girls.[65] Straightforward gifts to unmarried persons are not unlawful. Only if a charity provides employment specifically for unmarried persons would it be discriminating.

Also, as with the other exemptions, exemption from discrimination is not complete. It only applies when a charity is exercising a provision in its constitution which confers a benefit on persons of a certain sex. It will not exempt a charities from an act of sex discrimination which is unrelated to its charitable objects.

4.5.2(i) Meaning of "instrument"

The same conclusions drawn above in relation to other exemptions can be applied here, *viz.* that the exemption applies to any charitable provision whether it be in legislative document or private, formal written document. This approach is supported by the decision in *Hugh Jones v. St. Johns' College Cambridge* where it was held that college statutes were an instrument.[66] It is also supported by reference to Article 78 of the Order which speaks of "any trust deed or other instrument".[67]

4.5.2(ii) Timing and retrospective effect

There are no express provisions on the timing of the legislation or its retrospective effect. In line with the tenor of the other anti-discriminatory exemptions, it is submitted that that which would be deemed discriminatory before the coming into operation of the Order is not retrospectively deemed unlawful. Discriminatory acts which take place after the coming into operation of the Order will be unlawful, regardless of when the charitable instrument was made.

---

[65] *Re Cohen* (1919) 36 T.L.R. 16.
[66] *Hugh Jones v. St. Johns' College Cambridge* (1979) 123 Sol. Jo. 603.
[67] Art. 78(1) of the Sex Discrimination (N.I.) Order 1976.

4.5.3 Educational charities

Special provisions exist to permit educational charities which allow for sex discrimination in their constitution to remove any such clauses.[68] There are a number of prerequisites that such bodies must fulfil and a procedure to be followed before the Charities Branch can remove the discriminatory provision.

4.5.3(i) Prerequisites

The four prerequisites, which must be satisfied before Article 78 can apply, are as follows:

- Firstly, the provision must be contained in a trust deed or other instrument.[69] The usual inclusive interpretation of instrument will apply so that a legislative or private written document will both constitute instruments.
- Secondly, the provision concerns property which is applicable for or in connection with the provision of education.[70]
- Thirdly, the provision is in connection with education in one of five types of educational establishment.[71] These establishments are: grant aided educational establishments, independent schools, universities, the Ulster College or an establishment providing facilities for further education in respect of which contributions are paid to a body other than an Education and Library Board under Article 23(3)(b) of the Education and Libraries (N.I.) Order 1972.[72]
- The fourth prerequisite is that the provision restricts the benefits available to persons of one sex.[73]

The title of Article 78 refers to "educational charities" but there is no mention of charities in the body of the article itself. Specific exemptions already exist for single sex educational establishments and those which wish to become co-educational.[74] The court will be able to look at the title of the article to confirm that it will indeed apply to educational charities.

4.5.3(ii) Procedure

Applications can be made either by the trustees of the instrument or by those

---

[68] Art. 78 of the Sex Discrimination (N.I.) Order 1976.
[69] Art. 78(1) of the Sex Discrimination (N.I.) Order 1976.
[70] Art. 78(1)(a) of the Sex Discrimination (N.I.) Order 1976.
[71] Art. 78(1)(a) of the Sex Discrimination (N.I.) Order 1976.
[72] Art. 24(1)(a) of the Sex Discrimination (N.I.) Order 1976.
[73] Art. 78(1)(b) of the Sex Discrimination (N.I.) Order 1976.
[74] Arts. 27, 28 of the Sex Discrimination (N.I.) Order 1976.

responsible for the educational establishment. Those responsible for the educational establishment shall be one of five bodies, depending on the type of educational establishment it is, as set out in the previous section. These will be: the Education and Library Board/school governors, the proprietor, the governing body, the governors or the governing body.[75]

Applications must be made to the Charities Branch,[76] If the trust was created by gift or bequest within the 25 years preceding the application, the written consent of the donor / his personal representatives, or the personal representatives of the testator must be obtained.[77] The applicants must publish a notice containing the particulars of the proposed order and stating that representations may be made to the Charities Branch within a specified period.[78] A period of at least one month must be specified as the period in which representations can be made.[79] The Charities Branch may specify the way in which the applicants may publish this notice.[80] The cost of any publication can be defrayed out of the trust property.[81]

4.5.3(iii) Order made

The Charities Branch is obliged to take into account any representations made to it.[82] If they are satisfied that the removal or modification of the restriction would be conducive to the advancement of education without sex discrimination, it may modify the instrument to remove or modify the restriction or for any supplemental or incidental purposes.[83]

4.6 DISABILITY DISCRIMINATION

Under the Disability Discrimination Act 1995, discrimination against disabled people is unlawful. The Act applies throughout the United Kingdom, although Schedule 8 makes some minor modifications for Northern Ireland. A disability is described as "a physical or mental impairment which has a substantial and long term adverse effect on his ability to carry out normal day-to-day activities".[84] Discrimination also means victimisation, *i.e.* treating someone

---

[75] Art. 24 of the Sex Discrimination (N.I.) Order 1976.
[76] Art. 78(2) of the Sex Discrimination (N.I.) Order 1976.
[77] Art. 78(3) of the Sex Discrimination (N.I.) Order 1976.
[78] Art. 78(4) of the Sex Discrimination (N.I.) Order 1976.
[79] Art. 78(5) of the Sex Discrimination (N.I.) Order 1976.
[80] Art. 78(6) of the Sex Discrimination (N.I.) Order 1976.
[81] Art. 78(6) of the Sex Discrimination (N.I.) Order 1976.
[82] Art. 78(7) of the Sex Discrimination (N.I.) Order 1976.
[83] Art. 78(2) of the Sex Discrimination (N.I.) Order 1976.
[84] s. 1(1) of the Disability Discrimination Act 1995.

less favourably because they have initiated or helped in a claim of disability discrimination.[85]

4.6.1 Types of discrimination deemed unlawful

Disability discrimination only applies to direct not indirect discrimination.[86] It applies to discrimination in the employment field.[87] This includes discrimination against contract workers[88] and by trade organisations.[89] Discrimination also extends to discrimination in the provision of goods, facilities and services.[90] There are also various provisions relating to public transport.[91]

4.6.2 Exemptions for charities

The exemption for charities is contained in section 10 and is limited in its ambit to discrimination in the field of employment and not any other field.

There are two separate exemptions. The first is the usual one that charitable instruments which confer benefits on persons determined by reference to physical or mental capacity are not effected by the legislation in the employment field. The usual threefold test is present:

- Charity exercising a provision which confers benefits on persons due to their disability,
- This provision is contained in an instrument, and
- This provision is exclusively charitable in the law of Northern Ireland.[92]

The second exemption is implicit in the other pieces of legislation but is made explicit here. In the employment field, the Act does not make unlawful any act done by a charity in pursuance of its charitable purposes so far as these purposes are connected with persons determined by reference to a disability.[93]

4.6.2(i) Meaning of "instrument"

The legislation defines "charitable instrument" as meaning "an enactment or other instrument".[94] The same conclusions drawn with reference to other anti-

---

[85] s. 55 of the Disability Discrimination Act 1995.
[86] ss.5,13,19 of the Disability Discrimination Act 1995.
[87] Part II of the Disability Discrimination Act 1995.
[88] s. 12 of the Disability Discrimination Act 1995.
[89] s. 13 of the Disability Discrimination Act 1995.
[90] Part III of the Disability Discrimination Act 1995.
[91] Part V of the Disability Discrimination Act 1995.
[92] s. 10(1)(a) of the Disability Discrimination Act 1995.
[93] s. 10(1)(b)of the Disability Discrimination Act 1995.
[94] s. 10(3) of the Disability Discrimination Act 1995.

discrimination exemptions apply here, *viz.* that "instrument" can mean a legislative provision or a private formal written document.

4.6.2(ii) Timing and retrospective effect

Activities which would have been discriminatory before the coming into operation of the Disability Discrimination Act 1995 are not retrospectively made unlawful. The full rigours of the Order and the charitable exemption are applicable after the Order came into force. This is regardless of whether the discriminatory provision was made before or after the coming into effect of the Order.[95]

4.7 HUMAN RIGHTS

The full impact of the Human Rights Act 1998 is impossible to predict. In the area of charity law, as in all others, it will be some time before we know which of its provisions will present the greatest challenge to established law and practice.

4.7.1 Applicability of human rights norms

The United Kingdom has been a signatory to the European Convention on Human Rights and Fundamental Freedoms 1950 (the Convention) since 1953. The Human Rights Act 1998 incorporates the Convention into domestic law and came fully into force in Northern Ireland on October 2, 2000. Whilst any Northern Ireland Assembly is in existence, it is also subject to the Convention under the Northern Ireland Act 1998. Furthermore, the Good Friday Agreement and the Northern Ireland Act make provision for the creation of a Bill of Rights for Northern Ireland which may contain human rights additional to the Convention.

It was not necessary to wait for the implementation of the 1998 Act in order to rely on the protection available under the Convention. Case law indicates that the Convention could be used as an aid to interpretation, especially if the law was ambiguous on a point:

> "... the Convention is not, of course, law, though it is legitimate to consider its provisions in interpreting law, and naturally I give it full weight for this purpose."[46]

---

[95] s. 10(3) of the Disability Discrimination Act 1995.
[96] *Trawnick v. Ministry of Defence* (1984) 2 All E.R. 791 at 798, see also *Attorney General v. Guardian Newspapers (No. 2)* [1990] 1 A.C. 109 at 183 and *Derbyshire County Council v. Times Newspapers* [1992] Q.B. 770 at 812.

4.7.2 Human rights and political activity

Where a charity engages in campaigning or other such political activity for the purpose of promoting human rights then it should now find protection under the 1998 Act. Charities should now be free to develop cross community initiatives designed to bridge political divisions and consolidate the growth of a more civil society in Northern Ireland.

4.7.3 Human rights and religion

In the context of religion, the two most relevant Convention rights are Article 9, freedom of thought, conscience and religion, and Article 14, prohibition on discrimination. The creative nature of human rights jurisprudence has historically meant that a variety of rights can be used for purposes only tangentially relevant to their title.

Article 9 states that:

> 1. Everyone has the right to freedom of thought, conscience and religion; this right includes freedom to change his religion or belief and freedom, either alone or in community with others and in public or private, to manifest his religion or belief, in worship, teaching, practice and observance.

> 2. Freedom to manifest one's religion or beliefs shall be subject only to such limitations as are prescribed by law and are necessary in a democratic society in the interests of public safety, for the protection of public order, health or morals, or for the protection of the rights and freedom of others.

Article14 states that:

> "The enjoyment of the rights and freedoms set forth in this Convention shall be secured without discrimination on any ground such as sex, race, colour, language, religion, political or other opinion, national or social origin, association with a national minority, property, birth or other status."

The commonly accepted view is that it is wrong to discriminate between different religions. For example, if a state provides a privilege, right or benefit to one group then:

> "… it must treat all similar groups equally and provide them the same privileges, rights and benefits, unless there is justification to support the difference in treatment."[97]

the general view in charity law is that all religions are treated equally (see further, Chapter 10). No direct discrimination is permitted between them. However, it could be argued that there is indirect discrimination when the public benefit test as set out in Chapter 10 is considered. The argument is that the law

---

[97] See Francesca Quint and Thomas Spring, "Religion, Charity Law and Human Rights" (1999) 3 *Charity Law and Practice Review* 153.

indirectly discriminates against enclosed, primarily Roman Catholic, groups. It does this by providing a condition (open religious access/worship) which ostensibly applies to all religions. However, certain religions (*i.e.* Catholicism) due to their nature and belief structures find it more difficult to comply with this condition. The point remains to be litigated in the light of the Human Rights Act 1998.

4.7.4 Human rights and general charitable exemptions from discrimination

Article 14 of the Convention may have a broader effect than the definition of religion in common law. It also has the potential to scythe into the exemptions charities have from the various pieces of anti-discrimination legislation. The argument is that Article 14 prohibits discrimination on the grounds of sex, race, political opinion or religion (although not disability). Therefore, charities should not be entitled to operate partisan policies when selecting beneficiaries on any of these grounds.

However, Article 14 cannot act on its own; it has to attach itself to another right. This is a point for legal and/or judicial creativity. If a relevant human right can be found in which a charity is offering benefits which discriminate, then there will be a breach of Article 14. The right to freedom of religion is such an example. Another example is a right contained in a protocol to the Convention signed in 1952, which is the right to education.[98] The entry into force of the Human Rights Act 1998 may help clarify these issues.

---

[98] Art. 2, Protocol to the Convention on Human Rights and Fundamental Freedoms, Paris, 20.III.1952.

SECTION TWO

Administration

CHAPTER 5

The Administrative Agencies

5.1 INTRODUCTION

Charity law is largely administrative. Reserved for the courts are matters referred by the Attorney-General and/or by the Charities Branch where the issues are complex, involve a fine point of law, require interpretation or where a *cy-près* scheme concerning property valued at £50,000 is needed. Decisions of the Charities Branch can also be appealed to the High Court. Most issues affecting charities never reach the courts. They are filtered out and determined by one of the relevant administrative bodies.

A range of non-judicial *fora* is now available to settle issues relating to donors, charities and charitable activities. The Charities Branch will, on request, use its powers to give advice or make decisions upon many issues affecting the running of charities. The Inland Revenue will rule on whether or not the purposes and activities of an organisation are such as to warrant its recognition as a charity for tax exemption purposes. The Valuation and Lands Agency and, where appropriate, the Lands Tribunal will determine eligibility for rates exemption on charitable grounds.

Other non-judicial bodies exist to register the existence of certain types of charities and thereafter to set standards for good practice and require a degree of accountability in terms of how a charity is constituted, its aims and activities and an annual report presenting at least a statement of accounts. For example, the many charities with company status must satisfy the requirements of the Companies Registry Office. Other charities with the status of either an industrial and provident society or a friendly society must do so in relation to their respective Registries.

Both sets of non-judicial bodies play an important role in setting parameters for the practice standards of charities in Northern Ireland. However, certain questions arise. Is it really necessary to have so many of them? Would it be possible to co-ordinate the functions of the bodies within and between each set? Why are all bodies restricted to a reactive role? Should not one body be vested with the duty and the powers necessary to be pro-active in inspecting and monitoring charities in accordance with one fixed set of standards?

This chapter outlines the powers and duties of administrative agencies within the relevant statutory context and examines the co-ordination of their different areas of responsibility. It confines itself to a largely descriptive sketch of their respective roles and functions, leaving to later chapters a more particular consideration of the resulting implications for practice as illustrated by case law.

5.2 THE VOLUNTARY ACTIVITY UNIT

This government body was established, within the Department of Health and Social Services, in 1993[1] following recommendations to that effect made in the formative *Strategy*[2] document. In the words of J. Kearney,[3] the first director of the Voluntary Activity Unit (VAU), this broke new ground by providing:

> "a clear statement of the strategic aims of Northern Ireland departments in supporting the voluntary sector. These are:
>
> * to encourage, promote and support an independent, vigorous and cost-effective voluntary sector in the province;
> * to encourage and promote voluntary activity;
> * to ensure that maximum benefit is obtained from the resources which they make available to the voluntary sector;
> * to build on the experience of the voluntary sector in the development and advancement of departmental policy objectives, recognising the value of its independent perspective;
>
> a statement of the common and agreed principles underpinning all departments' support for the sector;
>
> a statement of the action which departments will take in pursuing the scope for securing greater consistency among their grant-making procedures and in developing good practice;
>
> a sectoral strategy for each area of business – for example, health and personal social services and rural development."[4]

Once established, the VAU embarked on an ambitious programme which included measures designed to ensure that all government departments in Northern Ireland, when framing policy initiatives, took into account their possible impact upon the voluntary sector. The VAU also assumed responsibility for the law relating to charities. Among its duties was, and continues to be, supervising the work of the Charities Branch. This entailed instituting a review of

---

[1] Announced by Sir Patrick Mayhew QC, MP on June 14, 1993 in the course of his address during a NICVA conference entitled *Partners or Adversaries – the Voluntary Sector's Developing Relations with Government and the Significance of the European Framework*.

[2] See Dept. of Health and Social Services, *Draft Strategy Statement on the Role and Aims of the Voluntary Activity Unit*, 1993. Also see, DHSS, *Strategy for the Support of the Voluntary Sector and for Community Development in Northern Ireland*, HMSO, Belfast, 1993.

[3] Currently, Visiting Professor at the Centre for Voluntary Action Studies, University of Ulster.

[4] See Kearney J., "The Development of Government Policy and its Strategy toward the Voluntary and Community Sectors" in Acheson, N., and Williamson, W., (eds.) *Voluntary Action and Social Policy in Northern Ireland*, Avebury, Aldershot, 1995, at p. 21.

charity law in Northern Ireland and publishing the resulting consultation proposal for a Draft Charities (N.I.) Order.

5.3 THE CHARITIES BRANCH

In Northern Ireland, the Charities Branch is that part of government administration charged with responsibility for the affairs of charities.[5] In England, the equivalent body is the Charity Commission. In Ireland, this responsibility falls to the Commissioners of Charitable Donations and Bequests. Their respective spheres of responsibility are very different.

The Charities Branch, strictly speaking, has no authority for independent action, it is merely the conduit through which the Department acts. It is the Department which is vested with authority and jurisdiction over charities. Administratively, however, the Department's powers are devolved to and exercised by the Charities Branch. In certain cases authority must be specifically delegated from within the Department but for most practical purposes it is the Charities Branch which deals with the day to day decisions. For the sake of consistency, the Charities Branch is referred to in this text as the agency with government responsibility for charities in Northern Ireland.

5.3.1 History of the Charities Branch

The responsibilities of the Charities Branch were formerly undertaken by the Commissioners of Charitable Donations and Bequests in Ireland. The latter body was set up and regulated under the auspices of a series of Charitable Donations and Bequests Acts (Ireland) 1844, 1867 and 1871. According to the Preamble to the 1844 Act its purpose was that:

> "... the pious intentions of charitable persons should not be defeated by the concealment and misapplication of their donations and bequests to public and private charities in Ireland."

The members of the Commissioners were then three judges and ten other persons, five of whom had to be Catholic.

After partition the functions of the Commissioners were transferred to the Ministry of Finance under section 1 and Schedule 1 of the Ministries of Northern Ireland Act (N.I.) 1921 and the Assignment of Functions Order of June 7, 1921. According to the courts, the Ministry is not exactly the "successor" of the Commissioners, but rather:

---

[5] Part I of the Charities Act (N.I.) 1964 is entitled "Powers of the Ministry of Finance as Charity Authority". The Ministry of Finance was historically the ministry under which the Charities Branch acted.

[6] *Re Townsend Street Belfast Presbyterian Endowment Trusts* [1954] N.I. 53, at p. 60.

"... the Ministry is the department responsible for the administration in Northern Ireland of the Irish service formerly administered by the Charity Commissioners."[6]

A Charities Advisory Committee, to be set up by an order of June 12, 1922 to assist the Ministry, never functioned.[7]

After the political partition of the island of Ireland, all the functions of the initial body remained in place. The Acts of 1844, 1867 and 1871 remained until they were repealed by the Charities Act (N.I.) 1964. This now provides the statutory source of authority for the functions of the Charities Branch.

The 1964 Act designated the Ministry of Finance as the body responsible for charity administration in Northern Ireland. In 1993 the responsibility for charity administration was statutorily transferred from the Ministry of Finance to the Department of Health and Social Services.[8] On December 2, 1999 the Department for Social Development was created[9] and the DHSS's functions were transferred to the Department for Social Development.[10] The Charities Branch now operates under the auspices of that Department.

5.3.2 General powers of the Charities Branch

The powers of this body are facilitative rather than regulatory in nature. It has described its responsibilities as follows:

> "Its main functions concern giving consent to the disposal of land or buildings by charity trustees, who usually cannot sell or otherwise dispose of such property without specific consent, and making Schemes to change the objects of charities whose original functions can no longer be carried out effectively.
>
> Apart from its specific functions under the legislation a major part of the Branch's work consists of giving informal advice to trustees and their solicitors."[11]

The Charities Branch exercises its powers to facilitate the better administration of charities in Northern Ireland. It also has powers to change the structure of charities, to protect charities both from external threats and internal abuses, and to monitor their performance. It can recover its costs from charities for any work carried out in managing their property or carrying out any of its functions under the 1964 Act.[12] It cannot recover its own or any government department's staff costs. In practice the only costs usually recovered are for placing adverts or notices in papers, etc. Other overhead costs would be too uneconomic to measure or recover.

---

[7] See Delany (1956).

[8] Department (Transfer of Functions) (No. 2) Order (N.I.) SI 1993/493

[9] Departments (N.I.) Order 1999.

[10] Departments (Transfer and Assignment of Functions) Order (N.I.) 1999.

[11] See Charities Branch, *Consultation Document on Charity Law in Northern Ireland*, DHSS, Belfast, 1995.

[12] See s. 33.

5.3.2(i) Advice

Under section 1 of the 1964 Act, the trustees of a charity may apply to the Department for a formal written opinion on any matter or question affecting the charity. The Charities Branch may give this advice under seal. If a trustee acts on this advice he is deemed to have acted in accordance with the terms of the trust, even if a court subsequently rules otherwise.[13] This provides some degree of protection for a trustee who is unclear as to the legal ramifications of his actions. This protection will not apply if he had been guilty of fraud or misrepresentation,[14] nor if the matter is already before the court.

In practice, the Charities Branch gives informal advice to charities and their solicitors on a day to day basis. This informal advice will provide a certain degree of protection for any trustee who relies upon it.

The Charities Branch could give advice to charities upon request under section 2 of the Charitable Bequests and Donations Act (Ireland) 1867. The advice then had to be authenticated by its seal.[15] The advice gave similar protection to non-fraudulent trustees. In England section 29 of the Charities Act 1993 authorises the Commission to give advice in a similar manner. The Commission is immune from civil proceedings based on the quality of the advice they give. For example, in *Mills* v. *Winchester Diocesan Board of Finance*[16] the court held that an action in negligence would not lie against the Commission for giving wrong advice. Further protection was given to the Commission by the decision in *Weth* v. *Attorney General*[17] which held that they need not be made defendants to an High Court appeal against one of their own orders. The plaintiffs had alleged bias and misconduct against the Commission, but since no relief could be had against the Commission, it was pointless to join it as a party to the appeal. Presumably the same protection would be extended to the Charities Branch in Northern Ireland.

5.3.2(ii) Scrutiny of wills

The Master (Probate and Matrimonial) is obliged to make an annual certified return to the Charities Branch of all charitable gifts to be applied or paid in Northern Ireland which are contained in wills.[18] The return must specify: the name of the testator, the names of the executors, the date of the will and the date of the grant of probate or letters of administration. In practice, rather than a certified return, the Probate and Matrimonial Office send the Charities Branch a copy of all wills containing charitable bequests.

---

[13] See s. 1(3).
[14] See s. 1(4).
[15] See s. 5 of the Charitable Bequests and Donations Act (Ireland) 1867.
[16] [1989] Ch. 428.
[17] Unreported, *The Times*, October 12, 1998.
[18] s. 30 of the Charities Act (N.I.) 1964.

This requirement provides the data for two further functions of the Charities Branch:

- Firstly, the provision of a statistical breakdown and analysis of charitable bequests. This is contained in the annual reports of the Charities Branch provided under section 34 of the Charities Act (N.I.) 1964.

- Secondly, there is a monitoring and compliance function under section 4 of the 1964 Act. The Charities Branch can require executors to furnish them with evidence that any charitable bequest in a will has been applied for the benefit of the charity. If the property is left for ill-defined purposes (*e.g.* "for such charities as my executors may select" or "for Masses") the Department may require the production of receipts to show that the bequest has been paid. In 1998 the Charities Branch asked for receipts in just one case.[19]

Sometimes property is bequeathed for the use of an individual during his or her life (a "life interest") with the provision that on death it is to pass to a charity. The Charities Branch may require the production of evidence, a certificate of awareness, to show that the charity concerned is aware of the existence of such a bequest. Once the charity knows about the bequest it must take responsibility for pursuing its interest. The Charities Branch has no further role.

There is no standard form for a "certificate of awareness". All that is needed is a document or series of documents providing evidence that the charity is aware of the bequest. This evidence may take the form of: a letter from the charity saying that it is aware of the bequest that will pass to it in due course; a letter from the charity saying that it has received a copy of the will; or a copy of the solicitor's letter explaining the bequest together with a letter of acknowledgement from the charity. Two certificates of awareness where asked for and received in 1998.[20]

Finally, the power to scrutinise wills also enables the Charities Branch to make an order requiring publication of charitable bequests.[21] Executors can be obliged to publish details of any charitable bequests in the manner indicated by the Charities Branch.

It is a criminal offence for an executor to fail to comply with any of the provisions relating to the scrutiny of wills.[22]

5.3.2(iii) Schemes of incorporation.

Under section 10 of the 1964 Act, a "scheme of incorporation" has the effect of turning the trustees of a charity (not the charity itself) into a body corporate

---

[19] Two in 1997, none in 1996.
[20] Three in 1997, five in 1996.
[21] Charities Act (N.I.) 1964, s. 4(1)(b).
[22] Charities Act (N.I.) 1964, s. 4(2).

with perpetual succession (see further, Chapters 6 and 16). This means that when new trustees are appointed the charity property vests in them automatically and there is no need for a formal deed of appointment of new trustees to be executed. This is of particular value to charities which hold large amounts of real property.

5.3.2(iv) Appointment of new trustees

Under section 12 of the 1964 Act, there is such a power of appointment. In normal circumstances the new trustees of a charity are appointed by the existing trustees, or if all the trustees have died, by the personal representatives of the last surviving trustee. However, the Charities Branch may appoint new trustees to a charity if there are no trustees or if they refuse to act or if they cannot be found.[23] In the case of some schools, the Department of Education, as a party to a school lease, may also be able to appoint trustees.

This power to make an order appointing new trustees is a measure of last resort and can only be used where the only alternative way of appointing new trustees would be by means of an application to the courts which would be excessively expensive for the charity. It cannot be used as an expedient alternative for applicants than trying to trace the personal representatives. It can only be used where an incumbent trustee wishes to be discharged or refuses to discharge their responsibilities. It cannot be used by Charities Branch to deal with incompetent or inefficient trustees.

The new trustees may be in addition to or in substitution for the old trustees. Detailed provisions exist, where the old trustees do not wish to be replaced, as to procedures and appeals.[24] Two orders were made under section 12 in 1998.[25]

5.3.2(v) Cy-près *schemes*

Under section 13 of the 1964 Act, such a scheme may be utilised to change the terms and/or purposes of a moribund charity so as to allow it to function more effectively. It is an established principle of law that the changes made must be the minimum necessary; the original purposes of the charity must be preserved as far as possible (see further, Chapter 19). Four schemes were made in 1998.[26]

---

[23] s. 12.

[24] See further s. 12(2) and s. 12(15); for the English equivalent rules see s. 18 and s. 48(6) of the Charities Act 1993. See also s. 17 of the Charitable Uses (Ir) Act 1763 and s. 3 of the Trustee Appointment Act 1850 for specialised rules on trustee appointment. See further, Chap. 6.

[25] Three in 1997, one in 1996.

[26] Six in 1997, ten in 1996.

5.3.2(vi) Misdescribed bequests

Under section 14 of the 1964 Act, where a testator has left a bequest of less than £2,500 to a charity in his or her will, but failed to describe the charity accurately, his personal representatives can deliver the bequest to the Charities Branch. They then have no further responsibility for the bequest and the Charities Branch becomes responsible for deciding which charity is to benefit from the bequest. This provision is really a way of avoiding having to make a *cy-près* scheme for such a small amount: a bequest of more than £2,500 in similar circumstances could only be dealt with by way of a *cy-près* scheme or a court scheme.

5.3.2(vii) Transfer of property

The Charities Branch may accept the transfer of charitable property to be held by itself on charitable trusts[27] or may accept any property whatsoever to be held on whatever charitable trusts the transferor directs.[28] The Charities Branch then becomes the sole trustee of the charity and the existing trustees are discharged and have no further responsibility for its future administration. This usually occurs in connection with the making of a *cy-près* scheme, though occasionally trustees will wish to be relieved of their duties because of age and will request that the Charities Branch assume full responsibility.

The Charities Branch is not obliged to accept a transfer under section 15 and before it does it will seek answers to the following questions:

(a) Are all the existing trustees agreeable to the proposed transfer? Theoretically, a two-thirds majority could insist on an application for a transfer under section 15 despite the wishes of the remainder.[29] The Charities Branch would be reluctant to accept a transfer in such circumstances.

(b) Can the Charities Branch administer the charity? It would be impractical for the Charities Branch to attempt to do so where specialist knowledge was required (*e.g.* a home for the elderly).

(c) Is the charity property in an acceptable form? The Charities Branch would almost certainly not accept a transfer of real property under section 15 because of the obvious administrative difficulties.

(d) Is all the necessary documentary evidence available: of the objectives and terms of the charity; and details of its administration. Examples of types of evidence would include: a *cy-près* scheme, if one is made; a copy of the will, if the charity is founded on a bequest, or of its deed of trust, constitution or other governing instrument; copies of correspondence, documents,

---

[27] Charities Act (N.I.) 1964, s. 15(1).

[28] s. 15(2).

[29] s. 26 of the Charities Act (N.I.) 1964 allows a two-thirds majority of trustees to act in certain circumstances, see further, Chap. 6.

> minutes of meetings etc, giving details of how the charity was set up and administered; a written statement by the trustees giving details of the charity's history and method of operation.

Having accepted the transfer, the Charities Branch can then appoint local administrators to run the trust.[30] Where the Charities Branch declines to exercise this power it is usually because:

- The trustees are trying to retain power while divesting themselves of responsibility, or
- The charity is moribund and the trustees should be applying for a new *cyprès* scheme, or
- Another mechanism, such as incorporation under section 10 or the provisions of Articles 3, 4 or 5 of the Charities (N.I.) Order 1987 would better serve the interests of the charitable trust.

Most often it declines to exercise this power for two reasons. Firstly it may encourage laxity in the remaining trustees if they feel that the Charities Branch has now taken over the running of the trust. Secondly, if the reason for the application is to facilitate the holding of property, other options exist, for example the trustees could become incorporated under section 10.

In England, the equivalent holding trustee is the Official Custodian for Charities, an officer of the Charity Commission.

5.3.2(viii) Receipts

Where a charitable gift has been made but for some reason there are no trustees to give a valid receipt of the gift (for example if they are all dead or cannot be found), the Charities Branch may accept the gift[31] and must then apply it for the purposes for which it was given.

5.3.2(ix) Protection of charity property

If charitable property is subject to court proceedings and is not being applied for the benefit of the charity, the Charities Branch may apply to court for that property. The Charities Branch must then apply that property in accordance with the direction of the court and the charitable trust.[32] The Charities Branch must give the Attorney General notice before it applies to court for this purpose.[33]

---

[30] s. 15(3).
[31] Charities Act (N.I.) 1964, s. 7.
[32] s. 8 *ibid.*
[33] s. 8(3).

5.3.2(x) Deposit of deeds

The deed or instruments of a charity can be deposited with the Charities Branch for safekeeping if the latter so consents.[34] The trustees or any persons having custody of the documents can apply to the Charities Branch to exercise this power. The Charities Branch may establish and maintain such facilities as it thinks necessary for this purpose.

5.3.2(xi) Annual report

The Charities Branch is obliged to prepare an annual report of its proceedings.[35] The report must contain details of: charitable bequests, *cy-près* schemes, constitutional amendments to charities investment funds, etc.

5.3.3 The power of disposal

The bulk of the work of the Charities Branch is concerned with exercising its powers, under sections 17 and 18 of the 1964 Act, to authorise trustees to dispose of charity property. These provisions grant trustees powers additional to those contained in the trust so long as they are authorised by the Charities Branch. Generally, the Charities Branch will exercise these powers if they are satisfied that their exercise would be for the benefit of the charity. Under section 21, the powers available in sections 17-20 may be applied with retrospective effect. There are nine basic types of case; the first four account for 95 per cent of cases.

5.3.3(i) Sale

Under section 18 of the 1964 Act, a straightforward sale of charity property (with or without a ground rent) can be authorised. This can apply to any type of charity property (other than some teachers' residences). In some cases, the power of sale may be applied for and granted where it is not strictly necessary in order to satisfy a purchaser about the charity's right to sell. In 1998 the Charities Branch authorised 29 sales, producing gross proceeds of £4,107,000.[36]

5.3.3(ii) Sale of teachers' residences

Uniquely, under Article 90 of the Education and Libraries (N.I.) Order 1986, a teacher's residence can be sold. In such a case the £50,000 *cy-près* limit does not apply. In order for a residence to qualify for Article 90 treatment it

---

[34] Charities Act (N.I.) 1964, s.28.
[35] Charities Act (N.I.) 1964, s.34.
[36] Thirty nine sales in 1997, thirty one in 1996.

must have been built with the aid of a statutory loan made by the Commissioners of Public Works in Ireland.

A second requirement of Article 90 is that the residence must be held "for an estate not limited by reference to any condition as to user". This means that if the residence is held under a lease made pursuant to the Leases for Schools (Ireland) Act 1881, which contains provisions for reversion when the property ceases to be used for the original purposes, it may not be possible to use Article 90.

5.3.3(iii) Surrender of lease

Under section 18 of the 1964 Act, there is a power for trustees who hold a property under a lease to surrender that lease and therefore the property to the lessor. This most often occurs in "Standard School Lease" cases. There were 13 surrenders of lease in 1998.[37]

5.3.3(iv) Lease

Under section 17 of the 1964 Act, there is a power enabling trustees to lease a part of their property. This they may do either for a few years (*e.g.* to raise money) or for a long period (*e.g.* to enable a school, youth club etc to be built). The lease can be a specific one such as a building, repairing or improving lease, or to allow for the working of any mines or minerals. In 1998 there were six leases authorised.[38]

5.3.3(v) Sale of contingent interest

Under section 18 of the 1964 Act, there is a power enabling a charity to sell its contingent interest. For example, someone may bequeath property by will to Mr A for his life, and on his death to Mr B absolutely, with the proviso that if A survives B the property is to go to a charity on A's death. In such cases the charity will sometimes wish to sell its contingent interest to A (who will also buy B's interest and thus secure the property for his children). This is generally similar to a normal sale except that the value of the charity's interest is dependent on the chances of B outliving A.

5.3.3(vi) Sale under governing instrument

In a few cases, charities which operate under court schemes or acts of parliament require the consent of the Charities Branch to sell, etc., their property.

---

[37] Eight in 1997 and six in 1996.
[38] Ten in 1997, six in 1996.

Since consent is not being given under the Charities Act (N.I.) 1964 it can be given by letter rather than by sealed application forms.

5.3.3(vii) Exchange of lands

In this case the trustees wish to exchange part of their lands for land belonging to someone else. Some payment may be involved to balance the transaction. There was one exchange of lands in 1998.[39]

5.3.3(viii) Mortgage

The trustees will require the consent of the Charities Branch if they wish to mortgage their property to a bank for the purposes of raising capital. The last mortgage authorised by the Charities Branch was in 1996.

5.3.3(ix) Miscellaneous powers concerning property

The Charities Branch can authorise a wide range of other actions by trustees concerning land belonging to a charity. They can authorise: digging or raising any stone, clay, gravel or other minerals;[40] cutting any timber;[41] making any new road, street, or laying any drains or sewers through the land;[42] erecting, repairing, altering, rebuilding or removing any existing buildings on the land;[43] or making any other improvements or alterations in the land.[44] The Charities Branch can also consent to the trustees redeeming any rent-charges on any land for which they receive or pay rent-charges.[45] The last redemption of a rent-charge authorised by the Charities Branch was in 1996.

5.3.3(x) Retrospective powers

All the above powers may be given retrospectively, *i.e.* after the transaction has been completed. This usually occurs where property has been disposed of without the prior consent of the Charities Branch and the purchaser subsequently discovers that his building society will not accept that he has a good title to the property until retrospective consent is obtained. Application for retrospective consent can only be made by the charity trustees. The valuation is taken at the time of sale.

---

[39] None in 1997 and one in 1996.
[40] Charities Act (N.I.) 1964, s.17(1)(b).
[41] Charities Act (N.I.) 1964, s.17(1)(c).
[42] Charities Act (N.I.) 1964, s.17(1)(d).
[43] Charities Act (N.I.) 1964, s.17(1)(e).
[44] Charities Act (N.I.) 1964, s.17(1)(f).
[45] Charities Act (N.I.) 1964, ss. 19, 20.

5.3.4 The power of disposal: procedure

The process whereby trustees apply for Charities Branch consent to dispose of property is as outlined below. Some steps may be taken concurrently.

5.3.4(i) Interest

What interest in the property do the trustees wish to dispose of, *i.e.* do they wish to apply for a power of sale, lease or surrender?

5.3.4(ii) Title

(a) Do the trustees actually own the property? In the case of church property it will sometimes turn out that the clergymen who purport to be the trustees have never been formally appointed.

(b) Are the right trustees applying? In a complicated case with several sets of trustees, there may be confusion as to who needs to apply for what.

(c) Do the trustees already have power to sell, etc? Sometimes the trustees already have powers of disposal contained in the title documents, or their constitution or other governing instrument. In which case the consent of the Charities Branch is not required.

(d) Is the property held upon a charitable trust, and if so, what is the nature of the trust? There may be an implied trust.

(e) Are there any unusual provisions in the title documents?

5.3.5 The power to change charities

The Charities Branch is authorised to change the constitution of charities and charitable gifts. These powers are contained both in the Charities (N.I.) Order 1987 and the Charities Act (N.I.) 1964.

The first such power is provided under Article 3 of the 1987 Order and allows the Charities Branch to concur in the alteration of the objects of old charities for the relief of poverty in a certain locality. The charity must be older than 50 years[46] and cannot be a corporate body.[47] The trustees must be of the opinion that the objects are now obsolete or useless due to the passing of time and that alteration of the objects is required to better effect the original intention.[48] They must take steps to obtain the approval of the founder of the

---

[46] Art. 3(1)(c).
[47] Art. 3(1)(b).
[48] Art. 3(2).

charity.[49] The trustees may then pass a unanimous[50] resolution to create objects which are as similar as possible to the old ones.[51] The trustees must inform the Charities Branch of the proposal. The Charities Branch then has three months to consider the alteration and either concur or reject it.[52] If it accepts, the resolution effects the alteration of the objects.[53]

Article 4 grants a power to small charities to transfer all their property to another charity, subject to the agreement of the Charities Branch. The charity must have a gross annual income of less than £200 and the transferee must accept the transfer in written form.[54] The transferor cannot be a corporate body.[55] The objects of the transferee must not be too dissimilar to the objects of the transferor[56] and the transferor must take reasonable steps to obtain the approval of the founder. The trustees must then pass a unanimous[57] resolution in the form set out in Schedule 2 of the Order. They must give public notice of this resolution if that would serve a useful purpose[58] and must give copies of it to the Charities Branch.[59] The latter has powers to investigate the matter[60] but must accept, refuse or adjourn the resolution[61] within three months. If it concurs, the transfer may take place.

In England these two provisions have been consolidated into section 74 of the Charities Act 1993. The charity must have an income of less than £5,000, not own any land and not be a corporate body.[62] Only a two thirds majority[63] and not unanimity is required by resolution to either transfer the property to another charity or alter the purposes of the charity. The trustees in England, unlike in Northern Ireland, also have the power to pass a resolution to alter the administration of a charity.[64]

The Charity Commission has produced guidelines on when and how this power to change the constitution of small charities should be exercised in "small charities".[65] Before this procedure is embarked upon, it recommends that the trustees consider:

---

[49] Art. 3(4).

[50] Art. 3(5).

[51] Art. 3(3).

[52] Art. 3(8).

[53] Art. 3(9).

[54] Art. 4(2).

[55] Art. 4(11).

[56] Art. 4(2)(b).

[57] Art. 4(4).

[58] Art. 4(5)(a).

[59] Art. 4(5)(b).

[60] Art. 4(6).

[61] Art. 4(7).

[62] Charities Act 1993, s. 74(1).

[63] *ibid.*, s.74(3).

[64] s. 74(2)(d).

[65] CC4 Small Charities, Transfer of Property, Alteration of Trusts, Expenditure of Capital (Charity Commission, 1999).

- The annual and predicted income of the charity.
- Value of the charity's assets and whether they could be more beneficially invested to increase income and capital.
- Whether the charity still serves useful purposes in its area.
- Whether there is another charity in the area with similar purposes with which the charity could be combined to increase effectiveness.
- Whether local needs could be better met by spending the charity's resources than by keeping their capital to produce an income.

Article 5 of the Charities (N.I.) Order 1987 makes provision for small charities to spend their capital as well as their income. The Charities Branch is required to monitor the exercise of this power, but can neither consent nor object to it being used. A charity must have a permanent endowment of less than £25, have no land and have income of less than £5 per year.[66] If the property is too small to allow any useful purpose to be fulfilled by only spending income, the trustees may pass a resolution removing any restrictions on capital expenditure.[67] That resolution must be unanimous[68] and be in a form set out in Schedule 3 to the 1987 Order. The trustees must first consider whether it would be better to make a transfer to a similar charity under Article 4 of the 1987 Order. The Charities Branch must be sent a copy of this resolution, but they cannot veto it.

In England and Wales, a similar English provision is contained in section 75 of the Charities Act 1993, though some differences exist. The charities which may apply must have an income of less than £1,000.[69] Only a two-thirds majority of trustees are required to support the resolution.[70] The Commission may require extra information from the trustees.[71] The most significant difference is that in England and Wales the Commission does not have a monitoring role but has an active interventionist role. It must concur with the resolution before it can have any effect.[72]

The other powers to change charities or charitable gifts have already been noted. The Charities Branch may create a scheme of incorporation for charitable trustees who wish to have a corporate status.[73] The Charities Branch has power to make *cy-près* schemes[74] and apply small failed gifts.[75] They may

---

[66] Art. 5(1).
[67] Art. 5(1).
[68] Art. 5(3).
[69] Charities Act 1993, s.75(1).
[70] *ibid.*, s.75(3).
[71] s. 75(5).
[72] s. 75(8).
[73] s. 10, and see further above.
[74] s. 13, 22, 23 and see further above and Chap. 19.
[75] s. 14 and see further above.

also make schemes to save gifts which are partly charitable and partly non charitable.[76]

5.3.6 The power to monitor charities

The powers and functions of the Charities Branch in relation to the monitoring of charities are embryonic. In Northern Ireland, trustees have a duty to keep proper books of account (*i.e.* accounting records) and to prepare periodical statements[77] consisting of either a receipts/payments statement or an income/expenditure statement.[78] The Charities Branch may direct any charity to also include a balance sheet in its statement of account if the value of its property exceeds £500.[79] The books of account and statements of account must be kept for at least seven years, unless the charity ceases to exist and the Charities Branch authorises a disposal of the accounts.[80]

In England, the detailed requirements to keep accounts and send annual returns to the Commissioners span the entirety of Part VI of the Charities Act 1993, from section 41 to section 49 as opposed to the one section in the corresponding Northern Ireland legislation. Accounting records (*i.e.* books of account) must be kept for at least six years.[81] The charity must also prepare annual statements of account[82] in a form prescribed by the Secretary of State in the Charities (Accounts and Reports) Regulations 1995 S.I. 1995/2724. These accounts are considerably more detailed than those required in Northern Ireland. Even the exemption for charities with an income of less than £100,000 per year[83] requires a receipts/payments account and a statement of assets and liabilities (*i.e.* a balance sheet). If the charity has income or expenditure of over £250,000 the accounts must be audited by a qualified auditor.[84] If the income or expenditure is over £10,000 the accounts must be examined by an independent examiner.[85] The Commission may order an audit if they think it desirable or if the audit/examination has not been made within ten months of the end of the accounting year.[86] Charities must submit annual reports to the Commissioners with the accounts annexed to them.[87] These ac-

---

[76] s. 24 and see further Chap. 15.

[77] s. 27.

[78] s. 27(1)(a).

[79] s. 27(1)(b); it has not given such a direction since at least 1979.

[80] s. 27(2). For professional accountancy regulations see SORP 2 – Statement of Recommended Practice for Accounting for Charities.

[81] Charities Act 1993, s.41.

[82] *ibid.*, s.42.

[83] s. 42(3) as modified by the Charities Act 1993 (Substitution of Sums) Order 1995 S.I. 1995/2696.

[84] s. 43(2).

[85] s. 43(3).

[86] s. 43(4)

[87] s. 45.

counts are open to public inspection.[88] A persistent failure to make annual returns is a criminal offence.[89]

5.3.7 The power to protect charities

The Charities Branch has the following regulatory powers:

(i) Where it appears that legal proceedings should be considered in relation to a charity, the Charities Branch may send a certificate to that effect, with explanatory particulars, to the Attorney-General.[90] The A-G may institute such proceedings as he considers proper.

(ii) The Charities Branch may itself institute proceedings to recover property which should be applied to charitable uses if the property is being concealed, misapplied or withheld.[91] It may, with the consent of the Attorney-General,[92] by order require copies of any books, records, deeds or papers relating to the charity.

(iii) Where there is alleged to be a breach of a charitable trust or the advice of the court is required in connection with a charity, the Charities Branch (having served notice of its intention on the Attorney-General) may apply for such relief as may be necessary.[93]

In the latter instance, any interested person can make such an application though they must first have the consent of the Attorney-General.[94] The Charities Branch must merely give notice to the Attorney-General of their intention to make this application.[95]

If the Charities Branch believe that charitable property is being concealed, misapplied or withheld it has certain limited powers of investigation.[96] It can require any person to furnish documents or copies of documents relating to the charity;[97] it may also inspect or copy, free of charge any document held by any public authority.[98] If anyone fails to comply with these requirements, the Charities Branch can apply to court for enforcement.[99]

If a charity is either bringing or defending a legal claim and they wish to

---

[88] s. 47.
[89] s. 49.
[90] Charities Act (N.I.) 1964, s.2.
[91] s. 16.
[92] s. 16(2). This power was previously contained in s.12 of the 1844 Act.
[93] See ss. 2, 3 and 29 of the Charities Act (N.I.) 1964.
[94] s. 29(3).
[95] s. 29(4).
[96] Charities Act (N.I.) 1964, s.3.
[97] s. 3(1).
[98] s. 3(2) of the Charities Act (N.I.) 1964, previously s. 21 of the Charitable Bequests and Donations Act (Ireland) 1867.
[99] Charities Act (N.I.) 1964, s.31.

settle it in advance of a court hearing, they may submit that proposal for compromise to the Charities Branch.[100] If the Charities Branch thinks that the proposal is for the benefit of the charity it may allow the compromise, with or without modification.[101] There was one such compromise in 1998.[102]

The Charities Branch can apply to take over the conduct of a legal claim concerning a charity on the ground of undue or improper delay of the party bringing the claim.[103] This can only be done if the action is for the administration of the estate of a testator who has left property for a charitable purpose. The Charities Branch must first give notice to the Attorney General of its intention to make this application.[104] The court may either transfer conduct of the action to the Charities Branch, or impose conditions on the persons currently conducting the claim in order to bring it to a speedy resolution.[105] The Charities Branch has further powers to protect a charity's interests in legal proceedings. It can request that a solicitor's bill of costs for work done for a charity be taxed by the Master of the Taxing Office of the High Court.[106] If the bill has already been paid it cannot be taxed unless the charges are, in the opinion of the Charities Branch exorbitant.[107] Nor can an order for taxation be made if there was an agreement in advance about remuneration or if a considerable period of time has elapsed since payment of the bill.[108]

5.3.8 Registration and regulation: the proposed powers of the Charities Branch

The DHSS review of charity law in Northern Ireland,[109] undertaken in 1995, made some modest but ultimately unsuccessful proposals for introducing legislative powers enabling the Charities Branch to supervise charities more authoritatively. The voluntary sector response to the Consultation Document was weighted against the Charities Branch proposals which were judged to be too intrusive.

---

[100] s. 5(1) and (2) of the Charities Act (N.I.) 1964.

[101] s. 5(3) replicating s. 3 of the 1867 Act.

[102] None in either 1997 nor in 1996.

[103] Charities Act (N.I.) 1964, s.6.

[104] s. 6(3).

[105] s. 6(2). This power also existed prior to 1964 under s. 14 of the 1871 Act.

[106] s. 9.

[107] s. 9(3)(a).

[108] s. 9(3)(b).

[109] See DHSS, *Consultation Document on Charity Law in Northern Ireland*, Charities Branch, Belfast, 1995. Note that this was not the first such attempt. In 1984 the Finance and Personnel Committee of the Northern Ireland Assembly recommended both that a register be established and that the powers of the Charity Commission (E & W) be extended to Northern Ireland.

5.3.8(i) Registration

After considering a number of different models, including extending the remit of the Charity Commission in England and Wales to this jurisdiction, it was proposed that a simple form of compulsory registration should be introduced specifically for Northern Ireland and be maintained by the Charities Branch. This would provide basic information on all charities, record any significant changes, allow for a degree of public access, permit a review of their registered details and facilitate an inter-agency exchange of information on charities. As explained in the Consultation Document:

> "Registration would not imply that a registered charity was guaranteed to be efficient, well managed and deserving of support, but rather that its objects and purposes were charitable in law."[110]

5.3.8(ii) Accounts, audits and annual reports arrangements

To address the lack of accountability it was proposed to introduce a requirement that the accounts of all charities with an annual income exceeding £10,000 should be subject to an independent audit. Charities Branch would be empowered through new regulations to specify, among other matters, the information required, the internal control systems to be adopted by charities and the right of access to charity accounts.

5.3.8(iii) Powers to control abuses

In order to equip the Charities Branch to intervene more directively in the affairs of charities where there is evidence of malpractice it was proposed that the Charities Branch should have such additional powers such as to require a charity, in certain circumstances, to change its name, and to disqualify certain persons from acting as trustees or company directors of charities.

5.3.8(iv) Powers in respect of administration

Many of the proposals for change centred on increasing the existing range of administrative powers vested in the Charities Branch. These proposals included new powers to assist in the winding up of charities, permit the disposal of charity property, amend the public notice requirements in respect of appointing new trustees, and the financial ceilings for Charity Branch involvement in *cy-près* and other schemes.

---

[110] *ibid.* at para 17.

5.3.8(v) Powers in respect of fundraising

Drawing attention to the need to make professional fundraisers more account-able to the charity on whose behalf they are collecting, the Consultation Document proposed that provisions be introduced to require a formal agreement between a specified charity and fundraiser as the basis for the latter's fundraising activities and related remuneration. Proposals also provided for the right of a charity to apply for a restraining injunction to prevent unauthorised collecting and to make it an offence to collect money on behalf of a body falsely claiming to be a registered charity.

5.3.8(vi) Powers in respect of charitable collections

By far the majority of the proposals sought to address deficiencies in the legislative framework governing charitable collections. They were primarily concerned with simplifying, consolidating and modernising the law in this context.

5.3.8(vii) Other powers

Proposals were also presented for the introduction of regulations enabling the Charities Branch to vary the investment limits currently restraining the investment opportunities for charities and amending the Educational Endowments Act 1885 so as to facilitate, where necessary, the winding up of related charities.

5.3.9 Registration and regulation: the actual powers of the Charity Commission

In England and Wales the Charity Commission:

> "… have the general function of promoting the effective use of charitable resources by encouraging the development of better methods of administration, by giving charity trustees information or advice on any matter affecting the charity and by investigating and checking abuses."[111]

The tripartite division into facilitating, monitoring and protecting functions is the same as in Northern Ireland. However, the jurisdictional differences in the degree of respective responsibilities are considerable.

Differences in substance exist under the facilitating and protecting functions (see above). These are usually differences of detail rather than of principle. For example, in Northern Ireland the legislation contains two sections governing the Charities Branch power to create schemes of incorporation for charitable trustees,[112] in England the equivalent provisions stretch to 13 sec-

---

[111] Charities Act 1993, s.1(3).
[112] Ss. 10 and 11.

tions.[113] But it is in relation to the monitoring function that the main differences exist.[114]

The most significant jurisdictional difference is the existence of a Charities Register in England and Wales, but not in Northern Ireland, in which the Charity Commission[115] registers certain charities. A number of charitable bodies are exempted from registration. These include universities and grant maintained schools, museums, Industrial and Provident Societies, Friendly Societies, charities with neither permanent endowments, land nor income over £1,000, places of worship, or charities for the advancement of religion in connection with major churches. In deciding whether or not to register a charity, the Commission is performing a quasi-judicial function. Registration is conclusive proof of charitable status.[116] The register contains particulars about the charity; its name, objects, bank account, area of benefit, and approximate annual income. The information on the register is kept up to date by way of the annual return for all charities whose income or expenditure is over £10,000.[117] The register is open to the public.[118] The significance of the register is twofold. Firstly it provides a vital monitoring tool. To gain registration a charity must submit its documentation to the Commission. Most charities must update this information on a yearly basis which provides a mechanism for the periodic review of charitable activity both by the Commission and the charity itself. Secondly, and going beyond the monitoring function, registration represents a centralised, specialised, harmonised and uniform system for attaining charitable status. In England, a charity need only make one substantive application to obtain charitable status. If it wishes tax exemption, it must apply to the Inland Revenue, but this is only a formality if it as already been registered with the Commission. The Commission provides certainty of charitable status.

In Northern Ireland the only comparable procedure is the letter issued by the Inland Revenue stating that a body is charitably exempt from income tax liability. An informal index of charities does exist in Northern Ireland; it is maintained by the Northern Ireland Council for Voluntary Action and is partly funded and used by the Charities Branch. In contrast to the English register, it is unofficial, non-governmental, voluntary, non-comprehensive and does not investigate nor affirm charitable status. It performs a valuable function in making some information on charities available, but it does not perform a monitoring function.

---

[113] Part VII Charities Act 1993, ss. 50–62.

[114] The present statutory focus and emphasis on monitoring in the Charities Act 1993 can be traced to the White Paper *Charities: A Framework for the Future*, Cmnd. 694, 1989.

[115] s. 3(5).

[116] s. 4(1).

[117] s. 48.

[118] It is accessible on the internet at http://www.charity-commission.gov.uk.

In Northern Ireland, the second important aspect of the monitoring function requires charities to prepare some form of accounting statement. This pales in comparison with English legislation which sets out substantial, detailed and precise requirements for accounts which must be submitted annually to the Commission and provides a compulsory external check on charities. The Charities Branch recognises the paucity of present accounting requirements and the desirability of more rigorous financial regulation:

> "These requirements are less stringent than those which apply in the rest of the UK and trustees of at least the larger and more active charities may wish to go a bit further than the Act requires, since trustees gave a general duty to act in the best interests of their charity and in some cases this might imply preparing more thorough accounts than are strictly required."[119]

A third power, which gives teeth to the monitoring function, is the right of the Commission to institute inquiries into a charity or a particular class of charities under section 8 of the Charities Act 1993. This is much broader than the comparable Charities Branch power which requires:

> "... reasonable grounds to believe that any property belonging to a charity or given for charitable purposes may have been concealed, misapplied or withheld."[120]

An inquiry can involve taking evidence on oath from witnesses.[121] It can require any person to furnish accounts and written statements on any germane matter, to furnish copies of documents they have in their possession and to attend at a specified time to produce these documents.[122] Legal proceedings can be instituted as a result of the findings of the inquiry which can be used as evidence in such proceedings.[123]

The Charity Commission also has further investigatory powers under sections 9–11 of the 1993 Act. As with inquiries, there is no need for evidence of fraudulent behaviour. It can seek information and documents from public and private sources. Section 10 is the only other provision in the Charities Act 1993 which applies to Northern Ireland. It states that the Commission may disclose information to and require information from:

> "... (a) any government department (including a Northern Ireland department); (b) any local authority; (c) any constable; (d) any other body or persons discharging functions of a public nature."[124]

---

[119] Charities Branch (1998) at p. 19.

[120] Charities Act (N.I.) 1964, s.3(1).

[121] Charities Act 1993, s.8(4).

[122] Charities Act 1993, s.8(3).

[123] s. 34 of the Charities Act 1993; for example, the case of *Jones v. Attorney General*, (1973) 3 All E.R. 518, resulted from such an inquiry.

[124] Charities Act 1993, s.10(6).

The protective function of the Commission has other aspects with no counterpart in Northern Ireland. These powers are operative after a section 8 inquiry has revealed mismanagement of a charity or that it is necessary for these powers to be activated.[125] A range of powers exist under section 18(1) to re-order the charity and to suspend the trustees. The Commission may also appoint a manager and receiver for the charity.[126] The exercise of these powers can be appealed to the High Court.[127]

5.4 THE INLAND REVENUE

Charities in Northern Ireland are not required to register with the Charity Commission in England and Wales. This is not because they are specifically excluded by section 3 of the Charities Act 1993 but because most of that statute does not extend to this jurisdiction. So, a charitable organisation in Northern Ireland will apply to the Inland Revenue seeking recognition as such, rather than registration, in order to claim tax exemptions and other financial benefits.

The Inland Revenue has a narrowly defined role in relation to charities. It considers and responds to applications from organisations, trusts or groups of persons claiming exemption from tax on the basis that they are charities. This body has no responsibilities in relation to the registration or regulation of charities. However, it does have a negative monitoring role in the sense that where it has notice that a charity has ceased or that its activities are no longer charitable then it can inspect that body and can remove an entitlement to tax exemption.

5.4.1 Revenue responsibilities

The Inland Revenue assess the eligibility of applicants for exemption in relation to income tax, capital gains tax, inheritance tax, stamp duty, value added tax, probate tax and sundry lesser liabilities. It does so by first establishing whether the activities of the applicant body come within one of the four heads of charity identified in the *Pemsel* case. Where this is confirmed it then examines the body's "governing instrument" to establish whether the income and property of the applicant body is exclusively and irrevocably committed to

---

[125] Charities Act 1993, s.18(1). Previously it was necessary that both these conditions should be satisfied (*i.e.* misapplication of property and necessary to use the provisions) before these further protective functions could operate. However, the Woodfield Report *Efficiency, Scrutiny and the Supervision of Charities* (1987) recommended relaxing this rule and these recommendations were duly enacted in the 1993 Act.
[126] See the Charities (Receiver and Manager) Regulations 1992 SI 1992/2355.
[127] Charities Act 1993, s.18(18).

charitable purposes. It will also require details regarding the body's account-ing period. If these tests are satisfied, the Inland Revenue is then in a position to issue a formal letter in which it states that the applicant body is recognised by it as a charity.

All applications from Northern Ireland are handled by the Inland Revenue (Charities) in Bootle, Merseyside in exactly the same way as claims from chari-ties in England and Wales.[128] The Inland Revenue will give a successful appli-cant a reference number (the only official number a Northern Ireland charity will possess) and a letter granting charitable status. This letter, for all practical purposes, provides the proof that the organisation is a charity and will: entitle it to the tax exemptions available to charities; support an application for ex-emption from rates of Value Added Tax (VAT); and support an application for permission to carry out street or house-to-house collections.

As well as having responsibility for granting or refusing such recognition, the Inland Revenue in Northern Ireland also plays a limited regulatory role by checking that income has, in fact, been applied exclusively for charitable pur-poses (or indeed applied at all rather than left to accumulate) and that claims for repayment of tax are properly substantiated. The Inland Revenue can also withdraw recognition where it appears that purposes are no longer exclusively charitable, for example where there has been an inappropriate alteration to a founding document or where the body's actual activities do not correspond to those in the founding document upon which charitable status was based.

5.5 Customs and Excise

Her Majesty's Customs and Excise regulate the imposition of VAT. It is the body which ultimately decides whether a charity is entitled to an exemption from VAT; such an exemption is largely self-regulating at the initial applica-tion stage.

5.6 The Valuation and Lands Agency

The Valuation and Lands Agency is the property valuation agency for North-ern Ireland. It maintains the Valuation Lists which contain details of the cur-rent rateable valuation of commercial properties (hereditaments and tenements), and of the rateable valuation of commercial, domestic and land properties from 1852. Included among its responsibilities is the duty to determine whether or not premises are entitled to exemption from rates on the grounds of charita-ble user by the occupier (see further, Chapter 21).

---

[128]   Charity Title Section, Inland Revenue (Charities), St John's House, Merton Road, Bootle, Merseyside L69 9BB.

5.6.1 The Lands Tribunal

This body was established by the Lands Tribunal and Compensation Act (N.I.) 1964 and its proceedings are governed by the Lands Tribunal Rules (N.I.) 1976 as amended. It is physically part of the Royal Courts of Justice in Belfast where it holds hearings and maintains offices. Hearings are in public and legal aid is available.

Among the functions of the Tribunal is the duty to hear appeals against rulings made by officers of the Valuation and Lands Agency regarding liability for rates. Where a charity wishes to claim exemption from liability for rates, as determined by such an officer, it will lodge an appeal to this Tribunal. Copies of written judgments maintained by the Tribunal provide invaluable guidance regarding the interpretation of eligibility for rateable exemption on charitable grounds (see further, Chapter 21).

5.7 THE REGISTRY OF COMPANIES

The registrar is responsible for maintaining the registry of companies; the many charities now incorporated are required to register.[129]

5.7.1 Registration requirements

Once the registrar is satisfied that the necessary statutory requirements have been met then the name of the company will be entered in the registry and a certificate of incorporation will be issued. Thereafter, annual returns including a statement of accounts must be made to the registrar. Failure to comply with the requirement to make annual returns will lead to a company being struck off the register.

5.7.2 The Companies Registration Office

The Companies Registration Office is open to public inspection. This provides one of the few legal mechanisms which allow for a measure of transparency in relation to the organisational structure, financial standing and activities of a charity.

5.8 OTHER REGISTRIES

A minority of charities are either industrial and provident societies or friendly societies and must register accordingly. In Northern Ireland, the Registry of

---

[129] The Registry, IDB House, 64 Chichester Street, Belfast.

Companies is also the Registry for Industrial and Provident Societies and is based at the same address. The Registry of Friendly Societies is based in London.[130]

5.9 THE NORTHERN IRELAND COUNCIL FOR VOLUNTARY ACTION

The Northern Ireland Council for Voluntary Action (NICVA) body promotes good practice among voluntary organisations, facilitates good governance and assists organisations to become formally established within an appropriate legal framework. In particular it provides a Charity Advice Service which makes available information on matters such as drawing up a constitution and claiming tax exemption. It has no regulatory responsibilities.

NICVA has an incidental but very useful role in relation to charities in Northern Ireland. It maintains an informal database of voluntary organisations including charities in Northern Ireland.[131] This does not bear comparison with the Charity Commission register. Firstly, the amount of information which NICVA is legally permitted to disclose to enquirers is very limited. Secondly, there is no enforceable obligation for charities to file annual reports and reports containing up-to-date information. Thirdly, there is no requirement to inform NICVA if a charity is to be wound up; indeed entries are often out-of-date, particularly in respect of contact details. Fourthly, the database is not limited to just charities, but also includes non-charitable voluntary groups. It also excludes some religious charities which do not have a social focus.

5.10 THE NATIONAL LOTTERY CHARITIES BOARD

The National Lottery Charities Board is the body charged with distributing money received by the National Lottery. It processes applications for funding and must determine if an applicant body is established for charitable, benevolent or philanthropic purposes.[132] It exercises an indirect regulatory role on Northern Ireland charities by forcing them to comply with the eligibility criteria if they wish to access funding.[133]

---

[130] Victory House, 30-34 Kingsway, London, WC2B 6ES.
[131] Known as "SectorNet", the organisations listed are encouraged to make annual returns to update the database in relation to matters such as their accounts, activities and other details. This information provides the basis for 'The State of the Sector' an annual NICVA report.
[132] National Lottery Act 1993, s.44.
[133] Hildon House, 30-34 Hill Street, Belfast, BT1 2LB.

5.11 THE NORTHERN IRELAND CENTRAL INVESTMENT FUND FOR CHARITIES (CIF)

This is a fund set up by the Department, similar to a unit trust, in which charities can invest their capital. The aim of the CIF is to maintain and increase the real value of the income and capital of charities, the emphasis being on a growing income. There are a number of other common investment funds under the ultimate authority of the Charities Branch (see further, Chapter 7). The main advantages of investment in the CIF, particularly for small charities are as follows:

(i) The trustees are saved the trouble and expense of having to obtain professional advice on how they should invest their capital and of having to vary their investments in response to market changes.

(ii) The CIF is not subject to the restrictions on the choice of investments which apply to most charities.

(iii) Any charity can invest in the CIF, even if its constitution forbids it from investing in any other type of equity-based investment.

(iv) The value of capital invested in the CIF is protected against inflation. This is very important to charities in view of the fact that their capital will remain invested indefinitely.

(v) The rate of return is good for a secure investment.

The CIF works on a system of shares, similar to a unit trust. Money coming in is held in the Consolidated Fund (a government bank account which earns interest) until the next date on which shares can be purchased. Dividends on the shares are paid six monthly on June 1 and December 1. Accounts Branch produces an introductory leaflet for prospective investors.

CHAPTER 6

Trusts and Charitable Trusts

6.1 INTRODUCTION

Equity and the law of trusts provide the foundations for modern charity law. Many of the principles now governing charitable trusts have a history which can be traced back to at least the sixteenth century. It is a subject which has often attracted academic and professional writers and a number of substantial and authoritative books are now in print to which those seeking an in-depth treatment can be confidently referred.[1]

This chapter examines the roots of charitable trusts and identifies their distinctive characteristics. It leaves to later (see Chapter 16) a discussion of the different legal structures available to frame the activities of charities and other voluntary organisations.

It should be noted that the law in England and Wales relating to trusts and trustees has undergone considerable change as a result of the Trustee Act 2000. The changes relate *inter alia* to powers of investment, delegation by trustees and duties owed to beneficiaries. There is no equivalent legislation in Northern Ireland although it may be the case that amending legislation will follow here in due course.

6.2 TRUSTS

The law of trusts provides the means whereby property may be held by one person for the benefit of another. As explained a century ago:

> ". . . if I give an estate to A upon condition that he shall apply the rents for the benefit of B, that is a gift in trust to all intents and purposes."[2]

This recognition that property can be divided into two components – the legal ownership and the beneficial ownership – is essentially a legal device providing for two different types of ownership in the same property. The trustee is the person who legally owns the property, the beneficiary is the person who

---

[1] In particular, see Keeton and Sheridan, *The Law of Trusts* (12th ed., Barry Rose Law Publishers Ltd., London, 1993) and Delany, H., *Equity and the Law of Trusts in Ireland* (Round Hall Sweet & Maxwell, Dublin, 1996). See also, Tudor, *Charities* (8th ed., London, Sweet & Maxwell, 1995), pp. 121-164 and Wylie, *Irish Land Law* (3rd ed., Butterworths, Dublin, 1997), pp. 511-595.

[2] See *Attorney General v. Wax Chandlers Co.* (1897) L.R. 6 H.L. 1 at p. 21.

benefits from the property. Legal recognition and enforcement for such a separation – of responsibilities vested in those controlling property from the rights of those ultimately entitled to enjoy the value of that property – has become extremely important and is now extensively used in many different forms. The law relating to charity is not wholly comprehensible unless there is some understanding of trusts.

6.2.1 Origins

In feudal times the ownership of land was all important. Feudalism, in a sense, was based on a system of land tenure. This ensured that land could not be wholly and absolutely owned by anyone; every "owner" held their rights as tenant to their lord. All such ownership was vested in the King as the ultimate lord and sovereign of his people and territory. Fealty to a lord and ultimately to the King, were tied to an estate in land.[3] Estates could be either freehold or leasehold. Several variations of the former were possible: an estate in "fee simple" conferred a good title in perpetuity; a "life estate" limited the title to the life of a particular person; an estate "pur autre vie" gave title to one person "for the life of another"; and an estate in "fee tail" restricted inheritance to the linear descendants of a particular person. Leasehold estates were defined and differentiated by length of tenure; weekly, monthly, yearly etc. Estates in land formed an ascending hierarchy, consisting of gradations of title from serf to lord, with final authority of ownership and disposal being vested in the King. This feudal system of land tenure provided the basis for imposing taxes and dues.

The concept of a "use" rather than an estate in land was developed in response to the rigidity of feudal land taxes. The transference of land to another for the latter's "use" was intended to avoid the liability that attached to actual ownership. It was employed not only to circumvent tax liability but also to facilitate gifts to religious bodies which, prior to the Statute of Mortmain 1391, would have been prohibited. Gifts of the latter variety were commonly made by landowners in return for masses being said for the salvation of their souls. It was a technical device, much abused and unenforceable through the common law courts, and of great concern to the lords who saw the basis for the feudal system being eroded and for whose protection the mortmain statutes were introduced.[4]

---

[3] The rigid hierarchical ordering of society that constituted feudalism was transplanted in the middle ages to this island with the armies of England. Feudalism took root where the writ of the King of England ran. Elsewhere the Brehon laws prevailed.

[4] See, for example, the Statute of Mortmain 1279 (7 Edw. 1, St 2), the Statute of Westminster III 1290 (18 Edw. 1) and in particular the Statute of Mortmain 1391 (15 Ric 2, c 5). Poynings Law 1495, a statute introduced by the Irish Parliament, applied the English Mortmain legislation to Ireland. It remained in effect until repealed by the Charities Act 1961.

The Court of Chancery, however, was prepared to give recognition to an equitable holding in land. The eventual evolution of the feudal concept of the "use"[5] into its modern manifestation as a "trust" was hastened by the Statute of Uses (Ireland) 1634[6] which gave statutory authority to the approach developed in the Court of Chancery where the transaction involved freehold land. The primary weakness in this legislation was its failure to address the situation where there was "a use upon a use" *i.e.* where land was conveyed "unto A and his heirs to the use of B and his heirs to the use of C and his heirs". The common law courts would refuse to recognise that any rights were thereby conferred upon C.[7] Again, the eventual willingness of the Court of Chancery to enforce such double uses[8] transferred to the common law courts and received statutory endorsement. In time the second use came to be treated by the courts as a trust and the conveyance of the beneficial interest in the land would typically be worded "unto and to the use of B in trust for C", where B was the trustee and C the beneficiary.

In this jurisdiction the statutory basis for the law governing trusts is now to be found largely in the Trustee Act (N.I.) 1958 augmented by legislation specific to company law and charity law.

6.2.2 Definition

There have been many attempts to define a trust.[9] One which has borne the test of time is the following definition offered by Keeton and Sheridan:

> "A trust is the relationship which arises whenever a person (called the trustee) is compelled in equity to hold property, whether real or personal, and whether by legal or equitable title, for the benefit of some persons (of whom he may be one and who are termed beneficiaries) or for some object permitted by law, in such a way that the real benefit accrues, not to the trustee, but to the beneficiaries or other objects of the trust."[10]

---

[5] It was Maitland who first remarked that "the modern trust developed from the ancient use". See further, Keane, R., *Equity and the Law of Trusts in the Republic of Ireland*, London, pp. 69-77.

[6] 10 Chas. 1, Sess 2, C.1. This extended to Ireland the provisions enacted earlier in England in the Statute of Uses 1535. For further information, see Holdsworth, *History of English Law*, vol. IV, pp. 438-9; Also, see Keeton and Sheridan, "The Development of the Law of Trusts" in *The Law of Trusts, op. cit.* at pp. 21–35.

[7] See *Tyrrell's (Jane) Case* (1557) 2 Dyer 155a; 73 E.R. 336. Also, see, *Girland v. Sharp* (1595) Cro. Eliz. 382.

[8] See *Sambach v. Dalston* (1634) Tothill 188, also reported as *Morris v. Darston* (1635) Nels. 30.

[9] See, for example, Hart (1899) 15 LQR 294; Underhill and Hayton, *The Law Relating to Trusts* (14th ed., 1987) at p. 1; and Pettit, *Equity and the Law of Trusts* (7th ed., 1993) at p. 24.

[10] See Keeton and Sheridan, *The Law of Trusts* (12th ed., 1993) at p. 3; a definition first formulated in a much earlier edition.

A trust provides a means whereby a donor can impose a legal requirement upon a trustee or trustees to receive, retain and utilise a gift for purposes specified by the donor. Such a trust will arise either during the lifetime of a donor by agreement or deed drawn up for that purpose or after death from the terms of a donor's will. An equitable remedy, confined at first to gifts of land, it has now gained full judicial and legislative recognition and has come to encompass all forms of property.

6.3 CREATION OF TRUSTS

A trust is an arrangement whereby one or more persons, operating under a legal document known as a "deed of trust", holds funds or property on behalf of another person or persons. However, a trust may also arise where one or more persons act on behalf of a wider group without any formal deed of trust being enacted. A trust is not subject to external controls. Trustees of charities, however, differ from other trustees in that they may call upon certain bodies for support. They are entitled to request the Charities Branch for assistance in the management of properties and other financial gifts entrusted to them for charitable purposes, or for changes to be effected in its objects. They are also entitled to seek the special protection traditionally offered by the Attorney-General to charitable trusts.

6.3.1 Technical formalities

As stated, most trusts are express trusts and are created either *inter vivos* or by will. Trusts may also be created without being formally expressed; implied or constructive trusts fall into this category. The formal requirements governing the creation of a trust are twofold: there are technical formalities relating to the method of creation; and there are those relating to the substance of the trust.

The former require that if the trust property is land, whether freehold or leasehold, then it should be properly evidenced. This is achieved by ensuring that the document creating the trust is in writing and signed.[11] A trust need not be in writing but the absence of such evidence that a trust has been declared, although not necessarily affect its validity, will make its existence more difficult to prove. In *Gilmurray v. Corr*,[12] for example, a declaration of trust was found to exist and to be enforceable despite an absence of written evidence. The courts will not allow non-compliance with the requirements of the Statute of Frauds (Ireland) 1695 to justify reneging on a contract, agreement or trust.

---

[11] s. 4 of the Statutes of Frauds (Ireland) 1695. Under s. 6 all subsequent dispositions of the beneficial interests must also be in writing and signed.

[12] [1978] N.I. 99.

Where written evidence exists, the trust need not be expressed in one document but may be collated from several documents;[13] nor does the evidence have to conform to any particular form of words.[14] If the trust property is of company shares, the trust must be made by deed and be registered.

6.3.2 Wills

If the trust is created by a will, it must comply with all relevant statutory formalities. This requires that a will be in writing, be signed by the testator (or by someone in his or her presence and at their direction), and that signature must be witnessed by two persons present at the same time. See the Wills and Administration Proceedings (N.I.) Order 194 for wills executed after the January 1, 1995 and the Wills Act 1837 for wills executed before that date.

6.3.3 Creation of trusts: substance

A trust must meet the "three certainties test" as formulated by O'Byrne J:

> "… in order that a trust may be created, the subject matter must be certain, the objects of the trust must be certain and the words relied on as creating the trust must have been used in an imperative sense so as to show that the testator intends to create an obligation."[15]

A charitable trust is entitled to breach the last certainty in two respects: its objects will always be purposes rather than persons;[16] and it may be expressed in terms which lack specificity.

6.3.3(i) Certainty of subject matter

A valid trust cannot be created unless the subject matter is specified with reasonable certainty. The subject matter is the property owned by the trust. If the property is not certain, the trust will not be created since it cannot be said upon what property it can "bite". It must be possible to ascertain the trust property and ascertain the apportionment, if any, of the property between the beneficiaries.[17] So, for example, "the bulk of my … residuary estate",[18] a blank cheque[19]

---

[13] See *Foster v. Hale* (1798) 3 Ves. 696.

[14] See *Foster v. Hale, op. cit.* where it was found in correspondence and *McBlain v. Cross* (1871) 25 L.T. 804 where it was in a telegram.

[15] See *Chambers v. Fahy* [1931] I.R. at p. 21. Also see, *Wright v. Atkyns* (1823) Turn & R. 143 *per* Lord Eldon at p. 157 and *Knight v. Knight* (1840) 3 Beav. 148, *per* Lord Langdale M.R. at p. 173.

[16] See *Morice v. Bishop of Durham* (1804), 9 Ves., J.399.

[17] See *Re King's Estate* (1888) 21 L.R. Ir. 273.

[18] See *Palmer v. Simmonds* (1854) 2 Drew 221.

[19] *Hartshorne v. Nicholson* (1858) 26 Beav. 58.

and instructions to "remember" certain persons[20] and "to reward ... my old servants and tenants according to their deserts"[21] have all been held to be insufficient.

Problems have arisen when the primary gift is void and the residuary/gift over is for a charitable purpose. If it cannot be said with certainty what proportion of the gift is to devolve to charity, then there is no certainty of subject matter. In the past, where gifts have concerned remainders of an estate, these have been particularly prone to failure. References to "the remaining part of what is left"[22] or to "such parts of ... my estate as she shall not have sold or disposed of"[23] have proved fatal. There seem to be three possible solutions. Firstly, to distribute equally between the charitable and non-charitable portions of the gift or *pari passu*; meaning that the charity will get half, making the subject matter certain.[24] The second, albeit little used, construction is that the gift-over fails unless the amount which would be required for the initial gift can be ascertained. The third possibility is that the entire gift goes to charity. In a case where the upkeep of tombs was found to indicate a void trust, with the gift-over to a charitable purpose, the court held "that the failure of the trust for the repair of the tomb is that the whole of the income becomes applicable for charitable purposes".[25]

More recently, where gifts concern intangible assets such as company shares, the court has held that the precise assets need not be specifically identified; sufficient certainty was achieved by identifying the quantum of shares in a named company.[26]

The requirements for certainty of subject matter and certainty of intention may, in practice, be closely related. As has been pointed out:

> "[T]he uncertainty of the subject of the gift has a reflex action upon the previous words, and throws doubt upon the intention of the testator, and seems to shew that he could not possibly have intended his words of confidence, hope, or whatever they may be ... to be imperative."[27]

6.3.3(ii) Certainty of objects

The objects, *i.e.* the people or purposes intended to benefit from the trust, must be sufficiently certain, the beneficiaries must be identifiable. In ordinary

---

[20] See *Bardswell v. Bardswell* (1838) 9 Sim 319.

[21] See *Knight v. Knight op. cit.*

[22] See *Sprange v. Barnard* (1789) 2 Bro. C.C. 585.

[23] See *Re Jones* [1898] 1 Ch. 438.

[24] See for example *Salusbury v. Denton* 1857) 3 K. & J. 529.

[25] *Re Rogerson* [1901] 1 Ch. 715 at p. 718, see also *Kelly v. Attorney General* [1917] I.R. 183.

[26] See *Hunter v. Moss* [1993] 1 W.L.R. 934 (D.C.); [1994] 1 W.L.R. 452 (C.A.).

[27] See *Mussoorie Bank Ltd. v. Raynor* (1882) 7 App. Cas. 321, *per* Sir Author Hobhouse at p. 330.

trust law the beneficiaries must in addition be a legal person, *i.e.* have a legal personality. This means that they can be natural persons or corporations. If a trust is charitable, this requirement is relaxed, a charitable trust can also be for an abstract purpose, but it must be an exclusively charitable purpose.[28] As the Privy Council explained in *Leahy v. Attorney General for New South Wales*[29]:

> "... a gift can be made to persons (including corporations) but it cannot be made to a purpose / object ... for a purpose cannot sue, but if it be charitable, the Attorney General can enforce it."[30]

The law goes even further than allowing a purpose to be the object of a charitable trust. It will not allow such a trust to fail due to a lack of certainty in its objects. The long-standing tradition of intervention in favour of charitable trusts was explained by Sir William Grant[31]:

> "There can be no trust, over the exercise of which this Court will not assume a control; for an uncontrollable power of disposition would be ownership, and not trust. If there be a clear trust, but for uncertain objects, the property, that is the subject of the trust, is undisposed of and the benefit of such trust must result to those, to whom the law gives the ownership in default of disposition by the former owner. But this doctrine does not hold good with regard to trusts for charity. Every other trust must have a definite object. There must be somebody, in whose favour the court can decree performance."

If trustees are to give effect to the intentions behind the trust then they, or the court, must be in a position to identify the objects or beneficiaries when the trust comes into operation. As Carswell J. has pointed out:

> "... it is necessary that the prospective beneficiaries should be sufficiently identifiable to satisfy the requirement of certainty of objects."[32]

The failure of a trust will often result from donor confusion between the requirements for creating a trust as opposed to conferring a power. Where the instrument discloses such an area of discretion that the gift may not vest, then clearly the donor has failed to create a trust. This is most likely to arise in the context of gifts to be distributed among members of a class. The dangers have been highlighted by Jenkins L.J. in *IRC v. Broadway Cottages Trust*[33]:

> "... a trust for such members of a given class of objects as the trustees shall select is void for uncertainty unless the whole range of objects eligible for selection is ascertained or capable of ascertainment."[34]

---

[28] *Re Brown* [1898] 1 I.R. 423, *per* Porter M.R. at p. 427.

[29] [1959] A.C. 457.

[30] *ibid.* at p. 479.

[31] See *Morice v. Bishop of Durham, op. cit.*, at pp. 404-405.

[32] See, *Re Dunlop* [1984] N.I. 408, *per* Carswell J. at p. 416.

[33] [1955] Ch. 20.

[34] *ibid.* at pp. 35-36.

This test has been termed the "complete list test" – *i.e.* it must be possible to draw up a complete list of beneficiaries. If this cannot be done, the gift will fail due to uncertainty.

Subsequently, the House of Lords in *McPhail v. Doulton*[35] retreated from this extreme approach when they ruled that a direction requiring a fund to be held on trust for the benefit of company staff and their "relatives and dependants" created a trust rather than a power. Lord Wilberforce then stated that "the trust is valid if it can be said with certainty that any given individual is or is not a member of the class".[36] This has been termed the "given postulant test" – can it be said with certainty that a given person is or is not a beneficiary?[37] Carswell J in *Re Dunlop* decided that this was most appropriate test for charitable trusts. He held that members of the Presbyterian Church in Ireland could be sufficiently identifiable "as long as it can be said at the time of selection that any given person comes within it".[38]

Failure may also be due to uncertainty surrounding the arrangements made by the donor regarding trust objects. For example, clear and definite provision for the vesting of the beneficial interest may not have been made.[39] Alternatively, as in *Re Waring's Will Trusts*,[40] a condition precedent may have been attached which is incapable of fulfilment by the intended beneficiary or cannot be satisfied without breaching the rule against perpetuities or a condition subsequent may threaten to divest the beneficiary of a gift already made.

Where there is clear evidence of an intention to benefit a charitable purpose then a scheme may be drawn up to correct or clarify the details, give effect to that intention and save the trust. Such a scheme is not to be confused with the exercise of *cy-près*. Whereas the latter permits the court or Charities Branch to alter the objects of a charitable trust in certain circumstances, the power to devise a scheme applies only to ensure that such a trust does not fail at the outset due to non-compliance with a minor aspect of the three certainties rule.

As with any rule, there are of course exceptions; certain non-charitable purpose trusts have been held to fulfil the requirement of certainty of objects. These include: trusts for building tombs and monuments,[41] trusts for the care of specific animals/pets,[42] trusts for the furtherance of fox-hunting and trusts for the saying of masses in private. These exceptions are very limited and unlikely to be extended.

The requirement of certainty of objects in relation to charitable trusts has,

---

[35] [1971] A.C. 424, see also *Re Gullbenkian's Settlements* (1970) A.C. 508.
[36] *ibid.* at p. 456.
[37] *ibid.*, also, see *McPhail v. Doulton* (1971) A.C. 424.
[38] *Re Dunlop* at p. 416.
[39] See *Harland v. Trigg* (1782) 1 Bro. C.C. 142. *Cf Re Bridgen* [1938] Ch. 205 (p. 114, *ante*).
[40] [1985] N.I. 105.
[41] *Re Hooper* [1932] 1 Ch. 38.
[42] *Pettingall v. Pettingall* (1842) 11 L.J. Ch. 176.

therefore, been transmuted into a requirement of certainty of charitable purposes. To this a *caveat* must be entered, it must be solely and exclusively for charitable purposes. According to Tudor:

> "... a trust must not only be declared in favour of objects of a charitable nature, but it must also be expressed that in its application it is *confined* to such objects."[43]

6.3.3(iii) Certainty of intention or words

There must be certainty of intention to create a trust, a clear indication that the donor sought to impose a binding obligation. The court will examine the substance and effect of the words used to establish whether they disclose the necessary certainty of intention. There is no particular form of words which conclusively indicate an intention to create a trust and the fact that the word "trust" is used will not in itself be decisive. The court will look to the intention behind the words used; giving effect to the principle that "equity looks to the intent rather than to the form". A lack of certainty in the use of words, however, will be fatal to the creation of a trust. The following examples are drawn from cases where uncertainty produced such results[44]:

> "... *feeling confident* that she will act justly to our children in dividing the same when no longer required by her.[45]
>
> ... *in full confidence* that she will do what is right as to the disposal thereof between my children.[46]
>
> ... *in the fullest trust and confidence* that she will carry out my wishes in the following particulars.[47]
>
> ... *it is my desire* that she allows A an annuity of £25 during her lifetime."[48]

The court will look for words indicating an imperative. It will be a matter of construction whether the court can discern an intention on the part of the donor to confer not an absolute gift upon a donee but a requirement that the latter hold the property on trust for another. In conducting this exercise the court will examine the entirety of the instrument in question.

The construction of any words attached to a gift will be closely examined. They will be tested to establish the motive for making the gift. This may indicate an intention to confer an absolute gift and the attached words can be regarded as merely precatory. Where words are used which refer simply to the

---

[43] Tudor at p. 134, my emphasis but see further Chap. 15 on techniques to avoid failure of gifts with partly charitable purposes.

[44] See further, Keeton and Sheridan (12th ed.), *op. cit.* at pp. 112-116.

[46] See *Mussoorie Bank Ltd. v. Raynor, op. cit.*

[46] See *Re Adams and Kensington Vestry* (1884) 27 Ch. D. 394.

[47] See *Re Williams* [1897] 2 Ch. 12.

[48] See *Re Diggles* (1888) 39 Ch. D. 253.

testator's "hopes", "desires", "wishes" and "confidence" then these are now usually construed as no more than a gloss on the true intent to be read in conjunction with other expressions of intention. Alternatively, the attached words may be construed as making a valid trust conditional in some way.

In Ireland and Northern Ireland the distinction between these various constructions has arisen in relation to trusts for the upkeep of family tombs; such trusts are not charitable, so courts have had to decide the effect a direction to maintain a tomb in good repair (see further, Chapter 10).

In the Irish case of *Roche* v. *McDermott*[49] the court held that such a direction only imposed a moral obligation and not a legally enforceable trust. The High Court in Northern Ireland followed this case in *Re Galway, Galway* v. *Incorporated Cripples Institutes, Peoples Palace and Homes of Rest*.[50] In that case the condition was quite definite and specific, to "keep my grave, tombstone and its appurtenances tidy and clean, cleaning and lettering tombstone and plinth say every five years". Nevertheless, Murphy L.J. agreed that the words in fact:

> "... merely created 'an honourable obligation' on his clients the charity, which was not legally enforceable but which his clients would voluntarily carry out."[51]

This illustrates the lenient judicial rules of construction applied to ensure that charitable gifts do not fail.

The same point arose again in *Re Steele, Northern Bank Executor and Trustee Company* v. *Linton*.[52] Murray J. had to decide if a condition to maintain a family burial plot was an attempt to create a legally enforceable condition or whether the words were merely precatory. Although he did not make any reference to *Re Galway*, Murray J. came to the same conclusion, *viz.* that the words were merely precatory and not legally enforceable. In reaching this decision he was swayed by the fact that the will "makes no gift-over of the trust property in the event of the grave condition being broken".[53] The testator had failed to make any direction regarding the future of the property in the event of the condition being unfulfilled, this indicated that the condition was an expression of hope, rather than an enforceable trust condition.

This point of law seems to be similar in England, both that precatory words do not create a trust[54] and that a direction for the upkeep of tombs will be construed as precatory. For example, *Re Brace*[55] was quoted with approval in *Re Steele* when it was noted that:

---

[49] [1901] 1 I.R. 394.

[50] [1943] N.I. 28.

[51] *ibid.* at p. 33.

[52] [1976] N.I. 66.

[53] *Re Steele* at p. 69

[54] See for example, *Re Adams and the Kensington Vestry* (1844) 27 Ch. D. 394, *Lambe* v. *Eames* (1871) 6 Ch. App. 597.

[55] [1954] 1 W.L.R. 955.

> "... the absence of a gift-over seems to me to point quite strongly to the conclusion that the words were not intended to be anything more than precatory."[56]

Furthermore, in the case of *Re Dalziel*[57] it was determined that directions to maintain tombs were to be construed to import only a moral obligation and not a legal one.

If a condition precedent is attached then, provided it can be satisfied without breaching the rule against perpetuities, the trust will be valid but in abeyance until the condition is fulfilled. Where a condition imposes a personal obligation upon the donee, thereby constraining the public benefit effect of the gift, the court will construe the net result as achieving a gift subject to a condition rather than creating a trust.[58]

The obligation to identify with some precision the exact property which a donor intends to give to charity can pose problems. This can often be the case with testamentary dispositions of residual property to religious or charitable causes. For example, the terminology "remembering always ... the Church of God and the poor"[59] has been held to be inadequate.

6.4 VOID TRUSTS

A trust is void if it is invalid *ab initio* and never comes into effect. This is most likely to occur if a trust is fundamentally flawed from the outset because it is in breach of a basic requirement. This could be because it contains terms offensive to public policy, is in breach of statute law or fails to comply with a governing rule of common law or equity. In such circumstances the trustees will then hold the property in question on a resulting trust basis for the settlor or for the estate.

6.4.1 Rule against perpetuities[60]

The law relating to property has always sought to facilitate freedom of disposition. This emphasis has often been in conflict with the intentions of landowners to ensure that their estates are preserved intact within the family for future generations. The rule against perpetuities expresses this tension. It was formulated by the courts to constrain the practice whereby some settlors contrived to tie up their estates indefinitely by providing for gifts of property to vest at some distant time in the future.

---

[56] [1954] 1 W.L.R. 955 at p. 958.

[57] (1943) Ch. 277.

[58] See *Jack v. Burnett* (1846) 12 Cl. & F. 812; *Att-Gen v. Cordwainers' Co.* (1833) 3 Myl. & K. 534; and *Att-Gen v. Christ's Hospital* (1830) 1 R. & M. 626.

[59] See *Curtis v. Rippon* (1820) 5 Madd. 434.

[60] See Wylie, *Irish Land Law, ibid.*, at pp. 305-348, for a detailed account of this rule.

6.4.1(i) General rule

If a gift is contingent on a certain event, and that event may or may not occur for a considerable period of time, the law will declare that contingency void. This is the rule against perpetuities. For example, in the case of a gift "to the first of my grandchildren to become a doctor", where such a grandchild is not even born, it may be a very long time, if ever, before the gift vests. The rule can take effect in two ways. If it is a condition precedent which is declared void, the gift will not vest in the donee at all. If it is a condition subsequent (*i.e.* to A and if A becomes a doctor, to B), it will depend on whether it is conditional or determinable. If conditional and the condition subsequent is void and the primary donee keeps the gift absolutely. If determinable and void, the gift is void *ab initio*, the primary donee is not entitled to it at all.

The period of time the law considers "too long" for a contingency is termed the perpetuity period. At common law the perpetuity period is "lives in being" plus 21 years. A life in being is someone who is alive at the date of the gift. Statute has created a simpler perpetuity period which can be utilised if the donor desires. Under the Perpetuities Act (N.I.) 1966, the perpetuity period can be up to 80 years as specified by the donee.[61]

The rule therefore is that a contingency which may vest outside the perpetuity period is void. Or as others have put it:

> "... no interest is good unless it must vest, if at all, not later than 21 years after some life in being at the creation of the interesty."[62]

The Perpetuities Act (N.I.) 1966 made several modifications to this rule. The most important was the introduction of the "wait and see" principle in section 3(1) which, somewhat torturously, states that instead of declaring such gifts void at the outset one must wait and see if they vest within the perpetuity period. If they do so they are valid; if not, then at the end of the perpetuity period, if the contingency is still possible, the gift is void.

The rule against perpetuities is a complex legal topic and this has merely been an attempt to sketch its parameters. It can and does have far reaching consequences in its application. Lowry J. in *Queens University Belfast* v. *Attorney General for Northern Ireland*[63] noted with approval the endorsement of the rule offered by the Law Reform Committee which likened the rule to:

> "... an unruly dog which, if not securely chained to its own kennel, is prone to wander into places where it ought not to be."[64]

---

[61] See s. 1(1) of the Perpetuities Act (N.I.) 1966.
[62] Gray, *The Rule Against Perpetuities*, 4th ed., s. 201.
[63] *Queens University Belfast* v. *Attorney General for Northern Ireland* [1966] N.I. 115.
[64] Fourth Report on Rule against Perpetuities (1956) at para. 34.

6.4.1(ii) Rule as it applies to charities

It has long been a fundamental and distinguishing characteristic of charities that a charitable trust can exist in perpetuity. This general exemption to the rule against perpetuities was intended to encourage donors by giving them the reassurance that gifts to charity would be applied for the purpose they intended until such time as the gift was entirely exhausted.

However, if the commencement of a charity is contingent on an event, then the normal rule against perpetuities applies.[65] If the charity will end upon some contingent event, again the normal rule against perpetuities applies; except where there is a gift to one charity with a condition that in case of default the gift then passes to another charity.[66] In that event, the rule against perpetuities will not apply and the contingency will be valid, even it if may cause the gift to vest outside the perpetuity period. This will be the case so long as no condition precedent intercedes. As expressed by Selborne L.C. in *Chamberlayne v. Brockett*[67]:

> "If the gift in trust for the charity is itself conditional upon a future and uncertain event, it is subject, in our judgment, to the same rules and principles as any other estate depending for its coming into existence upon a condition precedent. If the condition is never fulfilled, the estate never arises; if it is so remote and indefinite as to transgress the limits of time prescribed by the rules of law against perpetuities, the gift fails *ab initio*."[68]

This is the device suggested by Delaney to save gifts with a condition for the upkeep of a tomb.[69] Keeton and Sheridan suggest that the application of the rule against perpetuities to charities ends there. The authors have gone further to suggest that:

> "... the equity reports contain frequent misleading statements by judges upon the position of charities in relation to the perpetuity rule."[70]

Whether they would level this criticism at Lowry J. in *Queens University of Belfast* v. *Attorney General for Northern Ireland* is debatable. The issue in that case concerned payments made to the Board of Electors to implement the Musgrave Studentship Legacy. The legacy itself was charitable, but did the payments represent perpetual non-charitable payments? Lowry J. held that perpetual non-charitable payments would breach the rule against perpetuities. This is true in the general sense of the rule attempting to prevent the tying up of property in perpetuity, it is not strictly correct in the specific application of

---

[65] See *Re Macnamarra's Estate* [1943] I.R. 372.
[66] See *Christ's Hospital v. Granger* (1849) 1 Mac. & G. 460, also *Re Tyler* [1891] 3 Ch. 252.
[67] (1872) L.R. 8 Ch. 206.
[68] *ibid.* at p. 211.
[69] See, also, *Christ's Hospital v. Grainger* (1849) 1 Mac. & G. 460.
[70] Keeton and Sheridan (1983) at p. 246.

the rule to contingent interests. Arguably, reference to the rule against perpetual existence, rather than to the rule against perpetuities, would have been appropriate. On the actual facts of the case, the payments to the Electors were part of the administration costs of the trust and so could be subsumed within its perpetual, charitable framework and would therefore not be void.

6.4.2 Rule against inalienability

6.4.2(i) General rule

According to the dicta in *Re Richardson*[71] "the ancient principle of our property law is freedom of alienation".[72] The power of alienation is the power of an owner to sell his or her own property. Where a gift of property has an attached condition prohibiting sale, that condition is repugnant to the law and will be struck out as contrary to public policy. The roots of this rule stem from the laws against mortmain – literally preventing the "dead hands" of donors affecting the current use of land.

6.4.2(ii) Rule as it applies to charities

As was stated in *Re Richardson*:

> "The rule against inalienability of a fee simple estate does not apply to land given to a charity to be held by it on a perpetual charitable trust."[73]

This confirmed the earlier *obiter dictum* in *Re Steele* that it is:

> "… open to serious question whether this aspect of the doctrine of repugnancy has any application to a charitable trust."[74]

It is possible to attach a condition of non-sale to a gift to charity. This rule was established in *Chamberlayne* v. *Brockett*[75] and English text books confirm that:

> "… no gift for charitable purposes is void merely because it renders property inalienable in perpetuity."[76]

In the particular case of *Re Richardson* the land given to the National Trust could be inalienable in two ways. Firstly, through the common law charitable exemption. Secondly, through section 21 of the National Trust Act 1907 which

---

[71] *Re Richardson, Boyce v. National Trust for Places of Historic Interest of Natural Beauty* [1988] N.I. 86.
[72] *Re Richardson* at p. 89.
[73] *ibid.* at p. 92.
[74] *Re Steele* at p. 72.
[75] (1872) 8 Ch. App. 206.
[76] Megarry & Wade, *Law of Real Property*, 5th ed. at p. 300.

allows certain National Trust land to be held inalienably if certain procedures are followed.

The special rules relating to inalienability have been modified by statute (see further, Chapter 5 and the power of the Charities Branch to authorise various transactions involving land). Now charity land can be sold if authorised by the Charities Branch. If another statute states that land is held inalienably, this is still subject to the power of sale in section 18 of the Charities Act (N.I.) 1964. The only exception is land held inalienably by the National Trust. The Charities Branch has no power to authorise the sale of this land.[77] This power also existed prior to the Charities Act (N.I.) 1964 under the Charitable Bequests and Donations Act (Ireland) 1867, sections 14 to 18 and under the inherent power of the court in respect of charities.[78]

6.4.3 Rule against accumulations

This rule was framed to address the practice whereby settlors instructed trustees to invest a fund and accumulate income over a fixed period rather than give it directly to a beneficiary.[79] It applies to charities. In this jurisdiction the rule first found statutory endorsement in the Accumulations Act 1892 which limited the period for accumulation to the minority or minorities of any person who, if an adult, would be entitled under the trust. In the case of an unconditional gift to a charity, the effect of a direction to accumulate which breaches the rule was illustrated in *Shillington v. Portadown UDC*[80] where the gift vested immediately in the charity.

6.4.4 Rule in *Saunders v. Vautier*[81]

This rule is also directed against the settlor practice of tying up trust funds in order to accumulate income. It enables beneficiaries to end a trust by unanimously directing the trustees to do so and to distribute the trust property among all entitled. In *Harbin v. Masterman*[82] the House of Lords decided that directions for accumulating income on property given for charitable purposes was void; the rule in *Saunders v. Vautier* applied to charitable trusts.[83]

---

[77] s. 18(3) of the Charities Act (N.I.) 1964 as inserted by s. 2 of the Inalienable Lands Act (N.I.) 1966.

[78] See *Oldham Metropolitan Borough Council v. Attorney General* (1993) 2 All E.R. 432.

[79] See, for example, *Thellusson v. Woodford* (1799) 4 Ves. 227. This case resulted in Westminster passing the Accumulations Act 1800.

[80] [1911] 1 I.R. 247.

[81] (1841) 4 Beav. 115.

[82] (1871) L.R. 12 Eq. 559. *Harbin v. Mastermann* (1894) 2 Ch 184 in the Court of Appeal; affd. sub nom *Wharton v. Mastermann* (1895) A.C. 186 in the House of Lords.

[83] Followed in *Re Knapp* [1929] 1 Ch. 341 and *Re Blake* [1937] Ch 325, *sub nom Berry v. Green* [1938] A.C. 575.

6.5 VOIDABLE TRUSTS

If a trust is only voidable then it will come into effect and function as a fully valid trust unless and until a legal action is brought to have it "voided". Most often a trust is found to be voidable on grounds of mistake, misrepresentation, duress, undue influence or fraud. Where a trust has been contrived as a means of tying up assets, otherwise available to a creditor, then it will be voidable. As observed by Jessel M.R. in *Re Butterworth*[84]:

> "... a man is not entitled to go into a hazardous business, and immediately before doing so, settle all his property voluntarily, the object being this: "if I succeed in business, I make a fortune for myself. If I fail, I leave my creditors unpaid. They will bear the loss."[85]

6.6 TRUSTS AND OTHER FORMS OF LEGAL RELATIONSHIP

The legal device which permits separate sets of rights to be held in the same "property" is now well developed and by no means necessarily associated with trusts. While trusts provide the legal form governing almost all types of charitable activity, other forms may from time to time be relevant. To appreciate the particular appropriateness of charitable trusts it is necessary to consider the others.

6.6.1 Contract

A feature of modern business life for many charities is that, increasingly, they are becoming contractual partners with government bodies and/or other agencies. The distinction between charitable and contractual status is therefore of more than passing academic interest. The areas of difference and similarity between them are important and can be crucial when the terms of a contract threaten to compromise authorised charitable activity.

The differences are fundamental. A contractual relationship owes its origins to the common law unlike the trust which derives from equity. A contract is an agreement between two named parties, binding them to a specific exchange, is most usually time limited, depends upon valuable consideration being tendered and a breach is actionable only at the suit of one of the contracting parties. A trust, on the other hand, is quite different. It is an arrangement between three parties – the settlor (or testator), the trustee and the beneficiaries. It is grounded on the discretionary act of a donor, requires neither valuable consideration nor specified parties, may operate without time

---

[84] (1882) 19 Ch. D. 588.
[85] *ibid.* at p. 598.

constraints and is enforceable at the initiative of a beneficiary who was not a party to nor perhaps within the contemplation of the initial founding instrument. Whereas fulfilling a contract requires performance of specified terms, a trust may be validly executed despite non-completion of terms by application of *cy-près*. The rights of third parties to sue for a breach of obligation in the context of a trust but not of a contract is a particularly important difference. Also, of practical significance is the fact that debts are more readily recovered when a trustee becomes bankrupt than when this affects a contractual partner.

6.6.2 Agency

Again, modern business life requires many charities to engage in legal relationships which may take the form of trust or agency. The relationship between trustee and beneficiary and between principal and agent are similar in that in both a clear and firm non-profit duty rests on the subordinate parties (beneficiary and agent) who are also required to meet defined role specifications set by the primary parties (trustee and principal). Among the more obvious differences is the fact that the trust relationship is essentially proprietary in nature whereas agency is personal. This allows the agent in the latter relationship to impute to the principal a liability incurred in favour of a third party, which is not possible in the trustee/beneficiary relationship. An agent "stands in the shoes" of the principal and is obliged to give full and specific effect to the latter's directions. A trustee, on the other hand, is not so explicitly and directly bound by the wishes of either donor or beneficiary, their duty is simply to give effect to the terms of the trust. The two sets of relationships differ also in relation to any property involved: an agent may well be authorised to have dealings with the property of their principal but will not have ownership nor be in a position to give good title to another; a trustee can deal as owner with a donor's property.

6.6.3 Bailment

This has been defined as:

> "... the delivery of a chattel to another person for a limited purpose upon condition, express or implied, that it shall be returned to the bailor, or delivered to a third person at the bailor's order, when the purpose of the bailment has been carried out."[86]

Bailment owes its origins to the common law rather than to equity. It applies only to goods whereas a trust may apply to any property. There are other distinct points of difference. A donor divests himself of all rights in property

---

[86] See Keeton and Sheridan, *The Law of Trusts* (12th ed., Barry Rose, London, 1993), p. 13.

which are then held by the trustee as a full owner (subject to the conditions of the trust). A bailor, however, never relinquishes ownership as the bailee takes possession subject to the constraints of agreed purpose and time accompanied by the obligation to return the property in question. There is often a strong association between a contract and a bailment with the latter sometimes being made in pursuance of the former. There is less scope for overlap between trusts and bailment.

6.6.4 Power of appointment

This denotes the authority given to a named person or persons to nominate someone who will acquire ownership of specified property; again it is an arrangement between three parties. It provides only a power, exercisable at the discretion of the designated person who may choose not to use it.[87] Whereas a trust directs a trustee to give full effect to the terms of the trust, which may ultimately be enforceable through the courts, a power of appointment only equips a designated person to use their discretion.

6.6.5 Executor or administrator of a deceased's estate

The origins of the duties of a deceased's personal representative, whether as executor or administrator, lie in ecclesiastical law rather than equity. The actual duties, however, closely resemble those of a trustee. The primary duties of both are to gather in the property involved, manage it in accordance with the principles of good fiduciary practice while taking no personal profit. The roles differ as regards the scope of their authority to deal with third parties in relation to any property involved. While a trustee can only act jointly with other trustees to confer good title through sale to a third party, a personal representative can do so independently of others.[88]

The particular importance of the relationship between personal representative and trustee is that very often the same person will carry both roles successively and in that order. Indeed a personal representative holds the estate of the deceased as a trustee for the beneficiaries. The distinction between the two, although legislatively blurred, can be of real practical significance.[89]

---

[87] See *Brown v. Gregg* [1945] I.R. 224.

[88] See *Attenborough & Son v. Solomon* [1913] A.C. 76. Also, see, *Astbury v. Astbury* [1898] 2 Ch. 111.

[89] See *Attenborough & Son v. Solomon, op. cit.,* where liability turned on whether the defendant had been acting in the capacity of executor or trustee.

6.7 Types of Trust

A charitable trust is a species of trust. There are a number of different species within that genre. Each is therefore, to a greater or lesser extent, governed by characteristics common to all. A basic point of distinction between all trusts rests on a public/private division. With the exception of charitable trusts, all trusts are private in nature as they are established for the benefit of specific individuals or for small and well-defined classes of persons. Only charitable trusts are primarily intended to confer a public benefit.

6.7.1 Express trust

An express trust is one which is expressly declared by the settlor or testator. This may be done by instrument *inter vivos* or by will. All express trusts must contain the "three certainties" (see further, above), it may be either executed or executory and it does not require any particular form of words.[90] An executed trust is itself fully constituted so that no further instrument is required; the trust document contains a complete statement of the intentions of the settlor or testator and of the terms for giving effect to the trust. An executory trust contains only a broad statement of such intentions and of the means for giving effect to them; a further instrument is required to provide the details necessary to ascertain and implement the particular intentions of the settlor or testator.[91]

6.7.2 Resulting trust

An implied or resulting trust occurs when the beneficial interest in property reverts to the owner, or their representative, responsible for originally placing it in trust. They arise from the presumed intention of the originator of the trust to effect such a result. As has been explained:

> "… where it appears to have been the intention of the donor that the donee should not take beneficially, there will be a resulting trust in favour of the donor."[92]

The authority for a resulting trust rests with its originator, the courts merely give formal recognition to it.

Two different forms of resulting trust have been recognised: the automatic resulting trust; and the presumed resulting trust. The first refers to circumstances where there is a residual beneficial interest in property which has been

---

[90] The distinction between "executed" and "executory" was addressed in *Boswell v. Dillon* (1844) 6 Ir. Eq. R. 389 *per* Sugden L.C. at p. 392.

[91] See *Egerton v. Earl of Brownlow* (1853) HLC 1, 210.

[92] See *Vandervell v. IRC* [1967] 2 A.C. 291, *per* Lord Reid, quoting from Underhill (11th ed.) at p. 192.

made the subject of a trust. This may occur for reasons such as the failure of a trust due to illegality, uncertainty or lack of beneficiaries or from a surplus of funds remaining after the purposes of a trust have been met. The residue will then be held as a resulting trust for the benefit of the person, or representative, who declared the initial trust. The necessity to apply surplus funds by way of a resulting trust can occur in relation to funds raised by a charitable trust for the relief of disaster victims. Money contributed after the objects of the fund have been met may fall to be dealt with in this way.[93]

The second refers to a situation where a person acquires property from another voluntarily without consideration, or purchases property on behalf of another, and there is no documentary evidence as to the donor's intentions. It will then be presumed that the person holding the property is doing so on trust for the other. In the latter instance, the presumption may be rebutted by evidence of an intention to confer a gift or, depending on the nature of the relationship between the parties, may be displaced by the presumption of advancement.

6.7.3 Constructive trust

The intention of the donor is not determinative in establishing a constructive trust. The authority to do so lies with the court which can construct and impose a trust on all parties, guided by a concern for fairness, in order to resolve a disputed claim to ownership. It provides the means whereby the court can give effect to the principle that a legal owner of property should not be permitted to retain it where to do so would be inequitable or unjust; the fact that the legal owner has not acted improperly is beside the point.

Many constructive trusts arise out of fiduciary relationships, most often concerning leasehold interests. This context has provided the court with the opportunity to stress the obligation resting upon all who assume a trust responsibility for managing the property of others that they refrain from taking advantage of that position; it is inequitable to make a personal profit from a position of trust.[94]

There are also many circumstances where constructive trusts may arise despite the lack of a direct fiduciary relationship between the parties concerned. This will be the case, for example, when a vendor is holding title to property prior to transfer to a purchaser; the former holds the property on a constructive trust basis for the latter.[95] A similar relationship will also subsist between a mortgagee and mortgagor in respect of property mortgaged or in

---

[93] See *Re Trusts of Hobourn Aero Components Ltd's Air Raid Distress Fund* [1946] Ch. 86.

[94] See, for example, *Boardman v. Phipps* [1967] 2 A.C. 46; [1966] 3 All E.R. 721 and *Canadian Aero Services Ltd. v. O'Malley* (1974) 40 D.L.R. (3d) 371.

[95] See *Lysaght v. Edwards* (1876) 2 Ch. D. 499; *Tempany v. Hynes* [1976] I.R. 101.

respect of any surplus funds following the sale of that property. So, also, with spouses who make mutual wills or with third parties who assume a level of responsibility in respect of trust property; those who freely agree to assume obligations in respect of property, owned wholly or partially by another, will thereafter be deemed to be acting as a constructive trustee.

In the other jurisdictions of these islands there has been considerable judicial experimentation with the application of constructive trusts in the context of disputes regarding ownership of the family home; disputes between spouses and between a spouse and third parties. The use of both constructive and resulting trusts as a means of giving recognition to the beneficial interest of a housewife in property, to the purchase of which she has not financially contributed, has generated considerable case law in both England and Northern Ireland.[96] This dual usage of both types of trust has raised questions about the extent of any meaningful distinction between them. Hilary Delany offers the following useful summary:

> "The main distinction between resulting and constructive trusts is that in the case of the former, the courts assume that the creation of the trust was intended by the parties whereas in the latter instance a trust is imposed to satisfy the demands of justice and good conscience and may often be imposed in a manner contrary to the intentions of the individuals concerned. To the extent that there is no requirement to observe the formalities necessary in relation to express trusts in either case, there is often little practical significance in drawing a distinction between the two categories."[97]

6.7.4 Purpose trust

It can be briefly noted that other forms of purpose trusts exist in addition to charitable trusts. Unlike the latter, a purpose trust does not require an element of public benefit. Unlike a private trust, it is not intended to benefit an individual or a small well-defined class. There are a very limited number of private purpose trusts which can be valid: trusts for building tombs and monuments;[98] trusts for the care of specific animals/pets;[99] trusts for the furtherance of fox-hunting; and trusts for the saying of masses in private.

6.7.5 Charitable trust

Primarily, it is the fact that charitable trusts are established for purposes rather

---

[96] The leading case in this jurisdiction is *McFarlane v. McFarlane* [1972] N.I. 59.
[97] See Delany, H., *Equity and the Law of Trusts in Ireland* (Round Hall Sweet & Maxwell, Dublin, 1996), p. 62.
[98] *Re Hooper* [1932] 1 Ch. 38.
[99] *Pettingall v. Pettingall* (1842) 11 L.J. Ch. 176.

than for persons which sets them apart from other forms of trust. As has been observed:

> "... trusts for purposes rather than for human beings are rarely valid. They are regarded as difficult, perhaps impossible, to enforce, uncertain in their ambit and generally beyond the capacity of the court to control. In addition, they will very often contravene legal rules against creating perpetuities and inalienability. ... To this general doctrine the great exception is *charitable trusts* ... the distinctive feature of the charitable trust is that it is *for the public benefit*."[100]

This form of trust must be established for a recognised charitable purpose as defined by Lord Macnaghten in *Pemsel*.[101] It must, therefore, fit within one of the four *Pemsel* headings: relief of poverty; advancement of education; advancement of religion; or for charitable purposes other than those three. In addition, it must also be for the public benefit. The latter requirement prevents a charitable trust, unlike other forms, from being made in favour of named or specific beneficiaries.

The law governing charitable trusts is distinctive in that it has grown up around the central concern to identify and confirm the charitable intentions of donors and then ensure protection for their charitable donations. Once a trust has been confirmed as charitable, the law then makes available methods of enforcement not available in relation to other trusts: the Attorney-General, as protector of the public interest, may commence enforcement proceedings; the charitable organisation involved may do so; and the Charities Branch have certain statutory powers available to permit direct intervention.

The courts also lean towards saving a trust in which a charitable intent can be discerned. In circumstances where other trusts would fail, the courts will be guided by the principle expressed by Lord Loreburn:

> "... there is no better rule than that a benignant construction will be placed upon charitable trusts."[102]

Finally, a charitable trust may be saved by applying the *cy-près* doctrine. As explained by Delany:

> "Charitable trusts have traditionally enjoyed a number of advantages over other types of trust; they are not subject to requirements relating to certainty of objects nor do they depend on the existence of human beneficiaries to enforce them. Another crucial distinction is that charitable trusts may be perpetual in nature and enjoy a number of significant fiscal immunities in terms of exemptions from liability to various forms of taxation...Therefore for a trust to attain charitable status is a most desirable aim, not only because of the advantages referred to above, but also because it will facilitate the operation of *cy-près*

---

[100] Delany, H., *op. cit.* at p. 131.
[101] See *Commissioners of Income Tax v. Pemsel* [1891] A.C. 531.
[102] See *Weir v. Crum-Brown* [1908] A.C. 162 at 167.

jurisdiction should this become necessary. If a trust fails to qualify as charitable, this jurisdiction cannot be exercised and a bequest may fail as contravening the rule against perpetuities."[103]

See further, Chapter 19.

---

[103] See Delany, H., "Charitable Status and Cy-Près Jurisdiction: An Examination of Some of the Issues Raised in *In Re the Worth Library*" in N.I.L.Q., 1994.

CHAPTER 7

Trustees

7.1 INTRODUCTION

Trustees are crucial to the success of any trust. Honouring the terms of the trust is their fundamental responsibility. To that extent the obligations of all trustees are essentially the same. A considerable body of case law now exists to demonstrate the lengths the law is prepared to go in its protection of beneficiaries. The courts, over the centuries, have imposed an anomalous range of powers, liabilities and duties upon trustees in general.

However, there are some differences between trustees in general and those whose appointment arises in respect of charities. Legislation has imposed further duties with a particular application upon all those concerned with the:

> "... general control and management of the administration of the charity."[1]

A charity trustee may look to the Charities Branch or to the office of the Attorney-General for advice and assistance. For example, any person, such as a trustee, with the consent of the Attorney-General, may apply to the High Court for relief or directions relating to a charity and *cy-près* schemes are available only in a charitable context. This chapter deals with areas of similarity and difference in the responsibilities of charitable trustees and trustees in general. It focuses on the powers and duties of charitable trustees.

As noted in Chapter 6, the law in England and Wales relating to trusts and trustees had undergone considerable change as a result of the Trustee Act 2000. The changes relate *inter alia* to powers of investment, delegation by trustees and duties owed to beneficiaries. There is no equivalent legislation in Northern Ireland although it may be the case that amending legislation will follow here in due course.

7.2 DEFINITION OF TRUSTEES

The issue of who is a trustee, for the purposes of determining their responsibilities for the affairs of a charity, is one which has been fraught with difficulties.

---

[1] Charities Act (N.I.) 1964, s.35.

7.2.1 Definition under the Charities Act (N.I.) 1964

Section 35 of the Charities Act (N.I.) 1964 explains that:

> "... 'trustees', in relation to a charity, means the persons having the general control and management of the administration of the charity."

Two points can be made about this definition. Firstly, the legal definition of a charitable trustee is broader than that of an ordinary trustee. Orthodox trustees are defined as those holding the legal title to trust property under some form of a trust. However, there is no need for an actual trust before there can be charitable trustees. A director of a company is not a trustee, he is a director. A director of a charitable company is both a director and a charitable trustee. The office of charitable trustee does not depend for its existence on an actual trust, all that is required is the existence of a charity.

The second point is a related one. It does not matter what a person is called or what position they occupy. If they have general control over the charity, they are trustees. They need not be formally appointed under the trust deeds to be a charitable trustee.[2] If appointed to a charitable company the trustees will constitute the board of directors. If appointed to an unincorporated association they will be members of the executive or management committee.[3]

7.2.2 Extension of this definition into common law

The above cited definition is contained by and relates to the Charities Act (N.I.) 1964 and is therefore applicable to the powers, duties and liabilities referred to within that Act. No Northern Ireland case has raised the issue of whether this definition also applies beyond the precincts of the Act. Nor does any English case appear to have done so.

This can give rise to very real practice issues. For example, does the common law duty not to profit apply only to "orthodox" trustees or does it apply to all those connected with the general control and administration of the charity? Arguably, the latter is the case *i.e.* the full gamut of trustee responsibilities lies with those defined as trustees under the Charities Act (N.I.) 1964. The root of their duties is a fiduciary relationship and those charged with running charities should be held to be bound by a relationship of trust and confidence. This approach is implicit in the Charity Commission guidelines in CC3, Responsibilities of Charity Trustees (1999). The Commissioners utilise the section 35 definition and then go on to ascribe all the incidents of trusteeship to those falling within its broad spread.

---

[2] The position of "shadow directors" under Companies legislation is a good analogy.

[3] See *Affleck v. Newcastle Mind* (1999) I.C.R. 852; (1999) I.R.L.R. 405, holding that employees of a charitable unincorporated association were employed by its management committees, not by the entirety of its members.

7.3 APPOINTMENT OF A TRUSTEE

The interests of intended beneficiaries are protected by the appointment of trustees charged with safeguarding the property to be held on trust by them for the benefit of those beneficiaries.

7.3.1 Eligibility for appointment

Eligibility for appointment to the office of trustee in respect of a charitable trust is determined in the same way as for a private trust. A minor can be a trustee of land or other property in the Republic of Ireland or Northern Ireland. In England, a minor cannot legally own land.[4] A minor may not, however, act as an executor under a will.[5] Wylie suggests[6] that minors should not be trustees "as it has been often held by the courts that an infant [*i.e.* a minor] may lack capacity to act as trustee in terms of judgement and discretion". A bankrupt can be a trustee, though not the director of a charitable company, unless the court gives its consent.[7] A beneficiary or a relative or close friend of a beneficiary[8] may be appointed trustee. A trustee need not be resident within the jurisdiction,[9] as undesirable as this may prove to be in practice. Indeed, the courts have a well established reluctance to supervise a trustee resident outside the jurisdiction.[10] Although eligible for appointment as trustees, the above classes are open to be removed on the grounds set out in section 35 of the Trustee Act (N.I.) 1958.[11]

There are certain classes of trustee where eligibility is particularly contentious.

7.3.1(i) Corporations

A corporation can be a charitable trustee.[12] This can occur in two situations. Firstly, the corporation may be a standard trust corporation set up to administer trusts generally.[13] Secondly, it may be created specifically for that particular charitable trust. If a limited gift is given to a trust corporation, then a

---

[4] Law of Property Act 1925, s.20.

[5] Grattan, S., *Wills and Intestacy*, SLS, Belfast, 1995.

[6] Wylie, J.C.W., *op. cit.* at p. 1112.

[7] Art. 94(1) Companies (N.I.) Order 1989.

[8] See *Re Jackson's Trusts* (1874) 8 I.L.T.R. 174.

[9] See, for example, *Crofton v. Crofton* (1913) 47 I.L.T.R. 24.

[10] See *dicta* to that effect in *In re McCullough* [1966] N.I. 73, *per* Lowry J., see also *Goudiyo Mission v. Brahmachary* (1997) 4 All E.R. 957 on liability to supervise foreign charities.

[11] See further below.

[12] See, for example, *Incorporated Society v Richards* (1841) 1 Dr. & War. 258 at p. 302.

[13] See, for example, the Northern Bank Executor and Trustee Company Ltd. in *Re Dunwoodie* [1977] N.I. 141.

secondary trust may need to be created within that corporation to administer the gift. There are benefits in appointing a trust corporation as a trustee. For example, it can sometimes act alone rather than having to rely upon human trustees.[14] Where a corporation becomes a sole trustee due to its appointment by the court or Charities Branch, "the terms of the trust shall be treated as providing for or requiring the appointment of one trustee only".[15]

7.3.1(ii) State body

A local authority may be appointed trustee, for example, of open spaces under the Open Spaces Act 1906.

7.3.2 Ineligibility for appointment

There are circumstances in which a person will be ineligible to be appointed to a position which requires a high level of competence and trust. If, for example, a trustee is unable to exercise the degree of competence required because he or she is a minor, suffers from a learning disability, or is otherwise seriously incapacitated, then he or she will be unsuitable for appointment. If a person is an undischarged bankrupt, has previous convictions for fraud or theft, or has previously been disqualified from acting as a trustee or company director then again he or she will be rendered ineligible for appointment. All these criteria render a person ineligible in England and Wales under section 72 of the Charities Act 1993. No equivalent legislative provision exists in Northern Ireland.

7.3.3 Suitability for appointment

Trustee suitability, as opposed to eligibility, is not a matter addressed by any legislative provision. However, it is readily apparent that the selection of those who are to bear responsibility for the general control, management and administration of a charity should not be left to chance. In England and Wales, the Charity Commission has offered advice which has an equal application in this jurisdiction:

> "We recommend that trustees be selected for what they can contribute to the charity. They should not be appointed for their status or position in the community alone; this is the function of patrons. Trustees need to be able – and willing – to give time to the efficient administration of the charity and the fulfilment of its trusts. We recommend that they should be selected on the basis of their relevant experience and skills and need to be prepared to take an active part in the running of the charity."[16]

---

[14] *Re Duxbury's Secret Trusts* (1995) 1 W.L.R. 425.

[15] Charities Act (N.I.) 1964, s.12(15)(a).

[16] See Charity Commission for England and Wales, *Responsibilities of Charity Trustees* (leaflet CC3), Charity Commission, London, 1999, at pp. 4-5.

7.3.4 Power of appointment

Authority to appoint a trustee will be found in the initial trust instrument or in the Trustee Act (N.I.) 1958.

7.3.4(i) Governing instrument

This may take the form of a will, trust deed, conveyance, a scheme drawn up by the Charities Branch or by the court, a constitution, a Royal Charter or in a memorandum and accompanying articles in the case of a company. The instrument should clearly indicate the aims and rules for directing the charity and provide the trustees with the necessary powers for implementation.[17]

7.3.4(ii) The Trustee Act (N.I.) 1958

Section 35 of this statute, continuing the authority provided by section 10(1) of the Trustee Act 1893, deals with the appointment of replacement trustees. It provides that:

"(1) Where a trustee, either original or substituted, and whether appointed by a court or otherwise, is dead, or remains out of the United Kingdom for more than twelve months or desires to be discharged from all or any of the trusts or powers reposed in or conferred on him, or refuses or is unfit to act therein, then

(a) the person or persons nominated for the purpose of appointing new trustees by the instrument, if any, creating the trust, or

(b) if there is no such person, or no such person able and willing to act, then the surviving or continuing trustees or trustee for the time being, or the personal representative of the last surviving or continuing trustee,

may by writing appoint another person or persons to be a trustee or trustees in the place of the trustee dead, remaining out of the United Kingdom, desiring to be discharged, refusing or being unfit or being incapable, as aforesaid."

The trustee must remain outside the United Kingdom for an unbroken period of 12 months.[18] Trustees can be removed against their will under this power.[19] Refusal to act includes trustees who never accepted their office.[20] Being bankrupt can make a trustee unfit to act.[21]

---

[17] Where there are insufficient powers, but the charitable intention is clear, then the Charities Branch or the court may make good the deficiency; see, for example, *Re JW Laing Trust* [1984] Ch. 143.

[18] *Re Walker* (1901) 1 Ch. 259, return for one week prevented this power.

[19] *Re Storeham's Settlement Trusts* (1953) Ch. 59.

[20] *Re Hadley* (1851) 5 De G. & Sm. 67, see also *Re Birchall* (1889) 40 Ch. D. 436, *Noble v. Meymott* (1851) 14 Beav. 471.

[21] *Re Barker's Trusts* (1875) 1 Ch. D. 43, but see *Re Bridgman* (1860) 1 Drew & Sm. 164 where bankruptcy due to misfortune did not make a trustee unfit.

This statutory power must be exercised by writing and preferably by deed so as to facilitate the vesting of trust property as provided for in section 39 of the 1958 Act. In section 26 of this statute there is authority for existing trustees to delegate, by power of attorney, their responsibilities to another person of their choice (see Part 2: procedures).[22]

7.3.5 Manner of appointment

Trustees may be appointed to their office in various ways: by direction of the donor, by order of the court or by authority of the Charities Branch.

7.3.5(i) Appointment by donor

No particular formalities are required for the appointment of a trustee. However, most usually the appointment is made in an explicit statement to that effect by a donor in the will or trust deed which confers the gift. When no such express provision has been made then equitable doctrine may be called upon to ensure that "a trust shall not fail for want of a trustee".

7.3.5(ii) Appointment by the court

The court has a general power to appoint trustees.[23] The need to do so may arise in various circumstances including the death, incapacity, retirement or refusal to act of an appointed trustee.

7.3.5(iii) Appointment by the Charities Branch

The Charities Branch has the power to appoint new trustees under section 12 of the Charities Act (N.I.) 1964. It can exercise this power if it is necessary in the interests of the proper administration of the charity, and if appointment cannot conveniently be made otherwise. The trustees can ask for this power to be exercised, or if there are no trustees available, any person with an interest in the charity can request it. Alternatively, the Charities Branch may make an appointment of its own motion if no such application has been made by anyone else within a reasonable period.

The appointment can be in addition to, or in substitution for, existing trustees. The appointment can only be in substitution if the existing trustees desire it, or if they refuse to act in the administration of the charity. The appointment can be deemed effective in vesting all the necessary property in the new trus-

---

[22] For a fuller consideration of s. 35 of the Trustee Act (N.I.) 1958, see Carswell, R., *Trustee Act (N.I.) 1958*, (1964), Belfast.

[23] See *Pollock v. Ennis* [1921] 1 I.R. 181.

tee and making his appointment subject to the same powers, authorities and discretion as if he had been originally appointed under the trust.

The Charities Branch must give notice of at least one month of its intentions to appoint a new trustee. It must consider all relevant suggestions. It must give notice of the appointment within 14 days of making it. A person with an interest in the charity has 28 days from the date this notice is published to appeal it to the High Court.

An alternative way to appoint new trustees is under the *cy-près* procedure where the donor's intent to establish a trust is evident but no appointment of a trustee was made, then the Charities Branch may make good the donor's omission by itself supplying a trustee. Alternatively, where the donor's intent is clearly to make a charitable gift, generally and indefinitely, then the Charities Branch may employ the sign manual procedure to appoint the state as trustee.

7.3.5(iv) Appointment of the Charities Branch

Under section 12(3) of the Charities (N.I.) Act 1964 the Charities Branch may, with the consent of the Attorney-General, appoint itself as sole trustee in circumstances where:

> "there are no trustees of a charity or they cannot be found; and
>
> it appears to the Ministry that no suitable person is willing to be appointed. "

7.3.5(v) Appointment by remaining trustees

Under section 35 of the Trustee Act (N.I.) 1958, the remaining trustees can appoint new trustees. If no trustees remain, appointment can be by the personal representatives of the last surviving trustee.

7.3.6 Number appointed

While there is no maximum limit to the number of trustees that may be appointed to administer a trust, there is a minimum limit of one and usually there are at least two.

7.3.7 Effect of appointment

Where an appointment has been properly made, giving trustees full discretion, then the courts will not interfere.[24] However, the court will not release any funds which may have been lodged with it until the trustees submit an affidavit explaining how the funds are to be applied.[25]

---

[24] See *Richardson v. Murphy* [1903] 1 I.R. 227.
[25] See *Hagan v. Duff* (1889) 23 L.R. Ir. 516; *Blount v. Viditz* [1895] 1 I.R. 42; and *Warren v. Clancy* [1898] 1 I.R. 127.

7.3.8 Replacing trustees

The life of a trust may well exceed that of its trustees. In that event, the re-sponsibilities borne by an ex-trustee could simply be re-distributed among the remainder and no replacement would be needed. However, in those circum-stances which require a trustee to be replaced, then authority to do so will be sought firstly in the instrument establishing the trust. Where no such provision has been made it is then permissible to look to the court or to the Charities Branch.

7.3.8(i) Authority from governing instrument

In circumstances where a trustee has retired, died or otherwise needs to be replaced then the authority to make a new appointment may be found in the will or deed that gave rise to the trust. This instrument may have made provi-sion, by way of an express power, for a replacement to be appointed by a named person; to be exercised either in specified circumstances or at the lat-ter's discretion.

7.3.8(ii) Authority from the court

When appointing new trustees the court will seek to ascertain and be guided by the wishes of the donor as expressed in or inferred from the original trust instrument. Where possible the court will ensure that the new appointees are of the same religion as the original founder of the charity.[26] The court will not be deterred from making an appointment by the opposition of a surviving trustee.[27]

7.3.8(iii) Authority from the Charities Branch

The Charities Branch may, at the request of a charity, appoint trustees.[28] These appointments may be made either in substitution for, or in addition to, any existing trustee or trustees, or in circumstances where there are no existing trustees. When so doing the Charities Branch is statutorily required to give public notice of its intention on two occasions, in each case allowing 28 days for comment before proceeding. This can result in expensive delays for the charities concerned.

---

[26] See *Attorney-General v. Fitzgerald* (1851) 3 Ir. Jur. 37; *Attorney-General v. Drummond* (1842) 2 H.L.C. 837; and *Attorney-General v. Tottenham* (1870) 4 I.L.T.R. 689.

[27] See, for example, *Re Liddiard* (1880) 14 Ch. D. 310.

[28] S. 12 Charities Act (N.I.) 1964 and see further, above.

7.3.9 Disclaimer of appointment

Appointing a trustee is an act unaccompanied by any corresponding duty or power of enforcement. The prospective trustee has full discretion to decide whether or not to take up the appointment.[29] A disclaimer may be for any reason but should be made as soon as possible[30] and this can be achieved by deed to formally renounce the appointment or more simply by making a clear written or verbal declaration to that effect. A disclaimer must be total, absolute and in unambiguous language. Excessive delay will give rise to a rebuttable presumption of acquiescence. A prospective trustee, intending to disclaim, should take care not to become involved to any degree in decisions affecting trust property.[31]

Once the appointment is taken up a trustee is no longer free to disclaim (see further, below).

7.4 POWERS OF TRUSTEES

The powers of charitable trustees emanate from the instrument which established the trust and provided for their appointment. They are also empowered by statute, in particular by sections 12 to 39 of the Trustee Act (N.I.) 1958 and by the Charities Act (N.I.) 1964. Charitable trustees continue to share with other trustees the general powers derived from equity.

7.4.1 Vesting of powers

New trustees may be appointed under an express power or under the powers conferred by sections 35 and 36 of the 1958 Act.

7.4.2 Powers not vested

The powers of trustees are limited. Trustees have no powers, for example, in respect of the following:

- there is no power available to the trustees of a local charity for the relief of poverty enabling them to alter its objects, when circumstances suggest that this would be advisable;
- there is no legal mechanism available to trustees of a charity which has a low annual income enabling them to transfer its assets to a similar charity;

---

[29] See *Robinson v. Pett* (1734) 34 P. Wms. 249, *per* Lord Talbot at p. 251.

[30] But see, *Doe d. Chidgey v. Harris* (1847) 16 M. & W. 517; *Re Clout and Frewer's Contract* [1924] 2 Ch. 230 where a disclaimer, delayed for several years, was accepted because good reason was shown.

[31] See *James v. Frearson* (1842) 1 Y. & C.C.C. 370. *Cf. Orr v. Newton* (1791) 2 Cox 274. Also, see *Doyle v. Blake* (1804) 2 Sch. & Lef. 231.

- similarly, the trustees of a charity with a non-economic annual income are unable to simply liquidate its assets;

- there is no means whereby trustees can alter the memorandum of their charity, so that it ceases to be charitable, while ensuring that its property remains available for its original objects.

7.4.3 Power of sale, lease, etc.

At common law a charitable trustee had a recognised power to sell, lease, mortgage or otherwise deal with charity land.[32] In short, the trustee's capacity to deal with trust property was that of a legal owner.[33] Such power is now to be sought either in an express or implied direction[34] to that effect in the trust instrument, by authority of the court or by statutory provision.[35]

When exercising their powers the trustees should normally act with unanimity. Under section 26 of the Charities Act (N.I.) 1964, if there are four or more trustees certain actions may be performed by not less than two-thirds majority; rounding up if two-thirds is not an even number.[36] The actions which may be performed in this way are: making an application to the Charities Branch, entering contracts or giving assurances necessary for the disposing of charitable property, or exercising any power conferred upon them by the Charities Act (N.I.) 1964.[37]

Under sections 13 to 15 of the Trustee Act (N.I.) 1958, trustees may purchase or sell charity property unless expressly prohibited from doing so by the governing instrument of the trust. Under sections 17 and 18 of the 1964 Act, the Charities Branch may confer powers to lease, improve, sell, exchange or mortgage charity property subject to such conditions as it thinks fit (see further, Chapter 5). There is an onus on the trustee to ensure that any sale raises the best possible price for the trust beneficiaries.[38]

---

[32] See, for example, *Re Manchester New College* (1853) 16 Beav. 610, 628, 629; *Re Mason's Orphanage and London and North Western Railway Co.* [1896] 1 Ch. 596, 604; *Re Howard Street Congregational Chapel, Sheffield* [1913] 2 Ch. 690, 695.

[33] See *Burgess v. Wheate* (1759) 1 Eden 177, *per* Lord Northington at p. 251. See also, *Alexander v. Clarke* [1920] 1 I.R. 47 and *Re Murphy* [1957] NI 156.

[34] See *Re Murphy* [1957] N.I. 156 *per* Lord MacDermott L.C.J. for a case which examines the express and implied trustee power of sale.

[35] Charities Act (N.I.) 1964, ss. 17-21.

[36] S. 26(4).

[37] S. 26(3).

[38] See *Buttle v. Saunders* [1950] 2 All E.R. 193.

7.4.4 Power to insure

7.4.4(i) Property insurance

Under section 19 of the Trustee Act (N.I.) 1958, replicating section 18 of the Trustee Act 1893, trustees have a power to insure trust property "against loss or damage by fire, explosion, impact, lightning, thunderbolt, storm, tempest, flooding, subsidence or landslip". Buildings or any other trust property are equally insurable against these events. Section 19 confers a power to insure, it does not impose a duty[38] and allows payment of insurance premium out of the income of the trust; though the court can exceptionally allow payments of premium out of capital.[40] It is remarkable, both that the power to insure is so limited and that it is not a duty. Given the long standing acceptance that the most basic duty of the trustee is to conserve trust property it might be expected that this would be appropriately reinforced by a requirement to ensure comprehensive insurance in respect of all such property.

It is worth noting that the power to insure is, arguably, governed by the overriding duty to protect the trust property; at least in circumstances unforeseen when the trust was established and which require urgent action on the part of the trustees. As Romer L.J. has explained in *Re New*[41]:

> "In the management of a trust estate, it not infrequently happens that some peculiar state of circumstances arises for which provision is not expressly made by the trust instrument, and which renders it most desirable, and it may be even essential, for the benefit of the estate and in the interests of all the cestuis que trust, that certain acts should be done by the trustees which in ordinary circumstances they would have no power to do."

An approach which subsequently governed the decision of Powell J. in *Re Kinahan's Trusts*.[42] However, *Re New* concerned an ordinary trust. There is less scope for flexibility in the modification of charity trusts.

The Charity Commission has issued guidance on insurance generally for charities.[43] It recommends that buildings be insured for their full reinstatement value. However, Carswell suggests that the statutory power to insure is for the "full market value of the trust property, not replacement value".[44] The Commission recommend that the value of property insured should be reassessed every two to four years by a qualified building surveyor to ensure that the current figure is adequate.

---

[39] *Re McEacharn* (1911) 103 L.T. 900, see also *Bailey v. Gould* (1840) 4 Y. & C. 221, *Fry v. Fry* (1859) 27 Beav. 144.

[40] *Re Kinahan's Trusts* (1921) 1 I.R. 210, premiums paid out of capital for damage arising from riots.

[41] [1901] 2 Ch. 534 at p. 544.

[42] [1921] *op. cit.*

[43] See, Charity Commission 49, Charities and Insurance (1996).

[44] Carswell (1964) at p. 46.

The Charity Commission also recommends that contents insurance is purchased for all buildings occupied by a charity.

7.4.4(ii) Trustee indemnity insurance

Trustees may wish to have trustee indemnity insurance or liability insurance which protects them from any personal liability they may have for a breach of trust. It may be difficult to have the charity pay the premiums for this sort of insurance. Such insurance protects the trustees, it does not protect the charity. It may therefore be difficult to justify the expenditure. If trustees wish to avail themselves of this protection, it is advisable to enshrine this power to purchase trustee indemnity insurance in the charity's constitution.

If this power is not contained in the charity's constitution, trustees will face an uphill struggle to acquire appropriate authorisation. In England and Wales, the Charity Commission does have the power to authorise the purchase by the charity of trustee indemnity insurance. This is contained in section 16 of the Charities Act 1993 (power of the Commission to make schemes for the administration of the charity) and section 26 of that Act (power of the Commission to sanction administrative acts of a charity where expedient to do so). The Charities Branch do not have this general power in Northern Ireland.

The following are the only ways in which such a course of action may be authorised in Northern Ireland. Firstly, in the case of charitable trusts, the charity can apply to court to vary them. This can be done by invoking statutory powers[45] or under the courts inherent jurisdiction in relation to charities.[46] Secondly, if the charity is set up as an incorporated trust under section 10 of the Charities Act (N.I.) 1964, the trust can be amended by the Charities Branch. Thirdly, there is a power for a charitable company to purchase and maintain insurance for any officer or auditor of the company for any negligence, default, breach of duty or breach of trust.[47] In addition, a company can indemnify any officer or auditor of the company for any liability incurred in a successful defence of any proceedings.[48] According to the Charity Commission:

> "... we take the view that this provision[49] does not automatically authorise a charitable company to provide indemnity insurance for its trustees. This is be-

---

[45] Ss. 56 and 57 of the Trustee Act (N.I.) 1958.

[46] *Re Royal Society's Charitable Trust* [1956] Ch. 87 and see further below.

[47] Art. 318(3)(a) Companies (N.I.) Order 1986 as inserted by Art. 72 Companies (N.I.) (No. 2) Order 1990.

[48] Art. 318(3)(b) Companies (N.I.) Order 1986 as inserted by Art. 72 Companies (N.I.) (No. 2) Order 1990, no indemnities can be given for unsuccessful legal actions.

[49] S. 310(3)(a) Companies Act 1985. This is exactly replicated in the equivalent Northern Ireland legislation in Art. 318 Companies (N.I.) Order 1986 as amended.

cause the provision and maintenance of indemnity insurance for trustees confers a personal benefit on them. The trustees of a charitable company are usually precluded from personal benefit by a clause in the companies Memorandum of Association. An amendment to that clause would, therefore normally be required before the company could take advantage of section 310(3)(a)."[50]

The position therefore seems to be that charitable companies can purchase indemnity insurance provided that they modify their constitution to this end and the Charities Branch consent to alteration.[51]

The Charity Commission recommend that any trustee liability insurance policy contain the following exclusion clause:

"... the Insurers shall not be liable for loss arising from any act or omission which the trustee knew to be a breach of trust or breach of duty or which was committed by the trustee in reckless disregard of whether it was a breach of trust or breach of duty or not".[52]

The Charity Commission provides further general advice on the merits, disadvantages and modalities of trustee indemnity insurance in CC49, Charities and Insurance.

7.4.4(iii) Other insurance

Charities have a discretion, and in some cases an obligation to purchase other types of insurance. These are mentioned here for the sake of completeness: occupier's liability insurance to guard against those injured on the charity's premises, employer's liability insurance to protect against injury claims by employees, motor insurance, fidelity guarantee insurance to protect against theft by employees, Pluvius insurance to cover the cost of cancelled fundraising events, professional indemnity insurance to protect against claims made against the charity for negligent advice.

7.4.5 Power to initiate legal proceedings

In common with ordinary trustees, charitable trustees may commence legal proceedings. The trustee will have a duty to do so in circumstances, for example, where the trust property is under threat from the fraud, bankruptcy or incompetence of a third party.

---

[50] CC49, *op cit.* at p. 10.
[51] See further, Chap. 16 on the power to alter constitution of a charitable company with the consent of the Charities Branch under the Charities (N.I.) Order 1987.
[52] CC49 *op cit.*, at p. 9.

7.4.6 Power to vary trusts

A charitable constitution may contain within it the power to amend the constitution. Such a clause may not be acceptable to the Inland Revenue as it allows for the possibility of expenditure of funds on non-charitable purposes. The power of alteration has been mentioned briefly above. The power to alter the constitution of charitable companies is set out in more detail in Chapter 16. This section deals with variation of charitable trusts.

If the constitution does not provide the power to vary the trust, variation can only be effected by a court order. There are two possible sources of authority by which a trust can approve such a variation. The first is under the inherent and special jurisdiction over charities. The court "has also authority to direct a scheme in order to enforce [i.e. secure] the more complete attainment of those objects".[53] In *Re Royal Society's Charitable Trust*,[54] for example, the charity was the trustee of a large number of trust funds belonging to separate charities. It wished to consolidate them into one single fund to make administration easier. The court held that it could authorise a scheme to this end under its special charitable jurisdiction. Vaisey J. held that it could not do this if the trust was not charitable.

The second method to vary a charitable trust is statutory and is contained in sections 56 and 57 of the Trustee Act (N.I.) 1958. Section 56 allows the court to authorise any transaction concerning trust property which seems expedient. Section 57 allows the court to vary any trust. It was previously held, *per curiam* in *Re Royal Society's Charitable Trust* that the English equivalent to these provisions[55] could not apply to charitable trusts. This was overruled in *Re Shipwrecked Fishermen and Mariners' Royal Benevolent Society*[56] which concerned an application to vary the investment powers of a charity. Danckwerts J. held that this could be done by court order under the Trustee Act.

It is important to note that both these methods of varying a trust extend only to varying the administration of the trust. The courts have ruled that they cannot alter a charitable object, only its mode of attainment.[57] As explained in *Re Shipwrecked Fishermen*:

> "The situation is one where the court is being asked to do something purely in the administration of the trust. It is not altering the substantive trusts in anyway whatever, it is simply giving the trustees power, in the administration of the funds which they have under their control, to administer them in a more satisfactory and more effective way."[58]

---

[53] *Attorney General v. Sherborne Grammar School* (1854) 18 Beav. 256 at p. 280.
[54] [1956] Ch. 87.
[55] Trustee Act 1925, s.57.
[56] [1958] 1 Ch. 220.
[57] *Andrews v. M'Guffog* (1886) 11 App. Cas. 313 at p. 316.
[58] *op. cit.* at p. 228.

7.5 DUTIES OF TRUSTEES

There is an obligation to honour the terms upon which a donor has made a gift. This is placed upon the trustees but in the final instance it falls to be upheld by the courts. For centuries the courts, exercising their equity jurisdiction, have been attentive to the manner in which trustees give effect to their duties in respect of donors' wishes. A wealth of case law exists to illustrate the principles forged in the courts of equity to govern the duties of trustees; these largely apply to all trustees including those appointed in respect of charitable gifts.

7.5.1 To execute the terms of the trust

As has been said:

> "The primary duty of a trustee of a charitable trust, as of other trustees, is to carry out the trust according to the instructions of the founder so long as they are capable of fulfilment."[59]

In order to give effect to the purposes of the trust it is essential that the trustee first locates and becomes familiar with the trust governing instrument and all ancillary documentation. In *Hallows v. Lloyd*[60] the court observed:

> "I think that when persons are asked to become new trustees, they are bound to inquire of what the property consists that is proposed to be handed over to them, and what are the trusts. They ought also to look into the trust documents and papers to ascertain what notices appear among them of incumbrances and other matters affecting the trust."[61]

Advice subsequently reiterated by the Charity Commission:

> "Trustees can be effective only if they have a sound knowledge of the purposes of the charity, the trusts and procedures which govern the trustees' actions and the nature and condition of the property and resources of the charity. So every trustee (or person asked to be a trustee) needs to study the governing document or document of the charity."[62]

Expert advice may be needed on the correct execution of the trust.

The trustee has little scope for discretion, he or she is bound by the donor's directions. In so far as the directions are realisable they must be followed to the letter. Instances when the actions of trustees have failed to meet this standard include: the substitution of a more practical site for a hospital instead of

---

[59] See, Keeton & Sheridan, *The Modern Law of Charities* (4th ed., Barry Rose, London 1992), p. 349.

[60] (1888) 39 Ch. D. 686.

[61] *per* Kekewich J. at p. 691

[62] CC3, *Responsibilities of Charity Trustees* (1999) at p. 5.

the location specified by the donor;[63] the broadening of a donor's gift of a chapel to a school to permit the conferring of revenues upon villagers who were accustomed to the use of the chapel;[64] and the destruction of a church the maintenance for which the donor had left funds.[65] Where the trustee does have discretion then this must be exercised fairly.[66] When a discretionary decision is taken jointly by a majority of trustees this will be binding on the remainder.[67]

Two broad principles govern all trustee duties. In executing the terms of the trust the trustee is required to demonstrate both loyalty to the objects as set out in the governing instrument and impartiality when negotiating between the interests of trust beneficiaries. These can be seen in the duties of trustees as outlined below.

7.5.2 To manage trust assets

The essence of a trust is that the appointed trustee should exercise good stewardship in respect of the funds or other assets entrusted to him or her. This requires, in the first instance, that the trustee gather in and account for all trust property, inspect all relevant documents, ensuring that they are in order,[68] and ascertain whether the trust property is subject to any form of liability.[69] As stated by Christian J. in *Macnamara v. Carey*[70]:

> "The principle which stands out distinct and clear upon those authortities[71] is this: that it is not enough for a trustee to keep within the four corners of the deed, and perform literally what is there set down. The very first point to which he must direct his thoughts is the placing of the trust property in security; and, above all, the making it impossible that it shall ever fall under the control of unauthorised persons. If he, even by mere inaction, suffers a state of things to exist or to continue, which, however apparently at the time natural and harmless, results in the course of future events, in the fund getting under unauthorised control, even though it be *that* of a co-trustee only – still more that of the settlor himself – and loss follows, the trustee must make it good."

The warning is clear, a trustee must be pro-active from the moment of taking up appointment in taking such steps as may be necessary to satisfy himself that all documents are in order, all trust property is accounted for and is se-

---

[63] See *Re Weir Hospital* [1910] 2 Ch. 124.
[64] See *Attorney-General v. Earl of Mansfield* (1827) 2 Russ. 501.
[65] See *Ex parte Greenhouse* (1815) 1 Madd. 92; on appeal (1827) 1 Bligh N.S. 17.
[66] See *Re Beloved Wilkes Charity* (1851) 20 L.J. Ch. 588.
[67] See *Re Whiteley* [1910] 1 Ch. 600, 608.
[68] See *Macnamara v. Carey* [1867] I.R. 1 Eq. 9.
[69] See, for example, *Hallows v. Lloyd* (1888) 39 Ch. D. 686.
[70] *op. cit.*
[71] Referring to *Fenwick v. Greenwell* 10 Beav. 412, *Ghost v. Waller* 9 Beav. 497 and *Matheus v. Brise* 6 Beav. 239 among others.

cure. Where the trustee is a replacement appointee, taking up office some time after the trust was established, then he or she should also ensure that no breach of trust occurred prior to their appointment. Having taken up the appointment the trustee must ensure that all decisions taken fall fully within the objects of the charity.

Thereafter, subject to any directions in the trust instrument, the trustee must conserve and manage the property in such a way as to promote the best interests of the intended beneficiaries. This requires them to be cautious when investing trust funds: the short-term gains from business opportunities must not be allowed to compromise the long-term viability of trust funds.

Trustees have a duty to manage trust funds so as to ensure an equitable distribution of proceeds among all beneficiaries. Where a fund is intended to subsist for future generations of beneficiaries, this will entail taking such measures as may be necessary to avoid first generation beneficiaries benefiting at the expense of those with a future entitlement. The duty of a trustee to give effect to the purposes for which the trust was established can sometimes conflict with the more pressing obligation to be prudent in their management of trust assets. The standard rule should at all times prevail that no trustee should allow a situation to develop whereby their personal interests are in conflict with their duties as a trustee.

7.5.3 Duty to invest prudently

The obligations of a trustee may entail investing or re-investing trust funds. All trustees have a duty to invest the trust property wisely. The following advice offered by Murphy J. in *Stacey v. Branch*[72] has an equal application in this jurisdiction:

> "What is the nature of the duty imposed upon a trustee? A trustee must, of course, invest trust funds in the securities authorised by the settlement or by statute. To invest in any other securities would be of itself a breach of trust; but even with regard to those securities which are permissible, the trustee must take such care as a reasonably cautious man would take having regard not only to the interest of those who are entitled to the income but to the interest of those who will take in the future. In exercising his discretion a trustee must act honestly and must use as much diligence as a prudent man of business would exercise in dealing with his own affairs; in selecting an investment he must take as much care as a prudent man would in making an investment for the benefit of persons for whom he felt morally obliged to provide. Businessmen of ordinary prudence may, and frequently do, select investments which are more or less of a speculative character; but it is the duty of a trustee to confine himself not only to the class of investments which are permitted by the settlement or by statute, but to avoid all such investments of that class as are attended with hazard."

---

[72] [1995] 2 I.L.R.M. 136.

More general advice to charity trustees on how to make investment decisions has also been offered by Sir Donald Nicholls V.C.:

> "In most cases the best interests of the charity require that the trustees' choice of investments should be made solely on the basis of well-established investment criteria, having taken expert advice where appropriate, and having due regard to such matters as the need to diversify, the need to balance income against capital growth, and the need to balance risk against return."[73]

7.5.3(i) Investment authorised by the trust document

The primary source of authority to make investments will be contained in the trust document. The trust powers to invest will trump any contrary investment powers acquired by legislative intervention. It is usually thought desirable for trusts to contain an express power of investment due to the narrow width of permissible investments implied under statute. In this jurisdiction, the observation once made by Carswell J. remains valid:

> "The crying need for a wide power of investment in every properly drawn trust has now been considerably diminished with the passing of the Investments Act,[74] but its difficulties and limitations still make it very desirable to give the trustee greater freedom in drafting new trusts instruments."[75]

More recently, the government has taken the view that changing financial and economic conditions place a greater need for widely written express investment powers for trustees which go beyond those implied by statute:

> ". . . the law governing the powers and duties of trustees, particularly the relevent provisions of the Trustee Act 1925 and the Trustee Investments Act 1961 [the corresponding English legislation], has not kept pace with the evolving social and economic role which trusts now fulfil. This discrepancy has been brought into sharp focus by the fundamental changes in the conduct of investment business during the last ten years such as the introduction of the CREST system on the London Stock Exchange. The situation is now so serious that the view is widely held that it is very difficult for such trustees acting under the terms of trust instruments which make no specific provisions as to investment powers, to satisfy their paramount duty to act in the best interests of the beneficiaries of the trust".[76]

Whatever the express power may be, it remains subject to the overriding requirement to invest prudently as discussed above. For example, trustees should not lend trust funds solely on the security of a personal promise.[77]

---

[73] *Harries v. Church Commissioners* (1992) 1 W.L.R. 1241 at 1246.

[74] Trustee Investment Act 1961, see further below.

[75] Carswell (1964) *op cit.* at p. 171.

[76] From the Explanatory Notes to the Trustee Act 2000 (HMSO, 2000) at para. 6.

[77] *Holmes v. Dring* (1788) 2 Cox Eq. Cas. 1 and see *Khoo Tek Keong v. Ch'ng Joo Juan Neoh* [1934] A.C. 529 where unsecured loans were a breach of trust.

7.5.3(ii) Investment powers implied by statute

If no express investment powers are given to the trustees, a power to invest will be implied by legislation. The governing legislation is the Trustee Investment Act 1961. This Act, on its face, applies only to England and Wales. However, its ambit has been widened to include Northern Ireland by the Trustee Act (N.I.) 1958.[78] Section 1 of this Act states:

> "A trustee may, unless and until Parliament otherwise provides, invest trust funds in the manner in, and subject to the conditions upon, which a trustee in any part of Great Britain is under the Trustee Investment Act 1961, entitled to invest trust funds."

In outline, the Trustee Investment Act authorises investment in three separate categories. The first is a narrow range of investments not requiring advice; a list of which is contained in Schedule I, Part I of the Act. Broadly speaking these are various types of government bonds.[79] The second category is a narrow range of investments requiring advice, a list of which is contained in Schedule I, Part II of the Act. Broadly speaking these are government gilts, securities issued by various international banks, company debentures, building society deposits and mortgages on freehold land.[80] The third category is wider range investments requiring advice. A list of these is set out in Schedule I, Part III of the Act. Broadly speaking, these are shares in European Union companies with a capital of over £1,000,000 which have paid dividends on shares in each of the preceding five years.

The requirement for advice means that the trustees should obtain proper advice from a qualified person as to the suitability of a particular investment. The Trustee Act 2000 has effected major changes to trustee investment powers in England and Wales.

7.5.3(iii) Division of funds under statutory powers of investment

Initially, under the investment powers implied by the 1961 Act, there had to be a 50:50 division of the trust fund between narrow range and wider range investments. A tangled web of legislation has now produced the end result that:

> "... any division of a trust fund ... shall be made so that the value of the wider

---

[78] As amended by s. 1(1) of the Trustee Amendment Act (N.I.) 1962.

[79] Defence Bonds, National Savings Certificates, Ulster Savings Certificates, Ulster Development Bonds, National Development Bonds, British Savings Bonds, National Savings Income Bonds, National Savings Deposit Bonds, National Savings Indexed Income Bonds, National Savings Capital Bonds, National Savings FIRST Option Bonds, National Savings Premium Guaranteed Income Bonds and deposits in the National Savings Bank.

[80] For a comprehensive list see the Act as amended, or see Underhill and Hayton, *Law Relating to Trusts and Trustees* (1995) Butterworths at pp. 568–572.

range part of it at the time of the division bears to the then value of the narrower range part the proportion of three to one."[81]

In England, Wales and Scotland, the Trustee Investments Act 1961 was expressly modified by the Charities Act 1993. Under section 70 of the 1993 Act, the Secretary of State may allow the proportion of the investments between narrow and wide range investments to be varied from the minimum 50 per cent required for narrow range investments. The Secretary of State has further powers under section 71 of the 1993 Act to widen the powers of investment under the Trustee Investment Act 1961. He may make regulations specifying other investments which will be accessible to every charity, unless that power is expressly excluded by the trust document.

The Secretary of State exercised these powers in the Charities (Trustee Investments Act 1961) Order 1995 so that wider range investments should be three times the value of the narrower range. This order came into force on April 25, 1995. The next two legislative stages were synchronised. Firstly, the Charities (Trustee Investments Act 1961) Order 1996 repealed the 1995 Order of the same name. Secondly, the Trustee Investment (Division of Trust Funds) Order1996 stated that all trusts exercising the statutory power of investment should be in the ratio of three to one of wider range to narrower range investments. Both these Orders came into force on May 11, 1996.

The Trustee Investments (Division of Trust Fund) Order 1996 does apply to Northern Ireland, the other two Orders do not. The three to one rule therefore applies from at least May 11, 1996. An argument could also be made that the Charities (Trustee Investment Act 1961) Order 1995 applies, by implication, to Northern Ireland. This is because that Order modified the 1961 Act, and that Act applies to Northern Ireland by virtue of section 1 of the Trustee Act (N.I.) 1958. If that were the case, the three to one rule could apply from April 25, 1995.

The division of the trust fund into two parts takes place on the first occasion a wider range investment is made. One re-division can be made in the new three-to-one ratio after the changes made by the 1996 legislation. There is no requirement for the trust fund to remain in this ratio. Wider range investments are generally more remunerative and appreciate faster than narrower range ones. Withdrawals can be made from either the narrower or wider range funds.

The Charity Commission has produced further guidance on this topic for charitable trustees.[82]

---

[81] Art. 2 Trustee Investments (Division of Trust Fund) Order 1996.
[82] See CC32, *Trustee Investment Act 1961, A Guide* (1999).

7.5.3(iv) Variation of investment powers

Investment powers can be varied under section 56 of the Trustee Act (N.I.) 1958.[83] However, since statute implied a power of investment in the 1961 Act, the courts have been less willing to vary powers of investment.[84]

7.5.3(v) Common investment schemes

Section 25 of the Charities Act (N.I.) 1964 provides a specific provision to govern the power of investment of charities. The Charities Branch can create "common investment schemes" into which charities can invest their money. The Charities Branch can also create a "central investment fund"[85] for those charities of which it is the trustee. In addition, such a scheme is open for investment by all charities. As stated in section 25(12) Charities Act (N.I.) 1964:

> "... the powers of investment of every charity shall include power to participate in common investment schemes, unless power to do so is excluded by a provision in the trusts of the charity specifically referring to common investment schemes."

It is possible to invest all of a charity's money in a common investment fund without having to comply with the requirement of division into broad and narrow range investments.

There are currently four common investment schemes. The Central Investment Fund is run by the Department of Health and Social Services with an independent advisory committee and is open to any charity. The other three common investment schemes are separate from the Charities Branch and operate a more restrictive access policy. The Northern Ireland Health and Personal Social Services Charities Common Investment Fund is only available to charities whose trustee is a Health and Social Services Trust. The Eastern Health and Social Services Board Investment Fund can only be used by charities whose trustee is the Eastern Health and Social Services Board. This fund has been by and large superseded by the previous fund. The Representative Body Unit Trust (Northern Ireland) can only be used by a charity whose trustee is the Representative Church Body of the Church of Ireland.[86]

In England, similar provisions regarding "common investment funds"[87] exist. The difference is that the power to create such funds rests with the courts or the Commission, rather than the courts or the Charities Branch as in North-

---

[83] *Re Shipwrecked Fishermen and Mariners' Royal Benevolent Society* [1959] Ch. 220.

[84] *Re Cooper's Settlement* (1962) Ch. 826, *Re Kolb's Will Trusts* [1962] Ch. 531.

[85] S. 25(8) Charities Act (N.I.) 1964.

[86] See also the Charities Central Investment Fund Scheme (N.I.) 1965 and the Charities Central Investment Fund Order 1988.

[87] Charities Act 1993, s.24.

ern Ireland. In addition, there is no provision for a "central investment fund" for charities of which the Commission is trustee. Furthermore, there is one extra type of fund in England, the "common deposit fund"[88] which is a facility providing more security and stability by offering a fixed rate of return rather than a flexible one based on how the investment is performing. By press release on August 20, 1996, the Commission announced plans to create "green" common investment funds. These would allow charities with certain objects to invest in funds which to a certain extent were consonant with their ethical principles. Financial considerations would still be important, but greater weight would be given to non-financial grounds. See further below, on the conflict between trust purposes and investment decisions.

7.5.3(vi) Standard of care

There is an onus resting on any trustee to exercise due care when investing trust funds. When the investing trustee is acting in relation to charitable funds then, arguably, the law will require greater diligence than would be expected from the private management of personal funds. In the words of Lindley L.J.:

> "The duty of the trustee is not to take such care only as a prudent man would take if he had only himself to consider: the duty rather is to take such care as an ordinary prudent man would take if he were minded to make an investment for the benefit of other people for whom he felt morally bound to provide."[89]

Because it is constructed around a central concern to protect the charitable intentions and funds of donors, the law places a special onus on the trustees of charities to act with integrity and care when managing trust assets.

7.5.3(vii) Conflict between trust purposes and investment decisions

Trustees can sometimes be faced with a difficult balancing act. On the one hand they must approach investment options objectively, making decisions which are most likely to safeguard and increase trust assets. On the other hand they and the trust are established to further purposes designated by the donor in the originating trust instrument. In juggling these priorities the trustee is required to be guided by the best interests of the beneficiaries, rather than by personal bias.[90]

---

[88] Charities Act 1993, s.25.

[89] See *Learoyd v. Whitely* (1886) 33 Ch. D. 347 at p. 355 (*cf.* Keane, *op. cit.* 1988, at p. 110).

[90] See, for example, *Buttle v. Saunders* [1950] 2 All E.R. 193 where it was stated that trustees:

> ... have an overriding duty to obtain the best price which they can for their beneficiaries. ...

per Wynn-Parry J. at p. 195.

The leading case on this point is *Cowan v. Scargill*[91] which concerned the investment of the pension fund of mineworkers. Certain trustees (appointed by the National Union of Mineworkers) objected to investments being made in oil projects, overseas projects and the acquisition of land overseas. The objections were on a point of principle and also on the point that such investments would be inimical to the interests of mineworkers. Sir Robert Megarry V.C. held that the trustees had a duty to promote the provision of financial benefits and that their personal views or moral reservations on potential investments should not sway them. However, the court did realise that in "very rare" cases, the financial benefit of the beneficiaries may not be the paramount consideration. It cited the example of a trust for the benefit of teetotallers or pacifists who could vociferously object to alcohol or armaments investments:

> "… the beneficiaries might well consider that it was far better to receive less than to receive more money from what they consider to be evil and tainted resources."[92]

The court specifically considered this point in relation to charity trustees in the case of *Harries v. Church Commissioners for England*.[93] The case concerned the permissible extent of non-financial considerations for charitable investments. Sir Donald Nicholls V.C. made a number of important points which are worth quoting verbatim. Firstly, as regards any investment property:

> "… *prima facie* the purposes of the trust will be best served by the trustees seeking to obtain therefrom the maximum return … which is consistent with commercial prudence."[94]

However, he recognised that, in the minority of cases "… the objects of the charity are such that investments of a particular type would conflict with the aims of the charity."[95] In these circumstances then:

> "… if … trustees were satisfied that investing in a company engaged in a particular type of business would conflict with the very objects their charity is seeking to achieve, they should not so invest."[96]

The court pointed out that excluding a limited number of investments would not be to the financial detriment of the charity, since there would still remain a substantial range of available investments from which to choose.

A policy of excluding conflicting investments would seem logical and not in contravention of a duty of financial propriety. However, in the *Harries* case,

---

[91] [1985] 1 Ch. 270.
[92] *Cowan v. Scargill* [1985] Ch. 270 at p. 288.
[93] [1992] 1 W.L.R. 1241.
[94] *ibid.* at p. 1246
[95] *ibid.* at p. 1246.
[96] *ibid.* at p. 1246.

the court did acquiesce to an inclusionary investment policy whereby certain projects could be adopted because of their alignment with the purposes of the charity. The court did reject a fully inclusionary policy which would have bound the trustees to only those investments which furthered the purposes of the Church.

According to the Vice Chancellor, the trustees can refuse an investment in three circumstances. Firstly, if it would make potential beneficiaries unwilling to accept aid from the charity. Secondly, if an investment would alienate other potential donors to the charity. Thirdly, if the trust deed directed that non-financial criteria could be considered in investment decisions. However, trustees:

> "… must not use property held by them for investment purposes as a means for making moral statements at the expense of the charity of which they are trustees."[97]

On the precise facts of *Harries*, the court approved the "ethical investment policy" of the trustees. This avoided investments in tobacco, gambling, alcohol, armaments, newspapers or South Africa. It required environmental considerations in property investments and it sought out a small number of investments which responded positively to the Church's specified areas of social concern.

7.5.3(viii) Unauthorised investments

Where loss is incurred not because of poor judgment or bad luck but results from decisions taken by trustees acting outside the scope of their authority, then they will be liable to make good the loss to the trust property. They will not escape personal liability by claiming to have relied upon expert advice, where that advice is wrong-headed and perverse.[98]

7.5.4 To maintain proper records

There is an explicit statutory duty requiring trustees to keep proper accounts. Under section 27 of the Charities Act (N.I.) 1964:

> "(1) The trustees of a charity shall keep proper books of account with respect to the affairs of the charity, and the trustees of any charity who are not required by or under any other enactment to prepare periodical statements of account shall prepare consecutive statements of account each consisting of –
>
> (a) a receipts and payments or an income and expenditure account relating to a period of not more than fifteen months; and

---

[97] [1992] 1 W.L.R. 1241 at p. 1247.
[98] See *Re Beddoe* [1892] 1 Ch. 547 *per* Bowen L.J. at p. 562.

(b) if the value of the property belonging to the charity exceeds five hundred pounds, and the Ministry so directs, a balance sheet relating to the end of that period."

The charity trustees are required to preserve such records for at least seven years, unless the charity ceases to exist or is excused from doing so by the Charities Branch. The statutory requirement is minimal. The Charities Branch has never required a charity to produce such balance sheets. There is no enforcement mechanism to check if the income and expenditure account is prepared. The Charities Branch has recommended that the current requirements be enhanced.[99] In their advice to trustees they state:

"... the trustees of at least the larger and more active charities may wish to go a bit further than the Act requires, since trustees have a general duty to act in the best interests of their charity and in some cases this might imply preparing more thorough documents than are strictly required."[100]

The paucity of accounting regulation in Northern Ireland can be contrasted with the considerable requirements in England and Wales. All registered charities are required to submit annual accounts. If income or expenditure is over £10,000 a year, the accounts must be scrutinised by an independent person. If income or expenditure is over £250,000, the accounts must be audited by a registered auditor.[101]

The accounting profession has also produced a Statement of Recommended Practice on Accounting for Charities (SORP2 1995). This provides detailed technical guidance for producing accounts for charities.

The courts have long recognised that a legal obligation to maintain proper accounts rests on all trustees;[102] these need not be audited. A trustee is also under a more general obligation to provide the beneficiaries with such information concerning the affairs of the trust as may be reasonably required by them.[103] Such a beneficiary may inspect the records relating to the management of trust assets.[104]

---

[99] Consultation Document on Charity Law in Northern Ireland, Charities Branch, (1995) at p. 6,7.

[100] Northern Ireland Charities: A Guide for Trustees (1998) Charities Branch at p. 19.

[101] See further Part VI, Charities Act 1993, Charities Accounts and Reports Regulations 1995 SI 1995/2724 and CC52 Charities Accounts, Charities under the £10,000 threshold (1999), CC53 Charity Accounts: Accounting for the Larger Charity (1999), CC54 Charity Accounts: Accounting for the Smaller Charity (1999), CC55 Accruals Accounting for the Smaller Charity (1999), CCC56 The Carrying out of an Independent Examination (1996), CC57 Receipts and Payments Accounts Pack, CC58 Accruals Accounts Pack.

[102] See *Crawford v. Crawford* (1867) L.R. 1 Eq. 436.

[103] See *Low v. Bouverie* [1891] 3 Ch. 82 and *Moore v. McGlynn* [1894] 1 I.R. 74, 86 *per* Chatterton V.-C.

[104] See *O'Rourke v. Darbyshire* [1920] A.C. 581.

Re Londonderry's Settlement[105] concerned a request from beneficiaries that the trustees produce both minutes of meetings in which discretionary decisions were reached and copies of correspondence between trustees and individual beneficiaries. The court then held that trustees were not obliged to reveal those documents, of a confidential nature, which related to the exercise of their discretionary powers.

The general principle of disclosure, being applicable to all trusts, has a bearing also on charitable trusts; though in that context it may be more difficult to realise.

7.5.5 To apply trust assets for the benefit of beneficiaries

In addition to prudent stewardship of trust assets, the trustee must also make appropriate arrangements to distribute those assets, and/or the resulting proceeds, to the intended beneficiaries. This distribution must be both in keeping with the donor's intentions and in accordance with the law; a failure on either count will amount to a breach of trust. As noted in Tudor:[106]

> "... it is an obvious breach of trust for trustees to occasion the destruction of the trust property,[107] to alienate it improperly[108] or negligently to permit others to misappropriate it."[109]

7.5.6 Not to profit

There is a long-standing general rule that a person holding a fiduciary office must not acquire or seek to acquire any personal gain or advantage in the course of executing the responsibilities of that office. As Lord O'Hagan stated in *Armstrong v. Armstrong*[110]:

> "I think it is plain that a trustee, so making a commodity of his position, and gaining a profit which but for it he would not have secured, must be held, on general principles and for the safety of *cestius que trusts*, to retain that profit for the benefit of the trust estate."

A characteristic feature of the office of trustee is an acceptance by the latter that the appointment is one of honour carrying an obligation to serve the interests of the trust in a selfless manner; arguably, accentuated in the context of a

---

[105] [1965] Ch. 918.

[106] See *Charities, op. cit.*, at p. 254.

[107] *Ex parte Greenhouse* (1818) 1 Madd. 92, reversed on technical grounds, 1 Bli. (N.S.) 17, where trustees of a chapel had pulled down the chapel, sold the materials and converted a burial ground to other uses: "It is a breach of trust such as could not be expected in a Christian country", *per* Plumer V.-C. at p. 108.

[108] See *Att.-Gen. v. East Retford Corporation* (1838) 3 My. & Cr. 484; *Att.-Gen. v. Wisbech Corporation* (1842) 11 L.J. Ch. 412.

[100] See *Att.-Gen. v. Leicester Corporation* (1844) 7 Beav. 176.

[110] (1880) 7 L.R. Ir. 207 at p. 218.

charitable trust. Acceptance of appointment brings with it a duty that the trustee will not place his or her self in a position where a conflict might arise between their personal interests and those of the trust.[111] This basic rule has a myriad of permutations: trustees cannot use knowledge gained from their position to make a profit;[112] they cannot make a profit from an opportunity which arises by dint of their position;[113] nor can they allow their personal interest to conflict with their duty to the trust.[114]

The most important consequence in practical terms is that trustees cannot be paid for their work unless it is expressly authorised by the trust document or allowed by the court. If it is desired that trustees be paid, the trust document should therefore contain a charging clause.[115] The Inland Revenue may however, resile from any purportedly charitable trust which contains a charging clause. They may refuse to accept it as charitable as it allows the possibility of a private benefit accruing to individuals. The Charity Commission guidance is that "where the terms of the clause limit the remuneration to a reasonable sum for services provided as a trustee"[116] then the trust remains charitable. There are two principles which restrict trustee remuneration. The first is the equitable principle that a trustee should not profit from his fiduciary position. The second is the charitable principle that the charity should be for public and not private benefit.

If a charitable trust does not contain a charging clause, the trustees cannot be paid for their services. They cannot amend the trust themselves to give themselves the power of remuneration. In England and Wales, the Charity Commission can authorise payment. In Northern Ireland, only the court can do so. The factors which the Charity Commission, and presumably the court, take into consideration in deciding whether to authorise remuneration are: existing powers of remuneration, size of the charity, nature of charity's activities, degree of trustees involvement, specialist nature of skills required, and the comparative costs of obtaining specialist skills.[117]

There is a presumption that any acquisition by a trustee of benefits from beneficiaries will be presumed to derive from the former exercising undue influence over the latter.[118] Where that trustee is a solicitor the rule applies with particular force.[119]

---

[111] See, for example, *Bray v. Ford* [1896] A.C. 44.

[112] *Boardman v. Phipps* [1967] A.C. 45.

[113] *Regal (Hastings) Ltd. v. Gulliver* [1942] 1 All E.R. 378.

[114] *Aberdeen Railway Co v. Blaikie* (1854) 1 Macq. 461.

[115] For example see *Guinness plc v. Saunders* [1990] 1 All E.R. 652 where the defendant who was in a position analogous to a trustee had expended a considerable amount of effort to net his "beneficiaries" several million pounds, and yet could not be paid at all since payment was not expressly authorised by the trust documents.

[116] CC11, Remuneration of Charitable Trustees (1999) at p. 4.

[117] See further CC11, *op cit.*

[118] See *Provincial Bank of Ireland v. McKeever* [1941] I.R. 471.

[119] See *Edwards v. Meyrick* (1842) 2 Hare 60. But also see the rule in *Cradock v. Piper*

A trustee is, however, entitled under section 31 of the Trustee Act (N.I.) 1958, to remuneration for all out of pocket expenses reasonably incurred.[120] If the trust allows it, a professional trustee may be paid for their professional services. If a trustee is also an employee, he can be paid a salary. Trustees can only be employees if authorised by the trust document. A trustee who is being paid as an employee or for his services should take no part in any decisions or meeting concerning his remuneration. This would lead to a conflict between his personal interests in remuneration and his fiduciary responsibility to the trust to obtain the lowest price. Payment of professional trustees is now governed, in England and Wales, by the Trustee Act 2000.

7.5.7 Not to delegate

A delegate must not delegate or *delegatus non potest delegare*. It is in the nature of an appointment to the office of trustee that the latter undertake their responsibilities on the basis of trust personally vested in him or her. The trustee is honour bound to personally assume and give effect to their duties. This principle has been expressed by Lord Langdale in *Turner v. Corney*[121] as follows:

> "[T]rustees who take on themselves the management of property for the benefit of others have no right to shift their duty on to other persons; and if they employ an agent, they remain subject to the responsibility towards their *cestius que trust*, for whom they have undertaken the duty."[122]

However, this principle is not inflexible and the courts have conceded that delegation may occur in circumstances of "legal necessity" or "moral necessity".[123]

7.5.7(i) Appointment of agents

Delegation may occur by employing an agent such as a solicitor to undertake specialist responsibilities. Authority is provided for such an appointment in section 24 of the Trustee Act (N.I.) 1958 and it is possible that such a power or even a duty to that effect may have been provided in the governing instrument. Trustees appointing an agent must act in good faith, take such precautions as are reasonable to ensure appropriate skills, competence and honesty, and thereafter exercise such supervision as may be necessary.[124] When they have done

---

(1850) 1 Mac. & G. 664 which provides for an exception to the principle that a solicitor-trustee cannot charge the trust for services rendered as solicitor.

[120] See *Courtney v. Rumley* (1871) I.R. 6 Eq. 99.

[121] (1841) 5 Beav. 515.

[122] *ibid.* at p. 517.

[123] See *Ex parte Balchier* (1754) Amb. 218.

[124] See *Mendes v. Guedalla* (1862) 2 J. & H. 259, *per* Page Wood V.C. at p. 277.

so, but losses are nevertheless incurred, they may then be entitled to the protection of section 31 of the 1958 Act which holds a trustee accountable only for personal fault or default. As Kay J. explained in *Fry v. Tapson*[125]:

> "Trustees acting according to the ordinary course of business and employing agents, as a prudent man of business would do on his own behalf, are not liable for the default of an agent so employed."[126]

In such circumstances, the usual rules governing the reciprocal duties of principal and agent apply; the former may not wholly and fully devolve all responsibilities to the latter. Trustees, moreover, who can be shown to have demonstrated wilful default in the appointment or management of an agent, or in the retaining an unsuitable agent, will be held accountable for the consequences. Where delegation does occur, it is for the trustee alone to make that decision; the trustee is not permitted to delegate the responsibility or choices involved.

7.6 CONTROL OF TRUSTEES

The courts have powers to control or remove trustees. The court may exercise its discretionary powers available under its inherent jurisdiction to remove a trustee on the grounds of incompetence, dishonesty or being obstructive.[127]

Under section 12 of the Charities Act 1964 the Charities Branch may act to replace a trustee.

7.6.1 Breach of trust

Trustees will be liable to a charge of breach of trust if they either fail to discharge the duties of their office or if their actions are in excess of the authority conferred by their office. Any loss incurred to the trust property resulting from such a breach of trust must be made good by the trustee; any improper profits gained, whether or not loss resulted to the trust, must be made over to the trust. Liability for a breach of trust is actionable even though the trustee has since retired; if dead the action will lie against the estate of the deceased. Breaches of trust or mismanagement may provide grounds for judicial removal of trustees.

In keeping with the direct and personal nature of their appointment, a trustee will generally only be liable for acts or omissions for which he or she is personally responsible. There are two exceptions to this rule. Firstly, there

---

[125] (1884) 28 Ch. D. 268.
[126] *ibid.* at p. 270. See also, *dicta* to similar effect in *Re Weal* (1889) 42 Ch. D. 674, *per* Kekewich J. and in *Re Chapman* [1896] 2 Ch. 763, *per* Lindley L.J. at p. 776.
[127] See, for example, *Arnott v. Arnott* (1924) 58 I.L.T.R. 145.

may be liability on the part of a trustee for the actions or inactions of a fellow trustee[128] where it can be shown that culpability for wilful default or inactivity attaches to the former. Secondly, where two or more trustees are involved in a breach of trust then in law liability is joint and several; regardless of the actual proportional distribution of culpability each will be held personally and equally liable for the entire loss incurred.

However, in the words of Lindley L.J. in *Re Chapman*[129]:

> "... trustees acting honestly, with ordinary prudence and within the limits of their trust, are not liable for mere errors of judgment."[130]

Where trustees act improperly[131] or corruptly,[132] the court will hold them fully accountable.

It will be a good defence to a charge of breach of trust for the trustee to show that their actions were taken with the knowledge and permission of the beneficiaries. That this onus will not be lightly discharged is apparent from the comments of Westbury L.C. in *Farrant v. Blanchford*[133]:

> "Where a breach of trust has been committed, from which a trustee alleges that he has been released, it is incumbent on him to show that such release was given by the *cestui que trust* deliberately and advisedly with full knowledge of all the circumstances, and of his own rights and claims against the trustee. . . ."[134]

7.7 TERMINATION OF TRUSTEESHIP

A charitable trust may continue in perpetuity and with it will continue the role of trustees. Individual trustees, however, will change. The term of office of a trustee may terminate due to voluntary resignation, or to sudden incapacity or death, or due to the compulsory removal of a trustee.

7.7.1 Voluntary retirement

Trustees may not casually resile on the trust placed in them. Unless they initially decline, renounce or otherwise fail to take up their appointments they will be held to have accepted the responsibility of honouring the terms of their

---

[128] See *Townley v. Sherborne* (1634) J. Bridg. 35, 37.
[129] [1896] 2 Ch. 763.
[130] *ibid.* at p. 776.
[131] See *Att.-Gen. v. Boucherett* (1858) 25 Beav. 116.
[132] See *Att.-Gen. v. Glegg* (1738) Amb. 584; *Att.-Gen. v. Governors of Harrow School* (1754) 2 Ves. Sen. 551; *Waldo v. Caley* (1809) 16 Ves. 206, 212; *Ex parte Berkhampstead Free School* (1813) 2 V. & B. 134, 138; *Re Bedford Charity* (1833) 5 Sim. 578.
[133] (1863) 1 De G.J. & Sm. 107.
[134] *ibid.* at p. 119.

respective trusts. They are then expected to continue indefinitely. There are, however, some circumstances in which a trustee may retire.

Where the terms of appointment include an express provision for retirement then a trustee is fully entitled to retire at the specified time or age. In the absence of such provision a trustee can retire if all beneficiaries, *sui juris* and collectively entitled to the entire beneficial interest in the trust property, give their consent. Known as the rule in *Saunders* v. *Vautier*,[135] it was confirmed in *Wharton* v. *Masterman*[136] that this rule also applied to charitable trusts. If the object of charity is a legal entity, it can call for the gift to it to be made absolute. However, since most charitable trusts are for purposes, it may well be difficult to produce the necessary beneficiaries to call for a dissolution of the trust.

Alternatively, under section 38 of the 1958 Act, a trustee may retire with the consent of fellow trustees (attested to by deed) by making a declaration on deed to that effect, provided at least two trustees remain to administer the trust.

The retirement of a trustee may also be judicially sanctioned. This may follow as a consequence of the judicial appointment of new trustees under section 35 of the 1958 Act. Alternatively, a trustee may delegate their responsibilities to another person under section 26 of the 1958 Act. If a trustee is to be relieved of the burden of their office, the courts will require good reason to be shown. The court will grant such a request only where it is "inexpedient, difficult or impracticable" not to do so.

7.7.2 Incapacity or death of a trustee

Situations arise where a trustee is incapacitated,[137] dies[138] or is otherwise prevented from continuing to fulfil the duties of that office. The normal rules of survivorship then apply. Where necessary, replacement trustees may then be appointed by the Charities Branch or court (see further, above).

7.7.3 Removal of trustees

Traditionally, the power to remove and/or replace trustees was exercised by the Court of Chancery[139] using its inherent jurisdiction. This power was, and continues to be, available in circumstances where trustees behave with incompetence or dishonesty or obstruct the purposes of the trust.

---

[135] *Saunders v. Vautier* (1841) 4 Beav. 115.
[136] [1895] A.C. 186.
[137] See *In re Ledwich* (1843) 6 I.E.R. 561 and *In re Caldbeck's Trusts* (1874) 8 I.L.T.R. 119.
[138] See *Finlay v. Howard* (1842) 2 Dr. & War. 490.
[139] See Dickens, C., *Bleak House* for a memorable account of the dissipation of an estate due to the cost and time involved in that process.

7.7.3(i) Removal; wilful obstruction

In the leading Irish case of *Arnott v. Arnott*[140] the plaintiff sought the removal of his stepmother as trustee. Murnaghan J., then stated that the guiding principle for determining whether or not trustees should be removed was the welfare of the beneficiaries:

> "A trust is set up for the welfare of its beneficiaries. In my view, therefore, before determining whether or not any trustee should be removed from his or her office it is necessary to determine whether his continuation in that office will be detrimental to such welfare."

He found that long-standing and irreconcilable differences, existing between two members of the Arnott family, presented a threat to the future security of the trust. One trustee, the stepmother, constantly obstructed every decision taken by other trustees. In granting the order sought, Murnaghan J. held that the stepmother had persistently failed to give effect to the wishes of the donor, clearly expressed in the trust instrument, that the plaintiff should bear management responsibility for the family business.

7.7.3(ii) Removal; conflict of interest

The court's power of removal can also be brought to bear on trustees who place themselves in a position where there is a conflict of interest. It may be exercised regardless of whether or not trustees in such a position have in fact exploited it for personal advantage.

The decision in *Moore v. McGlynn*,[141] for example, provides authority for the view that where the duty of a trustee to further the best interests of trust beneficiaries is compromised by a conflict of interest then he or she may be removed. In that case, the defendant had established a business in competition with the one in respect of which he had been appointed trustee. In directing the trustee's removal, Chatterton V.C. explained:

> "... his new position disqualifies him from remaining any longer a trustee, and it would have been better for him to have procured his removal from trusteeship before setting up for himself. He should not be continued in a position where his duties and his self-interest may conflict."[142]

7.7.3(iii) Removal; other reasons

Authorisation for the removal of a trustee is available in other circumstances. The instrument creating the trust may expressly provide for the removal of a

---

[140] (1924) 58 I.L.T.R. 145.

[141] [1894] 1 I.R. 74.

[142] *ibid.* at p. 90.

trustee. The court is also empowered, under the terms of section 12 of the 1964 Act, to remove and replace on evidence of a trustee refusal or unfitness to act.

7.7.3(iv) Removal; the powers of the Charities Branch

The Charities Branch has no power to remove a trustee whose actions are demonstrably damaging to the interests of a charitable trust, this would have to be done by the court. In England and Wales, by way of contrast, the Charity Commission is empowered to remove not only a trustee but also any officer, agent or employee found to have perpetrated, facilitated or been aware of acts of mismanagement or misconduct.[143]

7.7.4 Bankruptcy

The bankruptcy of a testamentary trustee would not necessarily disqualify that person from administering a charitable trust. In *Re Wheeler*[144] the court drew a distinction between a trustee being unfit and being incapable of performing their duties. It held that bankruptcy itself would not prevent a trustee from continuing in office. The governing principle was expressed by Jessel M.R. in *Re Barker's Trusts*[145]:

> "… it is the duty of the Court to remove a bankrupt trustee who has trust money to receive or deal with, so that he cannot misappropriate it. There may be exceptions, under special circumstances, to that general rule; and it may be also be that where a trustee has no money to receive he ought not to be removed merely because he has become bankrupt; but I consider the general rule to be as I have stated. The reason is obvious. A necessitous man is more likely to be tempted to misappropriate trust funds than one who is wealthy; and besides, a man who has not shewn prudence in managing his own affairs is not likely to be successful in managing those of other people."

---

[143] See s. 8(1A) of the Charities Act 1992.
[144] [1896] 1 Ch. 315.
[145] (1875) 1 Ch. D. 43-44; as quoted in Keeton and Sheridan, *The Law of Trusts, op. cit.* at p. 260.

SECTION THREE

Charitable Purposes

CHAPTER 8

The Relief of Poverty

*"for the relief or maintenance of any manner of poor, succourless, distressed or
impotent person"*

(Statute of Pious Uses 1634)

"for the relief of aged, impotent and poor people"

(Statute of Charitable Uses 1601)

8.1 INTRODUCTION

Charity law has its origins in trusts for the relief of poverty. The governing
principles and an accompanying body of caselaw provide the foundations, the
entire moral basis, upon which the modern edifice of charity law has been
erected. Poverty, however, and the means of providing for its relief, are no
longer as readily susceptible to definition, classification and regulation as was
the case when the foundations first bedded down. The Dickensian approach to
poverty remains entrenched. A sophisticated national system of government
departments has long been charged with duties in respect of the relief of poverty. The remaining opportunities for individuals to make private contributions which supplement rather than supplant the public responsibilities of
statutory agencies are uncertain. The principles underpinning the public/pri-
vate interface in charity law are now, perhaps, being exposed to their most
fundamental challenge in relation to trusts for the relief of poverty.[1] J.C. Brady
drew attention to this problem when he referred to:

> "... the dangers inherent in a law of charity governed by its own internal logic
> and self-validating precedents, proceeding by analogy and rooted in a social
> system almost four hundred years old. The chief of these is the dislocation of
> the law from contemporary socio-economic realities. . . ."[2]

---

[1] In this context it should be noted that there is a specific problem of private charitable
hospitals and schools which move into the public sphere with the welfare state, *i.e. Re
Townsend Street*.

[2] N.I.L.Q., 1976, vol. 27, No 3, p 204. See, also, observations of Lord Greene M.R. in *Re
Compton* [1945] 1 Ch. 123 when, in relation to trusts for the relief of poverty, he said:
"Many trusts of this description have been carried out for generations on the faith that
they were charitable, and many testators have no doubt been guided by these decisions. The cases must at this date be regarded as good law, although they are, perhaps,
anomalous" (at p. 139).

It has to be said that there is considerable evidence to demonstrate that charities are not effectively addressing the problem of poverty in Northern Ireland. The statistical evidence indicates both that charitable giving per head of the population is higher in Northern Ireland than elsewhere in the U.K. and that so also is the level of poverty (in terms of low income, poor housing, dependency on state benefits etc.).[3]

The "public benefit" test, as interpreted by the courts, has been virtually nullified in its application to the relief of poverty. The recognition of charitable status, given originally by the courts in England to the "poor relations" class, has since been extended by analogy to such other classes as "poor employees" and "poor members". This trend has now reached the point where the courts are unlikely to rule that gifts to any other class will fail because of a failure to meet the public benefit test. So, in Northern Ireland, while the relevance of the "public benefit" test to gifts for the relief of poverty is reduced and the level of charitable donations is high, the actual prevalence of poverty continues to be more endemic than elsewhere in the U.K.

This chapter examines and explains the law and practice governing charitable trusts for the relief of poverty in Northern Ireland. Beginning with a brief consideration of the foundations laid by the two initial statues, attention is then given to the relevant definitions which are of crucial importance to this branch of charity law. This is followed by an examination of the classes of "the poor" and the types of gifts appropriate for their relief. Particular attention is given to determining the constituent ingredients of public benefit in this context.

8.2 THE STATUTORY FOUNDATIONS

There are differences between the Statute of Charitable Uses 1601 and the Statute of Pious Uses 1634. These have, from time to time, been pointed out and their significance explored by the judiciary. Some have a particular bearing upon how poverty is interpreted in the courts.

8.2.1 Statutory wording

The actual words used in the 1634 statute are different from those of the 1601 statute. In particular, whilst the 1601 statute refers to the "aged", the Irish statute refers to "succourless" and "distressed". In practice, the courts tend to discount the difference in wording. This was illustrated by the judgment of

---

[3] See, for example, the 1997/98 Northern Ireland family expenditure survey which concluded that households in this jurisdiction gave 19.6% more to charity than the U.K. average in cash terms and 40.3% more in terms of average weekly income.

Carswell J. in *Re Dunlop*[4] when he was called upon to determine whether "aged" came within the Northern Irish definition of charity. He stated that he:

> "... did not find it necessary to investigate the relationship between that [1601] statute and its Irish analogue of 1634 ... in which the wording of the preamble varies in a number of material respects, not least that concerning poverty."[5]

He considered himself bound by the authorities[6] which had by then established that the definition was the same for both statutes. He specifically held that in Northern Ireland "aged" was charitable under the first *Pemsel* head (see further, Chapter 12). A similar point could have arisen in *Re Lord Mayor of Belfast's Air Raid Distress Fund*.[7] The primary purpose of that fund was to relieve the distress of those affected by World War II air raids. The validity of this as charitable was accepted without question and no part of the judgement considered it. In Northern Ireland, the 1634 statute expressly mentions "distressed". Therefore, at least in theory, bodies which relieve the "distress" of their beneficiaries should find it easier to show they are charitable under the first head (see further, Chapter 12).

8.2.2 Construction of statutes

Whether the wording of the statutes should be construed conjunctively or disjunctively has been a perennial source of debate. A conjunctive construction holds that each element of the definition is a requisite and inseparable part of the whole. The use, therefore, of the word "and" implies that for the aged to benefit they must also be poor, and the impotent must also be aged. In contrast, the disjunctive approach holds that each element of the definition constitutes a separate and severable meaning of charity. Therefore, the use of the word "or" implies that to be charitable, a beneficiary may be either poor or old or distressed, etc.

The English statute appears on the surface to be conjunctive, "aged, impotent and poor people". This led the judiciary in some of the earlier cases to hold that poverty was a necessary prerequisite for gifts to the impotent or the aged. For example, in *Re Lucas*,[8] the court was of the view that a gift to old people of a parish would fail unless the court implied poverty into the gift.

A succession of English cases attacked this conjunctive approach. *Re Glyn*[9] concerned a gift of cottages to old working women. The court was able to

---

[4] [1984] N.I. 408.

[5] *ibid.* at p. 414.

[6] Citing, *Incorporated Society* v. *Richards* (1841) 1 Dr. & War. 258, *Attorney General v. Delaney* (1876) I.R. 10 C.L. 114 and in *Commissioners for Special Purposes of Income Tax v. Pemsel, op. cit.*

[7] [1962] N.I. 161.

[8] (1922) 2 Ch. 52.

[9] (1950) 66 T.L.R. 510.

imply poverty into the gift, but nevertheless took the disjunctive approach. Next, in *Re Robinson*,[10] the gift was to those aged over 65 and resident in a certain area. Vaisey J stated that "the gift is to the old people ... as a group of people who are within the Statute of Elizabeth, qualified not by poverty, sickness or impotence, but by age".[11] By 1983, it was taken as read by Gibson J. that "the words "aged, impotent and poor" must be read disjunctively".[12]

The Irish statute has an explicitly disjunctive approach, "poor, succourless, distressed <u>or</u> impotent persons". In Northern Ireland the only case on this point was *Re Dunlop*. In it Carswell J. expressly followed the reasoning of Gibson J. in the *Joseph Rowntree* case.[13] He held that a gift to "old Presbyterians" was charitable despite the fact that the Presbyterians in question, though old, were not necessarily also poor. He held that it would be as absurd to require the aged to be poor, as it would for the impotent to be aged, or the poor to be impotent. Carswell J.'s approach was based on English case law rather than the disjunctive Irish statute.

8.3 POVERTY

There are two requirements which must be fulfilled for an object to be charitable under this head. Firstly, it must be within the boundaries of the definition of poverty. Secondly, it must be directed at relieving some need which is an attribute of poverty. The question of "relief" will be considered under the public benefit test.

Sir Samuel Romilly[14] first gave judicial consideration to the meaning of poverty and to the means by which it was to be alleviated. As he saw it:

> "There are four objects, within one of which all Charity, to be administered in this Court, must fall: 1st, Relief of the indigent; in various ways: Money: Provisions: Education: Medical Assistance etc."

Subsequently, MacNaghten L.J. in *Commissioners for Special Purposes of Income Tax v. Pemsel*[15] endorsed "trusts for the relief of poverty" as clearly forming one of four categories of charitable trust. In *Pemsel*, it was said that "the popular conception of a charitable purpose covers the relief of any form of necessity, destitution or helplessness".[16] This approach was endorsed more

---

[10] [1951] Ch. 198.

[11] *ibid.* at p. 200.

[12] *Joseph Rowntree Memorial Trust Housing Association Ltd. v. Attorney General* [1978] 1 W.L.R. 910 at p. 171.

[13] Carswell J. also cited *Le Cras v. Perpetual Trustee Company* [1969] 1 A.C. 514.

[14] See *Morice v. Bishop of Durham* (1804) 9 Ves. 399 at p. 532.

[15] [1891] A.C. 531, 583.

[16] *op. cit.* at p. 572.

recently in *McGovern v. Attorney General*[17] where Slade J. commented that "this relief includes the relief of human suffering and distress".[18]

In the intervening century since *Pemsel*, the interpretation of what constitutes poverty may have changed but its current existence in Northern Ireland cannot be doubted. The challenging observation offered by J.C. Brady, more than two decades ago, remains relevant:

> "It would be fatuous to assert that the Welfare State has eliminated poverty and that private benefaction is no longer needed in Lord Macnaughten's first category but the new circumstances have altered the parameters of social need and deprivation. ... There is a growing body of what some might call radical opinion that traditional charity is a mere palliative which papers over the cracks in our society and does nothing to reduce the level of dependence of the poor and deprived on the philanthropy of others."[19]

Poverty is a relative term and the English dictionary does not provide a useful basis for defining it for the purposes of modern charity law. Case law, however, has drawn some parameters for its legal interpretation.

8.3.1 Degree or nature of poverty

Vaisey J. in *Re Coulthurst* considered that "poverty, it is well settled, is something far short of, or far wider than destitution: it includes straitened circumstances, financial stringency, pecuniary embarrassment and so forth".[20] Poverty, however, is not an absolute concept, it is relative to the individual poor person. When *Re Coulthurst* was appealed to the Court of Appeal, Evershed M.R. attempted a partial definition "it may not unfairly be paraphrased for present purposes as meaning persons who have to "go short" in the ordinary expectation of that term, due regard being had to their status in life and so forth".[21]

As explained by Viscount Simonds in *IRC v. Baddeley*[22] "there may be a good charity for the relief of persons who are not in grinding need or utter destitution" and a trust to provide for persons of limited or reduced means may come within the ambit of this category. In *Re Gardom*,[23] for example, a gift for the provision of a temporary residence for "ladies of limited means" was held to be charitable. As Eve J. commented although such persons were not destitute "there are degrees of poverty less acute than abject poverty or destitution".[24] The relative nature of poverty is illustrated by the wide range of

---

[17] [1982] 1 Ch. 321.
[18] *ibid.* at p. 333, the wording of the Irish statute makes it more amenable to this analysis.
[19] *op. cit.* at p. 205.
[20] *Re Coulthurst* [1951] Ch. 661 at p. 197.
[21] [1951] 1 T.L.R. 651, C.A. at p. 666.
[22] *op cit.*
[23] [1914] 1 Ch. 662.
[24] *ibid.* at 668.

cases associated with persons of professional standing such as out of work actors as in *In Re Lacy*[25] and *Re de Carteret*.[26]

8.3.2 Implication of poverty

A gift need not expressly state that it is for the poor, "such intention on the part of the donor may be implied from the nature of the gift looked at as a whole".[27] In *Re Dudgeon* it was stated "it is not absolutely necessary to find poverty expressed in so many words".[28] This is consonant with *Re Lucas*, "the court will look at the whole gift, and it if comes to the conclusion that the relief of poverty was meant, will give effect to it, although the word poverty is not to be found in it".[29]

A practical effect of this rule is that the smaller the gift the stronger the implication that it is for the poor. Another effect is that the court will look at the identity of the intended beneficiaries to see if it can imply poverty into their circumstances. In *Re Coulthurst*, "the status of "widows and orphaned children" suggests the possibility, or perhaps the probability of impecuniosity".[30] The breadth of this approach has been severely curtailed in Northern Ireland however. In *Attorney General v. Forde*, Andrews L.J. held that "our Irish courts will not extend the principle of implying the motive of the relief of poverty".[31]

8.3.3 To the poor in general

It was established at an early stage that a gift would not fail to be construed as charitable solely because the intended recipients were identified only in very general terms. In *Attorney-General v. Matthews*,[32] for example, a gift "to the poor generally" was held to be valid.

8.3.4 To a specific class of poor persons

A gift to specified poor persons will not satisfy the public benefit test. A gift made in favour of a class of poor persons, however, will satisfy this test (see, also, below). The class of poor may be appropriately defined by reference to a locality, to members of a particular religious faith/profession/nationality or to a particular line of descendants.

---

[25] [1899] 2 Ch. 149.
[26] [1933] Ch. 103.
[27] *Attorney General* v. *Forde* at p. 25.
[28] *Re Dudgeon* 74 L.T. (N.S.) 613.
[29] *Re Lucas* (1922) 2 Ch. 52 at p. 58.
[30] *op cit.*, at p. 197, but see below on gifts for widows.
[31] *Forde* at p. 26 and see below.
[32] (1677) 2 Lev. 167.

For example, gifts made to the poor of a specified town[33] or city[34] or of a particular religious denomination[35] have been upheld in the courts. So also have the following gifts been upheld: a gift to the poor in a particular parish;[36] a gift to a parish itself, the poor of the parish being intended;[37] and a gift to the poor maintained in a hospital.[38]

Similarly, gifts which are gender or status specific such as for the benefit of spinsters,[39] working men[40] or debtors[41] have all been upheld as charitable trusts. Although there are a great number of cases where valid charitable gifts have been made to tightly defined groups, many different permutations have been recognised by the courts, there are also limits to how specific a donor can be. For example, gifts to the employees of a firm for the benefit and maintenance of their families.[42]

8.3.5 To a specified class of poor persons in a specified locality

Locality based charitable gifts have long been recognised as valid provided the charitable intention directed the gift towards a class of persons, rather than particular individuals, whose poverty could be alleviated by that gift. For example, gifts made to the poor of a specified town[43] or city[44] or of a particular religious denomination[45] have been upheld in the courts.

The gifts were often directed towards a class of the poor in a parish. As Porter M.R. observed in *Browne v. King*:[46]

> "The word 'parish' has had weight attached to it in more than one case in England in determining charitable bequests. It has a peculiar force in an English will by reason of the parochial organisation by which the poor law is administered in England. That organisation does not exist in Ireland."

---

[33] See *Russell v. Kellett* (1855) 3 Sm. & G. 264; also, see, *Jones v. Williams* (1767) Amb. 651, 27 E.R. 422.

[34] See *Attorney-General v. Corporation of Exeter* (1827) 2 Russ. 45.

[35] See *AG v. Wansay* (1808) 15 Ves. 231; *Dawson v. Small* (1874) L.R. 18 Eq. 114; *Re Wall* (1889) 42 Ch. D. 510.

[36] See *Woodford v. Parkhurst* (1639) Duke 70 (378); see also, *AG v. Price* (1810) 17 Ves. 371, 34 E.R. 143.

[37] See *Attorney-General v. Webster* (1875) L.R. 20 Eq. 483.

[38] See *Corporation of Reading v. Lane* (1601) Duke 81 (361).

[39] See *Re Dudgeon* (1896) 74 L.T. 613.

[40] See *Guinness Trust (London Fund) v. West Ham Borough Council* [1959] 1 W.L.R. 233.

[41] See *A-G v. Painter-Stainers' Co* (1788) 2 Cox Eq. Cas. 51.

[42] See *Re Cullimore's Trusts* (1891) 27 L.R. Ir. 18.

[43] See *Russell v. Kellett* (1855) 3 Sm. & G. 264; also, see, *Jones v. Williams* (1767) Amb. 651, 27 E.R. 422.

[44] See *Attorney-General v. Corporation of Exeter* (1827) 2 Russ. 45.

[45] See *AG v. Wansay* (1808) 15 Ves. 231; *Dawson v. Small* (1874) L.R. 18 Eq. 114; *Re Wall* (1889) 42 Ch. D. 510.

[46] (1885) 17 L.R. Ir. 448.

The following gifts have been upheld: a gift to the poor in a particular parish;[47] a gift to a parish itself, the poor of the parish being intended;[48] a gift to the poor maintained in a hospital;[49] a gift "to the widows and orphans of the parish of L";[50] and a gift to "twenty aged widows and spinsters in the parish of Peterborough"[51] (see further, Chapter 12).

8.3.6 Gifts to widows

A divergence has arisen between the case law of Northern Ireland and the Republic of Ireland on the one hand, and the case law of England on the other, on the charitable status of gifts for widows. In England, gifts to widows are regarded as charitable.[52] A gift to the "widows and orphans of parish L" was held to be charitable.[53] In Ireland the reverse in the case.[54]

The Northern Ireland courts considered the meaning of poverty within the context of a gift to widows. In *Attorney General* v. *Forde*[55] a testator created a trust to give six houses, pay £10 per year for repairs, and pay £10 per year absolutely. The proposed beneficiaries of this trust were any six widows of men who had lived for five or more years on the testator's estates. The trust was created by codicil to a will in 1831. The issue before the court was whether this gift was for the relief of poverty. In the course of argument before the court the English cases were cited, "it is clear from the authorities that a gift to widows is a good charity, because the law supplies the word poor".[56] However, the court in *Forde* declined to follow the English cases which had held that "poverty" should be implied in gifts for widows. The judges in the Court of Appeal made reference to the Irish cases of *Browne* v. *King*[57] and *Re Cullimore's Trusts*.[58] The reason for different decisions in the Irish and English cases was attributed to the fact that:

> "… parishes have certain duties towards the poor in England which they have not here and poverty was implied from the terms of the gift".[59]

The result was that in Ireland and then in Northern Ireland the judiciary were

---

[47] See *Woodford v. Parkhurst* (1639) Duke 70 (378); see also, *AG v. Price* (1810) 17 Ves. 371, 34 E.R. 143.

[48] See *Attorney-General v. Webster* (1875) L.R. 20 Eq. 483.

[49] See *Corporation of Reading v. Lane* (1601) Duke 81 (361).

[50] See *Attorney-General v. Comber* (1824) 2 Sim. & Stu. 93.

[51] See *Thompson v. Corby* 27 Beav. 649.

[52] For example see *Re Coulthurst, op cit.*

[53] *Attorney General v. Comber* (1824) 2 Sim. & Stu. 93.

[54] *Re Cullimore's Trusts* 27 L.R.I. 18 and *Browne v. King* 17 L.R.I. 448.

[55] [1932] N.I. 1.

[56] *Forde* at p. 18.

[57] 17 L.R.I. 448.

[58] 27 L.R.I. 18.

[59] *Forde* at p. 33.

unable to import the word "poverty" into gifts for widows. Consequently such gifts were not charitable. The decision in *Forde* was followed in Northern Ireland by the stark pronouncement in the *Baptist Union* case that "a gift for the benefit of widows *simpliciter* is not charitable".[60]

8.3.7 Executor's interpretation

The fact that a donor has left to the executor or trustees the responsibility of interpreting that which might constitute "poverty" for the purposes of determining the recipients of a gift, does not itself have any effect on the validity of a gift for the relief of poverty. For example, in *Re Robinson*[61] a trust expressed to be for "the old people over sixty-five years" of a particular district "to be given as my trustees think best" was held to be charitable. So, also, in *Re Coulthurst*,[62] above, Vaisey J. ruled that the fact that the testator had left to a bank, which was acting as his trustees, the identification "at its absolute discretion" of possible recipients for a trust fund did not prevent the gift from being charitable.[63]

8.4 Charitable Intent

In common with all charitable trusts, a gift to provide for the relief of poverty must be made with a charitable intent if it is to come within the definition of charity.[64] Usually the purpose is stated with such clarity that there can be no doubt about the donor's charitable intent.[65] Where problems arise this is often due to an ambiguous or non-explicit use of language.

8.4.1 Ambiguous language

The language used by a donor when making the gift may be such that some ambiguity arises regarding his or her intentions. For example, the term "poor" may have been used simply as an adjective; where there is evidence that this was not the intention and provided there is a definite public benefit element then a trust will be held to be charitable.[66] Words of like meaning, such as

---

[60] *Baptist Union of Ireland (Northern) Corp. Ltd. v. Commissioners of Inland Revenue* [1945] N.I. 99 at p. 108.
[61] [1951] Ch. 198.
[62] *op cit.*
[63] See also, *Re Scarisbrick* [1951] Ch. 622 and *Re Cohen* [1973] 1 W.L.R. 415.
[64] Charitable intent being itself exposed to an objective test; see, for example *Re Pinion* [1965] Ch. 85 where such an intent did not prevent the court from objectively viewing the gift as non-charitable.
[65] See, for example, *Re Owens* [1929] 37 O.W.N. 97 and "very poor people".
[66] See *Oppenheim v. Tobacco Trust Ltd* [1951] A.C. 297.

"needy", are in this context considered to be synonymous with "poor" and are treated as meeting, equally satisfactorily, the evidential requirement for a donor's charitable intent.[67] Where the language used indicates that the meaning of "poor" is conditional upon a value judgement, as in "deserving poor", the courts have taken a firm line that the constraints imposed by the subjective condition are such that the definitional requirements of a charitable intention cannot be met.[68]

8.4.2 Implicit meaning

Although a donor failed to explicitly express a charitable intention, evidence may be admitted, by a constructive interpretation of the language used or by an examination of the context within which the gift was made, to show that nonetheless this intention was implicit. In *Gibson v. South American Stores (Gath and Chaves) Ltd.*,[69] for example, the form of words "necessitous and deserving" was interpreted as disclosing the donor's primary objective to confer a benefit upon persons in a "necessitous" state. Alternatively, the circumstances may disclose a charitable intention as in *Re Bingham*[70] where a gift expressed as being to a home "caring for aged women" was found to meet the requisite definitional requirements as the evidence showed that the testator had it in mind to provide for such persons because she was troubled by the non-existence of any such facility.

8.4.3 Objectively assessed as non-charitable

The purpose to be served by a gift may have been conceived as charitable by the donor but will not necessarily be viewed as such by the court. For example, the interjection of the word "deserving" in a term qualifying the purpose to be served by a gift has often opened the door for judicial re-appraisal of donor intentions. As Picarda explains[71]:

> "The word 'deserving' on the other hand does not necessarily connote poverty so that, whatever else it is, a trust to provide dowries for deserving Jewish girls is not for the relief of poverty.[72] Nor is a trust to advance deserving journalists a trust to relieve poverty."[73]

---

[67] See, for example, *Re Payne* (1954) 11 W.W.R. 424 (B.C.) and "needy" Imperial Veterans.

[68] See, for example, *Re Cohen* (1919) 36 T.L.R. and a trust to provide dowries for deserving Jewish girls.

[69] [1950] Ch. 177, C.A.

[70] [1951] N.Z.L.R. 491.

[71] See Picarda, H., *The Law and Practice Relating to Charities* (3rd ed., Butterworths, London, 1999), at p. 36.

[72] See *Re Cohen* (1919) 36 T.L.R. 16.

[73] See *Perpetual Trustee Co Ltd. v. John Fairfax & Sons Pty Ltd.* (1959) 76 W.N. N.S.W. 226.

Unless accompanied by the requisite charitable intent – whether explicit, implied or discerned by the court from the circumstances – a gift will be denied charitable status.

8.5 PUBLIC BENEFIT

There are two requirements which must both be satisfied under the public benefit test before an object is deemed charitable under the poverty head. The first is that the object must actually be of benefit to the public, *i.e.* it must be for the "relief" of poverty. The second is that the people who benefit are the public, or a sufficiently wide section of it. The definition of the public is different for poverty charities than for all other charities.

8.5.1 Benefit and the relief of poverty

The proposed charitable gift must provide an objectively verifiable benefit.[74] The persons to benefit must be the poor and the benefit must in some way be related to their being poor. In other words, the need which is being serviced must be in some way related to the condition of poverty. It is generally much easier to satisfy this requirement for poverty charities than for any other charities, the condition itself is the need. On the other hand, charities for the relief of the aged must show that they are relieving some particular need of the aged, rather than just providing them with money.[75]

Relieving the poverty of an individual is now presumed to be of benefit to the public. In *Re Scarsbrick* the court said that "the relief of poverty is of so altruistic a character that the public benefit may necessarily inferred".[76] In recent years the judiciary have greatly extended their recognition of the range of exceptions to the "public benefit" principle in the context of gifts for the relief of poverty. This development is a direct result of a judicial practice which has leant towards saving trusts under the heading of poverty where it seemed likely that they would otherwise fail. Where feasible, if a trust was in danger of not satisfying the more stringent public benefit test under the other *Pemsel* headings, then it would be saved under the poverty heading. Inevitably, this has resulted in an overall much more relaxed judicial approach towards public benefit in a poverty context.

However, the fact that not all gifts directed towards poor people necessarily assist in the alleviation of their poverty has often been judicially noted. For

---

[74] For example, see *Re Hummeltenberg, Beatty v. London Spiritualistic Alliance Ltd.* [1923] 1 Ch. 237.

[75] *Re Dunlop.*

[76] (1951) Ch. 622 at 639.

example, Harman J. in *Baddeley v. IRC*[77] commented that a gift to amuse the poor would not relieve them and would therefore not be considered charitable. In *Re Hadji Daeing Tahira binte Daeing Tedelleh's Estate*[78] it was held that the donor's gift, establishing a fund for the purpose of admitting the poor to dog races, would not relieve their poverty and so would not be charitable. In *Browne v. King*[79] a gift to be applied for the benefit of the children of the tenantry of an estate under the age of twelve years did not qualify as charitable because as Porter M.R. stated:

> "There is nothing to guide me in deciding that the gift is for children of poor persons, or persons in great need. The law imposes on parents the duty of supporting their children and there is nothing to satisfy me that the tenantry ... are not able to fulfil that obligation".

As the intended recipients had neither the capacity nor the responsibility to use the gift to relieve their poverty it failed.

The link between "impoverished circumstances", the nature of the gift and the capacity of that gift to actually ameliorate the poverty of the defined class of persons in those circumstances can be difficult to determine. In *Re Sanders' Will Trusts*[80] Harman J. held that a bequest to provide housing for the "working classes" and their families resident in a certain district did not qualify as a charitable trust. However, in *Re Niyazi's Will Trusts*,[81] Megarry V.-C. upheld as a valid charitable trust a gift "for the construction of or as a contribution towards the cost of a working men's hostel" in the town of Famagusta in Cyprus. Peter Gibson J. in *Joseph Rowntree Memorial Trust Housing Association Ltd. v. Attorney General*[82] stressed that the need which is to be relieved by the charitable gift must be attributable to the condition of the intended recipient. This ruling was made in the context of schemes to provide accommodation for disabled and elderly people but it would have equal application to trusts for the poor and would seem to rule out any gift which does not go towards relieving their condition of poverty.

8.5.1(i) Eligible recipients

It is a characteristic of charity law that, on the whole, a liberal and flexible judicial approach to the interpretation of contemporary social circumstances in the light of the principles embodied in seventeenth century legislation has enabled donors' charitable gifts to be applied for the public benefit. However,

---

[77] [1955] A.C. 572 at 585.
[78] (1947) 14 M.L.J. 62 at 63 (Singapore C.A.).
[79] (1885) 17 L.R. Ir. 448 at 456.
[80] [1954] Ch. 265.
[81] [1978] 1 W.L.R. 910.
[82] [1983] Ch. 159 at 171 (see, also *Dunlop*).

the conservative approach of the court in *Re Cole*[83] demonstrated the judicial capacity to also construe public benefit in a blinkered, traditional manner. This case concerned a gift of funds from the sale of houses which were to be used for the general benefit and welfare of the residents in a local authority home for deprived children. Harman J. ruled that the gift was not a charitable trust as the eligible children could be delinquent and refractory, the gift could be used for the purchase of luxury items such as a television and record player, and this would not be compatible with the objects as listed in the preamble to the Elizabethan statute. His decision was upheld by the Court of Appeal.

8.5.2 The public

It is also essential that the gift is not restricted to a specified group of poor individuals. The balance to be struck has been succinctly expressed in this jurisdiction as follows:

> "... the relief of poverty (including help for the aged and impotent) necessarily confers individual benefits upon the recipients of the donor's bounty. In order for it to constitute a public as opposed to a merely private benefaction, it has to include a public element, so that it transcends the conferring of benefit upon individuals selected by the donor and serves the wider purpose of benefiting the public weal by the provision of material assistance to classes of persons who require it by reason of their particular disability."[84]

The case of *Thomas v. Howell*[85] concerned a gift of £200 to each of ten poor clergymen of the Church of England, not holders of certain offices, as selected by a named friend or, in the event of the latter's death, by the executors. In reaching his decision, Mallins V.-C. stated the principle that a gift to named persons who happened to be poor would not be charitable and held that the principle applied in this case as much as if the poor clergymen who would be chosen had been specifically named. This case is a reference point both for the initial articulation of the principle and for its questionable application. The point, after all, was that the clergymen were not named and as a group of recipients formed a discrete class. The corollary to the principle is that a gift to a class of the poor will be charitable regardless of the size of that class.

In this branch of charity law, the legal requirements in respect of public benefit have been greatly relaxed due to judicial intervention. This was recognised by Simonds L.J. in *Oppenheim v. Tobacco Securities Trust Co Ltd.*[86]

---

[83] [1958] Ch. 877.

[84] *Re Dunlop* at p. 425.

[85] (1874) L.R. 18 Eq. 198. See also, *Re Wall* (1889) 42 Ch. D. 510, where the trust was established to provide annuities for Unitarians, over the age of 50, attending chapels in Bristol (*i.e.* a class within a class within a class). Kay J. upheld it as a charitable trust for the relief of poverty notwithstanding its very narrow application.

[86] [1951] A.C. 297.

where, in relation to the public benefit requirement, he commented that:

> "...the law of charity so far as it relates to 'the relief of aged, impotent and poor people' ... and to poverty trusts in general, has followed its own line. . . ."

8.5.3 Classes of "the poor"

The requirements of a charitable trust are satisfied by the implied public benefit dimension where a gift is made to a class of persons. The lack of such a dimension where the gift is to a group of individuals renders a gift non-charitable. The size of the class is not a determining factor[87] and the beneficiaries may form a class within a class.[88]

The distinguishing characteristic of charitable trusts is that they should confer a public rather than private benefit, or as expressed by Lord Greene M.R.[89]:

> "... a gift under which the beneficiaries are defined by reference to a purely personal relationship to a named *propositus*, cannot on principle be a valid charitable gift."

However, creative judicial interpretation of public benefit has been responsible for a broadening of the precedent established by the "poor relations" trusts. In this context, the cardinal principal of charity law has now been seriously undermined.

8.5.3(i) The poor relations trust

This is a trust where the donor or testator intends to make a gift for the benefit of poor relatives. The legal definition of a charitable gift to "poor relations" will not be satisfied by a donor who simply leaves a gift for a relative who happens to be poor. The law requires the gift to be in favour of a broad class of relatives, identified by degree of relationship (*e.g.* all nieces and nephews of the donor and spouse) rather than a specific group of individuals. So, for example, in *Re Compton*[90] a trust stated to be for the purpose of providing for the education of three named individuals was held not to be charitable.

Trusts for "poor relations" have long been recognised as forming an anomalous exception to the general rule that gifts where the beneficiaries are identified by a purely personal relationship to the would-be donor cannot be charitable gifts. As was explained by Evershed M.R. in *Re Scarisbrick*[91]:

---

[87] See *dicta* to that effect by Lord Greene M.R. in *Re Compton, op. cit.*, at p. 128.
[88] See, for example, *Baddeley, op cit.*, where the gift was to Methodists in a certain locality.
[89] See *Re Compton, op. cit.*, at p. 128.
[90] [1945] Ch. 123.
[91] [1951] Ch. 622, [1951] 1 All E.R. 822.

"The 'poor relations' cases may be justified on the basis that the relief of poverty is so altruistic a character that the public element may necessarily be inferred thereby; or they may be accepted as a hallowed, if illogical, exception."

This was a case where a trust to benefit such relations of the testatrix's son and daughters who in the opinion of the survivor of her children "shall be in needy circumstances" was held by the Court of Appeal to be a valid charitable trust. Jenkins L.J. in this case sought to make a distinction between an intention to relieve poverty among a class and an intention to relieve the poverty of particular individuals; the first being charitable and the second private. This, he acknowledged, was often a fine line to draw.[92] A further point made in this case was that no distinction should be drawn between trusts for the poor which are to be perpetual in nature and those having an immediate effect (a ruling which in effect over-ruled the earlier decision in *Attorney-General v. Price*[93] which rested on such a distinction).

The so-called "poor relations" trusts were recognised in a line of decisions which stretch back to the eighteenth century.[94] In *Issac v. Defriez* the court upheld gifts to beneficiaries required to be a poor relation of the testator and a poor relation of his wife selected by the trustees. In *White v. White*[95] Grant M.R. upheld as charitable a trust established for the purpose of providing apprenticeships for the poor relations in two specified families despite the obvious absence of any possible public benefit to the poor in general. Not, however, until the decision in *Gillam v. Taylor*[96] was the charitable status of gifts for poor relations put beyond doubt. That case concerned residual income which was to be distributed, according to need, among the descendants of a named uncle. Nowadays, the modification of the public benefit requirement in this category of charitable trust is well established.[97]

8.5.3(ii) Trusts for the benefit of "poor employees" and "poor members"

The principle governing the exception of "poor relations" has been extended to trusts for "poor employees". This is evidenced by cases such as: *Re Gosling*[98] where a gift for poor employees of a company was held to be charitable. The class of beneficiaries was determined by reference to their common rela-

---

[92] An opinion expressly endorsed by Chadwick J. in *Re Segleman* [1996] Ch. 171.

[93] (1810) 17 Ves. 371.

[94] See, for example: *A-G v. Bucknall* (1741) 2 Atk. 328; 26 E.R. 600; *Issac v. Defriez* (1754) Amb. 595; and *Brunsden v. Woolredge* (1765) Amb. 507, 27 E.R. 327 (Sewell M.R.).

[95] (1802) 7 Ves. 423, 32 E.R. 171.

[96] (1873) L.R. 16 Eq. 581 (Wickens V.-C.).

[97] See, *Gibson v. South American Stores* (Gath & Chaves) Ltd [1950] Ch. 177; *Re Scarisbrick* [1951] Ch. 622; *Dingle v. Turner* [1972] A.C. 601; *Re Cohen* [1973] 1 W.L.R. 415.

[98] (1900) 48 W.R. 300.

tionship to an institution. So also in *Re Rayner*[99] where income from a trust was to be applied for the benefit of employees of a specified company who had served for at least ten years and were permanently handicapped by age, accident, illness or otherwise from earning a living. Again, in *Gibson v. South American Stores (Gath & Chaves) Ltd.*[100] where it was held that gifts to poor employees were charitable[101] and in *Re Young* where gifts to members of a club who had fallen on "evil days"[102] were also charitable.

The principle has been extended to include trusts for "poor members": evidenced by cases such as *Spiller v. Maude*[103] concerning members of a theatrical society, and *Re Buck*[104] where the members belonged to the Commercial Travellers Society.[105]

8.5.3(ii)(a) Evidence of poverty

There must be irrefutable evidence of poverty. So, for example, in *Re Drummond*[106] a trust to provide for the holiday expenses of employees in a department of a particular store was found not to be charitable because:

> "... this is a trust for private individuals, a fluctuating body of private individuals it is true, but still private individuals."[107]

Again, in *Re Cullimore's Trusts*,[108] a trust for the benefit and maintenance of the families of employees of a firm was found not to be charitable. In the words of Porter M.R.:

> "Mere kindness, generosity, or benevolence on the testator's part is not enough to constitute a charitable purpose; there must also be an element of poverty or need on the part of the object, or else the gift must be dedicated to some purpose, such as education, religion or the like which the law regards as charitable. There is nothing here to show that the persons whom the testator meant to benefit were to be poor persons."

The *Gibson*[109] case concerned a trust established for the benefit of necessitous employees and their dependants and the ruling of Harman J., resting on a

---

[99] (1920) 122 L.T. 577 (Eve J.).
[100] [1950] Ch 177. Also, see, *Re Coulthurst* (1951) 1 Ch. 661.
[101] *Gibson v. South American Stores* (1950) Ch. 177,.
[102] [1955] 1 W.L.R 1269.
[103] (1881) 32 Ch. D. 158n.
[104] [1896] 2 Ch. 727.
[105] See also *Re Mead's Trust Deed* [1961] 1 W.L.R. 1244 and *Re Young* [1955] 1 W.L.R. 1269.
[106] [1914] 2 Ch. 90.
[107] *Re Drummond* at p. 97.
[108] (1891) 27 L.R. Ir. 18.
[109] *op. cit.*

requirement for an element of public benefit, was upheld by the Court of Appeal.

The House of Lords, in the leading case of *Dingle v. Turner*,[110] confirmed that trusts for the benefit of "poor employees" will be recognised as valid charitable trusts. After considering the case law, they came to the conclusion that there was an exception to the usual public benefit requirements in "poor relations" and "poor employees" cases – "the status of the 'poor relations' trusts as valid charitable trusts was recognised more than two hundred years ago".[111] In the words of Lord Cross:

> "The 'poor members' and 'poor employees' decisions were a natural development of the 'poor relations' decisions and to draw a distinction between different sorts of 'poverty' trusts would be quite illogical and could certainly not be said to be introducing 'greater harmony' into the law of charity. Moreover, though not as old as the 'poor relations' trusts, 'poor employees' trusts have been recognised as charities for many years; there are now a large number of such trusts in existence; and assuming, as one must, that they are properly administered in the sense that the benefits under them are only given to people who can fairly be said to be according to current standards, 'poor persons', to treat such trusts as charitable is not open to any practical objection."

However, gifts to named individuals will not be of benefit to the public.[112] More recently this approach has been reaffirmed in England by *Re Segelman*.[113] The gift in that case was to "poor and needy relations". The question for the court was whether it was a gift for the relief of poverty amongst a particular class, or a gift to particular poor people. Because of the fact that the class could grow as new relations were born, the court held it a valid charitable gift, even though it would only benefit a restricted class.

In this jurisdiction, Carswell J. in *Re Dunlop* considered the application of the approach taken by the House of Lords in *Dingle*. He recognised the validity of the exemption from the usual public benefit test. Even though there is a private relationship between employees or family members, they would still constitute a section of the public. Carswell J. then broke new ground. He considered whether this exemption would extend to the aged and impotent categories or whether it was solely confined to poverty. His decision was for the latter, "I consider that the House of Lords in *Dingle v. Turner* intended to circumscribe more closely and confine it to cases concerning the relief of actual poverty".[114] In Tudor it is suggested that *Re Dunlop* represents a divergence from the law as stated in *Dingle* and that the aged and impotent should

---

[110] [1972] A.C. 601 at 623.

[111] *ibid.* at p. 622.

[112] *ibid.* "merely a gift to particular poor persons, the relief of poverty among them being the motive of the gift" at p. 617.

[113] [1995] 3 All E.R. 676.

[114] *Re Dunlop, op cit.* at p. 423.

also benefit from this exemption. However, it is submitted that this criticism is not well founded. Carswell considered the cases[115] which suggested an exemption for the aged and impotent:

> "... in all of these cases in which gifts were left to aged persons ... or to impotent persons there was as sufficient public element by reason of the width of the class from which the potential beneficiaries were to be drawn."[116]

The position now seems to be that in cases of poverty, public benefit will be found in gifts to a very small class of people, even if they are linked by some private nexus. This approach by Lord Cross has since been extended, though not without attracting criticism,[117] to include poor members of a profession.

8.5.3(ii)(b) The personal nexus test

This test was introduced by the Court of Appeal in *Re Compton*[118] in an attempt to halt the broadening range of extensions to the personal relations trusts. In that case Greene L.J. suggested that:

> "... on principle a gift under which the beneficiaries are defined by reference to a purely personal relationship to a named *propositus* cannot ... be a valid charitable gift."[119]

This test was applied in *Re Hobourn Aero Components Ltd's Air Raid Distress Fund*[120] where the Court of Appeal held that a trust fund for the relief of employees of a company who had suffered damage and distress in air raids was not charitable because the fund in question was constituted from contributions made by employees of the company. The close link between donor and intended beneficiary was fatal to the charitable status of the gift. Both decisions were approved by the House of Lords in *Oppenheim*[121] where a gift to provide for the education of employees and former employees of the British American Tobacco Co. Ltd. was held not to be a charitable trust because the relationship nexus between donor and recipient was too close to properly allow for the necessary public benefit element. The rationale for this decision was expressed with firm clarity by Lord Cross as follows:

---

[115] *Joseph Rowntree, Re Lewis* (1955) Ch. 104, *Re Bradbury* (1950) 2 All E.R. 1150.

[116] *Re Dunlop, op cit.* at p. 423.

[117] See Goodman Committee on *Charity Law and Voluntary Organisations*, Chap. 11, para. 37.

[118] [1945] Ch 123. See, also, *Trustees of the Londonderry Presbyterian Church House v. IRC* [1946] N.I. 178 (N.I. C.A.) where MacDermott J. was of the view that not every class designated by reference to a personal quality was necessarily private; he considered that the personal quality needed to be one of bond or relationship.

[119] *ibid.* at p. 131.

[120] [1946] Ch. 194.

[121] *op cit.*

> "To establish a trust for the education of the children of employees in a company in which you are interested is no doubt a meritorious act; but however numerous the employees may be the purpose which you are seeking to achieve is not a public purpose. It is a company purpose and there is no reason why your fellow taxpayers should contribute to a scheme which by providing 'fringe benefits' for your employees will benefit the company by making their conditions of employment more attractive."[122]

However, the judicial attempt to impose a personal nexus test as a means of containing the growth in categories generated by the poor relations precedent was brought to an end by the decision in *Dingle v. Turner*.[123] Cross L.J., supported by his colleagues on the bench, observed that

> "... the question whether or not the potential beneficiaries of a trust can fairly be said to constitute a section of the public is a question of degree and cannot be by itself decisive of whether the trust is a charity. Much must depend on the purpose of the trust."

This pragmatic approach has restored opportunities for further growth in categories of charitable trusts deriving from the poor relations precedent.

8.5.3(ii)(c) Self-help trusts

One aspect of the personal nexus tests manifests itself in the rule that self-help trusts cannot be charitable.[124] Because they fail to satisfy the "distance" requirement of that test they will be invalid.

8.6 BOUNTY OR BARGAIN

The bounty or bargain test is relevant to all heads of charity, but has had the greatest judicial consideration in charities under the first head. The genesis of the test lies in the case of *Commissioners for Inland Revenue v. Society for the Relief of Widows and Orphans of Medical Men*[125] where it was stated:

> "... that does mean the relief of poverty by way of bounty; it does not mean the relief of poverty by way of bargain."[126]

---

[122] *ibid.*, at pp. 624–625.

[123] *op cit.* at p. 623.

[124] See, *Carne v. Long* (1860), 2 De G.F. & J. 75, 45 E.R. 550; *Re Hobourn Aero Companies op cit.*; *Ryan v. Forrest* [1946] Ch. 154, [1946] 1 All E.R. 501; *Lord Nuffield v. Inland Revenue Commissioners; Goodenough v. Inland Revenue Commissioners* (1946), 175 L.T. 465, 28 Tax Cas. 479; *Waterson v. Hendon Borough Council* [1959] 1 W.L.R. 985. [1959] 2 All E.R. 760 (Q.B.D.); *Re Clark's Trust* (1875) 1 Ch. D. 497, 45 L.J. Ch. 194; and *Re Mead's Trust Deed* [1961] 1 W.L.R. 1244, [1961] 2 All E.R. 836.

[125] (1926) 136 L.T. 60.

[126] *ibid.* at p. 65.

The Court of Appeal in Northern Ireland gave a detailed analysis of this test in the *Baptist Union*[127] case. The relevant facts were that Baptist ministers contributed to a fund which provided payments to: old ministers, incapacitated ministers and widows and orphans of ministers. The fund was augmented by voluntary donations from external sources. One issue was whether the character of the fund made it a mutual assurance fund, whereby benefits were gained by bargain, and consequently was not charitable. The court formulated a general principle and then some specific factors to assist in its decision. The general principle was that the fund "should be substantially, not necessarily absolutely, altruistic in character".[128] The specific factors to consider were:

• the terms of the contract binding the beneficiaries,

• the composition and source of the fund,

• whether the benefits were awarded as of right to the beneficiaries or whether they were discretionary,

• whether the beneficiaries had any control over the management of the fund.

Taking all these factors into account, the fact that the fund was managed by the Baptist Union and not the ministers, and that a substantial source of the fund was voluntary donations, the court held that it was charitable.

The bounty/bargain approach arose again in a minor way in three further Northern Ireland cases. In the *Musgrave Clinic*[129] case, the patients paid for their medical treatment. Did this make it bargain and not bounty? Thompson J. thought not – "payments by persons within the scope of the charge are not inconsistent with its being held to be charitable".[130] However, on the facts of that case, the hospital was not charitable. The hospitals in *Down Council*[131] also had paying patients. No argument was advanced that this made them non-charitable. Again, the school in *Campbell College*[132] received fees from its pupils. It was stated by McVeigh J. in the Court of Appeal that "the mere receipt of income from objects of the charity in respect of occupation is not *per se* and necessarily decisive against statutory exemption".[133] In the VAT context, payment of fees by pupils at a school will not necessarily change the nature of the school to business use.

In Northern Ireland, by the 1960s, it was therefore settled law that payments by beneficiaries for their benefits would not render a charity non-chari-

---

[127] *op. cit.*

[128] *Baptist Union , op cit.* at p. 122.

[129] *Governors of Royal Victoria Hospital (Musgrave Clinic) v. Commissioner of Valuation* (1939) 73 I.L.T.R. 236.

[130] *ibid.* at p. 237.

[131] *Down County Council v. Commissioner of Valuation* [1954] N.I. 173.

[132] *Campbell College v. Commissioner of Valuation* [1964] N.I. 107 in the Court of Appeal; [1964] N.I. 169 in the House of Lords.

[133] *Campbell College, op cit.* at p. 166.

table. In England the position was the same as illustrated by the hospital in *Re Resch*[134] which charged its patients but was still charitable. As was explained in *Joseph Rowntree* "the fact that the benefit given to them is in the form of a contract is immaterial to the charitable purpose in making the benefit available".[135] A contractual entitlement to the gift is thus different from the gift being made in the form of a contract. In addition, *Rowntree* decided that even if a beneficiary derived a profit from the charity, as long as that profit was incidental, it would not render it non-charitable.

MacDermott J, in *Baptist Union*, also considered some older English cases relating to "mutual benefit societies". In *Re Clark*,[136] for example the court concluded that a mutual society which paid old or sick members was not charitable. However, in *Pease v. Pattinson*[137] it held that a miners society which paid out to members who were old or sick was charitable though in *Cunnack v. Edwards*[138] a society which provided benefits to members' widows was held not to be charitable. MacDermott J was able to rationalise these somewhat conflicting English cases. He suggested that they:

> "… may have been intended to dissipate an idea that the element of mutual aid to be found in a friendly society could of itself give a charitable status to the common object."[139]

However, there does seem to be a slight divergence from the approach taken by the English cases. For example, in the case of *Spiller v. Maud*[140] which concerned a mutual benefit society for "decayed" actors or actresses, it was suggested that the source of the fund was irrelevant, what mattered was where the money was going. This conflicts with one of the factors underpinning the rationale relied upon by MacDermott J. *viz*. that the composition of the fund is a material issue. A further possible divergence occurs when the limits which are placed on bounty are considered. *Rowntree* stated that if a mutual society existed where all the members would be practically guaranteed of benefiting, it would be in the nature of an insurance fund and not a charity. However, the ministers in *Baptist Union* had a high possibility of benefiting and yet this was not placed as a barrier to the fund's charitable status.

8.7 TYPE OF GIFTS

Poverty may be relieved by many different types of gift and a wealth of caselaw

---

[134] *Re Resch's Will Trust* (1969) 1 A.C. 514.
[135] *Rowntree, op cit.* at p. 175.
[136] (1875) 1 Ch. D. 497.
[137] (1866) 32 Ch. D. 154.
[138] [1896] 2 Ch. D. 679.
[139] *Baptist Union, op cit.* at p. 114.
[140] (1881) 32 Ch. D. 158.

testifies to the wide range of methods recognised by the courts as appropriate for this purpose. To some extent social need has changed over time and the type of private benefaction appropriate to effect relief has changed accordingly. In the main, however, there is a striking similarity between contemporary types of gift and those which are recorded in caselaw dating back to the seventeenth century. They may be conveniently classified as gifts which provide either direct or indirect relief.

8.7.1 Direct relief

Almsgiving was the form of direct gift originally associated with the relief of poverty. This, in the words of the Nathan Committee[141]:

> "... was more a means to the salvation of the soul of the benefactor than an endeavour to diagnose and alleviate the needs of the beneficiary."

Gifts of money or of "necessaries" (*i.e.* food, clothing, fuel) have an immediate capacity to relieve poverty in the short-term and have long been used for that purpose. The courts have tended to question the efficacy of conferring financial benefits on the poor, as a method of alleviating their poverty, not just because a money gift can be misused by the recipient but also because in the words of Sir George Jessel M.R. in *Campden Charities*[142] "it tends to demoralise the poor and benefit no one". Gifts which are judged to have a more long-term uplifting effect by, for example, putting in place a new facility, or providing for apprenticeships or training, have received more emphatic judicial endorsement. Thus, over the centuries, the very many gifts for establishing a range of institutions and resource facilities have all been held to be charitable: soup kitchens,[143] almshouses,[144] hospitals, infirmaries or dispensaries,[145] asylums for the blind.[146] So also with gifts for apprenticing poor children[147] and for providing accommodation such as flats for the poor elderly,[148] homes for ladies in reduced circumstances[149] and homes for working girls.[150]

---

[141] See the Nathan Committee, *Report of the Committee on the Law and Practice relating to Charitable Trusts* (London: HMSO, 1952) Cmnd. 8710, para 36.

[142] (1881)) 18 Ch. D. 310 at 327.

[143] See *Biscoe v. Jackson* (1887) 35 Ch. D. 460.

[144] See *Harbin v. Masterman* [1894] 2 Ch. 184, C.A.

[145] See *Pelham v. Anderson* (1764) 2 Eden 296; *A-G v. Gascoigne* (1833) 2 My. & K. 647; and *Biscoe op cit.*

[146] See *Henshaw v. Atkinson* (1818) 3 Madd. 306.

[147] See *A-G v. Minshull* (1798) 4 Ves. 11 and *A-G v. Wansay* (1808) 15 Ves. 231.

[148] See *Re Cottam's Will Trusts* [1955] 1 W.LR.. 1299.

[149] See *Re Douglas* (1887) 35 Ch D 472, *Re Lacy* [1899] 2 Ch. 149; and *Spiller v. Maude* (1881) 32 Ch. D. 158n.

[150] See *Rolls v. Miller* (1884) 27 Ch. D. 71.

8.7.2 Indirect relief

A gift may be so framed that it does not give immediate relief from poverty but does so indirectly. So, for example, a gift may be directed towards supporting the carers who work with the poor by making provision for a rest home for nurses[151] and Christmas presents for nurses.[152] Gifts may also be given to organisations to aid their work with the poor, for example to religious communities which engage in poverty relief work,[153] to friendly societies obliged by their rules to work exclusively with the poor[154] and to the funds of a parish church to be used exclusively for the relief of the sick and poor.[155] A gift tending to promote the efficient administration of a trust for the relief of poverty is itself charitable.[156]

---

[151] See *Re White's Will Trusts* [1950] 1 All E.R. 528.
[152] See *Re Bernstein's Will Trusts* (1971) 115 Sol. Jo. 808.
[153] See *Cocks v. Manners* (1871) L.R. 12 Eq. 574 and *Re Delany* [1902] 2 Ch. 642.
[154] See *Re Buck* [1896] 2 Ch. 727.
[155] See *Re Garrard* [1907] 1 Ch. 382.
[156] See *Re Coxen* [1948] Ch. 747; *Re Charlesworth* (1910) 101 L.T. 908.

CHAPTER 9

The Advancement of Education

"For the erection, maintenance, or support of any college, school, lecture in divinity or in any of the liberal arts or sciences"

(Statute of Pious Uses 1634)

"Maintenance of ... schools of learning, free schools and scholars in universities ... for education and preferrment of orphans"

(Statute of Charitable Uses 1601)

9.1 INTRODUCTION

In Northern Ireland, history reveals that education and religion have been inextricably entangled. An historical study would show that very considerable amounts of charitable funding have flowed into the educational infrastructure of this jurisdiction; funnelled uncontroversially down clearly defined and very separate routes to advance either Protestant or Roman Catholic education. Arguably, this has contributed substantially to the legacy of community divisions which now impede the bedding down of civil society. Given the strategic significance of education to the polarisation of cultures in Northern Ireland, cases illustrating these tensions are noticeable by their absence. In particular, the absence of any high profile caselaw demonstrating charitable involvement in cross-community educational activity may reflect the level of such activity. In fact, this jurisdiction has produced no cases of great significance on matters of education. Six reported cases deal with educational charities, but none question the interpretation given to education. The unreported cases in the Lands Tribunal fare only slightly better at expanding the meaning of education. It is therefore necessary to look to English case law to fill in the gaps.

Some attempts have been made to craft a definition under which diverse educational activities can cohere. However, the simplest way to approach this topic is functionally rather than conceptually, by listing those activities which the law regards as educational as opposed to grafting specific cases onto a generalised conceptual framework. Any attempted logical ordering is further complicated by the fact that the courts have fused the definition of education with the first limb of the public benefit test, *i.e.* the definition of education comprises a requirement that it must be of a useful benefit to the public.

9.2 DEFINITIONS

The courts have noted the difference in wording between the two statutes and, surprisingly, have commented that this may cause a substantive difference between English and Northern Irish law. For example, the Court of Appeal in *Campbell College* drew attention to the fact that "the Irish Statute of Charitable Uses 1634 specifically refers to the 'liberal arts and sciences'".[1] The House of Lords went slightly further by holding that:

> "... the purpose of science, literature and the fine arts ... may well be coterminous in Ireland with the purposes of charity."[2]

One reason for this is the historical legislative favour bestowed upon the purposes of science, literature and the fine arts. For example, see the now repealed Scientific Societies Act 1843. There is also a specific rating exemption for bodies whose main objects are "charitable or are concerned with science, literature or the fine arts".[3] However, the development of the law in this jurisdiction on the concept of education has closely followed that in England.

9.2.1 The concept of education

It is possible to tease out and distinguish two strands within this concept which make it more explicable. The first strand is teaching and education in the broad sense of imparting knowledge or skills to others. The second strand is new learning, increasing and expanding existing knowledge. These two strands may be termed education and learning respectively. There is authority for this interpretation. In *Pemsel*[4] there is a reference to the "advancement of education", but earlier, in *Morice v. Bishop of Durham*,[5] the reference is to the "advancement of learning".

These two facets of education are evident in the different judicial attempts to define the concept. Buckley L.J. described education as "extending to the improvement of a useful branch of human knowledge and its public dissemination".[6] Along the same lines, Slade J. in *McGovern v. Attorney General*[7] described research into human rights as charitable as it was "manifestly a subject of study which is capable of adding usefully to the store of human knowledge".[8] Both these partial definitions are directed towards the second strand

---

[1] *Campbell College, op cit.* at p. 149.

[2] *ibid.* at p. 186.

[3] Art. 41(2)(d)(ii) Rates (NI) Order 1977.

[4] *Income Tax Special Purpose Commissioners v. Pemsel* (1891) A.C. 531.

[5] (1805) 9 Ves. 399.

[6] *Incorporated Council of Law Reporting for England and Wales v. Attorney General* (1971) 3 All E.R. 1029 at 1046).

[7] (1982) 1 Ch. 321.

[8] *McGovern, op cit.* at p. 353.

of "learning" in the sense of scientific advancement. Other examples of this strand can be found in case law. Promoting and encouraging the art of surgery is charitable,[9] as is advancing zoology and the study of animal physiology,[10] researching and studying Egyptology[11] and promoting the scientific study of law.[12] Northern Ireland has also produced an example of this strand. Lowry J. spoke of "the promotion and encouragement of research, a clearly charitable purpose".[13]

It is harder to find as firm a definition under the first strand. In *Re Mariette* it was said that no boy "can be properly educated unless at least as much attention is given to the development of his body as is given to the development of his mind".[14] This approach was reinforced in *Inland Revenue Commission v. McMullen*[15] which concerned a gift to:

> "... organise or provide ... facilities which will enable ... pupils of schools and universities in ... the United Kingdom to play association football or other games or sports and thereby assist in ensuring that due attention is given to the physical education and development of such pupils."

On final appeal to the House of Lords this gift was held to be charitable because education "when applied to the young" includes "instruction, training and practice containing ... spiritual, moral, mental and physical elements".[16]

Again, on this strand of education through instruction, the court in *Re Shaw's Will Trusts*[17] held charitable "promoting the education of Irish men and women and children to be better citizens in the various departments of secular life"[18] because, as explained by Vaisey J.:

> "... the promotion or encouragement of these arts and graces of life, which are, after all, perhaps the finest and best part of the human character."

The other five Northern Ireland educational cases have all been concerned with charities under this second strand. Other examples are the charitable status of the Boy Scout movement[19] and even the playing of chess.[20] There is much overlap between the two strands.

---

[9] *Royal College of Surgeons v. National Provincial Bank* (1952) 1 All E.R. 984.

[10] *Re Lopes, Bence-Jones v. Zoological Society* (1931) 2 Ch. 130.

[11] *Re British School of Egyptian Archaeology* (1954) 1 All E..R. 887.

[12] See *Council of Law Reporting, op cit.*

[13] *Queens University Belfast v. Attorney General for Northern Ireland* [1966] N.I. 115 at 118.

[14] *Re Mariette* (1915) 2 Ch. 284 at 288.

[15] [1981] A.C. 1 at 11.

[16] *ibid.* at 18.

[17] (1952) ALL E.R. 49.

[18] *Re Shaw's Will Trusts* (1952) All E.R. 49 at 52.

[19] *Re Webber* (1954) 1 W.L.R. 1500.

[20] *Re Dupree* (1945) Ch. 16.

9.2.2 The interpretation of education in practice

The courts have held fast to the view that if a trust is to be construed as one for the advancement of education then its intended purpose must be educational and not, for example, merely recreational (but see further, Chapter 14). Where the trust is expressed in terms of "general benefit" or "general welfare" this has been held to imply that it could be used for non- educational purposes and therefore must be denied charitable status.[21] As explained by Buckley L.J.[22] "educational" entails an "... improvement of a useful branch of human knowledge". The usefulness, or possible prospective usefulness, and to whom, of particular knowledge can be difficult to determine.

9.2.2(i) General educational purposes

A gift for the advancement of education in a general manner will usually be recognised as charitable. So, for example, a bequest for "educational ... purposes"[23] or a gift "for the benefit, and advancement, and propagation of education and learning in every part of the world"[24] or to finance "a body of persons established for the purpose of raising the artistic state of the country"[25] will be upheld. Similarly, a gift to schools,[26] or to colleges, either generally, or to found a scholarship[27] will be recognised as charitable under this heading. But if the purpose is expressed too generally then charitable status will be denied. In *Associated Artists Ltd. v. IRC*[28] it was held that the objects of an association, expressed as the presentation of classical, artistic, cultural and educational dramatic works, were so imprecise as to permit a range of activity, not all of which need be artistic, and it could not therefore be considered charitable.

9.2.2(ii) Specific educational purposes

The list of judicially approved charitable purposes in the context of trusts for the advancement of education is extensive. There has never been any doubt, for example, that a charitable trust would be for educational purposes if it provided for the study of subjects such as languages,[29] law,[30] medicine,[31] natural

---

[21] See *Re Cole* [1958] Ch. 877; also, see, *Re Sahal's Will Trusts* [1958] 1 W.L.R. 1243.

[22] See *Incorporated Council for Law Reporting for England and Wales v. Attorney General* [1972] 1 Ch. 73 at 102.

[23] See *Re Ward* [1941] Ch. 308.

[24] See *Whicker v. Hume* (1858) 7 H.L.C. 124.

[25] See *Royal Choral Society v. IRC* [1943] 2 ALL E.R. 101.

[26] See *Incorporated Society v. Richards* (1841) 4 Ir. Eq. R. 177.

[27] See *R v. Newman* (1684) 1 Lev. 284.

[28] [1956] 1 W.L.R. 752.

[29] See *A-G v. Flood* (1816) Hayes and Jo. App. xxi at xxxviii.

history,[32] archaeology,[33] economics,[34] theology,[35] religious instruction,[36] comparative religions,[37] agriculture,[38] mechanical sciences and engineering[39] or shorthand typewriting and book-keeping.[40]

However, the less vocational the subject the greater the judicial scepticism regarding its intrinsic educational value. So, for example, literature which is of no literary merit will not be viewed as educational and a trust to protect a testator's manuscripts will not be upheld as charitable;[41] though a biographical study may be viewed more positively.[42]

9.2.2(iii) Aesthetic educational purposes

Providing aesthetic education is charitable. No firm definition has been given of what precisely constitutes aesthetic education. It would seem to encompass the appreciation, promotion and development of art of a certain calibre, the cultivation of skills such as play and the imparting of civilised values. English courts have stated that "the education of artistic taste is one of the most important things in the development of a civilised human being".[43] That trust involved promoting fine quality choral work. Part of the trust in *Re Shaw's Will Trusts* was to provide masterpieces of fine art for the Irish. This was deemed to be:

> "... aesthetic education which is properly to be regarded as a branch of education ... the improvement of the mind of those subjected to that influence, is education in the best sense."[44]

A trust in very broad terms "to foster and promote the development of the arts

---

[30] See *Smith v. Kerr* [1902] 1 Ch. 774, C.A.
[31] See *Royal College of Surgeons of England v. National Provincial Bank Ltd.* [1952] A.C. 631.
[32] See *Re Mellody* [1918] 1 Ch. 228.
[33] See *Yates v. University College London* (1873) 8 Ch App 454; (1875) L.R. 7 H.L. 438; *Re British School of Egyptian Archaeology* [1954] 1 W.L.R. 546.
[34] See *Re Berridge* (1890) 63 LT 470, CA; *Re Corbett* (1921) 17 Tas. L.R. 139.
[35] See *Reagan* (1957) 8 DLR (2d) 541.
[36] See *A-G v. Sepney* (1804) 10 Ves 22.
[37] *Corrymeela Community v. Commissioner of Valuation* VR/1/1967.
[38] *Lylehill Young Farmers Club v. Commissioner of Valuation* VR/7/1981, *Trustees of the Agricultural Research Institute v. Commissioner of Valuation* VR/81+82/1967.
[39] See *Institution of Civil Engineers v. IRC* [1932] 1 K.B. 149; *Re Lambert* [1967] S.A.S.R. 19.
[40] See *Re Koettgen's Will Trusts* [1954] Ch. 252.
[41] See *Re Elmore* [1968] V.R. 390.
[42] See *Re Hamilton-Grey* (1938) 38 S.R. (N.S.W.) 262.
[43] *Royal Choral Society v. Inland Revenue Commissioners* (1943) 2 All E.R. 101 at 104.
[44] *Re Shaw's Will Trusts* (1952) 1 All E.R. 49 at 55.

in Northern Ireland and public participation in such development" has been held charitable.[45]

These are the broad conceptual brushstrokes of the theory of aesthetic education. The courts have also been adept in filling in the detail of specific charitable purposes. A gift to provide for the upkeep of ancient cottages so that modern craftsmen could learn from them is charitable.[46] Establishing art galleries and museums is charitable.[47] Exhibiting a collection of arms and antiques can be charitable.[48] Advancing or promoting literature is charitable.[49] As mentioned above, a choral society can be charitable[50] as can music generally.[51] Gifts to promote the training of singers of "serious music" have been held charitable[52] as has a gift to promote interest in a particular composer (Delius).[53]

In Northern Ireland it was argued that high quality art films could be the subject matter of an educational charity. The Lands Tribunal accepted that in theory such films could be charitable, but it held that the Queens Film Theatre also showed comedies and light entertainment films which were not of sufficient quality to deserve the epithet "art" or "charitable".[54] A trust to train individuals in the use of video equipment has been held not to be an educational charity, but only on the grounds of lack of public benefit.[55]

Theatres can be valid educational charities[56] but it will depend upon the quality of their productions. For example, the Lyric Players Theatre was obliged by its constitution to produce a certain type of play. The Lands Tribunal held that "the works staged by the appellants were chosen for their literary merit and educational value and their presentation was likely to improve the aesthetic education of people here".[57]

Assistance on the definition of aesthetic art may be derived from rating cases which seek exemption under the "fine art" exemption.[58] These show

---

[45] *Art and Research Exchange v. Commissioner of Valuation* VR/71/1980.

[46] *Re Cranstoun* (1932) 1 Ch. 537.

[47] *Re Holburne* (1885) 53 L.T. 212 and see *Re Town and Country Planning Act 1947, Crystal Palace Trustees v. Minister of Town and Country Planning* [1951] Ch. 132;and *Abbott v. Fraser* (1874) L.R. 6 P.C. 96.

[48] *Re Spence* (1938) 2 Ch. 96.

[49] *Re Hamilton-Grey* (1938) 38 S.R. (N.S.W.) 262 and *Re Hopkins' Will Trusts* [1965] Ch. 669.

[50] *Royal Choral Society v. Inland Revenue Commissioners* (1943) 2 All E.R. 101.

[51] *IRC v. Glasgow Musical Festival Association* [1926] S.C. 920; *Shillington v. Portadown Urban Council* [1911] 1 I.R. 247.

[52] *Re Levien* [1955] 3 All E.R. 35.

[53] See *Re Delius, Emmanuel v. Rosen* [1957] Ch. 299.

[54] *Queens Film Theatre v. Commissioner of Valuation* VR/44/1969.

[55] *Management Committee of Media Workshop v. Commissioner of Valuation* VR/74/1980.

[56] *Re Shakespeare Memorial Trust, Earl Lytton v. A-G* [1923] 2 Ch. 398, *Associated Artists v. Inland Revenue Commissioners* (1956) 1 WLR 752.

[57] *Lyric Players Theatre v. Commissioner of Valuation* VR/25/1970.

[58] Art. 41(2)(d) Rates (N.I.) Order 1977.

that it is not just instilling appreciation, but instructing in the practice which constitutes fine art. Furthermore, it is not just instructing the gifted, but instructing the mediocre and the amateur which is art. The Lands Tribunal has said "the conjunction of the aspects of technique and art in the context of what in its highest form is a fine art makes it wrong to conclude that the possible pursuit of lesser forms of art can essentially devalue the main purpose of the body".[59] In the past, photography was not regarded as a fine art.[60] At present, provided it has sufficient artistic aspirations, it will be fine art,

> "... it should be creative, make an impression in the mind of the beholder which is aesthetically satisfying, and have a form which remains to be seen, appreciated and judged."[61]

It is submitted that this reasoning will be relevant to the definition of aesthetic art in the educational and charitable sense.

In most cases concerning aesthetic education, the courts will need to be satisfied of the artistic content of a particular purpose. In certain cases, such as the commonly accepted academic conception of fine art, artistic quality will be assumed. In other, more modern art forms, artistic quality will have to be proved. If a work has no objectively verifiable artistic merit it cannot be construed as a proper object for charitable status. For example, there was no charity in foisting a donor's artefacts which were a "load of old junk" on the public.[62]

9.2.2(iv) A broadening interpretation of educational purposes

In recent years there has been a growing body of authority for the view that the ambit of trusts recognised as being for the advancement of education should not be confined to those which are educational only in the strictly formal sense of the word. Gifts for the purpose of promoting chess tournaments,[63] for annual outings for schoolchildren[64] and for the children of ex-servicemen belonging to a certain club[65] have been upheld as charitable. A trust to "advance that kind of education best calculated to make the English speaking people better known to each other" is charitable,[66] but a trust merely to spread knowledge about the United Kingdom is not.[67] To be charitable an educational trust

---

[59] *Lisburn Camera Club v. Commissioner of Valuation* VR/105/1978 at p. 8.

[60] *Royal Photographic Society of Great Britain v. City of Westminster and Cane (VO)* (1957-58) 6 R.R.C. 169.

[61] *Lisburn Camera Club v. Commissioner of Valuation* VR/105/1978 at p. 6.

[62] *Re Pinion* (1965) Ch. 85.

[63] See *Re Dupree's Deed Trusts* [1945] Ch. 16.

[64] See *Re Mellody* [1918] 1 Ch. 228.

[65] See *Re Ward's Estate* (1937) 81 Sol. Jo. 397.

[66] *English Speaking Union v. Westminster County Council* 4 R.R.C. 977.

[67] *British Council v. Commissioner of Valuation* VR/65/1980. However, although the Lands

must have intrinsic merit. The training of spiritualist mediums, for example, would not qualify.[68]

In *Re Shaw's Will Trusts*,[69] for example, George Bernard Shaw's wife had left property on trust for the "teaching, promotion and encouragement in Ireland of self-control, elocution, oratory, deportment, the arts of personal contact, of social intercourse and the other arts of public, private, professional and business life". Vaisey J found the gift to be charitable on the grounds that "education" included "not only teaching, but the promotion and encouragement of those arts and graces of life which are after all, perhaps the finest and best part of human character".[70] This view generously broadens the "benefit" criteria by identifying access to the "arts and graces of life" as a suitable charitable object.

9.2.3 Exceptions to definition

The only major restriction is that political activity and factional propaganda must be avoided. It is not charitable to lecture the public about the supposed virtues of a particular political party, but trying to get people to take an interest in constitutional history probably would be a charitable purpose. Unusual charities that qualify under this heading include Eton, the other public schools and the Flat Earth Society.

Sex education and advice on contraception and abortion are very controversial areas. In general, organisations operating in these fields can obtain charitable status if they are prepared to be careful in wording the purposes that appear in their governing instruments (see further, Chapter 12).

In this context, the recent Canadian case of *Vancouver Society of Immigrant and Visible Minority Women v. Minister of National Revenue*[71] is instructive because of its relevance to divided communities such as Northern Ireland in which charities could conceivably play a strategic role in facilitating the social inclusion of minority groups. The case concerned a society established in order to provide a mutual support base for women, mainly from Hong Kong, recently immigrated to Vancouver. The declared objects of the society were to:

(a) provide educational forums, classes, workshops, and seminars to immigrant women to enable them to secure employment;

(b) carry on political activities incidental and ancillary thereto that were not

---

Tribunal deemed such a body non-charitable in Northern Ireland, it has been deemed charitable by the Inland Revenue and registered as a charity by the Charity Commission.

[68] See *Re Hummeltenberg* [1923] 1 Ch. 237.

[69] [1952] Ch. 163 at p. 172.

[70] *Re Shaw, op cit.* at p. 55.

[71] (1999) 169 D.L.R. (4th) 34, SC.

supportive of, or in opposition to, any political party or candidate for public office;

(c) raise funds to carry out these purposes; and

(d) "provide services and to do all such other things that are incidental and
     conducive to the attainment of" those purposes.

The efforts of the society to achieve charitable status under the second *Pemsel*
head foundered on the grounds that (d) was so broad as to permit the pursuit
of non-educational objectives. The, perhaps enduring, significance of this
Supreme Court judgment lies in the finding made by Iacobucci J. that the
definition of "educational" could encompass the workshops, seminars etc which
the society provided. He further held that providing information and advice
for a narrowly defined purpose, such as attaining employment, was also advancing education. It is to be hoped that the reasoning which informed the
judgment made in that common law jurisdiction might in time guide judicial
determination of cases affecting the social exclusion of minority groups in
this jurisdiction.

9.2.4 The statutory definition of education

There is some statutory guidance as to what constitutes education in Northern
Ireland, although that guidance has had limited influence in shaping the definition of education. According to the Educational Endowments (Ireland) Act
1885:

> "... endowments for the payment of apprenticeship fees, or for marriage por-
> tions, or for the maintenance, nurture or clothing or otherwise for the benefit of
> poor children or young persons, shall be deemed to be and may be dealt with as
> educational endowments."[72]

That definition was stated to be only for the purposes of the Act and has not
been relied upon in any reported case in Northern Ireland.

As in the case of Catholic religious charities, there have been historical
doubts about the validity of gifts for Catholic education. For example, an Act
of 1782 (21 & 22 Geo. III c. 62) would not allow "the erection or endowment
of any popish university, college or endowed school". However, Delany points
out "the courts here have made no difficulty in recognising the validity of
bequests for the education of Roman Catholics".[73] As was noted in Chapter 4,
section 5(1) of the Government of Ireland Act 1920 removed any existing
legislative religious discrimination.

---

[72] See s. 10 of the Educational Endowments (Ireland) Act 1885.
[73] Delany (1956) at p. 33.

9.3 THE FORMAL EDUCATION SYSTEM

In its most pure and direct form, a gift for the advancement of education will be charitable if it is for the purpose of establishing a facility for educating others. Trusts for the purpose of founding such facilities have been upheld as charitable for hundreds of years.

9.3.1 Schools

Schools have always been held to be charitable in Northern Ireland. A schoolhouse set up by trust and run by a minister is charitable,[74] as is a school set up by a Presbyterian congregation.[75] A school for handicapped children was held charitable, probably both under the relief of the distressed/succourless head and for the advancement of education.[76] Schools run by nuns[77] have been held charitable as have schools run by monks.[78] Boarding schools were also held to be charitable in Enniskillen[79] and in Newry.[80] A school is charitable even if it charges its pupils.[81]

English cases are in harmony with these decisions. Providing "free or ragged schools for gutter children or for the poorest of the poor" is charitable,[82] as is providing schools for the children of the rich.[83]

Ancillary educational activities in schools have been held charitable in some cases. A school sanatorium is charitable.[84] Eton Fives courts for pupils are charitable.[85] A trust for an annual school treat or field day can be charitable.[86] Necessary ancillary activities to a school, such as a caretakers residence can also be charitable.[87]

---

[74] *Re Hardy, Nelson v. Attorney General* [1933] N.I. 150.

[75] *Re Townsend Street Belfast Presbyterian Endowment Trusts* [1954] N.I. 53.

[76] *Denmark v. Commissioner of Valuation for Northern Ireland* (1962) 28 Ir. Jur. Rep. 20.

[77] *Trustees of the Dominican Convent of the Holy Rosary v. Commissioner of Valuation* VR/23/1965, *Trustees of the Convent of Mercy, Newry v. Commissioner of Valuation* VR/10/1974.

[78] *Commissioner of Valuation v. Trustees of the Redemptorist Order, Commissioner of Valuation v. Trustees of the Newry Christian Brothers* [1971] N.I. 114 (the *Redemptorist* case)

[79] *Commissioner of Valuation for Northern Ireland v. Fermanagh Protestant Board of Education* [1970] N.I. 89, (the *Portora* case).

[80] *Redemptorists* case.

[81] *Campbell College v. Commissioner of Valuation* [1964] N.I. 107 in the Court of Appeal, [1964] N.I. 169 in the House of Lords.

[82] *Re Hedgman* (1870) 8 Ch. D 156.

[83] *Attorney General v. Lonsdale* (1827) 1 Sim. 105.

[84] *Re Harrow School Governors* (1927) 1 Ch. 556.

[85] *Re Mariette* (1915) 2 Ch. 284.

[86] *Re Mellody* (1918) 1 Ch. 228.

[87] *Governors of Victoria College Belfast v. Commissioner of Valuation* VR/17/1965.

In Northern Ireland the greatest controversy concerning schools has been with regard to whether they could be considered charitable for rating purposes. From at least 1854,[88] or possibly since 1838,[89] and for the next one hundred years, a school in any part of Ireland could gain charitable exemption from rates only if it provided education solely for the poor. The case of *Campbell College v. Commissioner of Valuation* went all the way to the House of Lords and the plaintiff's success, in ultimately acquiring exemption from rates for their school,[90] changed the law in this jurisdiction regarding charitable exemption from rates under this *Pemsel* head. Viscount Radcliffe, in the House of Lords, held that:

> "... the category of education is charitable in its own right, without any necessity to find an eleemosynary element in any particular form of education."[91]

"Charity" should be given its full and natural *Pemsel* meaning whenever possible.

The legal point was relatively minor, but the practical repercussions were large in granting schools exemption from rates. This landmark decision thereafter placed the law of Northern Ireland on a different footing from that of the Republic of Ireland regarding the eligibility of hereditaments for rates exemption on the grounds of their use for educational purposes.

9.3.1(i) Nursery schools, pre-school playgroups etc

Education begins at an early age and recognition is now given to this by acknowledgement that facilities with a child development dimension, catering for children before they enter the formal education system, may be eligible for charitable status. Northern Ireland, in recent years, has witnessed a virtual explosion in the number, variety and spread (socio-economic and cultural as well as geographic) of such facilities. These provide excellent adult opportunities for building neighbourly relationships and extending social networks, as well as opportunities for advancing the education of very small children. There are now a number of well-established bodies providing such facilities which have acquired charitable status and contribute greatly to building social cohesion in the fragmented communities of this jurisdiction.

9.3.1(ii) Integrated schools

The community divisions in Northern Ireland are reflected in its schools and

---

[88] Valuation (Ireland) Amendment Act 1854.
[89] Poor Relief (Ireland) Act 1838.
[90] *Campbell College v. Commissioner of Valuation* [1964] N.I. 107 in the Court of Appeal, [1964] N.I. 169 in the House of Lords.
[91] *Ibid.* at p. 175.

evident in what is arguably the most uniformed child population of any juris-diction in these islands. Whether the relationship between community divi-sion and segregation of schools into Catholic and Protestant is causal remains open to debate but there can be little doubt that educational apartheid does little to promote community cohesion. The movement to establish schools spe-cifically enabling both Catholic and Protestant children to be educated to-gether in the same classroom has been a particularly hopeful and increasingly successful initiative. The acquisition of charitable status by the organisation concerned illustrates the actual and potential contribution of charities to building a more inclusive society in this jurisdiction.

9.3.2 Teachers

Gifts to teachers are not necessarily charitable.[92] Accommodation provided for teachers may be charitable. Legislation provides that trusts for teachers residences are not subject to the usual *cy-près* limit for Charities Branch juris-diction.[93] Implicit in this is the view that such trusts can be charitable. Provid-ing a rest home for teachers can be charitable.[94] A considerable number of cases have asked whether such residences are entitled to the charitable ex-emption from rates. The short answer is that they are, if they directly facilitate the carrying out of educational duties (see further, Chapter 21).

9.3.3 Private education

Private endowment of education can take the form of trusts for establishing and/or maintaining schools which provide exclusively for the private educa-tion of minority sections of the school-aged population. In England, the fact that schools such as Eton which cater for the children of rich parents, should attract charitable status, has long been a matter of contention. But, it has never been a requirement that educational purposes should be for the benefit of the poor. A private school may permit fees to be paid but the trustees must not make a profit from the enterprise.[95] Within those constraints, it is of no signifi-cance that the educational facility restricts access either through levying fees or by offering specialist tuition.

---

[92] *R. v. Special Commissioners of Income Tax, ex parte Headmasters Conference* (1925) 41 T.L.R. 651.

[93] Education and Libraries (NI) Order 1986, s.90(7).

[94] See *Re Estlin* (1903) 72 L.J. Ch. 687.

[95] See *The Abbey, Malvern Wells Ltd. v. Ministry of Local Government and Planning* [1951] Ch. 728 where it was said that "it is well-established that education need not be provided free of charge in order to be charitable."

Gifts to schools "for the sons of gentlemen" have long been recognised as charitable trusts. As was explained by Leach V.-C.[96]:

> "The institution of a school for the sons of gentlemen is not, in proper language, a charity; but in the view of the Statute of Elizabeth, all schools of learning are to be considered."

While the law accepts the charitable nature of gifts to prestigious schools catering largely for privileged minorities, it must be acknowledged that the general public has a difficulty in sharing that view. Any application of the public benefit test which can result in affirming the charitable nature of elite institutions does give rise to scepticism and serves to emphasise a difference in perception between judiciary and the general public in what constitutes a charity.

Gifts to such schools for the purpose of providing for organised games have also been assured a sympathetic judicial hearing[97].

9.3.4 Universities etc

The practice of privately endowing fellowships,[98] scholarships[99] and university chairs is a well-worn route for establishing charitable trusts for educational purposes. Gifts given to found new departments or faculties within a college,[100] to learned societies[101] or institutions for the advancement of science[102] will be readily assured of charitable status. Universities are subject to the extra control and jurisdiction of Visitors.[103]

9.3.5 Students' unions

Students' unions have been held to be charitable.[104] Objections have been raised that if a student union is used by staff, there is too much private and not public benefit. However, the courts have held that such use:

> "... brings those who serve the university purposes into closer contact with the student body, and thus gives cohesion to University life in a manner which can benefit the purpose for which the university exists."[105]

---

[96] See *Attorney-General v. Lord Lonsdale* (1827) 1 Sim. 105.

[97] See *Re Mariette* [1915] 2 Ch. 284; and *Re Geere's Will Trusts (No. 2)* [1954] C.L.Y. 388.

[98] See *Attorney-General v. Whorwood* (1750) 1 Ves. 537.

[99] See *R v. Newman* (1684) 1 Lev. 284.

[100] See *Davenport v. Davenport Foundation* 222 P. 2d 11 (1950).

[101] See *British Museum Trustees v. White* (1826) 2 Sim. & St. 594.

[102] See *Weir v. Crum-Brown* [1908] A.C. 162.

[103] See further, Picarda (1995) Chapter 41.

[104] *President and Professors of Queens College Belfast v. Commissioner of Valuation* (1904) 38 I.L.T.R. 196.

[105] *Lord Mayor, Aldermen and Citizens of the City of Belfast v. Commissioner of Valuation* VR/17/1967 at p. 17.

London Hospital Medical College v. Inland Revenue Commissioners[106] held that a students' union whose sole function was the advancement of education was charitable.

9.3.6 Student accommodation

The authorities conflict on whether providing accommodation for students is charitable. The arguments for it are that it provides a stable and secure residence, and allowing students to share with each other in a studious environment is educational. The arguments against it are that accommodation is not *per se* a charitable activity. The High Court in Belfast has held that a trust to provide a hostel for female Protestant students and teachers and to grant bursaries to them is charitable.[107] No query was raised as to the charitable status of a hostel for overseas students in *Re Dominion Students' Hall Trust*.[108] However, the Lands Tribunal has held that a hall of residence for students of Queens University Belfast was not charitable, partly due to a vagueness of objects. In the trust, there was "intellectual discussion of an educational character, but only of such a vague and ill-defined nature that it would be virtually impossible for a court to execute such trusts".[109] When faced with a similar, but more clearly worded trust, the Lands Tribunal did not give a clear answer as to whether such accommodation was charitable. It held that the accommodation was not exempt from rates, but did not state whether or not it was a charity.[110] See further Chapter 21 for a consideration of this question in the rating context.

9.4 PUBLIC BENEFIT

The public benefit test is more difficult to satisfy in application to trusts for the advancement of education than to trusts for the relief of poverty or for the advancement of religion.

9.4.1 "Public"

Dissemination is an essential and distinguishing characteristic of a public trust for the advancement of education. As for other charitable purposes, the rules for determining when the "public" component is satisfied are neither fixed,

---

[106] *London Hospital Medical College* v. *Inland Revenue Commissioners* (1975) 1 W.L.R. 613.
[107] *Trustees of Aquinas Hall* (unreported, Chancery Division, February 24, 1972).
[108] *Re Dominion Students' Hall Trust* (1947) Ch. 183.
[109] *Trustees of Aquinas Hall* v. *Commissioner of Valuation* VR/50/1965 at p. 8.
[110] *Incorporated Governors of Riddell Hall* v. *Commissioner of Valuation* VR/33/1971.

precise nor readily applied. There are a number of influential English and Irish authorities which offer some guidance in this area.

9.4.1(i) Numbers

It was Lord Hardwicke L.C. in the eighteenth century who first declared that the hallmark of a public charity was its extensiveness.[111] But determining the minimum number necessary to meet an acceptable definition of "public" has proved to be difficult. In *Re Compton*,[112] for example, the Court of Appeal had no difficulty in finding that a trust to provide for the education of the descendants of three named individuals was too restrictive to be charitable. In the adjoining jurisdiction, Keane J. in *Re Worth Library*[113] was certain that three named persons was insufficient but could only suggest that to satisfy a definition of "public" the number should not be "negligible". The number that in fact actually derives a benefit should be distinguished from the number that might do so: to satisfy the "public" requirement it is crucial that there is the possibility of a significant number of beneficiaries; that only one person eventually benefits is beside the point. Gifts to uniformed societies with an "open-access" membership base, such as the girl guides and boy scouts;[114] have always been recognised as charitable.

9.4.1(ii) Class closure

It is essential that the size of the class can be ascertained. Where a gift is intended for the benefit of "descendants" there is potential for membership of such a class to be added to indefinitely. An issue then arises as to the point at which a line must be drawn beyond which no further descendants can be considered members of that class and thus potential beneficiaries. In *Re Compton*,[115] for example, the income from a trust for the education of descendants of three named persons was specifically directed to be paid "forever". In *Kilroy v. Parker*[116] it was expressly provided that the class was limited to those nieces and nephews "alive at the date of my death".

In this context the rule in *Andrews v. Partington*[117] is relevant. It states that the membership of a class should be treated as having closed at the death of the donor. Prior to the decision of the House of Lords in *Re Baden's Deed*

---

[111] See *Attorney-General v. Pearce* (1740) 2 Atk. 87.
[112] [1945] Ch. 123.
[113] [1994] 1 I.L.R.M. 161.
[114] See, *Re Alexander, The Times*, June 30, 1932, *per* Clauson J.; and *Re Webber* [1954] 1 W.L.R. 1500.
[115] *op. cit.*
[116] [1966] I.R. 309.
[117] (1791) 3 Bro. C.C. 401.

Trusts[118] it was generally accepted that the objects of a trust must be certain: the language employed must be certain; and the trustees must at any time be able to ascertain definitely the persons who would have a vested interest in the capital and income of the trust property. On the other hand where the trustees were not bound by a trust but merely had a power or discretion to confer or withhold a benefit then the requirement of certainty was recognised as being far less stringent.[119] As Upjohn L.J. explained in *Re Gulbenkian's Settlements*[120]:

> "...the rule is, that provided there is a valid gift over or trust in default of appointment ... a mere or bare power of appointment among a class is valid if you can with certainty say whether any given individual is or is not a member of the class; you do not have to be able to ascertain every member of the class."

In England and Wales, the authority of that statement ceased with the decision in *Re Baden's Deed Trusts* when the House of Lords held[121] that the test to be applied in determining the validity of imperative trusts was substantially the same as that applicable to discretionary trusts. Only if it can be said with certainty that any given individual is or is not a member of the class designated as potential beneficiaries will such a trust be valid. In Ireland, however, the judicial view is that the House of Lords decision is not to be preferred to the previously established caselaw. Both Budd J.[122] and Murphy J.[123] have declared that they will continue to place greater reliance on the established authorities than on the *ratio decedendi* of *Re Baden's Deed Trusts*.

The courts in this jurisdiction will be guided by the precedent established in the House of Lords decision. This marks a point of difference between the charity law of the two adjoining jurisdictions.

9.4.1(iii) Nexus of personal relationship

In some circumstances, the number of potential beneficiaries may be beside the point. For example, *Oppenheim v. Tobacco Securities Trust Co. Ltd*[124] concerned a trust established to provide for the education of the children of employees or former employees of a company and its subsidiaries (potentially in excess of 110,000). The House of Lords ruled that although the number of beneficiaries "must not be numerically negligible" they also must not form a

---

[118] [1971] A.C. 424.

[119] See, *Inland Revenue Commissioners v. Broadway Cottages Trust* [1955] Ch. 20; also see, *Re Gulbenkian's Settlements* [1970] A.C. 508.

[120] *op. cit.*, at p. 521.

[121] Specifically overruling, by a majority of three to two, the decision in *Inland Revenue Commissioners v. Broadway Cottages Trust* [1955] Ch. 20.

[122] See, *Kilroy v. Parker* [1966] I.R. 309.

[123] See, *Davoren decd., in the estate of, O'Byrne v. Davoren*, unreported, High Court, Budd J., May 13, 1994.

[124] [1951] A.C. 297.

group defined by a common relationship to a named *propositus*. As Lord Simonds expressed it:

> "...the quality which distinguishes them from other members of the community, so that they form by themselves a section of it, must be a quality which does not depend on their relationship to a particular individual."[125]

The beneficiaries were identified by the personal nexus of one employer; there was therefore no public benefit and the gift was not charitable.

An educational trust for the benefit of members of a particular family does not satisfy the public benefit test. The beneficiaries are defined by their relationship to a particular person or group.[126]

9.4.1(iv) The "founder's kin" rule

This rule has guided judicial determination of some cases which form an exception to the nexus of personal relationship test. In the words of H. Delany "... a gift to an educational institution which contains a direction that preference be given to the 'founder's kin' may constitute a charitable trust".[127] If the donor's primary intention is to achieve a *bona fide* educational purpose then a subsidiary condition favouring relatives may be attached without prejudice to the trust's charitable status provided, in the words of Lord Greene M.R. in *Re Compton*[128] that the preference is "merely a method of giving effect to this intention". It is crucial that the gift is expressed in terms which place a preference rather than an explicit directive in favour of the donor's kin. Where the gift is merely a disguised family trust established solely for the purpose of educating the donor's relatives, then it will not be accorded charitable status.[129]

9.4.2 "Benefit"

The authorities are clear that in addition to the public dissemination criteria, to be charitable a trust for the advancement of education must also have a purpose which meets criteria of "usefulness". Applying a "usefulness" test is fairly straightforward and satisfactory where a donor's intentions are to give effect to an educational objective which is manifestly either constructive or frivolous. Where those intentions are to further an objective which is more hobby than education then the test can be a very uncertain procedure.

---

[125] *ibid*. at p. 309.

[126] *Re Compton* (1945) Ch. 123.

[127] Delany, H., *Equity and the Law of Trusts in Ireland* (Round Hall Sweet & Maxwell, Dublin, 1996), at p. 260. See, for example, *Spencer v. All Souls College* (1762) Wilm. 163.

[128] [1945] Ch. 123 at 132.

[129] See *Caffoor v. Commissioner of Income Tax Colombo* [1961] A.C. 584.

That which is considered "useful", in the sense of serving the public interest, will vary according to the values informing a particular social context at any point in time. The case of *Re Shaw's Wills Trusts, National Provincial Bank Ltd v. National City Bank Ltd*[130] provides an interesting insight into the then prevailing cultural norms. In her will, Mrs Bernard Shaw established a trust for, among other things:

> "...the teaching, promotion and encouragement in Ireland of self-control, elocution, oratory, deportment, the arts of personal contact, of social intercourse and the other arts of public, private, professional and social life."

Vaisey J. upheld this as a valid charitable trust. But, distinctions of taste and artistic merit which may distinguish the fine arts from other art forms have often exercised judicial minds. While ballet dancing and folk dancing have received judicial recognition as inherently educational and meriting charitable status,[131] ballroom dancing has not.[132] In Ireland, Keane J., in *Re Worth Library*,[133] recently had cause to examine the requirement for a public benefit component in gifts for the advancement of education. He noted that:

> "... gifts for the advancement of education ... would embrace, not merely gifts to schools and universities and the endowment of university chairs and scholarships: 'education' has been given a broad meaning so far as to encompass gifts for the establishment of theatres, art galleries and museums and the promotion of literature and music. In every case, however, the element of public benefit must be present and, if the benefit extends to a section of the community only, that section must not be numerically negligible."[134]

He found that the gift of a library which is open to the public would be charitable[135] but not one restricted to those paying subscriptions.[136] So also would be a gift which was conducive to the attainment of a charitable object such as one for the purchase of books for Trinity College, Oxford[137] where it was held to be for the advancement of education. In this instance he expressed his view that the gift of a library, comprising a large and valuable collection of eighteenth century books, would be unlikely to meet a definition of "educational". The gift would fail the "public" test because access to the library was restricted "for the use, benefit and behoof of the physician, chaplain and surgeon for the time being of the said hospital...". It would also fail the "benefit" test because as he pointed out:

---

[130] [1952] Ch. 163.

[131] See *O'Sullivan v. English Folk Dance and Song Society* [1955] 1 W.L.R. 907.

[132] See *Linlithgow Town Council Entertainments Committee v. IRC*, 1953 S.L.T. 287.

[133] *op. cit.*

[134] *ibid.* at p. 193.

[135] Citing as his authority *Re Scowcroft, Ormrod v. Wilkinson* [1898] 2 Ch. 638 at 642.

[136] Citing *Carne v. Long* (1860) 2 De G.F. & J. 75 and *In re Prevost, Lloyds Bank Ltd. v. Barclay's Bank* [1930] 2 Ch. 383.

[137] See *Attorney General v. Marchant* (1866) L.R. 3 Eq. 424.

"... even if it could be said that the bequest was for educational purposes (and, given the insignificant proportion of the library devoted to medicine and surgery, that would involve some straining of the concept of 'education' even beyond the liberal limits of the modern decisions), it would be impossible to hold that this was an educational charity for the benefit of the public."

Facilities such as zoos,[138] public libraries,[139] museums[140] and botanical gardens[141] have also been recognised as appropriate objects for charitable trusts for the advancement of education.

The courts in England have had little difficulty in ruling that some donor intentions do not comply with usefulness criteria. For example, the compilation of lists of Derby winners[142] and the public exhibition of junk[143] have failed this test. The requirement of usefulness was also stressed in *Re De Noailles*[144] where it was remarked that:

"... the mere stuffing of information into a boy or girl may make them very priggish, but it does not make them of much use in life, unless they know how to apply that information for the purpose of being better citizens."[145]

9.5 TYPES OF CHARITABLE GIFTS FOR EDUCATIONAL PURPOSES

The courts have consistently and strenuously stated that education shouldn't he constrained into the narrow limits of purely academic, classroom based teaching. Lord Hailsham said that he would:

"... reject any idea which would cramp education within the school or university syllabus, confine it within the school or university campus, limit it to formal instruction, or render it devoid of pleasure in the exercise of skill."[146]

Accordingly, in addition to those gifts clearly directed towards servicing the formal education structure (see above), a range of gifts for ancillary purposes have also acquired charitable status.

---

[138] See *Re Lopes, Bence-Jones v. Zoological Society of London* [1931] 2 Ch. 130.

[139] See *Abbott v. Fraser* (1874) L.R. 6 P.C. 96; *Re Russell Institution* [1898] 2 Ch. 72; *Re Jones* [1898] 2 Ch. 83; and *Re Pitt-Rivers* [1902] 1 Ch. 403, C.A.

[140] See *Re Holburne* (1885) 53 L.T. 212; *Re Spence* [1938] 2 Ch. 96; *British Museum v. White* (1826) 2 Sim. & St. 594; and *Re Allsop* (1884) 1 TLR 4.

[141] See *Townley v. Bedwell* (1801) 6 Ves. 194; and *Harrison v. Southampton Corpn* (1854) 2 Sm. & G. 387.

[142] See *Brunyate* (1945) 61 L.Q.R. 268 at p. 273.

[143] See *Re Pinion* [1965] Ch. 85; and *Sutherland's Trustees v. Verschoyle* 1968 S.L.T. 43.

[144] (1916) 114 L.T. 1089.

[145] *ibid.* at 1094.

[146] *IRC v. McMullen* at p. 18.

9.5.1 Academic research

Trusts may be set-up for conducting research in, for example, veterinary matters.[147] A number of charities established solely for the purpose of conducting research are registered with the Charity Commission in London.

However, the public/private divide in academic research does present particular difficulties. These were addressed by Slade J. in *Re Besterman's Will Trusts*,[148] which concerned a bequest to a specified institute within Oxford University for the purpose of undertaking research on Voltaire, Rousseau and other authors of the Enlightenment and for such other relevant purposes and on such terms as the institute should consider appropriate. Slade J. found that the institute specialised in research and teaching in subjects relating to the Enlightenment period and held that the gift was charitable. In his judgment he identified three essential components of a charitable trust for research: the subject matter for research must be useful; the research results could be disseminated; and the trust must be for the benefit of the public, or for a significant section of it.

9.5.1(i) Dissemination of research findings

There is a school of thought which holds that the accumulation of knowledge is, in itself, essentially a private activity. In the celebrated case of *Re Shaw*,[149] for example, it was firmly held by Harman J. that a trust fund to provide for research into ways of improving the alphabet was not charitable partly because the testator had not provided a means for the research results to be used. As Harman J. explained:

> "... if the object be merely the increase of knowledge that is not in itself a charitable object unless it be combined with teaching or education."[150]

This approach was based to some extent on the decision of the House of Lords in *Whicker v. Hume*.[151] The view that research which provides only for an increase in the researcher's knowledge, is insufficient to qualify as charitable status, was challenged by Wilberforce J. in *Re Hopkins' Will Trusts*[152]:

> "I should be unwilling to treat [Harman J.'s words] as meaning that the promotion of academic research is not a charitable purpose unless the researcher were engaged in teaching or education in a conventional meaning. . . ."

---

[147] See *London University v. Yarrow* (1857) 1 De G. & J. 72.

[148] *The Times*, January 22, 1980.

[149] [1957] 1 W.L.R. 729; relying upon the House of Lords ruling in *Whicker v. Hume* (1858) 7 H.L. Cas. 124. See also, *Re Macduff* [1896] 2 Ch. 451 at 472-473, *per* Rigby L.J.

[150] *ibid.* at p. 737.

[151] (1858) 7 H.L. Cas. 124.

[152] [1965] Ch. 669.

However, in *Incorporated Council for Law Reporting for England and Wales v. Attorney General*,[153] the point was again made that storing information was insufficient to constitute education; it must also be disseminated.

9.5.1(ii) General usefulness of research findings

In *Hopkins*,[154] Wilberforce J. expressed his view that charitable research was of two types. It was:

> "... either of educational value to the researcher or must be directed as to lead to something which will pass into the store of educational material, or so as to improve the sum of communicable knowledge in an area which education may cover – education in this last context extending to the formation of literary taste and appreciation."[155]

This was a case which concerned a trust directed to a society for the purpose of enabling it to research a link between manuscripts written by Francis Bacon and William Shakespeare. While conceding the improbability that the research would produce any results of public benefit, Wilberforce J. nonetheless found that the trust was fulfilling an educational purpose and held it to be charitable.

9.5.2 Support services for educational establishments

Even where the purpose is not strictly educational but is to provide support for an educational establishment by founding, for example, a students union,[156] a rest home for teachers[157] and a nurses' home;[158] though note that residences as such are not charitable,[159] a swimming pool and hot water baths,[160] book prizes[161] and cash prizes[162] a trust may be upheld as charitable; provided it does not infringe indicators of charitable status.

A gift to found or to endow a college library will be charitable[163] provided it does not seek to make a profit.

---

[153] [1972] 1 Ch. 73.

[154] *op. cit.*

[155] *ibid.* at p. 680.

[156] See *London Hospital v. IRC* [1976] 1 W.L.R. 613.

[157] See *Re Estlin* (1903) 72 L.J. Ch. 687.

[158] See *Re White's Will Trusts, Tindall v. Board of Governors of United Sheffield Hospitals* [1951] 1 All E.R. 528.

[159] See *Heron v. Monaghen* (1888) 22 L.R. Ir. 532.

[160] See *Re Geere's Will Trusts (No. 2)* [1954] C.L.Y. 388.

[161] See *Re Mariette* [1915] 2 Ch. 284.

[162] See *Re Weaver* [1963] V.R. 256.

[163] See *A-G v. Marchant* (1866) L.R. 3 Eq. 424 at 430; and also see *Re Good* [1905] 2 Ch. 60.

9.5.3 Published law reports

The publication of law reports may qualify for charitable status but much will turn on whether it can be demonstrated that the content is educational and not merely informative, that they confer a public benefit and that they are published on a non-profit making basis. The teaching of law having been held to be charitable in *Smith v. Kerr*,[164] it was then successfully argued in *Incorporated Council of Law Reporting for England and Wales v. Attorney General*[165] that the publication of law reports was also charitable. The Council was a non-profit making body incorporated in 1870 to publish the important judgements of the courts. Law was regarded by the courts as a scientific subject of study, and it would be benefited by the dissemination of judge-made case law, "objects of the council are educational in that they result in the dissemination of information about the latest state of and development in the science of law".[166]

The case had broader significance as it showed the characteristics indicative of a subject which purported to be an educational charity. Sachs L.J. said the purpose of the reports was "to provide essential material for the study of the law – in the sense of acquiring knowledge of what the law is, how it is developing and how it applies to the enormous range of human activities which it affects".[167] If the word "law" could be meaningfully replaced with another object, that object would have a similar chance of being deemed educational.

9.6 GIVING EFFECT TO CHARITABLE GIFTS FOR EDUCATIONAL PURPOSES

Where there is doubt, the courts will lean in favour of finding that a donor has made a valid charitable trust to advance an educational purpose and will strive to find a means of giving effect to it.

9.6.1 Gift comprising charitable and non-charitable objects

The court, in *Re Litchfield*, held that because one object in a legacy was non-charitable, this was fatal to the entire gift.[168]

9.6.2 Gifts to professional bodies

In this context, the distinction between gifts which directly enhance the capac-

---

[164] (1902) 1 Ch. 774.
[165] (1971) 3 All E.R. 1029.
[166] *Council of Law Reporting, op cit.* at p. 1045.
[167] *ibid.* at p. 1039.
[168] See *Re Litchfield* [1961] A.L.R. 750.

ity of a body to achieve educational objectives and those which instead enable it to either cater for ancillary objectives or contribute towards its general effectiveness, has in the past been of crucial importance. However, the House of Lords in the *Royal College of Surgeons of England v. National Provincial Bank Ltd*,[169] reviewed the authorities and held that protecting the professional interests of College members was a natural ancillary objective which did not detract from the charitable status of the College.

---

[169] [1952] A.C. 631.

CHAPTER 10

The Advancement of Religion

"For the building, re-edifying or maintaining in repair any church ... for the maintenance of any minister and preacher of the Holy Word of God"

(Statute of Pious Uses 1634)

"For the repair of ... churches"

(Statute of Charitable Uses 1601)

10.1 INTRODUCTION

Religion in Northern Ireland has a long and troubled history. The role of charity law reflects its complicated social context.

In Northern Ireland religion has a different status from that prevailing in the other jurisdictions of these islands. For example, there is no equivalent to the declared constitutional preference for a particular religion which exists in the Republic of Ireland; nor is there any equivalent to the statutory presumption that gifts for religious purposes are for the public benefit. The relative preference given in law to the Church of England in the jurisdiction of England and Wales does not transfer to Northern Ireland; nor does the rich diversity of non-Christian culture extend, in comparable volume, to this jurisdiction. Religion, and charitable giving for the advancement of religious purposes, remain polarised around the twin monolithic blocks of Protestantism and Roman Catholicism. Religious organisations also retain their traditional place as the primary recipient of donations and bequests.

This chapter does not concern itself with the social role of religion in Northern Ireland. The possibly fascinating study of patterns in charitable giving as a means of advancing by proxy the relative social standing of particular religions, is similarly ignored. Instead the focus is on the actual practice of charity law under this *Pemsel*[1] head. Beginning with a brief outline of the historical background, the chapter then goes on to consider matters of definition, purpose and public benefit in the context of religion. This leads into an examination of the range of charitable gifts and related case law which constitutes the main part of this chapter.

---

[1] See *Income Tax Special Purposes Commissioners v. Pemsel* [1891] A.C. 531.

10.2 BACKGROUND

The law relating to charity under this head, as under all other *Pemsel* heads, has been largely shaped in the courts of England and Wales. Until its partition into two jurisdictions, the law was applied uniformly throughout Ireland. Since then certain jurisdictional differences have become apparent. The courts have warned of the dangers of relying on caselaw from the Republic of Ireland as "parts of the law relating to religious charities have developed along somewhat different lines".[2]

10.2.1 Statutory foundations

The Irish statute is much broader in its terms than the English equivalent, as it expressly mentions ministers as an object of charity. V.T.H. Delany[3] suggests a possible explanation for this. England in 1601 had undergone the social upheavel of the Reformation and a resulting shift in religious identity. The status of some ministers and religious bodies had changed and many had been declared illegal. Therefore a previously valid gift may subsequently have become void due to a turn in the religious tide. It was thought that the best way to preserve religious gifts was by giving them to a constant purpose. The repair of a church would be that constant, unchanging purpose regardless of whether it was being used for Catholic or Protestant services. Sir Francis Moor also eloquently explained why the English statue did not expand upon religious purposes:

> "… for religion being variable according to the pleasure of succeeding princes, that which at one time is held for orthodox may be at another accounted superstitious, and thus such lands are confiscated."[4]

However, it is unclear why Ireland had this much wider statutory definition of religious purposes. Perhaps it was because Protestantism was then the only established and formally recognised religion, and there were no gifts to those Catholic institutions which had converted into Protestant institutions.

Aside from this historical quirk, there seem to be little or no consequences in practice from the different wording of the two statutes. It is arguably easier to prove that gifts for ministers are charitable in Ireland than in England. For example, in one of the more important Northern Ireland cases on gifts to ministers it was said that a gift:

---

2   *Order of the Knights of St. Columbanus v. Commissioner of Valuation* VR/3/1996, (1997) 8 *Property Law Journal* 29 at p. 30.

3   Delany, V.T.H., *The Law Relating to Charities in Ireland* (1956, Dublin, Alex Thom & Co. Ltd).

4   Exposition on the Statute of 43 Elizabeth Concerning Charitable Uses, as contained in Duke, G., *Charitable Uses* (1676).

> "… would come within that part of the Statute of Charles which speaks of the 'maintenance of any preacher of the word of God'".[5]

However, the English courts have assiduously extended the meaning of religion to encompass everything within the wider Irish definition.

10.2.2 Current statutory framework

The statutory framework governing charitable activity for the advancement of religion, as with all other charitable activity, is provided by the Charities Act (Northern Ireland) 1964 and the Charities (Northern Ireland) Order 1987.

10.2.3 The European Convention for the Protection of Human Rights and Fundamental Freedoms 1950

This Convention guarantees religious freedom and prohibits discrimination on religious grounds. The principal Articles[6] in question are Articles 9 and 14. Article 9 provides that "everyone has the right to freedom of thought, conscience and religion"[7] "subject only to such limitations as are prescribed by law and are necessary in a democratic society in the interests of public safety, for the protection of public order, health or morals, or for the protection of the rights and freedoms of others".[8] Article 14 prohibits discrimination on the basis of, *inter alia*, "religion, political or other opinion". It has been argued that if the State provides fiscal and other benefits to one religion then the benefits must be made equally available to all belief structures covered by Article 9 unless good cause can be shown for not doing so.[9] As there are clearly both fiscal and other advantages accruing to charitable status, decisions regarding recognition under the religious head would need to ensure that no discrimination had been involved in reaching these decisions (see further, Chapter 4).

---

[5] See *Baptist Union, op. cit.* at p. 105.

[6] As listed in Schedule 1 of the Human Rights Act 1998.

[7] Art. 9(1).

[8] Art. 9(2).

[9] See Francesca Quint and Thomas Spring, "Religion, Charity Law and Human Rights", in *Charity Law & Practice Review*, Vol.5, Issue 3, 1999, pp. 153-186. They argue that if a state provides a privilege, right or benefit to one group then "it must treat all similar groups equally and provide them the same privileges, rights and benefits, unless there is justification to support the difference in treatment".

[10] See, Brady, J.C., *Religion and the Law of Charities in Ireland*, N.I.L.Q., Belfast, 1975, at p. xiii.

10.3 RELIGION

As J.C. Brady observed:

> "Religion is still inextricably interwoven with the whole fabric of life in Ireland and the Irishman's commitment to institutionalised Christianity is nowhere more clearly reflected than in his charitable benefactions."[10]

This comment is equally applicable to Northern Ireland. In a survey of charitable bequests carried out annually by the Charities Branch, religious bequests consistently outnumber the sum of all other charitable bequests.[11] This is reflected in the case law with a large number of religious charities involved in litigation. The approach of the courts to religion in Northern Ireland has been quite liberal and progressive as illustrated in particular by the judgments of Lord MacDermott L.C.J. in the leading Court of Appeal cases.[12] In Northern Ireland, religious charities are invariably Christian religions.[13]

10.3.1 Definition of religion

Although gifts under the religious head are the most common charitable gifts in Northern Ireland, no case here has attempted a precise definition of religion. Turning to the English cases for assistance, religion has been defined as:

> "… the promotion of spiritual teaching in a wide sense, and the maintenance of the doctrines on which it rests, and the observances that serve to promote and manifest it."[14]

It is clear from the cases that an essential prerequisite is a belief in the existence of a god. The view that the legal definition of religion could be satisfied by a system of belief not involving faith in a god was explicitly rejected by Dillon J. in *Re South Place Ethical Society*.[15] This case concerned a society

---

[11] For example, in 1997, there were 813 bequests for religious charities out of a total of 1,442 total charitable bequests. For more statistics, see *Charities Annual Report 1997*, Department of Health and Social Services.

[12] *Trustees of the City of Belfast Young Men's Christian Association v. Commissioner of Valuation* [1969] N.I. 3, *Commissioner of Valuation v. Trustees of the Redemptorist Order, Commissioner of Valuation v. Trustees of the Newry Christian Brothers* [1971] N.I. 114.

[13] Only one non-Christian case having been decided, a Hindu temple in *Trustees of the Indian Community Centre v. Commissioner of Valuation* VR/6/1988.

[14] *Keren Kayemeth Le Jisroel v. Inland Revenue Commissioners* (1931) 48 T.L.R. 459 at p. 477. But also see *Thornton v. Howe* (1862), 54 E.R. 1042, 31 Beav. 14 where, in a doubtful ruling, the court held that a trust for the printing, publishing and propagation of the sacred writings of the late Joanna Southcote (who claimed to have been made pregnant by the Holy Ghost and was to give birth to the second Messiah) was a valid charitable trust for a religious purpose.

[15] *Re South Place Ethical Society, Barralet v. Attorney General* [1980] 1 W.L.R. 1565; (1980) 124 S.J. 774; [1980] 3 All E.R. 918.

the objects of which included 'the study and dissemination of ethical principles and the cultivation of a rational religious sentiment'. As Dillon J. then explained:

> "Religion, as I see it, is concerned with man's relations with God and ethics are concerned with man's relations with man. The two are not the same and are not made the same by sincere inquiry into the question – what is God? If reason leads people not to accept Christianity or any known religion but they do believe in the excellence of qualities such as truth, beauty, and love, or believe in the platonic concept of the ideal, their belief may be to them the equivalent of a religion but viewed objectively they are not a religion."

An Australian court, adopting a broad view, declared the essential characteristics of religion to be: (a) belief in a supreme being and (b) a code of conduct to live in accordance with that belief.[16] However, whilst the English case law would agree with the first limb of belief in a supreme being, it differs in the second limb. English case law stresses worship of that supreme being rather than following a set of rules laid down by that being. The "two essential attributes of religion are faith and worship; faith in a god and worship of that god".[17] Worship is defined as "conduct indicative of reverence or veneration for that supreme being".[18] Worship is not regarded as merely any lawful means for formally observing the tenets of a cult.[19]

10.3.2 Equality of religions

The law holds that all religions are to be treated equally. It will not inquire into the inherent validity of any particular religion nor will it examine the relative merits of different religions.[20] As has been said:

> "... although this court might consider the opinions sought to be propagated foolish or even devoid of foundation, it would not, on that account declare it void."[21]

Again, in *R. v. Registrar General ex parte Segerdal*,[22] it was held that Buddhism was a religion even though it lacked a belief in a supreme being. The judicial view is that for a religion to be charitable it must be founded on a

---

[16] *Church of the New Faith v. Commissioner for Pay Roll Tax* (1983) 49 A.L.R. 65.
[17] *Re South Place Ethical Society, Barralet v. Attorney General* [1980] 3 All E.R. 918 at 924.
[18] *Application for Registration as a Charity by the Church of Scientology (England and Wales)*, Charity Commission Decision, November 17, 1999 at p. 24.
[19] *Fellowship of Humanity v. County of Almeda* 153 Cal. App. 2d673 (1957), formally rejected in the *Church of Scientology* Case *op. cit.*
[20] See *Thornton v. Howe* (1862), 31 Beav 14.
[21] *ibid.* at p. 20.
[22] [1970] 2 Q.B. 697.

belief in and reverence for a god or gods. Hinduism,[23] Islam and Judaism present few problems in theoretical terms. Buddhism presents no practical problems, but there are theoretical difficulties in that it covers a very wide spectrum of belief, from those who have a great deal in common with other religions to some who are more like the Masons than a religion, to hard-line Zen Buddhists who would firmly deny the existence of any sort of deity in the generally accepted sense.

The courts in Northern Ireland, in *Re Stewart's Will Trusts*,[24] had cause to consider a gift to Non-Subscribing Presbyterians some of whom may have been Unitarians. Although Unitarians would not profess to have a monolithic belief structure, in broad terms they believe that Jesus Christ was a man, there is no Trinity and no such place as hell. There had been some historic doubt as to whether gifts to Unitarians could be valid, much less charitable. Murray J. confirmed the equality of religious belief in *Re Stewart*. He cited the English case of *Shore v. Wilson*[25] as authority for the proposition that:

> "... it was recognised that by 1830 there could be a valid charitable trust for persons who held Unitarian beliefs."[26]

Recently, in line with a progressive and evolving approach to religion, faith healing has been deemed to be charitable where it was open to members of the public.[27] The broad principle was expressed by Walker L.C. in the Irish case of *O'Hanlon v. Logue*[28]:

> "... a gift for the advancement of 'religion' is a charitable gift; and that in applying this principle, the Court does not enter into an inquiry as to the truth or soundness of any religious doctrine, provided it be not contrary to morals or contain nothing contrary to law. All religions are equal in the eyes of the law... . Whether the subject of the gift be religious or for an educational purpose, the Court does not set up its own opinion. It is enough that it is not illegal, or contrary to public policy, or opposed to the settled principles of morality."

However, historically there has been some uncertainty regarding gifts for Roman Catholic purposes in Ireland. This was due to various statutes suppressing Catholicism[29] and the results can be seen in the cases considering gifts for masses and gifts to Roman Catholic bodies.

---

[23] See for example, *Trustees of the Indian Community Centre v. Commissioner of Valuation* VR/6/1988.

[24] (1983) 11 N.I.J.B.

[25] (1842) 8 E.R. 450.

[26] *Re Stewart, op cit.* at p. 12.

[27] *Funnell v. Stewart* [1996] 1 W.L.R. 288.

[28] [1906] 1 IR 247 at 259–260.

[29] See the effect of the Roman Catholic Relief Act 1829 and s 15 of the Charitable Donations and Bequests (Irl) Act 1844. See also, Brady, J., *Religion and the Law of Charities in Ireland*, 1976.

Although all religions are treated equally,[30] if a belief system has not been accredited with the status of a religion, it will attract adverse discrimination. The Church of Scientology was refused charitable status by the Charity Commission because its core practices of training and auditing (counselling) did not constitute worship of a supreme being.[31] This was the decision even though that body had already been deemed charitable in the USA and in Australia.[32]

10.3.3 Specific religion

A gift may be charitable even if it has been restricted to one specified religion. In *Copinger v. Crehane*[33] a gift "for the advancement and benefit of the Roman Catholic religion" was upheld as charitable. In *Re Bonnet dec'd.; Johnston v. Langheld*[34] the issue was whether the general charitable intention prompting a gift to the Lutheran Church should be interpreted as a gift to the Lutheran Church or to protestant churches in general. As the testator had been a member of the Lutheran Church the court held that it had been her intention to confer a benefit on that body. The reverse proposition is also true. If a gift is clearly stated and intended to go to a religious institution, the fact that the institution has not been named will not invalidate its charitable nature. As has been stated:

> "... a bequest to a religious institution, or for a religious purpose, is *prima facie* a bequest for a 'charitable' purpose, and that the law applicable to 'charitable' bequests, as distinguished from the law applicable to ordinary bequests, ought to be applied to a bequest to a religious institution, or for a religious purpose."[35]

If the gift deliberately discriminates against particular religions it may still be charitable as was demonstrated in *Re Lysaght; Hill v. Royal College of Surgeons of England*.[36] This case concerned a trust to establish a medical scholarship unavailable to both Roman Catholics and Jews. In explaining his decision to uphold the charitable status of the trust, Buckley L.J. said:

> "I accept that racial and religious discrimination is nowadays widely accepted as deplorable ... but I think that it is going much too far to say that the endowment of a charity, the beneficiaries of which are to be drawn from a particular faith or to exclude adherence to a particular faith is contrary to public policy. The testatrix's desire to exclude persons of the Jewish faith or of the Roman

---

[30] But see further consideration of this point in the human rights context, Chap. 4.

[31] *Application for Registration as a Charity by the Church of Scientology (England and Wales)*, Charity Commission Decision, November 17, 1999 at p. 24.

[32] *Church of the New Faith v. Commissioner for Pay Roll Tax* (1983) 49 A.L.R. 65.

[33] (1877) L.R. 11 Eq. 429.

[34] [1983] I.L.R.M. 359.

[35] See *Re White* [1893] 2 Ch. 41 at p. 52. Quoted with approval by Lord Hanworth M.R. in *Re Bain, Public Trustee v. Ross* [1930] 1 Ch. 224 at p. 231.

[36] [1966] Ch. 191, [1965] 2 All E.R. 888.

> Catholic faith from those eligible for the studentship in the present case appears to me to be unamiable, and ... undesirable, but it is not, I think, contrary to public policy."[37]

In Northern Ireland, by far the majority of donations and bequests made under this *Pemsel* head are restricted to furthering the purposes of a specified religion. In at least 90 per cent of instances a donor will have directed that their bequest is to benefit the Roman Catholic Church or a specified branch of a protestant church; a pattern firmly established for many generations. This homogenous use of bequests is different from that prevailing elsewhere in the United Kingdom where there is a greater spread of bequests among Christian and non-Christian religions.

10.3.4 Advancement of religion

A religious charity must not only be so constituted as to satisfy the legal definition of religion, including having objects or purposes of a religious nature, but its activities must also advance religion. It is not sufficient that a body adheres to religious purposes it must actively promote or advance the spiritual teachings or doctrines of that religion.

Advancement of religion is most clearly demonstrated in proselytising work. Spreading the gospel is charitable[38] as is spreading Christian principles.[39] The *Pemsel* case concerned the spreading of the tenets of the Moravian faith amongst heathens. A trust to 'advance the Christian gospel by spreading its message and to sustain and increase religious belief among service men and their families' is charitable.[40] A very liberal approach was adopted in Northern Ireland on this point. A trust which was meant, in a Christian context, to "stimulate the spiritual and cultural life of the church and the whole community, to promote radical thought and forward looking ideas in all aspects of life" was deemed charitable.[41]

In *Keren Kayemeth Le Jisroel, Ltd v. Inland Revenue Commissioners*[42] the advancement of religion arose for consideration in relation to a company which had been established with the primary object of acquiring land in the Holy Land for the purpose of enabling the settlement of Jews. The company argued that these objects could be regarded as advancing the Jewish religion because they would have enabled communities of Jews to be established. Lord Hanworth M.R. disagreed and explained:

---

[37] [1966] Ch. 191 at 206.
[38] *Re Lea* (1887) 34 Ch. D. 528.
[39] *Re Hood* [1931] 1 Ch. 240.
[40] *Sandes Soldiers' and Airmen's Homes v. Commissioner of Valuation* VR/7/1979.
[41] *Corrymeela Community v. Commissioner of Valuation* VR/1/1967 at 13.
[42] [1931] 2 K.B. 465; 100 L.J.K.B. 596; 145 L.T. 320; 47 T.L.R. 461; *affirmed* [1932] A.C. 650.

"... the promotion of religion means the promotion of the spiritual teaching in a wide sense, and the maintenance of the doctrines on which it rests, and the observance that serve to promote and manifest it."[43]

In *United Grand Lodge of Free and Accepted Masons of England and Wales v. Holborn Borough Council*[44] Donovan J considered whether the activities of freemasons could be said to advance religion. In concluding that they did not he reasoned:

"To advance religion means to promote it, to spread the message ever wider among mankind; to take some positive steps to sustain and increase religious belief; and these things are done in a variety of ways which may be comprehensively described as pastoral and missionary."[45]

Although freemasonry required its members to have faith in God and a belief in good works it did not advance or promote any particular religious beliefs and therefore was not itself a religious charity. They may have carried out good works, but they did not advance religion, "for a man may persuade his neighbour by example to lead a good life without at the same time leading him to religion".[46]

The Northern Ireland case of *Knights of Columbanus*[47] expanded and developed the rule that a religious charity needs to actually advance religious belief. The lay Roman Catholic order in that case were found to have three main objects. The first was to promote good works, *i.e.* practical assistance to the needy. The second was to sustain their own faith. The third was to become leaders in the lay community with a view to extending the influence of the order. The Lands Tribunal held that whilst the first and third objects may have been religious ones, they did not actually advance religion. With regards to the first object, the Tribunal Member, Curry held that "it does not follow that their setting of an example amounted to an advancing of religion".[48] With regards to the third object, "the promotion of faith must be regarded as an indirect result rather than a direct objective".[49]

10.4 Religious purposes

A gift expressed to be for "religious purposes" will normally be upheld as charitable. The Court of Appeal has ruled that:

---

[43] [1931] 2 K.B. 465 at 477.
[44] [1957] 1 W.L.R 1080; 121 J.P. 595; 101 S.J. 851; [1957] 3 All E.R. 281.
[45] [1957] 3 All E.R. 281 at 285.
[46] *ibid.*
[47] *Order of the Knights of St. Columbanus v. Commissioner of Valuation* VR/3/1996, (1997) 8 *Property Law Journal* p. 29.
[48] *ibid.* at p. 39
[49] *ibid.* at p. 39.

> "a bequest to a religious institution, or for a religious purpose, is prima facie a bequest for charitable purposes".[50]

Problems have arisen when the precise words "religious purposes" are not used. Even though such gifts may have a religious dimension, they are not necessarily charitable. Many gifts are deemed not charitable because they contain a mixture of charitable and non-charitable purposes. The narrowness of the meaning given to "religious purposes" can be contrasted with the breadth of meaning given to ancillary religious purposes. These purposes are not directly religious, but serve to promote and facilitate religious purposes. Finally, in this section, there is consideration of purposes which purport to be religious.

10.4.1 Mixture of charitable and non-charitable religious purposes

There have been numerous cases where trusts have failed due to their containing a mix of both charitable and other purposes. The basic rule was set out by Sir William Grant nearly two centuries ago, "the question is not whether the trustee may not apply it upon purposes strictly charitable, but whether he is bound so to apply it".[51] Where the gift is directed towards purposes which are all of a religious nature, the law has no difficulty in recognising it as wholly charitable. If a gift is expressed to be for both "charitable" and "religious" purposes, it will again be deemed charitable.[52]

The difficulty arises where the terms of the gift allow for the possibility that a non-charitable purpose might be exercised in accordance with those terms. Not every gift with a religious dimension is to be regarded as exclusively religious in the charitable sense. This is the meaning to be ascribed to the dictum of Fitzgibbon L.J. when he said that "every religious purpose is not necessarily charitable".[53] The case law in this field draws many points of semantic distinction. In *MacLaughlin* v. *Campbell*[54] there was a gift for "such Roman Catholic purposes in the parish of Coleraine and elsewhere as [my trustees] deem fit and proper". The gift was void as the court held there were Roman Catholic purposes which were not necessarily charitable. The Court of Appeal ruled that the gift would have a better chance of success if it had been expressed as being for the Roman Catholic Church. A gift for church purposes has been held charitable.[55]

---

[50] *Re White* (1893) 2 Ch. 41 at p. 52.
[51] *Morice v. Bishop of Durham* (1805) 9 Ves. 399.
[52] *Re Salter* (1911) 1 I.R. 289, but if a gift is expressed to be for "charitable, religious <u>or</u> other societies, institutions, persons or objects" it will fail *Re Davidson* [1909] 1 Ch. 567 (my emphasis).
[53] *MacLaughlin v. Campbell* [1906] 1 I.R. 588 at p. 597.
[54] *op. cit.*
[55] *Re Bain* [1930] 1 Ch. 224.

The leading case on this point is the decision of the House of Lords in *Farley* v. *Westminster Bank*[56] which concerned a trust for "parish work". The court held these words too large to be charitable, "parish work seems to me to be of such vague import as to go far beyond the ordinary meaning of charity, in this case in the sense of being a religious charity".[57] The gift therefore had to be void, following the ruling of Chatterton V.-C. in *Copinger v. Crehane* that "where there is discretion to apply it to charitable or to other purposes not charitable, and the trust is indefinite, the gift fails".[58]

Farley was followed in Northern Ireland in *Trustees of Cookstown Roman Catholic Church v. Commissioners of Inland Revenue*[59] which concerned a gift for "religious, educational and other parochial requirements". Sheil J. held that "if the words 'and other parochial' had been omitted from the trust it seems to me that it could successfully be maintained that the uses are charitable".[60] Parochial purposes are not charitable. However, courts have construed "parish gifts" as charitable by regarding them as "for the benefit of the parish for ecclesiastical purposes".[61]

A gift for the religious purposes of a convent will be charitable.[62] A gift for purposes "most conducive to the good of religion in this diocese" is not a gift for charitable religious purposes.[63]

The possibility remains of a whole trust failing to acquire charitable status because a part of it addresses, or allows for the possibility that it might address, a non-charitable purpose.

10.4.2 Ancillary religious purposes

A gift may be made not to a particular religious body but in support of a specified service or enterprise. The purpose must then be to advance religion and be clearly identified, but it need not be useful. In *Re Watson*[64] a gift to publish and disseminate certain religious works, which the court held to be of no intrinsic merit, was held to be charitable.

Bringing worshippers to church services is not directly religious, but it is a valid ancillary purpose, "the activity of transporting worshippers by bus to participate in church services is a purpose which directly facilitates the ad-

---

[56] *Farley v. Westminster Bank* (1939) A.C. 430.

[57] *ibid. per* Lord Atkin at p. 435.

[58] *Copinger v. Crehane* (1877) L.R. 11 Eq. 429 at 431, see also *Morice v. Bishop of Durham op. cit.*

[59] *Trustees of Cookstown Roman Catholic Church v. Commissioners of Inland Revenue* (1953) 34 T.C. 350.

[60] *ibid.* at p. 353.

[61] *Re Garrard* [1907] 1 Ch. 382.

[62] *Re Rickard, Harbison v. Meany* [1954] N.I. 100.

[63] *Dunne v. Byrne* [1912] A.C. 407.

[64] [1973] 1 W.L.R. 1472; 117 S.J. 792; [1973] 3 All E.R. 678.

vancement of religion".[65] Repairing such a fleet of buses to allow them to be used for the above purpose is too remote a use and is not charitable.[66] Providing meals and a social centre within which evangelism could be practised is "a discrete and sympathetic method of propagating the gospel".[67] Recreation can sometimes be construed as being ancillary to religion, see further below.

10.4.3 Purposes purporting to be religious purposes

It has proved difficult to draw a firm line discriminating between *bona fide* religious groups and fringe cults; a problem well illustrated by the case of the 'Moonies'. In July 1989 a group of witches in the US were accepted as constituting a *bona fide* religious group and therefore satisfied the legal definition of charitable status. Such groups have not yet sought charitable status in this jurisdiction.

Where a body is clearly not pursuing religious principles, perhaps explicitly promoting an atheist philosophy, the court will be obliged to hold that a gift to it cannot be for the advancement of religion and will deny it charitable status.[68] The court will treat with scepticism any claim from a society, cult or body which has a political agenda that it, or gifts to it, should attract charitable status.[69] In *R. v. Registrar General, ex parte Segerdal and Another*,[70] for example, the court considered a claim from the Church of Scientology that a chapel used by the Church should be exempt from rates on the grounds that it was a place of worship. Buckley L.J. examined the nature of the worship practised by the Church and rejected the claim with the explanation:

> "Worship I take to be something which must have some at least of the following characteristics: submission to the object worshipped, veneration of that object, praise, thanksgiving, prayer or intercession."

The Court of Appeal ruled that scientology was not a religion within the meaning of the Places of Worship Registration Act 1855. More recently, the Charity Commission has ruled that the Church of Scientology is not a charity.[71]

---

[65] *James McConnell and Trustees of the Metropolitan Church v. Commissioner of Valuation* VR/5/1988 at p. 13.

[66] *ibid.*

[67] *Sandes Soldiers' and Airmen's Home v. Commissioner of Valuation* VR/7/1979 at p. 8.

[68] *Bowman v. Secular Society* [1917] A.C. 406.

[69] For interesting American cases where the court examined the constituent characteristics of a religion, see *Malnak v. Yogi* 592 F. 2d 197 (1979); *Fellowship of Humanity v. County of Alameda* 153 Cal. App. 2d673 (1957); see also, *Re South Place Ethical Society* [1980] 1 W.L.R. 1565.

[70] [1970] 2 Q.B. 697; [1970] 3 W.L.R. 479; 114 S.J. 703; [1970] 3 All E.R. 886, C.A.

[71] *Church of Scientology op. cit.* It has also reviewed and removed the charitable status awarded to bodies such as the Pagan Federation and the Pagan Hospice and Funeral Trust on the grounds that paganism does not constitute a religion in the charitable sense; see, further, Harlow, J., "Pagans Stripped of Charity Status", *Sunday Times*, October 1, 1999.

10.5 THE PUBLIC BENEFIT TEST

The law in respect of the charitable status of religious bodies is somewhat different in the two jurisdictions on this island. In Northern Ireland, as in the rest of the U.K., such a religious body must have a demonstrable element of public benefit if it is to qualify for charity status. In the Republic of Ireland there is a statutory presumption[72] that a religious body is inherently of public benefit. So, whereas in the latter jurisdiction gifts to such bodies are automatically recognised as charitable, in the former this must be proven in the normal way.

There are three aspects of the public benefit test, as it applies to charities for the advancement of religion, which have traditionally presented most problems. Firstly, because donors invariably single out a particular religion as recipient, a question can arise as to whether such "positive discrimination" is in breach of the "public" aspect of the rule. Secondly, as the religion selected by the donor is invariably the one to which he or she belongs, this raises the possibility that the gift is in fact private rather than public. Thirdly, and controversially, it could be argued that because religious activity is essentially spiritual being based on functions of worship and the upholding of doctrines, any gift to advance religion is liable to fail the 'benefit' aspect of the test as it will be very difficult to identify the necessary public utility component.

10.5.1 The test

As with poverty, the public benefit test is relatively easy for religious charities. The decision in *Re Hetherington, Gibbs v. McDonnell*[73] provides authority for the view that all gifts for religious purposes are charitable and satisfy the public benefit test. In *Re White*[74] the court found valid an extremely vague gift "to the following religious societies *viz*. _____". No religious societies had been named by the testator, but the English Court of Appeal was able to assume that the various hurdles had been overcome. It concluded that:

> "... a bequest to a religious institution, or for a religious purpose, is *prima facie* a bequest for a 'charitable' purpose, and that the law applicable to 'charitable' bequests, as distinguished from the law applicable to ordinary bequests, ought to be applied to a bequest to a religious institution, or for a religious purpose."

The courts will assume the first limb in practically all religious gifts except those to contemplative religious orders and masses (see further, below). The nature of this benefit is twofold. Firstly, there is a direct benefit to the individual believers of that religion who enjoy the fruits of the particular gift.

---

[72] s. 45 of the Charities Act 1961.
[73] [1989] 2 All E.R. 129.
[74] [1893] 2 Ch. 41.

Secondly, there is the edifying effect of the gift on the public at large. The only difficulty arises under this limb of the public benefit test when gifts for enclosed, contemplative religious orders and gift for the saying of masses in private are considered.

The second limb of the public benefit test is also easily satisfied. Members of a religion are a sufficient section of the public. For example, the Plymouth Brethren were held to be a section of the public in *Holmes* v. *Attorney General*.[75] Indeed, it would be illogical to rule that advancing religion is charitable, but that in advancing it amongst its adherents, there is no public benefit. This would automatically deny status to some of the large, non-proselytising religions such as Judaism. The courts have also ruled that members of a particular religion in a certain area satisfy the public benefit test, for example, Roman Catholics in Cookstown.[76] Members of the armed forces serving at a particular barracks in Northern Ireland, together with their families and RUC personnel have also been deemed to be a section of the public for religious purposes.[77]

10.6 TYPES OF GIFT

A gift for the advancement of religion has traditionally taken one of several judicially accepted forms. These can be listed as gifts for the saying of masses, for the benefit of religious orders, for ministers, for the construction or refurbishment of churches, for the maintenance of tombs and gifts to ecclesiastic offices.

10.6.1 Gifts for the holding of religious services

The law relating to gifts intended to facilitate the holding of religious services, most usually the saying of masses, has had a long and troubled history in this jurisdiction.

10.6.1(i) Prohibition on chantries

A chantry is an endowment or chapel for the saying of Catholic masses for the repose of the soul of the dead. The Statute of Chantries[78] stated that such a mass was illegal because it fostered a superstitious belief in purgatory. In England, until 1919, gifts for chantries were not only non-charitable but were also

---

[75] *Holmes v. Attorney General* (1981) C.L.Y. 222.
[76] *Trustees of the Cookstown Roman Catholic Church v. Commissioners of Inland Revenue* (1953) 34 T.C. 350.
[77] *Sandes Soldiers' and Airmen's Home v. Commissioner of Valuation* VR/7/1979.
[78] Also termed the Statute of Superstitious Uses 1547 1 Edw. VI Cap. 14.

void. In that year the decision in *Bourne* v. *King*[79] held that chantries were not illegal and that gifts for them could be valid (although not necessarily charitable).

In Ireland the Statute of Chantries never applied. According to V.T.H. Delany there was:

"... nothing in the law or policy of the law in this country to interfere with the disposition of property for any purpose connected with the worship of the Roman Catholic religion."[80]

There has never been a case in Northern Ireland on the validity of gifts for chantries. It is unlikely that the law would find sufficient reason for determining that these were not valid charitable gifts.

10.6.1(ii) Public benefit in religious services – English case law

The objection to religious services being charitable has coalesced around the issue of religious services being held in private. This is because "the celebration of a religious rite in public does confer a sufficient public benefit because of the edifying and improving effect on members of the public who do attend".[81] If a religious rite is held in private, there is no public benefit. *Re Caus*[82] is authority for the view that such gifts will be charitable because they provide financial support for priests. As Luxmore J. then explained the public benefit test is satisfied on two grounds:

"... first, that it enables a ritual act to be performed which is recognised by a large proportion of Christian people to be the central act of their religion, and secondly, because it assists in the endowment of priests whose duty it is to perform that ritual act."[83]

Following the decision in *Cocks* v. *Manners*[84] and *Gilmour* v. *Coats*,[85] intercessory prayers in private are not charitable. Therefore a religious service from which the public are excluded is not charitable. It is now held to be charitable to have masses said, on the basis that it is edifying for the public to witness the procedure, not because of any supposed inherent value in the ceremony. To qualify for charitable status, therefore, the masses must be said in public.

Re Hetherington[86] went a long way towards saving gifts for masses which ran the risk of being contrary to the public benefit test. Browne-Wilkinson V.-

---

[79] *Bourne v. King* [1919] A.C. 815.
[80] Delany, V.T.H., (1956) at p. 58.
[81] *Re Hetherington, Gibbs v. McDonnell* (1989) 2 All E.R. 129 at p. 135.
[82] [1934] Ch. 162.
[83] *Ibid., per* Luxmore J. at p.170.
[84] (1871) 12 Eq. 574
[85] [1949] A.C. 246.
[86] *Re Hetherington, Gibbs v. McDonnell* (1989) 2 All E.R. 129.

C. assumed that a gift for masses would be charitable on the basis of support to priests and also that it would be heard in public. If the gift was silent as to the public/private point then it would be saved as "the gift is to be construed as a gift to be carried out only by the methods that are charitable, all non-charitable methods being excluded".[87]

10.6.1(iii) Irish case law

The Irish courts have, as might be expected, taken a different and more positive approach to the edifying effect of prayer and its public benefit. After some false starts,[88] the Irish Court of Appeal delivered the leading case of *O'Hanlon v. Logue*[89] The court held a gift for the 'celebration of masses for the repose of the souls of my late husband, my children and myself' charitable, regardless of whether or not the masses where said in public. The court further held that public benefit depended subjectively on the donor's belief of what was for the public benefit.[90]

10.6.1(iv) Northern Ireland case law

In Northern Ireland there has never been a case which has considered the charitable status of masses. Technically the Irish cases cited above provide the binding authority since they were pre-partition. *Re Hetherington* was only an English High Court decision and so could not overrule *O'Hanlon v. Logue*. However, it is submitted that the courts here would shy away from finding public benefit in a private mass. In line with their general policy, it is likely they would follow the approach of *Hetherington* and assume that masses were to be open to the public and therefore of public benefit, but if that masses were to be in private, the public benefit test would not be satisfied.

J.C. Brady has examined in some detail the application of the decision in *O'Hanlon v. Logue* to the law in Northern Ireland. As he states:

> "In the opinion of many Catholics the stairway from the Northern Ireland Court of Appeal to the House of Lords places bequests for masses in jeopardy unless the bequests are coupled with a direction for public celebration, such public celebration providing the element of public edification of which a court can take cognisance."[91]

---

[87] *Re Hetherington, Gibbs v. Mc Donnell* (1989) 2 All E.R. 129 at 135.

[88] *Attorney-General v. Delaney* (1875) I.R. 10; C.L. 104; 10 I.L.T.R. 34, *Kehoe v. Wilson* (1880) 7 L.R. Ir. 10.

[89] *O'Hanlon v. Logue* [1906] 1 I.R. 246

[90] Further authority for the charitable nature of masses in public or private came in *Re Gibbons, D'Alton v. Gibbons* [1917] 1 I.R. 448.

[91] Brady (1975) at p. 95.

The matter was considered by the Newark Committee[92] with the consensus emerging that there was no need to introduce legislative provisions in order to validate the rule in *O'Hanlon v. Logue*.

Brady concluded that private masses in Northern Ireland would not be held charitable, especially after *Gilmour v. Coates*[93] which "places that principle in jeopardy since their lordships seem firmly wedded to the view that the public efficacy of a trust for religious purposes is a matter for forensic proof".[94] For a full history and discussion of the law in this area see JC Brady, *Religion and the Law of Charities in Ireland*.[95]

10.6.2 Gifts for the benefit of religious orders

Again, as might perhaps be expected, the law in this jurisdiction has had difficulty in developing any consistent principled response to such charitable gifts.

10.6.2(i) Gifts to Roman Catholic orders of men

Gifts to Roman Catholic bodies presented a problem, particularly regarding gifts to religious orders of men. The Roman Catholic Relief Act 1829 stated that it is:

"... expedient to make provision for the gradual suppression and final prohibition of [Jesuits and other orders]."[96]

The Irish Court of Appeal in *MacLaughlin v. Campbell*[97] considered this provision as it applied to the Christian Brother order in Coleraine in pre-partition Ireland. Porter M.R. then held "the law says that a gift to them is void under the Roman Catholic Emancipation Act".[98] The Irish courts considered this law post-partition in *Re Byrne, Shaw v. Attorney General*[99] and held that anti-Catholic statutes had been impliedly repealed by section 5(2) of the Government of Ireland Act 1920[100] which stated that:

"... any existing enactment by which any penalty, disadvantage, or disability is

---

[92] Established in 1956, under chairmanship of Prof. Newark, to examine the law relating to charitable trusts in Northern Ireland.

[93] [1948] 1 All E.R. 521.

[94] Brady (1975) at p. xiv.

[95] Belfast, N.I.L.Q., 1975, chap 5, "Mass Bequests and Public Benefit; a Subjective Criterion". Also, see, by the same author, "Some Problems Touching the Nature of Bequests for Masses in Northern Ireland" (1968) 19 N.I.L.Q. 357 and (1974) 25 N.I.L.Q. 174.

[96] s. 28.

[97] [1906] I I.R. 588.

[98] *ibid.* at p. 593.

[99] [1935] I.R. 782.

[100] A statute of the United Kingdom Parliament.

imposed on account of religious belief or on a member of any religious order as such shall as from the appointed day, cease to have effect in Ireland."

No case has been reported in Northern Ireland on this point, but it is submitted that the courts here would follow the lead of *Re Byrne* in its interpretation of section 5(2). None of the cases concerning gifts to Roman Catholics in Northern Ireland have raised any issues regarding the legal status of that religion.

10.6.2(ii) English case law

In general terms, following the decision in *Re White*,[101] gifts for religious orders are charitable. However, this assumption is rebutted in the case of enclosed or cloistered religious orders since they fail the public benefit test. In *Cocks v. Manners*[102] Sir Wickens V.-C. held that the Dominican Convent, a contemplative order of nuns, was not charitable and explained:

> "A voluntary association of women for the purpose of working out their own salvation by religious exercises and self-denial seems to me to have none of the requisites of a charitable institution, whether the word 'charitable' is used in its popular sense or in its legal sense. It is said, in some of the cases, that religious purposes are charitable, but that can only be true as to religious services tending directly or indirectly towards the instruction or edification of the public; an annuity to an individual, so long as he spent his time in retirement and constant devotion, would not be charitable, nor would a gift to ten persons, so long as they lived together in retirement and performed acts of devotion, be charitable."[103]

This was very similar to the approach adopted in other rulings in that jurisdiction. For example, Rigby L.J. held that the Dominican Convent was not charitable as it abstained "even from good works as regards the outside public".[104] Then there was the ruling of Farwell J. who observed that there was no charity in attempting to save one's soul because charity, that is charity in law, was necessarily altruistic.[105]

Where a gift was made to, or for the use of, a closed contemplative religious order the court had been accustomed to finding that the public benefit requirement for charitable status was absent on the ground that private piety in a priory does not tend, directly or indirectly, to edify the public. In *Gilmour v. Coats*[106] the House of Lords placed their seal on this traditional interpretation,

---

[101] *op. cit.*

[102] [1871] 12 Eq. 574.

[103] *ibid.*, at p 585. See further, Wylie, J.C.W., *A Casebook on Equity & Trusts in Ireland* (2nd ed., Butterworths, Dublin, 1998) at pp. 908-917.

[104] See *Re Macduff; Macduff v. Macduff* [1896] 2 Ch. 451 at p. 474.

[105] See *Re Delany: Conoley v. Quick* [1902] 2 Ch. 642 at p. 648.

[106] [1949] AC 426. The point of departure can be traced to the ruling in *Cocks v. Manners* 12 E.Q. 574 as reinforced by *Dunne v. Byrne* [1912] A.C. 407.

applied an objective test and ruled that a gift to a Carmelite priory was not charitable because of an absence of the requisite public benefit. A variety of arguments were put forward and rebutted as to why the Priory was for the public benefit: intercessory prayers could not be legally proved as benefiting the public, the edification of the public by example of the nuns was too vague to be a public benefit, the fact that any woman could join the order was also not sufficient to constitute a public benefit.

10.6.2(iii) Irish case law

A significantly different approach has been developed by the Irish courts since partition. In *Munster and Leinster Bank v. Attorney General*[107] the court considered one of the arguments subsequently rejected in *Gilmour*, "example is sometimes better than precept, and the pattern of the self-sacrificing life may impress more than an indifferent sermon".[108] In *Re Howley*[109] the court, comparing the differences in society between Ireland and England, was of the view that:

> "... the assumption that the Irish public finds no edification in cloistered lives devoted to purely spiritual ends postulates a close assimilation of the Irish outlook to the English, not obviously warranted by the traditions and mores of the Irish people."[110]

10.6.2(iv) Northern Ireland case law

The leading case in this jurisdiction was a Court of Appeal decision on an application for rates exemption by two religious orders, *Commissioner of Valuation v. Trustees of the Redemptorist Order, Commissioner of Valuation v. Trustees of the Newry Christian Brothers*[111] (the *Redemptorist* case). The Redemptorist buildings were attached to Clonard monastery and used as a residence by priests and brothers who performed religious services both in the church and in the wider community. There was a considerable element of personal sanctification in their work, as part of their mission was to imitate Christ. The Christian Brothers' buildings were used as a residence for brothers who taught at a school. Once again there was an element of self-sanctification in the work of the order.

---

[107] [1940]) I.R. 19.

[108] *Munster, op. cit.* at p. 30, see also *Maguire v. Attorney General* (1943) I.R. 238 and s. 45(1) of the Charities Act 1961 "in determining whether or not a gift for the purpose of the advancement of religion is a valid charitable gift it shall be conclusively presumed that the purpose includes and will occasion public benefit".

[109] [1940] I.R. 109.

[110] *ibid.* at p. 113, see also *Attorney General v. Maguire, op cit.*

[111] *Commissioner of Valuation v. Trustees of the Redemptorist Order, Commissioner of Valuation v. Trustees of the Newry Christian Brothers* [1971] N.I. 114.

Lord MacDermott L.C.J. gave the leading judgement in the *Redemptorist* case. He did not separate out the public benefit issue and the exclusively charitable issue, but amalgamated them. He held that self-sanctification would not render the orders non-charitable. He went further and held that self-sanctification and shared living would assist the purpose of the orders. In the case of the Redemptorists, "bringing the gospel to the public by preaching or otherwise, can only gain by the spiritual quality of its messengers".[112] In the case of the Christian Brothers, "the communal life serves the educational purposes of the Order by strengthening and maintaining the religious basis for the teaching undertaken by the Order".[113] This was followed by the Lands Tribunal where Harrison QC, the President, held that the conventual life of nuns "can properly be regarded as renewing and deepening the spiritual resolution of the Little Sisters to carry on the work to which they have dedicated their lives".[114]

Lowry J. gave a concurring judgment in the *Redemptorist* case which, although not as progressive and liberal as that of his colleague, did continue the broad policy of generous treatment of religions. His concern was that the element of self-sanctification was not for public benefit and therefore the order was not established for exclusively charitable purposes. One possible solution was suggested by the Irish case of *Munster Bank* that self-sanctification was not the purpose of the orders, but merely a motive for their charitable work; the "so called primary object should not be treated as an object at all, but merely an ulterior motive".[115] But Lowry J rejected this solution as disingenuous, both the self-sanctification and charitable works were the professed purposes of the orders. He held instead both that the self-sanctification element was ancillary to the charitable purposes and that it was wholly coincident with them – "its significance cannot be viewed separately from the purpose of preparing the occupants for their work".[116]

The dissenting judge, Curran L.J. found the case too closely aligned with the facts of *Cocks* and *Gilmour*. He held that self-sanctification was not an ancillary aim and consequently there was no public benefit. He referred to another English case, "there is in truth, no 'charity' in attempting to save one's own soul. Charity is necessarily altruistic and involves the idea of aid or benefit to others".[117]

It may be argued that the sole aim of religion is the saving of souls, whether this involves the soul of the individual, the body of believers or the entire community. Supporting ministers, building churches, promoting public worship are all ultimately subservient to the end goal of salvation. The require-

---

[112] *Redemptorist, op cit.* at p. 138.
[113] *ibid.* at p. 132.
[114] *Congregation of the Little Sisters of the Assumption v. Commissioner of Valuation* VR/ 72/1967 at p. 6.
[115] *Munster Bank, op cit.* at p. 37.
[116] *Redemptorists, op cit.* at p. 170.
[117] *Re Delany* [1902] 2 Ch. D. 642 at p. 648.

ment of public benefit is in a way obfuscatory. This was alluded to by the court in *Gilmour* where the question was raised – how can prayers be legally proved to benefit the public? It may also be argued that religion gives rise to tangible and temporal benefits by raising moral standards and promoting good citizenship. In brief, it can be said that the courts have failed to face up to the full logic of their position on the advancement of religion. Sometimes they even deny it – "[the court] cannot, in my opinion derive the element of public benefit from the efficacy spiritual or temporal which, according to the faith of the testatrix, the religious act may possess".[118]

Lowry J.'s judgement is perceptive because he recognised the integral and inseparable element of self-sanctification in the work of all religious orders. This element would not of itself render a religious order non-charitable – "their use of the hereditaments is not rendered less charitable by the fact that the aim of the Orders, as well of the individuals is the personal sanctification of the members".[119]

The *Redemptorist* case was followed in *Trustees of the Congregation of the Poor Clares of the Immaculate Conception v. Commissioner of Valuation.*[120] Similarly to the *Redemptorist* case, it was a claim to exemption from rating by a religious order on the basis that their occupation of the convent was for exclusively charitable purposes. The order was an enclosed order, but it did carry out some "good works" in the outside community. The Court of Appeal held that it was not exempt because it failed the public benefit test, "the undoubted user of the convent for religious purposes lacked the public element essential to make that user charitable".[121] The court seemed to find that the external side of their work was not sufficient to make the self-sanctification side ancillary. The court also seemed to contradict the *Redemptorist* approach by not holding that the shared religious life increased the quality of their religious and community work outside the convent. The case is perhaps rationalised by looking at the degree of the external work carried out. The order of Poor Clares was bound by vows of poverty, chastity and obedience. The educational and poverty relief aspects were not sufficiently prominent to warrant public benefit being found. McVeigh L.J. described them as having a

---

[118] *Attorney General v. Delany* (1875) Ir. R. 10 C.L. 104 at p. 129.

[119] *Redemptorist, op. cit.* at p. 170, this view was reiterated by the Lands Tribunal, "the motive of each individual Little Sister in dedicating her life to the service of the sick poor involves the hope of personal sanctification through such service", *Congregation of the Little Sisters of the Assumption v. Commissioner of Valuation* VR/72/1967 at p. 6.

[120] *Trustees of the Congregation of Poor Clares of the Immaculate Conception v. Commissioner of Valuation* [1971] N.I. 174, see also *McLaughlin and Cosgrave v. Commissioner of Valuation* [1937] N.I. 174 and *Re Rickard* [1954] N.I. 100 which both held that a Sisters of Mercy convent whose purposes were not merely contemplative and who visited the sick, taught and gave aid to the poor was charitable.

[121] *Poor Clares, op cit.* at p. 176.

"fundamental religious life and discipline of a congregation of persons bound to live together, with limited access to the outside world, and dedicated by religious vows to the consecration of their lives"[122] (see., further, Chapter 21).

10.6.3 Gifts for the benefit of ministers

Gifts to ministers are charitable as being for the advancement of religion. For example, in *Re Foster*,[123] Bennet J. upheld a bequest of income to a society whose funds were applicable for the relief of infirm, sick and aged Roman Catholic priests who were members of that society. This he did because the gift indirectly advanced religion by making the ministry more efficient: old and sick clergy would find it easier to retire, thus making room for new blood in the ministry; and clergy could look forward to retirement with security, which would enable them to be more productive while in office. Again, rest homes for members of a religious community[124] and a gift of cottages for retired missionaries[125] have been found to be charitable.

The Court of Appeal in *Baptist Union of Ireland (Northern) Corporation Ltd.* v. *Commissioners of Inland Revenue*[126] gave a very wide latitude to gifts of this type (see also, Chapter 7). Those who were to benefit from the fund in question were: old ministers, incapacitated ministers, widows of ministers and those aged under eighteen who were orphans of ministers. The question in this context was whether the fund could be said to be for the advancement of religion. The court considered payments at varying degrees of remoteness from the religious purposes as stated in the Statute of Charles.

Firstly there were the gifts to active ministers. MacDermott J. held that these were charitable, primarily under the 1634 Statute, but also because:

> "... the maintenance of ministers and teachers of religion as such, has, I think always been charitable since the word acquired a legal meaning."[127]

This was followed in *Re Stewart*[128] which held that a gift to the Sustenation Fund (which provided an income to ministers) of the Non-Subscribing Presbyterian church was charitable.

Next there were gifts to retired ministers. MacDermott J. held that these were charitable for three reasons. Firstly:

> "... such a fund, I think, tends to make the ministry more efficient by making it easy for the sick and old to retire and give place to the young and healthy."[129]

---

[122] *ibid.* at p. 184.
[123] [1939] 1 Ch. 22.
[124] See *Re James* [1932] 2 Ch. 25.
[125] See *Re Macgregor* (1932) 32 S.R.N.S.W. 483.
[126] [1945] N.I. 99.
[127] *Baptist Union, op. cit.* at p. 105.
[128] *Re Stewart's Will Trusts* (1983) 11 N.I.J.B.
[129] Relying on the authority of *Re Forster, Gellatly v. Palmer* [1939] Ch. 22 at 25.

Secondly it would also:

> "… ease the minds of those actively engaged in the ministry to know that there is this fund to be used for their relief when they are overtaken by old age or struck down unexpectedly by sickness."[130]

Thirdly, by substituting the word "minister" for "missionary":

> "… it may well be that a gift providing for 'retired' missionaries may encourage people to take up missionary work."[131]

Finally, although MacDermott J. had been able to find authority for holding the previous two gifts as charitable, there was no authority regarding gifts to the widows and orphans of ministers. Nonetheless, continuing his very broad approach, he found the gift to be charitable by utilising the three reasons cited above, *viz.*: (a) it would make ministers more efficient as they would not have to work to provide money for their families in case they died, (b) it would free their minds from worrying about what would happen to their family if they died, and (c) it would make the ministry more attractive.

The *Baptist Union* case provides a good illustration of judicial flexibility and willingness to interpret gifts to ministers as charitable wherever possible. The final gift was quite remote from the purpose of advancing religion, and the bounty/bargain question was right on the edge of a bargain, yet the court was still able to hold the entire fund charitable. The law is the same in England with regard to active and retired ministers[132] though there seems to be no case on widows/orphans of ministers.

10.6.4 Gifts for religious buildings and their contents

Building and maintaining churches are within the express words of the Statute of Charles. In *Re Currie, McClelland v. Gamble*[133] a gift to the Victoria Hall Building Fund was held to be charitable. The fund was to provide for a new building in which members of a religious congregation could worship. Maintaining that new building would also be charitable, but the on the terms of the gift, it could not be construed as extending to maintenance of the hall. However, the gift was saved under the *cy-près* rules (see further, Chapter 19).

Re Steele[134] concerned a gift to maintain and repair a Church of Ireland parish church. That portion of the gift was valid though the gift as a whole failed because it had some impracticable conditions. Once again, the gift was saved by *cy-près*.

---

[130] *ibid.*
[131] *Re Mylne, Potter v. Dow* (1941) Ch. 204 at 206.
[132] See both *Re Forster* and *Re Mylne, op. cit.*
[133] [1985] N.I. 299.
[134] *Re Steele, Northern Bank Executor and Trust Company v. Linton* [1976] N.I. 66.

The gift in *Re Dunwoodie*[135] was of a carillon to be installed in the McCracken Memorial Church. The gift itself was charitable, though it was impossible to carry out, since the congregation decided it would be frivolous to spend a considerable amount of money on bells when there were more pressing demands. However, once again the court saved the gift by applying the *cy-près* rule.

Case law provides ample illustrations of the range of gifts, made for the benefit of churches and their fixtures, which have been upheld as charitable. These include gifts for the provision of ornaments in a church,[136] for the erection of a pulpit,[137] for an organ,[138] for the maintenance of a choir,[139] for the construction of an organ gallery,[140] for the repair of a parish churchyard,[141] for the repair of a rectory,[142] to provide stipends for organists[143] and choristers,[144] to repair memorial windows[145] and memorial tablets,[146] and a gift to a church *eo nomine*[147] and to a parish *eo nomine*.[148]

10.6.5 Gifts for the maintenance of tombs

V.T.H. Delany refers to the maintenance and repair of family tombs as "the posthumous gratification of one of the oldest sentiments of the human race".[149] The law makes a distinction between tombs which are physically within and part of the curtilege of a church and those which are set apart as individual private plots; the former acquiring charitable status and the latter not.

Gifts for the upkeep of graves and burial vaults etc, where the facility is an integral part of the fabric of a church, have always been upheld as charitable. Whether the gift was restricted to a particular grave[150] or provided for the maintenance of a whole cemetery,[151] the courts have had no difficulty in recognising the existence of an element of public benefit.

Where the gift is restricted to the upkeep of a specific grave or vault, de-

---

[135] [1977] N.I. 141.

[136] See *Hart v. Brewer* Cro. Eliz. 449.

[137] See *Sir Baptist Hender's Case*, Poph. 139.

[138] See *Attorney-General v. Oakover* (1736) cited: 1 Ves. Sen. 536.

[139] See *Re Palatine Estate Charity* (1888) 39 Ch. D. 54.

[140] See *Adam v. Cole* (1843) 6 Beav. 353.

[141] See *Re Vaughan* (1886) 33 Ch. D. 187.

[142] See *Attorney-General v. The Bishop of Chester* (1785) 1 Bro. C.C. 444.

[143] *Attorney General v. Oakover* (1736) 1 Ves. Sen. 536

[144] *Turner v. Ogden* (1787) 1 Cox. 316.

[145] *Hoare v. Osborne* (1866) L.R. 1 E.Q. 585.

[146] *Re Barker* (1909) 25 T.L.R. 753.

[147] See *Cresswell v. Cresswell* (1868) L.R. 6 Eq. 69.

[148] See *West v. Knight* (1670) 1 Ch. Ca. 134.

[149] Delany, V.T.H. (1956) at p. 44.

[150] See *Re Eighmie* [1935] Ch. 524.

[151] See *Re Vaughan, op. cit.*

tached from the main church buildings, then it will continue to be treated in law as fulfilling a private purpose, being of no public benefit and therefore not charitable.[152] For example, one of the trust conditions in *Re Steele* was for the upkeep of a family burial plot. Murray J then said that it is "well established that a trust for the upkeep of a private grave is not charitable".[153] The reason for this being that there is no benefit to the public in maintaining one grave as opposed to an entire graveyard. *Re Galway*[154] would also have held void a trust for the repair of the testator's grave for the same reason. In England the law similarly disallows charitable status in respect of gifts for the maintenance of family graves.[155] In *Re Pardoe*,[156] however, the court was prepared to admit that a very limited section of the public (pensioners who had lived in certain almshouses) would be sufficient to constitute the public benefit for the repair of graves. In England the law has also extended to include facilities for cremation as being charitable under this head.[157] There is nothing to indicate that that view would not be followed in Northern Ireland.

Delany suggested five ways in which a trust for the maintenance of a family tomb could be enforced. These may be condensed into the following four mechanisms.

10.6.5(i) Repair of tomb ancillary to repair of the church building

If the tomb forms part of the fabric of the church, then there will be a valid charitable trust for the repair of the church and tomb. The two parts of the gift will be indivisible. See for example *Re Manser*[158] and *Re Eighmie*.[159] The trust in *Re Steele* could not take advantage of this method since the grave was outside the church.

10.6.5(ii) Moral obligation only

The words could be construed as precatory, imposing only a moral and not a legal obligation to maintain the tomb (see also, Chapter 3).[160]

---

[152] See *Re Rigley's Trusts* (1866) 36 L.J. Ch. 147; *Toole v. Hamilton* [1901] 1 I.R. 383; and *Re McIntyre* (1930) 64 I.L.T.R. 179.

[153] *Re Steele, op. cit.* at p. 68.

[154] *Re Galway, Roche v. McDermott* (1901) 1 I.R. 394.

[155] For example, *Re Dalziel, op. cit.*

[156] (1906) 2 Ch. 184.

[157] *Scottish Burial Reform and Cremation Society v. Glasgow Corporation* (1968) A.C. 138.

[158] [1905] 1 Ch. 68.

[159] [1935] Ch. 524.

[160] For example *Re Galway, Roche v. McDermott* [1901] 1 I.R. 394.

10.6.5(iii) Double charity condition

This occurs where a gift to one charity is made on condition that the grave of the donor is maintained and in default, the gift goes to another charity. The condition can be enforced because both gifts are to charity, whereas it would otherwise be likely to fail for breaching rules against uncertainty, remoteness and perpetuities.[161] For example, in *Re Tyler*[162] it was held that a non-charitable condition attached to a charitable gift with a gift over to another charity could achieve the desired result. If the first charity failed to maintain the grave, the gift would then fall to the next charity upon the same conditions.

10.6.5(iv) Gift vests within perpetuity period

V.T.H. Delany also suggests that if a gift vests within the perpetuity period it will be valid.[163] In this case it would not be a trust to maintain the grave, since this would be a void purpose trust. It would be an absolute gift subject to the condition that the grave is to be maintained for the perpetuity period.

10.6.6 Gifts for missionary purposes

Religious organisations which send their members overseas to spread their religious beliefs have never had any difficulty in acquiring charitable status. Such work is sufficient in itself to satisfy the test of 'advancing' religion. The fact that most missionary work also entails the provision and maintenance of social care infrastructure is beside the point for the purposes of charitable status under this *Pemsel* head. However, as Cairns has pointed out[164]:

> "... a gift for 'missionary purposes' alone will be void since it may include non-charitable purposes, unless it can be inferred that missionary work in connection with a particular religion was intended."[165]

A gift for "missionary purposes" has been held to be too indefinite and failed.[166] Another Irish case concluded that 'missionary purposes' were not exclusively charitable.[167]

It is charitable to persuade people to convert from one religion to another, or even from one denomination to another within the same religion. Encouraging people to convert from a religion to any non-religious philosophy, however, is not charitable.

---

[161] See further, Chaps 6 and 7.

[162] [1891] 3 Ch. 252.

[163] See further, Chaps 6 and 7.

[164] See Cairns, E., *Charities: Law and Practice* (2nd ed., Sweet & Maxwell, London, 1993) at p. 13.

[165] See *Re Rees*, [1920] 2 Ch. 59.

[166] *Scott v. Brownrigg* 9 L.R. Ir. 246.

[167] *Jackson v. Attorney General* [1917] 1 I.R. 332.

10.6.7 Gifts to ecclesiastic offices

A preliminary question arises as to whether the gift is to an office holder or to the office itself. If it is a gift to a particular office holder for their own personal use, it is unlikely to be charitable. In *Donnellan v. O'Neill*[168] a gift for a cardinal for his own use and benefit was held not to be charitable. If the gift is to the office holder, not personally, but for a purpose, the words attached to the gift must be considered. There can either be gifts with absolute discretion resting with the recipient as to how to distribute, or there can be gifts with some sort of purpose expressly attached to them.

10.6.7(i) Gifts to individuals or offices

If the recipient of the gift is personally named, it is likely to be a gift to an individual. If the recipient is named by reference to their office, it is likely to be a gift to the office. If the gift is expressed to be for an office holder and his successors, it will almost always be construed as a gift to the office. The following have been held to be gifts to an office: gift to the minister for the time being,[169] gift to a minister and his successors,[170] gift to "persons in succession as holders of a particular religious office",[171] residuary gift to the bishop for the time being with remainder to his successors.[172] gift to vicar of Kington for the time being,[173] gift to the Archbishop of Brisbane and his successors[174] and a gift to the Reverend Mother or current superior of a Sisters of Mercy convent.[175]

10.6.7(ii) Absolute discretion to office holder

There are conflicting views on whether gifts to office holders, with absolute discretion to distribute, are exclusively charitable. The Privy Council have stated that:

> "… it is difficult to see on what principle a trust expressed in plain language … can be modified or limited in its scope by reference to the position [archbishop] or character of the trustee."[176]

However, Cozens-Hardy M.R. stated that :

---

[168] (1870) I.R. 5 Eq. 523.
[169] *Attorney General v. Sparks* (1753) Amb. 201.
[170] *Thornber v. Wilson* (1855) 3 Dr. 245.
[171] *Re Davidson, Minty v. Bourne* [1909] 1 Ch. 567 at 569.
[172] *Reddy v. Fitzmaurice* (1952) 86 I.L.T.R. 127.
[173] *Re Garrard* [1907] 1 Ch. 382.
[174] *Dunne v. Byrne* [1912] A.C. 407.
[175] *Re Rickard, Harbison v. Meany* [1954] N.I. 100.
[176] *Dunne v. Byrne* [1912] A.C. 407 at 410.

"... if you find in a will words indicating that a distribution is to be made by persons in succession as holders of a particular religious office, that goes far to establish – and, it may be, goes sufficiently far to establish – the fact the whole gift is charitable."[177]

Thus it would seem that if a gift is with absolute discretion to the office holder, it is charitable. If the gift allows for the possibility of non-charitable use, the fact that it is to an ecclesiastic office holder will not render it charitable. A residuary gift to a bishop was enough to attract charitable status.[178] A gift to a named priest and his successor 'for such purposes in the diocese as he wishes' was held charitable.[179]

The gift is charitable is because the office holder will be taken to distribute the gift in accordance with his office, as explained by Curran J.:

"... an absolute discretion to the Reverend Mother as to how the money is to be expended provided that it is applied to religious purposes for the benefit of the community."[180]

Re Garrard also held that a discretion to a vicar to distribute at his sole discretion was taken as meaning a discretion to distribute within a range of exclusively charitable purposes.[181] However, a gift of £10,000 "to his Holiness ... the Pope ... to use and apply at his sole discretion in the carrying out of his sacred office" failed.[182] And the fact that a priest was a trustee was not sufficient to make a gift charitable in *Mac Laughlin v. Campbell*.[183]

10.6.7(iii) Partial discretion to office holder

If a gift can be distributed among certain purposes, as set out by the donor, it will be considered in precisely the same fashion as any other gift. The fact that the recipient is an ecclesiastic office holder will not make a non-charitable purpose into a charitable one. So, if the possibility exists that the office holder may distribute in a non-charitable way, the gift will fail.[184]

---

[177] *Re Davidson, Minty v. Bourne* [1909] 1 Ch. 567 at 569.
[178] *Reddy v. Fitzmaurice* (1952) 86 I.L.T.R. 127.
[179] *Halpin v. Hannon* (1948) 82 I.L.T.R. 74, see also *Re Flinn* (1948) Ch. 241 and *Re Rumball* (1956) Ch. 105.
[180] *Re Rickard, Harbison v. Meany* [1954] N.I. 100 at 102.
[181] *Re Garrard* [1907] 1 Ch. 382.
[182] *Moore v. Pope Benedict XV* [1919] 1 I.R. 316.
[183] [1906] 1 I.R. 588.
[184] *Doe d. Toone v. Copestake* (1805) 6 East 328, *Re Davidson, Minty v. Bourne* [1909] 1 Ch. 567, *Farley v. Westminster Bank* [1939] A.C. 430, *Dunne v. Byrne* [1912] A.C. 407 and see further 10.4.1, Mixture of Charitable and Non-Charitable Purposes.

10.7 RECREATION

The question of recreation intrudes into religion and education and is now a separate head of charity under the Recreational Charities Act (NI) 1958 (see further, Chapter 14). Recreation within the limited confines of religion is, however, deserving of separate attention.

10.7.1 Recreation in a religious context

In Northern Ireland, the question as to whether recreation provided in a religious context is charitable has arisen in three reported cases.

The first and least important of these cases was *Commissioners of Valuation v. Trustees of Fisherwick Presbyterian Church*[185] which concerned a church hall used by church guild members to play badminton. They played approximately twice a week for six months of the year. Two reasons can be discerned for the decision that the hall was exempt from rating as being charitable under the religious head. Firstly, applying the *de minimis non curat lex* rule,[186] Moore L.C.J. held that "the playing of badminton in this hall forms a minor incident intended to assist the work of this church".[187] The underpinning rationale being that the playing of badminton was so inconsequential in the scheme of things that it could not serve to 'secularise' the church hall. However, the fact that badminton was played a total of 48 times per year on average seems to stretch any reasonable interpretation of a 'trifle' or a 'minor incident'. The second reason, discernible from the judgements of both Moore L.C.J. and Brown J., is that badminton attracts and involves young people in the work of the church. This is a purposive approach which looks towards the reason for an activity. As Brown J. put it, recreation affects young people by "interesting them with the work of the church and tying them, as it were, unofficially to it".[188]

The second case, *Trustees of the Londonderry Presbyterian Church House v. Commissioners of Inland Revenue*[189] was a tax exemption case which concerned buildings held in trust 'for helping in the religious, moral, social and recreative life' of those connected 'with the various Presbyterian Churches in the city of Londonderry'. The Court of Appeal held that the trust was not for exclusively religious purposes and therefore was not exempt from income tax. The court considered the *ratio decidendi* of the *Fisherwick* case. It had open to it the possibility of upholding and following the judicial approach in the latter case and held that the terms of the trust would facilitate the advancement

---

[185] [1927] N.I. 76.
[186] The law does not concern itself with trifles.
[187] *Fisherwick, op cit.* at p. 81.
[188] *ibid.*
[189] [1946] N.I. 178.

of religion by encouraging people to take a more active role in the life of the Presbyterian church. Instead, the court took part in some judicial revisionism, they held that the decision in *Fisherwick* was decided solely on the *de minimis* ground.[190] On that basis they could distinguish it from the present case. Having done so they then chose to follow instead the English cases of *Dunne* v. *Byrne*,[191] *Cocks* v. *Manners*[192] and *Farley* v. *Westminster Bank*.[193] This line of authority focused the issue on the question of 'could the buildings be used for non religious purposes?' as opposed to 'what would be for the advancement of religion?'. Thus, with these slightly shifted parameters, Andrews L.C.J. could say "activities or duties, as for example of a social character which, whilst indirectly furthering a religious purpose, are not directly religious".[194] Babington L.J. held that the trust was not religious as it could be used for non-charitable religious ends. Black J. held that the trust could be conducive to religion without being charitable.

Although this decision was strictly correct on the legal issues, it seems out of step with the broad though implicit policy thrust of the Northern Ireland judiciary, which is to give generous assistance to religious charities.

The third and most important is the *Trustees of the City of Belfast Young Men's Christian Association v. Commissioner of Valuation*[195] (the *YMCA* case). The Court of Appeal there reasserted the purposive approach first posited in a very adumbrated form in *Fisherwick*. The YMCA's trusts were to "endeavour to promote the improvement of the spiritual, mental and social condition of young men and the general extension of Christ's Kingdom". The case sought to claim that the grounds used as sports facilities by the YMCA were exempt from rating as being used for exclusively charitable purposes. The decision was that they were so exempt, except to the extent that they were used by outside bodies. The leading judgement was given by Lord MacDermott L.C.J. who had been one of the counsel involved in the *Fisherwick* case. However, no express reference was made to that case.

All the judgements in *YMCA* were extensive. MacDermott L.C.J. held the trusts charitable under an amalgam of religious, educational and sporting purposes and also under the Recreational Charities Act (NI) 1958. Curran L.J. held it charitable under the head of religion and education, though not under the Act. McVeigh L.J. held it charitable under the religious head and under the Act. In relation to the religion / recreation conjunction, two distinct common threads can be seen weaving through all three judgements. The first thread

---

[190] The court in *Armagh Infirmary, op cit.*, also came to the same decision.

[191] [1912] A.C. 407.

[192] (1871) L.R. 12 Eq. 574.

[193] [1939] A.C. 430.

[194] *op cit.* at p. 185.

[195] *Trustees of the City of Belfast Young Men's Christian Association v. Commissioner of Valuation* [1969] N.I. 3.

concerns the meaning of the phrase "exclusively charitable purposes". MacDermott L.C.J. took a very liberal approach to this phrase, he was able to construe the mental/physical/recreational aspects of the trust as being subordinate to the primary religious purpose. He held that "the paramount purpose of this trust is the advancement of Christ's Kingdom and that all else is intended to be ancillary and incidental to that end".[196]

The second common thread revives in part the discarded reasoning of *Fisherwick*. Recreation by itself can be for the advancement of religion. It attracts young people to join. Furthermore, according to MacDermott L.C.J. "organised recreational facilities tend to promote bodily health and fitness, endurance and self-discipline, and that these qualities are commonly accepted as the allies and adjuncts of wholesome religiosity".[197] The two other judges chose not to express any views on this proposition, content instead to hold that recreation could form a valid ancillary role to religion.

Other Northern Irish cases have recognised the validity of this 'religion in recreation' approach. The Lands Tribunal considered the charitable status of a church hall in which many social/recreative activities such as scouts, bowls, counselling and badminton were carried out. The Tribunal held that:

> "... most of these activities do not have a purely religious character but ... are organised as church activities. The need to provide instructional, recreational and social activities in the atmosphere and under the influence of a religious community has come to be recognised as a method of fostering and encouraging the advancement of religion."[198]

See also, *Sandes Soldiers' and Airmen's Home v. Commissioner of Valuation*[199] which provided social activities in a religious context. A trust which was "to promote the personal improvement of its members spiritually, intellectually, socially and physically and to play an effective part in the Lay Apostolate of Ireland" has also been held charitable.[200]

It would appear that no English case has gone this far in finding charitable the proselytising effects of recreation. The Court of Appeal in *YMCA* was able to reach its conclusion by relying on English cases which state that an exclusively charitable purpose will not be destroyed by ancillary non-charitable purposes. For example *Baddeley* v. *Inland Revenue Commissioners*[201] was cited – "if the dominant purpose of the trust is charitable in character the fact that the recreation is provided as an adjunct to that purpose does not destroy the character of the trust".[202] However, this quote was taken from the dissent-

---

[196] *op cit.* at p. 10.
[197] *op cit.* at p.13.
[198] *Trustees of the Belmont Church v. Commissioner of Valuation* VR/14/1965 at p. 5.
[199] *Sandes Soldiers' and Airmen's Home v. Commissioner of Valuation* VR/7/1979.
[200] *Catholic Young Men's Society v. Commissioner of Valuation* VR/40/1980.
[201] [1955] A.C. 572.
[202] *ibid.* at p. 600.

ing judgement of Lord Reid in *Baddeley*. The facts of that case were that a trust was created "for the promotion of the religious, social and physical well-being of persons resident ... [in a certain area who were] members or likely to become members of the Methodist church". The House of Lords held that this trust was not charitable as it could be used for non-charitable purposes.

Further authority was found in *Neville Estates* v. *Madden*[203] – "here the social activities are merely ancillary to the strictly religious activities ... in my judgement the purposes of the trust with which I am concerned are religious purposes- the social aspect is merely ancillary".[204] However these cases are only authority for the first thread on exclusively charitable purposes. They are not authority for the second thread, that recreation vitalises and reinforces religion.

---

[203] (1962) Ch. 832.
[204] *Neville Estates v. Madden, op cit.* at p. 852.

CHAPTER 11

Other Charitable Purposes

"For the erection, building, maintenance, or repair of any bridges, causeyes, cashes, paces, and highways within this realm"

(Statute of Pious Uses 1634)

"For repair of bridges, ports, havens causeways churches seabanks and highways,

some for education and preferment of orphans,

some for or towards relief stock or maintenance for houses of correction,

some for marriages of poor maids

some for supportation aid and help of young tradesmen, handicraftsmen and persons decayed,

and others for relief or redemption of prisoners or captives,

and for aid or ease of any poor inhabitant concerning payment of fifteens, setting out of soldiers and other taxes"

(Statute of Charitable Uses 1601)

11.1 INTRODUCTION

"Other charitable purposes" is not so much a category in its own right but rather a general safety net intended to cater for those activities which are clearly charitable but which do not readily fit within any of the other more specific categories. This fourth *Pemsel* head is a residual one, of charitable objects that cannot be conveniently fitted under the other heads. There is no guiding concept such as poverty, education or religion underlying this head, consequently judges have little principles to guide them on deciding whether a specified object is of general public utility. This has led V.T.H. Delany[1] to say of the fourth head:

> "... it provides one of the most outstanding examples in the law of endless technical distinctions which bear no relationship to reality or common sense, and which again and again succeed only in frustrating the intention of benevolently minded testators.[2]

---

[1] See Delany, V.T.H., *The Law Relating to Charities in Ireland* (1962).
[2] *ibid.* at p. 79.

An assessment echoed by the judiciary:

> "... the authorities ... upon whether particular trusts fall within or without Lord Macnaghten's fourth category baffle all efforts on my part to reconcile with one another."[3]

The House of Lords has also recognised the anomalous nature of the fourth head,

> "... this so called fourth class is incapable of further definition and can today hardly be regarded as more than a portmanteau to receive those objects which enlightened opinion would regard as qualifying."[4]

The legal basis of fourth head charities springs from the residue of the Statutes of Charles and Elizabeth after poverty, religion and education have been removed. In *Morice v. Bishop of Durham* they were classed as "objects of general public utility". Lord Macnaghten honestly, though cumbersomely referred to them as "other purposes beneficial to the community not falling under any of the preceding heads".[5]

Some activities have attracted such a body of caselaw that they are now commonly treated as separate and distinct species of the genre "other charitable purposes". In keeping with that approach the sub-categories of health (see Chapter 12), politics (see Chapter 13) and recreation (see Chapter 14) are dealt with elsewhere. This chapter sets out such definitions and governing principles as may apply but in the main concentrates on examining the various sub-groups which comprise this the most difficult of the *Pemsel* charitable headings.

11.2 DEFINITIONS

This is an area of law where definitions abound but little in the way of governing principle or commonality of function can be found.

11.2.1 The statutes

An obvious difference between the Statute of Charitable Uses 1601and the Statute of Pious Uses 1634 is that the English statute enumerates far more charitable objects under the fourth head. Whilst the statute of Charles stops at the "infrastructure" objects, the statute of Elizabeth goes on to list a wide variety of separate objects. Although this may have presented theoretical dif-

---

[3] *Trustees of Londonderry Presbyterian Church House v. Commissioners of Inland Revenue* at p. 187.
[4] *Scottish Burial Reform and Cremation Society v. Glasgow Corporation* [1967] 3 W.L.R. 1132 at 1137.
[5] *Pemsel, op cit.* at p. 583.

ficulties to Irish jurisprudence, in practice it has had no effect. Irish and Northern Irish courts have been content to appropriate the English charitable categories. No reported case has raised any objection based on the difference between the two statutes.

Some attempt at the etymology of the words of the Statute of Charles can be made. A "causeye" is the historical root of the word causeway, a raised road across a low or wet place. A "cash" (possibly from "cashel") probably refers to a wall which encloses a group of churches. A "pace" is a passage, pass or narrow way. Support for this view of the meaning of these words can be found in a Statute of Ireland of 1765 which refers to "the highways and cashes and paces and passages throughout the woods of this Kingdom".

A slight discrepancy has arisen over the role of statute and caselaw in determining new charitable purposes. The traditional position is that the law increases by analogy. A new purpose will be deemed charitable only if it is analogous to the objects set forth in the Preamble, or analogous to previously declared charitable objects. Kennedy J gave an illustration of this traditional approach – "only those objects of general public utility are charitable, in the legal sense of the term, which either are included in, or are analogous to, the objects mentioned in the Preamble to the Act."[6] The importance of case law in this approach has also been stressed – "what must be regarded is not the wording of the Preamble itself, but the effect of decisions given by the court as to its scope".[7]

A much broader approach has also been advocated. It relies less on analogy and more on an holistic approach, with the decided cases having less relevance. The Irish case of *Re Cranston*[8] provides an example, "any gift which proceeds from a philanthropic or benevolent motive ... and which will confer the supposed benefit without contravening law or morals will be charitable".[9] *National Anti-Vivisection Society v. IRC*[10] added to this list a further factor, that of enlightened public opinion:

> "... [the] concept of charity in a legal sense under the fourth head is towards tangible and objective benefits, and at least that approval by the common understanding of enlightened opinion for the time being is necessary before an intangible benefit can be taken to constitute a sufficient benefit to the community."[11]

---

[6] *Re Wedgwood* [1914] 1 Ch. 113 at p. 118, see also *Re South Place Ethical Society, Barralet v. Attorney General* [1980] 3 All E.R. 918 at p. 926, "the approach of analogy from what is stated in the Preamble to the Statute of Elizabeth or from what has already been held to be charitable within the fourth category".

[7] *Scottish Burial Reform and Cremation Society v. Glasgow Corporation* [1968] A.C. 138 at p. 154.

[8] [1898] I I.R. 431.

[9] *ibid.* at p. 446.

[10] [1948] A.C. 31.

[11] *ibid.* at p. 49.

Perhaps the strongest modern expression of this came in *Incorporated Council for Law Reporting for England and Wales v. Attorney General* where it was said "if a purpose is shown to be beneficial or of such utility it is prima facie charitable in law".[12] The Preamble still retains a role under this approach according to Russell LJ in *Council of Law Reporting*, it can be used to negative this *prima facie* charitable character. Logically, Russell LJ's approach causes some problems – the Preamble constitutes a partial list of charitable objects, if a new prima facie charitable object is discerned, how can the partial list exclude it?

The High Court in Northern Ireland has touched on this issue. In *Re Lester*[13] Megaw J considered the broad approach propounded in *Re Cranston* and found himself bound by it. To be charitable under the fourth head the purpose must be unselfish, public and either philanthropic or benevolent. However, as pointed out in Tudor,[14] there may be little practical difference between these approaches. If an object is prima facie charitable, it is highly likely that an analogy for it could be drawn from the Preamble or established cases.

11.2.2 "Charitable purposes"

In the words of Viscount Cave:

> "Lord Macnaghten did not mean that all trusts beneficial to the community are charitable, but there are certain charitable trusts which fall within that category, and accordingly to argue that because a trust is for a purpose beneficial to the community it is therefore a charitable trust is to turn round his sentence and give it a different meaning. . . . It is not enough to say that a trust is for public purposes beneficial to the community or for the public welfare, you must also show it to be a charitable trust."[15]

There has never been any suggestion that in order to qualify for charitable status under this heading a gift should be directed solely towards relief of the poor. Indeed, it was Lord Macnaghten in the *Pemsel* case who declared that trusts in this category:

> "... are not the less charitable in the eye of the law, because incidentally they benefit the rich as well as the poor, as indeed, every charity that deserves the name must do either directly or indirectly."[16]

As Lord Wrenbury later observed:

---

[12] *Incorporated Council for Law Reporting for England and Wales v. Attorney General* [1971] 3 All E.R. 1029 at 1036.

[13] [1940] N.I. 92.

[14] *op. cit.* at p. 90.

[15] See *Attorney General v. National Provincial and Union Bank of England Ltd.* [1924] A.C. 262 at 265.

[16] *op. cit.* at p. 583.

> "His [Lord Macnaghten's] fourth head does not contain the word 'poor'. He does not say 'beneficial to the poorer members of the community'; he says, 'beneficial to the community'. Did he mean his words to be confined to the poor? Education and religion, two of the heads which he had just mentioned, do not require any qualification of poverty to be introduced to give them validity. If he was going by general words to add a fourth class in which poverty must be an ingredient, he would surely have said so."[17]

It is at least certain that if the gift is exclusively directed towards the rich then it will not be charitable.

11.2.3 "Other" charitable purposes

The issue of when charitable purposes come within the "other" category, rather than under one of the three main *Pemsel* heads, is of recurring judicial and academic interest. The courts have always taken a strict view in interpreting that which constitutes a trust for "other purposes beneficial to the community" although in recent years some flexibility has become evident.[18] Dillon J., however, in *Re South Place Ethical Society*[19] has maintained that the presumptive approach advocated by Lord Russell, is not in line with previous caselaw. Instead, Dillon J. suggests, the process of determining whether or not a gift falls within the definition of a trust for other charitable purposes "is the approach of analogy from what is already stated in the preamble to the Statute of Elizabeth or from what has already been held to be charitable within the fourth category".[20]

11.3 PUBLIC BENEFIT

It has been held that it may seem anomalous to speak in terms of a public benefit in relation to this category as it is defined in terms of trusts for the benefit of the community.[21] Nevertheless, it is to this category that the interpretation of the public benefit test has been applied with most rigour.[22]

---

[17] See *Verge v. Somerville* [1924] A.C. 496 at 503.

[18] See *Incorporated Council for Law Reporting for England and Wales v. Attorney General, op. cit.* at p. 88 where Lord Russell suggests that if a purpose is beneficial to the community it is *prima facie* charitable in law.

[19] [1980] 1 WLR 1565.

[20] *ibid.* at 1574.

[21] See Hanbury and Martin, *Modern Equity* (14th ed., 1993), p. 420.

[22] See, comments of Babington L.J. in *Trustees of the Londonderry Presbyterian Church House v. Commissioners of Inland Revenue* [1946] N.I. 178, 196; Lord Simonds in *Williams v. I.R.C.* [1947] A.C. 447 and *I.R.C. v. Baddeley* [1955] A.C. 572 at 615 and of Lord Somervell in *I.R.C. v. Baddeley* [1955] A.C. 572 at 592 (although note the quite different conclusion reached by Lord Reid in *Baddeley* at pp. 612-613.

11.3.1 Test to be applied

The question as to whether the subjective opinion of the donor or the objective assessment of the court should determine whether a gift satisfies the public benefit test has been the subject of much debate.

Initially the subjective approach found favour with the judiciary in these islands. For example, in *Re Foveaux*,[23] which concerned a society for the benefit of animals, the court held that it was the belief of the society's creators which was the relevant belief in determining the public benefit. This approach has been dominant in Ireland both before and after Partition. It was most firmly endorsed by Fitzgibbon L.J. in *Re Cranston*[24] who argued that gifts for certain vegetarian societies were charitable and came within the category of gifts for other charitable purposes. He gave some consideration to the test to be applied by the court:

> "What is the tribunal which is to decide whether the object is a beneficent one? It cannot be the individual mind of the judge, for he may disagree *toto caelo* from the testator as to what is or is not beneficial. On the other hand, it cannot be the *vox populi*, for charities have been upheld for the benefit of insignificant sects and of peculiar people; it occurs to me that the answer must be: – that the benefit must be one which the founder believes to be of public advantage, and his belief must be at least rational, and not contrary either to the general law of the land, or to the principles of morality."[25]

This view, that the test should be subjective, was endorsed by Lord O'Brien L.C.J. in *Attorney-General v. Becher*[26] and by Barton J. in *Shillington v. Portadown U.D.C.*[27] the latter of whom upheld as charitable a gift which the donor wished to be used for the benefit of the residents of his native town and its locality. In reaching his decision Barton J took the view that if the donor believed the gift would be to "public advantage", and if this belief was both rational and legal, then there was no obstacle to the gift acquiring charitable status. In Ireland it is now accepted that the test is one which falls to be decided by the subjective intentions of a donor.[28]

In England and Wales, however, the courts gradually resiled from this approach. The gift in *Re Hummeltenberg*[29] was to train spiritualist mediums. The donor thought it would benefit the public, but the court held that public benefit could not be proved – "the question whether a gift is or may be operative for the public benefit is a question to be answered by the court forming an

---

[23] [1895] 2 Ch. 501.
[24] *op. cit.*
[25] *ibid.* at p. 446.
[26] [1910] 2 I.R. 251.
[27] [1911] 1 I.R. 247.
[28] See also, *Re Worth Library* [1994] I.L.R.M. 161, *per* Keane J. at p. 193.
[29] (1923) 1 Ch. 237.

opinion upon the evidence before it".[30] This decision was promptly followed in *Re Grove-Grady*[31] where it was stated that "the court must determine in each case whether the trusts are such that benefit to the community must necessarily result from their execution".[32]

In Northern Ireland it fell to Megaw J. in *Re Lester*[33] to decide between the two approaches. He held that the words of Fitzgibbon L.J. in *Re Cranston* were *obiter dicta* on this point, and that it was for the court to determine if a gift was for the public benefit. The objective approach is now applied in the courts of Northern Ireland and elsewhere in the United Kingdom[34] and marks a point of difference between the charity law of this and the adjoining jurisdiction.

11.3.2 "Public"

As in all four *Pemsel* categories of charitable trusts it is vital that a gift for other charitable purposes is potentially available to a significant number of beneficiaries, who are not linked in a private relationship nexus with the donor, if it is to be upheld as a charity.[35] In the words of Cairns:

> "It must be clear that the gift is not for the benefit of particular individuals since a gift for the benefit of individuals, however great their need, is a private rather than a public purpose and therefore not charitable. A gift for immediate distribution to the donor's next of kin will be interpreted as a gift for individuals and will not be charitable."[36]

Babington L.J. has commented that in this category "there can be no charity until it is shown that the gift is to or for the benefit of the public or a section of the public".[37] The "public" or section thereof which is to benefit must be identified with a degree of certainty.

In Northern Ireland, the judgment delivered in *Governors of Royal Victoria Hospital (Musgrave Clinic) v. Commissioners of Valuation*[38] illustrates the application of this principle. In England and Wales the decision of the House

---

[30] *ibid.* at p. 242.

[31] [1929] 1 Ch. 557.

[32] *ibid.* at p. 588, approved by the House of Lords in *National Anti-Vivisection Society, op cit.*

[33] *Re Lester, McCracken v. Law* [1940] N.I. 92.

[34] See *Re Hummeltenberg* [1923] 1 Ch. 237, *per* Russell J.; *Re Grove-Grady* [1929] 1 Ch. 557 at 572, *per* Lord Hanworth M.R.; and *Re Lester* [1940] N.I. 92, at 101–105.

[35] See *Oppenheim v. Tobacco Securities Trust Co. Ltd.* [1951] A.C. 297.

[36] See Cairns, E., *Charities: Law and Practice* (2nd ed., Sweet & Maxwell, London, 1993) at p. 18.

[37] See *Trustees of the Londonderry Presbyterian Church House v. Commissioners of Inland Revenue* [1946] N.I. 178 at 196–197; *Verge v. Somerville* [1924] A.C. 496; also, see *I.R.C. v. Baddeley* [1955] A.C. 572.

[38] (1939) 73 I.L.T.R. 236.

of Lords in *I.R.C. v. Baddeley*[39] confirmed that it was to prevail throughout the United Kingdom. However, the weight of authority both in Northern Ireland and England seems to suggest some equivocation. In this jurisdiction the proposition that a gift must be for the "entire community" was interpreted such that "it might be held to be a [fourth head] charity if the benefits were open and available to all persons".[40] While, in the House of Lords, the proposition was interpreted to mean that "if a charity falls within the fourth class, it must be for the benefit of the whole community or at least of all the inhabitants of a sufficient area".[41] The House of Lords went on to relent slightly on this strict test, if the nature of the gift was such that it could be enjoyed by all (*i.e.* a bridge) yet was restricted to a certain class (*i.e.* doctors), there would be no public benefit. If the gift was open to all, yet was such that it could only be effectively enjoyed by some (*i.e.* surgical instruments), then it would remain for the public benefit.

There is some evidence from caselaw to suggest that a strict interpretation of *Baddeley* may not be wholly in conformity with established authorities. In *Goodman v. Mayor of Saltash*,[42] for example, the court could find public benefit in a gift to "any particular class of such inhabitants.[43] In *Re Cohen*[44] a gift which would only benefit Jews was held to be charitable. Along similar lines, public benefit has been confirmed in gifts for Derry Presbyterians[45] and Cookstown Catholics.[46] Decisions after *Baddeley* are in a similar vein, with the courts finding gifts to lawyers,[47] ex-soldiers[48] and orphans[49] to be of public benefit.

11.3.3 "Benefit"

There is an emerging judicial consensus that the definition of "public" is in practice inextricably bound up with the purpose or "benefit" of a particular gift. Effectively, this means that the "benefit" quotient necessary to meet charitable status requirements will be different under each of the four *Pemsel* heads

---

[39] *Inland Revenue Commissioners v. Baddeley* (1955) A.C. 572.

[40] *op. cit.* at p. 238.

[41] *op. cit.* at p. 590.

[42] [1882] App. Cas. 633.

[43] *ibid.* at p. 642.

[44] *Re Cohen, National Provincial Bank v. Cohen* (1919) 36 T.L.R. 16.

[45] *Trustees of the Londonderry Presbyterian Church House v. Commissioners of Inland Revenue* [1946] N.I. 178.

[46] *Trustees of Cookstown Roman Catholic Church v. Commissioners of Inland Revenue* (1953) 34 T.C. 350.

[47] *Incorporated Council of Law Reporting for England and Wales v. Attorney General* [1971] 3 All E.R. 1029.

[48] *Royal British Legion Attendants Company v. Commissioner of Valuation* [1979] N.I. 138.

[49] See *Re Simpson, op cit.*

and will be most difficult to satisfy in the residual category "other charitable purposes". As Carswell J. explained in *Re Dunlop*[50]:

> "The essence of the charitable nature [of trusts within Lord Macnaghten's fourth category] is that the beneficiaries should not be a private class, nor should any limitations be placed upon the gift which would prevent the public as a whole from enjoying the advantage which the donor intends to provide for the benefit of all the public. It would be quite consonant with this concept that it should be more difficult for a trust under the fourth head to satisfy the requirements of public benefit, and that a bridge to be used only by Methodists should fail to qualify where a gift for the education of the children of members of that church might be a valid charity."[51]

This was a case where Carswell J. applied the public benefit test to a gift for the purpose of establishing a home for "Old Presbyterian Persons" and upheld it as a valid charitable trust. His decision was based upon a finding that "benefit" would accrue to those in need and that the group was sufficiently "public" and devoid of any personal relationship nexus to the donor. The fact that the benefit would be restricted to a narrowly defined category of potential beneficiaries did not negate its public utility.

11.4 TYPES OF CHARITABLE PURPOSE

Gifts under the fourth *Pemsel* head are almost impossible to classify. The caselaw being generated in some areas is growing in profusion and complexity to such an extent that require certain subjects to be treated separately e.g. "health" (see Chapter 12), "political purposes" (see Chapter 13) and "recreation" (see Chapter 14).

11.4.1 Gifts for the benefit of animals

A gift made for the purpose of conferring a benefit upon a particular animal cannot acquire charitable status.[52] However, if made for the benefit of a particular type of animal or for animals generally, then such a gift will be charitable. The related caselaw reveals a judicial rationale which at times finds it sufficient to ground charitable status on the intrinsic benefit of a gift to animals and at other times requires evidence that the true beneficiary is human.

---

[50] [1984] N.I. 408.

[51] *ibid.* at p. 426.

[52] See *Re Kelly* [1932] I.R. 255. However, a trustee may lawfully volunteer to give effect to the terms of such a trust provided the rule against perpetuities is not infringed; no enforcement procedure is possible. See, *Re Dean* (1889) 41 Ch. D. 552.

11.4.1(i) Animal as beneficiary

The reasoning for extending charitable status to gifts for animals probably originates in the expediency of costs for animal care being borne, where possible, by private rather than by public funds[53] which may also have been the original reasoning for upholding as charitable gifts to the Society for the Prevention of Cruelty to Animals.[54]

In England and Wales, unlike in Ireland,[55] the courts have not been based their decisions on a belief that the donor's intention to safeguard the welfare of animals was sufficient in itself to attract charitable status under this heading. For example, in *Re Grove Grady*,[56] Russell LJ expressed the opinion that the charitable status of gifts to animals depended upon whether or not they were of benefit to mankind.

11.4.1(ii) Human as beneficiary

It is charitable to relieve the suffering of animals, but not because to do so is a good thing in itself. The theoretical basis of the charitable status of animal charities is that either they are useful to mankind (in the case of domestic animals) or they elevate men's minds by stimulating humane and generous sentiments. The shift in emphasis towards regarding the true beneficiary of such gifts as being human rather than animal has become more pronounced in recent years. The fostering of public morality and the encouragement of philanthropic attitudes are viewed as the primary justification for regarding gifts to animals as charitable. This argument was advanced by Swifen Eady L.J. in *Re Wedgewood*[57] as follows:

> "A gift for the benefit and protection of animals tends to promote and encourage kindness towards them, to discourage cruelty, and to ameliorate the condition of the brute creation, and thus to stimulate humane and generous sentiments in man towards the lower animals, and by these means promote feelings of humanity and morality generally, repress brutality and thus elevate the human race."[58]

It was an argument which had already been expressed in Ireland by Holmes J. in *Re Cranston*[59] where, in reference to vegetarianism, he observed:

---

[53] See *London University v. Yarrow* (1857) 1 De G. & J. 72.

[54] See *Tatham v. Drummond* (1864) 4 De G.J. & Sm. 484.

[55] See for example: *Armstrong v. Reeves* (1890) 25 L.R. Ir. 325, *per* Chatterton V.-C.; *Swifte v. Colam* (1909) unreported, *per* Meredith M.R.; and *Swifte v. The Attorney-General* [1912] 1 I.R. 133, *per* Barton J.

[56] [1929] 1 Ch. 557 at 582.

[57] [1915] 1 Ch. 113.

[58] *ibid.* at p. 122.

[59] [1898] 1 IR 431. See, also, *Webb v. Oldfield* [1898] 1 I.R. 431.

"If it is beneficial to the community to promote virtue and to discourage vice, it must be beneficial to teach the duty of justice and fair treatment to the brute creation, and to repress one of the most revolting kinds of cruelty."[60]

This approach was also apparent in *Re Foveaux*[61] where it was said "cruelty is degrading to man" and that protecting animals does not just benefit the animals but is for "the advancement of morals and education among men".[62] Again, it surfaced in a judicial bias against trusts for those animals which had no demonstrable usefulness to mankind. For example, Kennedy L.J. in *Re Wedgwood*[63] thought that the protection of beasts of prey and mad dogs would not be charitable. The court in *Re Grove-Grady*[64] held that there was no public benefit in a wild bird sanctuary which would solely benefit animals.

The anthropocentric focus, at the expense if necessary of animal benefit, came to the fore when the vivisection question was litigated "the life and happiness of human beings must be preferred to that of animals".[65] In *Re Foveaux* the court had declared agitation against vivisection charitable, but this was strongly and unequivocally overruled by the House of Lords in the *National Anti-Vivisection Society* case. The moral benefit of abolishing vivisection would be completely outweighed by the medical loss. If vivisection were to be banned "the consequences would be calamitous to the community"[66] and the public benefit would be outweighed by the public detriment.[67]

11.4.1(iii) Type of benefit to animals

Domestic animals have traditionally been the favoured beneficiaries of charitable gifts. A case in Ireland, for example,[68] centered on a bequest of £4,000 Consolidated Stock upon trust, the income from which was to be applied exclusively for the benefit of "the Dublin Home for Starving and Forsaken Cats", was held to be charitable because cats are useful to man. In *Re Douglas*[69] the

---

[60] *ibid.* at p. 457.

[61] [1895] 2 Ch. 501.

[62] *ibid.* at p. 507.

[63] *op. cit.*

[64] *op. cit.*

[65] *National Anti-Vivisection Society v. Inland Revenue Commissioners* [1948] A.C. 32 at 48.

[66] *ibid.* at p. 63

[67] More recently affirmed by *Re Jenkin's Will Trusts* [1966] 1 Ch. 249 at 255 that it was impossible to prove public benefit – "the court cannot weigh the benefits to the community which result from using animals for vivisection and research against the benefits which would result to the community from preventing such practices".

[68] See *Swifte v. Attorney General* [1912] 1 I.R. 133. See also, *Swifte v. Colam* unreported, February 12, 1909, where the Master of the Rolls approved as charitable a gift "to be held by the Commissioners of Charitable Donations and Bequests upon trust to invest … for … the institution known as the Home for Starving and Forsaken Cats".

[69] (1887) 35 Ch. D. 472.

gift was to "a Home for Lost Dogs" and in *Re Moss*[70] it was "for the welfare of cats and kittens needing care and attention". Gifts may be expressed in more general terms, for example for the protection and benefit of animals,[71] for use by a society which professes such aims[72] and to institutions which provide a sanctuary for sick or unwanted animals.[73] Where the gift is expressed in such terms it is of no consequence whether the subjects are domestic pets or farm animals.

A body providing for the care, protection or treatment of animals will normally be eligible for charitable status, but not if it does so on a profit-making basis. The governing principle was explained by Russell L.J. in *Re Satterthwaite's Will Trusts*[74] in the context of gifts to animal hospitals:

> "*Prima facie*, an animal hospital is a charity, as being calculated to promote public morality by encouraging kindness, discouraging cruelty and stimulating humane sentiments to the benefit of mankind; but it lacks the quality of legal charity if it be carried on for private profit as a profession or occupation or trade."[75]

11.4.1(iv) Gifts not charitable

A gift expressed to be for the benefit of animals is not *per se* charitable. In addition to the possibility of failing for reasons of being a commercial enterprise[76] a gift may also fail to meet the standard public benefit test.[77] This was the case in *Re Grove-Grady*[78] where a gift from the testatrix was stated to be for the purpose of founding an animal benevolent society which would then establish a refuge for the preservation of "all animals, birds and other creatures not human". In denying the gift charitable status on the grounds of an absence of public benefit, Russell L.J. explained:

> "… it is merely a trust to secure that all animals in the area shall be free from molestation or destruction by man. It is not a trust directed to ensure absence or diminution of pain or cruelty in the destruction of animal life."[79]

The vivisection cases, in particular, provide frequently quoted examples of the animal/human benefit debate. The decision of the House of Lords in *Na-*

---

[70] [1949] 1 All E.R. 495.

[71] See *Re Wedgewood* [1915] 1 Ch 113; see also, *Re Green's Will Trusts* [1985] 3 All E.R. 455.

[72] See *Armstrong v. Reeves* (1890) 25 L.R. Ir. 325.

[73] See *Re Murawski's Will Trusts* [1971] 1 W.L.R. 707.

[74] [1966] 1 W.L.R. 277.

[75] *ibid.* at p. 284.

[76] See *Re Satterthwaite's Will Trusts op. cit.*

[77] See *Royal National Agricultural and Industrial Association v. Chester* (1974) 48 A.L.J.R. 304 which concerned a trust for improving the breeding and racing of homing pigeons.

[78] *op. cit.*

[79] *op. cit.* at p. 585.

tional Anti-Vivisection Society v. IRC[80] sharply contrasts with its predecessors in that the decision reversed the previous finding that the anti-vivisection objects of a society were charitable because they were conducive to the public benefit. In refuting this assertion the House of Lords held that vivisection offered long-term benefits to humanity which outweighed the incidental suffering in caused to animals. It may be argued that although the decisions of the judiciary turned on much the same facts, they arrived at opposite conclusions merely because they accurately reflected the prevailing values of their respective social contexts. This hardening in the relative weighting given to scientific research as opposed to liberal ideology as indicators of public benefit found further endorsement in the judgment of Buckley J. in *Re Jenkin's Will Trusts*[81] where he stated:

> "... the prohibiting of any forms of cruelty inherent in vivisection, however admirable that may be from an ethical point of view, is not a charitable activity in the contemplation of the law because the court cannot weigh the benefits of the community which result from using animals for vivisection and research against the benefits which would result to the community from preventing such practices."[82]

In Northern Ireland, the case of *Re Brown, Nesbitt v. Attorney General*[83] concerned a testator's gifts to certain societies for the benefit of animals, including the World League Against Vivisection and several vegetarian societies. The decision of Campbell J. followed the established English authorities and held that "prevention of vivisection is not a charitable purpose".[84]

11.4.2 Gift for the benefit of a locality

It is well established that the inhabitants of a specified locality such as a county or town may qualify as the collective beneficiaries of a charitable gift. Views to this effect were expressed with enduring authority by Selborne L.J. in *Goodman v. Saltash Corp*[85]:

> "A gift subject to a condition or trust for the benefit of the inhabitants of a parish or town, or of any particular class of such inhabitants, is (as I understand the law) a charitable trust."[86]

This case concerned an oyster fishery held on trust by the corporation subject

---

[80] [1948] A.C. 31.
[81] [1966] Ch. 249.
[82] *ibid.* at p. 255.
[83] unreported, Chancery Division, April 17, 1991.
[84] *Re Brown* at p. 2 of transcript.
[85] (1882) 7 App. Cas. 633 at p. 642.
[86] *ibid.* at p. 642. Subsequently applied in *Re Christchurch Inclosure Act* (1888) 38 Ch. D. 520.

to the condition that all owners of freehold tenements in the borough could exercise their ancient right to annually harvest oysters during the period Candlemas to Easter. The exercise of this right conflicted with that vested in the corporation and delegated to its lessees. The House of Lords held that when the corporation initially acquired its right it had done so subject to the trust in favour of the freehold owners and that this was a charitable trust which could not be rendered void on the grounds of having breached the rule against perpetuities.

11.4.2(i) Type of locality

This rule has been applied to confer charitable standing upon gifts to a wide range of localities. Examples of places so favoured are: to the freemen of the city of Norwich;[87] to the good of the county of Westmoreland and especially the parish of Lowther;[88] to trustees for "such charities and other public purposes as lawfully might be in the parish of Tadmarton" as they should think fit;[89] and to Stockton-on-Tees corporation for "a public hall".[90] While there are many instances of such gifts to localities defined as a named town, borough, county or parish there is also authority to show that a gift which defines the locality in terms of a country or nation may also be charitable. So, for example, Cottenham L.J. held a bequest "to the benefit and advantage of my beloved country, Great Britain" to be a good charitable gift.[91]

In Northern Ireland, Barton J. in *Shillington v. Portadown UDC*[92] ruled in favour of a testator's bequest to the residents of his native town and locality as a valid charitable gift. He explained the rationale for so ruling as follows:

> "He wished to benefit the residents of his native town and of its immediate locality. The benefits which he intended to confer on them were such as he believed to be of public advantage. That belief was rational and not contrary to the laws of the land or the principles of morality."[93]

The reminder that to be charitable in this context a gift must also conform to the usual rules was underlined by the decision of the Court of Appeal in *Trustees of Londonderry Presbyterian Church House v. Commissioners of Inland*

---

[87] See *Re Norwich Town Close Estate Charity* (1888) 40 Ch. D. 298.

[88] See *A-G v. Lonsdale* (1827) 1 Sim. 105.

[89] See *Dolan v. MacDermot* (1868) L.R. 3 Ch. App. 678.

[90] See *Re Spence* [1938] Ch. 96.

[91] See *Nightingale v. Goulbourn* (1847) 5 Hare 484. Followed in *Re Smith* [1932] 1 Ch. 153 where a bequest expressed to be "unto my country England to and for – own use and benefit absolutely" was held by Romer L.J. to be a valid charitable gift.

[92] [1911] 1 I.R. 247.

[93] *ibid.* at pp. 256-7 and also, *Attorney-General v. Dublin (Corporation of)* (1827) 2 Moll. 355; 1 Bligh N.S. 312. See, *Cookstown Roman Catholic Church v. CIR* (1953) 34 T.C. 350. *Cf* Albery, "Trusts for the Benefit of a Locality" (1940) 56 L.Q.R. 49.

Revenue.[94] In that case it was held that members of the Presbyterian Church in the city of Londonderry did not constitute a sufficient section of the public for the purposes of satisfying the definition of a charitable gift. The governing principle was explained by Eve J. in *Re Gwyon*[95]:

> "Limitation or specification of locality may prevent a charitable trust from being avoided for vagueness and uncertainty, but only when it has first been shown to be a charitable trust. A trust which is not a charitable trust cannot be changed into a charitable one by limiting the area in which it is to operate."[96]

A gift expressed to be for the benefit of a specified locality must identify that locality with sufficient precision so as to forestall the possibility of the gift being void due to uncertainty. However, it must also be defined in general terms (e.g. "for the use of", "to the benefit of" etc.) if it is to avoid being classified under an alternative *Pemsel* head. For example, in this jurisdiction many gifts are expressed to be for a specific locality, most usually a named parish, and are accompanied by a direction that the gift be used for a religious purpose such as the upkeep of a graveyard. This results in their charitable status falling to be determined under the heading of "gifts for the advancement of religion". Finally, it must also be defined with care to ensure that it is clearly providing for public rather than private benefit. The difficulties inherent in this exercise were graphically described in *IRC v. Educational Grants Association Ltd.*[97] by Lord Denning:

> "The inhabitants of a named place are a section of the community for this purpose: but the employees of a particular company are not. It follows that if a man sets up a trust *for the children of the inhabitants of Bourneville*, it will be held to be for the public benefit. But if he sets up a trust *for the children of those employed by Cadburys Ltd. at Bourneville*, it will be held to be for private benefit. In each case the beneficiaries will probably be identical, but in point of law the one trust is charitable and the other is not."[98]

11.4.2(ii) Type of gift

There is no consistency in the type of gifts which fall to be considered by the courts in this context. Arguably, the characteristic most likely to be common to such gifts is that each would have been unlikely to achieve charitable status if it were not given to a locality. This head of charity in particular affords many examples of judicial creativity in saving vague, generalised gifts as charitable where in another context they would surely fail.

---

[94] [1946] N.I. 178. Also, see, *Trustees of Cookstown Roman Catholic Church v. Commissioners of Inland Revenue* (1953) 34 T.C. 350.
[95] [1930] 1 Ch. 255.
[96] *ibid.* at p. 261.
[97] [1967] Ch. 993.
[98] *ibid.* at p. 1009.

In addition to rights to dredge for oysters,[99] the courts have also approved as charitable ancient rights of turbary (to cut turf)[100] and ancient grazing rights.[101] In Ireland, a gift "for the purpose of fostering, encouraging and providing the means of obtaining healthy recreation, including the teaching of singing in classes or choruses, for the residents of Portadown and the surrounding districts" was held charitable.[102]

In Northern Ireland the courts have had several opportunities to find a charitable trust under this head but have declined to do so. For example, in *Trustees of Londonderry Presbyterian Church House v. Commissioners of Inland Revenue*[103] a social centre for Presbyterians resident in Londonderry was argued to be charitable under the fourth head. The court found that they were a section of the public, but held that they could not place themselves under the fourth head as there was no analogous charitable object. Again, in *Trustees of Cookstown Roman Catholic Church v. Inland Revenue Commissioners*[104] Catholics resident in Cookstown were also found to be a sufficient section of the community and, it was argued, a trust for their benefit fell within the ruling given by Selborne L.J. in *Goodman v. Saltash Corp.* Sheil J. rejected this reasoning and held that *Goodman* had been effectively overruled by *Williams Trustees v. Commissioners of Inland Revenue*.[105] The latter case concerned a trust for the benefit of Welsh people living in London, the House of Lords held it was not for exclusively charitable purposes. Subsequent cases[106] have not regarded *Goodman* as being overruled. The Northern Ireland decisions[107] show a degree of caution about accepting the benefit to locality category as a good charitable purpose (see also, Chapter 8).

In England, the High Court recently made determined efforts to explain the rationale for construing gifts to a locality as charitable. In *Peggs v. Lamb*[108] Morrit J offered a benign interpretation of the donor's expressed purpose that "when the sum bequeathed comes to be used it is to be applied to charitable purposes".[109] He suggested that when a gift is expressed to generally benefit an area, it is to be construed that this benefit is to be enjoyed in a charitable way. Although the efforts of Morrit J. attempting this rationalisation are com-

---

[99] See *Goodman v. Saltash Corp. op. cit.*

[100] See *Re Christchurch Inclosure Act, op. cit.*

[101] See *Peggs v. Lamb* [1994] 2 W.L.R. 1.

[102] *Shillington v. Portadown Urban District Council* [1911] 1 I.R. 247.

[103] *op. cit.*

[104] (1953) 34 T.C. 350.

[105] [1947] A.C. 447.

[106] See, for example *Peggs v. Lamb, op. cit.* but also see *IRC v. Baddeley, op. cit.*

[107] See also *Governors of Royal Victoria Hospital (Musgrave Clinic) v. Commissioners of Valuation* (1939) 73 I.L.T.R. 236 which also arguably ruled out an object under this category.

[108] *op. cit.*

[109] *Re Smith* [1932] 1 Ch. 153 at 169.

mendable, it is submitted that they do not stand up when the case law in ana-lysed. The various types of gifts would not be charitable if they were a stand alone gift. It is not their inherently charitable nature which makes them valid gifts, it is the fact that they are applied to a certain area. The public benefit test consumes the charitable purposes test.

11.4.3 Agriculture

In Northern Ireland, the advancement of agriculture generally is charitable. This was the effect of the decision in *Pig Marketing Board v. Commissioners of Inland Revenue*.[110] The purposes of the Board included marketing pigs effi-ciently and regulating the pig industry. However, on the specific facts, the High Court held that the public benefit was not satisfied because the benefits disproportionately favoured the pig farmers – "the benefits conferred upon pig producers cannot in my opinion be left out of account as being merely incidental"[111] The court considered and upheld the validity of the ruling in *Commissioners of Inland Revenue v. Yorkshire Agricultural Society*[112] which had held that the advancement of agriculture was charitable.[113] This authority was subsequently confirmed in *Crystal Palace v. Minister of Town Planning*[114] which also held the promotion of industry, commerce and art to be charitable.

In this jurisdiction, an historical quirk has left the government holding the reins of a substantial trust for the advancement of agriculture. "Vaughan's Charity"[115] was formed as a private trust in 1780 with the object of promoting the advancement of agriculture in County Fermanagh. In 1936 the govern-ment assumed administrative control, although the charity receives no gov-ernment funding and retains the purposes set out by its founder. It distributes Mr Vaughan's beneficence by making study grants to young farmers. It has been subject of several pieces of legislation regulating it.[116]

11.4.4 Defence of the realm

By analogy with the maintenance of "maimed soldiers", "setting out of sol-diers" and repairing sea defences, the defence of the realm has also been held

---

[110] [1945] N.I. 155.
[111] *ibid.* at p. 160.
[112] [1928] K.B. 611.
[113] See also *Trustees of the Agricultural Research Institute of Northern Ireland v. Commis-sioner of Valuation* VR/81+82/1967, *Lylehill Young Farmers' Club v. Commissioner of Valuation* VR/7/1981 which both assumed the promotion of agriculture to be charita-ble.
[114] [1951] Ch. 132.
[115] So named after its founder George Vaughan.
[116] Vaughan's Charity (Administration) Act (NI) 1954, Vaughan's Charity Scheme (NI) Order 1973.

to be charitable.[117] As Lord Normand explained in *Inland Revenue Commissioners v. City of Glasgow Police Athletic Association*[118]: "gifts exclusively for the purpose of promoting the efficiency of the armed forces are good charitable gifts".[119]

In Northern Ireland the welfare of ex-soldiers is charitable. The company formed in *Royal British Legion Attendants Company v. Commissioner of Valuation*[120] had as its purposes the promotion of the employment and welfare of ex-soldiers. To this end they ran a car park staffed by an ex-soldier and an ex-merchant seaman. The Court of Appeal found this charitable because it would "encourage a person to join the Forces, raise his moral and efficiency while he is serving and help him ... when he returns to civilian life".[121] Some difficulties were caused by the inclusion of an ex-merchant seaman. Such people could join the Legion since, in times of war they could be required to perform military duties. However, technically they were not part of the armed forces. A solution was provided by reference to the decision in *Re Corbyn*[122] which had held that a trust for the Mercantile Marine was charitable, since a merchant navy was essential to a realm which could not produce enough food and essentials of life.

It has been explicitly held that "seamen were a sufficient section of the community at large to be an object of general public utility".[123]

In England the judiciary have made similar findings. For example, a trust for returning New South Wales soldiers after World War I was charitable because to do so would be "restoring them to their native land and giving them a fresh start in life".[124] Again, by analogy, promoting the efficiency of the police, encouraging their recruitment and preserving public order have all been held charitable. In *Inland Revenue Commissioners v. City of Glasgow Police Athletic Association*[125] the Glasgow police association applied for exemption from income tax for their annual sports meeting. The House of Lords held that "gifts or contributions exclusively for the purpose of promoting the efficiency of the police forces and the preservation of public order are by analogy charitable gifts".[126]

Gifts for private shooting clubs have been held charitable in the past on the

---

[117] See, for example, *Re Good* [1905] 2 Ch. 60 and *Re Gray* (1925) Ch. 362.

[118] [1953] A.C. 380.

[119] *ibid.* at p. 391.

[120] [1979] N.I. 138.

[121] *ibid.* at p. 146.

[122] [1941] Ch. 400.

[123] *Trustees of Stella Maris Residential Club for Seafarers v. Commissioner of Valuation* VR/37/1980 at 9, see also *Finch (Trustees of the Seamen's Mission) v. Poplar Metropolitan Borough Council* [1968] RA 208.

[124] *Verge v. Somerville* [1924] A.C. 496 at 506.

[125] *op. cit.*

[126] *ibid.* at p. 391.

basis that teaching Englishmen to shoot with particular weapons which are used in war for the destruction of their enemies is for the defence of the realm. This is why a gift to the National Rifle Association "for the teaching of shooting at moving objects in any manner they may think fit, so as to prevent as far as possible a catastrophe similar to that at Majuba Hill" was held charitable.[127] However, the Charity Commission has moved beyond this position and deemed such purposes not exclusively charitable:

> "The charitable purpose of promoting the security of nation and defence of the realm could not be carried out in the modern day by providing a restricted number of civilian members of a club with instruction and practice in shooting. In the aftermath of the Falklands and Gulf conflicts, it was seen that the skills required of modern uniformed personnel were quite different and clubs (whose principal concern was the benefit of members through recreational and sporting shooting) were in no sense a reserve for the armed forces."[128]

11.4.5 Commemoration

A war memorial may be charitable in Northern Ireland if it is purely symbolic. McVeigh J. tentatively suggested that this is because it "tends to the spiritual benefit of the community"[129] and may inspire others. He was guided in this by a decision of the Charity Commission that a statue of Duke of Wellington was charitable. He limited this decision to an extent by saying "memorials however, which are utilitarian, rather than purely commemorative and symbolic, appear to be charitable only if they can be justified on the ground of general public utility".[130]

In England, the Charity Commission has been happy to go further. The commemoration of dead police officers is charitable[131] for reasons similar to commemorating Earl Mountbatten; because to do so is "likely to foster patriotism and good citizenship, and to be an incentive to heroic and noble deeds".[132]

11.4.6 Orphans

The education and preferment of orphans is within the terms of the Statute of Elizabeth. No objection has been raised to such purposes being charitable in Northern Ireland. A gift to found a Protestant orphanage for boys at Hillmount was held charitable in *Re Simpson, Wallace v. Attorney General for Northern*

---

[127] *Re Stephens* (1892) 8 T.L.R. 792.
[128] *The Review of the Register of Charities*, RR1, Charity Commission (1999) at pp. 12–13.
[129] *Belfast Air Raid* at p. 174.
[130] *ibid.* at p. 175.
[131] [1984] Ch. Com. Rep. para. 17.
[132] [1981] Ch. Com. Rep. para. 68.

Ireland.[133] It seems the public benefit test will be satisfied if the beneficiaries are limited both by sex and religion. The care of orphans is also charitable in Ireland[134] as are children's homes in England.[135]

11.4.7 Natural heritage and beauty

The National Trust is charitable in Northern Ireland. The High Court in *Re Richardson*[136] agreed with the English reasoning[137] that "the permanent preservation of lands and tenements of beauty or historic interest for the benefit of the nation is a charitable purpose".[138] In England the preservation of old cottages was also held to be charitable in *Re Cranstoun*.[139]

11.4.8 Moral improvement

The objects of the Theosophical Society are (a) promote a universal brotherhood of man, (b) encourage the study of religion, philosophy and science and (c) investigate unexplained laws of nature. In Northern Ireland, *Re Lester*[140] held that some of these purposes were charitable, but unfortunately the court neglected to list which ones. An earlier case of *Macauley v. O'Donnell*[141] provides some assistance. It held that the second and third objects of the Theosophical Society promoted moral improvement and so were charitable. However, since the first purpose did not, the Society could not be deemed exclusively charitable.

The Anthroposophical Society (as founded by Rudolph Steiner) is charitable. In England it was judicially recognised as such in *Re Price*[142] on the grounds that "the teachings of Rudolph Steiner are directed to the mental or moral improvement of man". Mental or moral improvement has also been held charitable under the education head.[143]

A gift for the "furtherance of Conservative principles and religion and mental improvement" was held charitable in *Re Scowcroft*.[144] A gift for "the study and dissemination of ethical principles and the cultivation of rational

---

[133] [1974] N.I.J.B. Nov.

[134] *Jackson v. Attorney General* [1917] 1 I.R. 332.

[135] *Re Sahal's Will Trusts* [1958] 1 W.L.R. 1243.

[136] *Re Richardson, Boyce v. National Trust for Places of Historic Interest or Natural Beauty* [1988] N.I. 86, see also, *National Trust for Places of Historic Interest or Natural Beauty v. Commissioner of Valuation* VR/11-18/1971.

[137] *Re Verral, National Trust v. Attorney General* (1916) 1 Ch. 100.

[138] *Re Richardson, op cit.* at p. 92.

[139] [1932] 1 Ch. 537.

[140] *Re Lester, McCracken v. Law* [1940] N.I. 92.

[141] (1933), unreported.

[142] [1943] 2 All E.R. 505 at 510.

[143] See Chap. 9 and especially *Re Shaw*.

[144] [1898] 2 Ch. 638.

religious sentiment" is charitable as promoting the moral or spiritual welfare or improvement of the community.[145]

11.4.9 Reclamation of prostitutes

The Irish case of *Mahony v. Duggan*[146] illustrates the exceedingly broad scope of charitable activities under the fourth head. The case concerned a bequest "for the purpose of reclaiming fallen women in the city of Cork". The Master of the Rolls did not attempt to place this purpose within any particular head so it must be assumed he had the fourth in mind. He said "there may be as high, but there cannot be higher, purposes of charity than the reclamation of fallen women".[147]

11.4.10 Taxes

Assistance with the payment of taxes is within the words of the Statute of Elizabeth. In *Re Murphy's Trusts*[148] a charitable trust was created with the purpose of paying off Newry's debts and rates. In England, *Attorney General v. Bushby*[149] held that charitable objects under this category were not just restricted to payments of taxes of the poor.

11.4.11 Protection of lives and property

Following the "infrastructure" clauses in the preamble, the protection of lives and property is also charitable. For example a lifeboat is charitable[150] as is a fire brigade for the benefit of the public.[151]

11.4.12 Promotion of marriage

Promoting the "marriages of poor maids" is listed in the statute of Elizabeth. It would seem from the decision in *Re Cohen*[152] that the poverty requirement no longer applies. The bequest in that case was for deserving Jewish girls on their marriage. Mr Justice Petersen held that "deserving" did not mean "poor", but nevertheless "it tended to encourage marriage among Jews, and it was for the benefit of the Jewish religion".[153] Although this may tend towards the reli-

---

[145] *Re South Place Ethical Society, Barralet v. Attorney General* [1980] 3 All E.R. 918.
[146] [1883] 11 L.R. Ir. 260.
[147] *ibid.* at p. 264.
[148] [1967] N.I. 36.
[149] (1857) 24 Beav. 299.
[150] *Johnston v. Swann* (1818) 3 Mad. 457.
[151] *Re Wokingham Fire Brigade Trusts* [1951] Ch. 373.
[152] (1919) 36 T.L.R. 16.
[153] *Re Cohen* at p. 17.

gious head of charity, the case was presented and argued as a fourth head charity.

In Ireland, a bequest in *Re Charlton Charities*[154] to provide marriage portions for sons and daughters of labourers in counties Meath and Longford was held to be charitable.[155]

11.4.13 Law reports

As well as being charitable under the education head, law reports were also held to be charitable under the fourth head. As Russell L.J. explained in *Incorporated Council for Law Reporting for England and Wales v. Attorney General*[156] it is "beneficial to the community that reliable reports of judicial decisions of importance ... should be published".[157]

11.4.14 Justice

Surprisingly, the promotion of justice is not a charitable purpose under the fourth head. This may be due partly to the implied connotation of political purposes. Slade J. said in *McGovern v. Attorney General* that "the elimination of injustice has not as such ever been held to be a trust purpose which qualifies for the privileges afforded to charities by English law".[158]

11.4.15 Promoting ethical standards in business and corporate responsibility

The Charity Commission has recently ruled that "an organisation promoting high ethical standards and enabling employers and employees together to fulfil a business's responsibility to society (and helping employees in moral dilemmas)" was charitable.[159]

11.4.16 Promoting fair trade

A number of charitable and voluntary organisations promote fair trade as a part of their everyday activities. In the past, this has denied them exemption from rates under the charity shop exemption.[160] Fair trade is a trade system designed to maximise benefits to and minimise exploitation of third world

---

[154] (1879), unreported.

[155] See Hamilton (1881) who places this gift under the first head of relief of poverty. However, this was before the taxonomy of *Pemsel* was properly propounded.

[156] [1972] Ch 73.

[157] *ibid.* at p. 1034.

[158] [1982] 1 Ch. 321 at p. 354.

[159] *The Review of the Register of Charities*, RR1, Charity Commission (1999) at p. 13.

[160] Art. 41(2)(5) Rates (NI) Order 1977, see further, Chap. 21.

producers. An organisation created to promote and regulate fair trade marks was ruled to be charitable by the Charity Commission.[161] One objection was that there was too much private and commercial benefit in fair trade, but the Commission was satisfied that "there was a direct connection between the award of the fair trade mark and an actual and observable improvement of conditions in the third world".[162] Another objection which was not raised with the Commission is that fair trade programs can often stray into the political arena by lobbying for changes in an inequitable global trade structure.

11.4.17 Relief of unemployment

Northern Ireland has been quite progressive in recognising the relief of unemployment as a charitable objective. The Lands Tribunal has held that a company set up solely to promote new jobs and new enterprises would be charitable on the grounds that:

> "... business start-up advice to the unemployed, would seem to be charitable, as being for the relief of poverty."[163]

However, Ledcom, the company in that case also had as its main objects buying land to let to small businesses, advising small businesses and providing paid consultancy services. As these constituted a commercial undertaking with private benefit it was denied charitable exemption from rates. Similar reasons were advanced for refusal of charitable status in *Inland Revenue Commissioners v. Oldham Training and Enterprise Council*.[164] This is a particular area of vulnerability for organisations engaged in schemes to reduce pockets of unemployment. Not only is there a danger of breaching the public benefit test by focussing on a closely defined number of people and thus being more "private" than "public" but also such schemes tend to involve investments, small businesses and a degree of individual gain. Such activities can be fatal to charitable status.

The Charity Commission has now clarified and developed this area of law in RR3, *Charities for the Relief of Unemployment* (1999). The following activities are charitable:

• The provision of advice and training to unemployed individuals, concerning employment, self-employment, and the establishment of co-operative enterprises and the provision of CV writing, job search and job club facilities for them.

---

[161] *The Review of the Register of Charities*, RR1, Charity Commission (1999) at p. 13.

[162] *ibid.* at p. 14.

[163] *Larne Enterprise Development Company v. Commissioner of Valuation* VR/6/1995 at p. 8.

[164] *Inland Revenue Commissioners v. Oldham Training and Enterprise Council* [1996] S.T.C. 1218.

- The provision of practical support to unemployed people by way of accommodation, child care facilities or assistance with travel.

- The provision by charities of land and buildings at below market or subsidised rents to businesses starting up.

- The provision of capital grants or equipment to new businesses.

- The payment by a grant-making charity to an existing commercial business to take on additional staff from among unemployed people.

All of these activities remain subject to the public benefit test. If a person can no longer be considered as deserving of social security payments, then termination must be possible. Benefiting private individuals in the course of their trade is not charitable. Such charities must aim to make their beneficiaries ineligible for relief and provide arrangements, when this is achieved, to terminate assistance.

11.4.18 Promotion of urban and rural regeneration in deprived areas

In the latest review of the register, the Charity Commission has created a new category of charitable activity under the fourth head, the promotion of urban or rural regeneration in deprived areas. The ambit of this purpose is set out in detail in RR2, *Promotion of Urban and Rural Regeneration* (1999). It does not mean community development, but can be summarised as meaning:

> "… the maintenance or improvement of the physical, social and economic infrastructure and by assisting people who are at a disadvantage because of their social and economic circumstances."[165]

The requirement of deprivation must be objective. It can relate to high crime levels, high unemployment, poor public services, low income levels etc. Areas must be selected and delineated on this basis. The activities which can be carried out are the usual ones for recreation,[166] the relief of poverty[167] and the relief of unemployment.[168] They can also extend to:

- The provision of housing for those who are in conditions of need and the improvement of housing in the public sector or in charitable ownership provided that such power shall not extend to relieving the Northern Ireland Housing Executive of their statutory duty to provide or improve housing.

- The maintenance, improvement or provision of public amenities.

- The preservation of buildings or sites of historic or architectural importance.

- The protection or conservation of the environment.

---

[165] RR2, *Promotion of Urban and Rural Regeneration* (1999) at p. 2.
[166] See Chap. 14.
[167] See Chap. 8.
[168] See above.

- The provision of public health facilities and childcare.
- The promotion of safety and the prevention of crime.

As with charities for the relief of unemployment, once the beneficiaries no longer satisfy the criteria, there must be provision made to cease payment of benefits. Charities for the relief of unemployment and those for generating urban or rural renewal also share the same vulnerability to a challenge to their status based on a charge that commercial activity and some degree of private profit has been involved.

11.5 EXCEPTIONS

There are some activities which the courts will not countenance as charitable, even under the fourth *Pemsel* head.

11.5.1 Private clubs

Private clubs are not charitable because they confer no public benefit: in general an organisation which has as its primary aim the furtherance of the interests of its own members, cannot be charitable. Therefore, organisations such as the Masons, the Orange Order[169] and the Royal Black Preceptory fall outside the definition of charity on the grounds that they are mainly private clubs with no major element of public benefit. However, certain individual funds operated by them (*i.e.* the Masonic Widows' and Orphans' Fund) are charitable.

In general, an organisation that has as its primary aim the furtherance of the interests of its members cannot be charitable.

11.5.2 Overseas aid

Although it is charitable to raise money to provide equipment for the British army it would not be charitable to do this for foreign armed forces, even those of a current ally. A given activity may be charitable if carried out in the U.K. but not charitable if carried out abroad.

The latest Charity Commission guidelines on this point are that charities which provide benefits overseas are presumed to be charitable if their activities would be charitable if carried out in the United Kingdom. Only if there are good public policy reasons (for example the activities are actually illegal in the foreign country) will the Commission rule that the body is not a charity.[170]

---

[169] *Re Minis, Minis v. Attorney General for Northern Ireland* (unreported, Chancery Division, May 18, 1994).
[170] *The Review of the Register of Charities*, RR1, Charity Commission (1999).

The Inland Revenue operate a slightly different test from the tax perspective. Charity funds spent abroad will be deemed non-charitable expenditure unless the charity has taken reasonable steps to ensure the funds will be applied for charitable purposes.[171]

---

[171] Income and Corporation Tax Act 1988, s.506(3).

CHAPTER 12

Other Charitable Purposes:
Health and Welfare Services

12.1 INTRODUCTION

In Northern Ireland the existing infrastructure of health and welfare services, particularly hospitals, owes a great deal to the earlier contribution of charities and philanthropists. The patchwork legacy of facilities, resulting from the philanthropic endeavours of individuals, religious groups such as the Quakers and religious orders organised under the umbrella of the Roman Catholic Church, provided a foundation to support the building of the modern health and welfare services.

This chapter examines the law relating to charitable activity in the area of health and welfare services. Following a brief consideration of definitional matters, and the meaning and significance of the public benefit in this context, the focus is largely on the charitable role of hospitals and of gifts to them. Then the chapter deals with gifts to the sick and to those who may be otherwise termed "impotent" and "succourless".

Within a *Pemsel* style classification this chapter can be viewed as addressing an amalgamation of the first head under "aged and impotent" (Statute of Elizabeth), "succourless, distressed or impotent" (Statute of Charles) and of the fourth head under "maintenance of sick and maimed soldiers" (Statute of Elizabeth), "building, re-edifying, or maintaining in repair any ... hospital" (Statute of Charles). Alternatively, the dictum of Slade J could be applied and it may be seen as "a genus or division of charity not mentioned by Lord Macnaghten, of which poverty is merely a species, this genus includes the relief of human suffering and distress in all the various forms enumerated".[1]

12.2 DEFINITIONS

Recognition of a separate and distinct charitable heading entitled "the promotion of health" is now well-established in England and Wales.[2] The Charity

---

[1] *McGovern v. Attorney General* (1982) 1 Ch. 321 at 333.

[2] See, for example, Picarda, H., *The Law and Practice Relating to Charities* (Butterworths, London, 1995) and Keaton and Sheridan's *The Modern Law of Charities* (4th ed., Barry Rose, Chichester, 1992) where it is currently so treated.

Commissioners have recognised health as particular category of charitable activity. In an advisory leaflet[3] it includes within this category: the sick (including the mentally ill), convalescents, the disabled, the handicapped and the infirm. Arguably, a stronger case can be made for such a heading in this jurisdiction.

12.2.1 The disjunctive approach

The origins of charity law in this jurisdiction are rooted as much in the 1634 Act,[4] and the caselaw which it accumulated, as in the 1601 Act.[5] For three centuries or more, until Partition, this part of the island shared with the rest the consequences of judicial interpretation of the 1634 Act, as complemented by legislative and judicial initiatives emanating from the governing jurisdiction of England. The influence of the 1634 Act may have had an effect in shaping judicial determinations on this island and allowing a clearer focus on separate health matters than was possible in England.

A point which perennially arose in the construction of the statutes is whether they should be construed conjunctively or disjunctively. A conjunctive construction means that each element of the definition is a requisite and inseparable part of the whole. The use of the word "and" means that for the aged to benefit they must also be poor, and the impotent must also be aged. By way of contrast, the disjunctive approach holds that each element of the definition constitutes a separate and severable meaning of charity. The use of the word "or" means that to be charitable, a beneficiary can be either poor or old or distressed etc.

The problem has arisen because the Statute of Elizabeth uses the word "and". This led some of the earlier cases to hold that poverty was a necessary prerequisite for gifts to the impotent or the aged. For example, in *Re Lucas*,[6] the court was of the opinion that a gift to old people of a parish would fail unless the court implied poverty into the gift.

A succession of English cases attacked this conjunctive approach. In *Re Glyn*[7] concerned a gift of cottages to old working women. The court was able to imply poverty into the gift, but nevertheless took the disjunctive approach. Next was *Re Robinson*[8] where the gift was to the over 65s of a certain area. Vaisey J. stated that "the gift is to the old people ... as a group of people who are within the Statute of Elizabeth, qualified not by poverty, sickness or impo-

---

[3] See, CC6, *Charities for the Relief of Sickness* (1996).
[4] "An Act for the Maintenance and Execution of Pious Uses", 1634 (10 Car. 1 Sess. 3 Cap 1)
[5] The Charitable Uses Act, 1601 (43 Eliz. 1 c. 4).
[6] [1922] 2 Ch. 52.
[7] (1950) 66 TLR 510.
[8] [1951] Ch. 198.

tence, but by age".[9] By 1983, it was taken as read that "the words "aged, impotent and poor" must be read disjunctively".[10] In *Joseph Rowntree*, Gibson J. held that "It would be as absurd to require that the aged must be impotent or poor as to require the impotent to be aged or poor, or the poor to be aged or impotent".[11]

In Northern Ireland the only case to address this point was *Re Dunlop*.[12] In it Carswell J. expressly followed the reasoning of Gibson J. in the *Joseph Rowntree* case.[13] He held that a gift to "old Presbyterians" was charitable even though the old Presbyterians were not also poor. He also held that it would be as absurd to require the aged to be poor, as it would for the impotent to be aged, or the poor to be impotent. However, as the Irish statute uses the word "or" and not "and", there was therefore no possibility of arguing that a conjunctive construction was required. Could Carswell J have simply relied upon the Irish statute as authority for a disjunctive approach? Perhaps *Re Dunlop* simply falls between two stools. The Irish statute explicitly has a disjunctive approach, but does not mention "aged". The English statute explicitly mentions aged, but appears on the surface to be conjunctive. The easiest solution was to rely upon the English statute with a disjunctive interpretation.

Under the Irish statute the "poor", the "succourless", the "distressed" and the "impotent" have never been treated, for the purposes of charity law, as necessarily inter-linked groupings of potential beneficiaries within this category.[14] However, while there is some authority to suggest that a grant will be sufficiently charitable if directed simply towards a distinct category, for example "the mentally ill", the better view is that the defining condition should be accompanied by a clear need and the gift be directed to the alleviation of that composite set of circumstances.[15] The public benefit test must still be satisfied.

12.3 THE PUBLIC BENEFIT TEST

Time has altered the threshold for what may be construed as constituting public health. This has been recognised by the judiciary and was expressed as follows by Wright L.J. in *National Anti-Vivisection Society v. IRC*[16]:

---

[9] *Re Robinson, op cit.* at p. 200.

[10] *Joseph Rowntree, op cit.* at p. 171.

[11] See, *Joseph Rowntree Memorial Trust Housing Assoc. Ltd. v. A-G* [1983] Ch. 159.

[12] [1984] N.I. 408.

[13] Carswell J. also took authority from *Le Cras v. Perpetual Trustee Company* [1969] 1 A.C. 514.

[14] See *Barrington's Hospital v. Commissioner of Valuation* [1957] I.R. 299 at 320, *per* Kingsmill Moore J.; *Gleeson v. Attorney General*, High Court 1972, No. 2664 SP, *per* Kenny J., April 6, 1973; and *Re Worth Library* [1994] 1 I.L.R.M. 161 at 196.

[15] See, *Re Neal* (1966) 110 S.J. 549; and *Re Resch's Will Trusts* [1969] 1 A.C. 514.

[16] [1948] A.C. 31, *per* Wright L.J. at p. 42.

"... trusts [providing particular remedies thought to relieve the distress caused by advanced age, sickness, disability or poverty] may, as economic ideas and conditions and ideas of social service change, cease to be regarded as being for the benefit of the community. ..."

The court will not consider itself rigidly bound by precedent when determining whether a particular purpose is in fact charitable.

12.3.1 "Public"

The requirement that a hospital be open to the public, or a sufficient section of it, is a condition of charitable status. While it is not necessary that a hospital be used exclusively by the poor it cannot be charitable if used exclusively by the rich. Where public access is restricted by the imposition of admission fees then the degree to which this affects the balance between public and private patients will be a key factor in determining a hospital's claim to be a charity (see, further below). A hospital will satisfy this condition most convincingly when its wards are open as of right to all members of the public on the basis of need, is supported wholly or partially by public funds and is subject to a form of public control. If it is maintained entirely by fees levied in respect of all admissions then it will not satisfy the "public" arm of this test.

In *Needham v. Bowers*[17] a lunatic asylum was unendowed and received no appreciable subscriptions, but was maintained entirely from fees received. It was held not to be a charity for the purposes of the 1838 Act. The case was followed in Northern Ireland by *Governors of Royal Victoria Hospital (Musgrave Clinic) v. Commissioner of Valuation*.[18] The class of beneficiaries was quite constrained in that case. They had to be too wealthy to be admitted to the general wards, but too poor to pay the fees of a nursing home. Although it had been given buildings as a gift, it was to be self-supporting from the receipt of fees from patients. Thompson J. held that although:

"... payments by persons within the scope of the charge are not inconsistent with its being held to be charitable ... an institution founded by a benefaction but supported by paying patients [is not] charitable".[19]

The same principle of opportunity of access governs the eligibility of other health and welfare facilities for charitable status.

12.3.2 "Benefit"

In addition to providing for a certain breadth of access, a gift must also satisfy the "benefit" requirement if it is to be recognised as charitable. In this jurisdic-

---

[17] 21 Q.B.D. 436.
[18] (1939) 73 I.L.T.R. 236.
[19] *ibid.* at p. 238.

tion, Carswell J gave some consideration to this matter in *Re Dunlop*[20] a case which concerned a trust established to found a home for "Old Presbyterian persons". He then commented that it would be insufficient for the trust to merely "admit as beneficiaries any aged persons, whatever may be the amount of their resources and irrespective of their needs arising from their condition of advancing years".[21] His finding in favour of charitable status was grounded on evidence that the trust would be providing a form of sheltered accommodation appropriate to the needs of such elderly persons.

Sheltered accommodation for the elderly, disabled, mentally ill and other such groups often attract charitable gifts.

The relief of sickness is recognised as a charitable purpose; again, this is not confined to the sick who are also poor.[22] Nor is it confined to orthodox medical treatment. In *Funnell v. Stewart*[23] a bequest in favour of a faith healing group was found to be charitable. The fact that the care is not provided gratuitously will not affect eligibility for charitable status unless it is being run as a profit making business.

12.4 HOSPITALS

The reference in the 1634 statute to such charitable uses as "the building, re-edifying or maintaining in repair any ... hospital" perhaps accounts for the popularity on this island for gifts to establish or maintain hospitals. The law, however, has been largely exercised from two different perspectives. Firstly, there is a body of caselaw concerned with the charitable status of gifts to, or otherwise for the benefit of, hospitals. Secondly, over the past century or so a number of important judgments have been given relating to the claims of particular hospitals for exemption from liability for rates on the grounds of their charitable status. This chapter concerns the former (see Chapter 21 for the law relating to the latter). The distinction between the two is admittedly technical but as it is also long established and deeply entrenched it therefore has significant practice implications.

12.4.1 Gifts for hospitals

A gift to a hospital is *prima facie* a charitable gift. In England and Wales valid charitable gifts have included: a bequest for patients in named hospitals;[24]

---

[20] [1984] N.I. 408. See also, Dawson, *"Old Presbyterian Persons" – A Sufficient Section of the Public?* [1987] Conv. 114.
[21] *ibid.* at p. 414.
[22] See *Re Hillier, op. cit.*
[23] [1996] 1 W.L.R. 288.
[24] See *Re Roadley* [1930] 1 Ch. 524.

gifts for the endowment of hospital beds;[25] the endowing of ancillary hospital facilities.[26] The status of the hospital as a voluntary or state institution,[27] will not affect the validity of a charitable gift.

12.4.1(i) Charitable status and fee paying patients

There have been four cases in Northern Ireland on the charitable status of hospitals, three of which[28] have held the hospital to be charitable. The cases all concerned the question of whether the hospitals or various parts of them were exempt from rating as being used for exclusively charitable purposes. The specific decisions in the cases were: that a doctors house within the curtillage of the hospital was exempt for rates,[29] a matrons residence within the hospital was exempt,[30] and a nurses home 500 yards from a hospital was not exempt.[31] These cases have been superseded by later cases on rating and should be treated with some caution (see further, Chapter 21).

The presence of some fee-paying patients will not compromise the charitable status of a hospital.[32] In this jurisdiction the case of *Commissioner of Valuation v. Fisherwick Church Trustees*[33] illustrates this point, albeit in a valuation context.[34] If the patients are predominantly fee-paying then the hospital may well cease to be charitable. This will certainly be the case if it is conducted exclusively for the well-to-do as was demonstrated in *Governors of the Royal Victoria Hospital v. Commissioners of Valuation*[35] which concerned the status of the Musgrave clinic. To gain admittance, a patient had to be too wealthy to be admitted to the general wards and too poor to pay full private fees. They also had to be recommended by a staff member and pay some fees towards

---

[25] See *A-G v. Belgrave Hospital* [1910] 1 Ch. 73.

[26] See *Re Adams* [1968] Ch. 80.

[27] See, for example, *Re Frere* [1951] Ch 27 and *Re Perreyman* [1953] 1 All E.R. 223. Also, see *Re Hart, Whitman v. Eastern Trust Co* [1951] 2 DLR 30 and *Kytherian Association of Queensland v. Sklavos* [1959] A.L.R. 5.

[28] *Armagh County Infirmary Committee v. Commissioner of Valuation for Northern Ireland*, [1940] N.I. 1, *Commissioner of Valuation for Northern Ireland v. Committee of Management of Fermanagh County Hospital* [1947] N.I. 125 and *Down County Council v. Commissioner of Valuation for Northern Ireland* [1954] N.I. 173.

[29] *Armagh County Infirmary Committee v. Commissioner of Valuation for Northern Ireland, op. cit.*

[30] *Down County Council v. Commissioner of Valuation for Northern Ireland, op. cit.*

[31] *Fermanagh Hospital, op cit.*

[32] Relying on *Verge v. Somerville* [1924] A.C. 496.

[33] [1927] N.I. 76.

[34] Similarly in Ireland, see *Pembroke UDC v. Commissioner of Valuation* [1904] I.R. 429; *Clancy v. Commissioner of Valuation* [1911] 2 I.R. 173. See also, *University College Cork v. Commissioner of Valuation* [1911] 2 I.R. 593, [1912] 2 I.R. 328; and *O'Neill v. Commissioner of Valuation* [1914] 2 I.R. 447. See further, Chap. 21.

[35] 73 I.L.T.R. 236.

their cost of care. It was held that the hospital was not charitable because it was supported by private paying patients. However it was a decision of the Recorders Court and is now of questionable authority following case law developments on payments made by beneficiaries to charities.

This non-profit factor proved to be determinative when Lord Wilberforce in *Re Resch's Will Trusts*[36] came to consider the status of a gift to a hospital which admitted only "persons of means". He upheld the charitable status of the gift but conceded that he would be unable to do so where the functions of such a hospital were "carried on commercially, *i.e.* with a view to making profits for private individuals, or where the benefit provided was not for the public, or a sufficiently large section of the public to satisfy the necessary tests of public character".[37] Where, however, the hospital does make a profit but this is then re-invested in the facility, perhaps to refurbish wards or buy additional medical equipment etc, then its charitable nature remains uncompromised.

Subject to the caveat established regarding the *Musgrave clinic*, the position seems to be that non-profit making hospitals are charitable regardless of whether their patients pay. The law in England is the same[38] though it was overly stretched in *Re Dean's Will Trusts*[39] which declared charitable a gift to pay the travel expenses of relations to facilitate their visits to patients.

12.4.2 Ancillary purposes

A gift may still be charitable if given not to further the medical treatment functions of a hospital but to provide for ancillary services. Such charitable gifts have often been directed towards improving conditions for staff by, for example, providing for the advancement of nursing,[40] education,[41] training[42] and housing.[43] The governing rule has been that the intention of the gift must not be to confer a benefit upon individual members of staff, nor upon a professional body, but to improve the effectiveness of the hospital. In *Armagh County Infirmary Committee v. Commissioner of Valuation for Northern Ireland*[44] a gift to provide residential accommodation for a part-time surgeon on the site of his employing hospital was held to be charitable notwithstanding the possibility that the person in residence might use the premises for occasional dinner parties.

---

[36] [1969] 1 A.C. 514.
[37] *ibid.* at pp. 540-541.
[38] See, for example, *Re Roadely* [1930] 1 Ch. 524,
[39] [1950] 1 All E.R. 882.
[40] See *Royal College of Nursing v. St Marylebone Corp* [1959] 1 W.L.R. 1077.
[41] See *Re Osmund* [1944] Ch. 206 and the advancement of psychiatry.
[42] See *Re Webster* [1912] 1 Ch. 106.
[43] See *Re White's Will Trusts* [1951] 1 All E.R. 528.
[44] [1940] N.I. 1.

Ancillary purposes may extend to include charitable gifts to persons other than hospital staff. For example, gifts to provide accommodation for visiting relatives of patients[45] or resources to aid the comfort of patients have been held to be charitable.

12.4.3 Changes in ownership of hospitals

Government health policy in the twentieth century has brought about a gradual extension in the public provision of health care and a retreat in charitable provision. The Charity Commissioners state that:

> "... the NHS and other statutory services provide for many needs which in the past, used to be met by charities established for the relief of sickness or for the general benefit of the sick poor."[46]

This sea change is reflected by litigation in Northern Ireland. Two hospitals in *Down County Council v. Commissioner of Valuation*[47] moved from the charitable sector to the public sector under the Health Services Act (N.I.) 1948 and the Public Health (Tuberculosis) Act (N.I.) 1946. It was argued before Curran J. that this meant the hospitals were no longer charitable. He held that the constitutional changes meant a change in ownership, not in purpose. The hospitals remained charitable.

12.5 THE SICK OR OTHERWISE "IMPOTENT"

In England and Wales the word "impotent" has long been judicially accepted as an umbrella definition of eligibility for charitable status in the context of health and welfare. The extension of "impotent" to include categories of persons suffering from a wide range of different illnesses, disability, impairment and related types of facilities, housing and other resources has also been judicially adopted in this jurisdiction.

12.5.1 Gifts for the relief of the sick

In the words of Lord Wilberforce:

> "...the provision of medical care for the sick is, in modern times, accepted as a public benefit suitable to attract the privileges given to charitable institutions."[48]

---

[45] See *Dean's Will Trusts* [1950] 1 All E.R. 882, *per* Harman J., and a gift to a hospital: ... for the purpose of providing accommodation for the use of relative who come from a distance of patients who are critically ill.

[46] CC6, *Charities for The Relief of Sickness* (1996).

[47] [1954] N.I. 173.

[48] See *Re Resch's Will Trusts* [1969] 1 A.C. 514, *per* Lord Wilberforce at p. 540.

In England and Wales an extensive range of gifts have been judicially accepted as charitable, these include: a gift for the "sick and wounded"[49] for a home of rest for persons in a condition of strain[50] and for the maintenance of aged persons in a nursing home. It should be noted that gifts intended to promote good health, thereby avoiding the need to treat sickness, may also be deemed to be charitable.

With the increasing hegemony of the public sector in providing health care, the range of charitable activities which do not merely repeat public provision has diminished. Charitable provision should aim to complement public provision, not be a substitution for it. To this end, charities for the relief of sickness should ensure they are not merely duplicating public services and saving the public purse rather than providing extra services.

The Charity Commission has provided guidance for these circumstances.[51] They have created a series of lists of activities which complement official health service activities. They advise that the following items may be loaned or given: bedding, clothing, food for special diets, fuel or the equivalent savings stamp, heating appliances, medical or other aids and equipment (such items may be suitable for donation or loan to hospitals, clinics and GP surgeries), wheelchairs, televisions or TV licences, washing machines, prescription "season tickets". The following services could be provided: bathing, foot care, hair washing, shaving, help in the home, adaptations to the homes of the disabled, laundering, meals on wheels, nursing aid, physiotherapy, gardening, reading, exchange of library books, shopping, sitting-in, tape-recording for the housebound, child minding, outings and entertainment, travelling companions. Special arrangements which could be provided include: periods of rest or change or air, treatment at convalescent homes or health clinics, temporary relief for those having the care of a sick or handicapped person, help for relatives and friends to visit or care for patients, transport.

12.6 RELIEF OF THE AGED

The 1634 statute differs from its 1601 English counterpart in that it makes no actual mention of the "aged". However, both have long been construed as implying the same legislative intent to address the same headings of charity in like manner.[52]

---

[49] *Re Hillier, op. cit.*
[50] *Re Chaplin* [1933] Ch. 115.
[51] See CC6, *Charities for The Relief of Sickness*, (1996).
[52] See *Incorporated Society v. Richards* (1841) 1 Dr. & War. 258, *Attorney-General v. Delaney* (1876) I.R. 10 C.L. 114 and *Pemsel op. cit.*

12.6.1 "Aged"

In Northern Ireland there has never been any judicial case attempt to define "aged". In *Re Dunlop* the gift to "old Presbyterians" was considered sufficiently certain. A gift "to advance the object of providing a retirement home for vegetarians in the north of England"[53] was accepted as indisputably charitable by the High Court in Northern Ireland. It is unlikely that the courts would still agree with the view of Kay J. in *Re Wall*[54] that "men and women not under fifty years of age" adequately satisfies any modern definition of aged. The courts are more likely to concur with the decision in *Re Robinson*[55] that a gift for those aged over sixty five is a satisfactory estimate. In Tudor[56] it is argued that in view of today's better health care and increased longevity, "aged" should mean sixty years old or more. It is probable that a contemporary definition would be linked to the statutory interpretation of pensionable age.

12.6.2 "Relief"

The requirement of "relief" of the aged is slightly more difficult. The condition of proposed beneficiaries must be aged, and the nature of the gift must be to give relief to some need relevant to that condition. In *Re Dunlop*, Carswell J. said:

> "I lay some stress upon the word 'relief' because it seems to me of some significance in defining the limits of charitable purposes from which aged, impotent and poor people are to derive benefit."[57]

Carswell J. thereby recognised the qualification set out in *Joseph Rowntree Memorial Trust Hospital Association Ltd v. Attorney General*[58] that "the word "relief" implies that the persons in question have a need attributable to their condition as aged, impotent or poor persons which requires alleviating".[59] As expressed by Russell J. in *Re Lucas*:

> "I am not satisfied that the requirement of old age would of itself be sufficient to constitute the gift a good charitable bequest."[60]

To be construed as charitable, a gift for the aged must expressly aim to either relieve poverty or to relieve infirmities associated with ageing (*e.g.* lack of mobility, ill health etc). There is a well established line of cases offering au-

---

[53] See *Re Brown, Nesbitt v. Attorney General and Vegetarian Society*, unreported, April 17, 1991 at p. 6 of transcript.
[54] (1889) 42 Ch. D. 510.
[55] [1951] Ch. 198.
[56] *op. cit.*, p. 26.
[57] *Re Dunlop, op cit.* at p. 414.
[58] [1983] Ch. 159.
[59] *ibid.* at p. 171.
[60] [1922] 2 Ch. 52.

thority for the view that gifts for the purpose of constructing homes for the aged will meet the public benefit test by giving relief to the aged, but only if the intended recipients have needs appropriately related to the type of facility. The following gifts, for example, have been upheld as charitable within this category: a scheme to build self-contained dwellings for the elderly;[61] a trust to establish a home for "Old Presbyterian persons";[62] and a home for "old people over 65 years' resident in a specified locality.[63] Where it was intended that the residents would pay full costs then a gift to establish a home could not attain charitable status.[64] Likewise a gift to widows could not be charitable unless they were also old or poor.[65] Where a gift was to provide supplementary luxuries for residents, who would not otherwise be able to avail of same, then it was held to be charitable.[66]

Having become "aged" there is no necessity to be also indigent. A gift for the relief of the aged will be charitable even if the intended recipients are not poor[67] as will gifts to provide accommodation.[68] In England, as explained by Danckwerts J.[69]:

> "It has never been suggested that poor people must also be aged to be objects of charity, and there is no reason for holding that aged people must also be poor to come within the meaning of the preamble to the Statute."

However, a gift to provide money for the rich aged would fail since lack of money is not necessarily a need caused by old age, and furthermore, it does not require relief, since the beneficiaries already have that which the gift purports to provide.

12.7 ACCOMMODATION

12.7.1 Rest homes

"A home of rest for anyone who needs a home is *prima facie* a charitable object".[70]

---

[61] See *Joseph Rowntree Memorial Trust Hospital Association Ltd. v. Attorney-General, op cit.*
[63] See *Re Dunlop* [1984] N.I. 408.
[64] See *Re Robinson* [1951] Ch. 198.
[64] See *Re Clark House* (1972) 5 N.B.R. (2d) 431.
[65] See *A-G v. Northern Ireland v. Forde* [1932] NI 1.
[66] See *Martin v. Pelan* (1954) 13 W.W.R.N.S. 154.
[67] See for example, *Re Glyn's Will Trusts* (1950) 66 T.L.R. (Pt. 2) 510, and *Re Neal* (1966) 110 S.J. 549.
[68] See *Re Glyn's Will Trusts op. cit.*; *Re Bradbury* [1950] 2 All E.R. 1150n; and *Re Robinson, op. cit.*
[69] See *Re Glyn's Will Trusts, op. cit.*
[70] *per* Harrison QC, President of Lands Tribunal, *Incorporated Cripples Institute and Holiday Homes v. Commissioner of Valuation* VR/11/1965 at p. 13.

The provision of a rest home, as a support service for a defined group of persons with a need for such a service,[71] is charitable. Gifts have, accordingly, been granted charity status where the purpose was to establish a rest home for nurses,[72] members of a religious community[73] and lady teachers.[74] In these case it was established that the recipients were engaged in charitable activities, that their work would be assisted by the provision of a rest home and that they were in need of such a facility.

But it must be borne in mind, as Picarda has rightly observed[75] that while

> "... it would be wrong to assume that a rest home can only be charitable if it is confined to people carrying out charitable work. It must, however, be clear that such a home is intended for people who are truly in need of a rest home."

The public benefit test will be satisfied if the donor's intention is clearly to make provision for those in need. Such an intention may be explicitly expressed by the donor[76] where the facility was stated to be for "persons in need of rest by reason of the stress and strain caused or partly caused by the conditions in which they ordinarily live and/or work". It may be indicated by the use of a form of words such as "home of rest" or it may be implicit in the nature of the gift as when the intended beneficiaries are engaged in stressful work of a charitable nature.

The test will not be met by a gift to those without a need for it. As is often observed, a trust to establish a rest home for millionaires would fail.[77] Nor will it be met in the case of most nursing homes; a private nursing home, established and run on a profit making basis, is clearly not charitable.

In *Re Norgate*[78] the donor's gift of property to be used to establish a rest home for vegetarians, teetotallers, pacifists and conscientious objectors was held to be non-charitable because it was not evident that such a home would provide a congenial environment for a mix of persons with possibly mutually incompatible needs. The fact that a donor believed that his gift would have the effect of meeting the needs of the intended recipients would not affect the outcome. The terse good sense of Picarda's comment[79]:

> "... cranks are not a sufficient section of the public, so that a trust for the benefit of cranks will not be a trust for the public benefit. . . ."

---

[71] See *Re James* [1932] 2 Ch. 25 at 31, *per* Farwell J.
[72] See *Re White's Will Trusts* [1951] 1 All E.R. 528.
[73] See *Re James, op. cit.*
[74] See *Re Estlin* (1903) 72 L.J. Ch. 687.
[75] *op. cit.* at p. 112.
[76] See *Re Chaplin* [1933] Ch. 115.
[77] See *Re White's Will Trusts* [1951] 1 All E.R. 528 *per* Harman J. at p. 530.
[78] *The Times*, July 21, 1944; 88 Sol. Jo. 267n.
[79] *op. cit.* at p. 112.

would guide the judiciary in this jurisdiction, as elsewhere in the United Kingdom though not necessarily in Ireland, and ensure that charitable status was denied. In *Re Brown*[80] there is a sense that Campbell J. agreed with this view of "crank" in holding that gifts to "Vegetarian Retirement Homes Ltd and "Vegetarian Homes for Children" failed. However, he did hold that a gift to "Homes for Elderly Vegetarians Ltd" succeeded.

12.7.2 Children's homes

Orphans and orphanages have long been recognised as coming within the scope of both founding statutes. That they provide proper objects for charitable gifts has been illustrated, on this island, by two cases. Before Partition the court in *Jackson v. A-G*[81] held that "gifts to Presbyterian missions and orphans" were charitable. Subsequently and similarly, in *Baptist Union of Ireland (Northern) Corp Ltd. v. Commissioners of Inland Revenue*,[82] a gift which included missionaries and orphans among its intended beneficiaries, was also declared charitable. A gift to found a Protestant orphanage for boys was held charitable in *Re Simpson, Wallace v. Attorney General*.[83] It seems the public benefit test will be satisfied if the beneficiaries are limited both by gender and religion. More recently in England, gifts to statutory bodies to be used for the benefit of children in statutory care, have been held to be charitable.[84]

The English case of *Re Cole*[85] is often quoted to illustrate the law's concern to establish not just the eligibility of the intended beneficiary as a proper recipient of a charitable gift but also the appropriateness of that gift to the need of the intended beneficiary when viewed in the context of the relevant *Pemsel* heading. The case involved a gift to East Sussex county council "for the general benefit and general welfare of the children for the time being in Southdown House", which was a home for children accommodated under the powers of statutory care orders. At any point in time, some of the home's occupants would be children in care due to no fault of their own but to protect them from the abuse or neglect of adults, while others would be delinquents. In ruling that the gift was not charitable, Romer LJ declared:

> "I cannot regard the provision of television sets … for the benefit of such children as juvenile delinquents and refractory children … as coming within any conception of charity which is to be found in the preamble."[86]

---

[80] *op. cit.*
[81] [1917] 1 I.R. 332.
[82] [1945] N.I. 99.
[83] [1974] N.I.J.B. November.
[84] See *Re Sahal's Will Trusts* [1958] 1 W.L.R. 1243.
[85] [1958] Ch. 877.
[86] *op. cit.* at p. 888.

The problem is one of ensuring that the available recipients are both eligible beneficiaries by being within the scope of the donor's charitable intentions and have needs which may be appropriately met by the gift.

12.7.3 Holiday homes

Providing holiday homes for the "needy" has long been a popular charitable activity in Northern Ireland. The Lands Tribunal has given decisions in four cases on this subject. A wide variety of beneficiaries are comprised within the genus "needy". The rule, as expressed by Harrison Q.C., the President of the Tribunal, is that:

> "... a gift to provide and maintain a holiday home for handicapped or disabled persons would be a good charitable purpose within the spirit and intendment of the Irish Statute of Charitable Uses."[87]

Providing holiday accommodation for poor people (including children and old people) is also charitable.[88] Harrison, in *Incorporated Cripples' Institutes and Holiday Homes v. Commissioner of Valuation*[89] ruled that providing homes for cripples, neglected children, the working and neglected classes is charitable, and reiterated that it was charitable to "accommodate persons who are the proper objects of charity by providing an opportunity to take a holiday which they could otherwise not afford".[90] In this context, handicapped also includes mentally handicapped.[91]

12.8 RELIEF OF THE "IMPOTENT"

In its original context, the "impotent" were those persons rendered helpless and dependant by reason of physical disability (see also above). This remains the current interpretation which extends to accommodate, for example, those whose disability results from acts of war. Again, there is no necessity that the intended recipient be both disabled and poor,[92] though there must be some sense in which the gift relieves their situation and meets the public benefit

---

[87] *David Ravey v. Commissioner of Valuation* VR/28/1972 at p 5, although if provided by a private individual , without a trust, in his own dwelling house, it would not be charitable.

[88] *Trustees of Shankhill Road Mission v. Commissioner of Valuation* VR/21/1965.

[89] VR/5/1965.

[90] *ibid.* at p. 6.

[91] See the related case of *Incorporated Cripples' Institutes and Holiday Homes v Commissioner of Valuation* VR/6/1965, refused charitable status on other grounds.

[92] See, for example, *Sanderson's Trustee v. Edinburgh Royal Blind Asylum* [1919] 1 S.L.T. 39.

test. A gift which is for the benefit of persons both rich and poor[93] will be charitable but one which benefits only rich persons will not.[94]

12.8.1 Socially impotent

In Northern Ireland a wide meaning has been given to the term "impotent", so that it extends not just to those physically impotent but to those who are socially impotent. The Lands Tribunal accepted an argument put forward by Carswell (later Carswell L.C.J.) in which he described "alcoholics, ex prisoners, mentally inadequate or homeless men who could not accept the constraints imposed by society and how are impotent in the legal sense".[95] The case concerned what was then referred to as a lodging house but which might now be described as a hostel for those with special needs. The Tribunal, somewhat dismissively, defined its inhabitants as "virtually all are thriftless or improvident men who cannot properly manage what money they have, but spend it on drink, gambling or otherwise without thought for the morrow".[96] The Tribunal held that such a hostel was charitable. It helped the individual inhabitant by providing them with accommodation and it served the broader public benefit also.

There are many examples of a gift to a class of persons suffering from a common disability being confirmed as charitable.

12.8.2 Relief of the blind

The blind are, logically, a class of disabled persons within the broader grouping of "impotent". In England they are considered an object of charity under the first head.[97] In that jurisdiction the courts have held charitable, for example, a gift made for the benefit of 10 blind boys and 10 blind girls resident in a specified area.[98] Gifts to relieve the effects of particular forms of disability (*e.g.* blindness) through the development of related aids (*e.g.* Braille) will also be charitable whether on not the ultimate beneficiaries are rich or poor.[99]

In Northern Ireland, this approach has been extended to include the activities of an organisation dedicated to providing training for blind persons in a

---

[93] See *Jones v. Williams* (1767) Amb 651; *Verge v. Somerville* [1924] A.C. 496; *Karen Kayemeth le Jisroel Ltd. v. IRC* [1931] 2 KB 465.
[94] See *A-G v. Duke of Northumberland* (1877) 7 Ch. D. 745 at 753, *per* Sir George Jessel M.R.; *Re Macduff* [1896] 1 Ch. 451 at 471, C.A.
[95] *Incorporated Cripples' Institutes and Holiday Homes v. Commissioner of Valuation* VR/11/1965 at p. 6.
[96] *ibid.* at p. 3.
[97] For example, see *Re Lewis* (1955) Ch. 104.
[98] *ibid.* Also, see, *Re Elliott* (1910) 102 L.T. 528.
[99] See *John Brunyate* (1945) 61 L.Q.R. 268 at 272.

decision with important policy implications for persons anywhere in the United Kingdom suffering from any form of disability. A wide range of activities may be construed as charitable after the decision of the Court of Appeal in *Belfast Association for the Employment of the Industrious Blind v. Commissioners of Valuation*.[100] The association in that case was created for the amelioration of the condition of the blind by teaching skills and giving them employment. It had a factory where goods were made by blind people and it had a shop which sold both blind-produced and commercially purchased goods. The purpose of the selling of commercially purchased goods was twofold: (a) to increase profit generally and (b) to increase the viability of the shop to help sell blind-produced goods. All profits were used for the benefit of blind people.

The court did not dispute that the purposes of the organisation were exclusively charitable, in fact it was already exempt from income tax as a charity. The only point of contention was whether the shop was exempt from rating as being used for exclusively charitable purposes. The majority of the Court of Appeal (MacDermott L.C.J. dissenting) held that the shop was liable for rates because it sold non-blind produced goods. However, the organisation as a whole constituted a charity. Therefore, not just direct gifts to the blind, or funding into research for the blind, or material assistance for the blind are charitable, so to are gifts for training the blind, selling what they produce and providing employment for them (see also, Chaper 21).

12.8.3 Relief of substance abusers

Gifts to promote the curing of alcoholics or drug addicts, or to assist in the prevention of such addictions, are charitable.[101] Trusts to promote temperance by the introduction of legislation are political and therefore not charitable.[102]

12.8.4 Welfare of ex-soldiers

Following the decision in *Royal British Legion Attendants Company v. Commissioner of Valuation*[103] it appears that the welfare of ex-soldiers may have been assimilated into the definition of charitable under the first *Pemsel* head. This point was first mooted in the Privy Council case of *Verge v. Somerville*.[104] The Privy Council held the welfare of ex-soldiers charitable under the fourth head, but stated that it would have found it charitable under the first head if necessary. The court in the *Legion Attendants* case also took this safety net

---

[100] [1968] N.I. 21.
[101] See *Re Hood* [1931] 1 Ch. 240; *IRC v. Falkirk Temperance Café Trust* 1927 S.C. 261.
[102] See *IRC v. Temperance Council of Christian Churches of England and Wales* (1926) 136 L.T. 27.
[103] [1979] N.I. 138.
[104] (1924) A.C. 496.

approach, holding that the organisation was benefiting an ex-serviceman by providing him employment and was therefore charitable under the first and fourth head.[105]

---

[105] See further, Chap. 11 on fourth head charities for the army.

CHAPTER 13

Other Charitable Purposes: Politics

13.1 INTRODUCTION

Charitable status and political purposes are, in law, mutually exclusive.[1] This is a difficult moral proposition to sustain. Charitable purposes are and have always been symbiotically linked to the purposes of politicians. Charities, as champions of their respective causes, may be expected to contribute assertively to debates on issues affecting those causes. Arguably, it is a proposition with particularly unfortunate implications for the fragmented society of Northern Ireland where the political connotations of social disadvantage are often inescapable and where promoting peace and reconciliation is not a charitable purpose.

Political activity or inactivity often provides a focus for charitable activity. To confine charities to an independent and politically neutral stance, in a policy-creating context directly affecting the socially disadvantaged, is to insist that they revert to a stereotypical "soup-kitchen" role; treating the effects and ignoring the causes. Ironically, it is unlikely that charities ever adopted or were required to adopt such a politically neutral position in the past. In the Victorian era, many important initiatives resulting in policy changes by politicians were led by charities.

It is probable that the current prohibition on political activity has its origins in two quite separate principles. Firstly, in the principle that an organisation must be formed for exclusively charitable purposes if it is to attain charity status. It will be debarred from such status if it is evident that one of its primary purposes is to seek a change in government policy. Secondly, in the principle that charities should not become embroiled in party political disputes.

Efforts to sanitise or neuter the potential political activity of charities are probably doomed to failure as many are so long established, with power to control and disseminate authoritative research material commanding widespread public respect, that they will simply exercise political leverage more discretely. It may also be damaging to the fabric of democratic society to dumb down those who provide a voice for the socially excluded.

In Northern Ireland, the case for treating the relationship between charities

---

[1] *McGovern* v. *Attorney General* [1982] 1 Ch. 321. Some limited form of ancillary political activity may be permissible; see further, below.

and political activity as a distinct area of law is particularly strong. However, to do so entails dealing with the dearth of indigenous material, legislative and case law, which is usually relied upon to explicate law and practice. This absence of evidence that the law is relating to social need, in the context of charitable/political purposes, in the one northern European region most obviously likely to benefit from it, requires explanation. For that reason alone, despite the inherent difficulties, the subject warrants separate attention.

This chapter examines the complex manner in which the law relates to charitable status and political purposes. It begins by considering the definition of political purposes, the rights involved and the rationale for prohibiting charities from engaging in it.

13.2 RATIONALE, RIGHTS AND DEFINITIONS

A voluntary organisation seeking to acquire or retain charitable status, and all the attendant financial benefits, must avoid having political purposes and engaging in most forms of political activity. The proponents for and against this position rest their case ultimately on the same ground – it is necessary because it promotes the interests of democracy.

13.2.1 Rationale

The rationale underpinning the separation of charitable status from political activity has both theoretical and judicial components.

13.2.1(i) Theoretical rationale

The accepted rationale for denying charitable status to bodies pursuing political goals rests on several related arguments. They all essentially stem from the view that such activity subverts the established democratic political process. Because a charity has not submitted to the electoral system it is not publicly accountable. Because it is not usually internally organised in a democratic fashion it is seldom in a position to proclaim that other systems are unfair. It is therefore claimed that a charity has no mandate to represent issues before the "body politic". It is also suggested that the social value of a charity lies in the latter's independence which would be compromised if it became politicised. A corollary being that the legitimacy conferred on a charity by virtue of its formal recognition as such would, in the eyes of the general public, be extended to the cause it chose to espouse, with corresponding disadvantages for causes not championed by charities. Allied to this is the argument that it would be illogical for the state to defray the liability of an organisation to contribute towards the "public purse", thereby imposing a duty on others to make good the tax loss, only to find that by so doing it was subsidising the capacity of the organisation to undermine state policies. Again, by granting public monies to charities the state is channelling taxpayers' funds on a preferential basis, but it has no way of knowing which campaigns taxpayers support and which they do not.[2]

On the other hand, it could be argued that the business of charities is and always has been intimately related to the business of governments. Deprivation, homelessness, unemployment, civil liberties, animal rights, conservation and the myriad other issues which provide the *raison d'être* for charities are ultimately also political matters. The government of the day tackles the issues arising in accordance with its representative role in the political process. Charities do so in accordance with their participative role in that process. Both, arguably, are equally valid and complementary aspects of the same model of democratic politics.

The Charity Commission has recognised the validity of both these arguments:

> "On the one hand, many people think that charities should be allowed, and indeed have a duty, to campaign freely to change public policy on any issue if it is relevant to their work and if they have direct experience to offer. On the other hand, some argue that such campaigning is a misuse of charity funds, a misdirection of effort by charities and a misuse of the fiscal concessions from which charities benefit."[3]

The democratic vigour of a healthy society will be promoted and sustained where representative and participative bodies are not viewed as mutually exclusive but are instead enabled within a charity law framework to fully engage and commit their respective resources to addressing the same agenda of social need. As has been said:

> "... the existing situation needs to be reviewed, as the regulations governing charitable status and political activity are impractical, discriminatory and undemocratic."[4]

13.2.1(ii) Judicial rationale

The courts have accepted and indeed promoted the notion that charities cannot be established for political purposes. The rationale which they have advanced is different from the theoretical one stated above and is firmly grounded within the paradigm of charity law.

---

[2] See, further, Perri 6, *Restricting the Freedom of Speech of Charities: Do the Rationales Stand Up*. Also, see, *McGovern v. Attorney General* [1982] 1 Ch. 321, *per* Slade J. at p. 336.

[3] CC9 at p. 10.

[4] See, Burt , E., "Charities and Political Activity: Time to Re-think the Rules" in *The Political Quarterly*, vol. 69, no. 1, p. 23. Also, see, Dunn, A., "Charity Law as a Political Option for the Poor" in *Northern Ireland Legal Quarterly*, Belfast, vol. 50, no. 3, 1999, pp. 298–317.

The rationale is that political purposes cannot pass the public benefit test. There are two broad reasons are advanced. Firstly, it is not possible to say whether a political purpose will actually be of benefit. The court considered a company with a purpose of promoting a secular society in *Bowman* v. *Secular Society*.[5] It held that:

> "A trust for political objects has always been held invalid, not because it is illegal, for everyone is at liberty to advocate or promote by any lawful means a change in the law, but because the court has no means of judging whether a proposed change in the law will or will not be for the public benefit, and therefore cannot say that a gift to secure the change is a charitable gift."[6]

The first argument is an evidential one, but it is reinforced by the second which looks to the constitutional structure of the United Kingdom with its tripartite division of functions between the executive, parliament and the courts. Slade J. in *McGovern* v. *Attorney General*[7] held that the courts could not investigate whether political goals, such as changing laws, would be for the public benefit as to do so would be usurping the legislative authority of Parliament. Judges have neither the jurisdiction nor the competence to voice an opinion on the merit of a particular law, they merely apply it.

13.2.2 Rights

Charitable activity in its most traditional form was most typically associated with provision of care and shelter to the needy. As the State assumed more comprehensive responsibility for ensuring that basic levels of social care were being met, charitable activity became more concerned with complementing State service provision and on negotiating with the State on behalf of the socially disadvantaged. The latter activity – involving advocacy, representation and lobbying – is steadily bringing into sharp focus throughout the charity sector an underlying fault line between assertion of rights and delivery of services as appropriate methods of responding to social disadvantage.

13.2.2(i) Rights: international instruments

When considering advocacy rights it is necessary to bear in mind the wider context provided by the various international instruments which now bind this jurisdiction as others in the United Kingdom. These offer relevant benchmarks against which domestic policy must be measured.[8] In relation to freedom of expression, for example, the Universal Declaration of Human Rights 1948 states:

---

[5] [1917] A.C. 406.
[6] *ibid.* at p. 442.
[7] *op cit.*
[8] See for example, Art. 10(2) of the European Convention on Human Rights.

"Article 19: Everyone has the right to freedom of opinion and expression; this right includes freedom to hold opinions without interference and to seek, receive and impart information and ideas through any media and regardless of frontiers."

"Article 29(2): In the exercise of his rights and freedoms, everyone shall be subject only to such limitations as are determined by law solely for the purpose of securing due recognition and respect for the rights and freedoms of others, and of meeting the just requirements of morality, public order, and the general welfare of democratic society."

Freedom of association similarly finds international endorsement. Both Article 20 of the Universal Declaration of Human Rights and Article 22 of the International Convention on Civil and Political Rights provide specific recognition for the right of free association. Articles 10, 11, 17 and 18 of the European Convention on Human Rights deal explicitly with member states obligations to guarantee the freedoms of expression, assembly and association.

Charities, as much as persons, are entitled to avail of the protection provided by such rights (see further, Chapter 4).

13.2.3 Definitions

McCullough J. in *R. v. Radio Authority, ex parte Bull*[9] gave a sensible definition of when a matter can be construed as "political":

"Once the matter has become the subject of government policy, or once the need for legislation about it is advocated, particularly if the matter has become contentious, then, as it seems to me, it is open ... to treat it as political."[10]

13.2.3(i) Political activity

The exact range of conduct falling within the definition of "political activity" cannot be defined with any precision. It clearly includes any action undertaken in support of or in opposition to a particular political party or a candidate for a particular political office.[11] Equally clearly, it encompasses lobbying for or against specific laws, engaging in public advocacy or pursuing issue oriented litigation. However, individuals possess rights of freedom of speech and association; although there is some uncertainty about the degree to which these rights can be extended to organisations and, if so, the limits which may then be placed on the degree to which they can vest in charitable organisa-

---

[9] [1995] 4 All E.R. 481, [1998] Q.B. 294.

[10] *ibid.*, at p. 500.

[11] See, for example, *Re Jones* (1929) 45 T.L.R. 259 concerning a gift of land to the Conservative party.

tions. In the words of Cairns the following purposes are to be regarded as political and therefore not charitable:

> the furtherance of the interests of a political party;
>
> the procurement of changes in the law of a foreign country;
>
> the procurement of the reversal of government policy or of particular decisions of
>
> government or other authorities in this country or in a foreign country.[12]

13.3 VOLUNTARY ORGANISATIONS, CHARITIES AND POLITICS

The law insists that a line be drawn between the political activities of voluntary organisations *per se* and those which have acquired or are applying for charitable status.

13.3.1 Voluntary organisations

Voluntary organisations contribute to the political texture and vitality of society. They are strategically positioned to act as a bridgehead between government and the community by representing a wide range of groups or causes whose concerns would otherwise remain unheard by government. At the same time they remain available for consultation by government policy makers in search of practical and acceptable solutions to economic, social and environmental problems. In short, they generate a culture which permits the growth of participative democracy.

The current restrictions on political activity by charities result in some organisations being prevented from obtaining or retaining charitable status, or in choosing to forego it, even though they undertake charitable work. This denies them the substantial financial benefits of charitable status, including eligibility to receive funds from organisations which only support charities. Voluntary organisations as a whole can fulfil their responsibilities as part of the fabric of a modern democratic society only if the current restrictions governing the political activity of some are ended. Abolishing the restrictions would allow "non-charitable" voluntary organisations parity of access to the financial and other benefits of charitable status alongside their "charitable" counterparts, since "non-charitable" voluntary organisations will no longer be denied, or compelled to forego, charitable status on political grounds.

---

[12] See Cairns, E., *Charities: Law and Practice* (2nd ed., Sweet & Maxwell, London, 1993) at p. 25. In the adjoining jurisdiction, see *Colgan v. Independent Radio and Television Commission, Ireland and the Attorney General* [1999] 1 I.L.R.M. 22, *per* O'Sullivan J. at pp. 24–25.

It is open to question whether such a forced choice between freedom of speech and financial benefit should have to be made in a democratic society by voluntary organisations striving to alleviate need in that society.

13.3.2 Voluntary organisations and advocacy

Voluntary organisations often play an important role as "pressure groups" working to shape social, economic and environmental policies. They do so by providing a forum for the coherent expression of such fundamental rights as freedom of assembly and speech. They articulate the concerns of a diverse range of minority groups and thereby promote inclusiveness. For some groups, which may otherwise be defined as subversive and illegal, they provide a platform and a means whereby their grievances may be legitimately aired.

Arguably, recent years have witnessed a muting of dissent in the voluntary sector. The argument runs that the monitoring, lobbying and advocacy roles traditionally pursued by voluntary organisations in relation to the policies of government bodies have become suppressed. In England, Deakin has spoken of a danger of losing the distinctive nature of voluntary action:

> "The distinctive nature of voluntary action in our society is now in danger of being compromised as organisations move away from their original objectives and take on new roles defined for them by others"[13]

and both Deakin and Kemp fear a loss of independence:

> "Short-term contracts may threaten independence and the ability to speak out or campaign. And ... may lead to unhealthy dependencies."[14]

Referring to the partnership between the voluntary sector and government, both stress the need for equality and equability and need to maintain an advocacy role: "voluntary bodies must be free to be advocates even where they are also partners".[15] Several different reasons are advanced for this development. Firstly, that the contracting/partnership strategy pursued by the statutory agencies, has had the effect of persuading their voluntary partners that "biting the hand that feeds them" would not be conducive to a renewal of contractual arrangements. The remarks of Lord Astor of Hever, in a relatively recent House of Lords debate on the future of charities, apply with equal force to this jurisdiction:

---

[13] See the Commission on the Future of the Voluntary Sector in England, *Meeting the Challenge of Change: Voluntary Action into the 21ˢᵗ Century*, NCVO Publications, London, 1996 (also referred to as the Deakin Report).

[14] See the Commission on the Future of the Voluntary Sector in Scotland, *Head and Heart*, SCVO, Edinburgh, 1997 (also referred to as the Kemp Report), p.47, para. 6.5.5.

[15] Deakin (1996) pp.13-14.

"With so many of the charities' money coming from government sources, many charities lack genuine freedom of action."[16]

Secondly, it is argued that there has been a hardening of the judicial view that charitable status and lobbying for changes in the law are incompatible activities. Thirdly, it is suggested that at government level there has been a diverting of funds away from bodies which challenge or subvert contemporary politics. Other factors may also be playing a part: short-term funding from European sources is perhaps inducing a compliance culture in recipient bodies; the impact of the market economy on the voluntary sector, particularly competitive tendering for government contracts, is possibly fragmenting the capacity of similar organisations to co-ordinate their lobbying. It is also probable that the growth of umbrella bodies is reducing the number of independent voluntary sector voices, formalising and channelling their critical commentary, and perhaps opening up a new, direct and more discrete and internal dialogue between the voluntary sector and government policy and service providers. Further, it may be that the advocacy role traditionally borne by individual voluntary organisations is now perceived as the responsibility of other bodies such as those for Equal Opportunities, the Ombudsman or Law Centres etc.

Whatever its cause, it may be argued that the absence of a strong voice articulating the view from the voluntary sector inhibits a constructive democratic dialogue between state service providers and users. In England and Wales the related issues have generated vigorous debate.[17]

13.3.3 Voluntary organisations in Northern Ireland

The position of voluntary organisations in Northern Ireland is different from that of such organisations elsewhere in the United Kingdom in a number of important respects. Firstly, and most obviously, there has been the effect of thirty years of violence on the social infrastructure and, most importantly, on the sense of a shared community and willingness to build a civil society. Inevitably, many small local organisations are now as polarised and partisan as the communities they represent; they may well generate social capital within their constituencies but this often also serves to reinforce their separateness and fragment overall social cohesion. The voluntary sector in Northern Ireland cannot, thus, be viewed as sharing in the same collective values and strategic concerns typical of the sector elsewhere in the United Kingdom. Secondly, the absence of a local government tier of administration for two and a half decades has had a singular effect on the interface between the voluntary and statu-

---

[16] See HL Deb. vol. 586, col. 1213–1214, March 4, 1998.

[17] See, for example, the Labour Party Review of the Voluntary Sector *Building the Future Together: Labour's Policies for Partnership between Government and the Voluntary Sector*, 1997 and the Deakin and Kemp Reports each of which endorsed the contribution which voluntary organisations make to the democratic process.

tory sectors in Northern Ireland. In particular, the reliance upon government appointed boards led to a much stronger alliance between some of the larger voluntary organisations and government bodies than would be typical of other jurisdictions of the United Kingdom. Thirdly, the voluntary sector has provided the government with a conduit through which funds from Westminster and from the EC could be channelled and an expedient vehicle for delivering social care services to communities which were otherwise alienated from the State. This conferred status upon and vested real negotiating power in some mediating voluntary organisations. Together these and other factors point up the distinctiveness and relative importance of the voluntary sector in Northern Ireland when compared with other jurisdictions in the United Kingdom.

13.3.3(i) Funding arrangements

Voluntary organisations in Northern Ireland are very dependent upon government funding. As noted by the Department for Social Development:

> "Government in its various guises is the major source of funding for organisations and the most recent analysis of government funding of the sector found that a total of £189 million was delivered through 58 programmes in 1996/97. These included 30 European Structural Funds measures with a value of £64.6m, with £44 m made available to the Special Support Programme for Peace and Reconciliation."[18]

This dependency is much greater than is the case with their counterparts in England and Wales. In Northern Ireland, a survey conducted in 1995[19] revealed that 84 per cent of the income of a sample of voluntary organisations involved in delivering personal health and social care services was derived from public funding with a further 8 per cent from the sale of goods and services. A subsequent study in 1996/7,[20] drawing from a larger sample of similar organisations, showed that 76 per cent of such income was so sourced; 59 per cent being in the form of direct government grants or contracts. Research in England and Wales shows comparable figures of 26 per cent of income from grants and donations and 35 per cent from the sale of goods and services.

It may well be the case that such financial dependency on government is already accompanied in Northern Ireland by a greater degree of voluntary sector compliance with government policies than prevails elsewhere in the United Kingdom. That the government is actively pursuing measures to en-

---

[18] See Dept. for Social Development, *Consultation Document on Funding for the Voluntary and Community Sector*, Belfast, the Voluntary Activity Unit, April 2,000, para 1.

[19] See Social Services Inspectorate, *Adding Value: the Contribution of Voluntary Organisations to Health and Social Welfare*, Belfast, DHSS, 1998.

[20] See N.I.C.V.A., *The State of the Sector Two: Northern Ireland Voluntary Almanac*, Belfast, 1998.

sure a greater degree of future compliance is clear from the terms of reference of the inter-Departmental review group which produced the consultation document on funding. It firmly states its driving aim as:

"... the need to ensure that government funding (including European funding) of the sector aligns with government priorities."[21]

There must be some concern that such a policy will pose a threat to the independence of the sector and its capacity to advocate on behalf of those whose particular needs are not being met by government priorities.

13.3.4 Charities and the voluntary sector in Northern Ireland

The Northern Ireland Council for Voluntary Action (NICVA)[22] has provided a statistical map of the scale and scope of voluntary activities in Northern Ireland. It has also, since 1995, maintained *SectorNet* the most comprehensive, but entirely voluntary, database of the province's voluntary and community sector organisations. The Charities Branch of the Department for Social Development (previously the Department of Health and Social Services (DHSS)) has issued a number of helpful briefing and consultation papers.[23] From these valuable sources of data the following facts emerge to provide a picture of charities in Northern Ireland.

- In 1995 there were 3,095 charities known to the DHSS

- In 1997 private charitable giving totalled approx. £42m, corporate donations £4.4m,

- In 1996–97, the National Lottery Charities Board distributed £13.3m to 243 projects run by charities

- In 1996–97, the government gave £248m and foundations gave approx. £23m to voluntary and community organisations including charities.

Charities clearly play a prominent role in the voluntary sector in Northern

---

[21] *op cit.*, at p. 5. This resonates with similar long-standing policy concerns in England, see, for example: Woodfield, P., Binns, G., Hirst, R., and Neal, D., *Efficiency Scrutiny of the Supervision of Charities, Report of the Home Secretary and the Economic Secretary to the Treasury* (or 'the Woodfield Report'), London, HMSO, 1987; the National Audit Report Monitoring and Control of Charities in England and Wales, 1987; Report of the Public Accounts Committee, Monitoring and Control of Charities in England and Wales, 1988; and the resulting White Paper, Charities: a Framework for the Future (Cmnd 694), 1989. In this jurisdiction, see the *Adding Value* Report.

[22] See *State of the Sector* (first edition 1997, second 1998). However, more information is needed on matters such as; a profile of the sector by type of activity, type of legal form, duration and spread of organisations; on the on the extent of government funding; on the degree to which voluntary organisations engage in business activities; and on the scale of fundraising campaigns.

[23] See, for example, as *Northern Ireland Charities: A Guide for Trustees* (1997).

Ireland. In keeping with many other voluntary sector organisations, they have taken on and are being encouraged to take on an ever-increasing share of what would traditionally have been regarded as government service provision. Unlike, other voluntary organisations, however, charities are not free to bend their policies to suit government priorities. The law requires them to stay within their objects and retain their independence. There are grounds for concern if future funding arrangements and service delivery contracts are to flow from government bodies to charities in accordance with the latter's demonstrable compliance with the policies of the former.

13.3.5 Developments in the wider voluntary sector context

There have been two relatively recent U.K. experiments in the politics of the voluntary sector which may prove to be significant for the future of charities and charity law in Northern Ireland: "compacts" and "partnerships".

13.3.5(i) Compacts

The Deakin Report specifically recommended a concordat between central government and the voluntary sector, and the Labour Party made a General Election commitment to establish a "compact" which would establish the principles governing relations between central government and the sector, with a task force of ministers to oversee its implementation. Since Labour came to power in May 1997 four separate compacts (for England, Scotland, Wales and Northern Ireland) have been developed. The *Scottish Compact* was published in October 1998, the English Compact *Getting it Right Together* and the Compact for Wales were both published in November 1998. A similar Compact for Northern Ireland, entitled *Building Real Partnership* was laid before Parliament in December 1998. In this Compact the government pledges that:

> "It recognises, respects and supports the independence of the sector and its right to campaign within the law, to comment on and, where appropriate, to challenge Government policy."

Leaving aside the considerable caveat implied in "where appropriate" it remains the case that the Northern Ireland Compact together with the revised *Strategy for the Support of the Voluntary Sector and for Community Development in Northern Ireland*[24] have the potential to reshape the context within which charities and charity law have to operate; provided they are underpinned by a sound and practical programme of goals and objectives.

---

[24] D.H.S.S., 1993.

13.3.5(ii) The district partnerships

These are locally based forums comprising one-third representation from each of the following: business or for-profit bodies; community development and other non-profit bodies; and elected councillors. There are twenty-six such partnerships in Northern Ireland governed by a Partnership Board. Considerable funds have been made available to the partnerships by the EC on condition that each puts forward an agreed proposal for a project of benefit to its community. For example, under the European Special Support Programme for Peace and Reconciliation, approved by the European Parliament in April 1995, the European Commission granted 300m ecus and the governments of the United Kingdom and Ireland granted a further 100m ecus. This programme ran until 1997 and was then extended to 1999. The equal weighting of diverse interests in such forums provides an interesting and exciting demonstration of effective participative democracy. It remains to be seen whether these partnerships will be displaced by the new formal political structures or whether they will become consolidated as a mechanism for channelling small "p" politics to address local community needs. If the latter, then again the context for the role of charities and charity law will have changed.

13.4 CHANGING ROLE OF CHARITIES IN RELATION TO POLITICAL ISSUES

As the concept of "relative poverty" and the fact of fairly comprehensive health and social care programmes raise the threshold for charitable intervention within the northern European nations, so the role of their charities is changing. At least three major themes for future charitable activity are discernible. Firstly, there is a merging of social care service provision by charitable and government bodies. Secondly, the traditional role of charities though on the wane domestically is being revitalised and channelled into addressing third world poverty. Finally, the raised threshold of intervention is positioning charities to question the causes rather than to treat the effects of social disadvantage. Many charities now conduct, fund or utilise professional research programmes established to examine the myriad facets of social exclusion in contemporary western societies. This is necessarily opening up a more direct dialogue between charities and government.

13.4.1 An international perspective

The authors of a recent research project[25] carried out a survey of twenty-four

---

[25] See Perri 6 and Anita Randon, *Liberty, Charity and Politics: Non-Profit Law and Freedom of Speech,* Dartmouth, Aldershot, 1995.

countries to establish the nature of such links as might exist between the freedom of voluntary organisations to engage in campaiging and political activity and the prevailing type of civil law regime. They found that a clear distinction existed between countries with a charity law regime and those without it. As they state:

> "The majority of charity law countries are also characterised by a common law system ... At some stage in their history, all the charity law countries have followed the general approach which descends from the 1601 English Statute of Charitable Uses ... of the countries to constrain the campaigning activities of non-profit organisations specifically because of their organisational form or status, all were charity law, and ... originally common law, countries. *In other words, only the USA, Northern Ireland, Ireland, Canada, England and Wales, Australia, Scotland and India have specific constraints on campaigning by charities.*"[26]

All other non-charity law countries in their sample not only refrained from imposing any restrictions on campaigning by non-profit organisations but many openly encouraged their advocacy roles. More fundamentally, they state:

> "... no clear rationale was found to explain why campaigning by non-profit organisations is treated differently in charity and non-charity law countries."[27]

A common law legacy, and with it the differentiation between the *locus standi* of charities and other non-profit organisations, would seem to result in imposed constraints on political activity by charities. Northern Ireland is not alone in that respect.[28]

13.5 POLITICAL PURPOSES

The primary legal distinction, at the heart of the politics/charity interface, is

---

[26] *ibid.*, at pp. 5–6. Also note the observation made in the recent New Zealand case of *Re Collier* [1998] 1 N.Z.L.R. 81, regarding the non-charitable status of trusts for the benefit of political parties, that this:
... appears to be the agreed position throughout the common law world ...
per Hamond J. at p. 90.

[27] See, Perri 6 and Anita Randon, *Liberty, Charity and Politics: Non-Profit Law and Freedom of Speech, op. cit.* at p. 7.

[28] For further discussion on the political and social policy aspects of the relationship between charities and the law see, for example: Chesterman, M., *Charities, Trusts and Social Welfare*, Weidenfeld and Nicholson, London, (1979); Chisholm, L.B., "Politics and Charity: a Proposal for Peaceful Co-existence" in the *George Washington Law Review*, 1990, 58, 2, pp. 308–65; Gidron, B., Kramer, R.M. and Salamon, L.M. (eds.), *Government and the Third Sector: Emerging Relationships in Welfare States*, Jossey-Bass, San Francisco and Oxford, 1992; and Simon, J.G., "Foundations and Public Controversy: an Affirmative View" in Heimann, F., (ed.), *The Future of Foundations*, Spectrum Books, Prentice-Hall, Englewood Cliffs, New Jersey, 1973.

between bodies which have political purposes and bodies which engage in political activities. The tenor of the case law has always explicitly held that the former is not charitable. More recently and more realistically, *McGovern v. Attorney General* recognised that the latter could be charitable. Slade J held in that leading case that a charitable trust could use some political means to achieve its charitable ends. This approach has been expanded and developed considerably by the Charity Commission. It has issued guidance that ancillary political activities, carried out within defined parameters, will not vitiate charitable status.[29]

13.5.1 What are political purposes?

McCullough J. in *R. v. Radio Authority ex parte Bull*[30] gave a broad definition of what could be construed as political:

> "... once the matter has become the subject of government policy, or once the need for legislation is advocated, particularly if the matter is contentious, then, as it seems to me, it is open ... to treat it as political."[31]

Slade J. did not attempt a unifying conceptual definition in *McGovern v. Attorney General*,[32] instead he listed five things which were to be considered political purposes. These were:

(i)   to further the interests of a particular political party,

(ii) to procure changes in the laws of this country,

(iii) to bring about changes in the laws of a foreign country,

(iv) to bring about a reversal of government policy or of particular decisions of governmental authorities in this country,

(v)   to bring about a reversal of government policy or of particular decisions of governmental authorities in a foreign country.

This list was added to in *Re Koeppler's Will Trusts*[33]:

(vi) to oppose a particular change in the law or a change in a particular law.

As a leading case, the facts of *McGovern v. Attorney General* are worth stating. It concerned an attempt by Amnesty International to create a trust to have some of its work deemed charitable. The purposes of the trust were fourfold:

---

[29] CC9, *Political Activities and Campaigning by Charities*, (1999), CC9(a) *Political Activities and Campaigning by Local Community Charities*, (1996).
[30] [1995] 4 All E.R. 481, [1998] Q.B. 294.
[31] *ibid.* at p. 500.
[32] (1982) 1 Ch. 321.
[33] [1984] Ch. 243.

(a) looking after the needy, *i.e.* prisoners and ex-prisoners,

(b) promoting the abolition of capital and corporal punishment,

(c) researching and disseminating information on human rights,

(d) securing the release of political prisoners.

Slade J held that, although purposes (a) and (c) could be charitable, the other two were political. The political nature of these two contaminated the whole trust and the entire trust was void as being for political purposes. Other case law reinforces the summary of political purposes adopted by Slade J.

13.5.1(i) Political parties

Gifts for political parties are not charitable.[34] A gift for the "advancement and propagation of the teaching of socialised medicine" where this was very much in line with Labour Party principles is not charitable.[35] The case of *Re Hopkinson*[36] concerned a fund for the "advancement of adult education with particular reference to the education of men and women of all classes on the lines of the Labour Party's memorandum". Vaisey J., in dismissing the claim to charitable status, explained that:

> "... political propaganda masquerading – I do not use that term in any sinister sense – as education is not education within the statute of Elizabeth ... in other words it is not charitable."[37]

Some gifts, however, have escaped judicial disapproval even though they did, to all intents and purposes, further the interests of a particular political party. A gift for the maintenance of a village club and reading room "for the further-ance of Conservative principles and religious and mental improvement" was held charitable in *Re Scowcroft*.[38] The reasoning was based on a rather strained, conjunctive construction placed upon the words. It was only those Conserva-tive principles which promoted religious and moral improvement which were to be allowed. The latter case of *Bonar Law Memorial Trust v. IRC*[39] finds itself in greater alignment with the underlying rationale, by holding that a gift,

---

[34] *Goff v. Gurly* unreported, Supreme Court, April 24, 1980, gift to Fianna Fáil.

[35] *Re Bushnell* [1975] 1 W.L.R 1596.

[36] (1949) 1 All E.R. 346.

[37] *Re Hopkinson* [1949] 1 All E.R. 346, but see also the dubious authority of *Russel* v *Jackson* (1852) 10 Hare 204 which held that a socialist school could be charitable as long as socialism was not found to be subversive.

[38] [1898] 2 Ch. 638.

[39] (1933) 49 T.L.R. 220.

more explicitly expressed as being for the advancement of Conservative principles would not be charitable.[40]

Gifts with political themes may be charitable if they are bipartisan. A trust for the education of the public in political theory and forms of government is charitable.[41] In *Re Koeppler's Will Trusts*[42] it was held that a bequest to fund the holding of conferences with political themes can be charitable. The judge at first instance held that the ultimate purpose of that trust was to promote greater co-operation in Europe and the West. This would not be a charitable purpose.[43] However, the Court of Appeal held that the ultimate purpose was education in international relations through the holding of conferences.[44] This was a charitable purpose under the education head. There was no emphasis favouring the philosophy of a particular political party.

13.5.1(ii) Changing domestic law

A society which has as its object the total suppression of vivisection is a society with a political purpose and is therefore not charitable. This was the decision given by the House of Lords in *National Anti-Vivisection Society v. IRC*,[45] even though anti-vivisection and the protection of animals had previously been held charitable (see further, Chapter 11). One reason given was that courts could not pass comment on existing laws, "each court in deciding on the validity of a gift must decide on the principle that the law is right as it stands".[46]

Attempting to secularise society by lobbying for a change in the law is not charitable. Parker L.J. in *Bowman v. Secular Society Ltd.* stated that:

> "... the abolition of religious tests, the disestablishment of the Church, the secularisation of education, the alteration of the law touching religions or marriage or the observation of the Sabbath are purely political objects. Equity has always refused to recognise such objects as charitable."[47]

A body with the aim of increasing the restrictions on the sale of alcohol is a body with political purposes and is not charitable.[48]

Promoting existing law as opposed to lobbying for new laws is also politi-

---

[40] See also, *The Margaret Thatcher Foundation* (1991) Ch. Com. Rep. 39 App. D and political ideology passed off as education.

[41] *Re Trusts of the Arthur McDougall Fund* (1957) 1 W.L.R. 181.

[42] [1986] Ch. 423.

[43] [1984] Ch. 243

[44] [1986] Ch. 423.

[45] [1948] A.C. 32

[46] Tyssen on *Charitable Bequests*, 1st ed. at p. 176.

[47] (1917) AC 406 at p. 442.

[48] *IRC v. Temperance Council of Christian Churches of England and Wales* (1920) 10 T.C. 748, but see *IRC v. Falkirk Temperance Café Trust* [1927] S.C. 261.

cal.[49] However, promoting the enforcement of an existing law is not necessarily a political purpose. For example, promoting prosecutions or rewarding policemen in animal cruelty cases are charitable.[50]

It is possible to reconcile ostensible political purposes with charitable status. Charities can campaign against certain laws provided their goal is to educate the public to do voluntarily that which they may otherwise be statutorily required to do. For example, the purpose in *Jackson* v. *Phillips*[51] was to end slavery, not by changing the law, but by changing public sentiment through education. A gift to promote temperance, otherwise than by political means can be a valid charitable gift.[52]

13.5.1(iii) Changing foreign law

To pursue the abolition of capital and corporal punishment in foreign countries is to pursue a political purpose. Two reasons were advanced for this in the *McGovern* case. Firstly, the court would have no way of knowing if such an outcome would benefit the public. In this context, the public to be considered are the public of the United Kingdom according to Slade J acting on the authority of *Camille and Henry Dreyfus* v. *IRC*.[53] This seems open to question after the Charity Commission stated, in their latest review of the register that the public benefit test is now modified for charities which undertake activities overseas. The new test is to consider:

> "... whether they would be regarded as charities if their activities if their activities were confined to the United Kingdom and then deny charitable status only if there were good public policy reasons to do so, including whether or not the activities are legal in the country concerned."[54]

The second reason for denying charitable status is that such a body could damage diplomatic relations with that foreign country.

13.5.1(iv) Campaigning to change the policies of domestic or foreign governments

Students unions, renown for championing good causes and leading social protests against policies of the government of the day, have often been punished by judicial termination of charitable status. In *Baldry v. Feinbuck*[55] the court

---

[49] *Re Hopkinson* [1949] 1 All E.R. 346 at 350, *Re Koeppler's Will Trusts* (1984) Ch. 243 at 260.

[50] *Re Vallance* (1876) 2 Setons Judgements 1304, *Re Herrick* (1918) 52 I.L.T. 213.

[51] (1867) 96 Mass. (14 Allen) 539.

[52] *Re Hood* (1931) 1 Ch. 240.

[53] (1954) Ch. 672.

[54] RR1, *The Review of the Register of Charities*, (1999) at p. 13.

[55] [1972] 1 W.L.R. 552; (1971) 115 SJ 965; [1972] 2 All E.R. 81.

held that a students' union could not give financial support to a campaign against the Government's decision to end the supply of free milk to school-children. The students' union was an educational charity; the campaign was a "political" protest, and therefore could not be held to be a charitable activity. In *Webb v. O' Doherty and others*[56] the court ruled that a student's union could not campaign against the Gulf War. It was held that it was not charitable for the union to seek to influence public opinion against the Gulf War, or to use the union's funds to support a campaign against the Gulf War.

Some bodies have advanced the argument, relied upon in *Jackson v. Phillips*, that they are not attempting to change government policy, but are merely try-ing to educate the public on the issues. This argument was attempted in *Southwood v. Attorney General*[57] by a body known as Prodem (Project on Demilitarisation). The purported purposes of the body were "the advancement of the education of the public in the subject of militarism and disarmament". However, the court held that, upon investigation, the true aim of Prodem was to change the political stance of western governments on militarism.

The War on Want charity was investigated by the Charity Commission in the 1970s and again in 1987, as was Oxfam in 1991, to establish whether a charity could and should set up a non-charitable body to undertake its cam-paigning activities.

McGovern held that attempting to make a foreign government release pris-oners was a political purpose.

13.5.2 Peace and reconciliation as a political purpose

The promotion of peace and reconciliation has historically been a popular goal for voluntary organisations,[58] national governments[59] and international funders[60] in Northern Ireland. In this society, divided by religious and political affiliations, many bodies have formed with a goal of promoting inter-commu-nal or cross-border harmony. Law has been slow to react to this social pres-sure and has found difficulty in accrediting such bodies with charitable status, preferring instead the paradigm of political status. The courts have yet to hold that promoting peace and reconciliation is a charitable purpose. However, there are some possible loopholes.

---

[56] (1991) 3 Admin. L.R. 731, *The Times*, February 11, 1991. For the adjoining jurisdiction, see *Superintendent John V Ganly v. Henry Goff*, [1983] I.L.R.M. 425.

[57] *The Times*, October 26, 1998.

[58] For example, Co-operation Ireland.

[59] For example, the Education for Mutual Understanding program.

[60] For example, the European Union Peace and Reconciliation Fund.

13.5.2(i) Cross border bodies

A trust to improve relations between the Swedish and English peoples was held not charitable in *Anglo-Swedish Society* v. *IRC*.[61] A gift "for any purpose ... designed to strengthen the bonds of unity between the Union of South Africa and the Mother Country [England]" is not charitable but political according to *Re Strakosch*.[62] A goal of promoting greater international co-operation is not charitable.[63] A trust to "promote and aid the improvement of international relations and intercourse" is political not charitable.[64]

This substantial line of authority was followed in *British Council* v. *Commissioner of Valuation*[65] in Northern Ireland which held that:

> "... the promotion of closer cultural relationships between countries is a matter of prime importance and of great public utility, as well as being beneficial to the British Commonwealth as a whole, but it is not charitable by analogy with the spirit and intendment of that [1634] statute."[66]

It was then found that a body with the purposes of spreading knowledge about the United Kingdom and promoting closer cultural links between the United Kingdom and foreign countries by encouraging exchange visits was not charitable.

One case can be tentatively cited for the proposition that promoting peace is a charitable purpose. The issue in *Re Harwood*[67] was whether a number of gifts to non-existent bodies could be applied *cy-près*. The case concerned gifts to the Peace Society of Belfast and the Dublin Peace Society. The first question was whether these gifts were for charitable purposes. The court did not inquire, but merely assumed that these were valid charitable purposes. However, it must be said that *Re Harwood* is of limited value. Its reasoning is not explicit, or even deducible, and it was not followed in *Re Koeppler*.

Re Koeppler is itself another example of how cross border purposes can be charitable. If the purpose is merely, in a bipartisan and neutral manner, to educate the public about cross border co-operation, as opposed to promoting it, such a body could be charitable.

The final technique to make cross border relations charitable is that adopted in *Corrymeela Community* v. *Commissioner of Valuation*,[68] discussed more fully below.

---

[61] (1931) 47 TLR 295.
[62] [1949] Ch. 529.
[63] *Re Koeppler's Will Trusts, op. cit.*
[64] *Buxton* v. *Public Trustee* (1962) 41 T.C. 235.
[65] VR/65/1980.
[66] *ibid.* at p. 8.
[67] [1936] Ch. 285.
[68] VR/1/1967.

13.5.2(ii) Cross community relations

The other half of the trust in *Re Strakosch* was to "conduce to the appease-ment of racial feeling between the Dutch and English speaking sections of the South African community". The Court of Appeal held that this too was not a charitable purpose, "the problem of appeasing racial feeling within the com-munity is a political problem, perhaps primarily political".[69] However, this has now been overruled by the Charity Commission. It has held that:

> "... promoting good race relations, endeavouring to eliminate discrimination on grounds of race and encouraging equality of opportunity between persons of different racial groups were charitable purposes."[70]

As this decision may have important implications for Northern Ireland, it is worth examining its rationale and effect. The Commission looked at the ra-tionale behind *Re Strakosch*. This was that the court had no way of adjudging whether good race relations would be for the public benefit, it was a political question. Law and society have moved on since then, "the nation, through parliament, has already decided it is for the public benefit and the matter has ceased to be political".[71] Parliament did so through White Papers and legisla-tion.[72] Society has become more progressive in outlook and now "it is un-likely that any substantial body of opinion in England and Wales would not consider the promotion of good race relations to be a purpose beneficial to the community".[73]

It can be argued that this reasoning is equally applicable to Northern Ire-land in the context of religious and political division. Public opinion indicates that a substantial majority of the population view the promotion of good com-munity relations as a laudable aim. Parliament has responded, most recently with the Fair Employment and Treatment (N.I.) Order 1998, by a series of legislative attacks on discrimination. A broad reading of the Charity Commis-sion's decision supports this position. It stated that "the improvement of com-munity relations was a charitable purpose".[74]

A separate tack was adopted by the Lands Tribunal in *Corrymeela Com-munity v. Commissioner of Valuation*.[75] The case concerned a residential cen-tre in Ballycastle the purpose of which was partly to facilitate cross community

---

[69] *Re Strakosch* at p. 538.
[70] [1983] Ch. Comm. Rep. 9 para.15-20, "*The Promotion of Racial Harmony*" at para. 20.
[71] *Ibid.* at para. 18.
[72] For example, White Paper on Racial Discrimination, Cmnd. 8476 (1982) and in North-ern Ireland by the Race Relations (N.I.) Order 1997, see further Chapter 4 on Human Rights and Discrimination.
[73] *ibid.* at para. 18.
[74] *ibid.* at para. 15, see also RR1, *The Review of the Register of Charities* (1999) where a section is headed "good community relations".
[75] VR/1/1967.

relations. The Community itself had no single, concisely defined purpose. One purpose, as discerned by the Tribunal, was the:

> "... welding together of the different sections and classes in society whether in Northern Ireland, or nationally or on an international scale in a spirit of mutual understanding and tolerance in a Christian context."[76]

The Community had an avowedly religious framework. It was deemed charitable primarily under the religious head, but also under the education and fourth head. This finding is very much in harmony with the approach being developed by the Charity Commission in England and Wales and signposts the way for a more permissive interpretation of charitable status for bodies concerned to promote cross community relations in this jurisdiction.

13.6 POLITICAL ACTIVITIES

A charity may engage in political activities ancillary to its main charitable purposes without losing its special status. If its purpose is political, it is not a charity, but if it carries out some political activity as a means of furthering its non-political purposes, it remains a charity. Guidance from the courts on permissible political activity is scarce, what follows is mainly a summary of the Charity Commission guidance.[77] The genesis of the guidance springs from dictum of Slade J. in *McGovern v. Attorney General* which drew a distinction between a trust with political purposes and charitable trusts which used political means.

The underlying rule is that "trustees of a charity may do some things of a political nature as a means of achieving the purposes of the charity".[78] The political activity must be ancillary to, serve and be subordinate to the charity's purposes. For example, the charitable purpose of a student's union is educational: campaigning against the Gulf War[79] or the abolition of free milk to schoolchildren[80] is not ancillary to its educational purpose; but campaigning against university fees might be.[81] Thus, a charity can campaign for political change without necessarily endangering its status.

The Commission has added an element of good practice to their guidelines. The resources spent on political activities must be justified by a reason-

---

[76] *ibid.* at p. 4.
[77] See CC9, *Political Activities and Campaigning by Charities* (1999) and CC9(a), *Political Activities and Campaigning by Local Community Charities* (1996).
[78] CC9 at p. 8.
[79] *Webb v. O'Doherty, The Times,* February 11, 1991.
[80] *Baldry v. Feinbuck* [1972] 1 W.L.R. 552.
[81] See further, the guidance of the Attorney-General that it would be wrong for students' unions to offer financial support to political causes in foreign countries as opposed to merely debating the issues, (1983) Ch. Comm. Rep. 34.

able expectation that it will have a positive effect. Promoting views on a subject must be done in a reasoned and well argued way, not merely by polemics.

Charities are not allowed to advocate support for a particular political party solely because the latter has adopted a policy supported by the charity. If a charity has the same policy as a political party, it can still promote that policy, as long as its independence from the political party is explained and understood. All policies produced by charities should be based on reasoned argument and not merely emotion. Unless a restrictive medium is used (for example, billboards), arguments must be used to justify positions. As expressed by the Charity Commission:

> "... it would be unacceptable ... for a charity to seek to persuade government or the public on the basis of material which was *merely* emotive."[82]

13.6.1 Types of political activity

The Charity Commission has listed specific types of political activity and the circumstances and parameters within which this may be deemed permissible.

13.6.1(i) Influencing government and public opinion

Charities can exercise influence by using well-founded and researched arguments. They can inform the public on how politicians voted on certain issues, but only so the public can persuade politicians to change their stance through argument and not merely through public pressure. In practice, this would seem a difficult distinction to make, although it remains the one adopted by the Commission.

All attempts to influence must be by argument, not by the application of political or public pressure. For example, letter writing campaigns to politicians must set out the arguments rather than just request politicians to vote in a certain way.

13.6.1(ii) Legislation and public policy

Charities can respond to proposed legislation and support or oppose it. They can advocate or oppose changes in the law or public policy. They can supply relevant and balanced information for use in debates n parliament or elsewhere.

---

[82] CC9 at p. 12, their emphasis.

13.6.1(iii) Comment on public issues

Charities can comment on social, economic or political issues if these relate to their sphere of operations.

13.6.1(iv) Supporting political parties

Charities may not support political parties. They can support policies advocated by political parties if they maintain and appear to maintain their independence.

13.6.1(v) Acting with other bodies

Charities can affiliate with non-charitable bodies in a campaign. They can only do so if it will further the charities own charitable purposes. They cannot expend money on non-charitable purposes and may be required to disassociate themselves from parts of such a campaigning alliance.

12.6.1(vi) Providing information

Charities can provide information to politicians and may employ lobbyists to inform politicians on matter relevant to their purposes. However, the information should be accurate and not designed to support or oppose a particular political party.

13.6.1(vii) Forthcoming elections

Charities can comment on the policies of political parties as the latter prepare for elections. They can bring to the attention of candidates' matters which touch and concern the work of the charity. They cannot attempt to persuade the public to vote for or against a certain politician or political party. They must at all times remain within the constraints of electoral law.

13.6.1(viii) Conducting and publishing research

Research must be carried out scientifically, not merely to support the charities position. It must be accurate and cannot be disseminated if it is known to be flawed. The usual rules as to research in the educational context also apply.[83]

13.6.1(ix) Seeking government grants

Charities may lobby politicians to ensure that grants are paid to a charity.

---

[83] See further, Chap. 9.

13.6.1(x) Demonstrations and direct action

Demonstrations, rallies, pickets, etc. may go beyond promoting reasoned arguments and may detract from the charities special status. There are additional risks of public order offences or civil liability for events which are badly organised. As a general rule, the Charity Commission advise against recourse to such forms of protest.

If a charity does proceed, it should ensure that the following parameters are maintained. The demonstration should be thoroughly prepared, *i.e.* including liaison with police and other authorities. The demonstration should be peaceful and be under the control of the charity/its organisers at all times. It should be conducted in such a way as to avoid bringing the charity into disrepute (*i.e.* by being provocative, intimidatory or excessively disruptive). It should at all times remain within the law.

CHAPTER 14

Recreation

14.1 INTRODUCTION

Historically, recreation has never constituted a separate *Pemsel*[1] head of charity. It did not feature in the judicial deliberations of either *Pemsel* or *Morice v.
Bishop of Durham*[2] nor even expressly within the Statutes of 1601 or 1634.
The orthodox common law position has always been that recreation, of itself,
is not a charitable purpose. However, in recent years this position has been
steadily eroded. The courts will now recognise recreation as charitable in three
sets of circumstances: where it is ancillary to some other charitable purpose,
provided for the benefit of a locality, or is open air public recreation. The most
significant encroachment of recreation into the field of charity has been legislative, under the Recreational Charities Act (Northern Ireland) 1958.[3] It now
seems justifiable and necessary to consider recreation as a separate and distinct head of charity.

   This is a particularly untidy aspect of charity law. There are no governing
principles to determine the charitable status of recreation activities or facilities. Perhaps the only very evident characteristic is the lengths to which the
judiciary, in this as in other United Kingdom jurisdictions, will go to interpret
activities and facilities as recreational in order to save gifts as charitable. The
law relating to the charitable status of recreation may, in some instances, fall
to be considered under one of the *Pemsel* heads rather than in isolation.

   This chapter begins by examining the common law rule against recreation
and considering some of the exceptions to the rule. It then looks at the underpinning rationale and the effect of the Recreational Charities Act (Northern
Ireland) 1958. It concludes by analysing the role of the public benefit test in
the context of recreational charity.

14.2 COMMON LAW RULE AGAINST RECREATION

There is no rule that gifts for the provision of recreational facilities or to encourage particular sports, even if intended for the public benefit, merit chari-

---

[1] *Commissioners for Special Purposes of Income Tax v. Pemsel* [1891] A.C. 531.
[2] (1804) 9 Ves. 405.
[3] In England, the Recreational Charities Act 1958. In the Republic of Ireland there is no
equivalent legislation.

table status. The law was clear that gifts for the promotion of sports which served to entertain the participants or the spectators were neither within the "spirit or intendment" of the Preamble nor for the public benefit. In Northern Ireland, the Court of Appeal has held that:

"... the weight of authority is against holding recreation itself as a charitable purpose within the statute of Elizabeth."[4]

14.2.1 Competitive sports

A gift to encourage "mere sport and recreation"[5] was not be regarded by the courts as charitable *per se*. In the leading case of *Re Nottage*,[6] where a testator sought to encourage the sport of yacht racing by establishing a trust to provide prizes, Lindley L.J. explained the court's rationale for refusing charitable status in the following much quoted words:

"Now, I should say that every healthy sport is good for the nation – cricket, football, fencing, yachting or any other healthy exercise or recreation; but if it had been the idea of lawyers that a gift for the encouragement of such exercises is therefore charitable we should have heard of it before now."[7]

Where the dominant purpose of a donor's gift was to promote a competitive sport, as opposed to providing a general opportunity for healthy exercise, then charitable status was withheld.

The rationale for this approach is rooted in an established judicial view that if a sport is competitive then its primary purpose is to entertain the spectators, rather than develop the health of participants, and entertainment is not sufficient for the purposes of the public benefit test. On the strength of the reasoning in *Nottage*, gifts associated with fishing,[8] fox hunting,[9] cricket,[10] flying[11] and horse riding[12] have all been denied charitable status. The Charity Commissioners have concurred with this approach, holding that a gift for the Birchfield Harriers Athletics Club was not charitable[13] in law.

Locally, the playing of badminton was held to be, in itself, not a charitable

---

[4] *Commissioner of Valuation v. Lurgan Borough Council* [1968] N.I. 104 at 160.
[5] *City of Belfast Young Men's Christian Association v. Commissioner of Valuation* VR/19/ 1965 at p. 22.
[6] [1895] 2 Ch. 649.
[7] *ibid.* at pp. 655–656.
[8] See *Re Clifford* (1911) 106 L.T. 14.
[9] See *Peterborough Royal Foxhound Show Society v. IRC* [1936] 2 K.B. 497.
[10] See *Re Patten* [1929] 2 Ch. 276.
[11] See *Scottish Flying Club Ltd. v. IRC* [1935] S.C. 817.
[12] See *The Riding Establishments Advisory Associations Ltd.* [1965] Ch. Com. Rep. 30, App. C. 16.
[13] [1989] Ch. Com. Rep. para. 48, partly refused under the Recreational Charities Act 1958 as not open to the public at large.

activity.[14] A testator, when creating a "recreational" trust for Portadown, expressly excluded football and speed rowing from its ambit. Barton J found in favour of the trust, but agreed that the excluded activities were pure sport and non-charitable.[15] This, broadly speaking, continues to be the law.

14.2.2 Social facilities and recreation

Providing facilities for socialising and recreation in a social sense is also not charitable at common law. A trust for "helping in the religious, moral, social and recreative life" was held not charitable in *Trustees of the Londonderry Presbyterian Church House v. Commissioners of Inland Revenue*.[16] Another court, when commenting on that case, held that "it could not be shown that the trust was charitable in that it included social and recreational facilities"[17]. Unless it can come under one of the exemptions, just providing a club where people can meet and relax is not charitable. In *Royal British Legion Attendants Company v. Commissioner of Valuation*,[18] a trust would not be charitable if it were to "merely provide recreation and social intercourse".[19]

A town council entertainment's committee engaged in activities to improve the amenities of the town was deemed not to be established for charitable purposes.[20] While accepting that the purposes of the committee were for the public benefit, this was considered insufficient to qualify the committee as a charity; their activities were too wide to regard them as limited to charitable purposes.

14.3 EXCEPTIONS TO THE COMMON LAW RULE AGAINST RECREATION

There are four ways in which the common law rule against recreation can be avoided. Only two of them can truly be called exceptions in that they accept the applicability of the rule, then point to a specific exemption. The other two are not exceptions, but seek instead to deny the applicability of the rule in particular circumstances.

The first exception is that open air public recreational facilities are charitable. The second exception, linked to this, is that recreation for the benefit of a

---

[14] *Commissioner of Valuation v. Trustees of Fisherwick Presbyterian Church* [1927] N.I. 76.
[15] *Shillington v. Portadown Urban District Council* (1911) 1 I.R. 247.
[16] [1946] N.I. 178.
[17] *Belfast Air Raid* at p. 177.
[18] [1979] N.I. 138.
[19] *ibid.* at p. 146.
[20] See, *Linlithgow Town Council Entertainments Committee v. CIR* C.S. 1953, 35 T.C. 84.
[21] [1932] 1 Ch. 133, [1931] All E.R. Rep. 539.

locality is charitable. The third way to avoid the rule is to argue that recreation is being provided ancillary to a charitable purpose; this approach has generated a substantial body of case law. In England and Wales the cases have usually concerned situations where the primary charitable purpose is ostensibly education. In Northern Ireland, religion has been the favourite charitable purpose for which recreation has been held to be subsidiary. The fourth avoidance technique is the *de minimis* rule, that recreational facilities are negligible in terms of the total amount of charitable activities.

14.3.1 Outdoor public recreation

The Mortmain and Charitable Uses Act 1888 conferred charitable status upon gifts of land for use as places of public recreation. Its provisions allowed many gifts for such purposes to attain charitable status. For example, in *Re Hadden*[21] a gift for "the working people ... playing fields, parks, gymnasiums or other plans which will give recreation to as many people as possible" was held to be charitable.

The 1888 Act, now repealed,[22] never applied to Northern Ireland although the principle it established was judicially imported and had a bearing on caselaw in this jurisdiction. For example in *Commissioner of Valuation v. Lurgan Borough Council*[23] Lord MacDermott L.C.J., referring to the 1888 Act, commented:

"... it is, I think now well settled that the concept of a legal charity is substantially the same in this jurisdiction as in England."[24]

More specifically, section 6 of the 1888 Act designates parks for public recreation as falling within the definition of a charity. MacDermott L.C.J. would have held charitable a swimming pool if it had been "provided in the open air on land dedicated to the use and enjoyment of the public".[25] The spirit of the Act – that open air public recreation grounds are charitable – has now passed into the common law. In *Northern Ireland Housing Trust v. Commissioner of Valuation*,[26] the Lands Tribunal held that:

"... open air ground used for recreation is not a good charitable use unless it is shown that it is either for the public at large of for an appreciably important class of the community."[27]

This conclusion was based on a finding that if the public benefit test was satisfied, open air recreation would then be charitable at common law. This

---

[22] See s. 48 and Sched. 7 of the Charities Act 1960.
[23] [1968] N.I. 104.
[24] *ibid.* at p. 125.
[25] *ibid.* at p. 125.
[26] VR/21/1966 in the Lands Tribunal.
[27] *ibid.* at p. 12.

view was repeated in *Down District Council v. Commissioner of Valuation*[28] holding that a community centre for Drumaness village was not charitable at common law because it provided indoor recreation.[29]

That this is not the case in the adjoining jurisdiction apparent is from the decision in *Clancy v. Commissioner of Valuation.*[30]

There is now a considerable weight of authority, flowing from the Act of 1888, in favour of the charitable nature of outdoor public recreation. It has become difficult to sustain any contrary argument. However, it does seem slightly illogical to appropriate an English statute, which never applied to Northern Ireland, and which has long been repealed,[31] into the Northern Ireland definition of a charity. Such an argument was briefly made before the Lands Tribunal in the *YMCA*[32] case, but was disposed of peremptorily.

Some legislative validation of this position does exist in Northern Ireland. The Open Spaces Act 1906 remains in force at present, though it does not appear to have been cited in any of the recreation cases. The 1906 Act makes provision for public recreation grounds held on charitable trusts to be transferred to local authorities on those or similar trusts. Implicit in this is that outdoor public recreation grounds can be charitable.

14.3.2 Recreation ancillary to a charitable purpose

If recreational facilities are provided which are ancillary to a charitable purpose, then they form part and parcel of that charitable purpose and are not considered to be pure recreation. Therefore, the common law rule against recreation does not apply. Case law has consolidated the earlier common law approach favouring gifts ancillary to charitable purposes. In opinion of the House of Lords:

> "If the dominant purpose of the trust is charitable in character the fact that recreation is provided as an adjunct to that purpose does not destroy the charitable character of the trust."[33]

---

[28] *Down County Council v. Commissioner of Valuation* VR/8/1972.

[29] Although it was held charitable under the Recreational Charities Act (Northern Ireland) 1958, see further, below.

[30] [1911] 2 I.R. 173. See, Delany, H., *Equity and the Law of Trusts in Ireland* (Round Hall Sweet & Maxwell, Dublin, 1995):

> "While the question was not expressly considered, it would appear that the provision of recreational facilities for the benefit of the public, whether outdoor or indoor, would be regarded as charitable . . ."

at p. 289.

[31] By the Charities Act 1960.

[32] *op cit.*

[33] See, *IRC v. Baddeley, op. cit.* at p. 600, cited with approval by McVeigh L.J. (dissenting) in *Commrs of Valuation (NI) v. Lurgan Borough Council, op. cit.* See, also, *Re Mariette, op. cit. per* Eve J. at p. 288.

The Northern Ireland Court of Appeal in *City of Belfast YMCA v. Commissioner of Valuation*[34] considered at some length the question of recreation combined with other charitable purposes. From the judgments of the three judges in that case, two points emerge. Firstly, recreation can be an integral part of a charitable activity. The second and slightly different point is that recreation can be ancillary/incidental to a charitable purpose.

14.3.2(i) Ancillary to education

The most common charitable purpose to which recreation is usually appended is education. Practically all English case law on ancillary recreation is under the education head.

The leading case is the House of Lords decision in *Inland Revenue Commissioners v. McMullen.*[35] It concerned a trust by the Football Association for facilitating football and other sports at schools and universities. Its purpose was "to assist in ensuring that due attention is given to the physical education and development and occupation of their minds". The House of Lords held that although merely playing games would not be charitable, in this context, the purpose was the advancement of education. Lord Hailsham stated that the:

> "... purpose of the settlor is to promote the physical education and development of pupils at schools and universities as an addition to such part of their education as relates to their mental education."[36]

In reaching this conclusion, Lord Hailsham was swayed by the fact that the definition of education in the Education Act 1944 included physical education. The modern Northern Ireland curriculum must promote "the spiritual, moral, cultural, intellectual and physical development of pupils at the school".[37] Physical education is just as much education as is mental education.

One objection raised in *McMullen* was that the recreational facilities, although provided to pupils and students, were not being provided by an educational body. The House of Lords did not sustain this objection. The Court of Appeal in Northern Ireland have also held that a body which is not within the formal education system can nevertheless provide recreational facilities which are ancillary to the advancement of education. Referring to sports grounds owned and operated by the YMCA, Curran J. stated that:

> "... the promotion and advancement of physical fitness, as an adjunct to the education of the mind, falls within the charitable purpose of the promotion of education."[38]

---

[34] *op. cit.*
[35] [1981] A.C. 1.
[36] *ibid.* at p. 14.
[37] Art. 4(2)(a) Education Reform (NI) Order 1989.
[38] *YMCA* at p. 20.

The courts have previously held that physical recreation provided within and by a school is for the advancement of education. In *Re Mariette*[39] the court confirmed that a gift to build a "fives court" and provide prizes for athletics in a particular public school was charitable. The court held that no "boy can be properly educated unless at least as much attention is given to the development of his body as is given to the development of his mind".[40]

Gifts to encourage young people to play chess can be charitable.[41] Gifts for the boy scouts can be charitable applying this reasoning.[42] A gift for a swimming pool in a private college[43] and for athletic activities in a medical school[44] have been held charitable.

The argument has been advanced that the encouragement of sport and recreation should in itself be sufficient to attract charitable status, provided the public benefit requirement is satisfied.[45] This argument is currently receiving a sympathetic hearing in the courts of England and Wales, particularly in relation to sports such as skiing and rowing when young people are involved and where educational benefits may therefore be also claimed.

14.3.2(ii) Ancillary to aesthetic education

Social facilities, such as a lounge and bar may be ancillary to the charitable purpose of staging artistic plays. The Lands Tribunal has reasoned that such facilities are necessary in theatres as they allow opportunities for relaxation, for discussion of the plays, and they attract more people to the theatre. For all these reasons, they have been held ancillary to the advancement of aesthetic education.[46]

14.3.2(iii) Ancillary to religion

If recreational facilities are provided in such a way that they are subordinate to a religious purpose, they may be considered as merging with that religious purpose. This has been a popular construction in Northern Ireland, but it does have English precedents. In *Neville Estates v. Madden*[47] the court held that:

---

[39] [1915] 2 Ch. 284.

[40] *Re Mariette* at p. 288.

[41] *Re Dupree's Deed Trusts, Daley v. Lloyds Bank* [1945] Ch. 16, [1944] 2 All E.R. 443.

[42] *Re Webber* (1954) 1 W.L.R. 1500.

[43] *Re Geere's Will Trusts (No. 2)* (1954) C.L.Y. 388.

[44] *London Hospital Medical College v. Inland Revenue Commissioners* [1976] 1 W.L.R. 613.

[45] See, the Goodman Committee *Report on Charity Law and Voluntary Organisations* (1976).

[46] *Lyric Players Theatre v. Commissioner of Valuation* VR/25/1970.

[47] *Neville Estates v. Madden* [1962] Ch. 832.

"... here the social activities are merely ancillary to the strictly religious activities ... in my judgement the purposes of the trust with which I am concerned are religious purposes – the social aspect is merely ancillary."[48]

In the *YMCA* case, the Lands Tribunal held that:

"... the provision of recreational facilities at Bladon Drive is ancillary to the purposes of the Association, whether those purposes are regarded as religious purposes, or purposes of general public utility."[49]

A view subsequently endorsed in the Court of Appeal in the urbane judgment of Lord MacDermott L.C.J. who took the view that:

"... organised recreational facilities tend to promote bodily health and fitness, endurance, and self discipline, and that these qualities are commonly accepted as the allies and adjuncts of a wholesome religiosity."[50]

The playing fields in that case were furthermore ancillary to the advancement of religion because they attracted young people to the YMCA. McVeigh L.J. agreed with this construction, holding that, even though recreational facilities were being provided:

"... the whole tenor of the declaration in the trust deed seems to be of an overriding religious purpose and this is to my mind the paramount and controlling trust which pervades the deed."[51]

It had in fact been argued 40 years prior to the *YMCA* case that "there is no case that decides that the playing of games is for the advancement of religion".[52] The court rejected this argument and held that the playing of badminton in a church hall did not destroy its religious character. Two reasons were given. The first was that this sort of recreation could be ancillary to the work of the church. Brown J. held that:

"... most churches have a guild with the object of getting and keeping young people together, interesting them with the work of the church and tying them, as it were, unofficially to it."[53]

Further authority can be found in *Trustees of the Belmont Presbyterian Church v. Commissioner of Valuation*[54] where it was held that:

---

[48] *ibid.* at p.852.

[49] *YMCA* VR/19/1965 at p. 19.

[50] *YMCA* at p. 13.

[51] *ibid.* at p. 28.

[52] *Commissioner of Valuation v. Trustees of Fisherwick Presbyterian Church* [1927] N.I. 76 at 78. On a historical note, the barrister putting forward this argument is listed in the reports as Macdermott. It would appear that this was the same MacDermott who gave the exact opposite reasoning in deciding the *YMCA* case as Lord Chief Justice.

[53] *Ibid.* at p. 81. The second reason was the *de minimis* ground discussed below.

[54] VR/14/1965.

> "... the need to provide instructional, recreational and social activities in the atmosphere and under the influence of a religious community has come to be recognised as a method of fostering and encouraging the advancement of religion."[55]

The social facilities in that case included scouts, counselling, badminton and bowls.

The one case which is slightly at odds with this judicial current is *Trustees of the Londonderry Presbyterian Church House v. Commissioners of Inland Revenue*.[56] The trust in that case allowed for the use of buildings for religious and also for social and recreational purposes. The Court of Appeal held that with such a broadly worded trust, the building could be used for non-charitable purposes. This is correct within the context of the test of "exclusively charitable purposes" (see further Chapters 10 and 15). However, it did go on to state that:

> "... activities or duties, as for example of a social character which, whilst indirectly furthering a religious purpose, are not directly religious."[57]

Arguably, to show that social or recreational facilities are ancillary to the advancement of religion, some form of causal link must be shown. Two options seem possible: either that the facilities provided actively encourage or facilitate people to take part in a religious activity; or it must be shown that the recreation in itself promotes qualities which are beneficial to the advancement of religion. It is not enough merely to provide social/recreational facilities for those who happen to be members of a particular religion. The benefit to religion must be the primary, underlying concern, not a superficial one.

14.3.2(iv) Ancillary to the efficiency of the army

Where the donor's intention is not so much to encourage sport as an end in itself but to provide the means for achieving a public benefit then a gift may acquire charitable status. In *Re Gray*,[58] for example, such a gift was upheld as charitable on the grounds that it would serve to promote the efficiency of the army. As was then explained by Romer J.:

> "... it is to be observed that the particular sports specified were all healthy outdoor sports, indulgence in which might reasonably be supposed to encourage physical efficiency."[59]

The House of Lords confirmed this view by holding that "gifts exclusively for

---

[55] VR/14/1965 at p. 5.
[56] [1946] N.I. 178.
[57] *ibid.* at p. 185, *per* Andrews L.C.J.
[58] [1925] Ch. 363.
[59] *ibid.* at p. 365, see also *Re Good* [1905] 2 Ch. 60.

the purpose of promoting the efficiency of the armed forces are good charitable gifts".[60] See further Chapter 11 for gifts for the defence of the realm generally.

14.3.2(v) Ancillary to the efficiency of the police

Gifts for the promotion of law and order are charitable in the same way as gifts for the defence of the realm. The House of Lords has held, in *Inland Revenue Commissioners v. City of Glasgow Police Athletic Federation*[61] that:

> "... gifts or contributions exclusively for the purpose of promoting the efficiency of the police forces and the preservation of public order are ... charitable gifts."[62]

That case showed the importance of the distinction between ancillary and primary purposes. The Association failed to obtain charitable status because its primary purpose was "the non-charitable purpose of providing recreation to the members"[63] and therefore the recreation purpose was not incidental but an end in itself.

14.3.2(vi) Ancillary to other charitable purposes

Generally, where a gift is for the purpose of providing social or recreational facilities then it will not be regarded as charitable. However, where a clear public benefit can be established then charitable status will be upheld. This will be the case where the intended beneficiaries are, for example, the elderly, youth, handicapped or disadvantaged or where the application falls to be decided under one of the other *Pemsel* heads. Community centres, therefore, which have been established to provide services for those groups, will qualify for charitable exemption.

14.3.3 Negligible amount of recreation

If the amount of recreation is small in proportion to the total amount of charitable uses, then the recreation will be ignored and will not effect charitable status. This is just one application of the broad legal principle *de minimis non curat lex*, or "the law does not concern itself with trifles". It was applied in *Commissioner of Valuation v. Trustees of Fisherwick Presbyterian Church*[64]

---

[60] *Inland Revenue Commissioners v. City of Glasgow Police Athletic Federation* [1954] A.C. 380 at 391.
[61] *ibid.*
[62] *ibid.* at p. 391.
[63] *ibid.* at p. 395.
[64] *op cit.*

in the finding that "the playing of badminton in this hall forms a minor incident".[65]

14.3.4 Recreation for the benefit of a locality

Another exception to the common law rule has been developed in association with the "benefit to a locality" category under the fourth head. In *Shillington v. Portadown Urban District Council*[66] Barton J upheld a gift to an urban council which was made for the purpose of encouraging and providing a "means of healthy recreation" for the residents of a specified locality. He explained the grounds for his decision as follows:

> "The testator's purpose was a charitable or public purpose. He wished to benefit the residents of his native town and of its immediate neighbourhood. The benefits which he intended to confer on them were such as he believed to be of public advantage. That belief was rational and not contrary to the laws of the land or the principles of morality."[67]

In England, the courts took much the same approach. For example, the court in *Re Mann*[68] held charitable a building (used as a club and meeting hall) for the benefit of the inhabitants of Moreton-in-Marsh.

Where a gift was for the purpose of providing "playing fields, parks, gymnasiums or other plans which will give recreation to as many people as possible"[69] it was held to be charitable. So, also, where it was intended to provide a gift for "a public recreation ground for amateur activities" for the benefit of a particular parish.[70]

Where the trust is established explicitly for the purpose of carrying out public works or for providing public facilities such as a village club and reading room in a specified area[71] then charitable status will be awarded. A gift to a church council,[72] or to a town[73] will be upheld as charitable where the purposes are confined to general or public purposes beneficial to the community. However, a gift to a parish to be applied to "such public, benevolent or chari-

---

[65] [1927] N.I. 76 at 81. See also the judgment of Babington L.J. in the *Londonderry Church House* case agreeing with this approach.

[66] [1911] I.R. 247 at pp. 156–157.

[67] However, the case and principle are now of doubtful authority, firstly because the test of benefit is now objective and not that of the testator. Secondly, it was doubted by the Lands Tribunal, "but the case is not entirely satisfactory as it is difficult to discern the *ratio decidendi* which should be followed", *YMCA* VR/19/1965 at p. 21.

[68] *Re Mann Hardy v. Attorney-General* (1903) 1 Ch. 232.

[69] See, *Re Hadden* [1932] 1 Ch. 133.

[70] See, *Re Morgan* [1955] 1 W.L.R. 738.

[71] See, for example, *Re Scowcroft* [1898] 2 Ch. 638.

[72] See, *Re Norton's Will Trusts* [1948] 2 All E.R. 842.

[73] See, *Re Allen* [1905] 2 Ch. 400.

table purposes" as the trustees might think proper was construed disjunctively and was not regarded as charitable.[74]

14.4 THE RECREATIONAL CHARITIES ACT (NORTHERN IRELAND) 1958

This statute consolidated the charitable status of certain gifts for the provision of recreational facilities. In doing so, it has also firmly established a point of jurisdictional difference with the law in the Republic of Ireland which has no equivalent legislation.

14.4.1 Background

The narrow nature of the exemptions from the common law rule against recreation was highlighted by the ruling in *Inland Revenue Commissioners v. Baddeley*.[75] This leading case is instructive for its illumination of the key issues. It concerned the deeds for land on which a church, a hall and stores had been built. One trust was established:

> "... for the promotion of the religious social and physical well-being of persons resident in the County Boroughs of West Ham and Leyton in the County of Essex by the provision of facilities for religious services and instruction and for the social and physical training and recreation of such aforementioned persons who for the time being are in the opinion of [the leaders for the time being of the Stratford Newtown Methodist Mission] members or likely to become members of the Methodist Church and of insufficient means otherwise to enjoy the advantages provided by these presents and by promoting and encouraging all forms of such activities as are calculated to contribute to the health and well-being of such persons. Provided always that the trustees shall not at any time hereafter and so long as the trusts hereby declared shall not have totally failed use or permit the said property to be used either for physical recreation or any kind of game on Sundays, Christmas Days or Good Fridays, or for the sale or consumption of intoxicating drink."[76]

The trust was refused charitable status on two grounds. The first was that it was too widely worded to be constrained to purely charitable purposes. Acting to promote the moral, social and physical well being of the beneficiaries was not charitable. It was held to be a "community centre in which social intercourse

---

[74] See, *Houston v. Burns* [1918] A.C. 337.
[75] *Inland Revenue Commissioners v. Baddeley* [1955] A.C. 572.
[76] *ibid.*, see further, Keeton & Sheridan's *The Modern Law of Charities* (4th ed., Barry Rose, London, 1992) at p. 127 *et seq.*

and discreet festivity may go hand in hand with religious observance and instruction".[77] Recreational and social facilities were not charitable.[78]

The second reason for the refusal was the public benefit test. The House of Lords held that Methodists or potential Methodists in the area did not have a sufficiently public character. Lord Sommerwell held that:

> "... to be valid under this head [the trust] would normally be for the public or all members of the public who needed the help or facilities which the trust was to provide."[79]

This ruling raised doubts as to whether a large number of laudable organisations established for recreational purposes were in fact charitable, in particular, village halls, Women's Institutes, etc. The legislative response was to introduce specific legislation first in England and Wales, and subsequently in Northern Ireland, to put the matter beyond doubt. In the introduction to the Bill it was stated that it was designed to give:

> "... statutory recognition to the charitable nature of certain trusts and institutions which exist for the purposes of providing recreational or similar facilities, or whose purposes include the provision of such facilities in the interests of social welfare."

The English Parliament introduced the Recreational Charities Act 1958. In the same year Stormont enacted the Recreational Charities Act (Northern Ireland) 1958.

14.4.2 Overview of the Act

The Recreational Charities Act (Northern Ireland) 1958 is retrospective in effect as it explicitly confirmed the charitable status of the many such "trusts and institutions" already in existence.

The wording of the English and Northern Ireland statutes is precisely the same except in one respect. Section 2 of the English statute declared miners' welfare trusts, established by the Miners Welfare Fund or Coal Industry Social Welfare Organisation, to be charitable. There being no equivalent body in Northern Ireland, no such provision was necessary. Aside from this, the two statutes can be treated as one.

---

[77] See Viscount Simonds at p. 586.

[78] See *APP 8118* where the main object involved the promotion of the general social, recreational and economic interests of the people of ... and the promotion and encouragement of a community spirit among them. Exemption was refused on the grounds that "the objects appear to be analogous to those of the *Baddeley* case". Also, see, *APP 9658* where charitable exemption was refused on the grounds that "the provision of sporting and recreational facilities is not regarded as a charitable object".

[79] (1955) A.C. 572 at 615, see also Viscount Simonds, "it must be for the benefit of the whole community or at least all the inhabitants of a sufficient area" at p. 590.

The following are the requirements, under this legislation, for an object to be treated as a recreational charity:

- The object must provide/assist in the provision of facilities for recreation or leisure time occupation[80] and
- The facilities must be in the interests of social welfare[81] and
- There must be public benefit.[82]

In this context, "social welfare" means:

- Improving the conditions of life for the beneficiaries[83] and
- Beneficiaries have need of those facilities because of their youth, age, infirmity or disablement, poverty or social and economic circumstances[84] or
- Beneficiaries are the public or the female public at large.[85]

Section 1(3) explicitly states that the statute applies to village halls, community centres and women's institutes.

The definition and effect of each of these sub-sections and phrases is considered below.

14.4.3 Recreation/leisure time occupation

The object of a purported recreational charity must be to provide or assist in the provision of facilities for recreation or other leisure time occupation.[86] The case of *Incorporated Cripples Institutes and Holiday Homes v. Commissioner of Valuation*[87] gave some general guidelines on the parameters of this definition. Firstly, there is no requirement that recreation be a physical activity. The Tribunal held that:

> "... it does not seem to the Tribunal that Parliament contemplated only such recreational and leisure time facilities as involve physical activity and bodily exercise."[88]

Secondly, it can encompass both spectators and active participants in the activity. Thirdly, there is no requirement for it to be a mass or team activity. Finally, an element of residence does not automatically vitiate the recreational nature of an activity.

---

[80] s.1(1).
[81] s.1(1).
[82] s.1(1).
[83] s.1(2)(a).
[84] s.1(2)(b)(i).
[85] s.1(2)(b)(ii).
[86] s.1(1).
[87] VR/5/1965.
[88] *ibid.* at p. 9.

The following activities have all been held to be recreational: Gaelic games,[89] bingo,[90] dances,[91] art classes and gym training,[92] providing free traditional Indian meals,[93] sports grounds,[94] holiday homes,[95] pavilion and playing fields[96] and grounds for rugby and hockey.[97]

The Charity Commission has held that:

> "It is not a charitable purpose, even under the Recreational Charities Act 1958, to provide the services or a pub or social club (i.e. a members drinking club)."[98]

14.4.4 Social welfare

A condition precedent to acquiring charitable status under the 1958 Act is that the gift in question must fulfil a social welfare purpose.[99] The meaning of social welfare was broadly defined in *Commissioner of Valuation v. Lurgan Borough Council*[100] as being "to improve the physical and mental health of the members of society who make use of [the object]".[101] The following English definition was also approved in that case – "denotes a state of being well, whether in the physical, mental or material sense … it meant the well-being of individuals as members of society".[102]

14.4.5 Need of the listed classes

If the facilities are open to the public or female public at large, they will be provided in the interests of social welfare. If they are available to one of the listed classes, then acquiring charitable status under this legislation is condi-

---

[89] *Londonderry County Council v. Commissioner of Valuation and Trustees of the Newbridge Sean O'Leary Gaelic Centre* VR/21/1971, *Trustees of the Newbridge Sean O'Leary Gaelic Centre v. Commissioner of Valuation* VR/72/1980.
[90] *ibid.*
[91] *Lord Mayor, Aldermen and Citizens of the city of Belfast v. Commissioner of Valuation* VR/17/1967 where it was held that "the facilities for recreational dancing are to improve the conditions of life of the students for whom they are primarily intended" at p. 21.
[92] *Torr Heath Association v. Commissioner of Valuation* VR/15/1975.
[93] *Trustees of the Indian Community Centre v. Commissioner of Valuation* VR/7/1988.
[94] *YMCA op. cit.*
[95] *Incorporated Cripples Institutes and Holiday Homes v. Commissioner of Valuation* VR/5/1965.
[96] *Northern Ireland Housing Trust v. Commissioner of Valuation* VR/21/1966.
[97] *Trustees of Chambers Park v. Commissioner of Valuation* VR/16/1969, failing on public benefit grounds.
[98] CC27, *Providing Alcohol on Charity Premises*, (1996) at p. 4.
[99] s.1(1) Recreational Charities Act (Northern Ireland) 1958.
[100] *op. cit.*
[101] *ibid.* at p.151.
[102] *National Deposit Friendly Society v. Skegness Urban District Council* [1957] 2 Q.B. 573 at 581.

tional upon the gift meeting a need.[103] If the facilities are used by others not in that listed class, this part of the test is failed. Whether or not it does meet the need will be ascertained by applying an objective test; the fact that the donor subjectively believed and intended that this would be the effect of the gift is immaterial. In this respect the law differs from that applied by the courts in Ireland where a subjective test is sufficient. The listed classes are youth, age, infirmity or disablement, poverty or social and economic circumstances.

"Need" is not to be confused with "benefit". Facilities may benefit someone even though they are not in need of them. Need is a higher standard. The Lands Tribunal has stated that:

> "... 'need' of this character is not to be measured against the benefit which facilities confer but by the criterion, whether youth, age etc. that created that need."[104]

Curran L.J. in the Court of Appeal has held that everyone could be considered to be in need of facilities which improve their conditions of life, therefore, need means something more than basic human need. It means that the people in one of the listed classes have some difficulty accessing these facilities, more so than the general public.[105]

14.4.5(i) Youth

It is generally quite easy to show that the young have a need for recreational facilities. As has been explained:

> "... the young must have an outlet for their energies and enthusiasms which is socially acceptable and physically beneficial, and to fail to recognise this need can have disastrous results for individual young people and for the community as a whole."[106]

However, if the class is to be defined by youth, it is necessary that no other class be allowed to use the facilities.[107]

14.4.5(ii) Social and economic circumstances

When the legislation was being promulgated, Parliament said that, in considering the meaning of need due to social and economic circumstances, it meant those "cut off from home and life and social environment and are not in the

---

[103] s.1(2)(b)(i) Recreational Charities Act (Northern Ireland) 1958.

[104] *Lylehill Young Farmers Club v. Commissioner of Valuation* VR/7/1981 at p. 6.

[105] See judgment of Curran L.J. in the *YMCA* case, *op. cit.*

[106] *Londonderry County Council v. Commissioner of Valuation and Trustees of the Newbridge Sean O'Leary Gaelic Centre* VR/21/1971 at p. 9.

[107] *ibid.*

position to provide themselves with adequate facilities for spending their leisure".[108]

In *Northern Ireland Housing Trust v. Commissioner of Valuation*[109] the central issue concerned three community centres run by the N.I.H.T. for its tenants on certain housing estates. The community centres were for social intercourse and recreation and were found to fulfil valuable social functions. For reasons discussed below under the public benefit heading, the centres were held not to be charitable. The question of "need" was also discussed. Curran L.J. was ambivalent as to whether the social and economic circumstances of the tenants justified their need for recreational facilities. McVeigh L.J. tentatively accepted that worker tenants of the N.I.H.T. did have a need for this type of facility.

The question of "need" was somewhat clarified by the subsequent case of *Springhill Housing Action Committee v. Commissioner of Valuation*[110] which also concerned a community centre in a housing estate. This time the estate was Springhill in Belfast, an area of special social need. It was accepted by Gibson J. that the requirements of section 1(2)(b)(i) were satisfied, as residents of the estate had a need for those facilities due to their social and economic circumstances.

It has been argued by Girvan (now Girvan J.) that ethnicity counts as a social and economic circumstance, "an ethnic group should be entitled to meet for recreational purposes and to maintain Indian culture".[111] The Lands Tribunal agreed and held that lack of means to privately build a community centre was an economic circumstance that indicated the need for one.

The condition of being a university student is also one which can require the relief of need due to social and economic circumstances.[112]

14.4.5(iii) Other classes in need

Case law can offer no further guidance regarding the definition of other listed classes which may be in need of recreational facilities. The other classes are "age", "infirmity" or "disablement", or "poverty". It is probable that the common law definitions and principles will assist in setting out the ambit of these terms (see for example, Chapter 8 for poverty and Chapter 12 for age, infirmity or disablement).

---

[108] 582 House of Commons Official Report at 324, September 11, 1958.
[109] [1970] N.I. 208.
[110] [1983] 5 N.I.J.B.
[111] *Trustees of the Indian Community Centre v. Commissioner of Valuation* VR/6/1988 at p. 9.
[112] *Lord Mayor, Aldermen and Citizens of the city of Belfast v. Commissioner of Valuation* VR/17/1967.

14.4.6 Public/female public at large

Instead of providing facilities for those in need due to their being members of a listed class, facilities can be provided for the public or female public at large.[113] There was a suggestion by Walton J., the trial judge in *Inland Revenue Commissioners v. McMullen*[114] that, even where available to the public at large, facilities must assist deprived persons.[115] In the Court of Appeal, Bridge L.J. gave a dissenting judgement which disagreed with this proposition, "I cannot accept the judge's view that the interests of social welfare can only be served in relation to some "deprived" class".[116] The House of Lords did not consider the bearing of the Recreational Charities Act 1958, so the issue was left somewhat uncertain.

The issue arose again in the House of Lords in *Guild v. Inland Revenue Commissioners*.[117] It was then argued that facilities open to the public at large must demonstrably meet some social need. Lord Keith rejected this argument. He held that:

> "… it must necessarily be inferred that the persons for whom the facilities are primarily intended are not to be confined to those who have need of them by reason of one of the forms of social deprivation mentioned in sub-paragraph (a)."[118]

If facilities are provided for the female public, they satisfy the definition of social welfare. If they are for men only, they do not.[119] This distinction could be susceptible to challenge on the basis of sex discrimination under, for example, the Human Rights Act 1998 (see further, Chapter 4).

14.4.7 The public benefit test

The proviso to the Recreational Charities Act (Northern Ireland) 1958 is that it does not affect the requirement that the facilities must be for the public benefit.[120] The case of *Northern Ireland Housing Trust v. Commissioner of Valuation* was important for reiterating the requirement, which seemed to be missing from the majority judgement in *Commissioner of Valuation v. Lurgan Borough Council*, that the public benefit was an essential element of a recreational charity.

In the latter case, neither Lord MacDermott nor Curran L.J. mentioned public benefit, being content to hold that the requirement of section 1(2)(b)(ii)

---

[113] s.1(2)(b)(ii) Recreational Charities Act (Northern Ireland) 1958.
[114] [1978] 1 W.L.R. 664 at 675.
[115] *Inland Revenue Commissioners v. McMullen* (1978) 1 All E.R. 230 at 241.
[116] *Inland Revenue Commissioners v. McMullen* (1979) 1 All E.R. 588 at 597.
[117] (1992) 2 All E.R. 10.
[118] *ibid.* at p. 17.
[119] [1965] Ch. Comm. Rep. App. C–Wollerton Working Men's Club.
[120] s.1(1) of the Recreational Charities Act (Northern Ireland) 1958.

that the swimming pool be available to the public at large was satisfied. McVeigh L.J., the dissenting judge then held "I cannot hold that the facilities are available to the members or female members of the public at large".[121] He did, however, acknowledge that public benefit was a separate and distinct test to be fulfilled, even though he was unable to find the test satisfied because the people who were to benefit were not sufficiently well defined.

In *NIHT*, the majority of the Court of Appeal held that a community centre failed the test because the appellants could not establish how the centre was to benefit the public. McVeigh L.J. said that it:

> "… must be for the benefit of the community or of an appreciably important part of the community which must be sufficiently defined and identifiable by some quality of a public nature."[122]

This was an important reiteration that the public benefit test was just as much a part of the Recreational Charities Act (Northern Ireland) 1958 as for any other charitable purpose.[123]

The other point about public benefit under the Recreational Charities Act (Northern Ireland) 1958 is its relationship to the classes listed by need. There is authority in *Trustees of the Indian Community Centre v. Commissioner of Valuation*[124] that if the beneficiaries are defined by membership of one of the listed classes, this will satisfy the public benefit test.

Aside from these two points, the public benefit test is exactly the same for charities under the Recreational Charities Act (Northern Ireland) 1958 as it is for recreational charities at common law (see further, below).

14.4.8 Village halls, community centres and women's institutes

Section 1(3) of the Recreational Charities Act (Northern Ireland) 1958 states that it applies:

> "… in particular for the provision of facilities at village halls, community centres and women's institutes."

However, this does not mean that such bodies are automatically to be construed as recreational charities. No special exemption is given to them, they must still fulfil the legislative requirements in the same way as any other body.[125]

---

[121] *ibid.* at p. 152. See also the decision of the Charity Commission that the Birchfield Harriers Athletics Club was not charitable since its facilities were not open to the public at large, (1989) Ch. Com. Rep. para. 48.

[122] *N.I.H.T.* at p. 224; following the decision in *Oppenheim*.

[123] The Lands Tribunal had already made this finding in *Andrew Rowan Hamilton v. Commissioner of Valuation* VR/72/1965 that "this statute does not affect the principle that a trust to provide recreational facilities must be for the public benefit" at p. 6.

[124] For example, see the village hall in *Down District Council v. Commissioner of Valuation* VR/8/1972.

[125] *op. cit.*

14.5 PUBLIC BENEFIT

The public benefit remains a compulsory requirement for all recreational charities. Case law has not made any distinction between the public benefit test under common law and that under the Recreational Charities Act (Northern Ireland) 1958; the same test is applied to both. The usual caveat must be entered against the logic which says that if public benefit is satisfied under one head, *ergo*, it must be satisfied under another head.[126] Lord Cross has stated that public benefit is not a static concept but fluid depending upon the type of charity:

> "... in truth, the question whether or not the potential beneficiaries of a trust can fairly be said to constitute a section of the public is a question of degree and cannot be by itself decisive of the question whether the trust is a charity. Much depends upon the purpose of the trust."[127]

These sentiments were echoed by Gibson J. in the Northern Ireland Court of Appeal.[128]

However, the courts have found it advantageous to appropriate parts of the public benefit test under the "benefit to a locality" fourth head[129] charitable purpose. In particular, the *Springhill* case seemed to assimilate public benefit under the recreation head with public benefit under the benefit to a locality head.[130]

14.5.1 The "public"

The case law reveals several categories of beneficiary who could be considered to comprise the public. However, it is difficult to point to any overarching judicial definition. Perhaps the best attempt at a global exposition was given in argument to the Lands Tribunal where it was said that:

> "... trusts for recreational purposes must be for the benefit of the community at large, or the inhabitants of a particular geographical area (and possibly for a class determined by adherence of a particular religion or employment in a particular industry) but private benefit for a fluctuating body of individuals cannot ever qualify."[131]

---

[126] For example, "aged Presbyterians" are a section of the public for first head gifts, *Re Dunlop* [1984] N.I. 408, but "Londonderry Presbyterians" are not a section of the public for recreation gifts, *Londonderry Church House* case, *op. cit.*

[127] *ibid.* at p. 624.

[128] *Springhill Housing Action Committee v. Commissioner of Valuation* [1983] 5 N.I.J.B.

[129] See also, para. 11.4.2.

[130] Gibson J. cited *Wright v. Hobert* 9 Mod. 64, *Re Christchurch Enclosure Act* 38 Ch. D. 520, *Re Smith* [1932] 1 Ch. 153 and *Goodman v. Mayor of Saltash op. cit.* all leading cases under the benefit of a locality charitable purpose (see further, Chap. 11).

[131] *Andrew Rowan Hamilton v. Commissioner of Valuation* VR/72/1965 at p. 4.

Stronger authority exists, but it is less precise:

> "... a gift subject to a condition or trust for the benefit of the inhabitants of a parish or town, or any particular class of such inhabitants is (as I understand the law) a charitable trust."[132]

The rest of this section asks whether particular categories of beneficiaries may constitute the public. These categories are: all the residents of Northern Ireland, a class of residents of Northern Ireland, all the residents of a particular area, and a class of residents of a particular area. It then considers whether there is any minimum requirement as to number of beneficiaries. Finally, it assesses the distinction caused by a personal nexus or relationship which turns public benefaction into private benefaction.

14.5.2 The Northern Ireland public

No case has explicitly held that a gift to the entire Northern Ireland public is for the public benefit. However, it has been assumed without contradiction in all the cases that this is so. In England, a gift for all England was held charitable.[133]

14.5.3 Class of the Northern Ireland public

A class linked by shared ethnicity throughout Northern Ireland is a sufficiently important section of the public. The Lands Tribunal has held that Indians in Northern Ireland are a section of the public.[134] In that case the Lands Tribunal agreed with Tudor that:

> "... the trust is a charitable trust notwithstanding that the direct benefits are restricted to persons having special religious or professional or business qualifications which are not possessed by the members of the public at large."[135]

Young men in Northern Ireland have been held to be a section of the public sufficient to satisfy the public benefit test in the *YMCA*[136] case. University students have been held to be a section of the public[137] as they were in England.[138] The poor, the sick and the working classes are a section of the public.[139]

---

[132] *Goodman v. Mayor of Saltash* at p. 642.
[133] *Re Smith* (1932) 1 Ch. 153.
[134] *Trustees of the Indian Community Centre v. Commissioner of Valuation* VR/6/1988.
[135] Tudor, 6th ed. at p. 116.
[136] *op. cit.*
[137] *Lord Mayor, Aldermen and Citizens of City of Belfast v. Commissioner of Valuation* VR/17/1987.
[138] *Inland Revenue Commissioners v. McMullen op. cit.*
[139] *Incorporated Cripples Institutes and Holiday Homes v. Commissioner of Valuation* VR/5/1965.

14.5.4 Geographical area within Northern Ireland

There is ample authority for holding that recreation for the benefit of all the residents of a particular area is charitable. The Court of Appeal stated that a recreational trust for the benefit of residents in a housing estate would be charitable:

> "... there is no doubt that a trust for all the inhabitants of a designated place or area may in certain circumstances be charitable."[140]

The precise parameters of a "geographical area" are flexible. No case in Northern Ireland has failed the public benefit test because the area designated was too small. The following have been held to be geographical areas: Portadown and surrounding districts,[141] the Torr-Heath area of Belfast,[142] Newbridge district,[143] Drumaness village[144] and a housing estate in Belfast.[145]

Arguments have been posited that the boundaries of the geographical area should be set out with precision, so that all the beneficiaries are readily identifiable. McVeigh L.J. in a dissenting judgement in *Commissioner of Valuation v. Lurgan Borough Council* posed the question "whether the area in which the public are to be found is adequately defined".[146] He answered the question in the negative, holding that the catchment area of a swimming pool in Lurgan, used by those from within and without Lurgan was not sufficiently defined. However, other cases have taken a more relaxed approach to this question of identification. Sir Frank Harrison, in the Lands Tribunal stated:

> "... it is plain at least that if the beneficiaries are the residents of a particular parish, district, village, or neighbourhood, this would not render what otherwise would have been charitable, void for lack of definition."[147]

The survival of the very vaguely worded trust "for the residents of the town of Portadown and the surrounding districts" is testament to this lenient approach.[148]

---

[140] *Springhill Housing Action Committee v. Commissioner of Valuation* [1983] 5 N.I.J.B. at p. 7.
[141] *Shillington v. Portadown Urban District Council op. cit.*
[142] *Torr-Heath Community Association v. Commissioner of Valuation* VR/15/1975.
[143] *Londonderry County Council v. Commissioner of Valuation and Trustees of Sean O'Leary Gaelic Centre* VR/21/1971.
[144] *Down County Council v. Commissioner of Valuation.*
[145] *Springhill Housing Action Committee v. Commissioner of Valuation* [1983] 5 N.I.J.B. at p. 7.
[146] [1968] N.I. 104 at 156.
[147] *Torr-Heath Community Association v. Commissioner of Valuation* VR/15/1975 at p. 8.
[148] *Shillington v. Portadown Urban District Council op. cit.*

14.5.5 Class within a geographical area

The most difficult category of beneficiaries to fit within the public benefit test is the limited class within a geographical area. In essence, the court is being asked to find public benefit in a section of a section of the community. In theory, this is possible to show. The case of *Goodman v. Mayor of Saltash* stated that a trust for the benefit of the freemen of Saltash was charitable. The Lands Tribunal indicated, *obiter*, that a trust for the benefit of the youth of Newbridge would be charitable.[149]

The practical difficulty, however, is that a class within an area is usually construed as all members of the one body. This converts them from being a limited section of the public to being a private body of individuals. So, for example, a tennis club sought charitable status in *Andrew Rowan Hamilton v. Commissioner of Valuation*.[150] The club was ostensibly open to all individuals. The Tribunal held that the club was for the benefit of its members, not the public. The court was unable to find:

> "… any trust to be spelt out from the rules in favour of the inhabitants of a defined geographical area."[151]

The ruling was the same in *Trustees of Chambers Park, Portadown v. Commissioner of Valuation*.[152] That case concerned recreation grounds used by three different sports clubs. The Tribunal found that the grounds were there for the benefit of the clubs, not for the public.

14.5.6 Personal nexus

There will be no public benefit if the only link between the beneficiaries is a personal nexus. The House of Lords has stated:

> "… a group of persons may be numerous, but if the nexus between them is their personal relationship to a single *propositus* or to several *propositi*, they are neither the community nor a section of the community for charitable purposes."[153]

If the beneficiaries are identified by their relationship to the landowner of a housing estate then:

> "… this is not in my opinion a section of the community but a group of persons identified as tenants of the same landlord (and their families) and living on one estate."[154]

---

[149] *Londonderry County Council v. Commissioner of Valuation and Trustees of Sean O'Leary Gaelic Centre* VR/21/1971.

[150] VR/72/1965.

[151] *ibid.* at p. 5.

[152] VR/16/1969.

[153] *Oppenheim v. Tobacco Securities* [1951] A.C. 292 at 306.

[154] *Northern Ireland Housing Trust v. Commissioner of Valuation* at p. 229.

The nexus, the relationship was a private one, the beneficiaries were all tenants of the same landlord. The community centre in that case was not charitable. This decision was distinguished in *Springhill Housing Action Committee v. Commissioner of Valuation*. In the latter case the beneficiaries were then all living on an estate as tenants of the Housing Executive, but this was not a permanent relationship. It was envisaged that many of the tenants would eventually buy their houses. If so, they would still be entitled to use the community centre. The centre was for the benefit of the estate, not merely for the common tenants of one landlord, therefore there was no private nexus.

The gift must allow for the possibility of an appreciable number of the 'public' to access the recreational activity or facility in question. For example, where the objects involved teaching aviation skills it was conceded that the teaching of flying generally may be a purpose of benefit to the community but it could not be considered charitable when confined to members of the club.[155] An association set up on behalf of actors with a view to furthering their careers was denied charitable status as there was an insufficient public element.[156]

The point which is undecided at the moment is whether members of a certain religion in a certain area are the public or merely a private body of fluctuating individuals. In Northern Ireland, Presbyterians in Derry were held not to be the public in the *Londonderry Church House* case.[157] Babington L.J. stated:

> "The Presbyterian Church is not a section of the public. Its members, or those of its members to be benefited under this trust, are no doubt members of the public, but they are not a section of it anymore than were they workpeople in *Re Drummond, Ashworth v. Drummond*[158] and the trust is therefore not a trust for general public purposes but for a floating body of private individuals."[159]

Andrews L.J. concurring:

> "An institution formed for the benefit of its members is not an institution for the benefit of the public or of a section of the public. Lord Greene M.R. had indicated very clearly that a trust of a public character is one in which the benefici-

---

[155] See *Scottish Flying Club v. CIR* C.S. 1935, 20 T.C. 1. Also, see, *Master Mariners (Honourable Company of) v. CIR* K.B. 1932, 17 T.C. 298 where a company, incorporated under Royal Charter to provide a central representative body for the Merchant Navy service in relation, *inter alia*, to matters affecting the interests or status of its members, was held not to be established for charitable purposes only.

[156] See APP 12325. See, also, APP 12260 where charitable status was refused as the purpose of the group was primarily to represent the interests of its members. The main objects had stated it was established for the mutual assistance, welfare and advancement of its members. Thus this would be of direct benefit to the members in the practice of their profession but of marginal benefit to the public at large.

[157] [1946] T.C. 431; [1946] N.I. 178.

[158] [1914] 2 Ch. 90.

[159] *op. cit.* at 196.

aries do not enjoy the benefit when they receive it by virtue of their character as individuals, but by virtue of their membership of a specified class, the common quality uniting potential beneficiaries into the class being essentially an impersonal one."[160]

This was followed by *Baddeley* in which it was held that Methodists resident in a specified area were did not constitute "the public".

However, the Lands Tribunal has held that the Recreational Charities Act (Northern Ireland) 1958 changed the law:

"Viscount Simonds' reservation [in *Baddeley*] related to the class of beneficiaries being too narrow to constitute a section of the public, for example by adherence to a particular religion. After the 1958 Act even that reservation was swept away".[161]

14.5.7 Number of beneficiaries

There are no precise guidelines as to the minimum number of beneficiaries required, but they must not be numerically negligible. In the *Springhill* case Gibson J. stated:

"I know of no reason in principle which would fix a minimum number of beneficiaries in order that the benefit be regarded as public and therefore charitable."[162]

However, a key finding in the *Oppenheim* case had been that "the possible ... beneficiaries must not be numerically negligible".[163] The size of the class is a relevant factor in determining if it is a section of the public and, arguably, the statement by Gibson J. may have attenuated the *Oppenheim* principle. However, in analysing the case in detail, Gibson J. did look to the size of the class:

"... residents of a sizeable estate, is not so insignificant in numbers as to deprive it of its *prima facie* public character."[164]

---

[160] *ibid.* at 189.
[161] *Trustees of the Indian Community Centre v. Commissioner of Valuation* VR/6/1988 at p. 20.
[162] *Springhill* at p. 8.
[163] *Oppenheim* at p. 306.
[164] *Springhill* at p. 11.

CHAPTER 15

Exclusively Charitable Purposes

15.1 INTRODUCTION

The common law rule, that to be charitable an object or purpose must be exclusively for charitable purposes, has been a cornerstone in the development of the law relating to charity. But, when is a purpose charitable? If it can be placed within any of the categories set out in the preceding seven chapters of this section then a purpose is clearly charitable. If it straddles two or more of these categories then problems of definition arise. If a charitable and a non-charitable purpose appear together then this presents problems of exclusivity.

The courts and legislators have both sought to mitigate the effects of the exclusivity rule. Judicial interpretation of an accompanying non-charitable purpose as being variously – subsidiary, subordinate, incidental, consequential, coincident, motivated by or directly facilitating – the charitable purpose, has restricted the application of the rule. Parliament has also attempted to solve the problem of gifts failing because of non-charitable purposes by excising the offending clauses or construing them as solely charitable. These strategies have never wholly succeeded.

This chapter briefly examines the rule that in order for a gift to be construed in law as charitable it must be given for a purpose which is exclusively charitable.

15.2 CLASSIFICATION OF PURPOSES

The fact that a purpose straddles several categories will not necessarily prevent it from being construed as charitable. This was illustrated by the ruling of the Court of Appeal in Northern Ireland in the *Redemptorist* case[1] where the Christian Brothers were found to be charitable because:

> "... the main charitable purposes of the Brothers are not just the advancement of secular education or just the advancement of religion, but an amalgam of the two."[2]

Each element of the amalgamated purposes must be charitable. The same ap-

---

[1] See *Commissioner of Valuation v. Trustees of the Redemptorist Order, Commissioner of Valuation v. Trustees of the Newry Christian Brothers* [1971] N.I. 114.
[2] *ibid.* at p. 34.

proach was taken by MacDermott L.C.J. in the *YMCA* case.[3] It was not possible to compartmentalise the YMCA's purposes into discreet headings such as recreation, religion or education. The trust was charitable "as one comprehensive purpose rather than as a series of distinct purposes capable of being regarded in isolation".[4] The same approach is implicit in the *Baptist Union* case.[5] In that case, payments to ministers and their widows were charitable under the advancement of religion. Payments to their orphans, however, were also charitable as orphans were listed separately under the statute of Elizabeth.

15.3 JUDICIAL DEVICES FOR SAVING CHARITIES

A hallmark of the judicial approach towards gifts intended to give effect to a charitable purpose has been a marked tendency to adopt a benign interpretation of the donor's expressed intention so as to save the gift for charity.

15.3.1 Motive not purpose

If two purposes are expressed in a document and the first is not charitable, the courts can construe the first purpose as being merely the motive for the second purpose. So long as the second and true purpose is charitable, the first can then be discounted. In Northern Ireland there is little case law evidence that this doctrine has been employed to any real effect to save gifts. The doctrine was actually used in reverse in the *Londonderry Presbyterian* case[6] where the motive of the church was held to be charitable, to advance religion, but the methods it used were not. In reaching this conclusion, the court considered the ruling in *Keren Kayemeth Le Jisroel Ltd v. Inland Revenue Commissioners*[7] where the view was expressed that the law:

> "... looks at the nature of the transaction, it looks at the character of the activities, and it does not look behind these to what may be the motive."[8]

On this basis, the church hall was not entitled to the charitable exemption from rates.

Lowry J. considered the "motive not purpose" doctrine in the *Redemptorist* case. He referred to an Irish authority which stated that the "so called primary

---

[3] See *Trustees of the City of Belfast Young Men's Christian Association v. Commissioner of Valuation* [1969] N.I. 3.

[4] *ibid.* at p. 10.

[5] See *Baptist Union of Ireland (Northern) Corporation Ltd. v. Commissioners of Inland Revenue* [1945] N.I. 99.

[6] See *Trustees of the Londonderry Presbyterian Church House v. Commissioners of Inland Revenue* [1927] N.I. 76.

[7] [1932] A.C. 650.

[8] *ibid.* at p. 661.

object should not be treated as an object at all, but merely as ulterior motive".[9]
It was argued that the monks were motivated by self-sanctification (defined as
non-charitable as there was no public benefit) but their actions were nonetheless charitable (preaching, teaching, good works, etc.). Lowry J. accepted the
validity of the doctrine but rejected its application to the facts of the case.[10]
The self-sanctification was too important to their work to be regarded as merely
motive rather than purpose.

At times the English courts have also turned this doctrine on its head. In a
case concerning a religious gift to promote temperance and extinguish the
alcohol trade, instead of holding religion (charitable) as the motive and prohibition (non-charitable since political) as the purpose, the court viewed religion as the purpose and prohibition merely as a suggested way of carrying out
that purpose.[11]

15.3.2 Conjunctive construction

If there are two purposes, one charitable and the other not, the gift may be
saved if they are read conjunctively. For example 'religious and benevolent'
purposes can be construed as meaning only those purposes which are both
religious (charitable) and benevolent (non-charitable). Therefore, if the purposes must always be religious, the purposes are exclusively charitable.

Lowry J. also considered this approach in the *Redemptorists* case, where it
was suggested that "their work of public charity was so bound up with their
work of self-sanctification".[12] The two purposes were inseparable but could
not be saved by reading them conjunctively. The doctrine did not apply.

The doctrine has fared slightly better in England where a gift for "the furtherance of Conservative principles and religious and mental improvement"
was held to be charitable.[13] The conjunctive approach was applied: only those
Conservative principles were to be furthered which would also further religious and mental improvement. Since these were charitable, the gift was exclusively charitable.

15.3.3 Ancillary purposes

If a non-charitable purpose is of minimal importance it may not destroy the
charitable nature of the primary purpose. A veritable thesaurus of words has
been judicially compiled in furtherance of this doctrine: subsidiary, ancillary,

---

[9] *Munster and Leinster Bank v. Attorney General* [1940] I.R. 19 at 37.
[10] The validity of the doctrine was also accepted in the *Legion Attendants* case.
[11] *Re Hood* [1931] 1 Ch. 240.
[12] *Redemptorist* at p. 161.
[13] *Re Scowcroft* [1898] 2 Ch. 638.

subordinate, incidental, consequential and coincidental being among the more common.

In the High Court hearing of *Fermanagh Hospital*,[14] MacDermott J. stated that charitable purposes "must often necessitate the accomplishment of subordinate purposes so that the end in view may be attained". The Court of Appeal overruled his decision in 1947. The House of Lords subsequently overruled the Court of Appeal decision on its approach to rating law in 1965.[15] Three years later, MacDermott, then Lord Chief Justice, in *Industrious Blind*[16] cited with approval his earlier overruled judgement from the High Court in *Fermanagh Hospital*, thereby endorsing it as good law. In *Industrious Blind* the sale of goods made by blind persons in a shop was viewed as subordinate to the primary purpose of providing employment for the blind. However, given that the dictionary definition of subordinate is "of lesser importance" or "under the authority of another", it is submitted that "subordinate" is very close to the line which divides important from non-important purposes.

The construction 'incidental' seems to have found more favour as a means of giving effect to this doctrine. If a non-charitable purpose is wholly incidental to a charitable one, then the latter remains an exclusively charitable purpose. According to the dictionary, incidental means occurring as a minor accompaniment. In *Legion Attendants*,[17] the court was prepared to hold that the employment of an ex-sailor was incidental to the employment of an ex-soldier for the charitable purpose of providing for the welfare of ex-soldiers.[18] It took the view that if the purposes:

> "… are incidental to and consequent upon the way in which the charitable purpose for which alone the body was formed is carried on, the body is charitable."[19]

This reasoning is open to challenge on logical grounds: given that one ex-soldier and one ex-sailor were employed, employing one could not therefore be a minor accompaniment to employing the other.

In *Industrious Blind*, Curran L.J. held that selling goods produced by blind persons was incidental to the employment of blind persons.[20]

---

[14] Unreported, High Court, see *Belfast Association for Employment of the Industrious Blind v. Commissioner of Valuation for Northern Ireland* [1968] N.I. 21 for notes on the text of the judgment in this case.

[15] *Glasgow Corporation v. Johnstone* [1965] A.C. 609.

[16] *op. cit.*

[17] *Royal British Legion Attendants Company v. Commissioner of Valuation* [1979] N.I. 138.

[18] As will be recalled, this ruling was not strictly necessary as the court found that the welfare of sailors was also charitable.

[19] *Legion Attendants* at p. 143.

[20] See also, *Royal College of Nursing v. St. Marylebone Corporation* [1959] 3 All E.R. 663 which was cited in the *Legion Attendants* case.

Other constructions employed in furtherance of this doctrine include: "subsidiary" meaning of secondary importance; and "ancillary" meaning helping in a subsidiary way. If a purpose is subsidiary, then according to *Legion Attendants* it is a separate purpose and if non-charitable it will destroy the charitable purpose. However, according to *dicta* in *Industrious Blind* and English authorities, non-charitable ancillary purposes will not destroy a charitable purpose. Ancillary purposes are more favoured because they express a sense of working towards the primary charitable purpose, whereas subsidiary purposes can be separate and distinct purposes. This was recognised in *Legion Attendants* where it stated that the company's constitution expressed "a subsidiary, but not merely ancillary, object which permits a non-charitable application of the company's property".[21] However, it was more recently held in *Funell v. Stewart*[22] that private religious services carried out by a faith healing group were subsidiary to their public faith healing. The charitable nature of the latter was not vitiated by the non-charitable nature of the former. 'Subsidiary' purposes can therefore sometimes be defined as sufficiently unimportant not to destroy the exclusively charitable nature of a trust.

An incidental purpose can be viewed as charitable because it works towards furthering the paramount charitable purpose. This is the reason for some of the *dicta* in the *Redemptorist* and *YMCA* cases. Even if recreation was not charitable *per se* in *YMCA*, it was being harnessed to the advancement of religion. Similarly, non-charitable self-sanctification was harnessed to the advancement of religion and education in the *Redemptorist* case.

15.3.4 Results not purpose

If a non-charitable result flows from a charitable purpose, it will not render the purpose non-charitable. However, if the purpose of the charitable activity is to achieve the non-charitable result, the purpose is therefore not exclusively charitable. The courts in Northern Ireland, unlike their English counterparts, have not made this point explicitly. For example, in *Council of Law Reporting*[23] it was stated that:

> "… one must not confuse the results flowing from the achievement of a purpose with the purpose itself."[24]

15.3.5 Charitable purposes and rating

In this context, it may be briefly noted that different tests have been used to

---

[21] *Legion Attendants* at p. 144.

[22] [1996] 1 W.L.R. 288.

[23] See *Incorporated Council of Law Reporting for England and Wales v. Attorney General* [1971] 3 All E.R. 1029.

[24] *Council of Law Reporting* at p. 1039.

determine whether or not hereditaments have been occupied for charitable purposes. One is that of "mainly or exclusively" charitable purposes.[25] Another is that the hereditament is to "directly facilitate" the charitable activities[26] (see further, Chapter 21).

15.4 Legislative Validation of Charitable Purpose

The judicial leaning towards a benign interpretation of donor intention as a means of saving gifts for charity was complemented by a legislative intent to reinforce this approach by statutory provision.

15.4.1 Background

In spite of the various efforts made by judges to save gifts which included non-charitable purposes, inevitably a number failed. In England there were four prominent failures in the 1940s. *Chichester Diocesan Fund v. Simpson*[27] concerned a bequest for "charitable or benevolent" objects. Not all benevolent objects are charitable, therefore the gift failed as not being exclusively charitable. In *Re Diplock's Estate; Diplock v. Wintle*[28] the donor's gift of £250,000, "for such charitable or benevolent object or objects" as the trustees should at their discretion determine, was held to be invalid because "benevolent purposes" were not necessarily "charitable purposes".

In *Ellis v. Commissioners of Inland Revenue*[29] the trust included such general purposes as might be identified by a Roman Catholic bishop. Since not exclusively charitable, that trust (and potentially a huge number of similar religious ones) did not acquire charitable status. The decision in *Oxford Group v. Inland Revenue Commissioners*[30] was also viewed unfavourably.

Following these cases and the publication of the Nathan Report[31] the Charitable Trusts (Validation) Act 1954 and the Charitable Trusts (Validation) Act (N.I.) 1954 were enacted.

---

[25] s. 1(1) Rating and Valuation (Amendment) Act (N.I.) 1956, Rates (N.I.) Order 1977 Art. 41(2), and see *Mageean v. Commissioner of Valuation* [1960] N.I. 141.

[26] See *Poor Clares, YMCA, Industrious Blind* and now the Art. 41(4) Rates (N.I.) Order 1977.

[27] [1944] A.C. 341.

[28] [1948] Ch. 465, [1948] 2 All E.R. 318.

[29] [1949] 31 T.C. 178.

[30] [1949] 2 All E.R. 537.

[31] *Report of the Committee on the Law and Practice Relating to Charitable Trusts*, Cmd. 870; in Northern Ireland see the Newark Committee.

15.4.2 Charitable Trusts (Validation) Act (N.I.) 1954

This statute exactly replicates its earlier English counterpart. In the latter jurisdiction judges have criticised the wording of the statute, complaining of "considerable difficulty in following the language ... and in comprehending its true purpose and effect".[32] In a nutshell, the Act will apply to validate imperfect trust provisions, made before December 16, 1952, if they would otherwise be invalid, by declaring them to be exclusively charitable, so long as they have not already been applied to a non-charitable purpose. Because of its very limited temporal remit, the Act has decreasing relevance as time passes, indeed Keeton and Sheridan[33] have termed it moribund.

15.4.2(i) Imperfect trust provisions

The Act defines imperfect trust provisions somewhat torturously as:

> "... any provision declaring the objects for which the property is to be held or applied, and so describing those objects that, consistently with the terms of the provision, the property could be used exclusively for charitable purposes, but could nevertheless be used for purposes which are not charitable."[34]

Two points arise. Firstly, it need not be a trust, but can be any provision whereby property is to be given or used for a charitable purpose. Secondly, it will apply when there is not exclusively charitable purposes, but where the property could be applied to charitable or non-charitable ends.

15.4.2(ii) Validation

Under section 1(2) validation occurs in two ways:

(a) as respects the period before the commencement of this Act, as if the whole of the declared objects were charitable.

(b) as respects the period after that commencement, as if the provision had required the property to be held or applied for the declared objects in so far only as they authorise use for charitable purposes.

Therefore validation looks backwards, by declaring that the trust was charitable in the past, and looks forwards, by only authorising those future actions which are charitable.

15.4.2(iii) Operation of validating provisions

There are three important limitations on the scope of the Act.

---

[32] *Re Harpur's Will Trusts* [1962] Ch. 78 at 87.
[33] *op. cit.*
[34] Charitable Trusts (Validation) Act (N.I.) 1954, s.1(1).

Firstly, and most importantly, the Act will only validate some and not all imperfect trust provisions. It will apply "where apart from this Act, the disposition or covenant is invalid, but would be valid if the objects were exclusively charitable".[35] If an object is liable to income tax, or if a hereditament is liable to rating because it is not exclusively charitable, the Act will not apply. The Act will only apply if the disposition would be void unless it was charitable, for example if it would be a purpose trust,[36] or would breach the rule against perpetuities, or the rule against inalienability.[37] The Act will not operate solely to give fiscal advantage, it will only operate to save otherwise void dispositions.

Secondly, the Act will only apply to those imperfect trust provisions which take effect before December 16, 1952.[38] It has a retrospective effect and will not apply to trusts created after that date, which was when the Nathan report was published, as lawyers should then have known how to draft trust provisions so as to avoid the problem of not being exclusively charitable.

Thirdly, the Act will not apply if property "has been paid or conveyed to, or applied for the benefit of, the persons entitled by reason of the invalidity of the disposition in question".[39] If the trust has already been applied to non-charitable purposes, the Act will be unable to save it.

15.4.3 Section 24 of the Charities Act (N.I.) 1964

In England legislative validation is effectively confined to history. In Northern Ireland it was revived and is now continued by virtue of section 24 of the Charities Act (N.I.) 1964.[40] This legislative provision is clearer than as stated in the 1954 Act and differs from it in two major ways. Firstly, section 24 is not retrospective and therefore will not apply to dispositions before its commencement date of October 1, 1964. Secondly, the dispositions are validated by the Charities Branch or the court not simply by declaring them charitable, but by creating a scheme *i.e.* actually rewriting the terms of the provision. In a nutshell, section 24 applies to imperfect trusts which would otherwise be invalid because they were not exclusively charitable, and validates them by way of a scheme.

The combined effect of the two Acts has been to create a strange lacuna in the law. Trusts can be validated if created before December 16, 1952, or after October 1, 1964, but no legislation exists to correct trusts which fall between these two periods.

---

[35] s. 2(1).
[36] See Chaps 6, 7 and 16.
[37] See further Chaps 6 and 7.
[38] s. 1(2).
[39] s. 2(2).
[40] See further, Sheridan, L.A., *Cy-Près in the Cyxties: Imperfect Trusts* (1966) 17 N.I.L.Q. 235.

15.4.3(i) Imperfect trusts

An imperfect trust occurs where:

> "... property is given for purposes so described that, consistently with the terms of the gift the property could all be used for charitable purposes but could equally be used wholly or partly for purposes which are not charitable."[41]

In substance, this definition is the same as the 1954 Act, and like the Act, it will not just apply to trusts, but to any disposition of property.

15.4.3(ii) Validation

Validation will be by the court (or the Charities Branch if the property is worth less than £50,000) making a scheme for the disposition of the property.[42] By a scheme, the original disposition is effectively rewritten with the non-charitable purposes excised. In making the scheme, the court or Charities Branch must take into account "any predominant intention on the part of the donor to further a particular charitable purpose".[43] If the Charities Branch make the scheme, they have certain duties with regards giving notice to interested parties.[44]

15.4.3(iii) Operation of validating provisions

Unlike the 1954 Act, section 24 does not explicitly state whether it is to have a retrospective effect. Lowry J. considered this question in *Re McCullough*[45] where the testator made a bequest by will and died before the commencement of section 24. Lowry J. ruled that the bequest could not be validated; legislation only had retrospective effect if this was clearly indicated, as section 24 did not contain that clear indication it could not apply to trusts made before its commencement.

This decision was followed by Carswell L.J. in *Re Trusts of Carnmoney Orange Hall*.[46] A Samuel Moore had created a trust in 1904 in favour of Carnmoney Orange Hall. The hall was to be used, and was used:

> "... in connection with the Institution known as the Loyal Orange Institution of Ireland ... or for public or social meetings of any Protestant or charitable body or denomination the object and aims of which shall not in the opinion of the trustees be opposed to the principles of the said Loyal Orange Institution."

---

[41] Charities Act (N.I.) Act 1964, s.24(1)(a).

[42] s. 24(1).

[43] s. 24(2).

[44] s. 24(4), which imposes the requirements of s. 13 which governs notice when a *cy-près* scheme is being made (see further Chap. 19).

[45] [1966] N.I. 73.

[46] Unreported, May 12, 1994.

It was accepted by the parties that these were not exclusively charitable purposes. Section 24 could not apply because it could not retrospectively validate a trust. The 1954 Act could not apply because the property had already been applied to non-charitable uses. The trust was therefore void and the trustees held the hall absolutely. Although technically ruling against the trustees, Carswell L.J. effectively gave them what they wanted, by allowing them the freedom to redevelop the hall unfettered by the trusts.

As with the 1954 Act, the second limitation on the operation of section 24 is that it will only validate an object if it would otherwise be invalid.[47] It will not validate to avoid payment of taxes, etc.

The limitation of the previous Act, that validation will not occur if property has already been applied to non-charitable ends, is not mentioned in section 24. The tenor of section 24 suggests that *ex post facto* validation by scheme is possible. Even if non-charitable purposes have been pursued, arguably, a scheme can be made directing that in future only charitable purposes are authorised.

15.4.4 Flavour of charity

How much charity need an imperfect trust provision[48] or an imperfect trust[49] contain before it can be subject to validating legislation? To put the question another way, what flavour of charity must a disposition contain before it can be validated?

Two approaches have been posited:

- The narrow approach states that the legislation is "intended to cure dispositions whereby part of the trust fund is devoted to charitable purposes and part to purposes not charitable".[50] This looks at the mischief the legislation was intended to remedy, *i.e.* to declare charitable a gift expressed to be for 'charitable or benevolent' purposes.[51]

- The broad approach looks at the clear words of the statutes which do not impose any requirements as to "flavour of charity". The only requirement is that it is possible to apply the property for exclusively charitable purposes.

The English case of *Re Wykes*[52] recommended the broad approach by giving a natural construction to the words of the Act. *Leahy v. Attorney General for*

---

[47] s. 24(1)(b).

[48] Charitable Trusts (Validation) Act (N.I.) 1954.

[49] Charities Act (N.I.) Act 1964, s.24.

[50] *Re Gillingham Bus Disaster Fund* [1958] Ch. 300 at 306, affirmed on appeal that the legislation is "confined to cases where, among the declared objects for which the property is to be held or applied, one at least is charitable" [1959] Ch. 62 at 76.

[51] *Chichester Diocesan Fund v. Simpson* (1944) A.C. 341.

[52] [1963] Ch. 229.

New South Wales[53] also recommended the broad approach. The Privy Council in that case reasoned as follows: the previous law had required a precise use of words, the legislation was designed to save gifts which failed these formalities, where was the logic in construing the legislation as requiring a new "magic formulae" of words? In the opinion of text book writers "the flavour of charity need not be obtrusive, but it must be discernible to a discriminating palate".[54]

Northern Ireland chose the broad approach in *Re Mc Cullough*.[55] The gift was to the Provincial Grand Master of the Masons for such purposes as he thought fit. The testator did not list some charitable and some non-charitable purposes (*i.e.* failing the narrow approach test), but the gift could be applied for exclusively charitable purposes (*i.e.* passing the broad approach test). Lowry J. held it was not necessary to have purposes described which were partly charitable. However, he did not decide if a gift which was completely discretionary could be validated. There was a charitable flavour to the gift since the Masons did perform some philanthropic work, and the gift was to the Provincial Grand Master in that capacity, and not as a private individual.

---

[53] *op cit.*
[54] Keeton and Sheridan (1983) at p. 282.
[55] *op cit.*

SECTION FOUR

Charities

CHAPTER 16

Legal Forms for Charitable Activity

16.1 INTRODUCTION

Organised charitable activity requires a legal structure. Charitable trusts are one method of providing formal recognition for such activities in law. Other methods exist. The form best suited to the functions of any charity depends very much on its particular blend of funding sources, charitable purposes and its ethos. The range of legal structures available to serve as vehicles for charitable activity has long been a distinctive characteristic of this branch of the voluntary sector. Arguably, this has given charities the flexibility to adapt to changing circumstances, adjust their activities and deploy their resources in a manner unique to collective economic endeavour.

Establishing a charity will always necessitate certain prerequisites. Firstly, a gift of funds or other form of property is necessary. This may be acquired in a number of different ways ranging from the gift of a single contemporary donor to a heritage of innumerable bequests extending over centuries. The funds may be derived wholly or partially from sources such as fundraising activities, grants from government bodies, corporate donations, tax concessions or any combination of such public and private finances. They may be used wholly to cover overseas charitable activity. Secondly, in the words of Cairns:

> "A charity may be established by the completion of a formal governing instrument (declaration of trust, company memorandum and articles or constitution), under the terms of a will or by publishing an appeal for funds."[1]

Thirdly, the aims or purposes to be pursued by a charity as expressed in its governing instrument must conform to one of the four *Pemsel* heads and meet the public benefit test. They may be entirely focussed on the development needs of a third world country or the local needs of a housing estate. They may be given effect through activities as wide ranging as advocacy, contemplative religious orders or disaster relief. They may be of short or long-term duration.

The ethos of a charity can also be of importance. Its founder/s may have imbued it with particular principles such as those of mutuality, co-operative association or of public service. It could be embedded in the beliefs of a particular religion such as that of the Quakers, in the way of life of a religious

---

[1] See Cairns, E., *Charities: Law and Practice* (2nd ed., Sweet & Maxwell, 1993), p. 47.

order such as the Benedictines or the values of minority groups such as vegetarians.

These factors will determine the legal structure chosen to give effect to a charity's functions. This chapter examines the different forms available and the differences between them. It draws from the work of others who have written with authority on this subject.[2]

16.2 LEGISLATION, AIMS AND ETHOS

There is no legislation specifically governing the administrative framework for charities in Northern Ireland. Instead, charities must look to the legislation which governs the particular legal structure which they have adopted, usually in company or trust statutes. This legislation is not designed for charities, although it occasionally takes their special needs into account. The requirements regarding the aims of a charity, including the necessity for conformity between its aims and activities, regardless of its particular legal structure, are as important in this as in any of the neighbouring jurisdictions. Northern Ireland, as much as any other jurisdiction, is also experiencing the problems of preserving a charitable ethos in the corrosive context of a prevailing contract culture.

16.2.1 Legislation

All charitable activity is uniformly subject to the Charities Act of 1964 and the 1987 Order. All charities have equal access to the Inland Revenue for recognition as such to claim eligibility for tax exemption and to the Valuation and Lands Office for charitable exemption from rates. The legislation governing the organisational structure of charities, however, differs according to the type of structure. For example, the legislation governing status of a company limited by guarantee, not having a share capital, is the Companies (N.I.) Order 1986, the Companies (N.I.) Order 1990 and the Companies (No.2) (N.I.) Order 1990. Other structures such as housing associations are governed by the Friendly Societies Act 1992. The Industrial and Provident Societies Act (N.I.) 1969 relates specifically to such societies while certain anomalous forms of charities such as universities are subject to the provisions of their founding statutes.

16.2.2 Aims

A voluntary organisation must conform to certain standard requirements if it is to come within any legal definition of "charity". Most obviously, its pur-

---

[2]   In particular, Tudor, *Charities* (8th ed., London, Sweet & Maxwell, 1995), pp. 121–163.

poses must satisfy the public benefit test (see further, Chapter 1) without causing any ancillary and detrimental effects on society or the environment; mutual benefit societies, for example, are by definition not charities. Its aims
must be clearly stated.[3] The objects should not be so imprecise as to be unenforceable and they should be expressly stated from the outset, not expediently
adopted by the organisation at a later stage in order to acquire charitable recognition. The aims should also be both lawful[4] and exclusively charitable;
unless, in the latter instance, they are statutorily exempted. The persons designated as trustees (whether referred to as directors, governors, members of a
management or executive committee) should be clearly identified, in order
that responsibility and accountability for management of the charity's affairs
can be readily ascertained. Arrangements to ensure their independence when
representing the interests of the charity must be in place.

Crucially, the aims of a charity must be given effect by, and be wholly
reflected in, its activities. This conformity between charitable aims and charitable activities must be maintained and should be finally reinforced by conformity with charitable outputs. However, in practice, achieving such a seamless
continuity from purpose to results can present real problems. Many charities
find themselves in the position of contriving an artificial interpretation of the
nature or balance of their activities so as to satisfy the Inland Revenue or the
Charities Branch that they conform with declared charitable objects. Similar
pressures from potential funders can also result in charities tailoring their activities so as to be eligible for funds from various sources. Many charities also
find that over time their activities change and can diverge from the initial
interpretation given to the aims as stated in its founding documents. Where
activities have strayed far from aims then remedial action will be necessary to
correct the discrepancy. Where the aims of a charity allow for possible private
benefit,[5] perhaps in terms of conferring a professional or commercial advantage, it must be clear that this is incidental to and necessary for the fulfilment
of those aims. In addition it must be clear that the aims of the charity are not
such as would unduly restrict access to its facilities or services. In particular, it
cannot be confined to serve the interests of the rich; though they may also
benefit. Nor may the aims allow for the possibility of political activity[6] (see
also, Chapter 13).

---

[3] See for example, *Re Gott* [1944] Ch. 193, where the court ruled that the objects were not
clearly stated but, given clear evidence of charitable intent, it was able to remedy the
deficiency by providing the necessary details. See also, *Attorney General v. Mathieson*
[1907] 2 Ch. 383, for authority that trustees, in certain circumstances, may themselves
amend vague terms of a trust in order to clarify ill-defined objects.

[4] See *National Anti-Vivisection Society v. IRC* [1948] A.C. 31 and *Re Pinion* [1965] Ch.
85.

[5] See for example, *Williams' Trustees v. IRC* [1947] A.C. 447 and *IRC v. Educational
Grants Association Ltd.* [1967] Ch. 993.

[6] See *McGovern v. Attorney General* [1982] Ch. 321.

16.2.3 Ethos

The motivating force of altruism, prompting the birth of a charity, can be difficult to sustain. As it is forced to conform to the business environment in which it has to function and is induced to adopt many of the professional characteristics of government bodies upon which it is dependent for funding, there is an increasing danger that the philanthropic hallmarks of a charity will be steadily eroded. In particular, exposure to the "contract culture" and reliance upon paid staff rather than volunteers threaten to dilute the independence, creativity and advocacy traditionally associated with charities (see further, Chapters 17 and 18).

16.3 LEGAL FORMS FOR VOLUNTARY AND CHARITABLE ORGANISATIONS: HISTORICAL BACKGROUND

Voluntary organisations and charities share a common history; their development has been largely coterminous and exposed to much the same vicissitudes of politics, economics and religion. Not until the latter half of the nineteenth century, when legislation was introduced to facilitate and regulate the forming of companies, did legal forms for voluntary activity become clearly differentiated.

The legal status of voluntary organisations now takes a number of different forms: trusts, friendly societies, industrial and provident societies, unincorporated associations, and companies limited by guarantee without share capital. The most common modern forms are trusts, companies limited by guarantee and unincorporated associations.

16.4 LEGAL FORMS AND LEGAL PERSONALITY

Probably the most significant distinction between the varied legal forms a charity can adopt is whether the form has a legal personality which is separate and distinct from its members. If a legal form does not have a legal personality, then it does not exist in law and all actions are carried out, not by the charity itself, but by its members. On the other hand, if a charity has a legal personality then: it holds property in its own right not via its members, it is responsible and liable for its own tax, it sues and is sued in its own name, and it has a perpetual existence regardless of whether its creators/members die or change. Of most significance is the fact that members usually have limited liability; if the charity cannot pay its debts then creditors cannot seek the money from the members.[7] The corollary is true for charities which do not have a

---

[7] *Salomon v. Salomon* (1897) A.C. 22 illustrates some of these points in relation to a company's separate legal personality.

separate legal existence: all actions must be done by and for its members; it is the members who own the property and are sued, etc.

A separate legal personality exists if the charity is in some way incorporated or is a corporation. The following have a separate legal personality: companies, industrial and provident societies, some friendly societies, corporations established by Act of Parliament or Royal Charter, eleemosynary corporations and charities incorporated by a scheme of incorporation under section 10 of the Charities Act (N.I.) 1964. Trusts and unincorporated associations don't have a separate legal personality.

16.5 LEGAL FORMS WITHOUT SEPARATE LEGAL PERSONALITY

A voluntary organisation, for example a charity, without a legal personality may take one of several different forms.

16.5.1 Unincorporated associations

A voluntary organisation is most commonly constituted as an unincorporated association. In *Re Koeppler*[8] it was defined as:

> "… an association of persons bound together by identifiable rules and having an identifiable membership."[9]

The Charity Commission defines it as:

> "… an organisation consisting of a group of people who have decided to co-operate in furthering what the organisation is set up to do, and who have certain parts to play in its administration."[10]

No formalities are required to create an unincorporated association, though it is generally thought desirable to have some form of written constitution and contract of membership. Since an unincorporated association cannot hold property on its own behalf, it is necessary to have trustees or representatives hold it. Under section 15 of the Charities Act (N.I.) 1964 the trustees may transfer property to the Charities Branch which may then appoint and remove persons to administer or distribute it. Such persons need not be the original trustees. When property is transferred under section 15 the original trustees in effect surrender their interest in it and the Charities Branch thereafter is the trustee for all practical purposes. The Charities Branch therefore has the potential at least to act as a holding trustee, (see further, Chapter 5).

---

[8] [1985] 2 All E.R. 869.
[9] *ibid.* at p. 874. See further, Warburton, J., *Unincorporated Associations: Law and Practice* (2nd ed., London, Sweet & Maxwell, 1992).
[10] CC22, *Choosing and Preparing a Governing Document* (1999) at p. 7.

Many charities have commenced as unincorporated associations, and often this legal form has proved sufficient for their purposes; particularly where the charitable purpose is short-term and locally based. The Charity Commission suggests that an unincorporated association is appropriate where one or more of the following conditions are satisfied:

- Relatively small assets,
- Charity has a membership,
- Trustees elected to hold office for a fixed period by the members,
- Views of locals need to be represented via membership,
- Work of charity to be mainly carried out by members.[11]

Establishing an unincorporated association does not require adherence to any specific formal procedure. Best practice suggests a written constitution to be signed by officers of the association. The officers are the persons in charge of the charity. They can also be called the charity trustees or the executive or committee members. There should also be a meeting where the members adopt the constitution. A note should be made in the minutes of that meeting that the constitution has been adopted.

The Charities Branch will provide advice to assist an organisation meet the necessary formal requirements and become properly constituted as an unincorporated association. The Charity Law Association (England and Wales) also provide excellent and comprehensive guidance.[12]

A constitution is not essential but, if in existence, it should set out the name of the association, its aims and objectives and possibly provide details of the membership and management committee. It should outline matters such as membership eligibility and fees, the regularity and venue for meetings and provide for an annual general meeting.

In the absence of a written constitution or set of rules, a written or oral agreement between members will be sufficient evidence that they have formed an unincorporated association. As explained in *Thackrah; Thackrah v. Wilson*:

> "Before one can find an association, there must be some rules, either written or oral, by which those who are supposed to be members of it are tied together. I think that they would probably be written rules. There must be some constitution."[13]

Though legally binding as between members of the group any such constitution, set of rules or agreement has no effect on the group's external relations;

---

[11] CC22, *ibid*.

[12] See Charity Law Association Model Documents, *Charitable Association: Constitution for a Charitable Unincorporated Association*, drafted by Quint, F., 1997; available from the Charity Commission (see "Useful Addresses"), see also GD3, Model Constitution for a Charitable Unincorporated Association (1995), Charity Commission.

[13] [1939] 2 All E.R. 4 at p. 6.

i.e. it does not give the group a legal personality and therefore it is not subject to external legal controls.

In *Afleck v. Newcastle Mind*[14] the Employment Appeal Tribunal considered who would constitute the employers of staff employed by an unincorporated association. They ruled against the contention that all the subscribing members were the employers, and stated that the employers were the members of the management or executive committee.

16.5.2 Trusts

A trust is an arrangement whereby one or more persons, the trustees, operating under a legal document known as a "deed of trust" hold/s funds or property on behalf of another person or persons.[15] The essential point of distinction between trusts and other legal forms is that their *raison d'être* lies in the protection and use of designated property rather than in setting the rules for how individuals may be best organised to act collectively.

A charitable trust is a public trust, made with a charitable intention, for a purpose which complies with one of the four categories specified in *Pemsel* and satisfies the public benefit test. In this jurisdiction its legal status has not received specific statutory endorsement although the Inland Revenue will provide formal recognition for the purposes of awarding a right to tax exemption. Its governing instrument is a deed of trust.

There are two principal types of charitable trust. Firstly, there are those established by a benefactor, and perpetuated by investment generated income, which give effect to their objects by means of grants provided at trustee discretion. These are often associated with families; the Rowntree charitable trust being a good example. Secondly, there are charitable trusts established as service delivery agencies for a specified client group such as the elderly, disabled or mentally ill, which although established by philanthropic gift have come to depend upon contracts or grants provided by government bodies. In recent years as their work has grown in volume, complexity and has absorbed increasing numbers of paid professional staff, this type of trust has tended to make the transition to company status in order to limit liability. The distinction between the two types is no longer as distinct as formerly. A new type is emerging which is the charitable trust attached to a parent body. The "hiving off" of its charitable functions into a separate trust has become an accepted strategy for many social/health care client support agencies.

Trusts have been recognised as a valid legal form for giving effect to the charitable intentions and gifts of donors since at least the sixteenth century (see further, Chapter 6). The Charity Commission recommends that a trust may be appropriate where one or more of the following are satisfied:

---

[14] [1999] I.C.R. 852; [1999] I.R.L.R. 405.
[15] See further, Chaps. 6 and 7.

- Charity to be run by small number of people,
- No time limit on duration trustees may stay in office,
- New trustees appointed by remaining trustees,
- Charity not reliant on membership for its administration,
- Charity a grant-making body only,
- Land to be held on trust for permanent use of the charity,
- Restriction on spending of capital.[16]

Establishing a trust requires a declaratory document to be executed by being signed and dated. This must be done by the settlor/donor and by the first trustees if they are different people. The signatures must be authenticated by independent witnesses who must also provide their addresses. Once executed, the trust deed must be sent to the local Inland Revenue Stamp Office where it may attract stamp duty.

The Charities Branch will provide advice and access to model documents to assist an organisation meet the necessary formal requirements and become properly constituted as a charitable trust. The Charity Law Association (England and Wales) also provide excellent and comprehensive guidance.[17]

Establishing a properly constituted charitable trust requires adherence to the same requirements common to all trusts; the Inland Revenue will closely examine trusts claiming tax exemption on charitable grounds to ensure all formalities have been fully satisfied. The legislation governing the technical requirements for creating trusts in general has an equal application to charitable trusts. The trust must fulfil the three certainties and avoid rules against perpetuities, accumulations and inalienability (see further, Chapter 6). What distinguishes the setting up of such trusts from other legal forms is the relative speed, simplicity and lack of cost involved. However the requirements regarding the substance of the trust have a distinctive application in relation to those which are charities.

16.5.2(i) The rules against perpetuities and inalienability

Charitable trusts are essentially inalienable and perpetual. Where a gift is made to charity, unconditionally, then there is no problem. Any obstacle arising due to the mode specified to give effect to the gift can then be rectified by *cy-près*. However, charitable gifts are not immune to the effects of the rule against perpetuities. A gift to a charity will be in breach of the rule against perpetui-

---

[16] CC22, *ibid.*

[17] See Charity Law Association Model Documents, *Charitable Trust: Trust Deed for a Charitable Trust*, drafted by Quint, F., 1997; available from the Charity Commission (see, "Useful Addresses"), see also GD2, *Model Charitable Trust Deed*, (1998) Charity Commission for a draft trust.

ties if it is not framed so as to take effect within the perpetuity period. This is fixed at life or lives in being plus 21 years or just 21 years where there is no life in being (see further, Chapter 6). The rule will be breached in circumstances where there is a gift to a charity followed by a gift over to an individual or vice versa. In the latter instance, any attached condition precedent, with a capacity to defer the vesting of a charitable gift to a date beyond the perpetuity period, will be fatal to that gift.[18] Where there is a gift to a charity followed by a gift over to another charity the rule will not have application, unless a condition precedent intercedes.

16.5.2(ii) Advantages of charitable trusts

In this jurisdiction the importance of gifts to charitable trusts would be difficult to overestimate. Donors and testators have the security of knowing that the risk of a gift being invalidated is minimal due to the combined effect of its inherent perpetual nature, explicit statutory presumptions in its favour and judicial willingness to apply the *cy-près* doctrine. Tax exemptions add greatly to the value of the gift. The vigilance of the Attorney-General and the Charities Branch provide additional protection for charitable trusts.

P.J. Ford has usefully summarised the advantages and otherwise of charitable trusts as follows:

> "It is not a suitable form for a charitable body which is intended to become a members' organisation, nor for one likely to engage in providing services or to employ substantial members of staff. On the other hand, it is well-adapted to the management of assets held for charitable purposes either as a grant-making trust or as a trust ancillary to a service-providing charity constituted in another form. The trust is perhaps at its best as a 'charity vehicle' where the tasks to be performed are the management of substantial assets and the distribution of cash grants and where the administration of the trust will be undertaken by a small body of experienced trustees with ready access to professional advice."[19]

NICVA see the following as the advantages to a trust:

- continuity – because the same trustees will continue indefinitely they add continuity to the charity;

- independence – because the trustees are independent of their members they can act impartially without pressure being applied;

- confidentiality – because a trust is a private document it is not accessible to the public at large;

---

[18] See for example, *Re Lord Stratheden and Campbell* [1894] 3 Ch. 265. See also *Re Wood* [1949] Ch. 498; and *Re Mander* [1950] Ch. 547.

[19] See Barker, C.R., Ford, P.J., Moody S.R. and Elliot R.C., *Charity Law in Scotland* (W. Green, Sweet & Maxwell, Edinburgh, 1996) at p. 83.

- cost – because trusts are cheap to establish and manage; and
- certainty in that trust law is well defined so all parties know their duties.[20]

16.5.3 Friendly societies

A friendly society is a mutual assurance association. Under the Friendly Societies Act 1896 three types of friendly society were established: the Friendly Society, the Cattle Insurance Society and the Benevolent Society. Their legal standing was consolidated by the Friendly Societies Act of 1908 and became subject to regulation under the Friendly Societies Act (N.I.) 1970. That Act has now been repealed and they are now regulated by the Friendly Societies Act 1992; particularly under the powers provided by section 124 of that Act. Under the 1992 Act it is possible for friendly societies to be incorporated.

A friendly society which is exclusively charitable, may be used as a vehicle for charitable activity.

16.5.4 Benevolent societies

A benevolent society is a type of friendly society. It is the type most relevant to voluntary organisations. While the benevolent society is governed by statutory requirements, under the supervision of the Registrar of Friendly Societies, it does not provide a separate legal status for the organisation.

16.6 LEGAL FORMS WITH A SEPARATE LEGAL PERSONALITY

Any voluntary organisation, including a charity, can become incorporated. The effect of so doing is that it becomes duly registered as such with the relevant designated statutory body, it is made amenable to statutory requirements and the personal liability of its members, excluding board members, is thereafter limited. Once incorporated, an organisation may or may not have share capital; most voluntary organisations do not. There are several different types of incorporated voluntary organisations.

16.6.1 Charities incorporated by Royal Charter

The Crown's prerogative can be used to create, by Royal Charter, incorporated charities. Campbell College in Belfast, for example, is a charity for the advancement of education and was incorporated by Royal Charter in 1952.[21]

---

[20] NICVA Charity Advice Service, *Notes on Legal Structures*.

[21] See *Governors of the Campbell College Belfast v. County Court Judge of Down* [1964] N.I. 107. For an English example see *Attorney General v. National Hospital for Relief and Care of the Paralysed* (1904) 2 Ch. 252

Where a Northern Ireland court makes a scheme to modify a Royal Charter Charity, if that body applies to the government, the government may modify the Charter by secondary legislation.[22]

16.6.2 Industrial and provident societies

Industrial and provident societies were established by the Industrial and Provident Societies Acts of 1893 and 1894, as amended by the Act of 1913, and are supervised by the Registrar of Friendly Societies. The governing legislation in Northern Ireland is now the Industrial and Provident Societies Act (N.I.) 1969. This type of organisation is perhaps best considered as representing a cross between a registered company and an unincorporated association. It must comply with certain requirements. Firstly, it must be a society carrying on an industry, business or trade.[23] Secondly, it must either be a *bona fide* co-operative society or there must be some special reason why it shouldn't be registered as a company.[24] Thirdly its rules must include certain prescribed information.[25] And fourthly, its registered office must be situated within Northern Ireland.[26]

The constitution of such a society takes the form of rules of association in much the same way as an unincorporated body, but it is an incorporated body and enjoys the benefit of limited liability.[27] An industrial and provident society must have at least seven founder members.[28] It acquires legal personality by submitting its constitution to the Registrar of Industrial and Provident Societies. The legal capacity of the body is set out in its constitution. Beyond providing the information contained in Schedule 1, there is no prescribed form in which the rules must be prepared.

If it should wish to be charitable it must fulfil the usual requirements of having exclusive charitable objects and being for the public benefit. Portora school in Enniskillen, for example, established an industrial and provident society in order to manage housing accommodation for teachers at the school; this had charitable status.[29] Charitable registered housing associations commonly adopt this structure.

---

[22] See s. 15(2) Charities Act 1993, one of only two provisions of the English Charities Act which applies to Northern Ireland.

[23] s. 1(1)(a) Industrial and Provident Societies Act (N.I.) 1969

[24] s. 1(2) *ibid.*

[25] s. 1(1)(a)(ii) and Sch. I Part I, *ibid.*

[26] s. 1(1)(a)(iii), *ibid.*

[27] Barker, C., Ford, P., Moody, S. and Elliot, R. (eds.), *Charity Law in Scotland* (Green, Sweet & Maxwell, Edinburgh, 1996).

[28] s. 2 *ibid.*

[29] *Commissioner of Valuation for Northern Ireland v. Fermanagh Protestant Board of Education* [1970] N.I. 89; and also see *Rosemary Simmons Memorial Housing Association v. United Dominions Trust* [1986] 1 W.L.R. 1440.

16.6.3 Incorporated trustees

Under section 10 of the Charities Act (N.I.) 1964, charitable trustees can incorporate their trust. This has the effect of vesting all property of the trusts in the new body corporate. The method of incorporation is by a scheme drawn up by the Charities Branch. Sections 10(3) and 11 set out the provisions of those schemes and their effects. The purpose of incorporation is usually to allow the charity to hold property in its own right. Under section 10(4):

> "... every body corporate established by the scheme shall have a corporate seal and power to sue in its corporate name as well as power to do every act or thing necessary for the administration of the trusts applying to the charity."

However, it is important to note that incorporating the trustees does not confer limited liability. This is a disadvantage of the incorporated trust as compared to the other legal forms which have legal personality. The charity can own land on its own behalf, but the trustees are still personally liable for any debts incurred by it.

The previous legislation governing incorporated charitable trusts was the Charitable Trustees (Incorporation) Act (N.I.) 1961. This Act was repealed by the 1964 Act.

In England similar provisions exist under Part VII of the Charities Act 1993. That Act has a far greater degree of detail and regulation of such bodies. It comprises 14 sections as opposed to two sections in its Northern Irish equivalent. Incorporation is by way of a certificate of incorporation and not by a scheme and the Charity Commission has the power to dissolve the incorporated body.

By 1999, 33 schemes of incorporation had been created by the Charities Branch, though some were amendments of earlier schemes. A similar level of disinterest in incorporated trustees exists in England. According to the Charity Commission, there were 118 charitable trusts incorporated under the Charitable Trustees Incorporation Act 1872 until its replacement by the Charities Act 1993.[30]

16.6.4 Incorporated by statute

A charity can be incorporated by statute. This power is usually confined to entities which perform vital, semi-statutory functions, for example public utilities. However, it can also include charities. For example, an attempt was made under the Agricultural Marketing Act (N.I.) 1933 to establish the Pigs Marketing Board[31] as a charity under the legislative powers of the Northern Ireland Parliament, The attempt failed, but not because of any defect in the

---

[30] See further, CC43, *Incorporation of Charity Trustees* (1999).

[31] See *Pigs Marketing Board (N.I.) v. Commissioners of Inland Revenue* [1945] N.I. 155.

proposed legal structure of the putative charity nor due to any fault in the manner of its creation. However, the court did say that it would be difficult to regulate this sort of charity, since it would impinge upon questions of policy and government. The Northern Ireland Parliament has also legislated for a specific charity, Vaughan's Charity, and has provided schemes for its administration.[32] The National Trust is a statutory corporation set up under the National Trust Act 1907.[33]

The Belfast Charitable Society is perhaps the oldest charity in Northern Ireland. It was incorporated by an Act of the Irish Parliament in 1774[34] and since modified by various parliaments.[35] It has most recently been updated by a Local and Personal Act, the Belfast Charitable Society Act 1996. The objects of the Society are:

(a) to pursue all or any charitable activities which advance the interests or are for the benefit of persons appearing to the Society to be disadvantaged, primarily in Northern Ireland, including the care of the elderly, the relief of poverty, homelessness, distress, infirmity and sickness and providing for the educational and other needs of such persons; and

(b) to participate in and encourage all forms of co-operation among appropriate parties which are calculated to achieve any of the objects mentioned in paragraph (a) above.[36]

A charity, incorporated by statute, may be subject to special requirements before it can change its constitution. In *RSPCA v. Attorney-General*[37] Lloyd J. held that the RSPCA could make rule changes which effected administrative change without recourse to court. However, under the Royal Society for the Prevention to Cruelty to Animals Act 1932, any rule changes affecting its use of funds or property had to be confirmed by the High Court or by the Charity Commission.

---

[32] See Vaughan's Charity (Administration) Act (N.I.) 1954 and Vaughan's Charity Scheme (N.I.) Order 1973.

[33] See *Re Richardson, Boyce v. National Trust for Places of Historic Interest or Natural Beauty* [1988] N.I. 86. For an English example of charities incorporated by Act of Parliament see *Construction Industry Training Board v. Attorney General* [1973] Ch. 173.

[34] An Act for amending an Act made the last Session of Parliament, intitled, An Act for badging such Poor as shall be found unable to support themselves by Labour and otherwise providing for them, and for restraining such as shall be found able to support themselves by Labour and Industry, from begging 13 & 14 Geo. 3 C.46 (1774) (Ir.).

[35] See An Act for giving further Powers to the President and Assistants of the Charitable Society of the Town of Belfast, in the County of Antrim, to supply the said town with Water, and to improve their Estates, 57 Geo. 3 C. lvii (1817) and An Act to amend the several Acts relating to the Belfast Charitable Society, 3 & 4 Vict. C. lxxxvii (1840).

[36] s. 4, Belfast Charitable Act 1996 C. vi.

[37] Unreported, March 31, 1999, Chancery Division.

16.6.5 Eleemosynary corporations

Charities can be eleemosynary corporations. These are defined in Tudor as follows:

> "Eleemosynary corporations are those corporations constituted for the perpetual distribution of free alms and bounty of the founder to such persons as he has directed and are generally hospitals or colleges."[38]

They hold their corporate property upon charitable trusts.[39] A founder has complete discretion to order the affairs of such a corporation.[40] It is unclear if eleemosynary is a legally separate and distinct type of corporation, or merely a way to describe corporations which perform certain functions; although the latter seems the better view. For example, in *Royal British Legion Attendants Company v. Commissioners of Valuation*,[41] Lord Lowry L.C.J. spoke of the welfare element in the case as being eleemosynary while Lord Upjohn in *Campbell College*[42] defined eleemosynary as being connected with the relief of the poor.

It would appear that there are no eleemosynary corporations, in the strict sense, in Northern Ireland. This is borne out by the lack of a Northern Ireland case concerning an eleemosynary corporation. It is also borne out by legislation. The limitation period in actions for the recovery of land is 12 years.[43] In England, a similar period applies.[44] However, in the latter jurisdiction, special provisions apply to "actions brought by, or by a person claiming through, the Crown or any spiritual or eleemosynary corporation sole".[45] These special provisions are contained in Schedule I, Part II and are basically to the effect that the Crown and eleemosynary corporations have a limitation period of 30 years. In Northern Ireland, the Crown has a 30 year limitation period, but there is no mention of eleemosynary corporations in our legislation. A presumption is therefore raised that eleemosynary corporations are not the subject of legislation in Northern Ireland because they do not exist here.

16.7 COMPANY

A company is a body which is registered as such and whose memorandum of association and articles of association are lodged in the Companies Registra-

---

[38] See *Charities, op. cit.* at p. 163.
[39] See *Lydiatt v. Foach* (1700) 2 Vern. 410.
[40] See *Phillips v. Bury* (1788) 2 Tr. 346, 353; *Green v. Rutherforth* (1750) 1 Ves. S 462, 472; and *Spencer v. All Souls College* (1762) Wilm. Notes 163.
[41] [1979] N.I. 138.
[42] *Campbell College v. Commissioner of Valuation* [1964] N.I. 169 (H.L.).
[43] Art. 21, Limitation (N.I.) Order 1989.
[44] s. 15 Limitation Act 1980.
[45] s. 15(7) Limitation Act 1980.

tion Office. It is a separate legal entity with an existence independent from that of its members. Many unincorporated associations, as they grow in size and organisational complexity, make the transition to company status. The YMCA, for example, became a company limited by guarantee in 1960 after converting from an unincorporated association.

The Charities Branch will provide advice and access to model documents to assist an organisation meet the necessary formal requirements and become properly constituted as a company. The Charity Law Association (England and Wales) also provide excellent and comprehensive guidance.[46]

The Charity Commission recommends that it is appropriate to use the company structure where one or more of the following apply:

- The charity is to be quite large,
- It will employ a lot of staff,
- It will deliver charitable services under contractual agreements,
- It will regularly enter into commercial contracts,
- It will be a substantial owner of freehold or leasehold land or other property.[47]

16.7.1 Charitable company: definition

Article 47 of the Companies (N.I.) (No. 2) Order 1990 makes reference to a charitable company to which certain provisions of company law apply. A charitable company is one whose objects, as stated in its constitution, are exclusively charitable; all the objects must be charitable. As explained by Lowry L.C.J. in *Royal British Legion Attendants Company (Belfast) Ltd. v. Commissioner of Valuation*[48]:

> "... if a company is formed for a number of objects some of which ... permit expenditure on non-charitable activities ... the company is not formed for charitable purposes only."[49]

In that case, the objects of the company were: (a) to promote the employment of ex soldiers, (b) to promote the welfare of ex-soldiers and (c) to carry on a trade or business in connection with the above. Lowry L.C.J. held that object (c) was not a purpose "incidental to and consequent upon the way in which the

---

[46] See Charity Law Association Model Documents, *Charitable Company: Memorandum and Articles of Association for a Charitable Company Limited by Guarantee*, drafted by Quint, F., 1997; available from the Charity Commission (see "Useful Addresses") and see GD1 Model Memorandum and Articles of Association for a Charitable Company (1998) Charity Commission.

[47] CC22, *Choosing and Preparing a Governing Document* (1999).

[48] [1979] N.I. 138.

[49] *ibid.* at p. 143.

charitable purpose which alone the body was formed is carried on"[50] and consequently it was not a charitable company.[51]

A further aspect of this definition arises from the wording of Article 40 of the Companies (N.I.) Order 1986. This refers to the objects of a company being the "promotion of ... charity ... and anything incidental or conducive to any of those objects". The word "conducive" is different from the usual words requiring exclusivity of charitable objects. Following *Legion Attendants*, a company can be charitable if it has non-charitable objects which are ancillary or incidental. No case in Northern Ireland seems to be directly on this distinction between ancillary/incidental and "conducive". However, in *Dunne v. Byrne*,[52] it was held that "conducive to religion" was not the same as "for the advancement of religion". By analogy it would therefore appear to be possible to have a non-charitable company which nevertheless has charitable objects taking advantage of Article 40.

16.7.2 Types of company

Under Article 12(2) of the Companies (N.I.) Order 1986 three types of company can be distinguished: companies limited by shares, companies limited by guarantee and unlimited companies.

16.7.2(i) Company limited by shares

In a company limited by shares, members invest sums of money to purchase shares in the company. Shares can be bought and sold and their value may fluctuate depending upon market conditions. The maximum liability which a member/shareholder has to the company is the amount of money he still owes it for the purchase of his shares. This is by far the most common type of company but is rarely used by charities.

16.7.2(ii) Company limited by guarantee

Companies limited by guarantee were introduced by statute; they may or may not have share capital. In a company limited by guarantee, each member gains a stake in the company by means of guaranteeing a set sum of money to the company. This sum is fixed so there is no possibility of profit by the members by means of selling their stake. The maximum liability of the members is the amount of their guarantee. This type of company is favoured by charities since it grants limited liability and therefore restricts the liability of its members,

---

[50] *ibid.* at p. 143.
[51] See also, *Royal College of Nursing* v. *St Marylebone Corporation* [1959] 3 All E.R. 663 for an English case on the same issues.
[52] [1912] A.C. 407.

and yet also restricts the possibilities for trading ownership of the company by selling shares.

16.7.2(iii) Unlimited companies

The unlimited company is not the preferred structure in commercial and charitable organisations. The liability of its members is unlimited, so that if the company becomes insolvent, the members can be made personally liable for its unpaid debts.

16.7.3 Constituting a company

A fundamental requirement is that a memorandum and articles of association must be drafted. The memorandum of association, once registered, is binding upon all shareholders/members.[53] It must contain certain information:[54] the name of the company; an objects clause; declarations that it has a registered office in Northern Ireland, that the company is limited by guarantee and the amount of authorised capital *i.e.* the guarantees of members, subscribers clause *i.e.* the signature and addresses of the first shareholders together with signature and addresses of witnesses. The Department of Economic Development must give approval to certain names which suggest a link with government.[55] The usual form of articles of association are contained in Table A.[56] For companies limited by guarantee, the usual form of memorandum and articles of association are in Table C. These will apply unless the contrary is stated.

16.7.4 Regulation by company law

Company law comprises a formidable body of legislative provision and caselaw. The law governing the formal requirements of modern companies is now to be found in such statutes as: Companies (N.I.) Order 1986, Companies (N.I.) Order 1990, Companies (N.I.) (No. 2) Order 1990 and the Insolvency (N.I.) Order 1989. These contain provisions which impose a considerable regulatory burden. For example, a company must have a memorandum of association,[57] articles of association,[58] it must keep accounting records,[59] prepare

---

[53] Art. 25 Companies (N.I.) Order 1986.

[54] Art. 13 Companies (N.I.) Order 1986.

[55] Art. 39 Companies (N.I.) Order 1986.

[56] Companies (Tables A to F) Regulations (N.I.) 1986 (S.I. No. 264 of 1986).

[57] Art. 13 Companies (N.I.) Order 1986, a Memorandum of Association is the part of the constitution of a company regulating its relationship to the outside world.

[58] Art. 18 Companies (N.I.) Order 1986, the Articles of Association is the part of the constitution of a company regulating its relationship to its members and directors.

[59] Art. 229 Companies (N.I.) Order 1986.

directors[60] and auditors[61] reports. These apply generally to all forms of company including charitable companies. There are a number of books available on this specialist area of law to which reference should be made for standard information on aspects of company law.[62] However, broadly speaking, the main advantages of incorporation for a charity are as stated by Cairns[63]:

(i)   the power to alter the memorandum and articles;

(ii) the protection of limited liability;

(iii) the machinery for involving the members in the running of the charity; and

(iv) the corporate identity.

16.7.4(i) Basic requirements of companies

These are:

1.   To keep a register of members and directors

2.   To keep minutes of all meetings

3.   To hold an annual general meeting within 18 months of being incorporated and at least every fifteen months after that

4.   To make an annual return to the Companies Office within 60 days of the annual general meeting

5.   To keep proper accounts and submit audited accounts with the annual return

6.   To notify the Companies Office of any special resolutions and of any changes to the Memorandum and Articles

7.   To notify the Companies Office of any changes in the directors, the secretary, the auditors, or the registered office within 14 days of the change and of any change in the name (which must be approved by the Department).

16.7.4(ii) Directors of charitable companies

The requirement that company directors act in the best interests of their company applies with particular force in the context of charitable companies; the responsibility resting on a company director is every bit as onerous as that

---

[60] Art. 243 Companies (N.I.) Order 1986.
[61] Art. 244 Companies (N.I.) Order 1986.
[62] *Buckley on the Companies Acts* (Butterworths, 2000).
[63] See Cairns, E., *Charities: Law and Practice, op. cit.* at p. 52.

placed upon a trustee. As explained by Danckwerts J. in *Re French Hospital and Attorney-General*[64]:

> "The property of the charity is, of course, vested in and held by the corporation. It is a perpetual person which exists, however, only according to the rules of law, and it is not an actual person capable of acting on its own motion in any way whatever. It seems to me that in a case of this kind the court is bound to look at the real situation which exists in fact. It is obvious that the corporation is completely controlled ... by the governor, deputy governor and directors, and that those are the persons who in fact control the corporation and decide what shall be done. It is plain that those persons are as much in a fiduciary position as trustees in regard to any acts which are done respecting the corporation and its property. It is quite plain that it would be entirely illegal if they were simply to put the property, or the proceeds of the property of the corporation, into their pockets and make use of it for their own individual purposes or for their purposes as a whole, and not for the purposes of the charitable trust for which the property is held. Therefore it seems to me plain that they are, to all intents and purposes, bound by the rules which affect trustees."[65]

Directors are not permitted to profit from their position although they are entitled to proper recompense for out-of-pocket expenses and may claim fees, interest on money lent to the company and rent for premises. Legislation has introduced provisions making all directors personally liable for any company debts incurred as a consequence of wrongful or fraudulent trading. As charitable companies become increasingly involved in and dependent upon trading so too do their directors risk becoming the subject of such proceedings (see further, below).

16.7.5 Company law particular to charities

In addition to the standard requirements that affect all companies there are some which apply specifically to those which are charities.

16.7.5(i) Name of charitable company

A possible attraction for a charity to become a company limited by guarantee lies in the fact that companies of this type, and only this type, are permitted, under Article 40 of the Companies (N.I.) Order 1986,[66] to exclude the word "limited" or such derivatives as "Ltd" from its name and letter heading. To exercise this option the objects of such a company must be the "promotion of commerce, art, science, education, religion, charity or any profession and any-

---

[64] [1951] Ch. 567, [1951] 1 All E.R. 938; referred to in Chap. 15 of the Ontario Report.

[65] *ibid.*, at p. 570.

[66] English equivalent is s. 30 of the Companies Act 1985.

thing incidental or conducive to any of those objects".[67] The organisation must be non-profit distributing with no payment of dividends to members, and on dissolution all excess assets must go to a similar body or to a charity.[68] Additionally there is no need to send a list of the company's members to the registrar of companies every year.[69] This facility is often valued by charities as a means of avoiding being associated with the public image of big business and corporate finance.

Furthermore, such companies are exempt from the requirements as to "the publication of its name".[70] These publication requirements are not specifically enumerated in Article 40(7), but they seem to refer to Articles 356–357 of the Companies (N.I.) Order 1986, *viz.* name to appear outside its place of business, name to appear in its correspondence and name to appear on its company seal.[71] In England this exemption has been explicitly restricted by section 67 of the Charities Act 1993 which states that the exemption as to publication of the name will not effect duties under section 349(1)[72] to publish companies name in all of its correspondence.

Article 41 of the Companies (N.I.) Order 1986[73] provides safeguards against the abuse of the Article 40 exemptions. Companies cannot alter their constitution (*i.e.* their Memorandum of Association or Articles of Association) so as to cease compliance with the requirements of Article 40. The Department of Economic Development can require a company to add "ltd" or "limited" to its name if it breaches any requirements of Article 40. Article 41 also provides for fines in case of breaches.

The loophole created by the lack of any equivalent in this jurisdiction to section 67 of the Charities Act 1993 has been plugged to some extent by Article 9B of the Charities (N.I.) Order 1987.[74] Although the company is not required to publish its name on its correspondence, if the company's name does not contain the word "charity" or "charitable", then "the fact that the company is a charity shall be stated in English in legible characters"[75] on its business letters etc.

The combination of these legislative provisions has created a rather bizarre anomaly. Under Article 40(7) of the Companies (N.I.) Order 1986, cer-

---

[67] Art. 40(3)(a) Companies (N.I.) Order 1986, and see above for the effect of this definition.

[68] Art. 40(3)(b) Companies (N.I.) Order 1986.

[69] The duty is contained in Art. 372A of the Companies (N.I.) Order 1986, the exemption in Art. 40(7).

[70] Art. 40(7) Companies (N.I.) Order 1986.

[71] See Halsburys Statutes Vol. 8 (1999) reissue page 131 for support for this construction of the equivalent English rule in s. 30 Companies Act 1985.

[72] Northern Ireland equivalent is Art. 357 of the Companies (N.I.) Order 1986.

[73] English equivalent is s. 31 Companies Act 1985.

[74] As inserted by Art. 47 of the Companies (N.I.) (No. 2) Order 1990, English equivalent is s. 68 of the Charities Act 1993.

[75] Art. 9B(1) of the Charities (N.I.) Order 1987.

tain companies with charitable objects are exempt from publishing their name in their correspondence. But, under Article 9B of the Charities (N.I.) Order 1987, if their name does not include the word "charity" or "charitable", they must state on their correspondence that they are a charity. However, if their (non-appearing) name does include the word charity/charitable, they don't have to say they are charitable on their correspondence. The purpose of the provisions is to make others aware they are dealing with a charity. That effect can be avoided if a company's name contains the word charity/charitable.

On a practical level, it is usually thought desirable not to have the word "limited" as part of the company's name. This is because it denotes an air of commercialism which most charities wish to avoid.

16.7.5(ii) Alteration of objects

A charitable company cannot alter its objects without the consent of the Charities Branch.[76] Furthermore, if a charitable company makes some alteration to its constitution, thereby ceasing to be a charity, various safeguards under Article 9(1) come into play. For example, any property acquired or income received before the change in status must still be applied for charitable purposes after the change in status, unless the property was purchased for a reasonable amount (*i.e.* it will apply to donations, not commercial transactions).

Every company must be registered as such. It is thereafter required to file in the Companies Registration Office any changes made to its memorandum or articles of association.

16.7.5(iii) Limited capacity

The capacity of a charitable company is limited in the sense that its powers are restricted to those required to give effect to its charitable purposes. Strictly speaking it is legally bound to use its powers within the parameters set by its objects as stated in its constitution; it may only operate outside those parameters if it is reasonably necessary to do so in pursuance of matters ancillary to its objects.[77] Directors act as the agents of the company, are subject to its control as exercised through annual general meetings and are unable to act with full discretion. Actions taken which fall outside such limited capacity would be *ultra vires* the company's authority and may need to be challenged by injunction. The company itself could deny liability for the consequences while its directors could be held directly and personally liable.

The modern rule is that the "validity of an act done by a company shall not be called into question on the grounds of lack of capacity by reason of any-

---

[76] Art.9 Charities (N.I.) Order 1987.

[77] See, for example, *Dunne v. Byrne* [1912] A.C. 407, where "conducive to religion" was held not to be the same as "for the advancement of religion".

thing in the company's memorandum".[75] This rule also applies where directors have acted beyond their powers – despite this breach, if a third party acted in good faith, the company is bound by the *ultra vires* action of that director.[79]

Charities have a degree of immunity from this rule under Article 9A of the Charities (N.I.) Order 1987. A charitable company will not be bound by an *ultra vires* action unless the other party gives the full price and the other party does not know the charity is acting beyond its powers.[80] Alternatively, a charitable company will not be bound by an *ultra vires* action unless the third party does not know the company is a charity.[81]

The burden of proving any of these allegations lies on the party making them.[82] The charitable company cannot ratify any of these breaches of its constitution without the consent of the Charities Branch.[83]

16.7.5(iv) Audit exemption

The available audit exemptions differ for charitable and non-charitable companies. The exemptions are set out in the Companies (1986 Order) (Audit Exemption) Regulations (N.I.) 1995 SI 1995/128.[84] This modifies the primary legislation, the Companies (N.I.) Order 1986.

There are two types of exemption. The total exemption means there is no necessity for an audit.[85] The report exemption means a company is exempt from auditing its accounts if it prepares a report.[86] To satisfy the conditions for the total exemption, the company must[87]:

• Be a small company,

• Have a balance sheet value of less than £1.4 million and

• Have a turnover of less than £350,000, or, if a charitable company, have a gross income of less than £90,000.

To satisfy the conditions for a report exemption, the company must:

• Be a charitable company,

---

[78] Art. 45 Companies (N.I.) Order 1986, as inserted by Companies (N.I.) (No. 2) Order 1990.

[79] Art. 45A Companies (N.I.) Order 1986, as inserted by Companies (N.I.) (No. 2) Order 1990.

[80] Art. 9A(1) Charities (N.I.) Order 1987.

[81] *ibid.*

[82] Art. 9A(3) Charities (N.I.) Order 1987.

[83] Art. 9A(4) Charities (N.I.) Order 1987.

[84] As amended by the Companies (1986 Order) (Audit Exemption) (Amendment) Regulations (N.I.) 1997 SI 1997/500.

[85] Art. 257A (1) Companies (N.I.) Order 1986.

[86] Art. 257A (2) Companies (N.I.) Order 1986.

[87] Art. 257A (3) Companies (N.I.) Order 1986.

- Be a small company,
- Have a balance sheet value of less than £1.4 million,
- Have a gross income of between £90,000 and £250,000.

The report must be by an eligible reporting accountant and state that: the accounts are in accordance with the records, and the accounts satisfy the report conditions. The report must be signed by the reporting accountant.[88] The reporting accountant must be a member of an eligible body (*i.e.* a professionally qualified accountant).[89] The reporting accountant must not be ineligible on the grounds of lack of independence.[90]

16.7.6 Procedure

Companies are incorporated by filing all requisite documents and submitting a fee (currently £35) with the Companies Registrar and receiving a certificate of incorporation. Five documents must be lodged. Firstly, the name application form; indicating whether the name submitted has already been registered elsewhere in the United Kingdom. Secondly, the memorandum of association; this will have been signed by the subscribers and witnessed by witnesses. Thirdly, the articles of association. Fourthly, the statement of first directors and secretary with the location of the registered office on Form G21; containing the names, addresses, dates of birth, nationalities, occupations and consents of the first directors and secretary; signed by all the subscribers. Fifthly, the statutory declaration of compliance with requirements on application for registration of a company on Form G23; signed by a director or secretary of the company, or by a solicitor engaged in the formation of the company; made before a Commissioner for Oaths or someone having the powers of a Commissioner for Oaths (*i.e.* usually a solicitor).

It takes approximately one week from lodgment with the Companies Registrar to incorporation. A company must send its notice of accounting reference date to the Registrar within nine months of incorporation. All the lodgment documents together with the certificate of incorporation should be laid before the first meeting of the directors.

16.7.7 Differences between the company law of England and Northern Ireland

In addition to those already noted, there are several other miscellaneous differences between charitable company law in Northern Ireland and England and Wales.

---

[88] Art. 257C Companies (N.I.) Order 1986.
[89] Art. 257D Companies (N.I.) Order 1986.
[90] Art. 30 Companies (N.I.) Order 1990.

Firstly, English charities may be wound up and dissolved on the petition of the Attorney General or of the Charity Commission.[91] The Commission also has certain rights to be involved when a charitable company is being wound up.[92] Although the Attorney-General may impliedly have this power here, under the special jurisdiction over charities, it is not expressed in any legislation.

Secondly, the Charity Commission must consent to certain actions by a charitable company relating to payments to directors or to their service contracts.[93] No similar provision exists here in relation to the Charities Branch.

Finally the Commission may require an auditor to investigate and audit the accounts of any charitable company,[94] no similar provision exists in Northern Ireland.

16.8 GIFTS TO CHARITIES

The effect of any gift made to a charity depends very much upon the structure of the recipient charity.

16.8.1 Gifts to a charitable company

A gift to a charitable company may be given either absolutely or on trust. In the former case it will be wholly owned by the company and utilised in accordance with its own rules and objects. In the latter, the company will hold the gift on trust for specified charitable purposes.

It had been suggested[95] that charitable companies hold all their property on trust. No decision has been made on this point in Northern Ireland, but it is highly likely that the courts here would follow the ruling of Buckley J. in *Re Vernon's Will Trusts*[96] that:

> "... the natural construction is that the bequest is made to the corporate body as part of its general funds, that is to say beneficially and without the imposition of a trust."[97]

This case was subsequently supported by the decision in *Liverpool and District Hospital* v. *Attorney General*[98] that:

---

[91] See, s. 63 of the Charities Act 1993.
[92] *ibid.*
[93] See s. 66 Charities Act 1993.
[94] See s. 69 Charities Act 1993.
[95] *Soldiers', Sailors' and Airmens' Families Association* v. *Attorney General* [1968] 1 W.L.R. 313, and *Re French Protestant Hospital* [1951] Ch. 567.
[96] [1972] Ch. 300.
[97] *ibid.* at p. 303.
[98] [1981] 1 Ch. 193.

"… none of the authorities … establish that a company formed under the Companies Act 1948 for charitable purposes is a trustee in the strict sense of its corporate assets."[99]

This rule can produce harsh results as illustrated by *Re ARMS (Multiple Sclerosis Research) Ltd*[100] which concerned a charitable company in the process of being wound up. Several will bequests were received by the liquidator who applied to court to determine what should be done with them. The court held that there was nothing about the gifts to indicate they were given to the company on trust. Therefore they were absolute gifts to the company and were available to be used in satisfying the company's general creditors on the liquidation. The bequests were not to be applied to the charitable purposes of the company. While in this jurisdiction no decision has yet been made on this point, in effect, unless the donor specifies that the gift is to be held on trust for specified charitable purposes, separate from other property, then the presumption is that the company will take absolutely for use as it determines in giving effect to its objects. The position of a charitable company in relation to its assets is "analogous" to that of a trustee.[101]

16.8.2 Gifts to charitable unincorporated associations

Legal problems arise when a gift is made to an unincorporated association – who is the gift to? It cannot be a gift to the association, since the association does not exist at law. The court[102] has specified three possibilities: an absolute gift to all members as joint tenants at a fixed date;[103] a gift to existing members subject to the terms of their membership contracts;[104] or a gift to be held on trust or applied for the purposes of the association. It has been suggested that to this list should be added the possibility of a gift on trust for the members of the association for the time being.[105]

The courts in Northern Ireland courts have not had much opportunity to consider the issues which arise in relation to gifts to unincorporated associations. Only three reported cases[106] were directly concerned with the issue of

---

[99] *ibid.* at p. 209.

[100] [1997] 2 All E.R. 679.

[101] As noted in Tudor, *Charities, op. cit.* at p. 159 relying on *Liverpool and District Hospital for Diseases of the Heart v. Att.-Gen.* [1981] Ch. 193 at 209.

[102] See *Neville Estates Limited v. Madden* [1962] Ch. 832, *per* Cross J. at 849.

[103] See for example, *Re St James Club* (1852) 2 De G.M. & G. 385; *Murray v. Johnstone* (1896) 23 S.C. 981.

[104] See for example, *Re Recher's Will Trusts* [1972] Ch 526; *Re Grant's Will Trusts* [1980] 1 WLR 360.

[105] See Tudor, *Charities* (8th ed., Sweet & Maxwell, London, 1995) at p. 156. For case illustrations, see *Hogan v. Byrne* (1863) 13 I.C.L.R. 166 and *Stewart v. Green* (1871) I.R. 5 Eq. 470, *per* Christian L.J. at 481.

[106] *Re Lester, McCracken v. Law* [1940] N.I. 92 and *Re Rickard, Harbison v. Meany* [1954] N.I. 100, *Re Currie, McClelland v. Gamble* [1985] N.I. 299.

which possibility was most appropriate. Several other cases have been heard[107] concerning unincorporated associations, usually religious orders, but these have not considered the effect of a gift to such an association.

16.8.2(i) Gifts to members; past, present and future

The courts have experienced difficulties in determining the status of gifts in this context. *Re Lester*,[108] for example, concerned a gift to the Theosophical Society of Belfast. No society of that name existed, but there did exist three theosophical lodges in Belfast. The High Court held that the Society was not charitable, but that the gift was a valid gift to the members of the association at the time of the gift. *Re Lester* followed *Cocks v. Manners*[109] which had held that a gift to "the Dominican Convent at Carisbrocke" was non-charitable, but it was a valid gift to the members of that organisation existing at the time the gift was made.[110]

Religious orders came under judicial scrutiny again in *Leahy v. Attorney General for New South Wales*.[111] The gift in that case was a sheep-farm and the court had already decided that the objects were not exclusively charitable. The remaining question was whether it was a gift to its current members, or a gift to present members on trust for present and future members. In holding that it was the latter, the court took cognisance of the facts that: the nature of the gift meant it impracticable for each member of the unincorporated association to take their distributive share, the potential number of members meant that each individual share would be negligible, and that the gift was expressed to be for an Order and not for the Order's members. Since it was a non-charitable gift for future beneficiaries, it was void for uncertainty.

16.8.2(ii) Gifts for the purposes of the association

A charitable purpose is the only purpose which can take advantage of this construction; non-charitable purpose trusts are void. The courts tend to construe a gift to a charitable unincorporated association as a gift to be held on trust for the purposes of that association. The purposes of the unincorporated

---

[107] *McLaughlin & Cosgrove v. Commissioner of Valuation for Northern Ireland* [1937] N.I. 174, *Commissioner of Valuation* v. *Redemptorist Order, Commissioner of Valuation* v. *Trustees of the Newry Christian Brothers* [1971] N.I. 114, *Trustees of the Congregation of the Poor Clares of the Immaculate Conception* v. *Commissioner of Valuation* [1971] N.I. 174.

[108] [1940] N.I. 92.

[109] (1871) 12 Eq. 574.

[110] See also *Gilmour v. Coats* [1949] A.C. 426. Also, see *Carne v. Long* (1860) 2 De G. F. 75, 45 E.R. 550 where a gift to "… the trustees … of the Penzance Library … forever, for the use, benefit and support of the said library" was held to be invalid.

[111] *op. cit.*

association must be exclusively charitable. In such circumstances the gift is saved because:

> "If the gift is to be permitted to take effect at all it must be as a bequest for a purpose, *viz.* that charitable purpose which the named charity exists to serve."[112]

This approach rests on the premise that the members of an association have a contractual relationship which binds the membership, present and future, to pursue stated objectives. However, as H. Delany points out[113]:

> "... it is important to emphasise that the rules of the association must provide the necessary contractual element to the relationship between the members[114] and it is also necessary that the members have the requisite authority to divide the assets between themselves."[115]

In this jurisdiction, the gifts in *Re Rickard* were to the Superior of the Sisters of Mercy convent in Cookstown. These gifts were expressed to be for the religious purposes of the convent and the benefit of the nuns. Curran J. construed it as conferring:

> "... an absolute discretion to the Reverend Mother as to how the money is to be expended provided that it is applied to religious purposes for the benefit of the community."[116]

This is the language of a trust, yet Curran J. also construed it as a gift to the Reverend Mother. No reference was made to either *Re Lester* or *Cocks v. Manners* which could have saved the gift by construing it as a gift to current members of the convent.

More recently, in this jurisdiction, Carswell J. considered a gift to a church building fund in *Re Currie*. As he stated:

> "... gifts to unincorporated bodies may be regarded as gifts upon trust to carry out the purposes for which those bodies carried on their work."[117]

He then held that the gift created a trust for the charitable purpose of building a new church.

16.9 INSOLVENCY

The consequences for a charity should it become insolvent very much depend upon its legal structure. In this context there is a degree of jurisdictional dif-

---

[112] See *Re Vernon's Will Trusts* [1972] Ch. 300, *per* Buckley J. at 303. See also *Re Recher's Will Trusts* [1972] Ch. 526, *per* Brightman J. at 539.
[113] See *Equity and the Law of Trusts in Ireland, op. cit.*, at p. 235.
[114] See *Conservative and Unionist Central Office v. Burrell* [1982] 1 W.L.R. 522 at 525.
[115] See *Re Grant's Will Trusts* [1980] 1 W.L.R. 360.
[116] *Re Rickard, Harbison v. Meany* [1954] N.I. 100 at 102.
[117] *Re Currie* [1985] N.I. 299 at 305.

ference between the law in this jurisdiction and elsewhere in the United Kingdom.

16.9.1 Legal structures

As mentioned above, the law is quite unambiguous in terms of where liability lies when a charity becomes insolvent. If constituted as an unincorporated association then liability falls upon the trustees who enter into liabilities on behalf of the association. If it is a limited company then its debts must be borne by the organisation and not by either its directors or members. If limited by guarantee then its debts will be borne by its members to the limit specified in the charity's memorandum and articles of association. If a trust, then the trustees must make up the shortfall of any commitments they have entered into on behalf of the trust.

The protection afforded by incorporation can be lost in circumstances where there is evidence that any persons involved in the affairs of the insolvent charity conducted its business with intent to perpetrate a fraud.

16.9.2 Fraudulent trading

If, in the winding up of a company, it appears that any of its business has been carried on with a fraudulent purpose, the liquidator can apply to the High Court.[118] The court can then declare any defrauding party liable to make a contribution to the assets of the company. This liability can attach to any person who is party to the fraud, regardless of their position in the company.[119]

In practice it proved difficult to take advantage of this provision on fraudulent trading because of the high standard of proof necessary to prove fraud.

16.9.3 Wrongful trading

The provision on wrongful trading[120] was enacted to remedy the difficulties in fraudulent trading. It is for the liquidator, in the course of winding up, to apply to the High Court. The test is that at some time before the commencement of the winding up, the person concerned knew or ought to have concluded that there was no reasonable prospect of the company becoming insolvent.[121] This

---

[118] Art. 177 Insolvency (N.I.) Order 1989.

[119] See for example, *R. v. Grantham* [1984] 3 All E.R. 166 where it was held that an intent to defraud might be inferred if the person concerned obtained credit when he knew there was no good reason for thinking that funds would be available to pay the debt when it became due or shortly afterwards.

[120] Art. 178 Insolvency (N.I.) Order 1989.

[121] Art. 178(2) Insolvency (N.I.) Order 1989.

provision applies to directors or shadow directors (*i.e.* those concerned with the management of the company, not necessarily named as directors).[122]

The test is both objective and subjective: a director will be measured against the general knowledge, skill and experience that could be expected from a director in that position; if a director has more skill than usual, he or she will be judged against that particular level of skill.[123]

It should be noted that in Great Britain members of the management committee of an industrial and provident society cannot be held personally liable for wrongful trading. In Northern Ireland, however, they can be.

---

[122] Art. 178(7) Insolvency (N.I.) Order 1989.

[123] See *Norman v. Theodore Goddard* (1992) B.C.L.C. 1028; (1992) B.C.C. 14 where, in a case concerning a charitable company, the court held that a director is entitled to trust persons in a position of responsibility until there is reason to distrust them.

CHAPTER 17

Governance, Management and Accountability

17.1 INTRODUCTION

Legal form determines neither the good governance nor the proper management of a charity. Efficiency and probity, the quality of strategic and operational planning, together with the management of staff and resources to address
organisational objectives, are among the standards to be met regardless of
whether a charity is functioning within the structure of a company, trust, unincorporated association or other legal form. Liability for a breach of these standards does vary, however, according to how a charity is legally constituted.
Whether a charity takes the legal form of a charitable trust, unincorporated
association, a company or some other form such as a friendly society or industrial and provident society it is crucial that it has in place systems to ensure
good governance, management and accountability.

In the charity law of this jurisdiction, the single component most conspicuously absent is a regulatory system for facilitating transparency, monitoring
effectiveness and ensuring public accountability in relation to the activities of
charities whatever their legal form.

This chapter examines the requirements governing the arrangements made
both internally enabling charities give effect to their purposes and externally
enabling them to demonstrate probity and efficiency in their use of charitable
donations. It identifies and considers differences attributable to legal form. It
assesses the case for putting in place an overall regulatory system with inspection powers and duties in relation to all charities.

17.2 CONCEPTS

The concepts of "governance", "management" and "accountability" provide
relevant measures for examining the current operational difficulties facing
modern charities.

17.2.1 Governance

By "governance", in this context, is meant a charity's internal use of authority
in ways best suited to serving the functions and achieving the desired outcomes of its charitable activity.[1] This implies that a charity may not need to

---

[1] See further, for example, Rhodes, R.A.W., *Understanding Governance* (Buckingham,

conform to the traditional hierarchical business model with carefully structured levels of responsibility and authority. A charity in its simplest form has no need for a sophisticated system of governance. Beyond the necessary functional division between leadership and membership, all involved are united in pursuance of their collective charitable purpose. Whatever their legal structure, charities tend to conform to a common typology in that they are driven by a focused philanthropic endeavour which, infused throughout the organisation, permits and encourages overlapping board/staff functions. This serves to distinguish the *modus operandi* of charities from commercial companies which tend to be driven by market considerations and compartmentalise their organisational functions in order to permit a flexible response to arising opportunities.

As a charity grows and necessarily becomes more reliant upon complex organisational structures so its style of governance will change. In England, concern regarding the problems which may then emerge for any company, charitable or not, prompted the setting up of the Cadbury Committee. This committee reviewed the mechanisms for ensuring effective control over companies by shareholders, directors and auditors. As noted by C. Barker *et al*:

> "While drafted with the needs and interests of trading companies largely in mind, the Cadbury Committee's Code of Best Practice may be a useful starting point for any organisation looking to improve its own procedures on governance."[2]

Whatever its chosen style of governance, a distinctive consideration for every charity is that arrangements are put in place to ensure the independence of that system of governance.

17.2.2 Management

By "management" is meant the model for structuring the roles, functions and inter-relationships of those staff responsible for giving effect to a charity's purposes both internally and externally. In this context it refers to the compo-

---

Open University Press, 1996) and see also Adshead, M., and Quinn, B., "The Move from Government to Governance" in *Policy & Politics*, vol. 26 no. 2, pp. 209 – 225. Also, Gambling, T., and Jones, R., *The Financial Governance of Charities* (the Charities Aid Foundation, Kent, 1997). Note the definition offered by Hind, A., in *The Governance and Management of Charities* (Voluntary Sector Press, Hertfordshire, 1995): "... the process by which charities are guided, directed and controlled at a strategic level" (on jacket cover).

[2] See "Corporate Governance" in *Charity Law in Scotland, op. cit.*, at p. 36. As Sir A. Cadbury has explained, the Cadbury Code is:

> ... based on the principles which board structures and processes should aim to meet, rather than prescribing precisely the nature of those structures and processes. This is to meet the diversity of board situations and to encourage compliance with the spirit of the code and not simply with its letter.

sition of, and relationship between, the twin axes of authority characteristic of charities; the governing body and the operational staff. In relation to the former, it has been said that:

> "In general terms it has the ultimate authority to make decisions and to approve the actions taken by the organisation. By the same token it is responsible in law for those decisions and actions and accountable for the conduct of paid and voluntary staff and for the management of agency resources. A second general responsibility is to maintain the values and autonomy of the organisation."[3]

On this body rests the duty to ensure that the organisation conducts its affairs ethically, with fiscal probity, in accordance with the law, in pursuance of its charitable purposes and without straying beyond its objects. The Charity Commission for England and Wales has recently published indicators of effective management.[4] It suggests that the hallmarks of a well-run charity are that it:

> "is formally set up with clearly documented aims and rules by which it will be run, and which should include the legal powers it needs to achieve its aims;
>
> is run by a clearly identifiable body of people who take responsibility, and are accountable, for controlling the charity so that it is economically and effectively run;
>
> manages and accounts for its resources well;
>
> complies with all relevant legal and regulatory requirements;
>
> acts with respect to the legal and human rights of the individual;
>
> is able to show how its activities are, or will be, able to support its charitable aims;
>
> is open in the conduct of its affairs, except where there is a need to respect confidentiality;
>
> carries out its aims with regard to the requirements of those it is designed to serve, the community within which it operates and any relevant wishes of its donors; and
>
> conducts its external relations, fundraising and publicity in a way that enhances its own reputation and that of charities generally."

Among the distinctive characteristics of charities are the diversities in size, range and duration of management models. This rich diversity reflects differences in the nature and scale of modern charitable activity. Increasingly, also,

---

[3] See Harris, M., and Rochester, C., "Managing Relationships with Governing Bodies", in Osborne, S., (ed.), *Managing the Voluntary Sector*, Thompson Press, London, 1996, at p. 31. See also, Wise, D., *Performance Measurement for Charities*, ICSA Publishing, Hertfordshire, 1995.

[4] See Charity Commission, CC60 – *The Hallmarks of a Well-Run Charity*, London, July 1999.

charities are entering into contractual relationships with government bodies and/or other organisations. This imposes layers of administrative and professional requirements which can have the effect of blunting the independent advocacy role of a charity and blurring the distinction between it and other service delivery agencies. The results can be clearly seen in the convergence of management models employed within the social care field by business, government bodies and charities.

The independence of charities can also be blunted by dependency on funding. In Northern Ireland there is a higher degree of government funding for charities than in the rest of the United Kingdom. This may be accompanied by a greater perceived restriction on the freedom of charities to criticise government policies. Additionally, a non-government funder may have its own agenda and force a charity to bend their stated objects to comply with it.

17.2.3 Volunteers

Charities promote the involvement of caring people in service provision, stimulate public donation of funds and serve to consolidate civil society. Volunteering lies at the heart of charitable activity. Indeed, the giving of personal skill, time and energy for the benefit of others has traditionally been valued as being of greater charitable worth than the giving of funds. By engaging concerned individuals to ameliorate the disadvantages of others, charities generate a healthy, caring and responsible sense of community. The government has given a pledge to support the contribution of volunteers:

> "It recognises and values highly volunteering as an important expression of citizenship, as individuals contribute actively to the development of their communities and to meeting the needs of others, in a way which is complementary and of equal importance to financial investment."[5]

One reason why the government extends recognition to the contribution made by volunteers is because of the resulting saving to the cost of providing social care services. It has been estimated that in Northern Ireland in 1995 some 131,000 adults contributed 26.7 million volunteer hours at an estimated value of £202million.[6]

Volunteers have traditionally been seen as selflessly dedicated people in-

---

[5] See D.H.S.S., the Compact document, *op. cit.*, para 2.3. See also, *Giving Time, Getting Involved – A Strategy Report by the Working Group on the Active Community* (the Warner Report), Home Office, London, 1999. In the response from Northern Ireland to the latter document (see, *Active Community Initiative – Draft Northern Ireland Action Plan*) it is acknowledged that there is a need to introduce legislative provisions to facilitate volunteer activity:
> "Social policy and legislation must recognise the contributions made by people who give their time to community activities" (para 10, p. 5).

[6] See *Volunteering in Northern Ireland*, NIVDA, Belfast, Oct. 1995.

spired by altruism to work for no reward in order to advance charitable purposes. Many, perhaps the majority, of those currently working for charities still conform to this description. However, in the ever more complex and business oriented market in which charities now have to compete, there is increasingly a need for charities to both employ salaried professional staff and to exercise greater care in their use of volunteers. Many charities now have arrangements in place to provide for the training, supervision, payment of expenses and involvement in policy decisions of volunteers who would previously have been regarded as a resource which should be restricted largely to fundraising and similar activities.[7]

17.2.4 Accountability

By "accountability" is meant the obligation resting on the recipient of charitable donations and related tax exemptions to satisfy a public interest that the use of privileged funds complies with the highest standards of ethical and fiscal probity. It must be demonstrably evident that charities and all charitable activities honour the trust of donors and remain constantly governed by the public benefit principle and by their specific objects. Accountability requires systems to provide the means whereby charities, their activities and outcomes, can be identified, monitored and regularly measured against agreed standards. It implies the existence of a specific body, vested with regulating authority, to which charities are accountable, which differentiates between acceptable and non-acceptable activity and imposes sanctions in respect of the latter.[8]

17.3 GOVERNANCE AND MANAGEMENT; CHARITABLE COMPANIES

That a charity has the legal form of a charitable company, or an unincorporated association or a charitable trust is of considerable significance when it comes to applying the principles of governance and management. The individual liability of those with responsibility for the affairs of a charity is largely determined by how that charity is formally constituted.

17.3.1 Staffing structures

Companies and their directors are subject to both common law and statutory law. In particular, the Companies (N.I.) Orders 1986 and 1989 impose uniform

---

[7] See Ruddle, H., and Donoghue F., *The Organisation of Volunteering: a Study of Irish Voluntary Organisations in the Social Welfare Area*, Policy Research Centre, Dublin, 1995.

[8] See further, Kumar, S., "Accountability. What is it and do we need it?" in Osborne, S., (ed.) *Managing the Voluntary Sector, op. cit.*, pp. 237 – 252.

requirements upon the setting-up, functioning and winding-up of all companies.

All companies, whether charitable or not, are by definition required to adopt a corporate model of governance. This necessitates a clear distinction between the strategic planning functions of the board and the role of staff in implementing board decisions. The powers and duties of the board, as delineated in the articles of incorporation, should clearly give effect to this distinction. The actual process of governance in a charitable company will, however, differ in some significant respects from that typical of a commercial company.

17.3.1(i) Board/staff relationships

In a charitable company the board is much more likely to be highly involved in day-to-day management issues, and the staff in strategic planning, than would be the case in a commercial company. Moreover, in the former the roles of board and staff and the nature of their inter-relationship may evolve over time rather than be defined from the outset. In these respects, the fact that a charity is incorporated is incidental to its model of governance.

17.3.1(ii) Membership control

Because they are value driven, mission led organisations, usually with a heavy reliance upon the continued commitment of volunteers, charities tend to be more accountable to their members. This holds true whether the charity takes on the legal form of a trust, an unincorporated association or of a company.

17.3.2 Company directors

A comprehensive statutory code now affords protection to third parties by providing for transparency and accountability in relation to the appointment, decisions and discharge of company directors. Legislation now clearly distinguishes their legal standing from that of chief executive officers of unincorporated associations and charitable trusts.

17.3.2(i) Directors powers

A director is an executive officer of a company and as such is responsible for the day-to-day running of its affairs. He or she is most usually also the employee of the company. Their powers are derived from the collective will of company members as expressed in the company's memorandum and articles of association and asserted in general meetings.

17.3.2(ii) Directors duties; common law

At common law, the principal duties of company directors are fiduciary and to exercise due skill and care. Company directors have all the duties of charity trustees as set out in Chapter 7.

It has been suggested that their fiduciary duties can be summarised in the following set of three doctrines[9] :

> "they must exercise their powers for the benefit of the organisation and in good faith;
>
> they must not appropriate to themselves an opportunity which rightfully belongs to the organisation; and
>
> they must not put themselves in a position where their interests conflict, or may conflict, with those of the organisation."[10]

These most basic obligations require company directors to conduct themselves with honesty when dealing with a charity's internal and external affairs.

A company director also has a duty to act with diligence when conducting business on behalf of their charity. A reasonable standard of skill and care is required. This "reasonableness" standard is less than would be required of charitable trustees who are vested with a grave moral and legal responsibility to honour a donor's trust and protect the trust property. It is applied subjectively and requires that the actions of the director in question demonstrate the level of skill and care commensurate with someone of his or her knowledge and experience.[11]

17.3.2(iii) Directors duties; statutory

The Companies Orders govern the appointment, the powers and duties and the removal of company directors. These are standard statutory requirements applied uniformly to all companies. It makes no difference in law whether the company in question is charitable or commercial. The legislative intent is to protect staff and assets by requiring appropriate standards to be met and procedures to be implemented.

Statutory provisions governing the accounting responsibilities of directors are intended to provide the means whereby members of the company can satisfy themselves that the company is on a sound financial footing, their investments are secure and that procedures ensuring probity are in place.

---

[9] See Lynch, I., *Types of Directors; Eligibility for Appointment; Basic Legal Duties; Removal*. Paper presented to the Irish Centre for Commercial Studies, University College Dublin, (29.11.1990).

[10] See for example, *Aberdeen Railway Co. v. Blaikie Bros.* (1854) 1 Macq. 461, *per* Viscount Finlay at 471. See also *Cook v. Deeks* [1916] 1 A.C. 554, *Canadian Aero Service Ltd. v. O'Malley* (1974) 40 D.L.R. (3d) 371 and *Industrial Development Consultants v. Cooley* [1872] 1 W.L.R. 443.

[11] See for example, *Re City Equitable Fire Insurance Co Ltd.* [1925] Ch. 407. See also, *Re French Protestant Hospital* [1951] 1 Ch. 567.

17.3.3 Director liability

Many statutory provisions are concerned with the protection of third parties. Directors are bound by the objects of their charity. If they purport to take decisions on matters outside those objects, or not reasonably incidental to them, they will be acting *ultra vires*. In that event they and not the company will be directly liable for any loss incurred by a third party. The principle operates to protect the assets of the company as well as the interests of third parties. This was demonstrated in *Rosemary Simmons Memorial Housing Association Ltd v. United Dominions Trust Ltd*[12] where it was held that, in offering financial protection to another company, a housing association was jeopardising its own assets and thereby acting outside the scope of its charitable objects.

The liability of a director of a charity, operating from within the legal structure of a company, is governed by legislation. A layer of statutory responsibility is thereby added to a director's common law obligations (see further, Chapters 7 and 16). In particular, directors (and others) can be liable for wrongful or fraudulent trading (see 16.9.2 and 16.9.3).

17.4 GOVERNANCE, MANAGEMENT AND UNINCORPORATED ASSOCIATIONS

Decisions of members relating to internal organisational matters are governed by the contractual arrangements entered into when they established their association. External decisions, binding the association in relation to third parties, are governed by the normal obligations of contract law. The prospect of personal liability for debts incurred by the association or for contractual obligations entered into as a result of decisions taken by board or ordinary members without proper authority is a disincentive for establishing a charity within this legal form.

17.4.1 Responsibilities of management boards

The office bearers comprising the management board bear responsibility for the conduct of the affairs of that charity. Their roles and functions derive from the terms of their contractual relationship, which are usually expressed in a constitution.

The constitution should deal with the agreed structure of the organisation and provide for the procedure for appointing such office bearers as the secretary, treasurer and chairperson. The powers and duties of these office bearers and their terms of office should be clearly set out. Provision should be made for outlining the procedure for conducting committee meetings; how a quo-

---

[12] [1987] 1 All E.R. 281.

rum is to be formed, minutes taken, decisions made and records kept. An unincorporated association cannot hold property on its own behalf; it is necessary that trustees or representatives undertake this responsibility.

17.4.2 Duty to act within charity objects

Board members are bound by the objects of their charity. Their role and functions must be shaped to give effect to the powers provided by the charity's governing instrument within the ambit of its objects. There is a duty not to take any action which would lie outside the scope of the objects; to do so is to risk being the subject of proceedings for breach of trust and ultimate personal liability for making good any loss arising from charitable funds being misapplied. This implies that all board members should, at least, be familiar with the governing instruments of their charity.

The board acts as agents for the members of the association. As such it is authorised, on their behalf, to enter into such contracts and arrangements as may be necessary to give effect to the association's purposes. Provided the office bearers act within the authority conferred by virtue of their office in furthering those purposes then their decisions will be binding upon the members. If the association has been formed for the benefit of its members, then any property or other assets acquired by the board on behalf of the association, will be owned by the members in equal shares. Conversely, where the association has been established for the benefit of others then it is deemed to be held in trust for the purposes of the trust (see further, Chapters 7 and 16).

17.4.3 Responsibilities of members

Each member is held directly and personally responsible for any decision made or action taken by the organisation and is liable for any debt it may incur. Details of the organisation's membership or accounts are not a matter of public record; these are available only to its members. If branches of the association are established, the branch members serve as full members of the association and are bound by its rules. The constitution or rules of the association will normally outline procedures for enrolling or expelling members.

17.5 GOVERNANCE, MANAGEMENT AND CHARITABLE TRUSTS

In charitable trusts, like unincorporated associations, the internal legal relationships of office bearers and the management structure adopted are determined by the terms of their governing instruments. Similarly, external legal relationships are conducted by office bearers acting in a personal contractual capacity.

17.5.1 Trustees

The term "charitable trustees" can be misleading. Charitable trustees are defined as "the persons having the general control and management of the administration of the charity".[13] This is the same definition as adopted in England and Wales.[14] Whether the charity in question is formally constituted as a trust, a company, an unincorporated association or other legal form such as a friendly society, is of no relevance. Any person having any degree of control and management responsibility will be a charitable trustee. It is not confined to those who have a trust as the legal form to set up their charity. It has been used in a broad sense throughout this book, unless otherwise stated, to refer to anyone concerned with managing a charity, whether they be, trustees, company directors of management committees of unincorporated associations (see also, Chapter 7).

17.6 GOVERNANCE, MANAGEMENT AND OTHER LEGAL FORMS

Friendly societies and industrial and provident societies have their own discrete legislative frameworks. Issues relating to internal management and external accountability are subject to the rules contained in that legislation and to any specific provisions which may have been written in to their governing instruments. A consideration of matters relating to their governance and management is outside the scope of this book (see also, Chapter 16).

17.7 ACCOUNTABILITY: SYSTEMS FOR "CHARITY RECOGNITION"

Ensuring that charities are identifiable, that they exercise probity and accountability in the use of funds given or subsidised by the public, and that the related processes are transparent and readily amenable to public inspection, are important functions of government bodies. In Northern Ireland this responsibility, such as it is, is widely distributed. It can be located in varying degrees within the legislative framework and in the "charity recognition" role of certain government bodies.

17.7.1 The legislation

The law governing charities is unsatisfactory. The voluntary sector has greatly changed since the present legislation was introduced. It has been transformed from the role of substitute/supplement for State provision to becoming a ma-

---

[13] s. 35 Charities Act (N.I.) 1964.
[14] s. 97(1) Charities Act 1993.

jor service designer and provider. Statute law has not been similarly transformed.

The legal framework, within which this jurisdiction's many thousands of
charities now operate, is no longer appropriate to accommodate their needs
and regulate their activities. Within these islands the relevant legislation is
most dated in this jurisdiction. In England and Wales the law is as stated in the
Charities Acts 1992 and 1993. In Scotland the relevant legislation is the Law
Reform (Miscellaneous Provisions) (Scotland) Act 1990 and the Charities
Accounts (Scotland) Regulations 1992. In Ireland, the law is to be found in
the Charities Act 1961 as amended by the Charities Act 1973. In Northern
Ireland, however, the law remains largely framed by the Charities Act (N.I.)
1964 and the Charities (N.I.) Order 1987. The sophistication of modern charitable activity, notably in relation to professional fundraising, trading and political lobbying, is not adequately or appropriately addressed by this legislation.

17.7.2 The "charity recognition" role of government bodies

In Northern Ireland there is no statutory provision for the registration and
inspection of charities. Indeed "charitable status" is itself an uncertain legal
concept in the absence of any process for confirming the standing of a body as
a charity. No government body keeps a register of live charities and no statutory mechanisms exist for ensuring probity, requiring accountability, setting
and monitoring standards nor for ascertaining the effectiveness of charitable
activity. In particular there is no counterpart to the Charity Commission of
England and Wales which has the overall statutory duty of:

> "... promoting the effective use of charitable resources by encouraging the de-
> velopment of better methods of administration, by giving charity trustees infor-
> mation or advice on any matter affecting the charity and by investigating and
> checking abuses."[15]

In this jurisdiction there is no government body with equivalent statutory powers
to register, inspect and regulate charities. The emphasis is on providing official recognition for the charitable activities of organisations in order to facilitate their eligibility for tax exemption and thereby encourage the continuance
of such activity.

17.7.2(i) The Charities Branch

The role of the Charities Branch is largely advice giving and is facilitative
rather than regulatory in nature. It gives advice, assistance and guidance to
charities. It allows charities to change their constitutions, or exercise powers

---

[15] See further, Charity Commission for England and Wales, annual reports, The Stationery
Office, London.

not contained within those constitutions. Beyond this, it does not take a proactive role in monitoring and regulating the activities of charities.

17.7.2(ii) The Inland Revenue

As well as having responsibility for granting or refusing charitable recognition, the Revenue Commission also plays a limited regulatory role. This it does by withdrawing recognition where it appears that purposes are no longer exclusively charitable, for example where there has been an inappropriate alteration to a founding document or where the body's actual activities do not correspond to those in the founding document upon which charitable status was based. The Inland Revenue has occasionally inspected the financial accounts of charities in this jurisdiction and levied considerable fines where these have not been in order.

Otherwise, the Inland Revenue has no function in relation to the supervision of bodies granted charitable recognition for tax purposes. Any accounts furnished to it from registered charities are wholly confidential and not open to public scrutiny (see also, Chapter 5).

17.7.2(iii) The Valuation and Lands Agency

This body does have some limited regulatory powers. A charity must satisfy the V.L.A. that its purposes and use of property are charitable if it is to gain charitable exemption from rates. Very occasionally, the V.L.A. will inspect charities to ensure they are still complying with the exemption requirements.

17.7.2(iv) HM Customs and Excise

To gain any of the myriad exemptions from Value Added Tax, charities must satisfy the legislative requirements as monitored by Customs and Excise. These exemptions are largely self-regulating, the suppliers are liable for not charging VAT and it therefore falls to them to ensure that the exemption conditions are satisfied.

17.7.2(v) The Registrar of Companies

Charitable companies are required to register with the Registrar of Companies. This ensures that the first requirement of any regulatory system is met; the subjects are identifiable. Registration also requires the charity to declare its charitable purpose, lodge copies of its memorandum, articles or constitution and provide details regarding its organisational structure. Once registered, other statutory requirements then have to be met; for example, annual returns detailing accounts and notification of any change in name or of board membership. These statutory obligations again assist in the process of encouraging a degree of transparency and public accountability regarding the activities of charities. However, they are of course confined to those charities which are incorporated and while they place disclosure responsibilities on charities the statutory provisions do not place inspectoral or regulatory duties on the Registrar.

17.7.2(vi) The Royal Ulster Constabulary

The police currently play a statutory role in the issuing of permits for street and house to house collections. Otherwise, unless they have evidence that a crime has been committed, such as fraud or embezzlement, the police will have no cause to be involved in the affairs of a charity. Very occasionally the Fraud Squad will become involved. The police also have a role in screening people who work with charities connected with children.

17.8 Accountability: Charity Restraint

Although charities are not subject to formal regulatory systems, their activities are restrained by other less obvious influences. Among these are the requirements imposed by government funding bodies, the constraints of short-term contracts and what might be termed "ideological controls".

17.8.1 Restraint imposed by the funding role of government bodies

A great deal of charity funding comes from national or local government, particularly in the health and social care sector. Charities have become increasingly involved in the provision of welfare services which were previously provided by central government, and this has led to an increase in the number of service contracts entered into by charities with central and local government bodies – the so-called "contract culture".[16] Among the features of contract culture is the tendency for the principal party to impose general performance standards, with all the attendant administrative costs, upon the charity with which it has contracted. Government bodies are showing signs of wanting to streamline their dealings with charities and ensure compliance with the former's effectiveness indicators, standards of professional practice and output measures.

Concern has been expressed that some charities and other voluntary organisations are so dependent on State funding that they are in danger of becoming just an arm of the State. Moreover, the control exercised by funders is

---

[16] For further information on the "contract culture" see, for example, N.C.V.O., *The Contract Culture – The Challenge for Voluntary Organisations*, 1989; Warburton, J., and Morris, D. *Charities and the Contract Culture* [1991] Conv. 419.

such that by selecting some voluntary organisations for contracts they thereby de-select others which are then abandoned to sink or swim. This is in danger of becoming a process of virtual "colonisation" of "not for profit" bodies by government bodies, with survival guaranteed only for those favoured with government contracts because their agenda complies with government priorities.

The recent report of the Comptroller and Auditor General on the regulation and support of charities in England and Wales states that a third of charity income arises from contracts with government, government grants and tax relief.[17] These funding bodies impose their own form of regulation which is frequently additional to, or even in conflict with, the statutory provisions. Charities, heavily reliant upon funding provided by government bodies, can find their agendas for charitable activity being shaped to conform with their funder's priorities.

17.8.2 Ideological restraint

Advocacy and lobbying on behalf of the interests of their client group are activities traditionally associated with the role of charities. Society has come to expect and rely upon charities to assertively champion the cause of the underprivileged. The extent to which they may engage in advocacy (and trading) activity has, of course, always been subject to some legal constraint (the issue of "political" campaigning remains a hotly debated subject).[18] However, in order to obtain the necessary funding to continue their activities, charities may now be too willing to accept contracts which further restrict their advocacy role. Knight argues that the roles of service provision and user representation are so different that they should be separated out under different tax and legal frameworks:

> "Organisations that follow the state into new contracting arrangements can no longer think of themselves as sufficiently independent to warrant the adjective 'voluntary'. They could call themselves 'non-profits', 'third sector', 'contractors', or part of the 'third force' repeatedly described by senior civil servants and ministers as forming an important partner with state and private organisations in regeneration arrangements. 'True' or 'authentic' voluntary bodies, on the other hand, will remain independent, will eschew contracting arrangements, and will remain unfettered to be 'democracy seekers' in ways of their own choosing. This will be a 'first force' of voluntary action ... policy driven, rather than resource-led."[19]

---

[17] See Comptroller and Auditor General, *The Regulation and Support of Charities*, (1998), para.1.

[18] See *McGovern v. Attorney General* [1982] Ch. 321; Forder: "Too political to be charitable?" (1984) Conv. 263.

[19] See Knight, B., *Voluntary Action: Report for the Home Office*, HMSO, London, (1993), pp. 297-8.

The erosion of the independence of the voluntary sector also attracted concerned comment in the Deakin Report[20] and in the Kemp Report[21] (see further, Chapter 13)

17.9 ACCOUNTABILITY: SYSTEMS FOR REGULATING CHARITIES; THE EXPERIENCE IN ENGLAND

There is every reason to consider whether systems for registering, inspecting and regulating charities, such as those maintained by the Charity Commission in England and Wales,[22] should be introduced in this jurisdiction (see also, Chapter 2).

17.9.1 A statutory register

A register, such as that maintained by the Charity Commission, would provide a basic verified database of live charities and their activities. Arguably, this would fundamentally improve existing systems for supporting and regulating charitable activity in this jurisdiction.

17.9.1(i) Facilitating transparency and accountability

The Charity Commission's register is a central source from which information about charities can be readily and inexpensively obtained. An equivalent register in this jurisdiction would aid transparency and promote the public accountability of the charitable sector – the recipient of millions of pounds of "public" money in the form of freely offered donations from the general public and government-led funding in the form of service contracts and tax concessions. It would list those charities currently active and would provide the

---

[20] See the Commission on the Future of the Voluntary Sector in England, *Meeting the Challenge of Change: Voluntary Action into the 21st Century*, NCVO Publications, London, 1996.

[21] See the Commission on the Future of the Voluntary Sector in Scotland, *Head and Heart*, SCVO, Edinburgh, 1997. An additional factor is the short-term nature of many contracts which may lead to a further loss of independence by constraining the organisation's ability to speak out or campaign (see, Kemp, p. 47, para. 6.5.5).

[22] In England and Wales, systems for the registration and regulation of charities have a long history. Beginning with the Charitable Donations Registration Act 1812 which introduced a basic requirement for the registration of gifts, subsequent legislation (notably the Charitable Trusts Act 1853, the Charitable Trusts Amendment Act 1855 and the Charitable Trusts Act 1860) vested inspection powers in the Charity Commission and required charities to produce accounts. See further, the reports of the Brougham Commission in 1837 and the Nathan Commission in 1952. The current Charity Commission employs some 700 staff in three offices and provides an educational, advisory and a regulatory role in relation to charities throughout England and Wales.

information necessary for on-going monitoring and inspection. A register would also greatly assist the sector itself by providing a reliable yardstick of its activities.

17.9.1(ii) Revealing bogus charities

Arguably, a supplementary rationale for such a register lies in the need to ensure that only listed organisations are permitted to present as charities. The general public would then have ready access to a means for verifying the *bona fides* of a body or activity purporting to be charitable. The Charity Commission is empowered under section 6 of the Charities Act 1993 to police public opportuning by organisations purporting to be charities. Action can also be initiated by a *bona fide* charity to restrain another organisation from using its name and thereby passing itself off as a charity.[23]

The cost to the taxpayer of establishing and maintaining a register needs to be borne in mind and careful consideration would also need to be given to the kind of public information which the register would contain. For example, a register which provides information about the activities of a charity is perhaps less useful than one which gives verified quantitative information about the specific benefits conferred by a charity upon its beneficiaries. A register which is not backed up by fairly rigorous formal procedures for inspection and verification may not prove to be any more effective than existing administrative indexes in reducing fraud or inefficiency and providing reassurance to the general public. An integral part of this would be a requirement that charities submit annual accounts.

In England and Wales there are large numbers of exempted and excepted charities,[24] which are not required to register with the Charity Commission. This is unlikely to be a policy which this jurisdiction would wish to adopt. Arguably, all organisations, which solicit funds from the public or funding agencies, should be obliged to register.

---

[23] See for example, *British Legion v. British Legion (Street) Ltd.* [1931] 48 P.C. 55; and Dr Barnardo's Homes: *National Incorporated Association v. Barnardo Amalgamated Industries Ltd. and Jack Bernadout* [1949] 66 P.C. 103.

[24] The categories of charities exempted or excepted from registration in England and Wales are quite extensive. The following are exempted by s. 3 and Sched. 2 of the Charities Act 1993: major universities; grant maintained schools; higher and further education corporations; major museums and galleries; any institution administered by the Church Commission; and any Industrial and Provident or Friendly Society. The following are also exempted under s. 3 of the Charities Act 1993: charities with neither permanent endowments, land, nor income over £1,000; some voluntary schools; places of worship; and charities for the religious purposes of the major churches.

17.9.2 Disclosure of accounts

The public interest in ascertaining whether or not a charity is solvent, is on a sound financial footing and is conducting its financial affairs with probity cannot at present be satisfied. There are no accounting or filing requirements for charities which are not incorporated as companies.[25] Charities, which are so incorporated, must file an annual return at the Companies Registration Office, if they are limited by guarantee; although they are not required to detail expenses in any meaningful fashion. Where the charity in question is a company limited by shares, if it qualifies as a small company it need only file a balance sheet and related notes plus accounting policies. In practice many charities apply the standards outlined in the UK's Statement of Recommended Practice (SORP). There is a clear need to require all charities, whatever their legal form, to regularly file the accounts necessary to demonstrate the flow of income and expenditure and disclose assets and liabilities.

It is worth noting that 70 per cent of the 156,903 "main" charities registered in England and Wales have an income below the £10,000 limit.[26] They are therefore not required to routinely submit annual accounts and statutory annual returns to the Charity Commission, although they all are obliged to make accounts available to the Commission or members of the public on request. While this means that the charities in this income level band are subject to less scrutiny, it should be pointed out that they account for only 1.4 per cent of the registered charitable sector's total income.[27] Of the £18.4 billion total income of the main registered charities in England and Wales over 75 per cent is accounted for by the 1.73 per cent of registered charities with an income of £1 million and over.[28]

17.9.3 Regulatory duties

There is a need to increase the powers currently available in respect of charities and charitable activities. Those now exercisable at the discretion of the Charities Branch are insufficient. The public interest in an assurance that charities are conducting their affairs in accordance with proper standards must be satisfied.

It may well be that a distinction could usefully be made between supportive powers and inspection duties with the latter, perhaps, entrusted to an agency

---

[25] Except for the never enforced requirement in s. 30 of the Charities Act (N.I.) 1964 to prepare annual income and expenditure accounts.

[26] See CAF, *Dimensions of the Voluntary Sector* (1998), p. 17.

[27] *ibid.*

[28] See Charity Commission for England and Wales *Report of the Charity Commission for England and Wales for the Year 1997* (1998), p.12. In addition to the "main" charities there are some 28,000 subsidiary charities on the Charity Commission Register.

at "arm's length" remove from the former. Any new set of legislative provisions should require certain duties regarding registration, monitoring, inspection and regulation to be applied uniformly across the full range of legal structures available to charities. These could be extended in the form of powers enabling the inspection of organisations purporting to be charities but not recognised as such by the Inland Revenue (see also, Chapter 2).

CHAPTER 18

Fundraising

18.1 INTRODUCTION

Fundraising is vital to the survival of charities; for many it is their sole source of income. It is also an important means whereby members of the general public can express their philanthropic intentions. Arguably, the controls to be exercised in relation to the activities of donating and fundraising lie at the heart of charity law. If that is not right the law will lack overall coherence.

The relationship between donor and charity is one based on mutual trust and this is open to abuse. Charitable giving, after all, is the antithesis of *quid pro quo*. The donor gives without receiving anything in return. In a contract, consideration will flow from both parties but in a charitable donation consideration flows only from the donor. The need for supervision is therefore self-evident. There needs to be some mechanism to check that money is properly received and properly applied.

Ensuring probity, in the fundraising activities of charitable bodies, has become a complex task as charities increasingly rely upon professional fundraisers, commercial sponsorships and government partnerships. Electronic media such as telethons encourage the flow of funds across jurisdictions. While fundraising activities become more multi-media and trans-continental, the legislative framework remains predicated on collections being undertaken on a house-to-house or street basis. The question of how to provide for a system whereby organisations can be held accountable to donors for the proper use of gifts, without imposing an excessive additional administrative burden on those organisations, is a growing concern.

In England and Wales the law has moved radically and fairly comprehensively to provide a regulatory framework better fitted to modern fundraising practice. New legislation has been introduced to update and consolidate the many separate statutes dealing with collections. New legislation also addresses the particular issues raised by commercial sponsorship, lotteries and professional fundraising. Charities, charitable activities and practice issues are governed by the overall supervisory powers of the Charity Commission.

In Northern Ireland, by contrast, the law is increasingly being superseded by practice. In relation to public charitable collections, it is somewhat anachronistic and cumbersome. In relation to the modern techniques of charitable fundraising, the law is non-existent. There is now a real need for legislative intervention.

This chapter sets out the law currently governing fundraising in Northern

Ireland. It explains the procedures for implementing the law and offers some comment on their appropriateness. This is contrasted, where appropriate, with the more modern legislative provisions governing fundraising in England.

18.2 BACKGROUND

In the course of a generation the nature and scale of fundraising by and for charities has changed beyond recognition. The transformation has seen a switch from raffles to telethons from door-to-door collections to national lotteries. The volume, speed and frequency, the distances and the glamour accompanying modern fundraising could not have been predicted when the present legislative framework was introduced.

18.2.1 The "gift" relationship

It was Titmus who, in his seminal work *The Gift Relationship*,[1] first brought sociological expertise to bear on the nature of the relationship between donor and recipient in the context of philanthropic exchange. His examination of "giving" as a voluntary and altruistic act focused on blood donors. Since then much academic attention has been drawn to philanthropy in general.[2] As has been said:

> "The very voluntariness and optionality of private philanthropy gives it an important moral status ... a society without private philanthropy would be a morally impoverished society."[3]

18.2.2 Charitable giving

In this jurisdiction there has not been any professional examination of patterns in charitable giving. In other jurisdictions the fuelling of activity in the voluntary sector by means of charitable giving has attracted more sustained and systematic attention from researchers.[4]

---

[1] See Titmus, R., *The Gift Relationship* (London, Allen and Unwin, 1970).

[2] See for example, Frank, R., "Motivation, Cognition and Charitable Giving" in Schneewind, J.B., (ed.), *Giving: Western Ideas of Philanthropy*, Indiana University Press, Bloomington, 1996. Also, see: Banks, J., and Tanner, S., *The State of Donation: Household Gifts to Charity, 1974-96*, Institute for Fiscal Studies, London, 1997; Cheal, D., *The Gift Economy*, Cambridge University Press, Cambridge, 1988; and Halfpenny, P., and Lowe, D., *Individual Giving and Volunteering in Britain* (7th ed., Charities Aid Foundation, Kent, 1994).

[3] See Gerwirth, A., "Private Philanthropy and Positive Rights" in *Beneficence, Philanthropy and the Public Good*, eds. Paul, E., Miller, F., Paul, J., and Ahrens, J., Oxford, Basil Blackwell, 1987 at p. 78.

[4] For the U.K., see Charities Aid Foundation, *Charity Household Survey 1988/89*, Kent,

18.2.3 Collecting for charity

In Ireland, the Policy Research Centre in the course of its research programme reached some interesting conclusions regarding charitable fundraising in that jurisdiction which may well have an equal bearing on practice in Northern Ireland:

> "Irish people are generous relative to other European countries such as Britain and France. But charities need to note that fewer people gave in 1994 compared to 1992 and the average amount donated by those who did give was smaller than previously. Many also felt that there are now too many charities looking for money. Charities need also to be aware that while people are willing to give they see the Government as being primarily responsible for social need and do not want private giving to be used to allow Government abdicate their responsibility....
>
> 42% of the respondents believe that charities are not sufficiently accountable to the public for how money donated is spent ... respondents believe that Irish charities spend over two-and-a-half times what they consider to be an acceptable level on administration while overseas charities are believed to spend almost three-and-a-half times the acceptable level on costs.[5]

18.3 LEGAL REQUIREMENTS

There is no legislative requirement stating that only charitable bodies can raise funds. Any organisation can raise money through street collections. Any charitable, benevolent or philanthropic organisation can raise money by house to house collections. Beyond these two specific types of fundraising, there is no limit to the purposes for which funds can be raised; subject to the general prohibition on raising funds for purposes contrary to public policy and subject also to the prohibition on misrepresenting the purpose for which funds are being collected.

However, if an organisation wishes to take advantage of any of the tax benefits relating to donated money, its fundraising activity will only be accepted as being for charitable purposes if certain legal requirements are satisfied. Firstly, the organisation must show that it is a charity within the meaning given by the four *Pemsel*[6] headings. Secondly, it must also show that the funds raised are to be applied for charitable purposes. Thirdly, the fundraising activities must conform to specific statutory stipulations.

CAF, 1990; and see the subsequent on-going programme tracking charitable giving conducted by the National Council for Voluntary Organisations. For the U.S., see the *Journal of Contemporary Issues in Fundraising* (various issues).

[5] *op. cit.*, 1995, at pp. viii–x.

[6] See *Income Tax Special Purposes Commissioners v. Pemsel* [1891] A.C. 531.

18.3.1 The *Pemsel* test

Fundraising in itself is not necessarily a charitable activity. In order for it to be recognised as such the organisation responsible must be able to meet the fundamental requirement that its purposes can be brought within the traditional umbrella definition of charity. Where the fundraising is clearly in support of an organisation's charitable purposes, as defined by one of the *Pemsel* heads, then this test will be satisfied.

If an organisation specifies in its main object, the charitable purpose for which it wishes to fundraise (for example, to further cancer research, to provide a cardiac unit in a named hospital, etc.) then such organisation would be regarded as established for a charitable purpose. The requirements for determining whether an organisation is charitable are the same for all organisations (see for example, Chapter 1).

18.3.2 Applied exclusively for charitable purposes

Having satisfied the first arm of the test by coming within one of the four *Pemsel* heads, the next arm is that the income and property must be applied for charitable purposes only. One case, illustrative of the entailed difficulties, was *Lawrence v. CIR*[7] where an individual assigned copyright royalties under a publishing agreement to trustees on trust to make certain non-charitable payments and to apply the balance, if any, for specified charitable purposes. The court held that since the trust deed provided for prior obligations of a non-charitable nature which had not been fully met and only the balance, if any, of the income was applicable to charitable purposes, there was no entitlement to relief under the appropriate income tax legislation, which provided for relief in respect of income "applicable to charitable purposes only". Again, the case[8] concerned a fund established to benefit and assist those suffering from the effects of a certain disability. It was refused charitable exemption on two counts: the benefit was confined to those who had contributed to the fund; and the funds were not applied for charitable purposes only. The deed of trust allowed contributors the option of receiving an annual income provision [set amount] for general maintenance purposes, without the necessity to provide a medical certificate – once an initial medical certificate diagnosing the illness had already been obtained. Thus it was a mutual assistance fund benefiting contributors rather than the general public.

---

[7] K.B. (1940), 23 T.C. 333.
[8] APP 11990.

18.4 REGISTERING AND REGULATING FUNDRAISING ACTIVITIES

The fundraising activities of charities remain governed by three sets of statutes, each set addressing the activities listed in the statute headings. Firstly, the Collections in Streets or Public Places Regulations (N.I.) 1927 No. 120 and the Collections in Streets or Public Places Regulations (N.I.) 1963 No. 196. Secondly, the House to House Charitable Collections Act (N.I.) 1952. Finally, the Betting, Gaming, Lotteries and Amusements (N.I.) Order 1985. These are now too dated to adequately address the complexities of modern fundraising practice nor do they deal with the more fundamental issues of identifying the organisations and the activities which constitute fundraising for charitable purposes.

18.4.1 Registration

Northern Ireland, like Scotland but unlike England and Wales, has no system for registering charities. Among the disadvantages which flow from that fact is the absence of any readily accessed data base capable of verifying the *bona fides* of a person or body claiming to be fundraising for charitable purposes. All that exists are informal indexes of charities kept by NICVA, and to some extent by the Charities Branch, together with records maintained by the Inland Revenue in Bootle. Arguably, a statutory system is now required which could promote the accountability of charities by providing clear rules regarding the organisations required to register and an identified agency with specified duties and powers in respect of the registration process.

18.4.1(i) Eligibility for registration

The starting point for any new system of accountability is generally acknowledged to be provision for the registration of those bodies entitled to engage in fundraising activities. Any such registration system would be binding on all organisations which solicit funds from the public and from funding agencies. A parent body may or may not have responsibility for its constituent groups; an organisation could choose whether the parent body's registration would include all affiliated groups or whether each such group should register in its own right. A registered body would, thereby, be authorised to fundraise and be eligible to obtain tax exemption status from the Inland Revenue. However, this must be tempered by an acceptance that fundraising is not limited to charitable purposes.

18.4.1(ii) Registering authority

The introduction of a mandatory registration system will need to also provide for a registration body to implement the registration requirements. This will have to be an independent statutory body.

18.4.2 Regulation

Regulation of fundraising activities is currently left to the R.U.C. which, after granting the necessary permits, will rarely intervene unless presented with evidence of a crime such as fraud. The Charities Branch has no regulatory powers as such but it does have some albeit limited powers to intervene where concerns are brought to its attention.

18.5 STREET COLLECTIONS

This form of fundraising continues to be governed primarily by sets of very dated regulations.

18.5.1 Regulatory powers

Under the Police, Factories etc (Miscellaneous Provisions) Act 1916, the police have the power to make regulations governing street collections. The power will apply to circumstances where:

> "... persons may be permitted in any street or public place, within the police area, to collect money or sell articles for the benefit of charitable or other purposes."[9]

Two sets of regulations made by the police remain in force, the Collections in Streets or Public Places Regulations (N.I.) 1927 No. 120 and the Collections in Streets or Public Places Regulations (N.I.) 1963 No. 196 which amended the previous provisions only slightly. A street collection can only be carried out after a permit has been obtained from the RUC.

18.5.2 Application for a permit

Application should be made to the RUC station for the area in which the street collection is to be made.[10] However, a permit is not necessary if the collection is to be at an open-air meeting, notice of which has been given to the police at least 48 hours before the meeting is due to take place. Notice of a meeting is in a prescribed form[11] and must contain information on the objects of the charity and details about its officers. The police can, by counter-notice, prohibit collection at one of these open-air meetings.

Application for an ordinary permit is also in a prescribed form[12] and must give information on the charity, its purposes and the persons responsible for

---

[9] See s. 5(1) of the Police, Factories etc (Miscellaneous Provisions) Act 1916.
[10] r. 1 Collections in Streets or Public Places Regulations (N.I.) 1927.
[11] Sched. 2, *ibid*.
[12] Sched. 1

the collection. Application must be made by the first day of the month preceding the month of the proposed collection and must be signed by 3 people jointly responsible for the collection.[13] It is advisable to apply as early as possible, especially as there is competition for desirable times such as the week before Christmas. Applications for the following year can be lodged in January of the previous year, *i.e.* an application can be made up to two years in advance if it is for a Christmas collection.

The permit will authorise collections on given days and times[14] and in given streets or public places.[15]

18.5.3 Refusal or revocation of permission

The legislation does not contain within it any express powers for the police to refuse permission for collections. Presumably, a failure to comply with the regulations is a ground for refusing permission. Refusal on other grounds may be *ultra vires*. This is in marked contrast to the express statutory grounds for refusal in relation to house to house collections.

18.5.4 Purposes of the collection

A street collection can be for "charitable or other purposes". There is nothing to limit the purposes for which a street collection can be carried out. As long as the regulations are satisfied, a street collection can theoretically be for any purpose. One protective device could be the criminal offence of obtaining property by deception if the collector misrepresented the purposes of the collection.[16]

18.5.5 Conduct of the collection

Collections cannot take place on the carriageway of a street *i.e.* on the footpath not the road.[17] They cannot cause obstruction or annoyance to the public due to their location,[18] nor can collectors importune or annoy any person.[19] Collectors must occupy a stationary position[20] and cannot stand closer than 30 yards from each other.[21] Collectors cannot use a table which would cause an

---

[13] *op. cit.*, r. 2.
[14] *op. cit.*, r. 3.
[15] *op. cit.*, r. 4.
[16] s. 15 of the Theft Act (N.I.) 1969.
[17] *op. cit.*, r. 6.
[18] *op. cit.*, r. 6.
[19] *op. cit.*, r. 12.
[20] *op. cit.*, r. 7.
[21] *op. cit.*, r. 7.

obstruction or which is longer than 30 inches or wider than 20 inches.[22] Collectors cannot "use a box or other receptacle at the end of a pole intended to reach upper windows or roofs".[22] Collectors cannot be accompanied by an animal.[24] The collecting boxes must display prominently the name of the fund for which the collection is being conducted, the date of the collection and all boxes must be numbered.[25] Technically under these rules, any collection during a sponsored walk would be illegal, as would a collection by a blind person with a guide dog.

18.5.6 Collection or sale

The Collections in Streets or Public Places Regulations (N.I.) 1927 No. 120 replicate the language of the Act by speaking of the "collection of money or sale of any article".[26] Some charities seek to raise money by offering subscriptions/membership to members of the public for payment of a fee. It is unclear whether this comes within the ambit of the rules and therefore whether a permit is needed. A broad interpretation could construe the "sale of an article" as including the sale of membership benefits, such as a charity's newsletter. However, a narrow interpretation could construe the "sale of an article" as meaning the sale of a tangible item, not merely a right of membership. The narrow interpretation would appear to be the better one. Presently, charities do not seek permission for this sort of activity.

The rules do not apply to the:

> "... selling of articles ... where the articles are sold in the ordinary course of trade and for the purpose of earning a livelihood and no representation is made by or on behalf of the seller that any part of the proceeds of sale will be devoted to any charitable purposs."[27]

18.5.7 Street or public place

Street is defined so as to include "any highway and any public bridge, road, lane, footway, square, court, alley, or passage whether a thoroughfare or not".[28]

When the legislation was promulgated in 1916 and 1927, shopping centres were not a feature of everyday life in Northern Ireland. There is a question mark over whether they constitute a "public place" and therefore whether a permit is needed. On the basis that a public place is a place to which the public

---

[22] *op. cit.*, r. 9.

[23] *op. cit.*, r. 10.

[24] *op. cit.*, r. 11.

[25] *op. cit.*, r. 14.

[26] r. 1 of the Collections in Streets or Public Places Regulations (N.I.) 1927.

[27] s. 5(1)(b) of the 1916 Act and the *proviso* to r. 16 of the 1927 Regulations.

[28] s. 5(4) of the Police, Factories Etc. (Miscellaneous Provisions) Act 1916.

is allowed access, it is submitted that the current practice of the R.U.C. in relation to the granting of permits is correct. When the Charities Act 1992 in England was at the drafting stage, concern was expressed that regulation of public charitable collections should also extend to shopping centres. As a result, "public places" is defined by that Act as including "any place to which at any time when the appeal is being made members of the public have or are permitted to have access".[29] This definition then goes on to explicitly mention shopping precincts. It would be preferable if the Northern Ireland definition was similarly explicit.

However, in any event, as shopping centres own the premises and have the right to exclude people, it is also necessary to get their permission before any collection takes place.

18.5.8 Collectors

Collectors must be aged 16 or over. Collectors cannot be paid:

> "... no payment or reward shall be made to any collector or vendor, or other person connected with the promotion or conduct of such a collection or sale, for or in respect of services rendered in connection therewith."[30]

Collectors must have written authority from the permit holders to take part in the collection and they must produce this authority to the police on request.[31]

18.5.9 Accounting for money received

Contributors to the collection must place the money in collection boxes. These boxes must be securely sealed and numbered consecutively. Each collector must deliver these boxes to the person responsible for the collection.[32] Within two months of the collection, the person responsible for it must send a statement to the RUC.[33] This statement must be in a prescribed form[34] and give details of receipts and expenditure of the collection. The statement must be audited by a responsible independent person.[35] The charity must publish a short statement in a newspaper, as directed by the police, containing some basic details of the collection.[36]

---

[29] s. 65(8)(b) of the Charities Act 1992.
[30] r. 15 of the Collections in Streets or Public Places Regulations (N.I.) 1927.
[31] r. 5 *ibid.*
[32] *op. cit.*, r. 13.
[33] *op. cit.*, r. 16. The previous time limit was one month, it was extended to two months by r. 2(b) of the 1963 Regulations.
[34] Sched. 1.
[35] *op. cit.*, r. 16.
[36] *op. cit.* Rule 16.

18.5.10 Criminal offences

It is a criminal offence to breach any of the above regulations. The penalty is a fine of level 1 on the standard scale (up to £200). The matter is triable summarily in the magistrates court.

18.6 HOUSE TO HOUSE COLLECTIONS

House to house collections are authorised by statue and by ancillary regulations. This provides a legal framework which offers slightly more regulation than that imposed on street collections. However, the law in this jurisdiction bears little resemblance to that now prevailing in England and Wales where the laws on street and house to house collections have been consolidated in a new statute dealing with public charitable collections.

18.6.1 Regulatory powers

18.6.1(i) Regulation in Northern Ireland

House to house collections are governed by the House to House Charitable Collections Act (N.I.) 1952. Under section 5 of that Act, the Charities Branch can make further regulations. This they have done by issuing the House to House Charitable Collections Regulations (N.I.) 1952 No. 119 as amended by the House to House Charitable Collections Regulations (N.I.) 1953 No. 53.

In Northern Ireland a collection must be authorised, usually by a licence for which application is made to the R.U.C. Specific procedures are set out for the refusal or revocation of a licence. A distinction is drawn between the chief promoter, the promoters, and the collectors. The collection must be conducted in a certain way and all money raised must be accounted for. These provisions apply equally to collections of both money and other property.

18.6.1(ii) Regulation in England and Wales

In England and Wales, Part III of the Charities Act 1992 enacts and consolidates laws on public charitable collections. In overview, these laws are similar in principle to the piecemeal provisions on street collections and house to house collections which they amalgamate. Those repealed provisions are, in turn similar to the existing Northern Ireland provisions.

In England and Wales a public charitable collection must be authorised by a permit from a local authority or the Charity Commission. Public appeals incorporate both street collections, house collections and collections in other places to which the public are allowed access. Application must be made between one and six months before the first day the collection is due to take place and can last for up to 12 months. The local authority must consult the chief officer of police before making their decision to allow or refuse a permit. Refusal is on grounds similar to those in the house to house collection legislation in Northern Ireland, although section 69(1) of the Charities Act 1992 expressly provides that reasons for refusal will include public inconvenience, other conflicting collections and lack of authority of the collector to act for the charity. Appeals against refusal are to the magistrates court and not to the Charities Branch as in Northern Ireland. The Commission has the same power as the Charities Branch to allow collections across the entire country rather than requiring individual applications to all the separate local authorities.

18.6.2 Authority for a collection

The usual authority for a collection is a licence granted by the chief superintendent of police for the area in which the collection is made. Two further sources of authority are possible. A certificate may be granted by the R.U.C. if:

> "... that purpose is local in character and that the collection is likely to be completed within a short period of time."[37]

None of the following provisions apply to such collections, except for the criminal offences.[38] Schedule 1 of the Regulations gives the prescribed form for this certificate.

If the collection is intended to be Northern Ireland wide then, rather than applying to each individual Chief Superintendent of each area, one single application can be made instead to the Charities Branch. If that application is successful, the promoter is deemed to have a licence issued to him.[39]

18.6.3 Application for a licence

The promoter must apply to the chief superintendent of the area in which the collection is intended to take place.[40] Unlike a street collection which requires three applicants, house to house collection applications require only one. The application is in the form prescribed by Schedule 2 of the Regulations. A licence can then be granted for that area. The application must be made no later than the first day of the month preceding the month of the collection. The licence will usually last for 12 months, though it may be issued for a shorter period or extended for up to 18 months.[41]

---

[37] See s. 1(4) of the House to House Charitable Collections Act (N.I.) 1952.
[38] See s. 1(4) states the Act will not apply, r. 3(2) states the Regulations will not apply.
[39] See s. 3.
[40] See s. 2(1).
[41] See s. 2(2).

18.6.4 Refusal or revocation of licences

The R.U.C. may refuse a licence, or revoke a licence once it has been issued. They can do so on any of the following grounds:

- Amount applied to charity is inadequate as compared to the amount received (section 2(3)(a)).
- Persons concerned with the collection will receive excessive remuneration (section 2(3)(b)).
- The collection would facilitate offences under section 4(f) of the Vagrancy Act 1824 (section 2(3)(c)).[42]
- Licence holder is not a fit and proper person to hold the licence because he has been convicted of an offence involving fraud or dishonesty or any other offence listed in Schedule 1 of the Act (section 2(3)(d)).[43]
- Licence holder has not exercised due diligence to ensure collectors are fit and proper persons (section 2(3)(e)).
- Licence holder has not exercised due diligence to ensure collectors comply with the legislation (section 2(3)(e)).
- Licence holder has not exercised due diligence that no unauthorised persons have obtained official certificates or badges (section 2(3)(e)).
- Licence holder has failed to furnish information to police on any of the above matters (section 2(3)(f)).

The police must inform the person as to the reasons why the licence has been refused or revoked.[44] That person then has 14 days from the date notice was given to appeal that decision to the Charities Branch.[45]

18.6.5 Purposes of the collection

Unlike street collections, house to house collections can only be authorised if they are for "charitable, benevolent or philanthropic purposes".[46] The range of allowable purposes is narrower than all purposes, but broader than those which are merely charitable.

---

[42] This is the offence of "going about as a gatherer or collector of alms, or endeavouring to procure charitable contributions of any nature or kind, under any false or fraudulent pretence".

[43] These other offences include sexual offences, violent offences, offences under the street collections legislation or offences under the English House to House Collections Act 1939.

[44] s. 2(4).

[45] s. 2(5).

[46] s. 8 of the House to House Collections Act (N.I.) 1952.

18.6.6 Conduct of the collection

Collectors must have a badge of authority, in the prescribed form[47] and prominently displayed.[48] They must have a certificate of authority, in the prescribed form,[49] to be produced to the police or householder on demand.[50] Collectors must also give their name to the police on demand.[51] They must have either a marked box into which donations are placed, or a receipt book for recording all money received.[52] Alternatively, money can be collected by way of an envelope collection.[53] They must not importune or cause annoyance to any person or remain at a house if requested to leave by an occupant.[54]

18.6.7 Collectors

Collectors must be aged at least 16.[55] The only exception, under section 1(2), is where the collection is Northern Ireland wide and is conducted by a youth organisation. The collectors can then be under 16 years of age though they must be more than 12.[56] It is implicit that collectors or those concerned with the collection can be paid,[57] the reverse is the case for street collectors.

18.6.8 Duties of promoters

Promoters must exercise due diligence to ensure that collectors are fit and proper persons[58] and that they comply with all the requirements of the legislation.[59] They must also exercise due diligence to ensure that badges and certificates of authority have been correctly issued[60] and that such badges etc. are returned after the collection. It is the duty of the chief promoter to exercise due diligence to ensure that all badges etc. are destroyed when no longer needed for the purpose for which they were issued.[61]

---

[47] r. 6(1)(b) and Sch. 4 of the Regulations.
[48] r. 7(b).
[49] r. 6(1)(a) and Sch. 3 of the Regulations.
[50] r. 7(a).
[51] s. 6.
[52] r. 6(1)(c).
[53] r. 13.
[54] r. 9.
[55] r. 8.
[56] 1953 Regulations as amending r. 8 of the 1952 Regulations.
[57] See, s. 2(3)(b).
[58] r. 5(a).
[59] r. 5(b).
[60] r. 6(2)(a).
[61] r. 17.

18.6.9 Accounting for money received

Money can only be received in one of two ways. It must either be put into the collection box by the donor[62] or it must be given to the collector. If it is given to the collector, the date, amount and name of the donor must be entered in the receipt book with a copy being given to the donor.[63] All boxes and receipt books must be returned to the promoter when full, or requested or when the collection is complete.[64] Boxes can either be opened by the promoter and one other responsible person,[65] or opened by a bank official on his own.[66] The money in the boxes or the amount in the receipt books must be counted and entered on a list certified by the counter.[67]

The chief promoter must furnish an account of the collection to the police within one month of the expiry of the licence.[68] The only administrative crossover with the street collection legislation is that street collection accounts may be combined with house collection accounts if they are connected and the police agree.[69] The statement of account must be in a prescribed form[70] and certified by the chief promoter and an independent responsible person as auditor.[71] Vouchers for each item of expenditure and application of money must be included with the account[72] unless the auditor is a member of an incorporated society of accountants.[73]

18.6.10 Offences

The 1952 Act and its ancillary regulations make provision for several specific criminal offences. Promoting a collection without a licence contrary to section 1(2) is punishable by up to six months imprisonment and/or a level 3 fine on the standard scale (up to £1,000). The unlawful use of a charitable badge or certificate, contrary to section 5, is punishable by the same penalty as above. In England, the court in *R* v. *Davidson*[74] held that the unlawful use of a badge, etc. was not just limited to house to house collections. Collecting without a licence, contrary to section 1(3), is punishable by up to three months imprisonment and/or a level 2 fine (up to £500). A collector failing to give his name

---

[62] r. 10(1).
[63] r. 10(2).
[64] r. 11.
[65] r. 12(1).
[66] r. 12(2).
[67] r. 12(3) and (4).
[68] r. 14(1).
[69] r. 14(4).
[70] Sched. 5 of the Regulations.
[71] r. 15.
[72] r. 16(1).
[73] r. 16(2).
[74] [1972] 3 All E.R. 1121.

to a constable, contrary to section 6 is punishable by a level 1 fine (up to £200). All such offences are triable summarily.

18.7 GAMING AND LOTTERIES

The advent of lotteries, in particular the introduction of a national lottery, has transformed charitable fundraising.

18.7.1 Regulatory powers

The Betting, Gaming, Lotteries and Amusements (N.I.) Order 1985 and its associated subordinate legislation prescribe the circumstances in which gaming and lotteries will be deemed to be lawful for fundraising purposes. The 1985 Order, a relatively modern piece of legislation, replaces a statutory code which had prevailed since the early eighteenth century. It is a measure of the pace of change in modern fundraising practice that this statute required review 12 years after its introduction.[75]

18.7.2 Lotteries

If charities wish to raise money by way of a lottery, they are subject to the same rules as any other organisation.[76] In this jurisdiction the Lotteries Regulations (N.I.) 1994 provide the specific legal framework for charitable fundraising by means of lotteries.

The National Lottery Charities Board (NLCB) also provides an incidental regulatory function in relation to charities. All applicant charities seeking lottery funds, and very many do so, are required to submit to a formal screening process. This is quite rigorous and has unearthed many cases of irregularity which had escaped the attention of the Inland Revenue. There is a sense in which the NLCB has become a standard setting body which is directly influencing the legal structure and practice of charities in Northern Ireland (see also, Chapter 5).

18.8 OTHER FUNDRAISING METHODS

Advances in telecommunications have transformed the capacity and speed of modern fundraising. Charities now rely heavily upon the mass media, on professional fundraisers, celebrity entertainment events and on trading ventures

---

[75] See the D.H.S.S., *Consultation Paper on Casinos & Gaming, Betting, Lotteries and Amusements with Prizes*, Jan. 1997.

[76] See Charities Branch, *Northern Ireland Charities: A Guide for Trustees* (1998).

for generating resources. Traditional forms of fundraising such as raffles or collections still play a part in stimulating the generosity of local communities, but powerful national or multi-national televised appeals attract a far greater volume of funds in a concentrated period. This has brought with it complex legal problems which have yet to be addressed by statute.

18.8.1 Telethons

Telethons have become an extremely popular method of involving the general public in fundraising and of promoting awareness of deserving causes. However, at present such activity is outside statutory control. There is a need to introduce a registration and regulatory system to provide standards for the conducting of telethons, the keeping of proper records and auditing of accounts and to permit investigations where necessary.

18.8.2 Professional fundraisers

Charitable fundraising can be big business. Firms now employ full-time expert staff skilled in the art of generating public donations to worthy causes. Increasingly, charities are relying on the services of such professional fundraisers who are motivated by personal profit to collect money or solicit funds from the general public. This gives rise to certain issues. For example:

- Should all funds raised by a professional fundraiser be paid to the charity concerned before deduction of any remuneration or expenses?
- Should there be a fixed ceiling on payments by commission?
- Should professional fundraisers be required to furnish accounts within a fixed period of the termination of the promotion?
- Should all contracts entered into by a professional fundraiser with a charity be open to public inspection?

In England and Wales, new legislation now governs fundraising activities.[77] Part II of the Charities Act 1992 was introduced to prevent malpractice, in particular excessive remuneration of fundraisers, to give more information to donors, and to create greater clarity and transparency of relationship between charities and those who raise money on their behalf. The provisions apply not only to charitable but also to benevolent and philanthropic institutions. A professional fundraiser is defined as one who carries on a profit-making fundraising business or who solicits money for the benefit of a charitable institution. A commercial participator is one "who encourages purchases of goods or services on the grounds that some of the proceeds will go to charity".[78]

---

[77] See Picarda, *The Law and Practice relating to Charities* (1995), Chap. 45 for a comprehensive consideration of these provisions.

[78] *op cit.* at p. 586.

Professional fundraisers or commercial participators cannot act except in accordance with an agreement made with the charity. The agreement must contain certain prescribed information, *i.e.* details of the parties, duration of the agreement, details of remuneration, etc. Donors are entitled to a cooling off period and repayment in certain circumstances. This will apply if the payment is in response to a TV or radio appeal or other appeal made orally to the donor. If the size of the donation is over £50 and made in response to the actions of a professional fundraiser, the donor has seven days to cancel it.

In this jurisdiction, there is a need to introduce a registration and regulatory system to provide for the certifying of persons employed as professional fundraisers, to set standards for the terms under which they contract to charities and to ensure the proper auditing of all accounts. The system should provide for a register of such persons, a requirement that all activity be based on an explicit written contract with a named charity, mandatory disclosure requirements regarding amounts raised and remuneration paid, a cooling-off period, prompt payment of funds to charity, and submission of properly audited accounts. The cross-jurisdiction activities of fundraisers and the entailed movement of funds makes it a matter of growing concern that their activities be set within a regulatory legal framework.

18.8.3 Disaster appeals

Fundraising in the aftermath of a particular disaster gives rise to two distinct problems for charity law. Firstly, it is necessarily an activity intended to confer a benefit upon a restricted and clearly defined number of people; a question therefore arises as to whether this is in breach of the "public" branch of the public benefit test. Secondly, it follows that those who donate do not necessarily have a general charitable intention; a further question therefore arises as to *cy-près* may be used to dispose of any surplus funds.

It has long been accepted that fundraising does satisfy the "public" element of the public benefit test.[79] It is in the nature of an activity launched with a strong sense of urgency and involving many shocked and distressed people that, though undertaken with the best of intentions, it can encounter difficulties. As has been observed:

> "Action to set up a public appeal following some tragic accident or disaster or an occasion on which some special misfortune is brought to the public eye is generally taken with little time to prepare the ground. The community may well feel an urgent need to give practical expression to its sorrow and respect; and the response may well exceed expectations."[80]

---

[79] See *Re Lord Mayor of Belfast's Air Raid Distress Fund* [1962] N.I. 161.

[80] See the Attorney-General in *Charity Commission Report* (England and Wales), 1981, App. A as reprinted in the Charity Commission Leaflet CC40. See also, Suddards, R.W., Price, L., and Picarda, H., *Bradford Disaster Appeal: the Administration of an Appeal Fund*, 1986.

Fund-raising activity for the purpose of disaster relief must clearly specify the purpose for eliciting funds and ensure that all donations will be used exclusively for that purpose. In *Re Gillingham Bus Disaster Fund*,[81] for example, the appeal was expressed in such vague terms that the court held the trust to be void for uncertainty. The reason for a matter relating to a disaster fund coming before the courts tends to be because of surplus funds or because there is uncertainty regarding the extent of the class eligible for relief.

Under section 23 of the Charities Act 1964, a procedure is provided to dispose of funds, or of surplus funds, in circumstances where a public appeal has attracted donations which are not needed. After advertising for the donors to come forward, and making such enquiries as may be reasonable, the fund may be applied *cy-près* (see further, Chapter 19).

18.8.4 Trading

Charities are often engaged to a greater or lesser extent in trading as a means of fundraising. This activity, which can range from the seasonal selling of Christmas cards from a stall to a multi-national coffee import/export business, is not in itself charitable. Indeed, there is a very real legal tension between charitable activity and trading. Not only is a charity unable to claim tax relief on profits earned from trading, but significant and prolonged reliance upon trading can threaten charitable status. There are two different ways in which charities can develop trading functions:[82] either as small scale operations which are subordinate to and directly in furtherance of its primary purpose; or not as part of its primary purpose but to raise funds to be applied for charitable purposes. Where the charity relies heavily on its trading activities then these should be re-constituted within a separate company otherwise it may risk losing its charitable status.

The term "trade" has a non-technical meaning encompassing everyday interpretations such as manufacturing, catering, farming, mining, fishing etc. Activities such as running a restaurant open to outsiders,[83] selling books[84] and the renting of rooms for public entertainment[85] have all been held to come under the umbrella of charitable trading. As Cairns has pointed out:

> "Provided that the balance of the activities is towards charity rather than profit, the conduct of the trade is acceptable but it is a point to be decided on the particular facts of each case. Similar principles apply in cases where the non-charitable activities are inseparable from the primary purpose of the charity

---

[81] [1959] Ch. 62.

[82] See further, Inland Revenue, *Trading by Charities*, 1995.

[83] See *Grove v. Young Men's Christian Association* (1903) 4 T.C. 613.

[84] See *Religious Tract and Book Society of Scotland v. Forbes* (1896) 3 T.C. 415; see also, *Psalms and Hymns (Baptist) Trustees v. Whitwell* (1890) 3 T.C. 7.

[85] See *Coman v. Rotunda Hospital Dublin (Governors)* [1921] 1 A.C. 1.

such as the sale of goods made by disabled people in the charity's workshops, or the sale of Bibles and religious literature by charities established to advance the Christian religion."[86]

It is an open question whether or to what extent charities should compete in the open market; whether in direct competition with for-profit businesses or acting under contract or in partnership with government bodies. If by so doing a charity is able to remain squarely within its objects, retain its independence and generate income not otherwise available then arguably it should be encouraged to do so. However, there comes a point where sharp business acumen and a flair for entrepreneurial ventures threatens the integrity of the charitable ethos, at least in terms of public perception, and calls into question why such activity should be in effect subsidised by the public taxpayer.

As the law stands it is of the greatest importance that a charity is not distracted by trading opportunities from pursuing its objects, that it does not compromise its independence and that it does not place trust funds at risk by engaging in speculative business ventures (see further, Chapters 16 and 20).

---

[86] See Cairns, E., *Charities: Law and Practice, op. cit.* at p. 23.

CHAPTER 19

Cy-près

19.1 INTRODUCTION

"*Cy-près*", a Norman French expression, has been generally interpreted by the courts to mean "as near as possible".[1] The fact that it is advantageous to all concerned that a gift intended to be used for charitable purposes should acquire charity status explains the significance of the *cy-près* doctrine. There is an equitable presumption[2] that the charitable intentions of a donor should not be allowed to fail because of an inconsequential difficulty. This may be due to a mere technical illegality, an area of uncertainty, or perhaps a fundamental failure, to construct a trust or one of many other reasons which the donor may not have foreseen.[3] The legal significance of *cy-près* lies in its capacity to allow the High court or the Charities Branch, within certain parameters, to overcome legal technicalities and give effect to a donor's charitable intent.

This chapter examines the nature, history and current application of the *cy-près* doctrine. It considers matters of jurisdiction, administration and judicial interpretation. It explores how the doctrine is applied, the parameters for its application and assesses its significance. Mostly, however, this chapter concentrates on elucidating case law material to explain the current law and practice of *cy-près* in this jurisdiction.

19.2 DEVICES TO SAVE GIFTS

The law permits the use of at least four devices to save lapsed gifts of which the *cy-près* doctrine is by far the most important. Firstly, an obvious clerical or descriptive error can be summarily rectified. Secondly, a gift may be construed as a purpose trust. Thirdly, small failed gifts may be applied to other charities. Finally, a *cy-près* scheme may be drawn up to save a gift. Non-

---

[1] The etymological derivation of the phrase *cy-près* is either *ici pres* (near this) or *aussi pres* (as near as possible), *i.e.* "the intention of the donor must be ascertained and the new purposes should be those which most nearly give effect to that intention", Tudor (1995) at p. 444, see also *Re Lambeth Charities* (1853) 22 L.J. Ch. 959.
[2] See *dicta* of Lord Hanworth MR in *Re Watt* [1932] 2 Ch. 243 at 246.
[3] See for example, *Attorney-General v. Price* (1907) 24 T.L.R. 763. *Cf. T Doyle v. F O'Reilly & Ors.op. cit.*

charitable gifts can only use the first device, charitable gifts can use any. Most often a failure occurs as a consequence of a gift being given to a body which has ceased to exist.

19.2.1 Minor errors of description

There are three sources of the power to rectify errors so as to save a gift. The first is an inherent power of the court to correct minor clerical errors. This may occur where there has been a slight typographical error in naming a beneficiary, or the full name of an institution has perhaps been misspelled. For example, in *Re Brown*[4] a gift for the Resthaven Home of Healing was incorrectly described to be for the Resthaven Home for Hearing. The court had no difficulty correcting this mistake.

The second source is a relatively obscure common law doctrine known as *falsa demonstratio non nocet cum de corpore constat*, a misdescription of part will not render void an otherwise certain gift. Girvan J. applied this doctrine to Northern Ireland in *Re Robinson, Millar v. Ben Hardwick Memorial Fund*.[5] The case concerned a fund initially called the Ben Hardwick Transplant Fund. After the beneficiary died, the fund became the Ben Hardwick Memorial Fund, a charity registered in England.[6] The testatrix left money by will to the Transplant Fund. Girvan J. held that there was no need to exercise *cy-près* to save the gift as *falsa demonstratio* would suffice.

Historically *falsa demonstratio* had been applied "where any property in a will is sufficiently ascertained by the description, it passes by the devise, although all the particulars stated in the will with reference to it may not be true".[7] The theory that it rectifies an accurate description which contains some inaccurate detail was reiterated in the House of Lords, "the entirety which has been expressly and definitely given shall not be prejudiced by an imperfect and inaccurate enunciation of the particulars of the specific gift".[8] The decision in *Re Robinson* extends this principle somewhat to cases where a gift to a body has been accurately defined but that body has now been reconstituted.

The third source of the power to rectify errors of description is statutory. Article 29 of the Wills and Administration Proceedings (N.I.) Order 1994 states that where a will fails to carry out the testator's intentions due to a clerical error, or because of a failure to understand his instructions, the will may be rectified by the court after death. In England the same provision exists

---

[4] See *Re Brown, Nesbitt v. Attorney General* , unreported, Ch. D., April 12, 1991.
[5] Unreported, High Court, May 5, 1997.
[6] To digress slightly, the initial fund would have failed the public benefit test – "a specific gift for the benefit of Ben Hardwick's transplant operation would not have evinced an intention to benefit what in law would have constituted a charity" at p. 5 of transcript.
[7] *Doe d Dunning v. Cranstoun* (1840) 7 M. & W. 1 at 10.
[8] *West v. Lawday* (1865) 11 H.L. Cas. 315 at 384.

under section 20 of the Administration of Justice Act 1982 and was applied in *Re Segelman*[9] which concerned a testator's gift to his poor and needy relations, a list of whom was provided. The solicitor, when drafting the will, provided that if any of the named relations died their place could be taken by their children. This effectively excluded poor and needy relatives whose relatives were still alive. In so doing the solicitor had failed to carry out the testator's instructions and so the will was rectified because of its clerical error.

19.2.2 Purpose trusts

If the object of a gift is a defunct organisation whose purposes were charitable, the gift can be construed as a gift for those charitable purposes. In accordance with the rules for effectuating charitable intention, that purpose can then be fulfilled by the court providing the means to carry it out. This device was used with partial success in the Northern Ireland case of *Re Currie, McClelland v. Gamble*[10] concerning a gift to the Victoria Hall Building Fund. The purpose of that fund was to build a new place of worship for a religious congregation. After the will was made but before the testator died the congregation built the Crescent Church and transferred all remaining money into a fund for the upkeep of the new church. The testator died and the court was left with the issue of what to do with the gift. Carswell J. employed the purpose trust as a device to save the gift. He was able to construe the gift as one for the purpose of building a church; a valid charitable purpose. It was "tolerably clear that the testator's gift to the Treasurer of the Building Fund should be regarded as a gift to be held for the purposes for which the Building Fund was to be applied at the date of the will".[11] However, he then found that the purpose did not extend to maintaining the new church once built. As the purpose trust device was not capable of dealing with the next stage, Carswell J. had to turn to *cy-près*.

19.2.3 Small misdescribed gifts

Section 14 of the Charities Act (N.I.) 1964 has been described as the "poor man's *cy-près*". It will apply to gifts of under £2,500[12] in a will to an institution. Two conditions must be fulfilled, the personal representatives must be satisfied that no such institution exists[13] and that the testator intended to give the property to charity.[14] If the Charities Branch finds that these conditions

---

[9] [1995] 3 All E.R. 676.
[10] [1985] N.I. 299.
[11] *ibid.* at p. 305, as authority he cited *Re Finger's Will Trusts* [1972] Ch. 286 and *Re Vernon's Will Trusts* [1972] Ch. 300.
[12] As inserted by the Charities (N.I.) Order 1987, previously the limit was £250.
[13] See s. 14(1)(b)(i).
[14] See s. 14(1)(b)ii).

have been satisfied, it will then accept a transfer of the property in question from the personal representatives. The Charities Branch will then attempt to ascertain the specific charity which the testator intended to benefit.[15] Having done so, it can transfer the property to that charity,[16] or to a charity or charities of that class,[17] or to any charity generally[18] so long as the Attorney-General consents.

19.3 THE *CY-PRÈS* DOCTRINE

The classic statement defending the value of *cy-près* was made in the early nineteenth century by Lord Eldon:

> "... if the testator has manifested a general intention to give to charity, the failure of the particular mode in which the charity is to be effectuated shall not destroy the charity; but if the general intention is charity, the law will substitute another mode of devoting the property to charitable purposes."[19]

An alternative and more cynical view of the value of *cy-près* has also long prevailed in England. In *Bowman v. Secular Society*[20] it was stated that *cy-près* as a legal fiction was recognised by the courts because *cy-près* had "gone further than any other rule or canon of construction in defeating the real intention of testators".[21] These contradictory views of the role of the *cy-près* doctrine in the exercise of judicial discretion pervade the case law.

19.3.1 History

This ancient doctrine probably has its roots in Roman law[22] but became relevant to the development of charity law in these islands when introduced, among other rules of construction, to assist judicial interpretation of wills in the Ecclesiastical courts. These courts embraced with some enthusiasm the capacity of this doctrine to assist their policy of retaining for public rather than private benefit as much of a testator's estate as could be reasonably construed to be intended for charitable purposes. Where possible, when faced

---

[15] See s. 14(4).
[16] See s. 14(4)(a).
[17] See s. 14(4)(b).
[18] See s. 14(4)(c).
[19] *Moggridge v. Thackwell* (1803) 7 Ves. 36 at 69.
[20] (1917) AC 406.
[21] *ibid.* at p. 442. One particularly blatant example of this was a gift for holding Jewish religious services in *Da Costa v. De Paz* (1754) Amb. 228. When the gift failed, the court applying *cy-près* created a scheme for the gift to go to the Foundling Hospital as this was construed to be the presumed intention of the testator.
[22] See for example, Jolowicz, H.F., *Roman Foundations of Modern Law* (1957) pp. 138-139.

with a trust which would otherwise fail, these courts "discovered' a charitable intention on the part of the testator, judicial leniency was then exercised in favour of preserving the gift for charitable use and a *cy-près* scheme was prepared. The doctrine developed in keeping with "the religious notions entertained formerly in this country"[23]

In Northern Ireland, the courts have firmly rooted the concept in a religious source:

> "A charitable legacy was regarded as expiation for the testator's earthly sins, an act of piety which would help secure his salvation. To declare such a gift void was to raise an impediment in the way of the testator's soul on its heavenward path; to advance a supposed general charitable intention was to promote a spiritual end."[24]

In the United Kingdom, the *cy-près* doctrine has been exercised since at least the seventeenth century. As such, it predates other doctrines of law, in particular the doctrine of the resulting trust. A resulting trust operates to return money to the donor or another person when a gift fails or ends. If *cy-près* fails to save a gift, it will usually revert to the donor or the donor's estate on a resulting trust (see further, Chapter 6). Judges have suggested that if resulting trusts had originated first, *cy-près* would have had a very retarded development – "if the doctrine of resulting trusts had then been understood, the right of the heir-at-law would never, in all probability have been got over".[25]

19.3.2 The *cy-près* requirements

There are three pre-requisites for the application of this doctrine. Firstly, the intended recipient of the donor's gift must be a charity. Secondly, the circumstances in which the gift is being made must be legally recognised as a "*cy-près* occasion". Thirdly, depending on when the *cy-près* occasion occurred, there must either be a general charitable intention or an outright gift to charity.

19.3.2(i) Cy-près *and charitable status*

The *cy-près* doctrine applies only in the context of a gift for purposes which are recognised as charitable. Thus, the normal legal requirements must be fully satisfied.

The gift must clearly intend to confer a benefit and this must be demonstrably a benefit of a public nature.

---

[23] *Moggridge v. Thackwell* at p. 69.

[24] *Re Simpson, Wallace v. Attorney General for Northern Ireland* [1974] N.I.J.B. Nov. at p. 4.

[25] *Attorney General v. Mayor of Bristol* (1820) 2 J. & W. 294 at p. 307; the heir-at-law was the person entitled to the estate of the deceased under a resulting trust.

This public benefit test varies in the strictness of the proofs required under each of the four categories of charitable trusts. The courts in this jurisdiction adopt an objective approach, similar to that applied by their counterparts elsewhere in the United Kingdom, when determining whether or not a donor has demonstrated the requisite charitable intention. In the adjoining jurisdiction, the Irish courts have pursued an approach more sympathetic to the donor's interpretation of charitable purpose which has enabled them to use greater flexibility than is possible in the U.K.[26]

The requirement that a gift be charitable before its failure can instigate the *cy-près* procedure is well illustrated in the case law of this jurisdiction. In all but one of the Northern Ireland cases on *cy-près*, the original gift was charitable. In particular, the *ratio decidendi* of the Court of Appeal in *Attorney General for Northern Ireland* v. *Forde*[27] rested on a finding that *cy-près* could not operate because the initial gift to widows was not charitable. However, the court in *Re Brown* would seem to have demonstrated a readiness to deviate from that approach. In that case, one of the gifts was for an anti-vivisection society called the World League Against Vivisection. Campbell J., following established precedents, held that agitating against vivisection is not charitable (see also, Chapters 11 and 13). In theory, therefore, the appropriateness of *cy-près* was discounted at the first hurdle. However, Campbell J. continued with the rest of the *cy-près* tests before concluding with the decision that the gift failed on the ground that there was no general charitable intention.

The *cy-près* doctrine addresses only a deficiency in giving effect to charitable purpose; other defects (*e.g.* a failure to name a trustee or a failure in an aspect of administration) fall outside the remit of *cy-près* and remedies must be sought elsewhere. Nor will it be applied to make the donor's disposition more effective, or to accommodate a factor which the donor had clearly overlooked. If the disposition is capable of taking effect, however unsatisfactorily, then *cy-près* has no application.[28] Trustees have a duty to apply a gift *cy-près* where that is necessary.

The doctrine does not apply to foreign charities.[29] Indeed, it has been said[30] that there is the greatest doubt whether the courts have the power to prepare a scheme of *cy-près* to apply a gift, which had been intended for a charity within the jurisdiction but had not been successful due to a failure of purpose and objective, for the benefit of a charitable organisation based outside the jurisdiction. A gift made without the requisite charitable intent cannot be saved by *cy-près* and will fail. Where a disposition in favour of a charity fails then it

---

[26] See further, Delaney, H., *Charitable Status and Cy-Pres Jurisdiction: An Examination of Some of the Issues Raised in In Re the Worth Library, op. cit.* at fn. 6. See also, Sheridan, "Cy-près in the Cyxties" (1966) 17 N.I.L.Q. 235.

[27] [1932] N.I. 1.

[28] See for example, *Philpott v. St George's Hospital* (1859) 27 Beav. 107.

[29] See for example, *King v. Long* (1919) 53 I.L.T.R. 60.

[30] See Johnston J. in *Attorney-General v. Royal Hibernian Military School* (1929) 63 I.L.T.R.

will pass, as a resulting trust, to the residuary estate, thence to the donor's next-of-kin or representatives.

19.3.2(ii) Cy-près *"occasions'*

The courts of equity restricted the use of *cy-près* to "occasions" where it had become either impossible or impracticable to give effect to a donor's gift in the manner as he or she had intended. As Meredith J. has pointed out[31]:

> "Donors cannot be expected to provide expressly for more than the world and the times with which they are familiar. Accordingly, the perpetuity for which charities may endure throws upon the court the burden of providing for that which the donor did not foresee, in accordance with what it finds to be the underlying intention of the charity foundation."

The circumstances in which a *cy-près* scheme would be appropriate have since been considerably extended by the addition of instances as specified under section 22 of the 1964 Act and by the direction in that provision to "have regard to the spirit of the gift".[32]

The timing of the *cy-près* occasion is of vital importance. The requirements for *cy-près* depend on whether the failure occurs before or after the gift takes effect. The gift may fail *ab initio*, right from the start. Alternatively it may fail not when the gift is made (*i.e.* whenever the testator dies) but when the time comes for it to take effect.

19.3.2(iii) General charitable intention or outright gift to charity

If there is an initial failure then, for *cy-près* to succeed, there must be a general charitable intention.[33] If there is subsequent failure, all that must be shown is that the gift was an outright gift to charity.[34] Initial failure is the most common, and case law mainly addresses the question of whether there has been a general charitable intention, *i.e.* whether it can be inferred that an intention existed to promote charity generally in the gift, and that the particular purpose selected is representative rather than imperative. Wylie has suggested that the emphasis in this rule may be changing[35]:

> "The courts usually require that [the] donor exhibited a general charitable inten-

---

[31] See *Governors of Erasmus Smith Schools v. Attorney General and Others* (1932) 66 I.L.T.R. 57 at 61. Note, also, the distinction made by Meredith J., in this case, between motive and intention. See further 10.4.3ff.

[32] See further 10.4.4ff.

[33] See further 10.5ff.

[34] See further 10.5.2ff.

[35] See Wylie, J.C.W., *A Casebook on Equity & Trusts* (2nd ed.), Butterworths, Dublin, 1998) at p. 1000.

tion (see *Re Ffrench*[36]), although in more recent times the courts have tended to concentrate on the donor's 'paramount' intention (see *Re Currie*[37])."

An outright gift means that the gift has been irrevocably made to a charitable purpose and cannot be clawed back.

19.4 JURISDICTION FOR PREPARING A *CY-PRÈS* SCHEME

The *cy-près* doctrine is applied by the Charities Branch or by the High Court through the preparation of a scheme tailored to best give effect to the donor's intentions and to be most appropriate to the particular nature of the donor's gift. Responsibility for ordering a *cy-près* scheme to be prepared rests with the Charities Branch, under sections 13 and 24 of the 1964 Act, where the gift in question has a financial value of £50,000 or less. Where gifts are valued in excess of that amount then the responsibility passes to the court.

19.4.1 The Charities Branch and *cy-près* schemes

The powers of the Charities Branch in respect of *cy-près* administration were initially those conferred upon the Commissioners for Charitable Donations and Bequests by the Charitable Donations and Bequests (Ireland) Act 1844, extended under the 1871 Act and continued in this jurisdiction after partition. Before the Charities Act (N.I.) 1964, the monetary limits were governed by section 6 of the 1871 Act which granted the Charities Branch jurisdiction:

> "… whenever there shall be any charitable donation or bequest, not exceeding in amount the sum of £300, or in any case in which there shall be payable for any charitable or pious purposes any annual sum not exceeding £30."

The court, in *Ministry of Finance v. Attorney General for Northern Ireland*,[38] held that these were alternative tests. In that case the fund was valued at £361 and it produced an income of £12 annually. The *cy-près* jurisdiction of the Charities Branch was operative under the income head though if failed under the capital value head.

The power of the Charities Branch to make *cy-près* schemes is undoubtedly one of its most useful functions. However, in practice this power is circumscribed by restrictions which obstruct its potential usefulness.

19.4.1(i) Financial restrictions

Currently, the power of the Charities Branch to prepare schemes for applying

---

[36] *Re Ffrench, De Stacpoole v. Keller* [1941] I.R. 49.
[37] *Re Currie* [1985] N.I. 299.
[38] [1943] N.I. 83.

property *cy-près* is governed by section 22 of the Charities Act 1964, its jurisdiction being limited by the monetary value of the gift.[39] The Charities Branch
can act if the value of the property is less than £50,000.[40] Prior to 1987 the
limit was £5,000. In the Republic of Ireland, the equivalent limit is set at the
much more realistic level of £250,000. In England and Wales there is no upper
monetary limit on the power of the Charity Commission to make schemes.

Given the current value of property, the lower threshold in Northern Ireland has serious implications for charities needing *cy-près* schemes. Forcing
charities with assets worth more than £50,000 into the High Court is to impose them the necessity of accepting crippling costs.

Before making a scheme, the Charities Branch must comply with a number
of procedural points. They must give notice to people who would be interested in the charity that they are making a scheme.[41] The notice must contain
particulars of the proposed scheme.[42] At least 28 days must be allowed for
objections to the proposals to be made.[43] The Charities Branch is bound to
consider these objections[44] and may give out particulars of any modifications
to their proposals.[45] The Charities Branch can then create the scheme. Within
14 days of making the scheme, they must give notice of it to any interested
persons.[46] If anyone wishes to object to the scheme they have 28 days from the
date of notice of it to appeal to the High Court.[47] If an appeal is made, the
Charities Branch must, within seven days of that appeal give notice to the
Attorney-General.[48] Generally, the schemes drafted by the Charities Branch
are uncontroversial and have not generated any appeals in recent years.

19.4.1(ii) Other restrictions

In England and Wales, the Commission can make a scheme either by order of
the court or on the application of the charity.[49] Even if the charity has not
made such an application, but the Commission is satisfied that they are unreasonable in failing to do so, they can proceed as if the charity had made that
application.[50] The Commission can disclaim this concurrent jurisdiction in

---

[39] Although see below for educational and military charities.
[40] See s. 13(1) of the Charities Act (N.I.) 1964, as modified by the Charities (N.I.) Order
1987.
[41] See s. 13 (2) of the Charities Act (N.I.) 1964.
[42] See s. 13(3)(a).
[43] See s. 13(3)(b).
[44] See s. 13(4).
[45] See s. 13(5).
[46] See s. 13(6).
[47] See s. 13(8).
[48] See s. 13(9).
[49] See s. 16(4) of the Charities Act 1993.
[50] See s. 16(6) *ibid.*

favour of the court "in any case ... which, by reason of its contentious character, or of any special question of law or fact ... the Commission may consider
more fit to be adjudicated on by the court".[51] In practice, the Charities Branch
also avail of this rule. It will disclaim jurisdiction if there is not a consensus
among the parties or if there are novel points of law involved.

19.4.1(iii) No on-going management responsibility

Once a *cy-près* scheme has been drawn up responsibility for the management
of the donor's property passes to the trustees; neither the Charities Branch nor
the court retains any residual authority in respect of the matter; new problems
will require fresh applications. In the latter event, the application or consent of
the Attorney-General is probably necessary. Once an order applying a *cy-près*
scheme has been issued, with the approval of the Attorney-General, it will not
be altered by the court on the application of an interested party[52] but will
remain in effect until either distribution of the property has been completed,
or until a new scheme for disposal has been drawn up.[53]

19.4.2 Scope of *cy-près* schemes

The *cy-près* scheme should be used for those purposes which are as close as
possible to the failed purposes. In Northern Ireland the judiciary have warned
of the dangers of subverting the donor's intentions. The courts must:

> "... beware lest they may use the rules of law and construction to carry out, not
> the testator's intention but their own subconscious prejudices."[54]

Traditionally, *cy-près* extended to changing the purposes of a gift rather than
to changing its administrative provisions. In *Re Laing*[55] the purposes of the
gift were succeeding, but the trustees wished to change some of the administrative procedures. The court held that this could not be done by *cy-près*. In
Northern Ireland the law is different. The Charities Act (N.I.) 1964 includes
the traditional *cy-près* power to alter purposes, it also gives the power to alter
"the provisions and conditions governing the application of the property for
those purposes so as to secure that the property is applied as beneficially as
possible, consistently with the spirit of the gift".[56] There is no equivalent provision in the English charities legislation. In practice, however, there may not
be much difference between the two jurisdictions. The court in *Re Laing* was

---

[51] See s. 16(10) *ibid.*
[52] See *In re Sekeford* (1861) 5 L.T. 488.
[53] See *Re Betton's Charity* [1908] 1 Ch. 205.
[54] See *Attorney General v. Forde* [1932] N.I. 1 at 14.
[55] [1984] Ch. 143.
[56] See s. 22(3)(b).

able to alter the charities administrative provisions under its inherent jurisdiction over charities.

19.4.3 *Cy-près* occasions: under equity

The traditional grounds for a *cy-près* scheme have been continued by the 1964 Act. They remain relevant and important to present practice.

Most commonly, the circumstances where the mode designated to give effect to a donor's charitable intentions could be construed as either impossible or impracticable were: where there were insufficient funds; where there was no available or suitable site; where the gift was illegal or against public policy; where there was an impracticable condition; and where a charity was deprived of objects. These circumstances were all required to meet a strict definition of impossibility or impracticability. So, for example, in *Edinburgh Corporation v. Cranston's Trustees*[57] a gift to 12 poor persons meeting certain requirements, where only two could be found, was held not to satisfy the definition of impossibility. Nor would the definition of impracticability be met where it was evident that while the gift was not immediately practicable it would in due course become so.[58] Impossibility and impracticability were rigorously applied to restrict the availability of *cy-près*.

19.4.3(i) Insufficient funds

A common cause of difficulty arises where the donor's gift is insufficient to give effect to his or her charitable intentions. Where the donor has identified a number of objects, but has provided insufficient funds to distribute among them, the court may order a *cy-près* scheme to benefit the primary object. Gifts of money intended to benefit curates,[59] or a cottage hospital,[60] or a home for aged seamen,[61] or a public hall[62] have all been applied *cy-près* due to insufficient funds.

In Northern Ireland two cases have been reported in which there was an insufficiency of funds to carry out the purpose. In *Re Simpson*[63] the gift was to found an orphanage. Gibson J. held that the "funds available are quite inadequate to found and maintain a house such as was contemplated by the testatrix even with the benefit of government grants".[64] In *Re Dunlop*,[65] which

---

[57] [1960] S.C. 244; 8(I) Digest (Reissue) 334.
[58] See *e.g.*, *Re Tacon* [1958] Ch. 447, *per* Lord Evershed M.R. at pp. 453–454.
[59] See *Re Burton's Charity* [1938] 3 All E.R. 90.
[60] See *Re Whittaker* [1951] 2 T.L.R. 955.
[61] See *Hay v. Murdoch* [1952] W.N. 145.
[62] See *Parker v. Moseley* [1965] V.R. 580.
[63] See *Re Simpson, Wallace v. Attorney General* (1974) Nov. N.I.J.B.
[64] *ibid.* at p. 2.
[65] [1984] N.I. 408.

concerned a gift for a retirement home for Presbyterians, Carswell J. stated that because of the size of the fund "whereas the purposes set out in the will were practicable at the date of his death, they have now become impracticable to put into effect".[66]

19.4.3(ii) No available or suitable site

Certain charities need premises and these need to be sited in particular areas; homes for the elderly, soup kitchens, churches, etc. are usually intended to be established in and for the benefit of specified communities. It has often been the case that the charitable intention of a donor that funds left for the purpose of building a community facility in a particular location has been thwarted by the eventual lack of an available or suitable site or a site at a reasonable cost. Where the donor's gift is clearly inadequate to fulfil the stated purpose, and there is evidence that this was evident to the donor, then the courts may take the view that the donor lacked any genuine charitable intention. So, for example, in *Re White's Trusts*,[67] where the donor knowingly left an inadequate sum stated to be for the purpose of the erection of almshouses and a suitable site could not be found, the court held that the gift failed and fell into residue like a lapsed legacy. Where donor's gift is in the form of land, subject to a condition that it be used for a specific purpose, and it is eventually found to be unsuitable for that purpose, then again the gift will fail.

Where the court can detect a primary objective it may then order a *cy-près* scheme to re-direct a gift which has become impossible or impracticable as a site for the purposes designated by the donor, to be used instead for the benefit of that primary objective.[68]

19.4.3(iii) Gift illegal or against public policy

If the donor's intention is itself illegal or against public policy then the gift is automatically impossible. For example, in *Thrupp v. Collett*,[69] the court found that a gift of money to be used for the purpose of paying the fines of persons imprisoned for offences under the game laws was against public policy as it could only encourage the further commission of such offences; so the bequest failed. However, where the charitable intention is genuine but the prescribed mode of giving effect to it is illegal or against public policy then a *cy-près* scheme can be prepared to substitute a different means for complying with the

---

[66] *Re Dunlop* at p. 412.
[67] (1886) 33 Ch. D. 449.
[68] See for example, *A-G for New South Wales v. Perpetual Trustees Co. Ltd.* (1940) 63 C.L.R.
[69] (1858) 26 Beav. 125.

donor's intentions. For example, in *Attorney General v. Vint*,[70] the donor directed that all inmates of a workhouse aged 60 or over should be supplied with porter. The court found that the charitable intention was genuine but the means of giving effect to it was illegal as alcohol in such premises was prohibited. Accordingly, it was held that the donor's charitable intention would be appropriately satisfied by supplying the inmates with other consumables.

19.4.3(iv) Impossible or impracticable conditions

A gift will also fail if some condition in it cannot be fulfilled. In *Re Stewart*,[71] one of the conditions of the gift was that the recipient Non-Subscribing Presbyterian congregation should use the "unaltered hymnbooks". Some of the current hymnbooks contained hymns which had been altered to replace Trinitarian references with Unitarian ones. The testator's purpose was to discourage Unitarianism and this end could be served by having the hymns returned to their unadulterated, pre-Unitarian condition. However, the hymns had all been considerably altered in many ways from their historical origins, the Unitarian references were only minor examples of one particular modification. No such thing as an "unaltered hymnbook", in the sense of replicating exactly the original words and music of the composer, existed. The gift was therefore impossible to fulfil.

If the gift is conditional on a certain event, where there is a subsequent failure, the property can revert back to the donee.

As well as being objectively impossible, a gift can be subjectively impossible, *i.e.* made impossible by the refusal of the donee to carry out some condition. In *Re Dunwoodie*[72] a gift in Northern Ireland for a carillon of bells was refused by the church committee on the grounds that there were more pressing needs for money. Once the committee refused, the gift was impossible. Similarly, the gift in *McCormick* v. *Queen's University Belfast*[73] was conditional on the University creating an extra-mural centre in a particular building. When the university declined to accept the building the gift then failed and was returned to the donor. According to an English authority the "right of the donor to a return of the money arises when the trust is on the face of it contingent on the proposed institute being called into being".[74] Setting a condition that money is to be returned negatives an intention to make an outright gift to charity. This was reaffirmed in *Belfast Air Raid*:[75] "once a fund has vested for charitable

---

[70] (1850) 3 De G. & Sm. 704.
[71] [1983] 11 N.I.J.B.
[72] [1977] N.I. 141.
[73] [1958] N.I. 1.
[74] *Re University of London Medical Science Centre Institute Fund* (1909) 2 Ch. 1 at 8.
[75] *Re Lord Mayor of Belfast's Air Raid Distress Fund* [1962] N.I. 161.

trusts it cannot revert to the donor or his next-of-kin unless there is a condition express or implied for reverter in a limited time".[76]

The English courts have made similar findings. In *Re Dominion Students Hall Trust*[77] the charity was set up to house Commonwealth students in London. One condition was that only students of "European origin", *i.e.* white, could benefit. The charity no longer wished to have this condition so the court held that the charity had failed and could be applied *cy-près* by removing the condition. Along the same lines, a condition prohibiting Jews or Catholics from benefiting from medical scholarships meant that the Royal College of Surgeons had to decline a gift to it. Buckley J. held, in *Re Lysaght*,[78] that this provision would not make the gift void. However, the college trustees were entitled to decline it, and the gift therefore being impracticable, could be modified by deleting the discriminatory provision.[79] This case was approved in Northern Ireland by the ruling in *Re Currie*.[80]

A gift will fail if it is wholly subject to a condition which makes it impracticable to give effect to it. In such circumstances, a *cy-près* scheme is not possible.[81] However, where the condition attaches only to a subsidiary aspect of the gift then a *cy-près* scheme will be appropriate to modify the gift by removing the condition.

For example, in *Re McGwire*[82] Black J. had regard to the will as a whole and held that a general charitable intention was disclosed but that the particular charitable purpose which directed a gift to be conferred on the St Vincent de Paul Society was impracticable and should be disregarded. He explained:

> "If the paramount intention is general charity, a particular charitable purpose may be disregarded. . . . Thus the wearing of a black gown by a clergyman was eventually ignored in *In re Robinson, Wright v. Tugwell*,[83] and in *Brantham v. East Burgold*[84] the impossibility of chanting psalms was not allowed to deprive the poor of the bread a testator had left money to distribute. Likewise, in *In re Richardson's Will*[85] the stipulation in a bequest to provide lifeboats specifying a location that turned out inappropriate was sensibly treated as an inessential detail."

He ordered that the property in question should be applied *cy-près*.

---

[76] *ibid.* at p. 168, see also *Re Tacon* (1958) Ch. 447.

[77] [1947] Ch. 183.

[78] [1966] Ch. 191.

[79] As an aside, two observations are perhaps permissible. Firstly, that charities are to a certain extent exempt from anti-discriminatory legislation (see further, Chap. 4). Secondly, no voice was raised in protest that the gift also excluded women students.

[80] [1985] N.I. 299.

[81] See for example, *Re Mitchell's Will Trusts* (1966) 110 Sol. Jo. 291.

[82] [1900] 1 I.R. 200.

[83] [1923] 2 Ch. 332.

[84] (1794) cited 2 Ves. 388; 30 E.R. 687.

[85] (1888) 58 L.T. 45.

19.4.3(v) Charity deprived of objects

There is a considerable body of case law recording the efforts of donors to confer a benefit for a good cause but one which had in fact become redundant. So, charitable intentions to benefit such socially progressive causes as the abolition of slavery, the treatment of leprosy and the ending of imprisonment for debtors were all defeated by the fact that the cause had already been eradicated by the time the gift was to take effect. Where the donor has tied a gift specifically and exclusively to a charity which is or has become devoid of any objects then the gift must fail. Where the objects exist at the time when the gift takes effect but subsequently cease then a *cy-près* scheme may well be appropriate to re-direct the gift.

For example, in *Re Hardy*,[86] there was a gift of £100 per year to a school. After the Education Act (N.I.) 1923 the school became defunct and closed down. The gift therefore failed and could be applied *cy-près*. Again, in *Re Currie*[87] a gift for the purpose of building a new church hall failed because the new church had already been built.

The issue is slightly complicated if the institution still exists, but exists in a new form, under a new name, or has amalgamated with another. In *Re Brown*[88] there was a gift to the Vegetarian Retirement Homes Ltd. That organisation had ceased to exist and its functions had been undertaken by Homes for Elderly Vegetarians Ltd. Campbell J. held that the gift failed. He would not save it by construing it as a gift for Homes for Elderly Vegetarians Ltd and applying the gift *cy-près*. In England, such gifts have been treated more leniently. For example in *Re Lucas*[89] a gift was given for the benefit of the Crippled Children's Home at Lindley Moor. Although that house had closed down, it was held that the gift could be applied to the charity which used to run it. *Re Lucas* was upheld in Northern Ireland by Girvan J. in *Re Robinson* who then considered the effect of a charitable trust changing its constitution. He held that a gift to it would not fail since the trust continued to exist, albeit on different terms. Girvan J. also cautioned against charitable trusts unilaterally changing their constitution without the consent of the court.

19.4.4 *Cy-près* occasions: under the statute

Section 22 of the Charities Act (N.I.) 1964 sets out a number of carefully differentiated occasions when property may be applied *cy-près*. Some of these are additional to those established in the courts of equity which rested on impossibility or impracticability. In other instances they overlap or duplicate

---

[86] [1933] N.I. 150.

[87] *op. cit.*

[88] *op. cit.*

[89] [1948] Ch. 424.

grounds already established. An important principle, embodied and repeated in this section, is the requirement that in seeking to give effect to a donor's charitable intentions attention should be given "to the spirit of the gift". Exactly the same *cy-près* occasions exist in England and Wales under section 13 of the Charities Act 1993.[90]

19.4.4(i) Original purposes already fulfilled

Under section 22(1) a gift has failed:

(a) where the original purposes, in whole or in part –

(i) have been as far as may be fulfilled;

Where there are surplus funds remaining after the original purpose has been fulfilled then those funds may be applied *cy-près*; this provision merely continues the law as established by equity. In *Trusts of the Rectory of St John*,[91] for example, surplus funds remained after a donor's gift towards the maintenance of the choir and choral service in Cork city cathedral had been applied for that purpose. The court directed that the surplus be applied *cy-près* for the purchase of an organ which would be an appropriate extension of the donor's original purpose.

19.4.4(ii) Original purposes cannot be carried out

Under section 22(1) a gift has failed:

(a) where the original purposes, in whole or in part –

(ii) cannot be carried out, or not according to the directions given and to the spirit of the gift;

Where an original purpose was once capable of being carried out, but ceased to be so prior to the gift taking effect, then the courts will tend to view sympathetically a suggestion that the donor had a general charitable intention.[92] However, in the Republic of Ireland, the case of *Re Prescott*[93] provides some

---

[90] Which replicates the previous provisions of s. 13 of the Charities Act 1960.

[91] (1869) I.R. 3 Eq. 335. See also, *Doyle v. Attorney General High Court*, unreported, 1993, No. 612 Sp. (Carroll J.), February 22, 1995. This case concerned the opposition of the Attorney General to a scheme for the disposal of residual funds remaining after the death of the intended beneficiary of a fundraising campaign. It was contended that the planned distribution among seven charities did not sufficiently correspond to the purpose for which the funds were initially donated. The court agreed and drew up an alternative *cy-près* scheme which directed the funds to two charities intimately connected with the disease from which the deceased had suffered.

[92] See for example, *Re Welsh Hospital (Netley) Fund* [1921] 1 Ch. 655.

[93] [1990] 2 I.R. 342. See also *Re Doherty* (1930) 64 I.L.T.R. 50.

evidence of a reluctance to apply *cy-près* in circumstances where a donor's original purpose is no longer capable of being given effect. This was a case where the testatrix bequeathed her house to a Dublin parish of the "Russian Orthodox Church abroad". She added that if there were no members of that church living in Ireland then the house should be sold and the proceeds applied for the general purposes of the said church in England. However, even before she died the primary purpose of her charitable intention was incapable of being realised because the said parish had ceased to exist. After her death the executor applied to the court for directions as to how best to proceed. MacKenzie J. held that this was not a case where *cy-près* could be applied because the donor's charitable intention was not of a general nature but was restricted to conferring a benefit on a very specific body which had ceased to exist. The gift therefore lapsed.

Where the original purpose was never capable of being carried out, perhaps because the specified object of the donor's intention never existed,[94] then the judicial approach is more liberal. As Buckley J. commented in *Re Davis*[95]:

> "… where you find a gift to a charitable institution which never existed, the Court, which always leans in favour of a charity, is more ready to infer a general charitable intention than to infer the contrary."

In the adjoining jurisdiction the cases of *Re Royal Kilmainham Hospital*[96] and *Re Worth Library*[97] both provide excellent modern examples of how a donor's charitable intention to make an "out and out gift" can be applied *cy-près* when it is no longer possible to carry out the donor's original purpose. In the latter case, this proved possible despite a judicial finding that no general charitable intention could be ascertained.

Where the original purpose has simply been wrongly described, then again the court will make the corrections necessary to give effect to the donor's intentions.[98]

In England, the case of *Re Lepton*[99] shows how the *cy-près* provisions can be used to breathe new life into charities. A trust was created in 1716 with £3 per year to support a minister and the remainder, at that time £2, for the relief of the poor. By the 1970s the trust fund had profits of £800 per year, the minister still receiving only £3. The court held that the original purposes were not being carried out according to the spirit of the gift (*i.e.* under the equivalent of

---

[94] See for example, *Daly v. Attorney-General* (1860) 11 Ir. Ch. R. 41; *Re Geary's Trusts* (1890) 25 L.R. Ir. 171; *Re Mulcahy* [1931] I.R. 239.

[95] [1902] 1 Ch. 876 at 881.

[96] [1996] I.R. 451.

[97] [1995] 2 I.R. 301; [1994] I.L.R.M. 161.

[98] See *Re Geary's Trusts* (1890) 25 L.R. Ir. 171.

[99] [1972] Ch. 276.

section 22(1)(a)(ii)) and that a *cy-près* scheme for a new division between the minister and the poor should be directed.

19.4.4(iii) Original purposes already fulfilled

Under section 22(1) a gift has failed:

> (b) where the original purposes provide a use for part only of the property available by virtue of the gift;

This provision continued the law as established by equity. The case of *Merchant Taylor's Company v. Attorney-General*[100] provides an example of the circumstances where *cy-près* may be necessary. It concerned a testator who had devised property to a company, requiring it to apply the income to certain charitable purposes. On his death, it was discovered that excessive income had been so designated and the question arose as to how the balance should be applied. The court held that the company had no discretion to use the surplus as it saw fit but must apply it for the benefit of similar charitable purposes.

19.4.4(iv) Original purposes used in conjunction with other property

Under section 22(1) a gift has failed:

> "(c) where the property available by virtue of the gift and other property applicable for similar purposes can be more effectively used in conjunction and to that end can suitably, regard being had to the spirit of the gift, be made applicable to common purposes."

This circumstance was an entirely new justification for the preparation of *cy-près* schemes without any precedent in the courts of equity. It followed from a recommendation made by the Nathan Committee and was embodied in section 13(1)(c) of the English Charities Act 1960.[101] It provides for the possibility of using the *cy-près* procedure to merge several small charities where this would result in gifts being used to greater effect.

19.4.4(v) Original purposes refer to an area or class which has ceased to be suitable or practical

Under section 22(1) a gift has failed:

> "(d) where the original purposes were laid down by reference to an area which then was but has since ceased to be a unit for some other purpose, or by reference to a class of persons or to an area which has for any reason since ceased to be suitable, regard being had to the spirit of the gift, or be practical in administering the gift."

---

[100] (1871) LR 6 Ch. 512.
[101] See Nathan Report (1952) Cmnd 8710, para. 596.

This provision represents a statutory extension to the *cy-près* grounds recognised by the courts of equity. Where what was an achievable purpose has been thwarted (*e.g.* a gift to a specified parish which has since been subsumed into another parish) then the donor's gift may be permitted to follow the purpose by a *cy-près* scheme allowing a transfer to the new parish. This, for example, was the case in *Re Bloomfield's Bequest*[102] where a clergyman was found to be entitled to an endowment originally intended for the incumbent of a parish which had merged with his. However, where there has been such a change of circumstances, the court has some discretion to authorise the preparation of a *cy-près* scheme which may be incompatible with some of the charity's principles.[103] The reference to "a class of persons" enables the court to add the test of "unsuitability" to the established tests of "impossibility" and "impracticability" when considering whether the circumstances of a case warrant an application of the *cy-près* procedure.

19.4.4(vi) Original purposes adequately provided for

Under section 22(1) a gift has failed:

> (e) where the original purposes, in whole or in part, have, since they were laid down –

> > (i) been adequately provided for by other means.

This provision also, was a new statutory addition to circumstances recognised by the courts of equity. It addresses the situation where, typically, responsibility for a community facility established and maintained by voluntary effort is assumed by a statutory body. Instead of allowing the gift to pass to the state to defer general costs, the courts may order a *cy-près* scheme to re-direct the gift to benefit a cause similar to that specified by the donor.

19.4.4(vii) Original purposes ceased to be charitable

Under section 22(1) a gift has failed:

> (e) where the original purposes, in whole or in part, have, since they were laid down –

> > (ii) ceased, as being useless or harmful to the community or for other reasons to be in law charitable;

This was another entirely new addition to established *cy-près* occasions. It was not recognised by the courts of equity. Although there is no body of case law on the rare situations of charities which have ceased to engage in charita-

---

[102] (1920) 54 I.L.T.R. 213.
[103] See *Re Shillelagh Parochial School* [1900] 1 N.I.J.R. 206.

ble purposes, it has long been recognised that where an original purpose is impossible or illegal then the gift may be applied *cy-près*.[104] So a gift to "further the development of the Irish Republic" was held by a New York court to be against public policy as it was likely to draw the United States into difficult relations with the U.K., a friendly state.

Similarly, *cy-près* has been seen as appropriate in situations where the original purpose cannot be fulfilled because the intended recipient/s never existed or could not be identified.[105]

19.4.4(viii) Original purposes ceased in any other way to be suitable and effective

Under section 22(1) a gift has failed:

> (e) where the original purposes, in whole or in part, have, since they were laid down –
>
>> (iii) ceased in any other way to provide a suitable and effective method of using the property available by virtue of the gift, regard being had to the spirit of the gift.

Again, this type of situation was not one which was previously provided for in law. It is not enough that an alternative means of giving effect to the donor's purpose is available which would make more effective use of his gift. It must be shown that the actual means specified by the donor is no longer suitable or effective. In considering whether a limitation on the use of the gift, imposed by the donor, is of such a nature that it may be appropriately removed by a *cy-près* scheme, the Charities Branch will place great weight on "the spirit of the gift.

In this jurisdiction, the case of *Re Dunwoodie*[106] provides an illustration of the type of circumstance that would fall within the terms of this provision. This was a case that concerned the gift for the express purpose of installing bells in a specified Presbyterian Church. The Church did not want bells to be installed and the issue brought before the court was whether the gift could be applied *cy-près* for the benefit of the Church. Murray J. held that as the testatrix had shown a general intention to benefit the specific Church, the failure of her chosen method of doing so should not invalidate the gift which would be

---

[104] See for example, *Attorney-General v. Vint* (1850) 3 De G. & Sm. 704; *Incorporated Society v. Price* (1844) 1 Jon. & Lat. 498; and *Re Trusts of the Rectory of St John's* (1869) I.R. 3 Eq. 335.

[105] See for example, *Daly v. Attorney-General* (1860) 11 I.C.R. 41; *Re Quinlan's Trusts* (1876) 10 I.L.T. & S.J. 424; *Re Davis* [1902] 11 Ch. 876; *Re Harwood* [1936] 1 Ch. 285; *Re Knox* [1937] Ch. 109; *Pepper v. Attorney-General* as cited in (1878) 1 L.R. Ir. 116; and *Re Preston's Estate* [1951] Ch. 878.

[106] [1977] N.I. 141. In Ireland, see, *Representative Church Body v. Attorney General* [1988] I.R. 19.

applied *cy-près* (see, further below). Again, in *Re Steele*,[107] among the conditions attached to a gift of land to the Church of Ireland was a stipulation that the land should not be sold and that a caretaker was to occupy a house. Murray J. held that these conditions meant the property would cease to be used in an effective manner, consequently it was appropriate to apply the gift *cy-près* under section 22(1)(e)(iii).

In England, the equivalent to section 22(1)(e)(iii)[108] has been used in an attempt to resolve a dispute between members of a religious charity. The case of *Varsani v. Jesani*[109] resulted from a schism which had split the membership of a Hindu sect. The two rival branches applied for a scheme to exclude the other from worshipping at a temple. It was argued that the court should enquire into which side had broken faith with the original precepts of the sect, since this was a necessary prerequisite to the application of the *cy-près* jurisdiction. The Court of Appeal held that it was not necessary to show that the original purposes were impossible or impracticable. In a very sensible judgement they held that they could not arbitrate in matters of faith, but that it was plain that the original gift was not being used suitably or effectively. Consequently they ordered a *cy-près* scheme to divide the assets of the charity between the two branches of the sect.

19.4.5 Original purposes

Evidence as to what precisely are the "original purposes" of a gift is easier to garner for judges in Northern Ireland than for their English counterparts. Section 22(4) of the Charities Act (N.I.) 1964 states that the court or Charities Branch "may take into account the conduct, and any habits or actions, of the donor and any written or oral declarations made by him at any time in relation to the gift". There is no equivalent subsection in the English legislation. In *Re Lepton*[110] it was suggested that the "original purposes" should be ascertained by looking at the charitable purposes as a whole. In Northern Ireland, the approach is conducive to a more well-rounded view of the donor's intention by explicitly allowing the use of evidence extrinsic to explain the nature and context of the actual gift.

19.4.6 Widening geographical areas

Finally, the English legislation has an additional but minor clause which does not feature in the equivalent legislation of this jurisdiction. Section 13(4) of the Charities Act 1993 explicitly states that the geographical area of certain

---

[107] [1976] N.I. 66.
[108] s. 13(1)(e)(iii) of the Charities Act 1993.
[109] [1999] 1 W.L.R. 255.
[110] See *Re Lepton's Charity, Ambler v. Thomas* [1971] 1 All E.R. 799.

trusts can be widened. Schedule 3 of that Act lists these areas together with their possible enlargements. For example a gift for a certain district can be widened to include part of an adjacent district.

19.5 THE *CY-PRÈS* DOCTRINE AND A GENERAL CHARITABLE INTENTION

A general charitable intention, as opposed to one expressed in a particular form, is an essential pre-requisite for the preparation of a *cy-près* scheme. The difference being, as explained by Buckley J. in *Re Lysaght*[111]:

> "A general charitable intention, then, may be said to be a paramount intention on the part of a donor to effect some charitable purpose which the court can find a method of putting into operation, notwithstanding that it is impracticable to give effect to some direction by the donor which is not an essential part of his true intention – not, that is to say, part of his paramount intention.
>
> In contrast, a particular charitable intention exists where the donor means his charitable disposition to take effect if, but only if, it can be carried into effect in a particular specified way, for example, in connection with a particular school to be established at a particular place, *In re Wilson*,[112] or by establishing a home in a particular house: *In re Packe*."[113]

19.5.1 General charitable intention: the requirement

The rule is that the donor must have shown a general charitable intention in order for the *cy-près* jurisdiction to be applicable. There must be evidence that he or she was not intending to restrict the gift to a specific object to the exclusion of all others. In determining whether or not the donor had a general charitable intention the court will construe the document setting up the charitable trust as a whole.

It should also be noted that where the issue of the existence or otherwise of a donor's general charitable intention is not raised then, as in *Representative Church Body v. Attorney General*[114] (see below), it may be that the matter will be resolved by simple judicial approval of a *cy-près* scheme application.

19.5.1(i) Definition

Chatterton V.-C., in *Re Templemoyle Agricultural School*,[115] offered the following definition of this term and its significance:

---

[111] [1966] 1 Ch. 191, *per* Buckley J. at 202. Quoted by Carswell J. in *Re Currie* [1985] N.I. 299 in the course of a useful survey of judicial interpretations of "charitable intention".

[112] [1913] 1 Ch. 314 *per* Parker J.

[113] [1918] 1 Ch. 437.

[114] [1988] I.R. 19.

[115] (1869) I.R. 4 E.Q. 295 at 301.

"It does not mean merely an intention to give charity [*sic*] generally, without reference to any specified object, but it means an intention the substance of which is charitable, whether generally and without any specified object, in which case the Crown will prescribe the mode of effectuating it, or for an object more or less accurately specified, but with a mode of benefiting that object superadded, which cannot be lawfully or at all carried into execution, in which case the Court will carry out the substantial intention."

Basically, the more probable it is that the donor must have had a specific object in mind, to the exclusion of all possible others, then the stronger the likelihood that the court will find that a general charitable intention did not exist. It will, therefore be debarred from authorising the application of a *cy-près* scheme.

There are some indicators have in the past provided judicial guidance to determine appropriate circumstances for *cy-près*.

The first general rule is that the more specific the gift, the less likely there is a general charitable intention. In *Re Simpson*[116] the gift was simply for a Protestant orphanage for boys; with no provisions as to its constitution. The court held the testatrix "has not circumscribed the gift with stipulations or conditions which could be described as fundamental".[117] The gift was applied *cy-près*. In England, the case of *Re Harwood*[118] illustrates this point well. There were three gifts in that case, to the Wisbech Peace Society, Cambridge, to the Belfast Peace Society and to the Dublin Peace Society. The court held that, for the first gift "where the testator selects as the object of his bounty a particular entity and shows in the will itself some care to identify the particular society"[119] there could be no general charitable intention. This approach was applied to several of the gifts in *Re Brown*. For example, in the case of a gift to the Vegetarian Home for Children, "the testator has selected a particular charity and identified it and it ceased to exist in his lifetime. The gift is specific and therefore I do not find any general charitable intent and so the gift fails".[120]

The second rule is that if a gift is to an organisation which never existed, it is strong evidence of general charitable intention. In *Re Harwood,* the Belfast and Dublin Peace Societies had never existed. The judge found that this showed a general intention to benefit charity and that the particular mode was not fundamental. One of the gifts in *Re Brown* was to a body which never existed, however this was not taken as evidence of a general charitable intention, since the organisation was named with particular accuracy.

The third general rule can be expressed as "charity by association". If all

---

[116] *op. cit.*
[117] *Re Simpson* at p. 6.
[118] [1936] Ch. 285.
[119] *Re Harwood* at p. 287.
[120] *Re Brown* at p. 7 of transcript.

the gifts in a will are to charity, it is much easier to prove a general charitable intention. In *Re Simpson* the court gave weight to the fact that the only capital gifts in the will were to charity. In the English case of *Re Satterthwaite*[121] a gift was made to the London Animal Hospital, a body which no longer existed. As the majority of the remaining gifts in the will were to animal charities, the court was able to find a general charitable intention.

19.5.1(ii) Intention

It is the intention that is all important. The fact that the purpose has not been clearly and specifically identified will not prevent the making of a *cy-près* scheme if there is certainty that the donor had a charitable intention. Where there is such certainty then a *cy-près* scheme will be drawn up.

A general charitable intention is a condition precedent for an order of *cy-près*. The essence of a general charitable intention is that the specifics of a particular gift are subservient to the overriding or paramount charitable intention of the donor, so that if the particular gift fails, the property can be applied to a similar charitable object. As explained in *Re Willis*[122]:

> "... the failure of the particular mode in which the charitable intention is to be effectuated shall not imperil the charitable gift, if substantial intention is charitable, the court will substitute some other mode of carrying it into effect."[123]

Again, in *Re Lysaght*[124]:

> "... a paramount intention on the part of the donor to effect some charitable purpose which the court can find a method of putting into operation, notwithstanding that it is impracticable to give effect to some direction of the donor which is not an essential part of his true intention."[125]

Evidence of a donor's intention may be crucial. In determining the existence of a general charitable intention the court may have regard to the whole will or other instrument including the terms for distribution of all void gifts.[126] Oral evidence will be admitted, in the absence of written specific directions, to prove a donor's intentions.[127] Extrinsic evidence[128] or evidence as to the testator's family circumstances may also be taken into account.[129]

---

[121] [1966] 1 W.L.R. 277.
[122] [1921] 1 Ch. 44.
[123] *ibid.* at p. 54.
[124] [1966] 1 Ch. 191.
[125] *ibid.* at p. 202.
[126] See *Re McGwire* [1941] I.R 33.
[127] See *Re Watters* [1963] V.R. 256.
[128] See *Re Ulverston and District New Hospital Building Fund* [1956] Ch. 622.
[129] See *Re Simpson*, (1974) Nov. N.I.J.B.

19.5.1(iii) Primary and secondary purposes

Where the charitable intention is of secondary importance to a donor's primary purpose then this also will be insufficient to warrant a *cy-près* scheme. This was the case in *Re Ffrench; De Stacpoole v. Keller*[130] where the testatrix had devised Monivea castle "to the Irish Nation as a home for aged and indigent teachers". The Attorney-General applied for an order of *cy-près* on the grounds that insufficient funds existed to give effect to the testatrix's purpose. Gavan Duffy J., however, considered that:

> "... the will, far from showing charity as the paramount object of the gift, actually reveals the preservation of the Castle of Minevia and its extensive demesne and plantations, a non-charitable object, as the purpose on which Miss Ffrench had set her heart, and the plan for the charity in the Castle as quite subsidiary."

He held that the testatrix's purpose had been mainly to preserve the castle rather than to give effect to a charitable intention. The *cy-près* application failed. Where the evidence points to a lack of genuine charitable intention then the courts will decline to order a *cy-près* scheme.

19.5.1(iv) Conditions

Where a donor attaches a condition to a gift then a question arises as to its bearing on the exact nature of the charitable intention.

In Ireland, for example, in *In re the Worth Library*[131] Keane J considered the effect of the donor's instruction that the gift of the library be restricted to the physician, surgeon and chaplain of the hospital "who alone would have access to the room in which the library was housed". He concluded that as this was a condition "which the testator wished to be complied with to the letter" it was therefore a condition precedent to the vesting of the gift and, by clearly limiting the benefit of his gift in this way, the donor had obviated any possible interpretation of his intention as being to confer a public benefit.

In Northern Ireland, however, Murray J. in *Re Steele*[132] held that a condition requiring the upkeep of a family burial plot was merely a precatory condition which did not invalidate an otherwise charitable trust.

In England the case of *Re Lysaght*[133] provides a useful illustration of the effect of unreasonable conditions (see also above). The will of a testatrix made provision for students of the Royal College of Surgeons of England subject to certain conditions among which was the stipulation that the subjects be "not of the Jewish or Roman Catholic faith". The college would only accept the gift if that stipulation could be removed. Buckley J held that not to remove the

---

[130] [1941] I.R. 49. See also, *Re McGwire, op. cit.*
[131] [1994] 1 I.L.R.M. 161.
[132] *op. cit.*
[133] *op. cit.*

clause would nullify the paramount charitable intention of the donor. In order
to save the gift from failing due to the effect of a subsidiary clause, he directed
that a *cy-près* scheme be drawn up which would exclude that clause.

Again, in Northern Ireland, a similar approach is discernible in *Re Stewart's
Will Trusts*[134] where again a judicial direction was given that a subsidiary and
"ill-considered" clause could be removed because only then could effect be
given to the donor's primary charitable intention.

19.5.2 Exceptions to the general charitable intention requirement

Exceptions to the general charitable intention rule have been recognised because, as explained by Meredith J in *Governors of Erasmus Smith School v.
AG*[135]:

> "... donors cannot be expected to provide expressly for more than the world
> and the time with which they are familiar."

A more permissive approach to a retrospective analysis of the possible scope
of a donor's intentions was strengthened by the direction in section 22(1)(e)(iii)
of the 1964 Act that in interpreting a donor's original purposes regard should
be had "to the spirit of the gift".

19.5.2(i) Exceptions: supervening failure

Where a donor makes a gift, but subsequent circumstances either prevent the
gift from vesting or prevent it from continuing to vest, then the question of
whether or not the gift was initially made with a general charitable intent is
beside the point when considering the appropriateness of a *cy-près* scheme.
This may arise, as Wylie points out[136]:

> "... where the purpose ceases to exist after the gift (being an absolute one) has
> taken effect,[137] whether because an institution has ceased to exist or its objects
> have come to an end,[138] or where a surplus is left over after providing for a
> particular purpose."[139]

---

[134] [1983] N.I. 283.

[135] (1932) 66 I.L.T. 57.

[136] See Wylie, J.C.W., *Irish Land Law* (3rd ed., Butterworths, 1997), para. 9.1o7.

[137] See for example, *Munster and Leinster Bank Ltd v. AG* (1957), 91 I.L.T. 34. *Cf Re
Hardy* [1933] N.I. 150.

[138] See *McCormick v. QUB* [1958] N.I. 1; *Re The Worth Library* [1995] 2 I.R. 301. See
also, Hickling "Destination of Funds of Defunct Voluntary Organisations" (1966) 30
Conv. 117.

[139] See *Re Trusts of Rectory of St John in City of Cork* (1869) I.R. 3 Eq. 335; *Attorney-
General v. Forde* [1932] N.I. 1; *Re Royal Kilmainham Hospital* [1966] I.R. 451. See
also, Winder "The *Cy-près* Applications of Surplus Charitable Funds" (1941) 5 Conv.
198.

In *Re Slevin*,[140] for example, concerned a gift to an orphanage which had been in existence when the testator died. In principle, the money was therefore effectually dedicated to charity. When the estate came to be administered the orphanage had closed. The court held that it was a case of supervening failure.[141] In Northern Ireland, Murray J. in *In re Dunwoodie*[142] explained the significance of the "supervening failure" rule as follows:

> "There is an important difference between a charitable trust which is initially impossible or impracticable, i.e. impossible or impracticable as at the death of the testator, and a charitable trust which becomes impossible or impracticable after his death. As regards the former type, the property involved will not be applied *cy-près* unless the court finds that the testator had a general charitable intention, but as regards the second type – usually referred to as the case of supervening impossibility – the court will direct a *cy-près* application whether or not a general charitable intention can be found in the relevant will."

If a gift is made in a will, the relevant date to determine supervening failure is the date of death. If the gift is possible at death and subsequently becomes impossible, it is supervening failure.[143] If it is a gift in remainder or reversion, the relevant date is the date it vests in remainder or reversion.[144]

19.5.2(ii) Exceptions: "out and out" gifts

An absolute and perpetual (or "out and out') gift is excluded from the rule requiring evidence of a general charitable intention where the impossibility or impracticability of carrying out the intention only becomes evident after the donor's death. The operative date for determining whether or not such circumstances have arisen is the date of the testator's death. As stated in *Re Wright*[145]:

> "Once money is effectually dedicated to charity … residuary legatees are for ever excluded and no question of subsequent lapse, or anything analogous to lapse, between the date of the testators death and the time when money becomes available for actual application to the testator's purpose can affect the matter."[146]

When the property is given out and out to charity it cannot be claimed back at a later stage.

---

[140] [1891] 2 Ch. 236. In Ireland, see *Munster and Leinster Bank, Ltd. v. AG, op. cit.*

[141] *op. cit.*

[142] *op. cit.* at p.145.

[143] *Re White's Will Trusts* [1955] Ch. 188.

[144] *Re Tacon* [1958] Ch. 477.

[145] [1954] Ch. 347.

[146] *ibid.* at p. 364 cited with approval in Northern Ireland in *Re Dunwoodie, op. cit.* In Ireland, see, *Re Royal Kilmainham Hospital, op. cit., per* Budd J. at p. 469, quoted with approval by Keane J. in *Re The Worth Library, op. cit.*

In Northern Ireland two exceptions to this rule have been argued. Firstly if the gift is for a particular purpose which has been carried out it has been argued that the gift should revert back to the donors. This usually happens in the context of disaster appeals. Secondly if a gift is conditional on a certain event, it is argued that no outright gift has been made.

19.5.2(iii) Exceptions: the sign manual procedure

It may be evident that a donor had the requisite general charitable intention but that no appointment of a trustee was made. In such circumstances the state will be appointed trustee and the gift then administered in accordance with the sign manual procedure. This in fact occurred in the case of *Merrins v. AG*[147] where the testatrix, in a home made will, left property for "charity" but did not appoint a trustee. Black J. ordered the surviving executor to submit a memorial to the government for the ascertainment of "the government's will and pleasure" as to the application of the property.

19.6 CY-PRÈS, COMPLETED PURPOSES AND DISASTER APPEALS

If property is given to a certain purpose and that purpose is completed, the donor is entitled to a return of his property. In Tudor[148] it is stated that:

> "… in most cases, an identifiable donor with a particular charitable intention is entitled to the return of his contribution in full."[149]

In such situations there has been no outright gift to charity, merely a gift limited to a certain purpose and no other purpose. The gift has not failed, it has been successful, its purpose has been completed and the donor is entitled to the return of his gift. Considerable difficulties have arisen, both in Northern Ireland and in England, when this situation has occurred in the context of funds for disaster relief.

19.6.1 The *Belfast Air Raid*[150] case

In this Northern Ireland case the court gave detailed consideration to the issues involved. The fund in question was launched on April 16, 1941 and donations were received from that date. The trusts constituting the fund were created on April 22, 1941. The trusts declared the purpose as relieving the distress of those suffering due to the air raids and contained the power to

---

[147] [1945] 79 I.L.T. 121.
[148] Tudor (1995).
[149] *ibid.* at p. 421.
[150] *Re Lord Mayor of Belfast's Air Raid Distress Fund* [1962] N.I. 161.

distribute any surplus to other charitable ends. The post trust donations caused no legal problems. *Cy-près* would not arise since the trusts contained a power to devote the surplus to other charitable purposes, there was no failure. The difficulty was caused by donations received before the trusts were created.

It was argued that these donations were for a single charitable purpose (relieving air raid distress in Belfast) and that since that purpose was completed, the donors should be entitled to a return of their money. McVeigh J. disposed of this argument on two alternative grounds. Firstly, he held that the pre-April 22 donations were bound by that trust and, since it contained directions as to surplus, the money went as directed. He based this finding on English cases where large numbers of donors had contributed to funds. The courts had then held that, rather than attempting to ascertain the intentions of each individual donor, they would look to the intention of the people who created the fund. As stated in *Attorney General v. Clapham*,[151] where:

> "… such a direction is made by the persons in whom the property is vested, at or about the time when the sums have been raised, that declaration may reasonably be taken *prima facie* as a true exposition of the minds of the contributors."[152]

McVeigh J.'s alternative finding was that, if the pre-trust donations were not bound by the trust, there had been an outright gift to charity, that gift had now failed, therefore the money should be applied *cy-près*. McVeigh J., reflecting on the English case law, noted that "the law relating to this doctrine in relation to charities cannot be said to be in a very satisfactory state".[153]

19.6.2 The English cases

The decision in *Re North Devon and West Somerset Relief Fund Trusts*[154] lends most support to the outcome in *Belfast Air Raid*. The fund in that case was created for the relief of those who had suffered in the serious floods of 1952. Once that purpose was met there was a residual surplus; the facts were therefore analogous to *Belfast Air Raid*. The judge decided the donors had intended to make an out and out charitable gift and therefore the money would be applied *cy-près*. By contrast, *Re Ulverston and District New Hospital Building Trusts*[155] is more consonant with the principle that gifts for specific purposes should be returned to donors on failure of that purpose. The trusts were provided for the purpose of building a new hospital. When that became im-

---

[151] (1855) 4 De G., M. & G. 591. See also *Attorney General v. Mathieson* (1907) 2 Ch. 383 for a similar decision.
[152] *ibid.* at p. 626.
[153] *Belfast Air Raid* at p. 167.
[154] [1953] 1 W.L.R. 1260.
[155] [1956] Ch. 622.

possible (due to the National Health Service), the money was returned to the donors on a resulting trust.

19.6.3 Reconciling jurisdictional differences

The solution to reconciling these differences seems to be the timing of the failure/completion. In *Belfast Air Raid* the money had been applied to charitable ends, and after these failed, there was a surplus. In *Re Welsh Hospital*[156] the surplus of a fund created to build a hospital could be applied *cy-près*. In *Re Wokingham Fire Brigade Trusts*[157] there was a surplus of the fire brigade's funds after the fire brigade was disbanded and again the fund could be applied *cy-près*. In all these cases, the funds had already been applied in some way to the charitable purpose before that purpose failed or was completed. The judge in *Wokingham* said:

> "... in the event of a surplus being left over after that purpose had been duly fulfilled, any share in such surplus which might be regarded as representing his [i.e. the donor's] subscription or some part thereof should be permanently dedicated to charity."[158]

However, even this solution fails to satisfactorily explain the distinction between gifts which subsequently become incapable of completion and gifts whose purposes are subsequently completed.[159]

19.6.4 Anonymous donations; case law

What difference does it make to *cy-près* if the donors are anonymous? Two English cases dealing with initial failure have given divergent answers. In *Re Gillingham Bus Disaster Fund*[160] the court held that upon failure, money would revert to the donors on a resulting trust and if the donors were unidentified, the money would be paid into court. But in *Re West Sussex Constabulary Benevolent Fund*[161] the court held that anonymous donors give money as an absolute transfer and do not expect it back, therefore such gifts would be applied *cy-près* rather than be held by the court. In *Re Ulverston* it was held that where there were anonymous and identified donors contributing to the same fund, this was evidence that the identified donors were making an outright gift or had a general charitable intention.

---

[156] [1921] 1 Ch. 655.
[157] [1921] 1 Ch. 655.
[158] *ibid.*
[159] See further, the Attorney General's Guidelines on Disaster Appeals, reprinted as Charity Commission Leaflet CC40.
[160] [1959] Ch. 62.
[161] [1971] Ch. 1.

19.6.5 Anonymous donations; statute

Section 23 of the Charities Act (N.I.) 1964[162] was designed to address the problem of the failure of charitable gifts from anonymous donors. Although promulgated for the situation of initial failure, it is equally applicable to subsequent failure. It allows gifts to be applied *cy-près* if the following conditions are fulfilled.

- Initial gift was for a specific charitable purpose (section 23(1)) and,
- Donor cannot be found after reasonable advertisements and inquiries (section 23(1)(a)) or,
- Donor has provided a written disclaimer of his rights (section 23(1)(b)).

Certain donations are conclusively taken, without any adverts, etc., to have come from anonymous donors if they are:

- From cash collections which do not distinguish between the sources of money (section 23(2)(a)) or,
- From the proceeds of any lottery, competition, sale or similar money raising activity (section 23(2)(b)).

The courts or Charities Branch have the power to direct that other donations are similarly conclusively taken to be from anonymous donors, without any inquiries being necessary if:

- The size of the gift makes it uneconomical to attempt to find a donor to return it to (section 23(3)(a)) or,
- It would be unreasonable for the donor to expect money to be returned (section 23(3)(b)).

If the charity in question has made reasonable inquiries but failed to identify the donor, it must note what amount of money came from anonymous sources. If an anonymous donor subsequently comes forward, he can request a return of the money so long as not more than 6 months have elapsed from the date of the *cy-près* scheme being made.[163] These provisions are retrospective and apply to charitable gifts made before the commencement of the Act.[164]

The English equivalent provisions are effectively the same except that they are more detailed. In particular section 14(6) of the Charities Act 1993 states that if the anonymous donors come forward to make a claim, but insufficient money is present, they shall each be entitled to a proportion of their contribution. In addition, the Commission has the power to make regulations prescrib-

---

[162] In England, s. 14 of the Charities Act 1993 which contained provisions from s. 14 of the Charities Act 1960 as amended by s. 15 of the Charities Act 1992.
[163] See s. 23(4) of the Charities Act (N.I.) Act 1964.
[164] See s. 23(7).

ing the form, content and time limits for advertisements and inquiries regarding the anonymous donors.[165]

19.7 EDUCATIONAL CHARITIES

Legislation has attached three extra *cy-près* rules to educational charities.

19.7.1 Residential accommodation

The first rule is straightforward. Where a teacher's residence, owned for charitable educational purposes, is no longer required to further the functions of any school, there is no monetary limit to the *cy-près* rule.[166] This was an attempt to streamline administrative procedures. Most residences of this type were valued above the monetary jurisdiction of the Charities Branch. Whenever a charitable gift failed, the gift could only be applied *cy-près* on application to the court. Because there were a considerable number of this type of gift, dealing with similar issues, it was felt to be more efficient if they could be dealt with outside the jurisdiction of the court. Consequentially this provision was enacted in the Education Order. Most residences of this type have now been disposed of.

19.7.2 Alteration of original schemes

The second rule is technically not *cy-près* at all. The Educational Endowments (Ireland) Act 1885 sought to reorganise charitable donations under the education head. The power to make new schemes expired on August 31, 1897, but schemes made before then still exist and can and are altered. A scheme could have provided for its alteration by the Commissioners of Charitable Bequests and Donations for Ireland. After the Charities Branch assumed these functions, it now has the power to make schemes for altering such original schemes. In *Re Townsend Street Belfast Presbyterian Endowment Trusts*[167] the court gave judicial approval to the alteration of a scheme by the Charities Branch where the purposes of the educational charity had failed. It had been argued that the property should devolve *cy-près* as directed by the court but it was held that statutory provisions already existed for altering the purposes and therefore *cy-près* was not required.

---

[165] See the Charities (*Cy-près* Advertisements, Inquiries and Disclaimer) Regulations 1993.
[166] Art. 90(7) of the Education and Libraries (N.I.) Order 1986.
[167] [1954] N.I. 53.

19.7.3 Non-educational charities

The third rule creates a loophole in the law of *cy-près* which has not been used in any of the reported cases and has perhaps never been used. It states that a non-educational charity, whose purposes have in some way failed, may consent to the endowment being treated as an educational endowment. The failure of a gift, instead of resulting in a standard *cy-près* application, may allow the governing body of the endowment to apply it to educational purposes.

The initial gift need not even be charitable, as long as it fails it can be applied to a charity under the education head. In addition, the range of events constituting failure is arguably broader than the traditional *cy-près* definition. As stated in the statute, these will include cases where:

> "... there are no persons who are entitled to benefit out of the endowment, or if the purposes of the endowment have failed altogether, or have become obsolete or useless, or are otherwise sufficiently provided for, or are insignificant in comparison with the magnitude of the endowment, or are, in the opinion of the governing body, not substantially beneficial to the class of persons for whom such endowment was originally intended, or if it has been found impossible, either from the inadequacy of the endowment or the impracticable character of the founders intentions, to carry these into effect."[168]

The Charities Branch also has the power to consent to endowments being treated in this way.

19.8 Military Charities

Under section 149 of the Reserve Forces Act 1980 special *cy-près* rules exist for charities for the benefit of the reserve forces.

19.8.1 Application

This section applies to units of the Territorial Army, the Army Reserve or the Royal Auxiliary Air Force which are successor units to those which have been disbanded or amalgamated. Any charitable property held for the benefit of the old unit shall be held for the benefit of the successor unit.[169] This provision is not strictly speaking *cy-près*, but it does provide for a very straightforward application of a charitable gift when the designated object no longer exists. A copy of the warrant disbanding the old unit and designating the successor unit must be delivered to the Charities Branch as soon as it is made. Section 149(1) may be disapplied by the Charities Branch if they think it is not appropriate

---

[168] See s. 9 of the Educational Endowments (Ireland) Act 1885.
[169] See s. 149(1) of the Reserve Forces Act 1980.

that the successor unit benefits from the old unit's charity. The Charities Branch has six months, from the date of the warrant, to make this disapplying order.[170] Under this provision the charity itself, a trustee or an interested person can within the same period seek permission of the court to disapply. Under section 29(3) of the Charities Act (N.I.) 1964, the consent of the Attorney-General to make application is also required.

Cy-près proper can be applied under section 149(6) of the 1980 Act. *Cy-près* will occur either where an order to disapply section 149(1) has been made[171] or where the Secretary of State requests the Charities Branch to make provision for charitable property held for the benefit of a reserve unit which has disbanded.[172] In such circumstances, the £50,000 monetary limit to the jurisdiction of the Charities Branch is not relevant. The terms of section 149 will not apply if the interests of the charity in the property terminates whenever the unit disbands (*i.e.* they have a conditional interest), and another person becomes entitled to the property on the disbandment of that unit.[173]

Section 149 replicates almost exactly the provisions in section 147 of the equivalent English legislation. There is only one slight procedural difference: if a charity applies to the Charity Commission for permission to bring proceedings disapplying section 147(1) (charitable property automatically held for the benefit of the new unit), and the Commission does not grant permission within one month, it is deemed that permission has been refused.

---

[170] See s. 149(3).
[171] See s. 149(6)(a).
[172] See s. 149(6)(b).
[173] See s. 149(7).

CHAPTER 20

Tax Exemption

20.1 INTRODUCTION

The law places charitable trusts in a privileged position regarding taxation. All charities are eligible for tax relief. Eligibility for a range of tax exemptions has long been a primary reason for acquiring charitable status and it remains the case that there is little point in seeking recognition as a charity other than to claim tax exemption. But no one statute or statutory provision governs eligibility for relief, authority must be sought across the range of tax legislation. Nor is relief available in relation to all taxes, there are exceptions in relation to some aspects of value added tax.

The tax relief assiduously pursued by thousands of charities results in an annual loss of many millions of pounds to the Inland Revenue. The issue of whether this loss is sufficiently offset by the gains generated through charitable activity is a moot point. It has been stated that "freedom from taxation is not a form of subsidy".[1] Arguably, as both charities and the government spend money on public purposes, it is counter-productive to take from one to give to the other.

This chapter looks at the range of charitable exemptions from various taxes: income tax, capital gains tax, inheritance tax, stamp duty and value added tax. Of these, income tax is probably the most important both in terms of size, historical lineage and its use as gatekeeper for other exemptions. Rates, another form of tax, is sufficiently different to warrant being treated separately (see Chapter 21).

This chapter considers tax from the perspective of charity and donor, whether either be an individual or company. It also examines the changes to the system resulting from the *Getting Britain Giving*[2] initiative and culminating in the April 2000 budget.

20.2 TAX AND CHARITIES: HISTORY AND CONTEMPORARY STATUS

The association between charities and tax exemption has an extensive history.

---

[1] Tenth Report from the Expenditure Committee Session 1974-75, Charity Commissioners and their Accountability, Vol. II 250.
[2] Launched by the government on November 9, 1999 with effect from April 2000; see further, para. 20.3.2.

It is no coincidence that for the past century the most significant judgment in the charity law of this and other jurisdictions has been and remains the ruling given by the House of Lords in a case concerning tax exemption.[3] In recent years contention has grown regarding the privileged tax status of charities. There is a general concern that fiscal privileges be balanced by adequate systems for ensuring probity and accountability in the management of charity finances.

20.2.1 History

In feudal times, gifts were often made to religious/charitable institutions to be held for ever (mortmain) to avoid the payment of feudal dues. Typically the government would respond:

> "... no person, religious or other, whatsoever he be that will buy or sell any lands or tenements, or by any other craft or engine will presume to appropriate to himself, under pain of forfeiture of the same, whereby such lands or tenements may any wise come into mortmain."[4]

Exemption from liability for tax for bodies pursuing charitable purposes dates back to at least the mid-nineteenth century.[5] In England and Wales, judicial endorsement of statutory principle came with the decision in *Income Tax Special Purposes Commissioners v. Pemsel*[6] which confirmed that charitable status in itself conferred an automatic entitlement to tax exemption. This was followed by the decision of Palles C.B. in *Clancy v. Commissioner of Valuation*[7] which extended the House of Lords ruling to this island. Subsequent developments in the law relating to charities, whether initiated judicially or by legislation, have left the legal status of charities undisturbed. In this jurisdiction the legal standing of charities is given such recognition as they have solely through their relationship with the Inland Revenue.

20.2.2 Importance of the tax regime in Northern Ireland

Tax has a special importance in Northern Ireland since it constitutes the most significant source of charitable regulation. The Inland Revenue performs the function of a registration system by granting or recognising a body as having charitable status. In the submission of annual tax repayment claims and in the occasional auditing of accounts, it carries out a regulatory and monitoring

---

3   *Income Tax Special Purposes Commissioners v. Pemsel* [1891] A.C. 531.
4   7 Edw. I Stat. 2 *de viris religiosis.*
5   Such exemption has been dated to the introduction of income tax by William Pitt; specifically s. 5 of the Income Tax Act 1799; see, further, Tudor, *Charities* (8th ed., Sweet & Maxwell, 1995) at p. 282.
6   *op. cit.*
7   [1911] 2 I.R. 447.

role. In England and Wales, the Charity Commission to a certain degree have undertaken these functions, in Northern Ireland this remains with the taxing bodies.

20.3 THE PRINCIPLES AND POLICY GOVERNING CHARITY TAXATION

There are three basic principles, applying to all the various tax regimes, and there is now also a significant government policy initiative which is re-shaping charitable tax exemption.

20.3.1 The three principles

- Burden of proof. Charities *per se* do not enjoy any special rights to exemption from tax. Each must qualify for a specific exemption under the relevant legislation. The onus rests on each charity to bring itself within one of these exemptions otherwise it must, like any person, pay tax.[8]
- Interpretation of "charity". The *Pemsel*[9] case established that if an exemption was described as being for a "charity" then it applied to all charities without restriction. This reasoning was vigorously reasserted by the House of Lords in the Northern Ireland case of *Campbell College*[10] which held that "educational charity" in a rating context was not limited to education charities for the benefit of the poor. This single, unified meaning is now tempered by the constrained exemption for charities under the VAT legislation.
- Commonality of tax law throughout the United Kingdom. Except for rates, a common tax system exists for the entire United Kingdom. There is no tax legislation specific to Northern Ireland, only U.K. provisions which apply equally to Northern Ireland.

20.3.2 The *Getting Britain Giving* initiative

This initiative was launched on November 9, 1999 with effect from April 2000 by a government which explained that:

> "… *Getting Britain Giving* delivers a modernised charity tax system that will make tax breaks more extensive, easier to understand and therefore more attractive to people."[11]

---

[8] See for example, *Brighton College v. Marriot* (1925) 1 K.B. 313.
[9] *op cit.*
[10] *Campbell College v. Commissioner of Valuation* [1964] N.I. 169 (H.L.).
[11] Press release, November 9, 1999, Melanie Johnson M.P., Economic Secretary.

The initiative impacts mainly upon income tax and to a certain extent VAT. Broadly its effect is that:

- It replaces the Deed of Covenant scheme with the Gift Aid scheme.
- It reduces the £250 lower limit before Gift Aid can be used to zero.
- It removes the requirement for donors to sign a Gift Aid certificate.
- It removes the Give As You Earn maximum limit for charitable giving through employees payroll.
- It aligns VAT and income tax exemptions for charitable fundraising events.
- It extends the VAT exemptions for various charity activities/purchases.

20.4 INCOME TAX

20.4.1 The Inland Revenue

This body has responsibility for income tax, capital gains, inheritance and corporation tax. It receives applications, makes decisions and issues a tax reference number in relation to charitable status for tax purposes.

Following the introduction of the Self Assessment scheme, charities no longer have to submit annual accounts to the Inland Revenue. They only need do so in response to a request from FICO (Financial Intermediaries and Claims Office) (Audit and Compliance). From April 6, 2000, FICO introduced a new charity repayment claims form, R68 which must be completed and submitted annually to recover any payments charged to tax (see further, Procedures).

20.4.2 Applying for Inland Revenue recognition

Under section 506(1) of the Income and Corporation Tax Act 1988 a charity is defined as "any body of persons or trust established for charitable purposes only". Such a body must satisfy the Inland Revenue of the following before it can be recognised as a charity for tax purposes:

- The body must be established for exclusively charitable purposes. It must fit within one of the *Pemsel* heads or be a recreational charity (see Chapters 8–14). Most hospitals and schools have been granted charitable exemption because they qualify under the *Pemsel* criteria as do those public hospitals incorporated by Royal Charter as charitable organisations.
- A charity will not escape liability for tax unless it can show that the funds, or proportion of funds, on which exemption is sought are used exclusively for charitable purposes.
- A charity must be established within the jurisdiction if it is to qualify for tax exemption. This rule emanated from the *ratio decedendi* of the judgment given by the House of Lords in *Camille and Henry Dreyfus Foundation Inc.*

v. IRC.[12] As Jenkins L.J. stated in the Court of Appeal, and as approved by the House of Lords:

"The phrase to be construed is the whole phrase 'body of persons or trust established for charitable purposes only', and it must be construed in its context. Whether the claim for exemption is made on behalf of a body of persons or on behalf of a trust, the body or trust must be shown to be established for charitable purposes only, and that requirement must have the same quality in the case of a body of persons as it has in the case of a trust. I have already expressed the view that 'trust' in an Act of the United Kingdom means a trust taking effect and enforceable under the law of the United Kingdom. It follows that, in my opinion, a 'trust established for charitable purposes only' must mean here a trust taking effect and enforceable under the law of the United Kingdom and creating an obligation enforceable in the Courts of the United Kingdom to apply its funds for purposes which are, according to the law of the United Kingdom, exclusively charitable. I can attribute no different meaning to the phrase 'established for charitable purposes only' when applied to a body of persons. So applied, I think it is only satisfied by a body of persons which is under the law of the United Kingdom subject to an obligation enforceable in our Courts to apply its funds for purposes which are according to that law exclusively charitable."[13]

In practical terms, the Inland Revenue will consider the following factors to determine whether a body is established within the United Kingdom: place of residence of trustees; location of seat of administration; proper law applicable to the construction of the governing instrument of the institution; where the governing instrument was executed/company incorporated/constitution adopted; location of its assets; and where its funds are applied.[14]

See, further, Procedure for Applying for Tax Exemption, Section One, Procedure Four.

20.4.3 Appeals

Charitable exemption is not always granted; every year a significant number of applications from voluntary organisations are judged to be ineligible. Any person dissatisfied by a decision of the Inland Revenue can appeal[15] to either the General Commissioners or the Special Commissioners of the Inland Revenue.[16] Appeals must be brought to the Commissioners within 30 days.[17] Appeals can be brought out of time if there was a reasonable excuse and the

---

[12] [1955] 3 All E.R. 97, (1954) 36 T.C. 126.
[13] [1954] 2 All E.R. 466 at 486, 487.
[14] See further Claricoat, J., and Philips, H., *Charity Law A to Z: Key Questions Answered* (Jordans, Bristol, 1995) at p. 75.
[15] Taxes Management Act 1970, s. 31.
[16] Taxes Management Act 1970, ss. 44 and 46.
[17] Taxes Management Act 1970, s.30.

appeal was made thereafter without unreasonable delay.[18] If the Inland Revenue refuse to allow an appeal to be made out of time, that decision itself can be appealed to the Commissioners.[19] Once an appeal has been made, it cannot be withdrawn except with the consent of the Inland Revenue.[20] However, appeals can be settled by agreement.[21] Tax payments cannot be postponed just because an appeal is pending.[22] Appeal procedures are governed by legislation.[23]

An appeal lies from either the General Commissioners[24] of the Special Commissioners[25] to the Northern Ireland Court of Appeal.[26] Appeals to the Court of Appeal are on a point of law on a case stated. They must be brought within 30 days of a decision of the General Commissioners or within 56 days of a decision of the Special Commissioners.[27] A further appeal lies to the House of Lords.[28]

20.4.4 The exemptions

Once a charity is recognised as such by the Inland Revenue, it can take advantage of the various income tax exemptions. Tax exemption and charitable status are intimately related. There are very real financial benefits for those organisations which acquire charitable status and use this to claim exemption from income tax. For example, the Inland Revenue estimate that relief from income tax to charities in the tax year 1993–1994 amounted to £650 million.[29]

The rationale for charitable exemption from income tax is that activities, which otherwise would accrue profit for an organisation, are dedicated to public benefit by a charity and it would be counterproductive to impose taxes. As explained by Wylie:

> "...charities are exempted from income tax in respect of income from investment of the funds held by them for charitable purposes and on profits from trade if they are applied solely to the purpose of the charity and either the trade

---

[18] Taxes Management Act 1970, s.49.
[19] Taxes Management Act 1970, s.49(1).
[20] *R. v Income Tax Special Commissioners, ex parte Elmhirst* (1936) 1 K.B. 486, (1935) All E.R. Rep. 808.
[21] Taxes Management Act 1970, s.54.
[22] Taxes Management Act 1970, s.55.
[23] See Special Commissioners (Jurisdiction and Procedure) Regulations 1994, SI 1994/1811, the General Commissioners (Jurisdiction and Procedure) Regulations 1994, SI 1994/1812 and the General and Special Commissioners (Amendment of Enactments) Regulations 1994, SI 1994 /1813. For further guidance see IR 37, Appeals (1999).
[24] Taxes Management Act 1970, s.56.
[25] Taxes Management Act 1970, s.56A.
[26] Taxes Management Act 1970, s.58.
[27] See further s. 56A of the Taxes Management Act 1970.
[28] Taxes Management Act 1970, s.58(2C).
[29] Inland Revenue Statistics 1993, Table 1.6.

is the primary purpose or one of the primary purposes of the charity or it is mainly carried out by the beneficiaries of the charity."[30]

Section 505 of the Income and Corporation Tax Act 1988 sets out the principal income tax exemptions for charities. A pre-requisite is that the income must be applied to exclusively charitable purposes. If a charity adds income to its own funds or gives it to another charity, this is still an application to exclusively charitable purposes.[31]

The destination of income must therefore be charitable (but see below on the anti-avoidance provisions). If the source can also fit within one of the following categories, there will be an income tax exemption for the charity.

20.4.4(i) Profits from land

There is an exemption from Schedule A (income from land) and Schedule D (income from various sources) taxation for "any profits or gains arising in respect of rents or other receipts from an estate, interest or right in or over land".[32] The right to the rent etc. must be vested in a person for charitable purposes. The exemption will not apply to any development on land which is then sold as this is in the nature of a trading gain and is not exempt under section 505(1)(a).

20.4.4(ii) Interest, annuities or other annual payments

There is an exemption from Schedule D Case III for any interest, annuity or other annual payment, for example the payment of interest rates by banks or annual covenants, under section 505(1)(c)(ii). Annual payments must be income payments and not capital payments. The Inland Revenue has allowed an Extra Statutory Concession for bank interest which is not paid yearly.[33]

20.4.4(iii) Income from foreign securities or possessions

There are two separate exemptions for foreign income. Firstly, under section 505(1)(c)(iia), income from interest, annuities or other annual payments which would be treated as Schedule D Case III if it was generated within the United

---

[30] See Wylie, J.C.W., *Irish Land Law* (3rd ed.), Butterworths, 1997), para. 9.088; references to *Pharmaceutical Society of Ireland v. Special Commissioners of Income Tax* [1938] I.R. 203, *Baptist Union of Ireland v. CIR* [1945] N.I. 99, *Pig Marketing Board (N.I.) v. CIR* [1945] N.I. 155 and *Trustees of Londonderry Presbyterian Church House v. CIR* [1946] N.I. 178.

[31] *Inland Revenue Commissioners v. Slater (Helen) Charitable Trust Ltd.* [1982] Ch. 49 and now see s. 505(2) of the Income and Corporation Tax Act 1988 where one charity gives money to another charity.

[32] s. 505(1)(a).

[33] B9 Bank Interest, etc., received by Charities.

Kingdom, but comes from foreign securities or possessions, is exempt. Secondly, under section 505(1)(c)(iib), foreign income consisting of the dividends or other distributions of a company which would be treated under Schedule F if the company were resident in the United Kingdom, is also exempt.

20.4.4(iv) Income from company dividends

There is an exemption, under section 505(1)(c)(iii), from Schedule F income received as dividends or other distributions from United Kingdom companies.

20.4.4(v) Income from a trade

Income derived from trade is *prima facie* not tax exempt.[34] In general terms, if a charity receives trading income it must pay tax under Schedule D (usually Schedule D Case I). One way of avoiding this liability is to set up a trading subsidiary. Its profits are taxed and passed (*i.e.* by covenant or other agreement) to the charity which then reclaims the tax paid on the donation. This technique is known as profit shedding.

There are also a number of exemptions which allow a charity to trade directly and not pay tax on profits made. These exceptions come from a number of sources: statute, Extra Statutory Concessions and from the *Getting Britain Giving* initiative.

However, if a particular activity does not constitute a trade, then it is not necessary to find a related exemption. The most obvious and useful example of this is the sale by charities of donated goods. The essence of a trade is buying/manufacturing something then selling it. If goods are donated, the first element is not present. Rather than reselling for a profit, a charity is just realising the value of a donation. Sorting, cleaning and minor repairs do not destroy the non-trading nature of this activity, although substantially altering a donated good will do so.

Another activity on the borderline between trade and donation is business sponsorship of charities. If a charity merely acknowledges the receipt of money from the sponsor, this will not constitute a trade. But if this amounts to an advertisement on behalf of the sponsor, it will be a trade. Displaying corporate logo, corporate colours or mentioning corporate services, in return for donations from the business, is likely to be regarded by the Inland Revenue as a trading activity and will be taxable as such unless one of the other specific exemptions can be used.

If a charity is deemed to be trading and cannot rely on any of the following exemptions (or the preceding definitions of trade), it should set up some form of trading subsidiary and ensure that all costs are properly allocated and deducted from the trade before calculating taxable profit.

---

[34] See *Grove* v. *Young Men's Christian Association* (1903) 88 L.T. 696 which held that the profits of a commercial restaurant run by the YMCA was taxable as trading income.

The Charity Commission has produced guidance on trading activities for charities and the requirements to be satisfied before setting up a trading subsidiary.[35] Firstly, the charities constitution should contain an investment clause wide enough to allow it to set up a trading subsidiary. Secondly, the trading activity should not represent too risky a business venture for the charity. Charities have to bear in mind the extra costs of operating a subsidiary and complying with the requirements of the Companies Orders. There would need to be persons on the governing committee of both charity and subsidiary whose functions and duties do not overlap. Not all the charity trustees should be directors of the company, and not all directors of the company should be charity trustees. This will reduce the possible scope of conflict of interests. Charities should avoid guaranteeing any of the liabilities of the subsidiary company. The charity should not make unsecured or interest free loans to the subsidiary, to do so would breach the trustees duties to invest prudently on behalf of the charity. If a charity adopts a 100 per cent profit shedding approach to take advantage of the various tax exemptions, it may find itself having to provide cash injections to the subsidiary at intervals to maintain a supply of working capital. These cash injections should be justifiable investment decisions and accounted for as such. Alternatively, the subsidiary can adopt a profit retention approach and retain a certain level of profits to maintain its viability. The risk is that the subsidiary will not get its tax reliefs. If the charity supports its subsidiary by allowing it to use its land / staff or resources, this should be properly accounted for. The charity and its subsidiary should be kept clearly separate at all times.

20.4.4(vi) Trading exemption – primary purpose trade

No tax is payable on a trade exercised in the course of the actual carrying out of the primary purpose of the charity.[36] In the *Industrious Blind* case[37] a shop produced goods sold by blind people. The primary purpose of the charity was to promote the employment of blind people, it therefore had income tax exemption. The Inland Revenue provides the following examples of primary purpose trades[38]:

- Schools providing educational services in return for fees,
- Galleries holding exhibitions requesting entrance fees,
- Theatres selling tickets for plays,
- Hospitals selling medical services,
- Residential accommodation charities letting property etc.

---

[35] CC35 Charities and Trading (1999).
[36] s. 505(1)(e)(i) of the Income and Corporation Tax Act 1988.
[37] [1968] N.I. 21.
[38] Trading by Charities, CS2 (Inland Revenue 1998).

In addition, if a charity carries out a trade which is wholly ancillary to its primary purpose, it will also gain tax exemption for that trade. For example[39]:

- Galleries selling food in a cafeteria to visitors to the gallery,
- Schools selling crèche places for the children of its students,
- Schools letting accommodation to its students in return for rent.

The trade must be genuinely and objectively ancillary to the charitable purposes of the charity. It must also provide an income which is small in absolute terms and small relative to the overall income of the charity, *i.e.* 10 per cent.

20.4.4(vii) Trading exemption – employing the beneficiaries

No tax is payable if the work in connection with the trade is mainly carried out by the beneficiaries of the charity.[40] In the *Legion Attendants*[41] case the charity was set up to promote the employment of ex-servicemen. The profits from its car park trade were exempt from income tax. The Inland Revenue provide further examples[42]:

- A farm operated by students of an agricultural college,
- A restaurant operated by students as part of a catering course at a further education college.

20.4.4(viii) Trading exemption – agricultural shows

Agricultural societies are exempt from tax on the profits of any exhibition or show held for the purposes of the society which profits are applied solely to the purposes of the society.[43] An agricultural society is defined as "any society or institution established for the purposes of promoting the interests of agriculture, horticulture, livestock breeding or forestry.[44] Agricultural charities may be able to take advantage of this exemption (although there is no requirement that the agricultural society be a charity).

20.4.4(ix) Trading exemption – charity fundraising events

As part of the *Getting Britain Giving* initiative, the Inland Revenue has revised an Extra Statutory Concession, ESC C4 Charity Fund-raising Events. From April 2000, this ESC exempts charities from paying income tax on what would otherwise be a trading activity. It exempts charities from paying in-

---

[39] Trading by Charities, CS2 (Inland Revenue 1998).
[40] s. 505 (1)(e)(ii) of the Income and Corporation Tax Act 1988.
[41] [1979] N.I. 138.
[42] Trading by Charities, CS2 (Inland Revenue 1998).
[43] Income and Corporation Tax Act 1988, s.510.
[44] Income and Corporation Tax Act 1988, s.510(2).

come tax on fundraising events which are organised by them for the purpose of raising money and promoted as being for that purpose.[45] The profits must by transferred to charities or otherwise applied for charitable purposes.

The revised ESC expressly aligns the income tax concession to the VAT exemption contained in the Value Added Tax (Fund-raising events by charities and other qualifying bodies) Order 2000.[46] The purpose of the exemption is twofold: firstly, to widen the income tax exemption to charities raising money by a trading activity, secondly, to unify the VAT and income tax exemptions for those events.

20.4.4(x) Trading exemption – small trades

Section 46 of the Finance Act 2000, which came into effect in April 2000, introduced a new exemption from income tax for charities which raise money by trading activities. The existing exemptions still apply the new one applies only where the old ones do not and is designed to relieve the need for the setting up of trading subsidiaries and profit shedding if the trade is on a relatively small scale.[47]

There are two requirements for this exemption: the income must be applied solely for the purposes of the charity;[48] and either, the gross income from the trade must be less than the requisite limit,[49] or there must be have been a reasonable expectation at the beginning of the period that the gross income would not exceed that requisite limit.[50]

Three questions of definition arise from this. Firstly, there is the meaning of "gross income". It is defined as meaning "income before deduction of any expenses".[51] There is no definition of expenses in this context, *i.e.* if it is just limited to overheads and salary costs, or it if includes what would be termed costs of goods sold (*i.e.* the purchase price of goods which are then sold on). The Inland Revenue has elected to treat the term gross income as meaning turnover, *i.e.* all money received from sale of goods.[52]

Secondly, there is the meaning of a "requisite level" of gross income. The

---

[45] Schedule 9, Group 12, Value Added Tax Act 1994.

[46] See 20.9.2(ii) for the definition of a fundraising event.

[47] However, it will not exempt income received by virtue of s. 30 of the Taxes Management Act 1970, ss. 214, 412, 547(1)(b) and (6), 553(6), 660C, 677, 703, 776, 788, 790 and 804 of the Income and Corporation Tax Act 1988, para. 14 of Sch. 4 to the Finance (No.2) Act 1997, para. 52(4) of Sch. 18 and para. 13(7) to the Finance Act 1998. The Treasury can also, by order, specify other enactments to which it does not apply, see s. 46(2) Finance Act 2000.

[48] s. 46(3) Finance Act 2000.

[49] s. 46(3)(a) Finance Act 2000.

[50] s. 46(3)(b) Finance Act 2000.

[51] s. 46(6) Finance Act 2000.

[52] See s. 11, Getting Britain Giving: Inland Revenue Guidance Notes for Charities (2000, Inland Revenue).

requisite level is the higher of two figures. The first figure is a straightforward £5,000.[53] The second figure is the lesser of £50,000 or 25 per cent of all the charities incoming resources (*i.e.* grants, donations investments, etc.) for the period.[54] If the period in question is less than 12 months, the figures of £5,000 and £50,000 shall be proportionately reduced.[55]

In all circumstances, if trading income is up to £5,000, it will be tax exempt. If over £5,000 is raised by a trading activity, the charity will have to examine its total income from all sources. The requisite limit in this case will be 25 per cent of the charities incoming resources, subject to a maximum limit of £50,000. This means that a substantial part of small and medium sized trading activities will be tax exempt, but large trading charities will not be. The exemption is an all or nothing exemption.

Thirdly, there is the meaning of a "reasonable expectation" that gross income will not exceed the requisite limit. The term is not defined in the legislation, but at a practical level, it would seem to require an objectively verifiable belief that the limits would not be breached; either that trading income would be lower or income from other sources higher. The Inland Revenue has indicated that it will require such evidence as cash-flow forecasts, business plans, copies of previous years accounts etc.

20.4.4(xi) Trading and charity law

Charities must still operate within charity law. According to the Inland Revenue, the Charity Commission and the Treasury, this means that charities cannot engage in substantial, permanent trading activity.[56] As the Charity Commission has explained:

> "This is because of the general expectation that contributions made to a charity will be applied for its purposes or invested prudently, rather than being risked in trading activities which are undertaken simply to raise money."[57]

The model Charity Commission constitution, which prohibits "any substantial, permanent trading activity", will allow trading within the confines of the exceptions set out above (see also, Chapter 18).

20.4.4(xii) Income arising from a lottery

Any profits arising from a lottery are exempt from Income Tax under section 505(1)(f). The lottery must be conducted in accordance with the Betting, Gaming, Lotteries and Amusements (N.I.) Order 1985.

---

[53] s. 46(4)(a) Finance Act 2000.

[54] s. 46(4)(b) Finance Act 2000.

[55] s. 46(5) Finance Act 2000.

[56] See s. 11, Getting Britain Giving: Inland Revenue Guidance Notes for Charities (2000, Inland Revenue), Explanatory Note: s. 46 Finance Act 2000 at para. 10, HM Treasury.

[57] CC35 Charities and Trading (1999)at p. 4.

20.4.4(xiii) Anti-avoidance provisions

The Income and Corporation Tax Act 1988 contains provisions to prevent charities being used as a tax avoidance vehicle by individuals.[58] It does so by drawing a distinction between qualifying expenditure and non-qualifying expenditure: the former being defined as "expenditure incurred in that period for charitable purposes only";[59] the latter as every other kind of expenditure. If income exceeds qualifying expenditure, no relief shall be available for that part of the excess which does not exceed the non-qualifying expenditure. Three conditions must be satisfied to qualify under this anti-avoidance provision: the income of the charity must be greater than £10,000;[60] it must have incurred non-qualifying expenditure; and the income must exceed the qualifying expenditure.[61]

If two or more charities are acting in concert to avoid paying tax, the £10,000 threshold is not necessary.[62] If qualifying expenditure plus non-qualifying expenditure is higher than income, the Inland Revenue can treat some of the non-qualifying expenditure as being incurred in a previous year.

Qualifying expenditure receives further definition in section 506 and Sched. 20. If payment is made to a body outside the United Kingdom it is non-qualifying expenditure unless the charity has taken reasonable steps to ensure it will be applied for charitable purposes.[63] If the expenditure is by way of investment or loan it will not be qualifying expenditure unless it is a qualifying investment[64] or a qualifying loan.[65]

For these purposes a "qualifying investment" is either[66]:

- Narrow or broad range investments under the Trustee Investment Act 1961[67] except for certain mortgages.

- A common investment fund or common deposit fund created by either the Charity Commission or the Charities Branch.[68]

- An interest in land other than as security for a debt.

- Shares in a recognised stock exchange or in the Unlisted Securities Market.

- Unit trusts.

---

[58] See s. 505(3)–(8) and s. 506.
[59] s. 506(1).
[60] s. 505(3)(a).
[61] s. 505(3)(b).
[62] s. 505(7).
[63] s. 506(3).
[64] s. 506(4)(a) and Sch. 20 Part I.
[65] s. 506(4)(b) and Sch. 20 Part II.
[66] Sch. 20 Part I.
[67] See further Chaps. 6 and 7.
[68] *ibid.*

- Bank deposits paying interest at a commercial rate, unless the deposit is part of an arrangement to pay a loan to some person.

- Any other loan or investment which the Inland Revenue are satisfied is not made for avoidance of tax and is for the benefit of the charity.

For these purposes a "qualifying loan" is either a:[69]

- Loan made to another charity for charitable purposes only.

- Loan made to a beneficiary of a charity as part of its purposes.

- Money placed in a current account (unless, as above, it is part of an arrangement to make a loan to another person).

- Any other loan which the Inland Revenue is satisfied is not for tax avoidance and is for the benefit of the charity.

20.4.5 Gift Aid donations

The single most important change in the *Getting Britain Giving* initiative was to revise Gift Aid and turn it into the main vehicle for tax efficient charitable donations.

Donors can now give any amount, as a once-off gift or by periodical payments, and by making a Gift Aid declaration, they allow the charity to recover tax at the basic rate. The old Deed of Covenant scheme is largely superseded by Gift Aid, although an old Deed of Covenant will be treated as being a Gift Aid Compliant (s. 41 Finance Act 2000).

20.4.5(i) Gift Aid

This is now regulated by section 25 of the Finance Act 1990 as amended by the Finance Act 2000.[70] There is no minimum level before a gift can count as Gift Aid.[71] Old deeds of covenant are automatically Gift Aid compliant.[72] Gift Aid donations are treated as if income tax had already been deducted at the basic rated and as if the donor's basic rate was increased by an amount equal to the grossed up total of the gift.[73] If a donor pays income tax at the higher rate, he can recover the difference in these two rates from the Inland Revenue. If the donor does not pay tax, or pays it at the lower band rate, he must repay the tax reclaimed by the charity but not actually paid by him.

---

[69] Sch. 20 Part II.
[70] s. 39 of the Finance Act 2000.
[71] s. 39(3)(a) of the Finance Act 2000.
[72] *ibid.*
[73] s. 39(6) of the Finance Act 2000.

20.4.5(ii) Gift Aid declarations

The donor/charity must between them complete a Gift Aid declaration.[74] The Inland Revenue has made the regulations prescribing the format of the Gift Aid declaration under the Donations to Charity by Individuals (Appropriate Declarations) Regulations 2000.[75]

The Gift Aid declaration can be made in writing, by fax, in electronic form or by phone. There is no requirement for it to be signed (although this is advisable). The declaration can be prospective, applying to all current and future donations, or retrospective, applying to any donations made during the preceding six years. This is clearly procedural. The following prescribed information must be contained within the declaration:[76]

- Donor's name
- Donor's address
- Charity's name
- Description of the donation to which the declaration applies
- Declaration that the donation is to be treated as Gift Aid
- A note explaining the requirement that the donor must pay an amount of income or capital gains tax equal to the tax deducted from his donation
- Date of declaration.

The last two requirements are unnecessary if an oral declaration is given and this is followed with a written note to the donor containing all the items listed above (including the final two). It must, furthermore, state both the donor's right to cancel the declaration retrospectively and the date on which this written note was sent to the donor.

If a donor wishes to cancel a declaration, this can be done at any time. The declaration, unlike a deed of covenant, is not a legally binding obligation to give over a period of time. Cancellation means that tax cannot be reclaimed from the date of cancellation onwards. If an oral declaration is made, the donor has a period of 30 days after receipt of the written note to cancel the declaration. If cancellation occurs within this period, it is as if the declaration was never made. It may therefore be advisable for charities to delay making repayment claims until the 30 day period has elapsed.

The donor's name and address should be as full as possible. The declaration should state to which donation it applies, *i.e.* to the present one, a particular future one, or all donations from April 6.

---

[74] s. 25(1)(c) Finance Act 1990 as modified by s. 39(2) Finance Act 2000.
[75] S.I. No. 2074 of 2000.
[76] See appendices for a model Gift Aid Declaration.

20.4.5(iii) Records of Gift Aid declarations

For practical purposes, charities should be able to demonstrate an audit trail linking cash repayment claims to the donor.

Charitable companies must keep records for at least six years. Charitable trusts can keep them for a considerably shorter period, but it is recommended that they abide by the same requirement.[77]

20.4.5(iv) Donations by companies and individuals

Individuals make Gift Aid donations net of tax as explained above. A different system operates for companies making donations. Companies, from April 1, 2000 make donations to charities gross of tax. They will not make Gift Aid declarations and the charity will not reclaim tax on donations made by them. The company will deduct the gross donations from its profits before calculating its taxable profits.[78]

20.4.5(v) Donors who may use the Gift Aid scheme

The range of donors who can take advantage of Gift Aid has been widened. The usual donor will be one who is resident in the United Kingdom. The Finance Act 2000 extends this to a donor who "performs duties which by virtue of section 132(4)(a) of the Income and Corporation Taxes Act 1988 (crown employees serving overseas) are treated as being performed in the United Kingdom".[79] It also extends it to non-resident individuals who pay income or capital gains tax of an amount at least equal to the amount of tax being reclaimed by the charity[80] and to non-resident companies.[81]

20.4.5(vi) Future uses for deeds of covenant[82]

Deeds of covenant can still provide a mechanism for charitable giving. However, they can only be tax efficient it they also fulfil the requirements of Gift Aid declarations. It has been suggested that deeds will continue to be useful in two circumstances. Firstly, where there is a need for the donor or donee to create a legally binding obligation to give. Secondly, where a VAT registered

---

[77] See for example comments of Venables in Taxation News (2000) 6 *Charity Law and Practice Review* 227 at p. 245.

[78] s. 40 Finance Act 2000.

[79] s. 41(3)(c) Finance Act 2000 modifying s. 25(2)(i) of the Finance Act 1990.

[80] s. 41(3)(c) Finance Act 2000 modifying s. 25(2)(ii) of the Finance Act 1990.

[81] s. 40(3) Finance Act 2000 which removes s. 339(2) Income and Corporation Taxes Act 1988.

[82] See further, "Wither the Deed of Covenant?!", Julian Smith and Sam Macdonald (2000) 6 *Charity Law and Practice Review* 211.

trading subsidiary deals in donated goods.[83] There is a VAT exemption for the supply and sale of donated goods by trading subsidiaries of charities.[84] Such a subsidiary is now defined as a company that agrees to give all its profits to its parent charity. It has been suggested that a deed of covenant is the best way to show this agreement.[85]

20.4.5(vii) Donor benefit rules

If a charity gives a donor a benefit in return for a donation, and that benefit exceeds a certain level, then the donation will not count as Gift Aid.[86] The benefit to the donor cannot exceed either the relevant value level or the aggregate value level.[87] If the value of the gift does not exceed £100, the limit is 25 per cent of the value of the gift.[88] If the value of the gift is between £100 and £1,000, the limit is £25.[89] If the value of the gift is over £1,000, the limit is 2.5 per cent of the value of the gift.[90] If there is one benefit for one gift these rules apply. If there is more than one benefit in relation to one gift, it is the total value of all these benefits which must be considered.[91] The legislation then proceeds in more detail to consider how to "annualise" certain donations and benefits within these limits. If a benefit comes within these annualising provisions, it modifies the section 25(4) rule that total benefit must simply be added up. The annualising provisions apply:

- Where the benefit consists of the right to receive benefits at intervals over a period of less than 12 months, or
- Where the benefit relates to a period of less than 12 months, or
- Where the benefit is one of a series of benefits received at intervals in consequence of making a series of gifts at intervals of less than 12 months.[92]

The annualising provisions also apply if a once-off benefit is made as a consequence of making a donation which is one of a series of donations made at intervals of less than 12 months.[93] The annualising provisions essentially gross up the benefit of the donation to the equivalent annual benefit or donation by multiplying it by 365 and dividing by the number of days for which it is in effect.[94]

---

[83] *ibid.* at p. 217.
[84] See further 20.9.1(v) for details of VAT treatment.
[85] *ibid.* at p. 215.
[86] Finance Act 1990, s.25(2)(e).
[87] s. 25(2)(e) of the Finance Act 1990 as amended by s. 39(3) of the Finance Act 2000.
[88] Finance Act 1990, s.25(5A)(a).
[89] Finance Act 1990, s.25(5A)(b).
[90] Finance Act 1990, s.25(5A)(c).
[91] Finance Act 1990, s.25(4).
[92] Finance Act 1990, s.25(5B).
[93] Finance Act 1990, s.25(5C).
[94] Finance Act 1990, s.25(5D).

In addition, the value of the benefit cannot exceed the aggregate value limit. The value of benefits in consequence of all donations to a particular charity cannot exceed £250.[95] There is no annualising under the aggregate value limit.

"Benefit" means any item or service provided by the charity or a third party to the donor or any person connected to him in consequence of making the donation. Mere acknowledgements of the donation is not a benefit unless it amounts to an advertisement on behalf of the donor. Literature which is sent out to donors for the purpose of describing the work of the charity is not a benefit, so long as this literature is not normally sold to the public.

The Finance Act 2000 also exempts certain things from being regarded as a benefit to donors in relation to charities whose sole or main purpose is either the preservation of property or the conservation of wildlife for the public benefit.[96] The only benefits which are exempted in relation to those charities are free/reduced rights of admission, as a consequence of the donation, to view the property/wildlife whose preservation/conservation is the sole or main purpose of the charity.[97] However, the opportunity to make donations so as to attract these admission rights must be available to all the members of the public.[98] The "right of admission" refers to the admission of the person making the gift or any member of his family.[99]

In valuing benefit, the charity should attempt a market valuation. If the benefit is on sale to the non-donating public, the value of the benefit should be readily identifiable. Otherwise, the charity should estimate the normal sale price. If an item is sold at a charity auction, the benefit to the donor will generally exceed the sale price. In these cases, the charity should again assess the market value of the benefit. Occasionally, the charity may decide that the benefit of the donor of a particular gift is excessive, and the gift will therefore not be Gift Aid compliant. In this case, prior to, or at the time of the gift, it can request the donor to split the payment. Part of the payment can be regarded as an outright donation with no related benefit and will therefore be Gift Aid compliant. The other part will be regarded as a straightforward payment in return for benefit and therefore attracting Gift Aid tax exemption. The advantage of splitting payments in this way is that at least some of the donation will gain tax exemption.

---

[95] Finance Act 1990, s.25(2)(e).

[96] Finance Act 1990, s.25(5F).

[97] Finance Act 1990, s.25(5E).

[98] Finance Act 1990, s.25(5E).

[99] According to Venables, the Inland Revenue guidance which limits this to spouses is open to challenge on grounds of discrimination, Taxation News (2000) 6 *Charity Law and Practice Review* 227 at 248.

20.4.5(viii) Transitional arrangements

The Finance Act 2000 ends the separate regime for deeds of covenant and places them within the Gift Aid regime.[100] All existing deeds of covenant are deemed to be Gift Aid compliant. The new regime applies to all donations made or falling due after April 6, 2000. If a deed of covenant payment falls due before April 6, 2000, even if paid after that date, the old rules apply.

20.4.6 Other donations

The Getting Britain Giving initiative also revised some of the other vehicles for charitable giving. It extended the Give As You Earn scheme. It introduced a new exemption for gifts of stocks and shares. The Millennium Gift Aid scheme was not greatly affected, but is a scheme which has a very finite life span.

20.4.6(i) Give As You Earn

Give As You Earn (GAYE), or Payroll Giving as it is also known, is a scheme to promote tax efficient charitable giving by employees who pay tax under the PAYE scheme.[101] The employee informs the employer how much he wishes to donate, and that amount is deducted from gross pay before calculation of tax (although after calculation of National Insurance Contributions). The employer forwards the money to a Payroll Giving Agency which then forwards it to the charity of the employee's choice.

The Finance Act 2000 made two significant changes. Firstly, there is no longer an upper limit on the amount which can be donated.[102] Secondly, the government will add an extra 10 per cent on to all GAYE donations[103] for all donations made between April 6, 2000 and April 6, 2003. The Payroll Giving Agencies pay out this extra 10 per cent supplement then reclaim it from the government.[104]

The Payroll Giving Agencies are approved by the Inland Revenue and a list of such is available. Currently the only agency in Northern Ireland is the Northern Ireland Council of Voluntary Action. The government is strongly supportive of the GAYE scheme, both in terms of providing the 10 per cent supplement and also in terms of extolling its benefits to employers.[105] The

---

[100] s. 41 Finance Act 2000.

[101] Income and Corporation Taxes Act 1988, s.202.

[102] s. 38(5) of the Finance Act 2000 modifying s. 202 of the Income and Corporation Taxes Act 1988.

[103] s. 38(1) of the Finance Act 2000.

[104] s. 38(2) of the Finance Act 2000.

[105] For example, in Payroll Giving: A Guide for Employers, the Revenue states "it shows that you care about your staff – offering them the benefits of Payroll Giving can help to build better employee relations and attract the right people to come and work for you".

scheme is voluntary, both for employers to set up and for employees to join or leave as they desire. It falls outside of the deed of covenant and Gift Aid schemes.

20.4.6(ii) Millennium Gift Aid

Millennium Gift Aid is governed mainly by the old Gift Aid rules.[107] It applied to certain donations between July 1998 and December 31, 2000. The Finance Act 2000 made little change to Millennium Gift Aid. In practical terms, it has been superseded by the much more flexible Gift Aid scheme.[107]

20.4.6(iii) Gifts of shares and securities to charities

A new income tax exemption has been created for donors who wish to donate certain qualifying investments to charities.[108] They will be able to deduct the value of the investment from their income tax before calculating tax payable.[109] If a company makes the donation, it will be able to deduct its value from its income before calculating corporation tax.[110]

There are a number of requirements to fulfil before the tax exemption can be utilised. Firstly, the donor must give the gift "otherwise than by way of a bargain made at arm's length".[111] In practical terms, it must be either a gift or a sale at an undervalue. Secondly, the relief will only apply to gifts by individuals after April 6, 2000 or gifts by companies after April 1, 2000.[112] Thirdly, only certain "qualifying investments" can be donated. These are[113]:

- Shares or securities which are listed or dealt with on a recognised stock exchange (including the Alternative Investment Market)

- Units in an authorised unit trust

- Shares in an open-ended investment company

- An interest in an off-shore fund.

The value of the gift is: its market value,[114] plus the incidental costs of disposing of the investment,[115] minus any consideration received for the gift,[116] mi-

---

[106] Finance Act 1998, s.48.

[107] See s. 42 Finance Act 2000 for consequential amendments to Millenium Gift Aid.

[108] s. 587B of the Income and Corporation Taxes Act 1988 as inserted by s. 43 of the Finance Act 2000.

[109] Income and Corporation Taxes Act 1988, s. 587B(2)(a)(i).

[110] Income and Corporation Taxes Act 1988, s. 587B(2)(a)(ii).

[111] Income and Corporation Taxes Act 1988, s.587B(1).

[112] s. 43(3) Finance Act 2000.

[113] Income and Corporation Taxes Act 1988, s.587B(9).

[114] Income and Corporation Taxes Act 1988, s.587B(4)(a).

[115] Income and Corporation Taxes Act 1988, s.587B(6).

[116] Income and Corporation Taxes Act 1988, s.587B(4)(b).

nus the value of any benefits received by the donor or a connected person in return for making the donation.[117]

This new relief is in addition to existing capital gains tax relief. Charities do not reclaim tax on these donations. The tax benefit is to the donor who can reduce the amount of his income which is chargeable to income or corporation tax.

The Treasury claim two advantages in this new tax relief for qualifying investments:

> "They are generally high quality, readily realisable assets which will be of value to charities.
>
> They generally have an easily identifiable valuation which can be adopted for the purposes of tax relief – this will minimise the costs of valuation for both the donor and the Inland Revenue."[118]

20.4.6(iv) Loans to charities

The Finance Act 2000 states that loans by individuals to charities do not constitute "settlements" for the purposes of the anti-avoidance legislation[119] in so far as there is no consideration (or only interest as consideration) for the loan.[120] This relaxation applies to income arising on loans after April 6, 2000, regardless of whether the loan is made before of after that date. It has been criticised because: it only applies to individuals who lend, not companies; it does not apply to loans made to charitable trading subsidiaries; and because it will not apply where the lendor obtains a benefit (*i.e.* redemption on repayment of the loan) other than the interest payments.[121]

20.4.6(v) Gifts to charities from settlor interested trusts

As part of the Getting Britain Giving initiative, to the extent that this sort of gift is made to a charity, the anti-avoidance provisions in Chapter 1A of Part XV of the Income and Corporation Taxes Act 1988, do not apply.[122] The income must be given from a U.K. resident trust. According to Venables "there is no justification for this requirement which is no doubt generated by a general prejudice against non U.K. resident trusts".[123] The income must either be

---

[117] Income and Corporation Taxes Act 1988, s.587B(8).
[118] Treasury Guidance Note on s. 43 Finance Act 2000.
[119] Chapter 1A of Part XV, Income and Corporation Taxes Act 1988, ss. 660A to 600B.
[120] s. 45(1) of the Finance Act 2000.
[121] See Taxation News, Robert Venables QC, (2000) 6 *Charity Law and Practice Review* 227.
[122] s. 44 of the Finance Act 2000.
[123] Taxation News, Robert Venables QC, (2000) 6 *Charity Law and Practice Review* 227 at 228.

given to the charity (*i.e.* under a discretionary trust),[124] or be income to which it is entitled to (*i.e.* a straightforward non-discretionary trust).[125] If the trust income comes from more than one source, and the trust income is greater than the income given to the charity, the gift to the charity is rated proportionally between those sources.[126] However, if the trust states that the income from one particular source is to go to the charity, it will be deemed that the income comes form that particular source.[127] The new relaxation provides that trust management expenses are apportioned between charitable and non-charitable ends so that the proportion of expenses which relate to charitable donations are allowable for tax purposes.

20.5 CAPITAL GAINS TAX

Capital Gains Tax is governed by the Taxation of Chargeable Gains Act 1992. Under section 256(1) of the Act, charities are exempt from Capital Gains Tax if the gain is applied to charitable purposes. If the property ceases to be held for charitable purposes, the trustees are treated as if they disposed of it and immediately re-acquired it at its market value.[128] The charity is not to be taken as having made a profit on disposal.[129]

From the donor's perspective a charity (*i.e.* otherwise than by a bargain at arm's length), is treated under section 257(2) as being a disposal for which neither a gain or a loss is made. Therefore the individual will not become liable to Capital Gains Tax in respect of any gifts of property which have appreciated in value since their acquisition.

20.6 INHERITANCE TAX

Inheritance Tax is only payable by natural persons, therefore charities will never have to pay it. If a donor makes a bequest to a charity, that bequest will be exempt from Inheritance Tax under section 23 of the Inheritance Tax Act 1984. Under the Finance Act 1983 all lifetime or death transfers are completely exempt. The gift must be for exclusively charitable purposes.[130] There

---

[124] s. 44 (1)(a) of the Finance Act 2000.

[125] s. 44 (1)(b) of the Finance Act 2000.

[126] s. 44 (2) of the Finance Act 2000.

[127] s. 44(3) of the Finance Act 2000.

[128] s. 256(2)(a) of the Taxation of Chargeable Gains Act 1992.

[129] See also Extra Statutory Concession D 47 Temporary Loss of Charitable Status due to Reverter of School and Other Sites for provisions which affect England but not Northern Ireland.

[130] s. 23(1) of the Inheritance Tax Act 1984.

will be no exemption if the gift is for a limited period[131] or the donor reserves to himself some interest in the property for less than full consideration.[132]

20.7 STAMP DUTY

Stamp duty is not payable if a conveyance or transfer on sale, voluntary disposition or lease is to a trust of body of persons established for exclusively charitable purposes.[133]

20.8 VALUE ADDED TAX

Value added tax is an indirect tax on the supply of goods and services.[134] It is charged by the supplier of goods and services if his turnover is over the annual limit.[135] The current rate of VAT is 17.5 per cent.[136] It is only charged if the supply is in furtherance of a business. There are a number of supplies which are exempt from VAT[137] and a number which are zero rated for VAT.[138] The VAT law in force in this jurisdiction is subject to the overriding requirements of the Sixth EC VAT Directive. If there are inconsistencies between the mandatory provisions of that Directive and national law, the Directive applies.

There is no automatic exemption from VAT for charities. This has long been a bone of contention for charities. The other criticism has been the complexity of the system. The government has taken some cognisance of this criticism and the *Getting Britain Giving* initiative also attempted to both simplify and expand the system for charities.

20.8.1 Rudiments of Value Added Tax

20.8.1(i) Supplies

To supply means to furnish or to serve.[139] The supply must be for some consideration.[140] Even if no profit is made or intended to be made in relation to

---

[131] s. 23(3).
[132] s. 23(4).
[133] s. 129 of the Finance Act 1982.
[134] s. 1(1) Value Added Tax Act 1994.
[135] Currently £52,000 per year as amended by the VAT (Increase of Registration Limits) Order 2000, S.I. No. 804 of 2000 with effect from April 1, 2000.
[136] From April 1, 1991, prior to this it was 15%.
[137] s. 31 Value Added Tax Act 1994.
[138] s. 30 Value Added Tax Act 1994.
[139] *Williams v. Pearce* (1916) 114 L.T. 989.
[140] s.5(2)(a) Value Added Tax Act 1994.

the supply, if consideration is paid, it will be deemed to be a taxable supply.[141] However, if a supply is made gratuitously, a subsequent voluntary payment will not bring it within the scope of VAT.[142]

20.8.1(ii) Business

For a supply to be taxable, it must satisfy three requirements. It must be made by a taxable person. It must be made within the United Kingdom. It must also be made in the course or furtherance of any business carried on by the taxable person.[143] The requirement of "business" has proved most difficult for charities.

General guidance on the meaning of business was given in *Customs and Excise Commissioners v. Morrison's Academy Boarding Houses Association*[144] where a business was held to be "predominantly concerned with the making of taxable supplies to consumers for a consideration".[145] A business must possess some degree of continuity. The absence of a profit motive does not mean that an activity is not a business.[146]

Activities which are no more than a voluntary service to the community are not business activities.[147]

20.8.1(iii) Registration

Charities only need to register for VAT (and charge VAT on supplies) if their turnover from business activities in the previous 12 months is above the annual limit. From April 1, 2000, that limit is £52,000.[148] If charities are making taxable supplies below this limit they can voluntarily choose to register. As discussed below, zero-rated supplies will be considered to be taxable supplies, exempt supplies will not.

As a result of the *Getting Britain Giving* initiative, the threshold below which charities (and other businesses) do not have to account for VAT when they de-register is raised from £250 to £1,000.

---

[141] *Heart of Variety Ltd. v. Customs and Excise Commissioners* (1975) VATTR 103.
[142] *Warwick Masonic Rooms Ltd. v. Customs and Excise Commissioners* (1979) VAT decision 839.
[143] s. 4(1) Value Added Tax Act 1994.
[144] [1978] S.T.C. 1.
[145] *ibid.* at p. 6.
[146] *Customs and Excise Commissioners v. Lord Fisher* [1981] 2 All E.R. 147.
[147] *Greater London Red Cross Blood Transfusion Service v. Customs and Excise Commissioners* (1983) VATTR 241.
[148] Value Added Tax (Increase of Registration Limits) Order 2000, S.I. No. 804 of 2000.

20.8.2 Common charitable activities and business status

20.8.2(i) Membership facilities of an association

The provision by a club, association or organisation (for a subscription or other consideration) of the facilities or advantages available to members is a business.[149] The meaning of "facilities" or "advantages" was discussed in *Customs and Excise Commissioners v. British Field Sports Society*.[150] If some of the services provided are exempt or zero rated, the subscription fee can be apportioned between these and the taxable services.[151]

The VAT authorities have provided some further guidance on this issue of subscription payments being a facility or an advantage to members, and thereby making a charity a business.[152]

20.8.2(ii) Admission charges

Admitting persons to any premises for a consideration is a business activity.[153] It is possible to charge a certain level for admission to premises which is standard rated, then request an extra amount as a voluntary donation in addition to the required entry charge. This extra amount will be regarded as outside the scope of if the following conditions are satisfied[154]:

- It is clearly stated on all publicity material, including tickets, that anyone paying minimum charge will be admitted without further payment;

- The extra payment does not give any particular benefit;

- The extent of further contributions is ultimately left to the ticket holders to decide, even it the organiser indicates a desired level of donation;

- For film or theatre performances, concerts, sporting fixtures, etc the minimum charge is not less than the usual price of the particular seats at a normal commercial event of the same type; and

- For dances, dinners and similar functions, the minimum total sum upon which

---

[149] s. 94(2)(a) Value Added Tax Act 1994 and see, for example, *Royal Ulster Constabulary Athletics Association Ltd v. Customs and Excise Commissioners* (1989) VATTR 17, *Friends of the Ironbridge Gorge Museum v. Customs and Excise Commissioners* (1991) VATTR 97, *Northamptonshire Football Association v. Customs and Excise Commissioners* (1995) VAT decision 12936.

[150] (1999) S.T.C. 315.

[151] *Customs and Excise Commissioners v. Automobile Association* [1974] 1 All E.R. 1257, [1975] S.T.C. 192, *Barton v. Customs and Excise Commissioners* [1974] 3 All E.R. 337, (1974) S.T.C. 200 and *Trewby v. Customs and Excise Commissioners* (1976) 2 All E.R. 199, (1976) S.T.C. 122.

[152] See further, VAT Notice 701/1/95 Charities.

[153] s. 94(2)(b) Value Added Tax Act 1994, see for example, *Eric Taylor Deceased Testimonial Match Committee v Customs and Excise Commissioners* (1975) VATTR 8.

[154] Vat Notice 701/1/95 Charities.

organisers will be liable to VAT will not be less than their total costs incurred in arranging the event.

In *Glasgow's Miles Better Mid Summer 5th Anniversary Ball*,[155] an admission fee of £20 plus a "minimum voluntary contribution" of £30 failed this test. It implied that the £30 was a compulsory not a voluntary requirement.

20.8.2(iii) Third party advertisements promulgated by charities

If a charity prints an advertisement in its brochure, programme, annual report or similar publication, in return for a consideration, this is a business activity. There is an Extra Statutory Concession if more than 50 per cent of the advertisements come from private individuals. This concession allows all consideration from all advertisers to be treated as donations by the advertisers. Selling advertising space to commercial organisations is regarded as business even if the advertisements make no specific reference to trading activities. If over 50 per cent of advertising is not from private individuals, all advertisements are within the scope of VAT. If over 50 per cent is from private individuals, all advertisements are outside the scope of VAT.[156] The purchase by charities of certain types of advertisements is a separate issue and is considered below under one of the zero-rating reliefs.

20.8.2(iv) Welfare services

Supplying "welfare services" in return for consideration is a business activity. Subject to certain requirements, the provision by a charity of welfare services at below cost is an exempt supply, see further below. Examples of welfare services include residential care for elderly and disabled people, providing accommodation in hostels for the homeless and in children's homes, meals in day care centres and children in care

20.8.2(v) Financial investment income

The receipt of interest from banks, building societies etc is a non-business activity. Dividends received on shares are outside the scope of VAT and regarded as part of a charity's non-business income. Share dealing by charities is not a business activity. Any VAT incurred with the acquisition or disposal of shares, or the management of investments cannot be treated as input tax and therefore cannot be reclaimed on a VAT return. In *National Society for the Prevention of Cruelty to Children*[157] the tribunal held that even though the

---

[155] (4460).
[156] See further VAT Notice 701/1/95 Charities.
[157] [1992] VATTR 417 (9325).

charity's investment activities had a turnover of over £7 million, it did not amount to a business as the charity was not primarily concerned with those supplies.[158]

20.8.2(vi) Sponsorship

Sponsorship by a company can either be business or non-business. If the charity merely provides a simple acknowledgement of the contribution of the sponsor, the receipt of the sponsorship money is not a business activity. If the contribution is made on condition that the company's name or trading logo is advertised or promoted, it is a business activity. If the company receives some other benefit (for example free tickets, preferential booking rights or free advertising space in a charity event programme, it is a business activity. Some supplies of this sort by the charity may be exempt if they are part of a fund-raising event (see further, para. 20.9.2(ii)).

20.8.2(vii) Secondment of staff

The secondment or loan of staff by a charity is a business activity rated at the standard rate even if the staff are supplied at below cost. However, there is an Extra Statutory Concession where staff are seconded from one charity / non-profit making body to another. This will be an exempt supply if the employee is only engaged in non-business activities in both the lendor and lendee charity and if the consideration for the supply does not exceed the normal remuneration (*i.e.* the wages normally paid by the lendor charity to its seconded staff).

20.8.2(viii) Affinity credit card schemes

Affinity credit card schemes are generally regarded as partly business and partly non-business. The charity allows its name and logo to be used on a credit card of a financial institution. It also usually allows the institution to access its members/mailing list and endorses the credit card. In return, the charity receives a fixed amount whenever the credit card is first used, and a percentage of all retail spending made with the card. There should be a clear separation between the use of charity logo and name (which is outside the scope of VAT) and the access to members / promotional activity which is business. Provided this is done, Customs and Excise will take the view that the percentage payments are donations by the financial institution and are outside the scope of VAT. They will also regard approximately 80 per cent of the fixed

---

[158] See also *The Wellcome Trust Ltd v. Commissioners of Customs and Excise*, CJEC (1996) S.T.C. 945.

sum for first use as outside the scope of VAT. The charity will therefore not be liable for VAT on these sizeable portions of income. To take advantage of this, there should be two separate contracts dealing with the two separate services provided by the charity.

20.8.2(ix) Miscellaneous activities

Certain activities by charities are automatically deemed to be non-business.[159] Receiving donations from legacies or other voluntary contributions from the public is not a business activity. Even if the donor receives something like an emblem or badge in return for a donation, it remains non-business. Receiving grants which are not consideration for services rendered is not a business activity. Performing a service which is free of charge is not a business activity *e.g.* first aid at public functions, sea rescue, religious rites of worship.

Sales of goods by charities are business activities. Sales of donated goods are business activities.[160] However, sales of donated goods are zero-rated.[161] Hiring out charity run buildings (*i.e.* village halls) is a business activity. However, this is an exempt supply.[162]

20.8.2(x) Likelihood of charities being VAT registered

In the majority of cases, charities will not have to become VAT registered and charge VAT on supplies they make. This is because they are unlikely to pass the necessary hurdles. Firstly, they are unlikely to be regarded as a business because they will be distributing to beneficiaries without seeking payment in return. Secondly, if they are a business, the supplies they will be making may well be exempt or zero-rated. Thirdly, even if they are making non-exempt business supplies, it is unlikely that these will be over the £52,000 annual threshold.

20.9 SUPPLIES TO CHARITIES

With the usual position therefore being that charities will not be VAT registered, their only point of contact with the Customs and Excise will be VAT charged on supplies to them. There are a number of specific VAT exemptions charities can utilise. The following two sections describe zero rated and exempt supplies to charities.

---

[159] See further VAT Notice 701/1/95 Charities.
[160] Contrast this with the income tax approach which regards this activity as merely realising the value of a donation and not a trading activity.
[161] See further below.
[162] See further below.

20.9.1 Zero-rated supplies to and by charities

VAT is chargeable on zero-rated supplies, but it is chargeable at the rate of 0 per cent. Charities do not have to pay VAT on zero-rated supplies made to them. Charities do not have to charge VAT on zero-rated supplies made by them. However, they can reclaim VAT paid on supplies received by them in relation to zero-rated supplies made by them.

These supplies are listed within Schedule 8 of the Value Added Tax Act 1994. There are reliefs for books for the blind, buildings, sea rescue equipment, charity funded medical equipment, some disabled aids, exported goods, advertising and donated goods.

20.9.1(i) Books for the blind

The supply to the Royal National Institute for the Blind, the National Listening Library or other similar charities of certain items is zero-rated.[163] These include all sound recording equipment, including parts and accessories to be used by the blind or severely handicapped. In addition, the supply to a charity of radios or tape-playing/recording apparatus which are solely for gratuitous loan to the blind are zero-rated.[164] The zero-rating does not apply to cassette tapes. The charity should supply a certificate to the supplier (see VAT notice 701/1/95 Annex F for a suggested certificate) in order to take advantage of the relief.

20.9.1(ii) Construction of buildings

The supply of services made in the course of the construction of a building intended for use solely for a relevant charitable purpose is zero-rated.[165] For the meaning of "the course of" construction see *Customs and Excise Commissioners* v *St Mary's Roman Catholic High School*.[166] The supply of building materials by a supplier of services which satisfies the above test is also zero-rated.[167] Some items are specifically excluded: prefabricated furniture (except kitchen furniture), materials for the construction of furniture (except kitchen furniture), most electrical or gas appliances (except heaters, air regulators, alarm/safety equipment and lifts), and carpets.[168] VAT Notice 708 Buildings and Construction gives a comprehensive list of zero-rated services. The supply of the services of an architect, surveyor or other person acting in a supervisory capacity are not zero-rated.[169]

---

[163] Schedule 8, Group 4, Item 1 VAT 1994.
[164] Schedule 8, Group 4, Item 2 VAT 1994.
[165] Schedule 8, Group 5, Item 2 Value Added Tax Act 1994.
[166] (1996) S.T.C. 1091.
[167] Schedule 8, Group 5, Item 4 Value Added Tax Act 1994.
[168] Schedule 8, Group 5, Note 22 Value Added Tax Act 1994.
[169] Schedule 8, Group 5, Item 2 Value Added Tax Act 1994.

A "relevant charitable purpose" means any use by a charity so long as it is not in the course of a business, or use as a village hall or similarly in providing social or recreational facilities for a local community.[170] Three points arise from this definition of "relevant charitable purpose". Firstly, charities who are applying for this relief will have to satisfy Customs and Excise that their intended use of the premises is not a business use. Secondly, that the actual use need not be charitable, so long as it is a use by the charity. Thirdly, the use as a village hall can be a business use.[171]

If part of the building only is intended to be used for a relevant charitable purpose, the supplies can be apportioned between it and the non-qualifying part so that the proportion of the supplies which relates to the qualifying part is zero-rated.[172] The zero-rating will not apply unless the person in receipt of the supply gives the supplier a certificate stating that the supply relates to a relevant charitable purpose.[173]

The construction of a building does not include the conversion, reconstruction or alteration of an existing building.[174] Nor does it include enlarging or extending existing buildings, except to the extent that it constitutes an independent annex.[175] An independent annex to an existing building can qualify provided it is capable of functioning independently from the existing building. The main/only access to the annex cannot be via the existing building and the main (or only) access to the existing building cannot be via the annex.[176]

There is also zero-rating for the first grant of a major interest by a person constructing a building intended for use solely for a relevant charitable purpose.[177] A major interest means the fee simple or a lease of at least 21 years. The major interest must be in any part of the building or its site.

There is a related Extra Statutory Concession[178] for charities which wish to convert one of its buildings into residential accommodation but is prevented by legal constraints from granting a major interest in that accommodation. The concession allows the charity to recover VAT incurred on the conversion works.[179]

---

[170] Schedule 8, Group 5, Note 6 Value Added Tax Act 1994.
[171] For applications of the relevant charitable purpose rule, see *Newtownbutler Playgroup Ltd. v. Customs and Excise Commissioners* (1995) VAT decision 13741, *Jubilee Hall Recreation Centre v. Customs and Excise Commissioners, Customs and Excise Commissioners v. St. Dunstan's Educational Foundation* (1999) STC 381.
[172] Schedule 8, Group 5, Note 11 Value Added Tax Act 1994.
[173] Schedule 8, Group 5, Note 12 Value Added Tax Act 1994 see VAT Notice 708 Buildings and Construction Appendix A for a precedent certificate.
[174] Schedule 8, Group 5, Note 16(a) Value Added Tax Act 1994.
[175] Schedule 8, Group 5, Note 16(a) and(b) Value Added Tax Act 1994.
[176] Schedule 8, Group 5, Note 17 Value Added Tax Act 1994.
[177] Schedule 8, Group 5, Note 1 Value Added Tax Act 1994.
[178] News Release 15/96, announced on March 13, 1996.
[179] See further VAT Notice 708 Buildings and Construction at Section 4.4.

Charities can also recover VAT chargeable on the supply or acquisition of goods used in connection with the construction of certain work.[180] This relief applies broadly where the charity carries out the construction work itself, otherwise than in the course of a business. Charities can recover VAT on building materials which are incorporated into the building or the site. They must reclaim the VAT from Customs and Excise within three months of the completion of the construction.[181]

20.9.1(iii) Sea rescue equipment

The supply, repair and maintenance of certain seas rescue equipment to a charity which provides rescue or assistance at sea is zero-rated.[182] The recipient of the supply must give a certificate to the supplier stating the name and address of the recipient and a statement that the supply satisfies Schedule 8, Group 8, Item 3 VAT1994.[183]

20.9.1(iv) Drugs, medicines and aids for the handicapped

The supply to a charity of various items which are to be made available to handicapped people, by sale or otherwise, for their domestic use is zero-rated.[184] A complete list is contained within Item 2. The items are generally medical, surgical or mechanical devices designed specifically for use by handicapped persons. The zero-rating extends to installing the equipment.[185]

There is also zero-rating for supplies to charities by adapting goods[186] or repairing said goods.[187] Supplying ramp construction or door widening services to a charity for the purpose of facilitating a handicapped person's movement within a building is zero-rated.[188] The supply to a charity of a service of providing, extending or adapting a bathroom, washroom or lavatory for use by handicapped persons, either in residential accommodation or in a day care centre where at least 20 per cent of the users are handicapped is zero-rated. The provision, adaptation etc must be necessary by reason of the condition of the handicapped persons.[189] There is also zero-rating for washroom or lavato-

---

[180] s. 35 Value Added Tax Act 1994, see also VAT Notice 708 Buildings and Construction.
[181] See VAT Notice 719 for details on how to make a repayment claim.
[182] Schedule 8, Group 8, Item 3 Value Added Tax Act 1994.
[183] Schedule 8, Group 8, Note 3 Value Added Tax Act 1994 and see VAT Notice 701/1/95 Charities Annex G for a suggested format.
[184] Schedule 8, Group 12, Item 2 Value Added Tax Act 1994.
[185] Schedule 8, Group 12, Item 7 Value Added Tax Act 1994.
[186] Schedule 8, Group 12, Item 4 Value Added Tax Act 1994.
[187] Schedule 8, Group 12, Item 5 Value Added Tax Act 1994.
[188] Schedule 8, Group 12, Item 9 Value Added Tax Act 1994.
[189] Schedule 8, Group 12, Item 11 Value Added Tax Act 1994 as inserted by the Value Added Tax (Charities and Aids for the Handicapped) Order 2000, part of the Getting Britain Giving initiative.

ries for use by the handicapped in a building used principally by the charity for charitable purposes.[190] The supply to a charity, providing accommodation or a day centre for handicapped persons, of the services required in installing a lift for handicapped persons is zero-rated[191] as is the supply of personal alarm systems to charities for handicapped persons.[192]

20.9.1(v) Sale of donated goods

The sale or letting of donated goods by a charity is zero-rated.[193] The zero-rating has recently been extended by the *Getting Britain Giving* initiative.[194] The sale or letting of donated goods by a "profits to charity person" is also zero rated.[195] A "profits to charity person" means a trading subsidiary of a charity which passes all its profits to its charitable parent. The passing of profits must either be agreed in writing (although a deed is not necessary) or otherwise payable (i.e. by Gift Aid) to the charity.[196] It is to be noted that there is no requirement that the profits to charity person be a subsidiary of the charity, just that its profits are payable to the charity.

There are a number of anti-avoidance provisions. The goods must have been donated to the charity for the purpose of sale, letting or export by it. To be able to donate goods implies that the donor has title to the goods. The court has struck down an attempt to use subsidiary companies as a device to avoid paying VAT on certain goods.[197] The goods must be continually relet, and it they are not to be relet, they must be sold, exported or destroyed.[198] Whilst not being let, they cannot be use for any purpose other than being available for letting sale or export.[199] The donation cannot be made as a result of prior arrangements relating to the goods made between the parties to the sale/letting or between the donor and either of those parties.[200]

The goods must be available to either the general public or to two or more "specified persons".[201] A "specified person" is defined as either a handicapped

---

[190] Schedule 8, Group 12, Item 12 Value Added Tax Act 1994.

[191] Schedule 8, Group 12, Item 17 Value Added Tax Act 1994.

[192] Schedule 8, Group 12, Item 19 Value Added Tax Act 1994.

[193] Schedule 8, Group 15, Item 1 Value Added Tax Act 1994.

[194] See Value Added Tax (Charities and Aids for the Handicapped) Order 2000, SI 2000/805.

[195] Schedule 8, Group 15, Item 1A Value Added Tax Act 1994 as modified by the above Order.

[196] Schedule 8, Group 15, Note 1E Value Added Tax Act 1994.

[197] See *University of Wales College, Newport v. Customs and Excise Commissioners* (1998) B.V.C. 2082; (1997) V. & D.R. 417.

[198] Schedule 8, Group 15, Note 1C Value Added Tax Act 1994.

[199] Schedule 8, Group 15, Note 1B Value Added Tax Act 1994.

[200] Schedule 8, Group 15, Note 1 Value Added Tax Act 1994.

[201] Schedule 8, Group 15, Item 1 Value Added Tax Act 1994.

person or a person in receipt of certain specified means-tested benefits.[202] Handicapped "means chronically sick or disabled".[203] The specified benefits are: income support, housing benefit, council tax benefit, income based Job Seekers Allowance, working families tax credit or disabled persons tax credit.

As well as the sale or letting *by* the charity[204] or the profits to charity person[205] of donated goods being zero-rated, the donation *to* them is also exempt.[206] The donation must be for the purposes of either sale, letting or export by the charity or profits to charity person.

20.9.1(vi) Export of goods by a charity

The export of any goods by a charity to a place outside the member states of the European Union is zero-rated.[207]

20.9.1(vii) Charity funded equipment for medical and veterinary uses

The supply of "relevant goods" which will be donated to nominated "eligible bodies" are zero rated if the goods are purchased with charitable funds or with money from voluntary contributions.[208] The supply of "relevant goods" to "eligible bodies" are zero-rated if the eligible body pays for the goods with funds from a charity or with money from voluntary contributions.[209] The supply of "relevant goods" to an "eligible body" which is a charitable institution providing care or medical or surgical treatment for handicapped persons is zero-rated.[210] Customs and Excise have prepared extensive lists of particular items which can qualify.[211] These should be referred to determine whether a specific item is a qualifying one.

In cases where the goods supplied are donated to a nominated eligible body under Item 4, if that body is not a charity, it cannot have contributed either in whole or in part to the funds used to purchase the goods.[212] In cases where the goods are supplied to an eligible body under Item 5, if that body is not a charity, it cannot have contributed either in whole or in part to the funds used to purchase those goods.[213]

---

[202] Schedule 8, Group 15, Note 1C Value Added Tax Act 1994.
[203] Schedule 8, Group 15, Note 5 Value Added Tax Act 1994.
[204] Schedule 8, Group 15, Item 1 Value Added Tax Act 1994.
[205] Schedule 8, Group 15, Item 1A Value Added Tax Act 1994.
[206] Schedule 8, Group 15, Item 2 Value Added Tax Act 1994.
[207] Schedule 8, Group 15, Item 3 Value Added Tax Act 1994.
[208] Schedule 8, Group 15, Item 4 Value Added Tax Act 1994.
[209] Schedule 8, Group 15, Item 5 Value Added Tax Act 1994.
[210] Schedule 8, Group 15, Item 5 Value Added Tax Act 1994.
[211] VAT Notice 701/6/97 Charity Funded Equipment for Medical, Veterinary etc. Uses
[212] Schedule 8, Group 15, Note 6 Value Added Tax Act 1994.
[213] Schedule 8, Group 15, Note 7 Value Added Tax Act 1994.

The supply of these goods also includes their letting or hire.[214] The supply of repair and maintenance services for relevant goods owned by an eligible body is also zero-rated.[215] The supply of goods in connection with this repair and maintenance is zero-rated too.[216] However, as with the purchase and letting reliefs, these supplies must be paid for with funds which have been provided for by a charity or with voluntary contributions.[217] If the owner of the goods repaired is not a charity, the owner cannot contribute in whole or in part to those funds.[218]

Customs and Excise have granted an Extra Statutory Concession[219] in this area. Relevant goods are those supplied to: a charity whose sole purpose and function is to provide a range of care services to meet the personal needs of handicapped people, or a charity which provides transport services predominantly to handicapped people, are zero-rated. The repair and maintenance of these goods is also zero-rated. In order to take advantage of this concession, a charity must be able to demonstrate it meets these requirements by way of:

- its charitable aims and objectives,
- its publicity and advertising material,
- any documents it has issued for the purposes of obtaining funding,
- its day to day operations and,
- any other relevant information.

In practice, this concession is designed for motor vehicles which are specially adapted for use by handicapped persons.[220]

The "relevant goods" which have been alluded to above are listed precisely both in the legislation[221] and even more precisely in the VAT Guidance.[222] Relevant goods are[223]:

- Medical, scientific, computer, video, sterilising, laboratory or refrigeration equipment for use in medical or veterinary research, training, diagnosis or treatment;
- Ambulances;
- Parts or accessories for any of the above;

---

[214] Schedule 8, Group 15, Note 8 Value Added Tax Act 1994.
[215] Schedule 8, Group 15, Item 6 Value Added Tax Act 1994.
[216] Schedule 8, Group 15, Item 7 Value Added Tax Act 1994.
[217] Schedule 8, Group 15, Note 8(a) Value Added Tax Act 1994.
[218] Schedule 8, Group 15, Note 8(b) Value Added Tax Act 1994.
[219] Extra Statutory Concession of June 16, 1997.
[220] See Customs and Excise Business Brief 13/97 of June 16, 1997 and VAT Information Sheet 8/98 for further details on this concession.
[221] Schedule 8, Group 15, Note 3 Value Added Tax Act 1994.
[222] VAT Notice 701/6/97, Charity Funded Equipment for medical, veterinary, etc., uses at Section 5.3 and Appendix F.
[223] Schedule 8, Group 15, Note 3 Value Added Tax Act 1994.

- Goods in Schedule 8, Group 12, Item 2 (see above 20.9.1(iv) Drugs, Medicines and Aids for the Handicapped);
- Motor vehicles designed or substantially altered for carrying handicapped people in wheelchairs (subject to certain minimum requirements as to numbers of wheelchair places as opposed to numbers of ordinary places);
- Motor vehicles (not necessarily adapted) (with between seven and 50 seats) for use by an eligible body providing for care for blind, deaf, mentally handicapped or terminally sick persons mainly to transport such persons;
- Telecommunication, aural, visual, light enhancing or heat detecting equipment solely for use for the purpose of rescue or first aid services undertaken by a charity providing these services.

These definitions have been further refined by the VAT authorities. Equipment means articles designed for a specific purpose. Disposable items are still articles even though they are only designed to be used once. Consumables are not articles. Goods like liquids, powders, sheets, pellets, granules or other bulk materials are not equipment. Medical equipment encompasses items designed for use in the diagnosis or treatment of patients. Scientific equipment means equipment which performs a scientific function, not which works on a scientific principle. Computer equipment means computer hardware and includes servers, screens, keyboards and disks. It includes off the shelf but not custom made software. Video equipment includes recording and playback equipment. Laboratory equipment means goods designed specifically for use in a laboratory (even though ultimately the goods may not be used there). Refrigeration equipment includes all cooling and freezing equipment whether of an industrial type, special design for specific purpose, or the common domestic fridge. Ambulance means an emergency vehicle used for transporting injured people or animals. Medical or veterinary research means original research into disease and injury of humans or animals. Medical and veterinary training means the training of doctors, nurses, surgeons or other professionals involved in diagnosis or treatment. The training must include an aspect of practical application of the theory. Medical and veterinary diagnosis and treatment means the diagnosis and treatment of a physical or mental abnormality by a medical or paramedical practitioner or by a veterinary surgeon.

An eligible body means:[224]

- A Health and Social Services Boards in Northern Ireland (together with their equivalent in the rest of the U.K.),
- A hospital whose activities are not carried on for profit,
- A research institution whose activities are not carried on for profit,
- The Northern Ireland Central Services Agency for Health and Social Services,

---

[224] Schedule 8, Group 15, Note 4 Value Added Tax Act 1994.

- A National Health Service Trust,
- A Primary Care Trust
- A charitable institution providing rescue or first-aid services,
- A charitable institution providing care or medical or surgical treatment for handicapped persons.

The last category is only satisfied if the charity provides the said facilities in a relevant establishment and the majority of persons who benefit from those facilities are handicapped.[225] A relevant establishment is a day centre so long as it is not primarily a day centre for activities which are social and recreational.[226] A relevant establishment can also be an institution which is regulated in some way by any enactment.[227] The goods must either be used in that relevant establishment,[228] unless the charity provides the medical care to the handicapped persons in their own home, the goods are used in connection with that care and the goods are medical, scientific, computer, video, sterilising, laboratory or refrigeration equipment for use in medical treatment.

20.9.1(viii) Charity advertising

The supply to a charity of advertising time and space in a medium which communicates to the public is zero-rated.[229] The supply to a charity of design and production services connected with such an advertisement is zero-rated[230] as is the supply of goods closely related to those services.[231]

The advertisements must be directed to the public. It does not apply where the recipients of the advertising are selected by or on behalf of the charity. "Selected" includes being selected by address, phone number, email or by random selection. The relief will therefore not apply to telesales or direct mail or email. Examples of acceptable forms of communication include television, cinema, billboards, sides of buses, newspapers, printed publications, reverse of tickets etc.[232] The reliefs apply to supplies made to the charity of someone else's advertising time and space. They do no apply to advertisements in the charities own magazine, notice boards, publication etc. Websites are specifically excluded from this relief, "none of the items 8 to 8C includes a supply

---

[225] Schedule 8, Group 15, Note 4A Value Added Tax Act 1994.
[226] Schedule 8, Group 15, Note 4B(a) Value Added Tax Act 1994.
[227] Schedule 8, Group 15, Note 4B(b) Value Added Tax Act 1994.
[228] Schedule 8, Group 15, Note 5A Value Added Tax Act 1994.
[229] Schedule 8, Group 15, Item 8 as modified by the Value Added Tax (Charities and Aids for the Handicapped) Order 2000, SI 2000/805.
[230] Schedule 8, Group 15, Item 8B Value Added Tax Act 1994.
[231] Schedule 8, Group 15, Item 8C Value Added Tax Act 1994.
[232] Draft VAT Notice 701/58 Charity Advertising and Goods Connected with Collecting Donations, Appendix C for further examples.

used to create, or to contribute to a website which is the charity's own. For this purpose, a website is a charity's own even though hosted by another person".[233] Nor does the relief apply to supplies of good which a charity uses for making its own advertisements.[234]

Customs and Excise have indicated a degree of flexibility in determining the applicability of this relief.[235] Liability is to a certain extent determined in reverse. If a proposed advertisement is intended to be publicised the preceding design and production work will be zero-rated. If a charity intended to use an advertisement, but subsequently did not, it can retrospectively obtain zero-rating on production costs already incurred. Charities cannot obtain retrospective relief on goods and services purchased for another purpose but then subsequently used for a qualifying advertisement. Charities should fill in a declaration to the supplier of the zero-rated supplies.[236]

20.9.1(ix) Goods used by charities in connection with collecting monetary donations

There is a proposed Extra Statutory Concession for certain goods used by charities in collecting monetary donations.[237] The concession will zero-rate three categories of goods supplied to charities: certain printed stationery, collection boxes and lapel stickers or similar tokens.

Charities should fill in a declaration to the supplier of the zero-rated supply.[238]

20.9.1(x) Medical or veterinary research or medicinal products

The supply to a charity of a substance directly used for synthesising or testing in the course of medical or veterinary research is zero-rated.[239] Medical and veterinary research means activities which are directed towards opening up new areas of knowledge or understanding, or initial development of new techniques, rather than towards mere quantitative additions to human knowledge.

---

[233] Schedule 8, Group 15, Note 10B Value Added Tax Act 1994.

[234] Schedule 8, Group 15, Note 10C Value Added Tax Act 1994.

[235] Draft VAT Notice 701/58 Charity Advertising and Goods Connected with Collecting Donations.

[236] Draft VAT Notice 701/58 Charity Advertising and Goods Connected with Collecting Donations.

[237] See Draft VAT Notice 701/58 Charity Advertising and Goods Connected with Collecting Donations, Appendix B Printed Matter and Certain Other Supplies to Assist with the Collection of Donations.

[238] Draft VAT Notice 701/58 Charity Advertising and Goods Connected with Collecting Donations, Appendix E.

[239] Schedule 8, Group 15, Item 10 Value Added Tax Act 1994.

Certain other supplies to charities which are either: providing care, medical or surgical treatment to animals or humans, or which are engaged in medical or veterinary research are zero-rated.[240] The supply must be of medicinal products used solely by the charity in such care, treatment or research. A medicinal product is any substance or article used wholly or mainly for being administered to humans/animals for a medicinal purpose, or for use as an ingredient in preparing same.[241] It does not include any instrument, apparatus or appliance. Substance means any natural or artificial substance, either solid, liquid or gas.[242] Administer means administering orally, by injection, or by external application and either with or without any other substance being used as a vehicle.[243] Medicinal purpose means a use for treating or preventing disease, diagnosing disease or ascertaining physiological condition; contraception; inducing anaesthesia; or otherwise bringing about some alteration in the physical or physiological state of the patient or animal.[244] Ingredient includes anything which is the sole active ingredient of that substance as manufactured or prepared.[245]

The charity should supply a certificate to the supplier of these goods stating that they should be zero-rated.[246]

20.9.2 Exempt supplies

Exempt supplies are not treated as taxable supplies.[247] No VAT is charged on these supplies and no VAT can be recovered for taxable supplies received in relation to them. Schedule 9 of the Value Added Tax Act 1994 provides a list of exempt supplies.[248] The *Getting Britain Giving* initiative widened the scope of the exemption for fundraising events by charities. The other exempt supply is the provision of welfare services by charities.

20.9.2(i) Welfare services

The supply, otherwise than for profit, by a charity, of welfare services and goods supplied in connection therewith is exempt.[249]

Welfare services means services directly connected with[250]:

---

[240] Schedule 8, Group 15, Item 9 Value Added Tax Act 1994.
[241] Schedule 8, Group 15, Note 11 Value Added Tax Act 1994.
[242] Medicines Act 1968, s.132.
[243] Medicines Act 1968, s.130.
[244] Medicines Act 1968, s.130(2).
[245] Medicines Act 1968, s.130.
[246] VAT Notice 701/1/95 Charities, Annex I.
[247] Value Added Tax Act 1994, s.4(2).
[248] See also s. 31 Value Added Tax Act 1994.
[249] Schedule 9, Group 7, Item 9 Value Added Tax Act 1994.
[250] Schedule 9, Group 7, Note 6 Value Added Tax Act 1994.

- The provision of care, treatment or instruction designed to promote the physical or mental welfare or elderly, sick, distressed or disabled persons; or
- The protection of children or young persons; or
- The provision of spiritual welfare by a religious institution as part of a course of instruction or a retreat, not being a course or retreated designed primarily to provide recreation or a holiday.

Welfare means financial and other assistance given to people in need. It must be of help and benefit to the recipient. It should be given rather than sold (although nominal charges are acceptable).

The supply of accommodation or catering is not exempt unless it is ancillary to the provision of care, treatment or instruction.[251] Supplying catering to elderly residents in sheltered accommodation can be ancillary.[252] Supplying hotel accommodation and catering to cancer patients and their families can be ancillary.[253]

In *Customs and Excise Commissioners* v. *Bell Concord Educational Trust Ltd*[254] the Court of Appeal held that surpluses raised on the activity can be applied in the furtherance of the activity which generated the surplus. However, surpluses raised cannot be applied to any other activity, even if that activity is also charitable. There is authority for saying that the making of profit is irrelevant provided it is only a subsidiary object which allows the main object to be fulfilled.[255] For a Northern Ireland approach to the meaning of "not established or conducted for profit" see *Larne Enterprise Development Co. v. Commissioner of Valuation.*[256]

Care means some form of continuing personal contact in looking after, helping or supervising people. It also includes domestic help services (*i.e.* cooking, cleaning and shopping) provided to people who have major difficulty carrying out key daily living tasks.[257] Some form of assessment of needs should be carried out to determine if the recipient is unable to carry out routine domestic tasks. The assessment should be carried out by someone with suitable training or experience (although not necessarily someone who is medically qualified).[258]

---

[251] Schedule 9, Group 7, Note 7 Value Added Tax Act 1994.

[252] *Viewpoint Housing Association Ltd.* (13148).

[253] *Trustees for the Macmillan Cancer Trust* (1998) VATDR 289 (15603).

[254] [1989] S.T.C. 264.

[255] *National Deposit Friendly Society Trustees* v. *Skegness Urban District Council* (1959) AC 293 at p. 319, 320, (1958) All ER 601 at p. 612.

[256] VR/6/1995, see further Chap 21.

[257] *Watford and District Old People's Housing Association Ltd. (t/a Watford Help in the Home Service)* [1998] VATDR 477 (15660).

[258] See VAT Information Sheet 6/99, March 1999, Customs and Excise Business Brief 24/98, December 2, 1998, and Customs and Excise Business Brief 4/99, February 16, 1999.

Supplies of food and drink by charities from trolleys, canteens or shops are business, but exempt when connected with the welfare of those in hospital, prison, etc.[259] The supply, otherwise than for profit, of goods and services incidental to the provision of spiritual welfare, by a religious community to a resident member of that community in return for a subscription or other consideration paid as a condition of membership is an exempt supply.[260] This exemption is slightly different to the one listed above.

There is also an Extra Statutory Concession for welfare services and related goods supplied by charities at consistently "below cost" to distressed people for the relief of distress. Such supplies are also exempt. The subsidy should be as the result of a deliberate policy, not inefficient trading.

If a charity delivers meals on wheels as the agent of a local authority, it is part of that authority's non-business activities, even if the recipient makes a payment. If the charity charges the local authority, this is the taxable supply of a delivery service and not a welfare supply by the charity.[261]

20.9.2(ii) Fundraising events by charities

The supply of goods and services by a charity in connection with a fundraising event is VAT exempt.[262] The law has recently been updated with effect from April 1, 2000 by the Value Added Tax (Fundraising Events by Charities and other Qualifying Bodies) Order 2000, SI 2000/802. The purpose of the amendment was to extend the exemption and bring it into alignment with the income tax exemption on fundraising as part of the *Getting Britain Giving* initiative.[263]

The event must be organised for charitable purposes. The primary purpose must be to raise money and it must be promoted as being primarily for that purpose.

The event must be organised either by the charity, by two or more charities jointly, by a qualifying body, or by a qualifying body and a charity jointly.[264] The scope of what constitutes an event is not set out in the legislation. It includes an event wholly or partly accessed by means of electronic communication.[265] Customs and Excise give the following examples: balls, discos, performances, festivals, exhibitions, bazaars, games, fireworks, meals, auctions, etc.[266]

---

[269] VAT Notice 701/1/95 Charities.

[260] Schedule 9, Group 7, Item 10 Value Added Tax Act 1994.

[261] VAT Notice 701/1/95 Charities, see further Tolley's VAT Guide.

[262] Schedule 9, Group 12 Value Added Tax Act 1994.

[263] See further, para. 20.4.4(ix) Trading Exemption – Charity Fundraising Events

[264] Qualifying bodies are necessarily charities and are defined in Group 9 Item1, Group 10 and Group 13 Item 2, see further Schedule 9, Group 12, Note 3 Value Added Tax Act 1994.

[265] Schedule 9, Group 12, Note 1 Value Added Tax Act 1994, *i.e.* web based events.

[266] VAT Notice 701/59 Exemption for Fundraising Events held by Charities and other Qualifying Bodies.

No more than 15 events of the same kind can be held in any one location by the charity in a year.[267] In *Northern Ireland Council for Voluntary Activity*[268] the tribunal held that a week of fundraising activities including several performances of a play could be described as a single fundraising event.[269] Location means the geographical area where the fundraising activity takes place. If gross undertakings of an event are under £1,000, it will not count towards the 15 event limit.[270]

If the financial year is shorter than 12 months, there is provision in the legislation to adjust the figure of 15 proportionately over that shorter time period.[271]

The scope of the exemption is wide. It applies to all supplies made by the charity in the course of the event. However, it does not apply to supplies made to the charity, *i.e.* the charity cannot reclaim VAT incurred in making purchases in relation to the event. Exempt supplies include[272]:

- All admission charges.

- Sale of commemorative brochures.

- Sale of advertising space in those brochures.

- Other items sold by the charity at the event, for example tee shirts, auctioned goods etc.

- Sponsorship payments directly connected with the event.

If accommodation in connection with the event is supplied by the charity organising, or a charity connected with that charity, and that accommodation is more than incidental to the event, the event does not qualify for the exemption.[273] Accommodation is only incidental if it does not exceed two nights and also does not qualify under the Tour Operators Margin Scheme.[274] Fundraising holidays and day trips will therefore generally not be VAT exempt.

There is a catch-all restriction on the scope of this exemption. It does not include a supply "which would be likely to create distortions of competition such as to place a commercial enterprise carried on by a taxable person at a

---

[267] Schedule 9, Group 12, Note 4 Value Added Tax Act 1994.

[268] (1991) VATTR 32 (5451).

[269] See also *Reading Cricket and Hockey Club* (13656) holding that a three day real ale and jazz festival, planned as a single event was a single event, even though separate tickets had been sold for each evening.

[270] Schedule 9, Group 12, Note 5Draft VAT Notice 701/58 Charity Advertising and Goods Connected with Collecting Donations..

[271] Schedule 9, Group 12, Note 6 Value Added Tax Act 1994.

[272] VAT Notice 701/59 Exemption for Fundraising Events held by Charities and other Qualifying Bodies.

[273] Schedule 9, Group 12, Note 8 Value Added Tax Act 1994.

[274] s. 53 and Schedule 9, Group 12, Note 9 Value Added Tax Act 1994.

disadvantage".[275] According to Customs and Excise "customs will only use this measure where there is potential to distort the relief".[276]

20.9.2(iii) Other exempt supplies

There are a range of other exempt supplies. They do not apply specifically to charities, but charities may be able to avail of some of them. These are the supply of land,[277] insurance,[278] betting, gaming and lotteries,[279] education,[280] burial and cremation,[281] sports, sports competitions and physical education,[282] works of art[283] and supply of cultural services *i.e.* admission to galleries, theatres, zoos, and concerts of a cultural nature.[284]

20.9.3 Fuel supplies to charities

The supply of fuel, electricity and heat to charities is chargeable at the reduced rate of 5 per cent.[285] The supply must be for qualifying use. A qualifying use is either domestic use or use by a charity otherwise than in the course or furtherance of a business.[286]

Fuel in outline means solid fuel, piped gas, or fuel oil etc. It does not apply to any road fuel gas.[287] If at least 60 per cent of the goods are for a qualifying use, the entirety shall be treated as a supply for a qualifying use.

Independent schools and other schools which are charities, but which charge fees to their pupils will constitute a business. Fuel and power supplied to them will be at the standard rate of 17.5 per cent. However, the lower rate applies where the fuel and power are for separate residential accommodation for the students.[288]

---

[275] Schedule 9, Group 12, Note 11 Value Added Tax Act 1994.
[276] VAT Notice 701/59 Exemption for Fundraising Events held by Charities and other Qualifying Bodies.
[277] Schedule 9 Group 1 Value Added Tax Act 1994.
[278] Schedule 9 Group 2 Value Added Tax Act 1994.
[279] Schedule 9 Group 4 Value Added Tax Act 1994.
[280] Schedule 9 Group 6 Value Added Tax Act 1994.
[281] Schedule 9 Group 8 Value Added Tax Act 1994.
[282] Schedule 9 Group 10 Value Added Tax Act 1994.
[283] Schedule 9 Group 11 Value Added Tax Act 1994.
[284] Schedule 9 Group 13 Value Added Tax Act 1994.
[285] s. 2(1A) and Schedule A1 Value Added Tax Act 1994, before the 31/8/97 the rate was the reduced rate of 8%.
[286] See above sections 20.9.1 (ii) and 20.9.2 Common Charitable Activities and Business Status.
[287] Schedule A1, Note 4(2).
[288] VAT Notice 701/19/95.

CHAPTER 21

Rates Exemption

21.1 INTRODUCTION

Northern Ireland charities or, perhaps, those bodies claiming to be charities, are at their most litigious when it comes to rating law. This is well illustrated by the fact that the Commissioner of Valuation has been a party to 19 out of the 47 reported[1] cases on issues concerning charities in Northern Ireland. A statistic that becomes even more telling when one considers that the Supreme Court is not the body which makes the initial decision on rating. First, there is the administrative decision taken by the District Valuer; then further rights of appeal exist to the Commissioner of Valuation and to the Lands Tribunal; and then, on points of law, to the Court of Appeal and beyond. Even after the filter of three appeal procedures, rating still constitutes the single most litigated aspect of charity law in Northern Ireland.

This chapter examines the law relating to charitable exemption from rateability. It begins by considering the historical background, the relevant legislative provisions and the effect given to them by the courts and the Lands Tribunal. It then considers the meaning and the bearing of two key concepts, "charitable occupation" and "charitable use" as determinants of eligibility for charitable exemption from rates. The bulk of the chapter, however, concentrates on the case law. Rates exemption forms a discrete, fairly self-contained, sub-division of charity law which has attracted a good deal of commentary.[2]

21.2 LEGISLATIVE HISTORY

The eligibility of charitable trusts to claim exemption from the general duty to pay rates on property dates from the late eighteenth and early nineteenth cen-

---

[1] That is the High Court or the Court of Appeal, depending on whether a case was initiated before or after the creation of the Lands Tribunal.

[2] See for example, Delany, *Rating Exemption on the Ground of Charitable or Public Use* (1960) 13 N.I.L.Q. 316; Carswell, *Rating Exemption and Charitable Purposes* (1965) 16 N.I.L.Q. 88; Lowry, *Some reflections on Ratings* (1966) 17 N.I.L.Q. 256; Brady, *Charitable Purposes and Ratings Exemption in Ireland* (1968) 3 Ir. Jur. (N.S.) 114; Brady, *House of Lords, Charities and Rating Relief in Northern Ireland* (1973) 24 N.I.L.Q. 106.

turies.[3] For most of the intervening years the law carefully distinguished the grounds enabling an organisation to acquire charitable status from the grounds enabling it to acquire charitable exemption from liability to pay rates on its premises.

The provisions of the Poor Relief (Ireland) Act 1838 introduced a new poor law and with it a new system to pay for the relief of poverty throughout the island. The poor rate was levied by the board of guardians under powers provided by this Act. It also provided grounds under which premises could claim exemption from liability for rates. Legislative provisions from that time, together with related case precedents, exercised a determining influence on the application of the law to charitable exemption from rates in both jurisdictions on this island until comparatively recently. However, in recent decades important jurisdictional differences have arisen in the law governing rates. In Ireland the distinct difference between the law governing the interpretation of "charitable" in the context of exemption from rateability and in the more general context of determining the nature of an organisation's activities is scrupulously maintained. There is no equivalent differentiation in the law of this jurisdiction nor elsewhere in the U.K.

21.2.1 The Valuation Act 1773

This stated that no hospitals, public infirmaries, alms houses, charity schools, public work houses, custom houses, or the offices appurtenant thereto, and no public exchanges, mayoralty houses, public market houses, shambles for the sale of flesh or fish, the King's barracks and guard houses, the public coal yards and gaols and houses of correction should be included in any valuation or charged with any rates or taxes. The statutory exemption for public buildings in Ireland never applied in England; Marsh's Library in Dublin was exempted[4] and so was the Armagh Observatory.[5] The Valuation Act 1831 exempted houses, lands and tenements "which by any law or usage have been heretofore exempted". In 1832 the words "of a public nature or used for charitable purposes" were introduced and subsequently narrowed in their application by the valuers, the legal profession and the courts.

21.2.2 The Poor Relief (Ireland) Act 1838

Entitled "An Act for the more effective relief of the destitute poor in Ireland", the statute directed that funds necessary to give effect to this purpose were to be raised by imposing an annual levy upon the occupiers of rateable

---

[3] See the Valuation Act 1773 the Poor Relief (Ireland) Act 1838, the Valuation (Ireland) Act 1852, the Valuation (Ireland) Act 1854 and the Scientific Societies Act 1843.

[4] See 6 Anne C. 19 (1707).

[5] See 31 Geo. 3 C. 46 (1791).

hereditaments. Section 61 provided for the making and levying of rates and section 71 required payment to be made by the occupier. Section 63 was all important. It specified the hereditaments deemed to be rateable subject to the following exemption clause:

"Provided also, that no church, chapel, or other building exclusively devoted to religious worship or exclusively used for the education of the poor; nor any burial ground or cemetery; nor any infirmary, hospital, charity school, or other building used exclusively for charitable purposes, nor any building, land, or hereditament dedicated to or used for public purposes, shall be rateable, except where any private profit or use shall be directly derived therefrom, in which case the person deriving such profit or use shall be liable to be rated as an occupier according to the annual value of such profit or use. "

This clause provided the grounds for the many applications since received by the courts from religious, health and educational establishments seeking exemption from rateable liability.

21.2.3 The Valuation (Ireland) Acts 1852 and 1854

The relevant provision of section 2 of the 1854 Act was as follows:

"In making out the Lists or Tables of valuation ... the Commissioner of Valuation shall distinguish all hereditaments and tenements, or portions of same, of a public nature, or used for charitable purposes or for the purposes of science, literature, and the fine arts ... and all such hereditaments or tenements, or portions of the same, so distinguished, shall, so long as they shall continue to be of a public nature, and occupied for the public service, or used for the purposes aforesaid, be deemed exempt from assessment for the relief of the destitute poor in Ireland and for Grand Jury and County Rates."

These provisions replaced the almost identical provisions of section 15 of the Valuation Act 1852, repealed by section 1 of the 1854 Act. Section 16 of the 1852 Act, in so far as it was relevant, provided as follows:

"For the purposes of such valuation, no hereditaments or tenements, or portions of the same, shall be deemed to be of a public nature, or used for such charitable ... purposes as hereinbefore specified, within the meaning of this Act, unless such hereditaments or tenements, or portions of the same respectively, shall be altogether of a public nature, or used exclusively for such charitable ... purposes aforesaid. . . ."

In the adjoining jurisdiction this remains the governing statutory framework for determining eligibility for charitable exemption from rates. In Northern Ireland these legislative provisions survived for over one hundred years until their piecemeal modification in the Rating and Valuation (Amendment) Act (N.I.) 1956 and the root and branch reform of the Rates (N.I.) Order 1972 leading to the current legislation, the Rates (N.I.) Order 1977.

21.3 CASE LAW HISTORY

Case law discloses a range of problems and anomalies. The root of many of
these problems lay in the Byzantine complexities, constructions and interde-
pendency of the legislative legacy. This was noted in the Northern Ireland
Court of Appeal by McVeigh J. when he stated that the:

> "... pursuit of the grounds for a logical decision traps the mind in a web of
> authorities and statutes from the study of which it struggles out tired and bewil-
> dered."[6]

It is significant that in this jurisdiction, following the major changes in rating
in 1972 and to a lesser extent in1977, only two cases have been appealed
through the courts compared with 17 during the preceding 57 years.

21.3.1 Charitable purposes and *Pemsel*

Income Tax Special Purposes Commissioner v. Pemsel[7] was a landmark case
in the development of charity law. The decision, which laid the foundations
for charitable tax exemption, also continues to provide the basis for contemporary rates valuation. The House of Lords then ruled that charitable status in
itself conferred an automatic entitlement to income tax exemption and should
not be subject to a restrictive interpretation. A trust was to be deemed charitable if it came within one of four "heads': a trust to relieve poverty; trusts for
the advancement of education; trusts for the advancement of religion; and
trusts beneficial to the community not falling under any of the preceding heads.

   On this island, some judiciary at the outset seem to have granted exemption on a similar liberal interpretation of what constituted "charitable purposes".
So, for example, in *The Guardians of Belfast Union v. Ryan*[8] a Christian Brothers' School was exempted even though it admitted some fee-paying pupils.
This approach was briefly consolidated by the decision of Palles C.B. in *Clancy
v. Commissioner of Valuation*[9] which extended the House of Lords ruling to
this island and applied it to exemption for liability for rates. Palles C.B. considered that the interpretation of "charitable purposes" was as construed by
Lord Macnaghten in *Pemsel's* case and expressed his view as follows:

> "The uniform current of authority in this country has been based (and I think,
> rightly) on the word "charitable" as used in this section (*i.e.* section 2 of the
> 1854 Act) being construed in the large sense in which that word is generally

---

6   *Governors of the Campbell College, Belfast v. County Court Judge of Down* [1964] N.I.
    107 at 146.
7   [1891] A.C. 53; see, further, Chap 1.
8   (1894), unreported, Lyons' Valuation Cases, 23. See also, *Guardians of Limerick Union
    v. Slattery* (1892), unreported, Lyons' Valuation Cases, 23.
9   [1911] 2 I.R. 447.

used in our law – in the sense in which it had been held to be used in the Legacy Duty Act and in the Income Tax Acts – upon it not being restricted merely to the relief of poverty."[10]

However, this view was resisted by his colleagues. In cases such as *Trustees of Magee College v. Commissioner of Valuation*[11] the judiciary had already demonstrated a preference for a more restrictive interpretation and with some exceptions[12] continued to do so.[13] In time this hardened into an approach which held that hereditaments were not charitably exempt from rates unless used exclusively for charitable purposes.[14]

21.3.2 Construing the statutes

The rationale for construing charity in a narrow sense is that by so doing the various individual statues may be viewed as forming one single code. More precisely, the requirement for exemption in section 2 of the 1854 Act was controlled by section 63 of the 1838 Act. To construe these two provisions as setting forth a single, unified code is to reason that when section 2 stated that "hereditaments used for charitable purposes" were exempt, what it actually meant was that the various uses enumerated in section 63 were exempt.

In *Guardians of Londonderry Union v. Londonderry Bridge Commissioners*[15] the issue before the court was whether a bridge was exempt from rates. The court held that the 1838 Act provided the actual exemption, the 1854 Act merely provided the technique for measuring the value of property. Together these two Acts formed a complete code:

> "... the Valuation Acts ... [are] only to provide a machinery for valuing property according to the standards provided by the existing legislation."[16]

The *Clancy*[17] case took a different approach, holding that "charity" was to receive its wide, common law meaning. However, this interpretation was ex-

---

[10] See *Commissioners for Special Purposes of Income Tax v. Pemsel* [1891] A.C. 531.

[11] (1871) I.R. 4 C.L. 438. See also *Guardians of Waterford Union v. Commissioner of Valuation* [1896] 2 I.R. 538.

[12] See for example, *Trustees of Leper Hospital v. Corporation of Waterford* (1883) 17 I.L.T.R. 88, *Ex parte Hayes* (1881) 8 L.R. Ir. 196 and *Ulster Society for Deaf and Dumb v. Commissioner of Valuation* (1904) 38 I.L.T.R. 150.

[13] See *Trustees of Harold's Cross Parochial Hall v. Commissioner of Valuation* (1886) unreported, Lyons' Valuation Cases 26 and *Trustees of Union Hall v. Londonderry Corporation* (1892) 28 L.R. Ir. 100.

[14] See for example, *The Dublin Cemeteries Committee v. Commissioner of Valuation* [1897] 2 I.R. 157, *per* Holmes J. at 170 and *O'Neill v. Commissioner of Valuation*, [1914] 2 I.R. 173, *per* Palles CB.

[15] (1868) I.R. 2 C.L. 577

[16] *ibid.* at p. 586.

[17] *op. cit.*

cised in *O'Neill v. Commissioner of Valuation, Council of Alexandra College v. Commissioner of Valuation*[18] where the court held that, taking section 63 into account, educational charities were not exempt unless they provided education for the poor. The case was followed by the Irish Supreme Court, which held that exempt school buildings "would not include those belonging to the appellants unless used for the education of the poor".[19] This is still the position in the Republic of Ireland.

In Northern Ireland, the courts in *Trustees of St. MacNissis College* v. *Commissioner of Valuation*[20] recognised and followed the authority of the *Londonderry Bridge* case. In this jurisdiction, therefore, the definition of charity in a rating context was narrowly interpreted, in particular it only allowed exemptions to educational charities if they provided education exclusively for the poor. This remained the law for more than a century until the *Campbell College* case.

21.3.3 Charitable purposes: user and *O'Connell*[21]

A number of cases have concerned the right to charitable exemption of an hereditament which is used for purposes ancillary, rather than central, to a charitable purpose. This issue was recognised in *Commissioner of Valuation v. O'Connell* where Palles C.B. stated:

> "I desire to be distinctly understood as not deciding that if the main purpose for which a building is used is a charitable one, as is that of a hospital for the gratuitous healing of the poor, the residence therein, as part of their duty, of nurses or a resident physician would necessarily render the use not 'exclusively for charitable purposes'. I should be prepared to hold quite the contrary. But in the present case, in my opinion, this house was provided for the benefit and convenience of the parish priest, and not as imposing upon him the personal obligation of residence there which medical gentlemen and nurses may be subjected to."[22]

In that case and others[23] the court held that there was not an exclusive use of the premises in question for charitable purposes.

---

[18] [1914] 2 I.R. 447.
[19] *McGahan v. Commissioner of Valuation* (1934) 1 I.R. 736 at 749, see now *Clonmel Mental Hospital v. Commissioner of Valuation* [1958] I.R. 381 construing these two Acts as one Act.
[20] [1957] N.I. 25.
[21] [1906] 2 I.R. 479.
[22] [1906] 2 I.R. 479.
[23] See, *Dore v. Commissioner of Valuation* (1916) 50 I.L.T.R. 105 and *McKenna v. Commissioner of Valuation* (1915) 49 I.L.T.R. 103.

21.3.4 Residential occupation and *Fermanagh Hospital*[24]

The decision in this case consolidated a long line of Irish authorities in sup-port of the proposition that in determining whether or not a hereditament was eligible for rates exemption, on the grounds that it was used exclusively for charitable purposes, it was the character of the occupation alone which was decisive. It was not possible to look beyond the immediate hereditament. Thus if the hereditament in question was a residential home for staff who worked in a nearby charitable institution, such as a hospital, it should be treated as a residence and be liable for rates, rather than be treated as an extension of the functions of the charity.

21.3.5 Wholly and exclusively charitable

The statutes explicitly stated that the use made of the premises must be exclu-sively charitable. Any non-charitable use completely destroyed the charitable status; 100 per cent charitable use qualified for a 100 per cent exemption but 90 per cent charitable use would result in 0 per cent exemption.

21.4 THE "RATING CASE OF THE CENTURY"[25]

In Northern Ireland many of the above principles came under sustained attack in the last half of the twentieth century. In particular, the 1960s proved to be an important decade for the development of rating case law. The first major de-velopment came with the decision in the *Campbell College* case.

21.4.1 The *Campbell College* case

Campbell College was a fee-paying school set up by trust. It did not provide education exclusively for the poor. For many years it, like many other schools, had been paying rates and decided to appeal against liability on the grounds of charitable exemption. The county court, at first instance, ruled that Campbell College was not entitled to the charitable exemption and this was confirmed on appeal to the Court of Appeal.[26] However, the appeal to the House of Lords[27] was successful.

The Court of Appeal had relied upon the construction of section 63 of the

---

[24] *Commissioner of Valuation for Northern Ireland v. Committee of Management of Fer-managh County Hospital* [1947] N.I. 125.

[25] See Lowry J., commenting on the Campbell College case in *Some Reflections on Rating*, N.I.L.Q., vol. 17, no 2, 1966.

[26] *Governors of the Campbell College v. County Court Judge of Down* [1964] N.I. 107.

[27] *Campbell College v. Commissioner of Valuation* [1964] N.I. 169. In this context, see also, *Moon v. London County Council* [1931] A.C. 151 at 167 *et seq.*

Poor Relief (Irl.) Act 1838 and section 2 of the Valuation (Ir.) Act 1854 noted above *viz.* that the charitable educational exemption was limited to education of the poor. It considered itself bound both by authority and the weight of a century of uniform practice.

The House of Lords reversed this decision on several grounds. Firstly, they held that section 2 of the 1854 Act was an independent, stand-alone provision which clearly granted exemption to all charities. Lord Reid stated " I see no ground for holding that its [1854 Act] terms must be controlled by any of the earlier Acts".[28] Secondly, and in the same vein, the later Acts trumped the earlier Acts to the extent that there was inconsistency. Thirdly, "charity" should be given its wide, *Pemsel* meaning rather than the narrow interpretation which had until then prevailed. Fourthly, that the earlier Irish authorities had been wrongly decided. Finally, the fact that a law had been wrongly applied for one hundred years was no reason to continue to misapply it.

Campbell College was a very important case for two reasons. The first, narrow reason was that all educational hereditaments were thereafter potentially exempt from rates, regardless of whether or not their provision was exclusively for the poor; this led ultimately to the exclusions listed in Schedule 13 of the Rates (N.I.) Order 1977. The second, broader reason was that the courts avoided a limited definition of charity. Charity was to be given its full, *Pemsel* style definition.

21.5 CURRENT PRINCIPLES OF RATING EXEMPTION

The current legislation governing charitable exemption from rates is to be found in Article 41 of the Rates (N.I.) Order 1977 (which largely replicates Article 41 of the Rates (N.I.) Order 1972). It is much more extensive than the preceding historical legislation and also codifies many points raised in case law. It has been fleshed out by a number of leading cases from both within and without Northern Ireland which have also helped set out the governing principles.

21.5.1 Apportionment

Charities are exempt from rates to the extent that they use the hereditament for charitable purposes. The value of the hereditament is apportioned between exempt and non-exempt uses.

The test under the old legislation was "used exclusively for such charitable … purposes" whereas under the new legislation it is "used wholly or mainly for charitable purposes".[29] The Commissioner of Valuation is specifically

---

[28] *ibid.* at p. 173.
[29] See, respectively, s. 16 of the 1854 Act and Art. 41(2)(c)(ii) Rates (N.I.) Order 1977.

directed under Article 41(3) of the Rates (N.I.) Order 1977 to apportion the value of the property between charitable and non-charitable uses.

Therefore, if an hereditament is used 80 per cent for charitable purposes, it will gain an 80 per cent rates exemption. Under the old law, without apportionment, unless a hereditament was used 100 per cent for charitable purposes, it would not gain any exemption.

21.5.2 Occupation and use

The fundamental principle of rating exemption remains the same under the old and modern legislation. A two-fold test must be satisfied. A hereditament must by occupied by a charity and it must be used for charitable purposes.[30] This two-fold test holds for all the charitable and quasi-charitable exemptions. The only exception is that hereditaments used for charitable purposes under the Recreational Charities Act (Northern Ireland) 1958 do not have to satisfy an occupier test.[31]

The definition of a charity, under the Rates (N.I.) Order 1977 is a "body established for charitable purposes only".[32] It might, therefore, be argued that the two-fold test is tautologous, if a body was established for exclusively charitable purposes, then any use it made of its property must automatically be charitable. The appellants relied upon this interpretation in *Incorporated Governors of Riddell Hall v. Commissioner of Valuation*,[33] but were unsuccessful. It is possible for a charity to make a non-charitable use of its property. For example a charity could raise money by selling goods in a shop. It would remain a charity, but its use of the shop would be commercial not charitable.[34]

21.5.3 Occupier

The first requirement of the two-stage test is that the hereditament must be occupied by a charity; this is not always self-evident, particularly from a rating perspective. Case law has produced detailed specific guidance for certain factual situations to help determine who is the occupier, but no broad governing principles. The guidance given in *William McPeake, Trustee of Hibernian Hall v. Commissioner of Valuation*[35] came close to articulating general principles. The case concerned the rateability of a hall owned by the Ancient Order

---

Apportionment was first introduced by s. 2 of the Rating and Valuation (Amendment) Act (N.I.) 1956 which stated that if a hereditament is used mainly but not exclusively for charitable purposes, one can apportion its value to the extent that it is used for charitable purposes.

[30] Art. 41(2)(c) Rates (N.I.) Order 1977.

[31] Art. 41(2)(e) Rates (N.I.) Order 1977.

[32] Art. 41(9) Rates (N.I.) Order 1977.

[33] VR/33/1971.

[34] But see further below on the specific rating exemption for charity shops.

[35] VR/6/1966.

of Hibernians and used by a local school as a classroom. The school paid rent and the Order only used the hall for meetings for approximately ½ an hour every month. The Lands Tribunal held that the Order was the occupier and must pay rates. The rationale of the Tribunal was that the Order still controlled the use of the hall.

If the charity is using a hereditament as its offices, it is occupied by the charity. If the work of the charity is carried out from there, the occupier remains the charity. If people are living in the hereditament, this can confuse the issue. Use of the property by the objects of the charity does not detract from charitable occupier. For example, if homeless people live in a hostel, the charity and not they are regarded as the occupiers.[36] If an employee is living in the hereditament, the nature of the relationship must be examined.

21.5.3(i) Employee and employer

If an employee lives in the hereditament, is that person the occupier or is the charitable employer the occupier? The courts in Northern Ireland have wrestled with this problem innumerable times and have variously held that: occupation by teachers within the curtillage of the school was exempt[37] and so too was occupation by a vice-principal in premises close to a school, though similar occupation by ordinary teachers was not;[38] occupation by a doctor within the curtillage of the hospital was exempt[39] as was occupation by a matron but not occupation by nurses 500 yards away from the hospital;[40] occupation by nuns in a convent was not exempt[41] and neither was occupation by a priest,[42] by a religious order of monks to assist in their teaching and preaching,[43] nor occupation by a sexton of premises which were part of a church.[44]

---

[36] *Incorporated Cripples' Institutes and Holiday Homes v. Commissioner of Valuation* VR/12/1965, see also *Trustees of the Civil Servant Benevolent Fund v. Commissioner of Valuation* VR/50/1978.

[37] *Denmark v. Commissioner of Valuation for Northern Ireland* (1962) 28 Ir. Jur. Rep. 20

[38] *Commissioner of Valuation for Northern Ireland v. Fermanagh Protestant Board of Education* [1970] N.I. 189 by the C.A. and [1970] N.I. 135 by the House of Lords.

[39] *Armagh County Infirmary Committee v. Commissioner of Valuation for Northern Ireland* [1940] N.I. 1.

[40] *Commissioner of Valuation for Northern Ireland v. Committee of Management of Fermanagh County Hospital* [1947] N.I. 125

[41] *McLaughlin and Cosgrove v. Commissioner of Valuation for Northern Ireland* [1932] N.I. 174, *Trustees of the Congregation of the Poor Clares of the Immaculate Conception v. Commissioner of Valuation* [1971] N.I. 174, but see *Trustees of the Dominican Convent of the Holy Rosary v. Commissioner of Valuation* VR/23/1965.

[42] *Commissioner of Valuation v. O'Connell* [1906] 2 I.R. 479, approved in Northern Ireland by *McLaughlin*, but see *Trustees of the Belmont Presbyterian Church v. Commissioner of Valuation* VR/44/1968, *Reed v. Cattermole* [1937] 1 K.B. 613 and *Commissioners of Inland Revenue v. Leckie* (1940) S.C. 343.

[43] The *Redemptorist* case.

[44] *Mulholland v. Commissioner of Valuation* [1936] 70 I.L.T.R. 253, but see *Trustees of*

The Lands Tribunal has held that where caretakers lived in a home for the sick the charity was the occupier[45] as when a school caretaker lived in a house in grammar school premises[46] or primary school premises.[47] A house used by a gravedigger was deemed occupied by the charity.[48] However, employees of an agricultural institute who lived on farm grounds were deemed to be in occupation to the exclusion of their employer.[49] Some warders of the National Trust were deemed to be in occupation of their houses, whereas, for others, the National Trust was in occupation.[50]

The courts eventually formulated a specific test to determine whether the employee or the employer was in occupation. The root of the test is the distinction between privilege and obligation. If the employee resides in the hereditament as a benefit of his office, he is the occupier. If the employee is under a duty to reside, the employer is the occupier.

The leading case is a House of Lords decision on Scottish rating exemption, *Glasgow Corporation v. Johnstone*.[51] It concerned the residential occupation by a sexton of part of a church. The House of Lords held that:

> "... if the servant is given the privilege of residing ... the occupation is that of the servant. ... If, on the other hand, the servant is genuinely obliged by his master for the purposes of his master's business or if it is necessary for the servant to reside in the house for the better performance of his services the occupation will be that of the master."[52]

There are three possible situations. The first is that the employee is obliged by the contract of employment to live in the premises. The contractual obligation can be express or implied and it can be found by parol evidence.[53] The employee's residence must also be of material assistance, or otherwise support

---

the Belmont Presbyterian Church v. Commissioner of Valuation VR/14/1965, *Education Board of Coleraine Presbytery, Trustees of New Row Presbyterian Church v. Commissioner of Valuation* VR/36/1969 and *Trustees of Seagoe Presbyterian Church v. Commissioner of Valuation* VR/8/1970.

[45] *Trustees of Shankhill Road Mission v. Commissioner of Valuation* VR/21/1965.
[46] *Governors of Victoria College Belfast v. Commissioner of Valuation* VR/17/1965.
[47] *Governors of Victoria College Belfast v. Commissioner of Valuation* VR/16/1965.
[48] *Hugh Kirker v. Commissioner of Valuation* VR/19/1981, affirmed on appeal by the Court of Appeal at (1983) 12 N.I.J.B.
[49] *Trustees of the Agricultural Research Institute v. Commissioner of Valuation* VR/81+82/1967.
[50] *National Trust for Places of Historic Interest and Natural Beauty v. Commissioner of Valuation* VR/11-18/1971.
[51] [1965] A.C. 609.
[52] *ibid.* at p. 626.
[53] For example of use of parol evidence, see *Education Board of Coleraine Presbytery, Trustees of New Row Presbyterian Church v. Commissioner of Valuation,* "there was an express term in the parol contract of employment ... that she must live in the sexton's house" VR/36/1969 at p. 9.

the better performance of his duties. In this case there is a genuine obligation to reside and the employer is the occupier.

In the second situation, the employee is not obliged under the contract to reside, but it is necessary or essential for him to do so. The necessity stems from the nature of the employment. In this case also, there is a genuine obligation to reside and the employer is the occupier. It must be necessary to reside, not just be of material assistance.

The third situation covers all other circumstances of employee residence. The employee occupies as payment for his services. He lives there on his own behalf, not on behalf of his employer. He and not his employer is the occupier.

An analysis of the cases gives examples of how these principles are applied in practice. If a caretaker resides in an hereditament they must show some sort of reason why it either assists their duties or is necessary. Being available to provide emergence cover is of material assistance.[54] It is also of material assistance for a school caretaker to reside on the premises to: prevent fires, start up the boilers and attend to the security of the school and its pupils.[55] A sexton's residence next to a church is of material assistance to the church as he can open/close it and protect it from intruders at all times.[56] However, if a sexton is not obliged by his contract to live on the premises, then it is:

> "... not essential for the discharge of his duties that he should live on the premises – it was merely convenient and made for the efficient performance of his duties."[57]

In the *Portora* case,[58] the House of Lords considered the position of teachers living in premises provided by a school. There was no contractual obligation to reside, therefore the charity had to show that it was essential or necessary for them so to reside. Both the House of Lords and the Northern Ireland Court of Appeal held that it was essential for the vice-principal to have his house on school grounds and within 100 yards of the school buildings. The courts had regard to his duty to receive visitors and parents at his house and the need for high quality teaching on site. However, with regard to six ordinary teachers at the school, Curran L.J. held that there is:

---

[54] *Trustees of Shankill Road Mission v. Commissioner of Valuation* VR/21/1965.

[55] *Governors of Victoria College Belfast v. Commissioner of Valuation* VR/17/1965.

[56] *Trustees of the Belmont Presbyterian Church v. Commissioner of Valuation* VR/14/1965, *Trustees of Seagoe Presbyterian Church v. Commissioner of Valuation* VR/8/1970, or across the road from the church, *Education Board of Coleraine Presbytery, Trustees of New Row Presbyterian Church v. Commissioner of Valuation* VR/36/1969.

[57] *Mulholland v. Commissioner of Valuation* (1936) 70 I.L.T.R. 253 at 254, see also the *National Trust* case for various facts making some residence material assist in duties but others not.

[58] *Commissioner of Valuation v. Fermanagh Protestant Board of Education* [1970] N.I. 134, in the Court of Appeal [1970] N.I. 89.

> "... no such cogent evidence that it is necessary for the purposes of the school that the masters living in Castle Lane should reside in the houses in question."[59]

This was the view of the majority in both courts.[60]

21.5.3(ii) Religious occupiers

The courts have been much exercised by issues relating to occupation by religious orders and religious office holders – is the individual the occupier, or is his occupation representative of his order or religious superiors? The Lands Tribunal has held that, although the minister/church relationship is not the same as the employee/employer one, it was sufficiently analogous to apply the *Glasgow Corporation v. Johnstone* test.[61] The underlying principle is the same: if a minister or member of a religious order is obliged to live in the hereditament, his occupation is not beneficial, but representative of the charity that owns it.[62] This decision is equally applicable to members of religious orders.[63]

Legislation has since introduced some modifications which would seem to have satisfactorily resolved the principal areas of dispute. Article 41(8) of the Rates (N.I.) Order 1977 makes specific provision for hereditaments owned by religious bodies. There are a number of prerequisites before the Order will apply. Firstly, a religious body (or trustees for a religious body) must own an interest in the hereditament. Secondly, it must either be used or be made available for use as a residence for certain people. The "certain people" are defined as "the persons from time to time holding any full time office as clergyman or minister of any religious denomination".[64] Its use must be as a residence from which to carry out the duties of the office.

The scope of Article 41(8), therefore, does not embrace all religious occupiers, only clergymen or ministers. It will not extend to members of religious orders. The dictionary definition of minister is "a person, especially an ordained one, with a certain liturgical ministry or function; a member of the clergy ... responsible for leading or co-ordinating, preaching, public worship and pastoral care in a particular church, chapel, community etc.".[65]

If these conditions are satisfied, the hereditament will automatically pass both the "occupier" test and the "use" test (see further below). It will also

---

[59] In the Court of Appeal, *ibid.* at p. 119.

[60] The Rates (N.I.) Order 1977 states that residential occupation is only 50 per cent exempt: Art. 41(3)(a), and Art. 21.5.4(vi).

[61] *Trustees of the Belmont Presbyterian Church v. Commissioner of Valuation* VR/44/1968.

[62] See for example *Reed v. Cattermole* [1937] 1 K.B. 613, "he lives there for the purposes of the church as part of the obligation which he owes to the church as part of his service" at p 620.

[63] *Trustees of the Dominican Convent of the Holy Rosary v. Commissioner of Valuation* VR/23/1965.

[64] Art. 41(8)(a) Rates (N.I.) Order 1977.

[65] New Oxford Shorter English Dictionary.

automatically be deemed to be occupied for "domestic purposes" with the consequence that the hereditament will be 50 per cent exempt from rates (see further below for the meaning of "domestic purposes").

21.5.3(iii) Effect of occupation agreements

The nature of an occupation agreement between employee and employer may assist in deciding who is the occupier. The Lands Tribunal and Court of Appeal considered this point in *Hugh Kirker v. Commissioner of Valuation*[66] but came to no firm decision. It is submitted that if there is a service tenancy, then the employee has exclusive possession of the hereditament because he is self-employed/employed under a contract of service and it is his occupation and not that of his employer. However, if there is a service occupancy (*i.e.* a licence to occupy under a contract of service), it is submitted that the employee is occupying on his employer's behalf and that the employer is more likely to be the occupier.

21.5.3(iv) Occupation by bodies not individuals

To gain the exemption, the occupier must be a charity. A charity is defined as a "body established for charitable purposes".[67] In interpreting the phrase "occupied by a body" in relation to one of the several charitable exemptions,[68] the Lands Tribunal held that "as an individual he could not qualify as a body".[69] That case concerned an application by an M.P. for exemption from rates for his constituency surgery. One reason for refusal was that individual occupiers could not take advantage of the exemption, only bodies.

The case law which the legislation codified illustrates both the rationale for the rule and a method of avoiding it. There is no exemption for individuals purporting to be charitable occupiers:

> "If it is merely by his own volition and not by the law, that he is deprived of a benefit which he might have received, then there is a potential beneficial occupation and he is liable to be rated in respect of it."[70]

In *David Ravey v. Commissioner of Valuation*[71] the Tribunal found that the appellant had dedicated his life to God. Almost every month for 20 years he had been taking handicapped children into his family home for a holiday but he was still refused charitable exemption from rates. There was no legal com-

---

[66] VR/19/1981 and (1983) 12 NIJB respectively.
[67] Art. 41(9) Rates (N.I.) Order 1977.
[68] Under Art. 41(2)(f) Rates (N.I.) Order 1977.
[69] *Cecil Walker MP* v. *Commissioner of Valuation* VR/47/1985.
[70] *Winstanley* v. *North Manchester Overseers* [1970] A.C. 7 at 14.
[71] VR/28/1972.

pulsion upon him to do what he was doing; a lack of obligation made it impossible for an individual to be a charitable occupier. The case also addressed the way to avoid this problem, it stressed:

> "… the importance to an individual who wished to used his dwelling house for charitable purposes, of having an appropriate declaration of trust and trustees to execute the trust purposes, if he desired to have the premises distinguished as exempt."[72]

21.5.4 Charitable use

The second part of the two-stage test is the requirement that the hereditament be used for charitable purposes. If the activities carried out in the hereditament constitute the final stage in the delivery of benefits to the objects of the charity, then this test is satisfied. If they are no more than a stepping stone on the way to delivering benefits to those objects, the test is slightly more difficult. This can be illustrated as follows: feeding the poor, teaching, giving religious services, etc., are all end results of charities; but cooking food, preparing lesson plans, putting on religious vestments, etc., are all only steps in that process. The latter are insufficient to constitute the purpose of the charity. The legal test is that an ancillary activity will be regarded as charitable if it directly facilitates the main charitable activity.

This sub-section also looks at whether a use for profit can ever be a charitable use. It then asks whose use is to be considered and whether it is permissible to look beyond the hereditament in question to ascertain whether the activity in the hereditament constitutes a charitable use.

21.5.4(i) Ancillary charitable uses

As has been said:

> "If the use which the charity makes of the premises is directly to facilitate the carrying out of its mains charitable purposes, that is, in my view, sufficient to satisfy the requirement that the premises are used for charitable purposes."[73]

The case law is full of similar judicial pronouncements. Perhaps the most expansive of these was made in *Oxfam v. City of Birmingham District Council*[74] where it was said:

> "I consider that user 'for charitable purposes' denotes user in the actual carrying out of the charitable purposes: that may include doing something which is a necessary or essential or incidental part of, or which directly facilitates, or which

---

[72] *ibid.* at p 7.
[73] *Glasgow Corporation v. Johnstone op. cit.* at p 621.
[74] [1975] 2 All E.R. 289.

is ancillary to, what is being done in the actual carrying out of the charitable purpose."[75]

There has to be a strong, causal link between the activities in the hereditament and the charitable purposes of the occupier.

The employee residence cases are relevant also under the "directly to facilitate" test. Residence by objects (*i.e.* the homeless) of a charity is a charitable use. Residence by employees is not, unless such residence directly facilitates the work of the charity. The courts look at exactly the same facts in determining "directly to facilitate" as they do when determining "material assistance" or "necessary to reside" under the occupier test.

Therefore, it there are security concerns regarding certain premises, a resident employee will directly facilitate the charity by keeping the premises safe. Residence by a warden will directly facilitate charitable purposes if he is available to look after wildfowl on the site at any time.[76] However, there must be a reason why the particular hereditament directly facilitates the work of the charity; for example, because of its proximity. If an employee only works part time, it is more difficult to show that his residence is ancillary to the charitable purposes.[77]

21.5.4(ii) Use for profit

A use for profit is prima facie not a charitable use. So if a charity rents out an hereditament, this is a use for profit and not a charitable use. It does not matter to whom it is rented nor how nominal is the rent.[78] It is irrelevant that any profit made will be ploughed back into the charity and ultimately be used for charitable purposes. It is actual use which is relevant. It would be unfair to other businesses if charities were granted rates exemption when engaged in normal commercial activities. The Lands Tribunal has stated:

"... it is the use of the hereditaments and not the destination and use of moneys [*sic*] derived from that use which is decisive."[79]

This principle is now enshrined in legislation:

"... any use (whether by way of letting or otherwise) for profit shall not be treated as a use for [charitable] purposes ... unless it directly facilitates the carrying out of those purposes."[80]

---

[75] *ibid.* at p 302.

[76] *National Trust op. cit.*

[77] *National Trust* case *op. cit.*

[78] *Incorporated Cripples' Institute and Holiday Homes v. Commissioner of Valuation* VR/ 6/1965.

[79] *Incorporated Cripples' Institute and Holiday Homes v. Commissioner of Valuation* VR/ 6/1965 at p 4.

[80] Art. 41(4) Rates (N.I.) Order 1977.

If the purpose of a charity is to provide employment for ex-servicemen, the fact that it rents out car parks staffed by such beneficiaries will not stop it from being a charitable use, even though the car park may be a commercial enterprise.[81] The Northern Ireland Court of Appeal came close to granting exemption to another use for profit in *Belfast Association for the Industrious Blind v. Commissioner of Valuation*.[82] The hereditament in that case was a shop in which goods produced by blind workers were sold together with commercially purchased goods. The Association was a charity set up to ameliorate the condition of the blind by teaching them skills and giving them employment. Lord MacDermott L.C.J., in a dissenting judgement held that the shop was used for charitable purposes. The sale of the commercially purchased goods was not to merely make a profit, but to attract more custom to the shop and broaden the range of goods sold and therefore increase the viability of the operation. The rest of the Court of Appeal found that the shop made excessive private profit and refused exemption.

The English High Court in *Wynn v. Skegness Urban District Council*[83] in a creative judgment was able to find charitable use in a letting. The case concerned a charitable holiday centre for miners and their families. The trustees had power to rent out surplus rooms to members of the public to help meet the maintenance costs. Ungoed-Thomas J held that this was not a use for profit but was to directly facilitate the charitable purposes of providing holiday accommodation for miners. It was an economic provision to meet maintenance costs, not to provide cash for the centre:

> "... the admission of the public, it seems to me, is so dovetailed into the purposes and overriding use of the centre for qualified persons and is, in its function, subsidiary, in the eyes of the trustees to that use and so directly and physically associated with that use, that in my judgement it falls within the *Glasgow* principle."[84]

It is submitted that this proposition is difficult to sustain. The holiday homes open to the public were being let to generate income, which may have been eventually destined for maintaining the centre, but the actual use was a commercial one. In Northern Ireland, the Lands Tribunal acknowledged the validity of the *Wynn* case, but stated that there is:

> "... [no] principle that money raising activities, in premises subject to charitable trusts, designed to keep the accounts of the trustees in balance either in

---

[81] *Royal British Legion Attendants Company v. Commissioner of Valuation* [1979] N.I. 138.

[82] [1968] N.I. 21.

[83] [1966] 3 All E.R. 336.

[84] *ibid.* at p. 344.

relation to those premises or generally, can, as a matter of fact, be held to be wholly ancillary to the charitable purposes of those truste."[85]

That case concerned a charitable holiday home under the first *Pemsel* head which was let out during the winter months. This was held to be a use for profit.

21.5.4 (iii) Exemption for charity shops

The decision in *Oxfam v. Birmingham City District Council*[86] was welcomed by those traders who competed with charities but received with dismay by the latter. It held that "charity shops", in which donated goods were sold, did not make a charitable use of their premises. In England and Wales this was remedied by the Rating (Charity Shops) Act 1976.[87] In Northern Ireland it was remedied by the Rates (N.I.) Order 1977.

Article 41(5) of the Rates (N.I.) Order 1977 states that an hereditament:

> "... shall be treated as used for charitable purposes to the extent that it is used for the sale of goods donated to charity, so long as the proceeds of sale (after deduction of expenses) are applied for the purposes of a charity."

A charity shop must be able to show a percentage of goods sold from donated and non-donated sources. It only gains exemption for the percentage sold which are of donated goods. With the recent Charity Commission decision that fair trade is a charitable purpose,[88] it remains to be seen whether charity shops will be exempt to the extent they sell fair trade goods; any change in the law will, however, necessitate alteration to Article 41.

21.5.4(iv) Relevant use

The relevant use is the use the occupier makes of the hereditament. The first point which flows from this is that the use made of the hereditament by a resident employee for his own purposes is irrelevant. As long as his residence directly facilitates the charitable purpose of the occupier, any additional use is not considered. Therefore, if an employee works part-time and sometimes uses the hereditament for non-charitable purposes, this use is ignored. The only use which is considered is the use made by the employee on behalf of his employer.[89]

---

[85] *Incorporated Cripples' Institute and Holiday Homes v. Commissioner of Valuation* VR/5/1965 at p. 8.

[86] [1976] A.C. 126.

[87] Now, s. 64(10) of the Local Government Finance Act 1988.

[88] See further Chap. 11. See, also, Inland Revenue, *Trading by Charities*, 1995.

[89] *Trustees of Seagoe Parish Church, Portadown v. Commissioner of Valuation* VR/81/1970.

The second point is whether a charitable use can be made of the premises which is not within the charitable purposes of the occupier? The Rates Order states that the hereditament must be "used wholly or mainly for charitable purposes (whether of that charity or that and other charities)".[90] This indicates at least that some of the use must be for the purposes of the occupying charity. In one of the *Incorporated Cripples*[91] cases, the holiday home was used by the Eastern Special Care Committee as a holiday home for the handicapped. As has been seen, the Lands Tribunal ignored that charitable use and looked to the use the occupiers were making. Their use was letting out the home. This was non-charitable and therefore not exempt.

21.5.4(v) Residential use

Employees residing in a hereditament must first pass the occupier test. They must then pass the use test of "directly to facilitate". Even if they reach this stage, the legislation has reduced the relief available.

"Domestic purposes" are defined as:

> "... the purposes of providing living accommodation for one or more than one person who is a member or employee of a body by or on behalf of which the hereditament is occupied."[92]

If an hereditament is occupied for domestic purposes, it only is allowed a 50 per cent exemption.[93] An employee is defined as someone who is employed under a contract of service.[94] The *Hugh Kirker*[95] case applied the traditional test to distinguish between a contract of service and a contract for services.[96] That case also showed how difficult it would be to show employee occupation which could not be described as being for domestic purposes.

21.5.4(vi) Looking beyond the hereditament

The Northern Ireland Court of Appeal had given clear authority that one looks only to the actual use of the hereditament and not beyond it:

> "... the user of each unit must be ascertained by an inspection of the hereditament itself and an enquiry as to the persons in actual occupation."[97]

---

[90] Art. 41(2)(c)(ii) Rates (N.I.) Order 1977. Though it should be noted that the case in question preceded the introduction of the Rates (N.I.) Order 1972.

[91] *Incorporated Cripples' Institute and Holiday Homes* v. *Commissioner of Valuation* VR/6/1965

[92] Art. 41(9) Rates (N.I.) Order 1977.

[93] Art. 41(3)(a) Rates (N.I.) Order 1977.

[94] Art. 41(9) Rates (N.I.) Order 1977.

[95] *Hugh Kirker* v. *Commissioner of Valuation, op cit.*

[96] See, for example, *Harvey on Industrial Relations and Employment Law* (2000, Butterworths, London).

[97] *Fermanagh Hospital* at p. 131.

In *Glasgow Corporation*,[98] however, the court looked beyond the individual hereditament to see in what context it was being used. It drew from the example of nurses in a hospital:

> "I cannot think it would be right or that it is the intention of the Act [Local Government (Miscellaneous Provisions etc.) (Scotland) Act 1962] to draw a line between the wards where they perform their charitable function of nursing the sick, and the places where they eat, rest and sleep."[99]

This is now fully part of charity law in Northern Ireland. The Court of Appeal in the *Industrious Blind* case stated that one could look beyond the hereditament and that *Fermanagh Hospital* had been overruled. In the *Portora* case in the Court of Appeal, Curran L.J. thought that some part of the *Fermanagh Hospital* case still stood, but the other judges disagreed, McVeigh L.J. held "the reasoning in the *Fermanagh* case is inconsistent with that in the *Glasgow Corporation* case".[100] If confirmation was required it was given a third time by the Court of Appeal in the *Redemptorist* case when it ruled that *Fermanagh Hospital* was no longer good law.

21.5.5 The Article 41 exemptions

There are a number of different exemptions from rates set out in the Rates (N.I.) Order 1977. They can be utilised by churches, charities, quasi-charities, recreational charities, partially recreational charities and others. This subsection examines the requirements of each of the exemptions relevant to charities and then briefly mentions other exemptions.

21.5.5(i) Churches and church halls

There is an exemption for:

> "(b) any hereditament which consists of either or both of the following –
>
> (i) a church, chapel or similar building occupied by a religious body and used for the purposes of public religious worship;
>
> (ii) a church hall, chapel hall or similar building occupied by a religious body and used for purposes connected with that body or for purposes of any charity;
>
> together in either case with buildings ancillary thereto."[101]

---

[98] *op cit.*
[99] *op cit.* at p. 621.
[100] *Commissioner of Valuation for Northern Ireland v. Fermanagh Protestant Board of Education* [1970] N.I. 89 at p. 127.
[101] Art. 41(2)(b) Rates (N.I.) Order 1977.

In *Mageean v. Commissioner of Valuation*[102] it was held that the Roman Catholic chaplaincy at Queens University Belfast performed the functions of a church hall and was therefore exempt. Lord MacDermott L.C.J. defined a church hall as a building "used to further the work or meet the needs of a group or community of worshippers associated for the purposes of their religion".[103] There was no need for such a hall to be linked to a place of public worship.

Under the old legislation[104] the exemption did not apply to buildings ancillary to a church hall, only buildings ancillary to a church. The sexton's residence in *Trustees of the Belmont Presbyterian Church v. Commissioner of Valuation*[105] would have failed this test under that law. However, the 1977 Order is broader in ambit.

The Lands Tribunal went so far as to hold that the Corrymeela Community centre was exempt as being a church hall.[106] However, this should be treated as *obiter* as it had already been held charitable on other grounds.

21.5.5(ii) Charities

There is an exemption for:

> "(c) any hereditament, other than a hereditament to which sub-paragraph (b) applies, which –
>
> (i) is occupied by a charity; and
> (ii) is used wholly or mainly for charitable purposes (whether of that charity or that and other charities)."[107]

There is an interface at this point between rating law and Inland Revenue law. The question is usually – if the Revenue has recognised the body as a charity, is this conclusive for the "occupier" stage of the two-stage rating test? The Valuation and Lands Agency generally accept the findings of the Inland Revenue as conclusive; there has not been any instance in recent years where the assessment of the VLA has differed from that made by the Inland Revenue. However, although a positive assessment made by the latter agency is undoubtedly a very significant indicator in favour of a body also being treated as charitable within rating law, the VLA are not bound to so accept the findings of the Revenue; an approach endorsed by the case law. In *British Council v. Commissioner of Valuation*[108] the corporation was a charity registered with

---

[102] [1960] N.I. 141. In the judgment, reference was made to people meeting "under the influence and atmosphere of religion".

[103] *ibid.* at p. 152.

[104] Rating and Valuation (Amendment) Act (N.I.) 1956.

[105] VR/14/1965.

[106] *Corrymeela Community v. Commissioner of Valuation* VR/1/1967.

[107] Art. 41(2)(c) Rates (N.I.) Order 1977.

[108] VR/65/1980.

the Charity Commissioners and recognised as having charitable status for tax purposes by the Inland Revenue. Nevertheless, the Lands Tribunal held that it was not a charity and failed the charitable occupier test.[109] In *Trustees of the Civil Service Benevolent Fund v. Commissioner of Valuation*[110] the fact that the Inland Revenue had recognised the trust in question as charitable did not prevent the Lands Tribunal from conducting its own investigation. The latter body did not routinely accept the finding of the former and did not consider itself bound by the earlier decision. The ruling was made explicit in *Lyric Players' Theatre v. Commissioner of Valuation* where Higgins J. stated that "the attitude of the Revenue Authorities in this respect is not binding on the Tribunal".[111] Arguably, however, while accepting that a decision of the Charity Commission to grant charitable status cannot be challenged it is open to question whether the lack of any decision or a decision to deny such status may not be investigated and determined.

In practice, a body which can show evidence of status from the Inland Revenue will generally satisfy the occupier test.

21.5.5(iii) Quasi-charities

There is an exemption for:

> "(d) any hereditament, other than a hereditament to which sub-paragraph (b) applies, which is occupied by a body –
>
> (i)   which is not established or conducted for profit; and
> (ii) whose main objects are charitable or are concerned with science, literature or the fine arts;
>
> where the hereditament is used wholly or mainly for purposes of those main objects."[112]

The two fundamental requirements are also relevant in this context. The hereditament must be occupied by a certain body and it must be wholly or mainly used for the purposes of that body. Article 41(2)(d), a hurdle easier to overcome than Article 41(2)(c), widens the scope of the exemptions to what may be called "quasi charities". The body must first show that it is not established or conducted for profit. This point was conceded in *Royal British Legion Attendants Company v. Commissioner of Valuation*.[113] In that case, all surplus

---

[109] See also *Trustees of Newtownards Young Farmers Club v. Commissioner of Valuation* VR/41/1966 for another body recognised as charitable by the Inland Revenue, but refused charitable status by the Tribunal.
[110] VR/50/1978.
[111] VR/25/1970 at p. 8.
[112] Art. 41(2)(d) Rates (N.I.) Order 1977.
[113] [1979] N.I. 138.

profit made by the company was reinvested in the company and any assets remaining on dissolution were to be transferred to another charity.

However, it is to be noted that the legislative requirement is "not conducted for profit" as opposed to "non-profit distributing". The fact that no person receives a profit from a body does not mean it is not conducted for profit. In *Larne Enterprise Development Co. v. Commissioner of Valuation*,[114] the Lands Tribunal held that:

> "… although any surplus was ploughed back in and members did not nor could not benefit, the objects and conduct of the company itself … could only lead to the conclusion that it was established and conducted for profit."[115]

The crucial object, making the company non-charitable, was that it provided business and consultancy services for a fee. If it had stopped at the stage of merely providing advice, even for a fee, it may have retained the exemption. But providing professional business services meant it was conducted for a profit.

The second requirement is that the body's main objects must be charitable, or are concerned with science, literature or the fine arts. This widens the scope of the charitable exemption in two ways. Firstly, it broadens exemption to include bodies which are not exclusively but only mainly charitable. Secondly, it extends exemption to science, literature and the fine arts.

It will be recalled that the third fundamental requirement of a charity is that it be established for exclusively charitable purposes.[116] Article 41(2)(d) relaxes this and allows those bodies whose purposes are only mainly charitable. This may be illustrated by further reference to the *Legion Attendants*[117] case. The company had three objects: to promote the employment of ex-soldiers, to promote the welfare of ex-soldiers, and to undertake trade or business in furtherance of those two objects. The Court of Appeal held that the first two objects were charitable, but that the third one was not. The third object could not be regarded as ancillary to the first two, but was an independent object. Therefore, the company was not charitable. However, the third object was not a main object, only a subsidiary one, therefore the company was exempt as a quasi charity.

This principle is echoed in the exemption for science, literature and the fine arts. Previously, under the Scientific Societies Act 1843, the exemption was for "any society instituted for the purposes of science, literature or the fine arts exclusively".[117] Under the new legislation, it is enough to show it is mainly if not exclusively so connected.

---

[114] VR/6/1995.
[115] *ibid.* at p. 10.
[116] See further Chap 1.
[117] *Royal British Legion Attendants Company v. Commissioner of Valuation* [1979] N.I. 138.
[118] s. 1 of the Scientific Societies Act 1843.

The second way that Article 41(2)(d) widens the availability of the exemption is by recognising other categories of exempt objects. These are science, literature or the fine arts (see further, Chapter 9, particularly on aesthetic education, for definition of literature and fine art). Fine art was defined by the Lands Tribunal as follows:

> "… it should be creative, make an impression upon the mind of the beholder which is aesthetically satisfying, and have a form which remains to be seen, appreciated and judged."[119]

Photography can be a fine art. Science, however, is somewhat circuitously defined as something capable of proof by scientific methods.[120] The only case reported in Northern Ireland on this issue was *Belfast Psychical Society* v. *Commissioner of Valuation*.[121] This concerned a club interested in psychical and supernatural phenomena such as thought transference. The Lands Tribunal held that its methods of investigation were not sufficiently scientific to warrant exemption.

21.5.5(iv) Recreational charities

There is an exemption for:

> (e) any hereditament which is used wholly or mainly for purposes which are declared to be charitable by the Recreational Charities Act (Northern Ireland) 1958.[122]

See Chapter 14 for the meaning of recreation. This provision specifically places recreation within the sphere of rating exemption. The Recreational Charities Act (Northern Ireland) 1958 states that "it shall be and be deemed always to have been charitable to provide. . . ."[123] Arguably, if these purposes are deemed charitable, then they are automatically included within Article 41(2)(d) and there is therefore no need to do so a second time in Article 41(2)(e).

The other point about this exemption is that it removes one leg of the fundamental occupier/use test. All that is necessary is to show charitable use, not charitable occupation. It is therefore theoretically possible to make use of land in accordance with the Recreational Charities Act (Northern Ireland) 1958, but yet to make a commercial gain at the same time.

---

[119] *Lisburn Camera Club v. Commissioner of Valuation* VR/105/1978 at p 6. See, also, *Art and Research Exchange v. Commissioner of Valuation*[1] and *Management Committee of the Media Workshop v. Commissioner of Valuation*[1].

[120] *Institute for the Comparative Study of History, Philosophy and the Sciences v. Castle (VO)* (1957) 50 Rating and Income Tax 409.

[121] VR/13/1976.

[122] Art. 41(2)(e) Rates (N.I.) Order 1977.

[123] s. 1(1) of the Recreational Charities Act (Northern Ireland) 1958.

21.5.5(v) Partial recreational use

There is an exemption for:

> "(f) any hereditament, other than a hereditament to which sub-paragraph (e) applies –
>
> > (i) which is occupied by a body that is not established or conducted for profit; and
> >
> > (ii) which is used, either by the occupying body or by some other person (whether that person is a charity or not), to an extent of not less than 10 per cent for purposes which are declared by the Recreational Charities Act (Northern Ireland) 1958 to be charitable; and
> >
> > (iii) which use is made available by the occupying body for that use –
> >
> > > (aa) where the use is by that body, subject to charges, if any, not more than necessary to defray reasonable expenses actually incurred by the body by reason of that use, or
> > >
> > > (bb) where the use is not by that body, for a consideration, if any, not more than necessary to defray such expenses."[124]

The two stage occupier/use test is reasserted once more under Article 41(2)(f). The occupier must not be a body conducted for profit. The use must be at least 10 per cent recreational under the Recreational Charities Act (Northern Ireland) 1958. If charges are made for such use, they must be only enough to cover reasonable expenses. The use of the hereditament is apportioned under Article 41(3) between recreational and non-recreational uses.

The Rates (N.I.) Order 1977 explains in detail how to calculate and apportion exempt and non-exempt use under this exemption in Article 41(10). Use is specifically stated to include both use by the occupier for recreational purposes and use by any other body for those purposes. A comparison is required between the number of "sessions" actually devoted to use for such purposes during the year and the total number of "sessions" that might reasonably be expected to be available for all active uses in that year. There is no benefit, therefore, in an occupier disclaiming all non-recreational use and letting the hereditament go unused. The apportionment is carried out on the basis of actual recreational use versus non-recreational use and non-use combined. This "part recreational" approach was introduced in order to address the position of the many hereditament, such as Orange halls and Hibernian halls, which would fail on any strict application of the occupier test but may well be used for quasi-charitable purposes.

The legislation then goes on to define "session". A session is a period of time in which the hereditament is used or may be available for use. If a hereditament is made up of several parts such that each part can be used concurrently, each actual or possible concurrent use is treated as a session. A continuous period of between two and six hours is treated as one session.

---

[124] Art. 41(2)(f) Rates (N.I.) Order 1977.

Between six and 10 hours is two sessions, between 10 and 14 hours is three sessions, etc. When calculating the total number of sessions which might be available for use (*i.e.* in order to work out the apportionment between actual recreational use and possible total use), the Commissioner of Valuation must have regard to all the circumstances, in particular the location of the hereditament and the actual or potential demand in the neighbourhood for activities which the hereditament is, or might be, suitable.

Further legislation has been introduced to make this exemption more precisely calculated and regulated. The Recreational Charities (Record of Use) Regulations (N.I.) 1979 No. 156 applies where an occupier wishes to apply for rates exemption under Article 41(2)(f). The occupier must keep a record of uses in a prescribed form in a record book. As stipulated in the regulations, the:

> "... record of each active use of the hereditament shall be made or completed as soon as is reasonably practicable after the conclusion of that use and shall be authenticated by the signature of the person keeping the record."[125]

The Commissioner of Valuation or someone authorised by him can request the record book and must be given it within a reasonable time.[126] This person may make a copy of the information in the record book.[127]

The information to be contained in the record book is set out in the Schedule to the Regulations and is as follows: date, persons using the premises (including the occupying body), use for recreational charity (*i.e.* nature of the activity), use for other purposes (*i.e.* nature of the activity), time of commencing and finishing, charges made for use, expenses incurred (lighting, heating, cleaning and others), and signature.

The Lands Tribunal has reinforced the view that this record book is compulsory. It refused to hear the case of *Trustees of Newbridge Sean O'Leary Gaelic Centre v. Commissioner of Valuation*[128] for two reasons. Firstly the appellants attempted to change their grounds of appeal from the Commissioner of Valuation to the Lands Tribunal. Secondly, because they did not have a record book. Sir Frank Harrison, the Member said "the Tribunal consider it proper to state its view that this requirement is mandatory".[129]

21.5.5(vi) Other exemptions

Two further exemptions are contained within Article 41. They are not charitable exemptions and are mentioned here only for the sake of completeness. There is an exemption for hereditaments altogether of a public nature which

---

[125] Reg. 3(3) Recreational Charities (Record of Use) Regulations (N.I.) 1979 No. 156.
[126] Reg. 4(1) *ibid.*
[127] Reg. 4(3) *ibid.*
[128] VR/72/1980.
[129] *ibid.* at p. 3.

are occupied and used for purposes of the public service,[130] *e.g.* public toilets, leisure centres etc. There is also an exemption for hereditaments used for residential accommodation for those with an illness or disability. This was amended by the Rates (Amendment) (N.I.) Order 1994 to substitute "rebates" instead of "exemptions" in certain circumstances.[131]

21.6 PROCEDURE

As previously stated, rating decisions are made in the first instance by the District Valuers of the Valuation and Lands Agency (VLA). If a body is aggrieved by that decision, it can appeal to the Commissioner of Valuation. Further rights of appeal lie to the Lands Tribunal and then, on points of law only, to the Court of Appeal and beyond.

21.6.1 The agencies

The total annual rates bill for Northern Ireland is approximately £490 million. It is estimated that the charitable exemption proportion amounts to 5 per cent. On average, two cases a year are appealed to the Lands Tribunal; charity cases are proportionately over-represented in the total of appeals heard by the Tribunal. The majority of these cases were in the 1960s and 1970s. Following the introduction of the 1972 and 1977 Orders the number of annual appeals declined; in the 1990s' there were very few appeals.

The onus on obtaining the exemption rests with the charity. It must apply for exemption to the local VLA office. Charities, in common with other bodies, should submit all evidence necessary to support a claim. It should include the following: Inland Revenue exemption certificate, its constitution, the names of the people involved in the charity and their respective roles; and a synopsis of the activities carried out in the hereditament. All applications should be made promptly.

The VLA look to an Inland Revenue reference number as evidence of charitable status. The District Valuer will then consider the application and is required to make his decision within three months, though longer periods are permissible if it is a complex case. In making their decisions, District Valuers will be guided by the established body of case law. If dissatisfied with the decision of the District Valuer, the charity can appeal to the Commissioner, etc.

---

[130] Art. 41(2)(a) Rates (N.I.) Order 1977; see, for example, *Commissioner of Valuation v. Lurgan Borough Council* [1968] N.I. 104.

[131] The amendment was necessitated by a case brought by Moyle District Council asserting that "exemption" was inappropriate as they and other councils received no compensation from central government to offset the revenues lost due to charitable exemptions. The case was settled on terms that provided for the law to be amended. The authors are grateful to Mr M Curry of the Lands Tribunal for drawing our attention to this matter.

CHAPTER 22

Dissolving a Charity

22.1 INTRODUCTION

There are some very practical reasons why a charity may have to terminate or be terminated. To some extent these vary according to the legal structure of the charity. It has been said that dissolution of a charity may occur in the following circumstances:

- on the distribution of all its assets for charitable purposes;
- on the transfer of all its assets to another charity;
- at the expiration of the permitted time in the case of a "time" charity, or on the occurrence of an event giving rise to a gift over to non-charitable purposes.[1]

However, it has also been said that: "A charity once established does not die, though the nature may be changed".[2]

This chapter considers the conceptual difficulties which arise in relation to the prospect of termination. It then outlines the circumstances and manner in which a charity may be discontinued.

22.2 TERMINATION

The concept of termination in relation to a charity is open to doubt.[3] The *Pemsel* heads signify four immutable areas for charitable activity. Once the purposes of a donor's gift have been established as addressing one of those areas, and a related trust fund has been set up, the law then provides for the indefinite continuation of that charitable trust. In legal theory, charitable trusts are immortal and are designed to have perpetual existence. A donor's decision to commit funds exclusively to charity through trusts, absolutely and perpetually, has been treated in equity and by modern statute law as inherently inviolable.

---

[1] See Cairns, E., *Charities: Law and Practice* (2nd ed., Sweet & Maxwell, London, 1993) at p. 191.
[2] See *National Anti-Vivisection Society v. Inland Revenue* [1948] A.C. 31, *per* Lord Simonds at p. 74. Also, see, *Re Faraker* [1912] 2 Ch. 488, *per* Farwell, J., at p. 495.
[3] For discussion on this point see, for example, Tudor, *Charities* (Sweet & Maxwell, London, 1995), p. 452 *ante*.

526

The rationale for this approach would seem to lie in the public benefit principle. Having verified a philanthropic gift as bringing funds into the public domain for the public benefit, the law will lend its support to a gift continuing to serve that function until such time as the particular *Pemsel* head no longer requires charitable activity. Indeed, the singular claim of this type of trust to such continuation was recognised by its exclusion from the rule against inalienability and for most purposes from the rule against perpetuities. In any consideration of charity termination, however, a distinction must be drawn between the cessation of its legal structure and its charitable content. While the first may be readily extinguished the latter will often survive that termination and continue within a different legal structure; a process which most frequently occurs in order to render the charity more effective.

22.2.1 Prevention

The focus of the Charities Act (N.I.) 1964 is on preventing charities from terminating. The various administrative decisions which the Charities Branch can make are all designed to rescue charities or make them more charitable. If a charity is being dilatory in prosecuting an action, the Charities Branch can assume responsibility for it.[4] If charitable trust funds in court are "not being applied for the benefit of the charity" the Charities Branch can apply to assume responsibility for them.[5] The Charities Branch can facilitate the metamorphosis of a charity into an incorporated trusteeship.[6] If a charity has become untenable due to a lack of trustees, the Charities Branch can appoint new ones.[7] The Charities Branch can accept the transfer of charitable property from trustees, thus allowing the charity to continue.[8] If a gift would fail because it is partly charitable and partly non-charitable, the Charities Act (N.I.) 1964 allows a scheme to be drawn up to save it.[9]

The Charities (N.I.) Order 1987 continues this policy with more measures to ensure that charities continue, albeit in a different form. Old charities for the relief of poverty in a certain area, whose objects are now obsolete, can apply to the Charities Branch to have them modified.[10] Small charities can transfer their property (therefore ensuring survival of the charity in a changed form).[11] The only provision which facilitates termination of a charity is Article 5 of the Charities (N.I.) Order 1987. This provides that where a charity has

---

[4]   Charities Act (N.I.) 1964, s.6.
[5]   Charities Act (N.I.) 1964, s.8.
[6]   Charities Act (N.I.) 1964, s.10.
[7]   Charities Act (N.I.) 1964, s.12.
[8]   Charities Act (N.I.) 1964, s.15
[9]   s. 24 of the Charities Act (N.I.) 1964, and see further Chap. 19.
[10] Art. 3 Charities (N.I.) Order 1987.
[11] Art. 4 Charities (N.I.) Order 1987.

a permanent endowment of less than £25, no land and an income of less than £5 per year, it can pass a resolution allowing it to divest itself of its capital as well as its income. If all the capital is spent, there is no more property to which the charity can attach.

Probably the most significant legal device available to ensure that charities do not die is the *cy-près* scheme.[12]

The legislative intent behind all these provisions is to provide trustees with access to the additional authority necessary for good management and to prevent the failure of charities. Apart from Article 5 of the Charities (N.I.) Order 1987, these powers conspicuously fail to address any necessity for charity termination. The thrust of the legislation, and the role of both court and Charities Branch, is to support the charitable intent of a donor and to protect charities. The emphasis is very much on facilitating the continuation of a charity.

22.2.2 Variation rather than termination

In this jurisdiction, legislative initiative has ensured that wide powers are available to the court and the Charities Branch enabling their intervention in circumstances where a variation of the manner in which effect is given to a charity would forestall its termination.

22.2.2(i) Where a charity's purposes are fulfilled

Under section 22(1) of the Charities Act 1964 the doctrine of *cy-près* will apply to save a charity which has fulfilled the purposes for which it was established. This permits the charity to continue but in pursuance of other purposes. Such express statutory authority is required to protect trustees from what might otherwise be unlawful action. Charity trustees are bound to ensure that funds continue to be applied in furtherance of the charity's objects; trustees who take steps resulting in a charity's funds passing to another charity risk being exposed to a charge of breach of trust.

In *Trusts of the Rectory of St John*[13] the funds remaining after completion of the charity objectives and after all the donor's intentions had been satisfied were applied *cy-près* to achieve an ancillary and necessary objective. Re-directing surplus funds to address an extension of the initial charity objects is an appropriate use of *cy-près*.[14]

Cy-près is not the only means whereby the funds of an extant charity can be re-directed. Authority for such action may be provided in a charity's governing instrument. A great many charities are incorporated and in the process of becoming so a charity will, almost invariably, have included a standard

---

[12] s. 22 of the Charities Act (N.I.) 1964, see further below, see in more detail Chap. 19.
[13] [1898] I.R. 3 Eq. 335.
[14] See *Attorney-General v. Earl of Winchelsea* (1791) 3 Bro. C.C. 373.

clause in its memorandum making provision for its assets to be transferred to another named charity or to one of a defined type in the event of its dissolution. Such a dissolution clause gives trustees some flexibility: if a charity winds up without such a clause, any remaining assets are likely to be applied *cy-près*; if it winds up using such a clause, the trustees' choice of recipient for any remaining assets is unlikely to be challenged unless it is clearly inappropriate. Those charities constituted as trusts or unincorporated associations may not have made, or have been able to make, such arrangements (see further, below).

22.2.2(ii) Where a charity's purposes cannot be fulfilled

It may be the case that the charitable intentions of a donor cannot be fulfilled because they are impossible, impracticable or illegal. The fund may have already vested in trustees, and a legal structure established for the charity, before the facts rendering it incapable of fulfilment came to light. In such circumstances the trustees or the Charities Branch may petition the court for the trust funds to be applied *cy-près*.[15]

22.2.2(iii) Other circumstances

Under section 22 of the Charities Act 1964 a wide range of circumstances, including instances where charities have ceased or their funds would be more effectively used for other purposes, are now identified as appropriate for *cy-près* schemes. Under section 13(1) of the 1964 Act, as amended by the 1987 Order, the Charities Branch had authority to create *cy-près* schemes, up to a financial limit of £50,000, above which jurisdiction passed to the court. The statutory broadening of the *cy-près* doctrine, together with raising the financial ceiling for Charities Branch application of schemes to £50,000 in 1987, have certainly increased the opportunities for varying the use for which donor funds are given to charities. However, there is one statutory caveat which stands as a reminder of the judicial approach in the courts of equity. Under section 22(1) when applying a *cy-près* scheme regard must be given to "the spirit of the gift". The donor's intentions continue to be relevant.

A charity may also be altered in ways falling short of changing its charitable purposes. This may be permitted by its governing instrument,[16] by statute[17] or by less formal methods.[18] A charity may, for example, amalgamate

---

[15] See s. 8 of the Charitable Donations and Bequests Act 1867, as amended by s. 7 of the Charitable Donations and Bequests Act 1871 and now consolidated in ss. 13 and 22 of the Charities Act 1964.

[16] See *Re Bagshaw* [1954] 1 W.L.R. 238.

[17] See *Re Donald* [1909] 2 Ch. 410.

[18] See *Re Joy* (1888) 60 L.T. 175.

with another allowing the funds from the first to be transferred. As charities become active players in today's modern business environment so they are becoming exposed to the same risks and opportunities of mergers and takeovers experienced by other public and private corporations in an adversarial marketplace.

22.2.3 Termination by trustees acting under express authority

It is not unusual for trustees to be expressly vested with authority by the governing instrument to terminate the charity.[19] This power may be explicitly provided in circumstances where a charity is established to meet a short-term objective, such as disaster relief. The termination of the charity will, in such cases, have been foreseen from its inception. Once the intended goal has been met then the trustees will be expected to make the necessary formal arrangements for the charity to cease to exist. Included among such arrangements will be directions for the disposal of any residual funds and any capital or other assets.

22.2.4 Termination by authority of beneficiaries

A trust can be terminated by the collective action of its trustees and beneficiaries. In the absence of trustee co-operation, the beneficiaries can achieve dissolution by requiring the trustees to surrender all trust property. This is known as the rule in *Saunders v. Vautier*.[20] This strategy necessitates all beneficiaries to be *sui juris* and to be collectively entitled to the whole of the beneficial interest. Charitable trusts do not readily lend themselves to this type of termination. The rule does, in theory, apply to charities.[21] However, it will not apply if there is a gift to a charity which is to be ascertained in *futuro*.[22] Logically it may be difficult to determine who are the beneficiaries who can agree to termination of a charitable trust. Since charities are for the public benefit, it is difficult to argue how a number of private individuals can terminate it.

22.2.5 Termination due to lack of funds

A charity can only subsist for so long as there are funds to give effect to its purposes. Once its source of funds is exhausted it must cease. As was explained in *Re Withall*[23] by Clauson J.:

---

[19] See *Re Roberts* [1963] 1 W.L.R. 406, *per* Wilberforce J. at p. 413.
[20] (1841) 4 Beav 115.
[21] *Wharton v. Masterman* (1895) A.C. 186.
[22] *Re Jeffries* [1936] 2 All E.R. 626, see also Delaney (1962) at pp. 132-134.
[23] [1932] 2 Ch. 236.

"... if the work of an institution such as the Margate Cottage Hospital is being carried on by those who are voluntarily administering its affairs, without funds, from day to day on such bounty as it can obtain, when those administrators cease for lack of means to carry on the work, the work ceases, there are no longer any persons associated for the purposes of the work, and there are no funds dedicated to the work which was therefore carried on: in such circumstances in a full and true sense that institution in my view has ceased to exist."[24]

This situation may also arise where a donor intends to establish or maintain a number of charities but provides insufficient funds. The court will then direct that if one of these charities should cease to exist the portion allotted to it should be transferred to the others.[25] It may come about because the trustees decide to give effect to the objects of the charity by immediately distributing trust property among intended beneficiaries (as above in charities established for disaster relief).

22.2.6 Termination due to cessation of objects

The object or objects for which a charity was established may simply have ceased to exist. In such circumstances, a general charitable intention will most usually be inferred and any surplus funds will be applied *cy-près*.[26] Where such an inference cannot be made then there is some authority for the view that a resulting trust will arise.[27]

22.2.7 Termination following collapse of "parent" organisation

Where the objects of a charity are entirely dependent upon another agency then, in the event of the latter ceasing to exist, for whatever reason, the charity will also terminate.[28] It may prove to be the case that the objects of the charity can in fact be continued independently of the failed agency. The charity will then survive the death of the principal organisation.[29]

22.3 TERMINATION AND TYPE OF LEGAL STRUCTURE

Termination of the legal structure formed to give effect to a charity will not necessarily end the life of that charity. The consequences for the charity con-

---

[24] *ibid.*, at p. 241. See also, Tudor, *Charities, op. cit.* at p. 453.
[25] See *Re Evans' Charities* (1858) 10 I.C.R. 271.
[26] See *Re Prison Charities* (1873) L.R. 16 Eq. 129 and *Re Camden Charities* (1881) 18 Ch. D. 310.
[27] See *Re Stanford* [1924] 1 Ch 73; doubt has been cast on the wisdom of this approach by Simonds J in *Re Royce* [1940] Ch. 514.
[28] See *Re Rymer* [1895] 1 Ch. 19.
[29] See *Re Finger's Will Trust* [1972] Ch. 286.

cerned will depend to some degree on whether it is housed within a charitable trust, an unincorporated association or a company limited by guarantee.

22.3.1 Charitable trust

As has been said:

> "It is in relation to charitable trusts that the general proposition that a charity cannot die is most powerful."[30]

In this jurisdiction there is no specific statutory power to authorise the dissolution of a charitable trust. The Charities Branch may, however, exercise their statutory powers to advise and assist trustees who find themselves in the position of having to terminate a charity.

The termination of a charitable trust may be voluntary or involuntary. Most usually, in either case, it occurs because a charitable trust no longer has funds.

22.3.1(i) Voluntary termination

In addition to the instances mentioned above, a charity may cease to have funds not because these have been wholly expended in addressing its objects but because its trustees have chosen to transfer all funds to another charity. This may be achieved at trustee initiative where authority to do so has been provided by an express power in the governing trust instrument. Otherwise, the authority must be sought in the powers available to the Charities Branch under the 1964 Act. Such a transfer of funds is most likely to occur when a charity wishes to transform its legal status from a charitable trust to a company. On completion of transfer, the charitable trust will then cease to exist.

Where a transfer or distribution of funds is contemplated, trustees must first meet all trust liabilities. A full settlement of all accounts must precede any trustee action likely to place trust assets beyond the reach of possible claims by creditors. Where trustees are operating within the legal framework of a charitable trust, as opposed to a company, they are then personally liable for debts incurred by and on behalf of the charity. They may avoid personal liability where those debts were properly incurred and where no action has been taken to obstruct creditors access to trust assets.[31]

22.3.1(ii) Involuntary termination

A charity may cease to have funds because trust property is wholly liable to the claims of creditors. Termination of a charitable trust will occur involuntary in circumstances which would amount to bankruptcy if it had been consti-

---

[30] See Tudor, *Charities,* 1995, *op. cit.* at p. 454.
[31] See *Ex parte Garland* (1804) 10 Ves. 110.

tuted as a company. Where there are no remaining trust assets, the trustees of a charitable trust will be personally and individually liable to the creditors for debts incurred by the charity.

22.3.2 Unincorporated association

The termination of an unincorporated association seldom entails the termination of a charity. Most often the reason for such action is to provide a more effective legal vehicle to carry forward the purposes of the charity. As part of a strategy to achieve this the members may decide to substitute a company for the unincorporated association which provided the initial legal structure for the charity. Having transferred all trust funds to the company and vested it with full responsibility for giving effect to the charity, the unincorporated association then terminates.

However, as noted above, the termination of an unincorporated association will necessitate the simultaneous cessation of a charity in circumstances where the latter is either wholly dependant upon the former and it ceases[32] or if its funds are exhausted.

22.3.2(i) Voluntary termination

This may be achieved by activating a formal provision to that effect, written into the rules of the association at the time of its formation. When establishing an unincorporated association it is now customary for the members to ensure that the rules contain a provision allowing for such a voluntary dissolution. This would empower the executive committee to convene a special general meeting for that purpose, having served advance notice on all members. Then by resolution, usually requiring a two-thirds majority, the association may be formally dissolved.[33]

In the absence of such a formal procedure, the members may still achieve a voluntary termination simply by undoing the contractual agreement which forms the only legal basis for binding them into an association. This could be accomplished by the parties to the initial contract formally and specifically agreeing to dissolve their association.[34]

---

[32] See *Re Vernon's Will Trusts* [1972] 1 Ch. 300 at 303.

[33] See *Re Tean Friendly Association* (1914) 58 S.J. 234 for authority that the converse is also true; where no such provision exists it is not possible for the members to use the resolution procedure.

[34] See *Re William Denby & Sons* [1971] 1 W.L.R. 973 which provides authority for the view that the resolution must be specifically for dissolution.

22.3.2(ii) Involuntary termination

An unincorporated association may be terminated by the court either in response to a petition from a majority of members requesting such action or on
evidence provided by any person that the association can no longer properly
function. The High Court, exercising the discretionary powers available under its equitable jurisdiction, can then direct the winding-up of any such unincorporated association.[35]

22.3.2(iii) Spontaneous dissolution

As pointed out in Tudor[36]:

> "A charitable association can become dissolved by ceasing all of its activities.[37]
> This will only occur where the objects of the association are dependent upon a
> particular place or institution and not where the objects of the charity are wider
> purposes. If the particular institution which is the essence of the charity closes
> down or is destroyed or if a particular place becomes impracticable to use, the
> charitable unincorporated association will be dissolved without action by the
> members or the court.[38] Spontaneous dissolution will not occur if the charitable
> association merely becomes inactive[39] or if its objects are to carry out particular
> purposes for which the existence of a particular institution or place is not essen-
> tial."

22.3.2(iv) Assets

Where a power to dissolve by member resolution is provided in the rules of an
unincorporated association this will invariably be accompanied by a clause
addressing the matter of disposal of residual assets. This will usually stipulate
that, following settling of all *bona fide* claims, they should be transferred to a
charity with similar objects. Alternatively, where the contract stipulates other
arrangements, these must be adhered to, or, in the absence of explicit terms,
the assets must be divided equally among the members.

   If dissolution occurs in any other way then a *cy-près* scheme will be drawn
up either by the Charities Branch or by the court to dispose of any remaining
assets.

---

[35] See *Re Lead Company's Workmen's Fund Society* [1904] 2 Ch. 196.

[36] See *Charities, op. cit.*, p. 457.

[37] See, *Re William Denby & Son, op. cit.* Sere also *Re GKN Bolts and Nuts Ltd. (Automo-
tive Division) Birmingham Works Sports and Social Club* [1982] 1 W.L.R. 774.

[38] See *Re Slater's Will Trusts* [1964] 1 Ch. 512 at 527 and [1974] Conv. 187 at 191 (J.E.
Martin).

[39] See *Re GKN Bolts and Nuts Ltd., op. cit.* at p. 860.

22.3.3 Company limited by guarantee

The termination of any company, whether charitable or not, follows the same pattern and is governed by the same body of company law and accompanying rules and regulations. The resulting effect on charitable companies has been noted in Tudor[40]:

> "Charitable companies limited by guarantee provide the major exception to the rule that charities never die. Property of a charitable company is usually construed as being held beneficially rather than on trust for the purposes of the company. Accordingly, the dissolution of the company will also cause the termination of the charity."[41]

The exception is the company limited by guarantee which is holding some or all of its property on trust for either general or specific purposes.[42] Then the dissolution of the company will not necessarily cause the termination of the charity.

Reference to standard academic books[43] is suggested for those seeking general information on the voluntary and involuntary winding up of companies.

22.4 TERMINATION, THE COURT AND PUBLIC BODIES

The involvement of the court, Charities Branch or other agency is far from certain on the dissolution of a charity. Unlike the situation in England and Wales, there is no statutory requirement that a charity serve notice of termination on a public body.[44] This has led to a situation where there is no definitive record of those charities which are still active.

22.4.1 Termination and the court

The traditional equitable jurisdiction of the court may well be called upon in a situation where an incorporated charity with significant assets terminates or is terminated. It was Slade J. in *Liverpool & District Hospital for Diseases of the Heart v. Attorney-General*[45] who ruled on the court's jurisdiction in such circumstances. As he then stated:

---

[40] See *Charities, op. cit.*, p. 457.
[41] See *Re Stevenson's Will Trusts* [1970] 1 Ch. 16, 26.
[42] See *Re Meyers* [1951] Ch. 534.
[43] For example, Forde, M., *Company Law, op. cit.*
[44] s. 3(7)(b) of the Charities Act 1993 requires final trustees to serve such notice upon the Charity Commission which must then remove that charity from its register.
[45] [1981] 1 Ch. 193, [1981] 1 All E.R. 994; referred to in the Ontario Report, *op. cit.*, at Chap. 15.

"[Authorities] establish that [a company formed for charitable purposes] is in a position analogous to that of a trustee in relation to its corporate assets, such as ordinarily give rise to the jurisdiction of the court to intervene in its affairs."[46]

22.4.2 Termination and the Charities Branch

The powers of this body in relation to the termination of charities are limited. Where a charity is being wound up, the trustees have a duty under section 22(6) of the 1964 Act to apply for a *cy-près* scheme to be drawn up in certain circumstances; such action will of course involve the Charities Branch. Under Articles 3, 4 and 5 of the Charities (N.I.) Order 1987 the Charities Branch also has some limited capacity to permit the winding-up small charities in specified circumstances. However, the Charities Branch is not statutorily charged with any general duties in respect of charities which, for whatever reason, cease to function. Perhaps in most cases it will not even be aware that a charity has ceased as there is no formal mechanism for serving notice to that effect. Where a charitable trust eventually fails, and this fact has been brought to the attention of the Charities Branch then it is empowered to frame a *cy-près* scheme to direct the use of residual funds and/or property to purposes compatible with the donor's charitable intention. The Charities Branch is also empowered to authorise the sale of charity property (see further, Chapter 5).

22.4.3 Termination and the Inland Revenue

Again, there is no legal obligation placed on a charity to notify the Inland Revenue of its pending termination nor to ensure that the name of the charity is withdrawn from any list of charities maintained by that agency.

---

[46] *ibid.* at p. 209.

PART TWO

The Procedures

SECTION ONE

Inland Revenue Procedures

Giving to Charity by Businesses

This procedure, together with details regarding the required supporting documentation, is set out in the Inland Revenue 'Clubs and Charities Series' leaflet IR64.

Further relevant information can be found in the following Inland Revenue documents:

- IR65   Giving to charity by individuals

- IR178   Giving shares and securities to charity

- Helpsheet IR295   Relief for gifts and similar transactions

- CGT1   Capital gains tax. An introduction

Many leaflets are available on the Internet at www.inlandrevenue.gov.uk

From April 6, 2000, tax relief on gifts to charities can be claimed in respect of: gifts of money; gifts of shares and securities; gifts of assets; and gifts of employees' time. Tax relief is also available on sponsorship payments to charity.

1(A) The Gifts of Money Procedure

Businesses can get tax relief when they give money, whether as a one-off or a regular payment. From April 2000, all gifts of money qualify for tax relief under the Gift Aid scheme. There is no longer separate tax relief for payments to charity under a deed of covenant. There is no limit to the amount which the business can give, but the way you get tax relief will depend on whether the business is a company, sole trade or partnership.

How does a company get relief?
If your company decides to give money to charity, it simply makes the payment through Gift Aid and deducts the amount when working out its profits for corporation tax purposes. You make the full payment to the charity. You do not need to deduct any tax from the payment and the charity does not claim back any tax on the gift. You no longer have to provide a Gift Aid certificate to the charity nor provide a new form of declaration. If your company has no corporation tax liability in an accounting period, there are special rules regarding how any loss created by the donation can be used. You should contact the Inland Revenue office that deals with your company's corporation tax affairs if you need further information on this point.

If you are a close company, generally one under the control of five or less people, there is a limit on the benefit which the company, or a person connected with the company, can receive from the charity in return for the payment. An explanation of connected persons is set out in our leaflet CGT 1 'Capital gains tax. An introduction'. The limits on benefits are set out on page 3 of this leaflet.

How do sole traders get relief?
If you are trading on your own account, you can give through Gift Aid as any individual taxpayer would. Your gift will be treated as paid out of taxed income and the charity will reclaim basic rate tax on it from the Inland Revenue. If you are a higher rate taxpayer, you can get relief on the difference between the basic rate and the higher rate of tax on the gross amount of your gift. You simply enter the details of the gift on your Income Tax Self Assessment return. You will need to make a Gift Aid declaration to the charity. The charity may supply you with its own Gift Aid declaration form .

How do partnerships get relief?
We treat any gift by a partnership as made by the individual partners. We will treat you and your partners as each giving an equal share of the gift, unless you tell us that the partnership has decided to split the gift in a different way. We will treat your gift as paid out of your taxed income and the charity will reclaim basic rate tax on it from us. If you are a higher rate taxpayer, you can get relief on the difference between the basic rate and the higher rate of tax on the gross amount of your share of the gift.

Unless one partner has power, under the partnership agreement or some other document, to make a Gift Aid declaration on behalf of the partnership, each partner will need to make a Gift Aid declaration in favour of the charity. This can be done on one declaration, providing the name and address of each partner is shown. In Scotland, where partnerships have a legal personality, a partner may make a Gift Aid declaration on behalf of the partnership simply showing the partnership's name and address.

What evidence do I need of the payment to the charity?
If required, you will need to provide us with reasonable evidence of all the payments you have made to charities in the year in the same way as for other items in your Self Assessment tax return. A cancelled cheque, an entry in a bank or credit card statement, or an acknowledgement from the charity would suffice.

What are the limits on the benefits I can receive in respect of my gift?
The following table sets out the maximum benefits an individual, partner, or close company donor is allowed to receive in any tax year in respect of gifts to anyone charity. Your business can make gifts to as many charities as you choose.

Amount of donation	Value of benefits
£0–100	25% of the value of the gift
£101–1,000	£25
£1,001–10,000	2.5% of the value of the gift

The total benefits must not exceed £250.

1(B) The Gifts of Shares or Securities Procedure

Businesses can get tax relief for gifts to charity of certain shares and securities. This is in addition to the relief you can claim for them when calculating capital gains (see our Helpsheet IR 295 'Relief for gifts and similar transactions').

How does the tax relief apply?
You can claim this relief if you give to a charity, or sell to a charity at less than market value, any qualifying shares or securities. However, a company cannot get relief for a gift of its own shares.

What shares or securities qualify?
The following categories qualify

- shares and securities listed or dealt in on the UK stock exchange, including the Alternative Investment Market
- shares and securities listed or dealt in on recognised foreign stock exchanges
- units in an authorised unit trust
- shares in a U.K. open-ended investment company
- holdings in certain foreign collective investment schemes.

If in doubt, we can tell you whether the shares or securities will qualify for relief.

How do I calculate the amount of relief?
The amount you can deduct from the business' profits is

- the market value of the shares or securities at the date of disposal, **plus**
- ny incidental costs of disposing of the shares (broker's fees, etc.), **less**
- any money or the value of any other benefits the business, or a person connected with the business, receives from the charity as a result of you giving the shares to the charity.

How do I claim the relief?
Calculate the amount as above. Deduct that figure in working out the busi-

ness' profits for corporation tax purposes in the accounting period in which the disposal takes place. The amount should be entered on your Corporation Tax Self Assessment return as a charge.

If you are a partner or sole trader, deduct the amount when working out your income for the tax year in which the disposal takes place for your Income Tax Self Assessment return.

What date should I take as the date of disposal for the purpose of establishing the market value of the shares or securities?
The date on which you transfer ownership of the shares to the charity. In the majority of cases, that will be the date you sign the stock transfer document. There is further information to help you identify the market value at that date in our leaflet IR 178 'Giving shares and securities to charity'.

1(C) The Gifts of Assets Procedure

Gifts of equipment or trading stock to charity

What qualifies for relief?
The gift must be an article which is either
- an item manufactured or sold in the course of your trade, or
- machinery or plant used in the course of your trade.

You can get relief if you are a trading company, a sole trader, or a trading partnership.

How do I get relief?
When you give away an article manufactured or sold in the course of your trade, the normal treatment is to include the market value of the gift as a trading receipt when calculating your profits for tax purposes. Where such articles are given to a charity, nothing is included as a trading receipt. In that way, you get relief for the cost of the article in calculating the taxable profits of the trade.

In the case of machinery or plant used in the course of your trade, treat it as having been disposed of at nil value for capital allowances purposes (rather than at market value, as would otherwise be the case). The total capital allowances given to you in respect of the article will be equal to its cost.

1(D) The Gifts of Employees' Time Procedure

Secondment of employees to charity

Who can get this relief?
Trading or investment companies, sole traders, or trading partnerships.

What sort of secondments qualify?
The secondment of an employee to work for a charity on a temporary basis.

How do I get relief?
Deduct any costs you incur in connection with the employment of the person on — secondment (including his or her salary) in calculating your taxable profits for tax purposes.

1(E) The Sponsorship Procedure

Who can get relief?
Trading companies, sole traders, or trading partnerships.

What relief is available?
Relief is available for payments to sponsor a charitable activity, provided the payments are made wholly and exclusively for the purpose of your trade, and are not of a capital nature. (Capital expenditure is expenditure incurred for the purpose of acquiring, improving, or extending an asset held for use in the business.)

What sort of payments might qualify?
A payment made to get publicity for your name or product, which represents a reasonable return for the amount paid. Whether a payment qualifies for relief will depend on the facts. If you are in doubt, contact your Tax Office.

How do I get relief?
You deduct the sponsorship payments in calculating your trading profits for tax purposes.

What happens if sponsorship payments do not meet the conditions for relief?
No relief is available unless all the conditions are met. For example, if you make a – sponsorship payment to a charitable activity which results in your business acquiring an asset of the charity (for instance, office equipment or vehicles), you cannot deduct the payment when calculating the trading profits of the business for tax purposes. Similarly, if you make a payment partly for commercial reasons and partly for charitable reasons, you cannot deduct it in calculating the trading profits of the business for tax purposes. However, you might be able to get relief for such payments as Gift Aid donations. If you are in doubt about how we will treat a particular payment for tax purposes, ask your Tax Office before making it.

Giving to Charity by Individuals

This procedure, together with details regarding the required supporting documentation, is set out in the Inland Revenue 'Clubs and Charities Series' leaflet IR65.

Further relevant information can be found in the following Inland Revenue documents:

- IR64   Giving to charity by business

- IR178   Giving shares and securities to charity

- Helpsheet IR295   Relief for gifts and similar transactions

- CGT1   Capital gains tax. An introduction

- P/PG/1   Payroll Giving – a guide for employers

- P/PG/1   Payroll Giving – a guide for employees

Many leaflets are available on the Internet at www.inlandrevenue.gov.uk

From April 6, 2000, there are three procedures available for claiming tax relief on gifts to UK charities: under Gift Aid; through a Payroll Giving Scheme run by an employer; and by making a gift of shares or securities.

2(A) The Gift Aid Procedure

If you pay tax, Gift Aid is a scheme by which you can give a sum of money to charity and the charity can reclaim from the Inland Revenue basic rate tax on your gift. That increases the value of the gift you make to the charity. For example, if you give £10 using Gift Aid in the tax year 2000/01, that gift is worth £12.82 to the charity.

You can make payments by cash, cheque, postal order, direct debit, standing order, debit or credit card or even in a foreign currency (including the Euro).

Subject to a few rules, you can give any amount, large or small, regular or one-off, and the charity can reclaim the tax.

If you are a higher rate taxpayer, you can claim relief on the difference between the basic rate and higher rate of tax.

If you do not pay tax, you should **not** use Gift Aid.

How does my gift qualify for Gift Aid?
You must

- pay at least as much tax as the charities will reclaim on your gifts in the tax year in which you make them (tax credits on dividend income will count towards the tax paid). The tax year runs from 6 April in one year to 5 April in the next. See below.
- make a declaration to the charity that you want your gift to be treated as a Gift Aid donation.
- not receive excessive benefits in return for your gift.

Have I paid sufficient tax?
When you give money to a charity under Gift Aid, the charity will reclaim basic rate tax on that money. You must therefore pay an amount of tax in that tax year at least equal to the tax the charities will reclaim. That tax can be income tax or capital gains tax at any rate. Even if you only pay tax at the 10% starting rate, that tax can cover the tax the charity reclaims on the gift.

You can calculate the amount of tax the charity recovers by simply multiplying the amount of your gift by

$$\frac{\text{the basic rate of income tax}}{100 \text{ minus the basic rate}}$$

With the basic rate at 22%, the charity reclaims 22/78ths of your gift.

Example
During the tax year you give a total of £400 to various charities.

Under Gift Aid, we treat this sum as a gift made net of basic rate tax (*i.e.* after tax has been taken off at the basic rate).

With the basic rate at 22%, the charities reclaim £112.82 (£400 x 22/78) and your gross gift is worth £512.82 (£400 + £112.82) to them.

If you have paid less tax than £112.82, you should not make the donation under Gift Aid. You should simply give the money to the charity and not sign the Gift Aid declaration. If you do sign the declaration, so that the charity recovers tax on the donation, you may have to pay any excess to the Revenue.

If you are a starting rate (10%) or basic rate (22%) taxpayer and you have paid tax (income or capital gains) at least equal to the £112.82 claimed by the charity, there is nothing further for you to pay.

What if I am a higher rate taxpayer?
The charity reclaims tax on your gift only at the basic rate, even if you are a higher rate payer. If you are a higher rate taxpayer, you can claim the difference (18% in 2000/01) between the higher rate of tax of 40% and the basic rate of tax of 22% in your Self Assessment return.

So, in the example above, you may reclaim higher rate relief of £92.30 (£512.82 @ 18%) on your gross donation of £512.82.

Can I count tax paid on my dividend income?
Yes. Tax credits on dividend income can be used to cover tax reclaimed by the charity.

What about tax deducted from my savings?
If tax is deducted from bank or building society interest you receive, you can use that .. to cover the tax on the gift, provided you have not reclaimed it. If you have reclaimed that tax, then you must not use it to cover the tax on your gift.

Why do I need to give a declaration?
The declaration is the charity's authority to reclaim tax from the Inland Revenue on your gift. By giving the declaration, you are confirming that you understand this.

How do I make a declaration?
In writing or orally. Usually, the charity will provide a written declaration form.

All you need to do is:

- enter your name and address
- enter the name of the charity
- make clear whether the declaration covers just this gift or others as well (already made or to be made later)
- make clear that you want the gift or gifts to be within the Gift Aid scheme.

The charity will often complete some, or all, of the details for you. You then just complete any remaining details and send the form to the charity.

You can give a written declaration to a charity by post, fax, or e-mail.

You can also make a declaration by telephone or in person. In this case, the charity will take a note of your details, as above, and send you a written record. All you need do is check that the details are correct.

Can I withdraw a declaration?
If, for any reason, you decide that your gift should not be within Gift Aid – perhaps you realise that you will not pay enough tax to cover the tax reclaimed by the charity – then you have 30 days from the date of the written record sent to you after making an oral declaration, to tell the charity and withdraw it. Your withdrawal will cancel the declaration with effect from the date the declaration was made. If you make a written declaration your cancellation will only take effect from the date you notify the charity.

Do I have to make a declaration with every gift?
No. You can specify in one declaration as many gifts for whatever period you wish — for example, it can cover gifts you might already have made to a particular charity since 6 April, 2000 or it can cover the gifts you make in the future.

What if I no longer want my gifts to be within Gift Aid?
If you wish to stop your donations or if you think that your gifts should no longer be within Gift Aid because you no longer pay sufficient tax to cover the tax that the charity reclaims, you can cancel your declaration at any time. The cancellation will take effect from the time the charity receives your letter.

Can I get any benefits in return for my gift?
Some charities, particularly those which have membership schemes, like to acknowledge your donation with some small gift in return, such as a book. That is fine as long as whatever the charity gives you (or anyone connected with you, such as a relative) in return for your donation is within the limits below.

You can receive benefits up to certain limits in each tax year. The maximum value of the benefits you can receive in return for your donation to a particular charity are as follows.

Amount of donation	Value of benefits
£0–100	25% of the donation
£101–1,000	£25
1001–10,000	2.5% of the donation
Over £10,000	£250

The total benefits you receive from one charity in the same tax year must not exceed £250.

If you receive benefits which exceed the above figures, the donations will not be within Gift Aid. That means that the charity will not be able to reclaim basic rate tax and you will not be able to claim any higher rate relief on your gift.

Can I pay my membership subscriptions through Gift Aid?
You can pay membership subscriptions to a charity through Gift Aid, provided any membership benefits you receive do not exceed the limits above. However, you can disregard free or reduced entry to view heritage property or wildlife, the preservation of which is the charity's main aim.

Can I use Gift Aid when I buy things from a charity?
No. You can use Gift Aid only for outright gifts to charity. You must not use Gift Aid for payments to buy goods or services -for example, Christmas cards or other goods from a charity shop.

Can I pay my children s educational fees under Gift Aid
No. A child's or student's fees at a school or college which is a charity cannot be donated under Gift Aid. This is because, whether paid by a parent or any other person, the payment would be made for services and not as an outright gift to a charity.

Other Gift Aid issues

What about money paid under my existing deed of covenant?
If you had a covenant in existence at April 5, 2000, you can continue to make the payments due under that deed of covenant, without completing a Gift Aid declaration, until that deed expires. The charity will claim tax back under the Gift Aid scheme. If you make additional gifts, above your commitment under the deed, you must give the charity a declaration to cover those gifts if you want it to be able to recover the tax on them.

What should I do when my deed expires?
You can bring your regular payments to charity within the Gift Aid scheme, simply by making a declaration. You do not need to execute a further deed of covenant, but can set up a standing order. If you prefer to execute a further deed of covenant, you will also need to make a declaration to enable the charity to reclaim tax.

Can I pay my membership subscriptions through Gift Aid?
You can pay membership subscriptions to a charity through Gift Aid, provided any membership benefits you receive do not exceed the limits above. However, you can disregard free or reduced entry to view heritage property or wildlife, the preservation of which is the charity's main aim.

Can I use Gift Aid when I buy things from a charity?
No. You can use Gift Aid only for outright gifts to charity. You must not use Gift Aid for payments to buy goods or services -for example, Christmas cards or other goods from a charity shop.

Can I pay my children s educational fees under Gift Aid
No. A child's or student's fees at a school or college which is a charity cannot be donated under Gift Aid. This is because, whether paid by a parent or any other person, the payment would be made for services and not as an outright gift to a charity.

Other Gift Aid issues

What about money paid under my existing deed of covenant?
If you had a covenant in existence at April 5, 2000, you can continue to make the payments due under that deed of covenant, without completing a Gift Aid declaration, until that deed expires. The charity will claim tax back under the Gift Aid scheme. If you make additional gifts, above your commitment under the deed, you must give the charity a declaration to cover those gifts if you want it to be able to recover the tax on them.

What should I do when my deed expires?
You can bring your regular payments to charity within the Gift Aid scheme, simply by making a declaration. You do not need to execute a further deed of covenant, but can set up a standing order. If you prefer to execute a further deed of covenant, you will also need to make a declaration to enable the charity to reclaim tax.

Can I use Gift Aid to pay the proceeds of fund-raising events to charity?
If you have simply collected money from other people, such as on a flag day, you have not given the money yourself, and the other people have not made a declaration to the charity that they are taxpayers, so the payment is not made under Gift Aid. However, if you have been sponsored for an event, and each sponsor has signed a Gift Aid declaration, then the charity can recover the tax on the amounts covered by declarations. Charities may produce sponsorship forms for this.

Does a gift I make jointly with someone else qualify for Gift Aid?
Yes, but you must tell the charity how much is from each of you. You will both need to give declarations if the whole amount is to qualify.

If I make a loan to a charity and write it off later, can that count as a Gift Aid payment?
No. Gifts must take the form of payment of a sum of money to qualify for relief under Gift Aid.

If I give the charity money to buy something from me, does that qualify for Gift
No. Gifts linked to a purchase from you (or someone connected with you) do not qualify for relief.

I already give to charity through Payroll Giving, Can I use Gift Aid as well?
Yes, but not on donations given under the Payroll Giving scheme. You get tax relief only once on each type of gift you make.

Can I use charity vouchers to make Gift Aid donations?
Some organisations, which are charities themselves, offer charity accounts and provide you with a charity card or charity "cheque book" of vouchers so that you can give directly to the charities of your choice. In this case, you give your money to the organisation issuing the charity card or vouchers. They will ask you for a declaration and will reclaim basic rate tax on your gift. The value of your charity account or the vouchers issued to you will include the tax reclaimed.

Is there any restriction on the number of charities I can give to?
No. You can give to as many charities as you like.

Can I get relief for a gift to a foreign charity?
No. Gift Aid applies only to gifts to charities established in the UK, but many foreign charities are established in the UK through branches.

Can I make a Gift Aid payment to a UK charity if I do not live in the UK?
In certain circumstances. You may do so if you are a Crown employee serving overseas (typically as a serving member of the armed forces, or a diplomat). You can also use Gift Aid if you are not a UK resident but you make your gift out of income or gains charged to UK tax.

Can trustees make payments under Gift Aid out of a trust?
No. Gift Aid is for gifts by individuals and companies only.

2(B) The Payroll Giving Scheme Procedure

What is Payroll Giving?
It's a simple way for you to give regularly to charity from your pay and get tax relief on your gifts. The Government is adding a further 10 per cent to all such donations for three years from April 2000.

Does my employer have to offer a Payroll Giving scheme?
No. But if your employer doesn't run a scheme, you might want to ask if he would be willing to start one. Your employer can find out more about running a scheme by calling the number at the front of this leaflet.

Can all employees join in Payroll Giving?
Yes, provided you are an employee or pensioner and your employer deducts Pay As You Earn tax from your pay or pension.

How much or how little can I give?
There are no limits on how much or how little you can give. It is entirely up to you.

How does Payroll Giving work?
You authorise your employer to deduct your gift from your pay. Every month your employer pays it over to a Payroll Giving agency approved by the Inland Revenue. The agency then distributes the money to the charity or charities of your choice. Some agencies can provide you with a charity card or cheque book so that you can give directly to any charity whenever you want to.

How do I get tax relief?
Because your employer deducts your gift from your pay or pension before Pay As You Earn tax is worked out, you pay tax only on the balance. This means that you get your tax relief immediately at your highest rate of tax. (The amount you pay in National Insurance contributions is not affected.)

Example

Basic rate taxpayer
You authorise a monthly deduction of	£10.00	
You save income tax at 22%	2.20	
Net cost to you		£7.80

Higher rate taxpayer
You authorise a monthly deduction of	£10.00	
You save income tax at 40%	£4.00	
Net cost to you		£6.00

Charity
Charity receives	£10.00	
Plus 10% Government supplement (until April 2003)	£1.00	
Total		£11.00

Can I give to any charity?
Yes, you can give to any UK charity and you may give to more than one if you wish. You can nominate a large, national charity or a smaller, local one. You can nominate your church, village hall, Parent Teacher Association or Scout group, etc, providing they are charities.

Will my employer have to know which charity I want to support?
No, you can keep your choice confidential if you wish. The Payroll Giving agency will provide you with a charity nomination form which you can complete and return direct to the agency. Alternatively, you may prefer to use the charity card or cheque book option described above.

Can I change the charities I wish to support?
Yes, by simply telling the Payroll Giving agency.

Can I stop giving?
Yes, at any time. Simply tell your employer's payroll department.

Can I ask for a refund of my donations?
No, once your employer has deducted a gift from your pay, it must go to charity.

Will the Payroll Giving agency deduct a handling charge?
The agency is a charity in its own right. It may deduct a small fee -usually no more than 4 per cent or 35p per donation, whichever is the greater -to meet administration costs. Some employers will pay the agency's charges so that the full amount of your gift can go to your chosen charity.

Will this affect the other gifts I make to charity?
No, you can make any other gifts you want to – for example, under Gift Aid.

Is more information available?
Yes, there is the P/PG/2 'Payroll Giving – a guide for employees' and the P/PG/1 'Payroll Giving -a guide for employers' available from the Inland Revenue. These give more information about the scheme and can be obtained by calling the number at the front of this leaflet. The guide for employers contains a list of all the approved Payroll Giving agencies. It also contains a list of promotional fundraising organisations which will help employers set up and run a Payroll Giving scheme.

2(C) The Gifts of Shares and Securities Procedure

As well as giving money through Gift Aid and Payroll Giving, you can also get income tax relief for gifts to charity of certain shares and securities. You get this relief in addition to the relief for gifts to charity of shares, securities and other assets when calculating capital gains.

When does the tax relief apply?
You can claim this relief if you give, or sell at less than market value, any qualifying investments to a charity.

What is a qualifying investment?

The following investments qualify for the tax relief

• shares and securities listed or dealt in on the UK Stock Exchange, including the Alternative Investment Market

- shares or securities listed or dealt in on any overseas recognised stock exchange
- units in an authorised unit trust (A.U.T)
  - shares in a U.K. open-ended investment company (O.E.I.C.)
- holdings in certain foreign collective investment schemes (foreign equivalents of A.U.T.s and O.E.I.C.s).

If in doubt, Inland Revenue (Charities) can tell you whether your shares or securities will qualify.

How do I calculate and claim the relief?
You deduct the amount from your income for the tax year in which the gift takes place.

The amount you can deduct is

- the market value of the shares or securities at the date of the gift, plus
- any incidental costs of transferring the shares (such as broker's fees or stamp duty), less
- any disposal proceeds or other money or the value of any other benefits you, or a person connected with you (such as a relative), receive in consequence of your giving or selling the shares to the charity.

You can claim relief, at your highest rate of tax, on your Self Assessment return. If you do not usually receive a tax return, you should write to your Tax Office and let them know about your gift.

If you decide to give some shares to charity, our leaflet IR178 'Giving shares & securities to charity' will tell you more about what you need to do and how to calculate and claim the tax relief.

Further information

Inheritance tax
Outright gifts and bequests to UK charities are completely free of inheritance tax.

Capital gains tax
You are not liable to capital gains tax when you make a gift of assets, such as land or stocks and shares, to charity, even if the asset is worth more when you donate it than when you acquired it.

Our leaflet C.G.T.1. 'Capital gains tax. An introduction' gives you more details about capital gains tax.

Contact with the Tax Office
This leaflet does not cover every point. If you have any questions, the staff at

your local Inland Revenue Enquiry Centre or Tax Office will be happy to answer them. They can also give you the other leaflets listed on the inside front cover.

Drawing Up Gift Aid Declarations

MODEL GIFT AID DECLARATION

Name of Charity ....

Details of Donor

Title .... Forename(s) .... Surname ....

Address ....

....

.... Post Code........................

I want the charity to treat

　　*the enclosed donation of £ ....

　　*the donation(s) of £ .... which I made on ..../ ..../ ....

　　*all donations I make from the date of this declaration until I notify you otherwise

　　*all donations I have made since 6 April 2000, and all donations I make from the date of this declaration until I notify you otherwise

as Gift Aid donations.

NB. Charities do not have to include all these statements on their declarations, but can choose whichever is appropriate.

See overleaf for notes.

Notes

1. You must pay an amount of income tax and/or capital gains tax at least equal to the tax that the charity reclaims on your donations in the tax year (currently 28p for each £1 you give).

2. You can cancel this declaration at any time by notifying the charity.

3. If in the future your circumstances change and you no longer pay tax on your income and capital gains equal to the tax that the charity reclaims, you can cancel your declaration (see note 1).

4. If you pay tax at the higher rate you can claim further tax relief in your Self-Assessment tax return.

5. If you are unsure whether your donations qualify for Gift Aid tax relief, ask the charity. Or ask your local tax office for leaflet IR 65.

6. Please notify the charity if you change your name or address.

PROCEDURE 4

Applying to the Inland Revenue for Recognition of Charitable Status

There is no formal application form for charities to fill in when applying for a charity recognition number and exemption from tax from the Inland Revenue.

What follows are suggestions from the Inland Revenue on how best to make an application. The best practice is to send off full documentation. Charities should send in:

- the governing instrument,
- a synopsis of their activities,
- any promotional material already generated,
- any literature they have produced, and
- full contact details with a contact name.

The Inland Revenues aims to reply within 28 days, either with a decision, or an acknowledgement that the application for exemption has been received.

The Revenue often suggests changes which can be made to constitutions to make them charitable. Before the Charity Commissioners were set up in 1960, the Revenue performed the role of advice giver to charities on status. They still retain this role where the Charity Commissioners are not involved. If more major changes would be required from the applicant, the Inland Revenue often refers applicants to the Northern Ireland Council on Voluntary Action.

Whenever exemption is granted, the Revenue sends out a letter with a reference number and a charities help-line.

Charities Branch Procedures

The Charities Branch prefers not to use standard forms. It responds on a case-by-case basis to queries, customising relevant forms and procedures to fit the particular needs of each charity. It does, however, have in place fixed procedures enabling small charities to alter objects, transfer assets or expend capital under the powers provided by Articles 3, 4 and 5 of the Charities Order 1987. These procedures are set out below.

Further relevant information can be found in the following Charities Branch documents:

- Northern Ireland Charities: A Guide for Trustees (10th ed.), 2000
- Northern Ireland Charities: A Guide for Trustees – Supplement No 1, 1995
- Charities Annual Report
- Summary of the Charities Act (N.I.) 1964 and the Charities (N.I.) Order 1987
- Summaries of the Charities Acts 1992 and 1993
- Summary of the Law Reform (Miscellaneous Provisions) Scotland Act 1990

Anyone wishing to apply for the exercise of the Department's powers under the Charities Act (N.I.) 1964 or other charity legislation should in the first instance contact Charities Branch explaining what they want to do. Charities Branch will then either:

- send them the appropriate forms and a note of any additional information, copy title documents etc. required; or
- invite them to write in with a formal application, telling them what additional information, copy title deeds etc. are required.

The Charities Branch welcomes informal inquiries from trustees or solicitors before the submission of formal applications.

Small Charities: Alteration of Objectives Procedure

Under Article 3 of the Charities (Northern Ireland) Order 1987 the trustees of a local charity for the relief of poverty may alter its objects provided that: -

1. Its sole or primary object is the relief of poverty; and

2. It is established for purposes directed wholly or mainly to the benefit of a particular area (e.g. a county) in Northern Ireland; and

3. At least 50 years have passed since its foundation; and

4. It is not a company or other body corporate; and

5. The trustees have unanimously resolved to alter the charity's objects and given notice of their intention to the Department for Social Development in the. form required by the Order (a copy is attached); and

6. The Department has concurred with that resolution.

Prior Consideration
Before passing the resolution referred to above the trustees must have come to the unanimous conclusion:

a. that the objects of the charity may fairly be considered obsolete, or lacking in usefulness, or impossible of achievement, having regard to the period that has elapsed since the charity was founded, the social and economic changes that have taken place in that period, and any other circumstances relevant to the functioning and administration of the charity; and

b. that an alteration of the charity's objects is required so that the charity's resources may be applied to better effect consistently with the spirit of the original gift; and

c. that the proposed new objects (which must be charitable) are not so different in character from those of the existing charity that the proposed alteration would be an unjustifiable departure from the intentions of its founder or violate the spirit of the gift.

Founder's Approval
The trustees must take any reasonable steps open to them to secure the approval of any person who can be identified as the founder of the charity .[1]

Public Notice
After passing the resolution the trustees must give public notice that they have done so, unless ; they are of the opinion that this would serve no useful purpose. It is up to the trustees to decide what form of public notice is reasonable and justified in the light of the charity's resources and the extent of its area of benefit.

Copy of Resolution to be sent to the Department
Having passed the resolution the trustees must send a copy to the Department at the address below, together with the following documents:

1.   A copy of their charity's Deed of Trust or other governing instrument.

2.   Documentary evidence, such as a copy of a Deed of Appointment of New Trustees, to establish who the trustees are, and copies of the death certificates of any of those trustees who are deceased.

3.   A statement, in the form of a letter, setting out the trustees' reasons for wishing to alter the charity's purposes, and the reasons for the particular choice of new purposes, and giving details of how public notice of the resolution was given.

If the trustees encounter difficulties in obtaining any of the above documents they should contact the Department's Charities Branch for advice on how to proceed.

Department's Action
Within a period of three months from receipt of the resolution the Department must either:

1.   give the trustees written notice that it requires further time to consider the case;

2.   give the trustees written notice that it concurs with the resolution; or

3.   give the trustees written notice that it does not concur with the resolution.

The Department may require the trustees to provide any further information which it feels is necessary and may take into consideration any representations made by interested parties.

Subsequent Procedure
If the Department does not concur with the resolution the alteration of the

---

[1]   This is the requirement under Article 3(4) referred to in the Form of Resolution.

charity's objects cannot proceed. If it does concur then the alteration will take place with effect from a date specified by the Department.

FORM OF RESOLUTION BY CHARITY TRUSTEES UNDER ARTICLE 3

Introductory

We are the trustees of the Charity, being a charity to which Article 3 of the Charities (Northern Ireland) Order 1987 applies. We are of the opinion –

*(a) that the objects of the charity may fairly be considered obsolete or lacking in usefulness, or impossible of achievement, having regard to the period that has elapsed since the charity was founded, the social and economic changes that have taken place in that period and other circumstances relative to the functioning and administration of the charity, as follows *(relevant circumstances, if any to be specified)* and

(b) that an alteration of the charity's objects, as set out in *(here specify the applicable trust instrument)* is required in order that the charity's resources may be applied to better effect, consistently with the spirit of the original gift.

*Delete any words or phrases not applicable.

Alternative objects, being in law charitable, are specified in the schedule to this resolution and are in our opinion not so far dissimilar in character to those of the original charitable gift that this modification of the charity's trusts would constitute an unjustifiable departure from the intentions of the founder of the charity, or violate the spirit of the gift.

We have complied with Article 3(4) of the Charities (Northern Ireland) Order 1987

Resolution
We, the trustees of this charity, under and in pursuance of Article 3 of the Charities (Northern Ireland) Order 1987, hereby resolve that the trusts of the charity be modified by replacing the objects set out in the trust instrument by the alternative objects specified in the schedule.

Signed.   TRUSTEES OF THE CHARITY

Date

Schedule to this Resolution

ALTERNATIVE OBJECTS PROPOSED TO REPLACE THOSE SET OUT IN THE TRUST INSTRUMENT

Small Charities: Transfer of Assets Procedure

Under Article 4 of the Charities (Northern Ireland) Order 1987 a small charity may be wound up and its assets transferred to another similar charity if:

1. Its gross income in the last accounting period (of not less than 12 and not more than 15 months) was £200 or less; and

2. It is not a company or other body corporate; and

3. The trustees have unanimously resolved to transfer the charity's assets and given notice of their intention to the Department for Social Development in the form required by the Order (a copy is attached); and

4. The Department has concurred with that resolution.

Prior Considerations
Before passing the resolution referred to above, the trustees must:

1. obtain written confirmation from the trustees of the receiving charity that they are willing to accept the transfer .

2. be of the unanimous opinion that the objects for which the transferred property would be held by the receiving charity would not be so dissimilar to the objects of the existing charity as to depart unjustifiably from the intentions of its founder, or violate the spirit of the gift;

3. take any reasonable steps open to them to secure the approval to the proposed transfer of any person who can be identified as the founder of the charity.[2]

Public Notice
After passing the resolution the trustees must give public notice that they have done so unless they are of the opinion that this would serve no useful purpose. It is up to the trustees to decide what form of public notice is reasonable and justified in the light of the charity's resources and the extent of its area of benefit.

---

[2] This is the requirement under Article 4(3) referred to in the Form of Resolution.

Copy of resolution to be sent to the Department

Having passed the resolution the trustees must send a copy to the Department at the address below, together with the following documents:

1. A copy of their charity's Deed of Trust or other governing instrument.

2. A copy of the receiving charity's Deed of Trust or other governing instrument.

3. Documentary evidence, such as a copy of a Deed of Appointment of New Trustees, to establish who the trustees are, and copies of the death certificates of any of those trustees who are deceased.

4. A statement, in the form of a letter, setting out the trustees' reasons for wishing to transfer the charity assets and giving details of how public notice of the resolution was given.

If the trustees encounter difficulties in obtaining any of the above documents they should contact the Department's Charities Branch for advice on how to proceed.

Department's Action

Within a period of three months from receipt of the resolution the Department must either:

1. give the trustees written notice that it requires further time to consider the case;

2. give the trustees written notice that it concurs with the resolution; or

3. give the trustees written notice that it does not concur with the resolution.

The Department may require the trustees to provide any further information which it feels is necessary and may take into consideration any representations made by interested parties.

Subsequent Procedure

If the Department does not concur with the resolution the transfer cannot proceed. If it does concur then the trustees may make arrangements for the transfer.

It is important to note that the transfer is not achieved automatically through the Department's concurrence with the resolution. It is suggested that the trustees should seek the advice of their legal advisers as to exactly what steps will be necessary to give the receiving charity good title to the charity's assets, particularly if these include land. The assets must be distinguished into capital and income in accordance with Article 4(9) of the Order and the trustees of the receiving charity should be told how much of the property being transferred to them can be expended and how much must be retained as capital.

FORM OF RESOLUTION BY CHARITY TRUSTEES
UNDER ARTICLE 4

Introductory

We are the trustees of the   Charity, of which the gross income in the preceding accounting period was £   .

We think it expedient that the whole property of the charity be transferred to another charity, to be held and applied for, and as property of, that other charity.

We have obtained from the trustees of the *(here name proposed transferee charity)* written confirmation that they are willing to accept a transfer of property under Article 4 of the Charities (Northern Ireland) Order 1987.

We have formed the opinion that the objects of the   Charity are not so far dissimilar in character to those of the original charitable gift that the proposed transfer would constitute an unjustifiable departure from the intentions of the founder of the Charity, or violate the spirit of the gift.

We have complied with Article 4(3) of the Charities (Northern Ireland) Order 1987.

Resolution

We, the trustees of the   Charity, under and in pursuance of Article 4 of the Charities (Northern Ireland) Order 1987, hereby resolve that the whole property of the charity, including its permanent endowment, be transferred to the   Charity.

Signed: TRUSTEES OF THE CHARITY

Date:

Small Charities: Expending Capital Procedure

Under Article 5 of the Charities (Northern Ireland) Order 1987 a small charity may spend its capital if the following conditions are met:

1. Its capital endowment is worth £25 or less and does not include land or any interest in land; and

2. Its gross income during the last accounting period (of not less than 12 and not more than 15 months) was £5 or less; and

3. The trustees have unanimously resolved that the charity may spend its capital as income and given notice of their intention to the Department for Social Development in the form required by the Order (a copy is attached).

Prior Considerations
Before passing the resolution referred to above, the trustees must be of the opinion that the assets of the charity are too small in relation to its objects for any useful purpose to be achieved by the expenditure of income alone. They must also consider whether there is any reasonable possibility of transferring the charity's property to another charity under Article 4 of the Charities (Northern Ireland) Order 1987 although they do not have to undertake such a transfer if they consider that it would be unacceptably costly.[3]

Copy of resolution to be sent to the Department
Having passed the resolution the trustees must send a copy to the Department at the address given below.

Expenditure of Capital
Once the Department has acknowledged receipt of the resolution, the trustees are free to expend the charity's capital for its purposes.

---

[3] This is the requirement under Article 5(2) referred to in the Form of Resolution.

FORM OF RESOLUTION BY CHARITY TRUSTEES
UNDER ARTICLE 5

Introductory

We are the trustees of the   Charity.

The value of the charity's permanent endowment is £   (or thereabouts), and the endowment does not consist of or comprise land or any interest in land, and its gross income in the last preceding accounting period was £   .

We are of the opinion that the property of the charity is too small, in relation to its objects, for any useful purpose to be achieved by the expenditure of income alone.

We have complied with Article 5(2) of the Charities (Northern Ireland) Order 1987.

Resolution

We, the trustees of the said charity, under and in pursuance of Article 5 of the Charities (Northern Ireland) Order 1987, hereby resolve that the charity ought to be freed from any restrictions imposed by law with respect to expenditure of capital.

Signed: TRUSTEES OF THE CHARITY

Date

Appendices

Charities Branch Consultation Document: Proposals for Changes to Charity Legislation in Northern Ireland

REGISTRATION OF CHARITIES

13. In framing proposals, the Department considered a number of models for maintaining a register of charities in Northern Ireland. These included:

    (a) The extension to Northern Ireland of the remit of the Charity Commission in England and Wales. Apart from the question of whether it would be appropriate for the Home Office and the Commission to assume responsibility for charities in Northern Ireland, given the resultant loss of local supervision and control, the cost involved would be likely to be prohibitive.

    (b) The introduction of a system of registration similar to that in England and Wales, but maintained by the Department. This would be equally expensive.

    (c) The Scottish model, where the Inland Revenue would be required to disclose to members of the public, on request, information about an organisation's charitable status for tax purposes. This might be less expensive than the above options, but it is not suitable for charities in Northern Ireland because the only Inland Revenue Offices which could operate the system are in Edinburgh and Merseyside. In addition, not all charities in Northern Ireland will be on the Inland Revenue's database.

    (d) A "soliciting register", based on elements of practice in the USA and on a proposal put forward but not acted upon in the Republic of Ireland, which would require only those charities wishing to collect money from the public at large to register. This approach would concentrate supervisory effort on those charities which may be expected to cause most concern in terms of fundraising, but it would not provide a comprehensive register .

    (e) A variant devised specifically for Northern Ireland, with a register of all charities maintained by the Department.

14. It was decided to adopt proposal (e). Our proposed model, based on what we believe to be appropriate for Northern Ireland, realistic in resource terms, and balanced in terms of the impact on charities, particularly small charities, is one on the lines set out below.

15. The Department proposes that a simple form of register should be introduced and maintained by the Department, on the following lines:

(a) Compulsory registration for all charities without exception, phased in over a period of time for existing charities and, on their foundation, for new charities. In view of the large numbers of separate charitable funds held by some corporate trustees, simplified arrangements will be made for the registration of these charities.

(b) The Department would have power to refuse to register, or remove from the register, a body which it considers is not, or has ceased to be, a charity, and to note on the register whether a charity is in breach of any requirement made by the Department. In practice, it would be a condition of registration that the body concerned has obtained charitable status for tax purposes from the Inland Revenue, or can demonstrate a valid case for not obtaining such status. Such a case might be based on the fact that a charity has no taxable income or gains, or on religious or philosophical grounds.

(c) The information held in respect of each charity registered would include:
    (i)   The name and address of the charity.
    (ii)   Abbreviated, colloquial, and alternative names.
    (iii) A short summary of the charity's objects.
    (iv) The names and addresses of the trustees and officers. (These will not be made available to the public).
    (v)   The name and address of a public contact point (normally the secretary).
    (vi) The date of the last accounts provided.
    (vii) The annual income and amount spent on the charity's objects.
    (viii) A miscellaneous comments section, to be used by the Department to note matters of interest.

(d) Where two or more charities have the same name, or names so similar as to lead to confusion, the Department would have power to require one or more of them to change its name.

(e) The Department would have the power to direct that two or more charities having the same trustees should be treated as a single charity for the purposes of the legislation. This is intended to simplify the registration process for trustees who hold multiple similar charities.

(f) Charities with an annual income over £1,000 (other than religious charities and schools) would be required to make an annual return updating their registration record. Charities with incomes of less than £1,000 a year (and religious charities and schools) would be exempted from annual returns.

(g) All charities would be obliged to inform the Department of any major change in their circumstances, such as a change of name or address or income level, and of their winding-up or moving outside Northern Ireland.

(h) All charities would be required to submit their annual accounts and reports to the Department on request, but not routinely.

(i) The Department would have the right to review individual charities" registration records to ensure they are accurate and up-to-date.

16. The proposed register would, therefore, amount to a list of bodies whose purposes were accepted as being charitable in law. It would:

(a) provide a database which could be used to:
    (i) provide the public with contact points for charities with which they. wish to correspond, for example, to obtain copies of annual accounts r and reports;
    (ii) generate statistics about the size and nature of the charitable sector;
    (iii) identify specific charities which meet given criteria, for example, for a potential donor who wishes to give money for a specific purpose;
    (iv) provide information for use by the Department in the discharge of its lead responsibility for promoting efficiency and effectiveness in the voluntary sector (of which charities are a part), for example, in promoting training for trustees;

(b) provide a source of information for the discharge of the Department's charity supervision activities.

17. Registration would not imply that a registered charity was guaranteed to be a efficient, well managed and deserving of support, but rather that its objects and purposes were charitable in law.

18. The Department proposes that it should have the power to charge fees for registration and for amending registration details.

19. The Department proposes that it should have power to exchange information about charities with the R.U.C., the Inland Revenue and other government departments and agencies.

ACCOUNTS, AUDITS AND ANNUAL REPORTS
ARRANGEMENTS

20. Section 27 of the Charities Act (N.I.) 1964 requires charities to "keep proper books of account" and prepare annual accounts consisting of either a receipts and payments or income and expenditure account, as the trustees decide, and, if the charity's capital exceeds £500 and the Department so directs, an end-of-year balance sheet.

21. There is no obligation to supply copies of accounts to the public or to the Department except where the Department has reasonable grounds to believe that charity property has been concealed, misapplied or withheld and the Attorney-General agrees that it is entitled to demand the accounts.

22. The preparation of annual accounts, subject where appropriate to independent examination and audit, is an important means of demonstrating accountability for charities. The Department proposes, therefore, that there should continue to be a statutory requirement on the trustees of Northern Ireland charities to prepare annual accounts. The objective would be to keep the burden placed on charities to the minimum necessary to ensure that they are properly supervised. To this end, the form and minimum content of the accounts would be prescribed by regulations, and would vary for charities of different sizes. As a minimum, an end-of-year balance sheet (or a statement of assets and liabilities in the case of smaller charities) would be mandatory in all cases.

23. In relation to audit requirements, the Department proposes that there should be a requirement for all charities whose annual gross income exceeds a prescribed level to have an annual audit of their accounts, as follows:-

Income or Expenditure	Audit
Less than £10,000	None
£10,000–£100,000	Independent examination
£100,000–£250,000	Full audit if the Department requires, otherwise independent examination
£250,000	Full audit.

24. "Independent examination" means an examination by an individual appointed by, but having no connection with, the trustees of a charity. The individual must be "suitable for the circumstances of the charity", but need not be professionally qualified. For charities in the £100,000-£250,000 band, the individual must have accountancy experience.

25. In the preparation of their accounts, charities and their accountants would be expected to draw on existing guidance on good practice, for example, the

Statement of Recommended Practice on accounting by charities (S.O.R.P.2) produced by the Charity Commission for England and Wales.

26. The requirements imposed in relation to reporting and accounting arrangements would be without prejudice to those imposed by any other legislation or a charity's own constitution. For example, a charity which is a limited company would still have to comply with the requirements of the Companies (Northern Ireland) Order 1982.

27. All charities would have to prepare an annual report giving details of the charity's constitution and objectives, together with a review of its activities during the year, likely future developments, and particulars of any connected bodies.

28. All charities would be placed under a duty to establish and maintain effective systems of internal controls for controlling their financial activities.

29. It is proposed that the Department should have the power to make regulations:

    (a) varying the income levels specified above;

    (b) specifying the form of annual accounts and reports;

    (c) specifying the information to be included in annual accounts and reports;

    (d) specifying the accounting principles to be followed in annual accounts;

    (e) prescribing a minimum system of internal controls which charities must maintain, or different systems for different types of charity; and

    (f) specifying the qualifications, duties, and rights of access to information of auditors and independent examiners, and entitling them to require information and explanations from past or present trustees or employees of charities.

30. Charities would not be required to submit annual accounts to any central supervisory body. They would, however, be obliged to furnish to the Department and members of the public, on request, copies of their annual accounts (suitably audited depending on size) and annual report. They would be entitled to charge members of the public, though not the Department, an appropriate fee to cover costs.

31. It is proposed that the Department should have power to exempt charities from the public right of access to their reports and accounts. This power would only be used in exceptional circumstances where the charity concerned could make a strong case for concerns about the security of their staff and/or beneficiaries. In these circumstances the charities exempted would be required to submit their reports and/or accounts to the Department on a confidential basis.

32. Charities would continue to be required to retain their accounting records for seven years, and this requirement would be extended to include any records needed to substantiate their annual accounts for the years in question.

POWERS TO CONTROL ABUSES

33. The Department's powers to supervise and control charities" activities are limited and most cases where a charity comes under suspicion of malpractice are dealt with by the R.U.C. under the criminal law relating to theft or fraud. The Department's involvement lies with the rare cases in which an allegation is made that a charity is being mismanaged but the criminal law has not been broken. In such a case the Department can apply to the courts for action to be taken against such a charity if necessary. It is felt that certain additional powers are required, as discussed below.

34. The Department proposes that it should have the power to require a charity to change its name where:

    (a) this name is the same as, or similar to, the name of another charity which was founded earlier; or

    (b) this name is likely to mislead the public as to the charity's purposes or activities; or

    (c) this name is likely to falsely give the impression that the charity is connected in some way with any government department or local or other public authority or any other body of persons or individual.

35. The Department proposes that a person should be disqualified from being a charity trustee if:

    (a) he has been convicted of any offence involving dishonesty or deception; or

    (b) he is an undischarged bankrupt; or

    (c) he has been removed from office as a charity trustee by the Charity Commission for England and Wales, the Commissioners of Charitable Donations and Bequests for Ireland, or any Court in the U.K. or Ireland; or

(d) he is disqualified from being a company director.

It is also proposed that the Department should have the power to waive disqualification on any of the above grounds in exceptional cases.

POWERS WITH RESPECT TO THE ADMINISTRATION OF CHARITIES

SMALL CHARITIES

36. Existing legislation permitting the winding-up of small charities in certain circumstances (Articles 3,4 and 5 of the Charities (Northern Ireland) Order 1987) is quite limited in its extent. The Department proposes to amend the existing provisions so that:-

(a) a charity whose income is less than £5,000 pa could alter its purposes or transfer its assets to another charity; and

(b) a charity whose income is less than £1,000 pa could expend its capital.

The net effect of these changes would be to simplify the system, increase the maximum size of the charity that can use it, and extend it to charities that hold land.

DISPOSAL OF CHARITY PROPERTY

37. The Department proposes that charities should in general be allowed to dispose of property without the consent of the Department or the Court if they fulfil a number of requirements in relation to obtaining professional valuations, advertising the sale, and ensuring that the terms of sale are the best obtainable. Certain disposals (e.g. where the purchaser has some connection with the charity) would still require consent.

38. Some charities do not currently require a power of sale from the Department in order to sell property. Occasionally, however, they may apply for such a power because the purchaser is reluctant to accept that it is unnecessary or the transaction is in some way unusual. The Department's policy is to grant power of sale, even if it is unnecessary, if this will assist the charity. If the preceding proposal is adopted it appears that a specific power would be required to allow the Department to grant power of sale where it is not strictly required.

39. The Department proposes to introduce such a power which could be used at the charity's request and if it appears to the Department to be in the charity's interests.

PUBLIC NOTICE

40. When appointing new trustees for a charity, or making a scheme to alter its objects, the Department is required by the existing legislation to give public notice of its intention on two occasions, in each case allowing 28 days for public comment before proceeding. This delays the making of schemes and can impose considerable costs on charities (who bear the cost of publication). In general the public respond to only about 5% of first notices, and no comments have ever been received in response to a second notice.

41. Cases sometimes arise in which there is no possibility of anyone being in a position to comment on or object to a scheme, for example, where a scheme is making purely technical changes to the way in which a charity operates such as changing the examination results necessary to qualify for a scholarship in response to changes in the examination system. In these cases the notices serve no purpose.

42. The Department proposes, therefore, to amend the legislation to require only one notice to be given, and to allow the Department to dispense with notices altogether where, in its opinion, they would serve no useful purpose.

DORMANT BANK ACCOUNTS

43. The Department proposes to introduce a provision empowering it to transfer bank and building society accounts belonging to charities to other similar charities where the account has not been used for five years and the charity trustees cannot be traced

SCRUTINY OF WILLS

44. Under the existing legislation the Probate Registry is required to send copies of all Wills containing charitable bequests to the Department, which may require the executors to produce receipts from the charities concerned. No evidence of misbehaviour by executors has ever been revealed in the exercise of this role.

45. The Department proposes to abolish the automatic aspects of this function, while retaining the Department's right to ask for all or any copy Wills containing charitable " bequests if spot checks are considered to be necessary.

REVISION OF MONETARY LIMITS

46. The monetary limits listed below define the maximum value of charity property with which the Department can deal in the circumstances described; charities with more valuable property can only be dealt with by the courts:

(a) Power to make *Cy Près* Schemes to change the purposes of a charity under section 13 of the Charities Act (N.I.) 1964 – Limit £50,000.

(b) Power to apply misdescribed charitable bequests to an appropriate charity under section 14 of the Charities Act (N.I.) 1964 – Limit £2,500.

(c) Power to make schemes to apply property given for mixed purposes to charitable purposes under section 24 of the Charities Act (N.I.) 1964 – Limit £50,000.

47. Powers to make *Cy Près* Schemes and schemes for property given for mixed purposes have proved popular with trustees, since they save the charity concerned the cost of an application to the Court. No such scheme made by the Department has ever been the subject of legal challenge.

48. The Department proposes that the limits on its powers to make such schemes should be abolished, giving the Department unlimited jurisdiction. This would not affect a charity's right to apply to the Court for such a scheme if it felt this would serve its interests better than an application to the Department.

49. Power to deal with misdescribed bequests is most often regarded as providing a simpler alternative to a *Cy Près* Scheme in cases where it is usually obvious which charity the testator meant to benefit although he got its name or address wrong. However, it also covers very rare cases where a *Cy Près* Scheme cannot readily be made.

50. The Department proposes, therefore, that the limit on the Department's power to deal with such cases should be abolished, giving the Department unlimited jurisdiction, subject to the Attorney-General's consent to the Department's proposals in each case.

FUND RAISING

51. Professional fund-raisers are a recent development in the charity field and their activities are not closely regulated in Northern Ireland. The Department proposes to introduce a range of provisions making professional fund-raisers much more accountable to the charities on whose behalf they are collecting. In brief, they would provide that:

(a) A professional fundraiser could only collect on behalf of a charity if he has a formal agreement with it to that effect.

(b) A professional fundraiser must indicate which charity he is collecting for and how his remuneration is to be calculated.

(c) A charity could apply to the Courts to issue an injunction preventing unauthorised fundraising on its behalf.

(d) It would be an offence to collect money for an institution which is not a registered charity by falsely claiming that it is.

CHARITABLE COLLECTIONS

52. The legislation governing street collections is the Police, Factories etc {Miscellaneous Provisions) Act 1916 and the Regulations made under that Act, while the legislation governing house-to-house collections is the House-to-House Charitable Collections Act (N.I.) 1952 and the Regulations made under that Act.

53. All street and local house-to-house collections must be licensed by the R.U.C. In the case of province-wide house-to-house collections only, the Department may issue an 8 exemption order permitting a charity to collect without having to approach the R.U.C. In practice exemption orders are only issued after consultation with the R.U.C.

54. The Department proposes to simplify these arrangements by replacing the present categories of street and house to house collections with a single new definition of "public charitable collections" and introducing the licensing system described below.

55. Public charitable collections would be equivalent to the existing street and house-to-house collections, and would also embrace other types of collection that are technically illegal at present or that may evolve in the future. A public charitable collection would be defined as a charitable appeal which is made in any public place or by means of visits from house to house. A house for the purposes of this legislation would include a place of business. A charitable appeal would mean an appeal to the public to give money or property (whether or not they receive a consideration in return) which represents that all or some of the proceeds are to be applied for charitable, benevolent or philanthropic purposes.

A public place would include any highway, any open place to which the public has access, and any enclosed place to which the public has access, such as a public house, station, airport or shopping precinct. It would not include:

(a) collections made at public meetings;

(b) collections made on church property;

(c) collections made by means of unattended collection receptacles on private property;

(d) collections made in any place to which the public must always pay to gain access (but this would not apply to an event for which an entrance fee is charged which takes place in an enclosed space to which the public has access at other times); or

(e) collections made in any place to which the public are permitted to have access only for the purposes of the appeal in question.

Collections made by individuals on their own behalf (*i.e.* begging) or collections made for purposes which are not charitable, benevolent or philanthropic would continue to be dealt with by the R.U.C. under existing separate legislation.

56. All public charitable collections would have to receive approval from the R.U.C. (the Divisional Commander in whose area of responsibility the collection is to take place) by means of a permit which would authorise a specific charity to collect in a specific location or locations on a specific date or dates.

57. Where a large scale collection was planned, the charity would apply to the R.U.C. (the Assistant Chief Constable, Belfast) for a permit which would authorise the collection throughout Northern Ireland or in a specified area and save the charity the trouble of applying separately to each R.U.C. district.

58. An application for a permit would have to be made in writing in English (or a translation into English supplied at the applicant's expense) in a form specified in regulations made under the legislation. Minimum and maximum periods of notice could be specified in regulations made under the legislation. The R.U.C. would have power to accept an application at periods of notice other than those specified in regulations if they thought fit. Every application would have to include the following information:

(a) The full names, home addresses, telephone numbers and dates of birth of the trustees of the charity or the persons organising the collection or of the person responsible for carrying out the collection, if not a trustee.

(b) A full description of the manner in which the collection is to be carried out.

(c) The precise purposes for which the proceeds of the collection are to be applied.

(d) The locations in which and the date or dates on which it is proposed to hold the collection.

(e) Such details as the R.U.C. may require in relation to any previous collections carried out by or on behalf of the charity concerned, or for the same purpose.

(f) Such details as the R.U.C. may require in relation to any organisation (whether it is located in Northern Ireland or elsewhere and whether or not it is a charity) with which the charity or other organisation on whose behalf a permit is being sought is connected.

(g) If required by the R.U.C., a list of the names, home addresses and dates of birth of all the persons who are to act as collectors.

(h) Such other information as may be specified in regulations made under the legislation.

59. The R.U.C. would be able to charge a fee or different fees for issuing a permit, and could exempt individual charities or classes of charities from payment of such fees. The level of such fees would be specified in regulations made under the legislation.

60. When considering whether to grant a permit the R.U.C. could make enquiries about the charity, its trustees and staff, the persons organising the collection, the person responsible for carrying out the collection, individual collectors, and the history of any previous collections with which any of these persons were connected.

61. The R.U.C. could determine that certain specific charities should be given preference when it comes to deciding which charities should be allowed to collect on specific dates and in specific areas. (This relates to, for example, the British Legion Remembrance Day or the Salvation Army Christmas collections).

62. The R.U.C. could issue or refuse to issue a permit. Where one was issued, the R.U.C. could attach such conditions to it as they thought fit. Without affecting the generality of the foregoing, such conditions could concern the time or place of a collection, or the manner in which it is carried out, or the persons who may act as collectors. The grounds upon which the R.U.C. could refuse to issue a permit would include:

(a) The proposed collection would cause undue inconvenience to the public, or might present a risk of injury to the public or the persons carrying out the collection.

(b) Another collection has already been authorised to take place on the day and in the area concerned.

(c) It appears that the amount likely to be applied for the charitable, benevolent or philanthropic purposes of the collection would be small in absolute terms, or inadequate in relation to the amount actually collected given the nature of the collection, or less than 90% of the total amount collected.

(d) It appears that any person would be likely to receive an excessive amount by way of remuneration in connection with the collection.

(e) Any of the charity's trustees or staff, or any person connected with the collection has been convicted in any jurisdiction of an offence involving dishonesty, or any offence of a kind the commission of which would in the R.U.C.'s opinion be facilitated by the issue of a permit. A conviction for an offence of the types specified may be taken into account regardless of whether it is a spent conviction.

(f) The trustees of the charity concerned have not authorised the collection.

(g) It appears that in relation to any other collection for charitable, benevolent or philanthropic purposes the trustees of the charity, the persons organising the collection or the person responsible for carrying out the proposed collection failed to exercise due diligence to ensure that such collection was carried out efficiently or in accordance with any relevant legislation or regulations.

(h) Two collections for the charity concerned, or for a similar or related charity, or for the same charitable, benevolent or philanthropic purpose have been carried out in the same or a similar geographical area in the twelve months preceding the date on which the proposed collection is to be held.

(i) The trustees or staff of the charity, the persons organising the collection or the person responsible for carrying out the collection have refused or neglected to provide the R.U.C. with any information reasonably required for the purposes of investigating or considering any of the matters specified above, or have supplied false or misleading information.

(j) The trustees of the charity, the persons organising the collection or the a person responsible for carrying out the collection are not resident in Northern Ireland.

(k) The R.U.C. has reasonable grounds to believe that the issue of a permit might lead to or expedite the commission of any criminal offence.

63. Where the R.U.C. had reason to believe that there had been a change in the circumstances which prevailed when a permit was issued, or that the information furnished in connection with an application for a permit was false in a material fact or that there was or was likely to be a breach of any condition attached to a permit they could withdraw or attach additional conditions to the relevant permit.

64. Where the R.U.C. refused to issue, or attached conditions to, a permit they would inform the applicant of the reasons for this decision in writing. The applicant could appeal against their decision to the Magistrates Court provided that he did so within 28 days.

65. The Department proposes that it should be an offence to:

   (a) Organise, promote, carry out or take part in a collection which is subject to the new legislation if a permit has not been issued authorising it.

   (b) Fail to comply with any regulations made under the legislation.

   (c) Falsely represent to any person that a collection is being carried out for a charitable, benevolent or philanthropic purpose.

   (d) Make use of a prescribed badge or certificate of authority in the course of a collection to which it does not relate.

   (e) Make use of any device, badge, certificate or other document so nearly resembling a prescribed badge or certificate of authority as to be calculated to mislead.

   (f) Fail to identify oneself to a member of the R.U.C. when acting as a collector if required to do so under the provisions of the legislation.

   (g) Supply false or misleading information to the R.U.C. in connection with an application for a permit or a requirement contained in the legislation or regulations made thereunder.

66. The penalties for the above offences would be as follows:-

   (a) Imprisonment for a term not exceeding 6 months or a fine not exceeding £1,000 or both.

   (b) Imprisonment for a term not exceeding 6 months or a fine not exceeding £1,000 or both.

   (c) A fine not exceeding £100.

   (d) A fine not exceeding £100.

   (e) A fine not exceeding £100.

(f) A fine not exceeding £100.

(g) Imprisonment for a term not exceeding 6 months or a fine not exceeding £1,000 or both.

67. The Department proposes that it should have the power to make regulations prescribing anything which requires to be prescribed for the purposes of the legislation and for regulating the manner in which collections are carried out including, but not limited to:

(a) Requiring and regulating the use by collectors and the form and content of prescribed badges and certificates of authority and the use, custody, production and return thereof, and requiring collectors to carry and display their badges and carry their certificates of authority at all times while carrying out a collection or being in possession of money collected, and on demand by a member of the R.U.C. or any occupant of any house or the owner, tenant or proprietor of any other premises visited in the course of a collection to produce their badges and certificates of authority.

(b) Prohibiting persons below a prescribed age from acting as collectors and prohibiting others from causing them to act as collectors. However, the general age regulations may include exemptions or variations in respect of members of specified organisations.

(c) Preventing annoyance, nuisance or inconvenience to the public or risk of injury to the public or collectors.

(d) Prescribing information to be furnished to the R.U.C. about the costs, expenses, proceeds and the application of the proceeds of collections.

(e) Prescribing the level of fees in connection with the issue of a permit and the circumstances in which individual charities or classes of charities may be exempted from payment of such fees.

(f) Specifying the minimum period of notice which must, and the maximum period of notice which may, be given by an applicant between the receipt by the R.U.C. of an application for a permit and the proposed date of the collection

(g) Specifying the form and content of accounts required to be produced under this legislation, and how such accounts are to be audited, certified or witnessed.

68. The Department proposes that:

(a) Any member of the R.U.C. could require any person whom he believed to be acting as a collector for any charitable, benevolent or philanthropic purpose to immediately declare his full name, home address and date of birth, and could arrest him if this was necessary to establish his identity.

(b) If a collection to which the legislation applies was carried out without a permit having been properly obtained, the R.U.C. could seize the proceeds of the said collection.

(c) Where any collector carrying out a public charitable collection was in breach of any of the regulations governing such collections {including, but not limited to, those relating to the carrying of badges and certificates of authority) any member of the R.U.C. could seize any money in his possession which was or appeared to be the proceeds of such collection.

(d) Following any collection for which a permit had been issued, the person to whom the permit was granted would have to supply the R.U.C. with accounts showing how much was raised by the collection and how it was applied.

THE ROLES OF THE ATTORNEY-GENERAL AND THE COURT

69. The Department proposes that there should be no change in the arrangements by which certain of the Department's powers require the Department to consult the Attorney-General before taking action: these arrangements provide a valuable oversight of the Department's activities.

70. In view of the cost of Court proceedings, and to reduce the burden on the Court system, it is desirable that the number of applications to the Court by or about charities should be minimised. The majority of such applications are likely to concern *Cy Près* Schemes, and the number could be reduced by increasing the Department's jurisdiction to make such Schemes: this point is addressed above under "Revision of Monetary Limits".

CHARITIES' INVESTMENT POWERS

71. The Trustee Investments Act 1961 which was extended to cover Northern Ireland by the Trustee (Amendment) Act (N.I.) 1962 defines the investments which can be used by charities and divides them into two groups; narrower-range (basically gilts) and wider-range (basically equities). Unless it has a contrary power in its constitution, a charity must invest at least 50% of its capital in narrower-range investments.

72. Most new charities include a clause in their constitutions allowing them to use any of the investments listed in the 1961 Act without having to follow the 50% narrower-range rule. It is felt by many people in the charity sector that the 50% narrower-range rule is unduly restrictive in modern financial circumstances and is rather patronising to trustees.

73. The Department proposes that it should have the power to make regulations varying the narrower- and wider-range limits and allowing charities to invest property in investments not otherwise allowed in Northern Ireland.

EDUCATIONAL ENDOWMENTS SCHEMES

74. These Schemes were originally made towards the end of the last century under the Educational Endowments (Ireland) Act 1885 for the government of certain educational charities. From time to time these Schemes require amendment, and this is done under the provisions of the 1885 Act rather than under the more recent charity legislation. At present it is difficult for the 100 or so affected charities to be wound up.

75. The Department proposes to amend the 1885 Act to allow the Department to make Schemes, on the application of the Trustees, to wind up these charities and apply their assets to other similar purposes.

MINOR AMENDMENTS

76. The Department proposes to make a number of minor amendments that which would have the following effects:

(a) Ensuring that charitable companies cannot amend their constitutions so as to allow charitable funds to be used for non-charitable purposes.

(b) Transferring the Department of Finance and Personnel's charities functions under the Consumer Credit Act 1974 and the Reserve Forces Act 1980 to the Department of Health and Social Services.

(c) Allowing the Department to share and exchange information about charities with other government bodies, including the Inland Revenue.

APPENDIX 2

Select Bibliography

Books

Barker, C.R., Ford, P.J., Moody, S.R. and Elliot, R.C., *Charity Law in Scotland* (W Green/Sweet & Maxwell, Edinburgh, 1996).

Brady, J.C., *Religion and the Law of Charities in Ireland* (W & S Magowan, Belfast, 1975).

Chesterman, M., *Charities, Trusts and Social Welfare* (Weidenfeld and Nicholson, London, 1979).

Cracknell, D.G., *Law Relating to Charities* (2nd ed., Oyez Longman, London, 1982).

Delany, H., *Equity and the Law of Trusts in Ireland* (Round Hall Sweet & Maxwell, Dublin, 1996 (2nd ed., 1999)).

Delany, V.T.H., *The Law Relating to Charities* (Alex Thompson, Dublin, 1956, 1962).

Gidron, B., Kramer, R.M. and Salamon, L.M. (eds.) *Government and the Third Sector: Emerging Relationships in Welfare States* (Jossey-Bass, San Francisco and Oxford, 1992).

Halfpenny, P., and Lowe, D., *Individual Giving and Volunteering in Britain* (7th ed., Charities Aid Foundation, Kent, 1994).

Hamilton, F.A.P., *The Law Relating to Charities in Ireland* (E. Ponsonby, Dublin, 1881).

Hind, A., in *The Governance and Management of Charities* (Voluntary Sector Press, Hertfordshire, 1995).

Jones, *History of the Law of Charity 1532-1827* (Cambridge University Press, London, 1969).

Keeton and Sheridan, *The Law of Trusts* (12th ed., Barry Rose Law Publishers Ltd., London, 1993).

Luxton, P., *Charity Fund-Raising and the Public Interest: an Anglo-American Legal Perspective* (Avebury, Aldershot, 1992).

O'Halloran, K., *Charity Law* (Round Hall Sweet & Maxwell, Dublin, 2000).

Perri 6 and Anita Randon, *Liberty, Charity and Politics: Non-Profit Law and Freedom of Speech* (Dartmouth, Aldershot, 1995).

Pettit, *Equity and the Law of Trusts* (7th ed., 1993).

Picarda, H., *The Law and Practice Relating to Charities* (3rd ed., Butterworths, London, 1999).

Rhodes, R.A.W., *Understanding Governance* (Buckingham, Open University Press, 1996).

591

Sheridan, L.A., *The Modern Law of Charities* (Barry Rose Law Publishers Ltd, Chichester, 1992).

Titmus, R., *The Gift Relationship* (Allen and Unwin, London, 1970).

Underhill and Hayton, *The Law Relating to Trusts* (14th ed., 1987).

Warburton J., *Tudor on Charities*, (8th ed., Sweet & Maxwell, London, 1995).

Wise, D., *Performance Measurement for Charities* (ICSA Publishing, Hertfordshire, 1995).

Journal Articles, Book Chapters & Conference Papers

Adshead, M., and Quinn, B., "The Move from Government to Governance" in *Policy & Politics*, vol. 26 no. 2, pp. 209–225.

Acheson, N., and Williamson, A., *Voluntary Action and Social Policy in Northern Ireland* (Aldershot, Avebury, 1995).

Barker, C.R., "Religion and Charity Law" in *The Juridical Review*, Edinburgh, 1999, Part 5, pp. 303–315.

Brady, J.C., "Some Problems Touching the Nature of Bequests for Masses in Northern Ireland" (1968) 19 N.I.L.Q., 357 and (1974) 25 N.I.L.Q. 174.

Brady, J.C., *Charitable Purposes and Ratings Exemption in Ireland* (1968) 3 Ir. Jur. (N.S.) 114, 1968.

Brady, J.C., *House of Lords, Charities and Rating Relief in Northern Ireland* (1973) 24 N.I.L.Q. 106.

Brady, J.C., *The Law of Charity and Judicial Responsiveness to Changing Social Need* (1976) 27 N.I.L.Q., 198.

Burt , E., "Charities and Political Activity: Time to Re-think the Rules" in *The Political Quarterly*, vol. 69, no. 1, p. 23.

Carswell, *Rating Exemption and Charitable Purposes* (1965) 16 N.I.L.Q. 88.

Cheal, D., *The Gift Economy* (Cambridge University Press, Cambridge, 1988).

Chisholm, L.B., "Politics and Charity: a Proposal for Peaceful Co-existence" in the *George Washington Law Review*, 1990, 58, 2, pp. 308–65.

Dawson, N., *"Old Presbyterian Persons" – A Sufficient Section of the Public* [1987] Conv. 114.

Dawson, N., *"Cy-près*: Means, Motive and Opportunity and Other Matters', in *Northern Ireland Legal Quarterly* (1988) Belfast, 39, p. 177.

Delany, H., "Charitable Status and *Cy-près* Jurisdiction: An Examination of Some of the Issues Raised in *Re the Worth Library*' (1994) N.I.L.Q. 45, Belfast.

Delany, H., *Rating Exemption on the Ground of Charitable or Public Use* (1960) 13 N.I.L.Q. 316.

Dunn, A., "Charity Law as a Political Option for the Poor" in (1999) N.I.L.Q. 50, Belfast, pp. 298–317.

Forder, "Too political to be charitable?" (1984) Conveyancer 263.

Frank, R., 'Motivation, Cognition and Charitable Giving" in Schneewind, J.B., (ed.), *Giving: Western Ideas of Philanthropy* (Indiana University Press, Bloomington, 1996).

Gerwirth, A., "Private Philanthropy and Positive Rights" in *Beneficence, Philanthropy and the Public Good*, Paul, E., Miller, F., Paul, J., and Ahrens, J., (eds.), (Basil Blackwell, Oxford, 1987).

Harris, M., and Rochester, C., "Managing Relationships with Governing Bodies', in Osborne, S., (ed.) (1996), *Managing the Voluntary Sector*, Thompson Press, London, at p. 31.

Lowry J., *Some Reflections on Rating* (1966) 17 N.I.L.Q., No. 2.

National Council for Voluntary Organisations, *The Contract Culture – The Challenge for Voluntary Organisations*, 1989; "Charities and the Contract Culture" in *Charity Law in Scotland, op. cit.*, pp. 208–228.

O'Halloran, K., *The Role of Charity Law in Creating an Enabling Environment for Private Philanthropy in N Ireland*, International Journal of Not-for-Profit Law, Washington, vol. 1 issue 3, 1999.

O'Halloran, K. & Breen, O., *Charity Law in Ireland and Northern Ireland: Registration and Regulation*, in Irish Law Times, Dublin, no 1, vol. 18, pp 6-14, 2000.

O'Halloran, K. & Barker, C., *Charity Law in Scotland and Northern Ireland: a comparative study*, International Journal of Not-for-Profit Law, Washington, vol. 1, issue 5, 2000.

Simon, J.G., "Foundations and Public Controversy: an Affirmative View" in Heimann, F., (ed.) *The Future of Foundations*, Spectrum Books, Prentice-Hall, Englewood Cliffs, New Jersey, 1973.

Quint, F., and Spring, T., "Religion, Charity Law and Human Rights', in *Charity Law & Practice Review*, Vol.5, Issue 3, 1999, pp. 153-186.

Wood, M., "Is Governing Board Behaviour Cyclical?" in *Non-profit Management and Leadership*, vol. 3(2), 1992, pp. 139-163.

Reports, White Papers

Banks, J., and Tanner, S., *The State of Donation: Household Gifts to Charity, 1974-96*, Institute for Fiscal Studies, London, 1997.

Charities Aid Foundation, *Charity Household Survey 1988/89*, Kent, CAF, 1990; Charity Commission (England and Wales), *The Hallmarks of a Well-Run Charity*, (leaflet CC60), London, July 1999.

Charity Commission (England and Wales), *Responsibilities of Charity Trustees* (leaflet CC3), Charity Commission, London, 1994.

Charity Commission (England and Wales), *Report of the Charity Commission for England and Wales for the Year 1997*, 1998.

Commission on the Future of the Voluntary Sector in England, *Meeting the Challenge of Change: Voluntary Action into the 21st Century*, (the Deakin Report), NCVO Publications, London, 1996.

Commission on the Future of the Voluntary Sector in Scotland, *Head and Heart* (the Kemp Report), SCVO, Edinburgh, 1997.

DHSS, *Building Real Partnership: Compact Between Government and the Voluntary and Community Sector in Northern Ireland*, Belfast, 1998.

Gambling, T., and Jones, R., *The Financial Governance of Charities*, the Charities Aid Foundation, Kent, 1997.

Goodman Committee *Report on Charity Law and Voluntary Organisations* (1976).

Government White Paper, *Charities: A Framework for the Future*, Cmnd 694, 1989.

Knight, B., *Voluntary Action: Report for the Home Office*, HMSO, London, 1993.

Nathan Committee, *Report of the Committee on the Law and Practice relating to Charitable Trusts*, HMSO, London, Cmnd. 8710, 1952.

National Council for Voluntary Organisations, *Charity Law Review Project: Update Briefing Paper*, London, May 1999.

National Council for Voluntary Organisations, *Lotteries and Gaming: Voluntary Organisations and the Law*, and also *Malpractice in Fundraising for Charity*, NCVO, London, 1986.

The International Centre for Not-for-Profit Law, *Handbook on Good Practices for Laws Relating to Non-Governmental Organisations* (Draft), Washington, D.C., U.S.A., May 1997.

Winder "The *Cy Près* Applications of Surplus Charitable Funds" (1941) 5 Conv 198.

Woodfield, P., Binns, G., Hirst, R. and Neal, D., *Efficiency Scrutiny of the Supervision of Charities, Report to the Home Secretary and the Economic Secretary to the Treasury*, HMSO, 1987.

APPENDIX 3

Useful Addresses

Association of Voluntary Action Research in Ireland
The Secretary,
Centre for Voluntary Action Studies,
University of Ulster,
Cromore Rd.,
Coleraine,
Co Londonderry,
N Ireland.
Tel. 028 7032 4882,
Fax. 028 7032 4881.

Centre for Voluntary Action Studies
Faculty of Social and Health Sciences and Education,
University of Ulster,
Cromore Rd.,
Coleraine,
Co Londonderry,
N Ireland.
Tel. 028 7032 4882,
Fax. 028 7032 4881.

Charities Aid Foundation
Sterling House,
150/152 High St.,
Tonbridge,
Kent, TN9 2JD.
Tel. 01732 358234.

Charities Branch
Voluntary Activity Unit,
Dept for Social Development,
5th Floor,
Churchill House,
Victoria Square,
Belfast, BT1 4SD.
Tel. 028 9052 2780,
Fax. 028 9052 2799.

Charity Commission
St Alban's House,
57-60 Haymarket,
London,
SW1Y 4QX.
Tel. 0171 210 4556.

Charity Law Association
c/o Paisner & Co.,
Bouverie House,
154 Fleet Street,
London,
EC4A 2DQ.

Charity Law Research Unit
Dept of Law,
University of Dundee
Scotland,
DD1 4HN.
Tel. 01382 344461
Fax. 01382 226905.

Charity Law Unit
Faculty of Law,
University of Liverpool,
Liverpool,
L69 3BX,
Tel. 0151 794 2825.

Commissioners of Charitable Donations and Bequests
12 Clare St.,
Dublin 2.
Tel. 01 6766095
Fax. 01 6766001.

Customs & Excise
Custom House,
Queen's Square,
Belfast,
BT1 3EU.
Tel. 0345 125730
Fax. 028 9056 2972.

Dept of Finance and Personnel
Rating Policy Branch,
Rathgael House,
Balloo Annexe,
Bangor,
BT19 7NA.
Tel. 028 9185 8091.

Dept for Social Development
Castle Buildings,
Stormont,
Belfast,
BT43 SQQ.
Tel. 028 9052 2305.

Inland Revenue (Charities)
Charity Title Section,
St John's House,
Merton Rd.,
Bootle,
Merseyside,
L69 9BB.
Tel. 0151 472 6053 or 6029
Fax. 0151 472 6268.

Institute of Charity Fundraising Managers (ICFM)
208, Market Towers,
1 Nine Elms Lane,
London,
SW8 5NQ.
Tel. 0171 627 3436/3508.

International Centre for Not-For-Profit Law
733 15th Street, NW,
Suite 420,
Washington,
DC 20005,
USA.
Tel. 202-624-0766,
Fax. 202-624-0767.

Lands Tribunal
Law Courts,
Chichester St.,
Belfast 1.
Tel. 028 9032 7703
Fax. 028 9054 6187.

National Council for Voluntary Organisations
Regents Wharf
8 All Saints Street,
London N1 9RL.
Tel. 020 7713 6161
Fax. 020 7713 6300.

National Lotteries Charities Board
Hildon House,
30-34 Hill St.,
Belfast,
BT1 2LB.

Northern Ireland Council for Voluntary Action (NICVA)
61 Duncairn Gardens,
Belfast,
BT15 2GB.
Tel. 028 90877777.

Northern Ireland Voluntary Trust (NIVT)
22, Mount Charles,
Belfast,
BT7 1NZ.
Tel. 028 9024 5927
Fax. 028 9032 9839.

Office of Law Reform
Lancashire House,
Linenhall St.,
Belfast.
Tel. 028 9054
Fax. 028 9054 2909.

Ombudsman
Progressive House,
33, Wellington Place,
Belfast,
BT1 6HN.
Tel. 0800 343424
Fax. 028 9023 4912.

Probate Office
Royal Courts of Justice,
PO Box 410,
Chichester St.,
Belfast,
BT1 3JF.
Tel. 028 9026 2400.

Registry of Companies
IDB House,
64, Chichester St.,
Belfast.

Registry of Friendly Societies
15, Marlborough St.,
London,
W1V 1AF.
Tel. 0171 437 9992.

Scottish Council for Voluntary Organisations
18/19 Claremont Crescent,
Edinburgh,
EH7 4QD.
Tel. 0131 556 3882
Fax. 0131 556 0279.

Valuation & Lands Agency
Rating,
Queen's Court,
55-66 Upper Queen St.,
Belfast,
BT1 6FD.
Tel. 028 9054 3922
Fax. 028 9054 3930.

VAT Registration Unit
PO Box 40,
Carnbane Way,
Damolly,
Newry,
Co Down,
BT35 6PJ.
Tel. 0345 112 114.

Wales Council for Voluntary Action
Llys Ifor,
Crescent Rd.,
Caerffli,
CF8 1XL.
Tel. 01222 869224.

Index